Travels with Mina Loy

Travels with Mina Loy

NAVIGATING THE AVANT-GARDE

Suzanne W. Churchill, Linda A. Kinnahan,
and Susan Rosenbaum

LEVER
PRESS

Lever Press (leverpress.org) is a publisher of pathbreaking scholarship. Supported by a consortium of higher education institutions focused on, and renowned for, excellence in both research and teaching, our press is grounded on three essential commitments: to be a digitally native press, to be a peer-reviewed, open access press that charges no fees to either authors or their institutions, and to be a press aligned with the liberal arts ethos.

The complete manuscript of this work was subjected to a partly closed ("single blind") review process. For more information, please see our Peer Review Commitments and Guidelines at https://www.leverpress.org/peerreview

DOI: https://doi.org/10.3998/mpub.13250636
Print ISBN: 978-1-64315-105-2
Open access ISBN: 978-1-64315-106-9

Library of Congress Control Number: 2025947184

Published in the United States of America by Lever Press, in partnership with Michigan Publishing.

Cover image: Mina Loy, *Lady Reading*. Private collection. Reprinted with Roger Conover's permission.

Contents

Member Institution Acknowledgments

Lever Press is a collective effort. This work was made possible by the generous support of Lever Press member libraries from the following institutions:

Amherst College
Bard College
Bennington College
Berea College
Boston College
Bowdoin College
Carleton College
Claremont Colleges
Claremont Graduate University
Claremont McKenna College
Colby College
Davidson College
Denison University
DePauw University
Grinnell College
Hamilton College
Hampshire College
Harvey Mudd College
Haverford College
Hollins University
Iowa State University
Keck Graduate Institute
Knox College
Lafayette College
Macalester College
Middlebury College
Norwich University
Pitzer College
Pomona College
Randolph-Macon College
Rollins College
Santa Clara University
Scripps College
Smith College
Susquehanna University
Swarthmore College

Tilburg University
Trinity University
Union College
University at Buffalo (SUNY)
University of Delaware
University of Rhode Island
University of Sheffield
University of Texas at Austin
University of Vermont
Vassar College
Washington and Lee University
Whitman College
Williams College
Yale University

List of Figures and Permissions

Unless otherwise specified, all images reprinted with Roger Conover's permission.

PREFACE

INTRODUCTION

CHAPTER 1: NAVIGATING THE AVANT-GARDE WITH MINA LOY

CHAPTER 2: LOY'S ITALIAN *BAEDEKER*

CHAPTER 3: LOY TAKES THE STAGE

CHAPTER 4: LOY AND THE MUSEUM WITHOUT WALLS

CODA: COLLECTING MINA LOY

Preface

Roger Conover

> *It matters not that in our own location we may have travelled a million miles in that desolate dimension—inwards.*
>
> – Mina Loy

SCENE 1

Mina Loy is with her daughter Joella. They are sitting on a bed, in Paris, in a room bereft of charm. Both are looking down, but the gaze, the hands, the placement of feet are entirely different. Mina's hands are purposeful. She is busy at something. Is she darning? Beading? Threading? Hard to tell. It's 1929; she is not texting. Joella is sitting at the other end of the bed—bored, impatient. Twenty-two years of age, she holds between her legs the stick that has long been her companion; she had polio as a child. Now she stares abjectly floorward. *When will mother be done? Does she even know I'm here? What is she making now?* Joella thinks these things, but doesn't say them. *Get me out of here.*

Six decades pass.

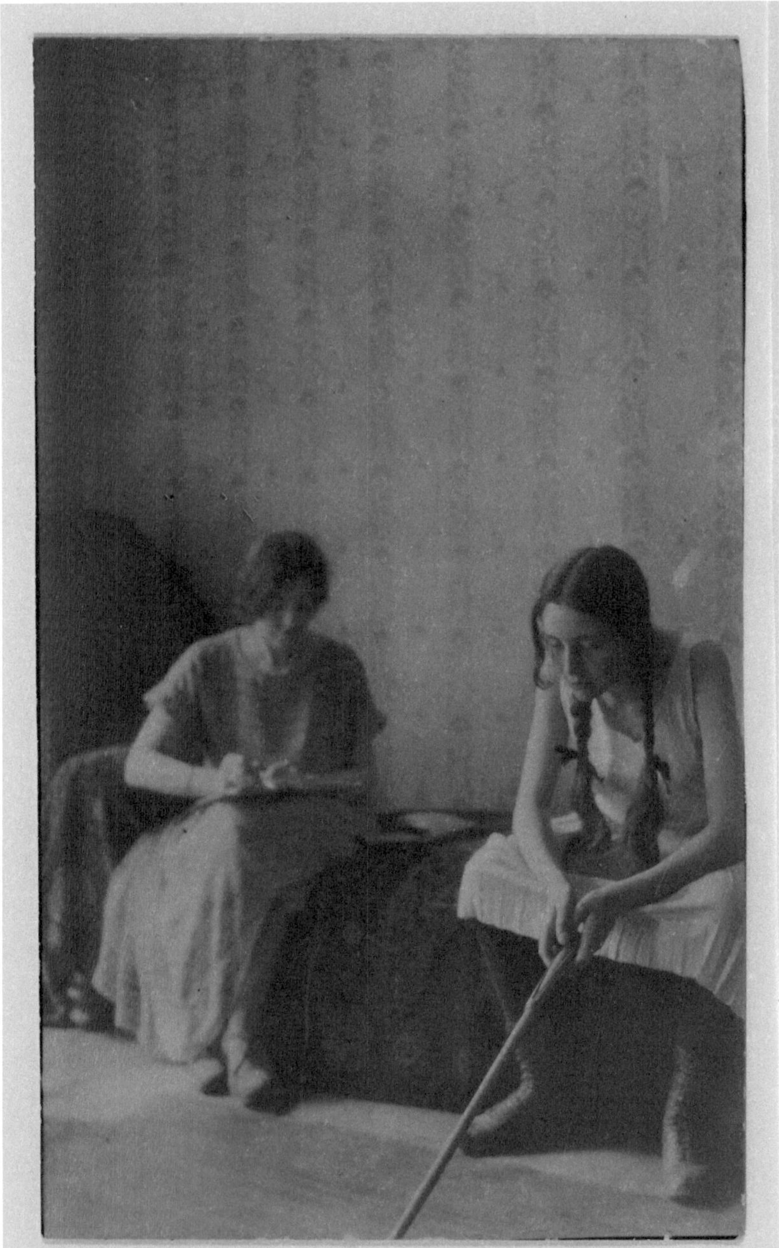

Figure P.1. Mina Loy and her daughter Joella at home in Paris, 1929. Private collection.

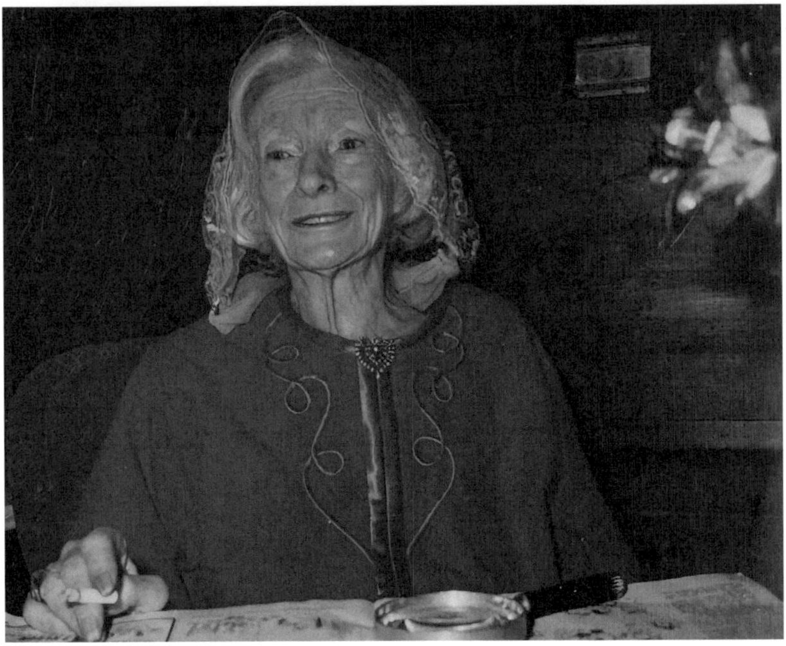

Figure P.2. Mina Loy at home in Aspen, Colorado, 1964. Private collection.

I meet the erstwhile girl Joella as an older woman. When I ask her what she remembers most about her mother, she immediately starts complaining about Mina's constant smoking. "She never emptied her ashtrays, and she never stopped making art trash." She goes on about Mina, asking me what I find so fascinating about her. "She was just Mama Mina." She passes me the photo of the two of them. "Take it," she says, handing it over like a piece of evidence. "I don't miss those days."

SCENE 2

Another photograph, also taken in Paris. In this one, Mina Loy oozes charisma. She is not sitting on a bed. She is kneeling on the sidewalk in front of the notorious Jockey Club. She is positioned strategically, with perfect surround sense. She knows where the other players are and makes herself the vertex of the image. She looks at Man Ray with delight, loving the fact that he inverts the optics by doing his meta thing—taking a picture of

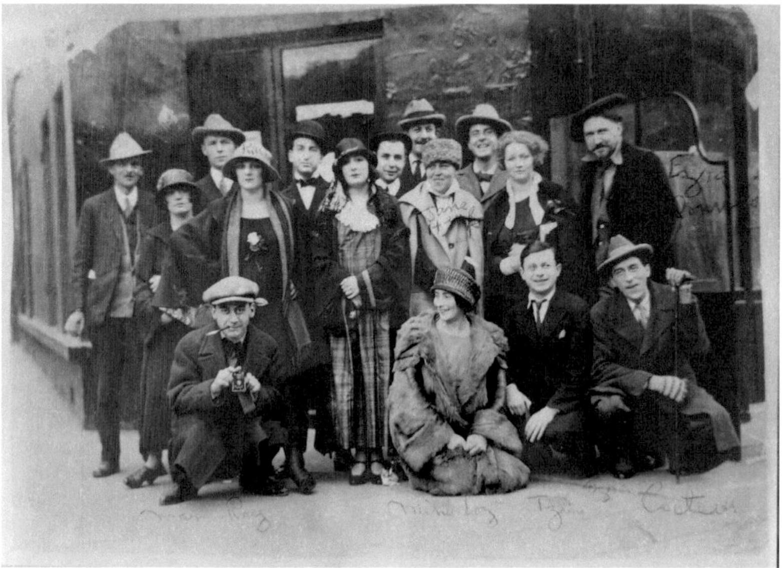

Figure P.3. Mina Loy in front of the Jockey Club, Paris, 1923 (with Man Ray, Tristan Tzara, Jean Cocteau, Kiki, Jane Heap, Margaret Anderson, Ezra Pound, Bill Bird, Hilaire Hiler, Curtiss Moffit, and others). Janet Flanner/Solita Solano Collection, Library of Congress.

the photographer taking a picture of everyone else. Everyone else except Mina. She resists capture. She transforms the entire picture by making it just about her and Man Ray. Their dramaturgy commands the play and creates a mousetrap scenario, a private game within a public display. She is all light, front and center, marginalizing Tristan Tzara and Jean Cocteau who sit shadowed to her left. Tzara looks stilted next to her; hatless. Margaret Anderson stands directly behind her, the only other person in the photo who ignores the camera. She too looks elsewhere but doesn't see what Mina sees. Ezra Pound is his own situation, standing a bit off from the rest. But not as far off as Mina Loy's confidant and "admirant" Marcel Duchamp, who is completely offstage. He doesn't do group portraits. Mina Loy evokes him in her raccoon coat.

Mina and Marcel. Two art bandits, disarming systems and opening latches.

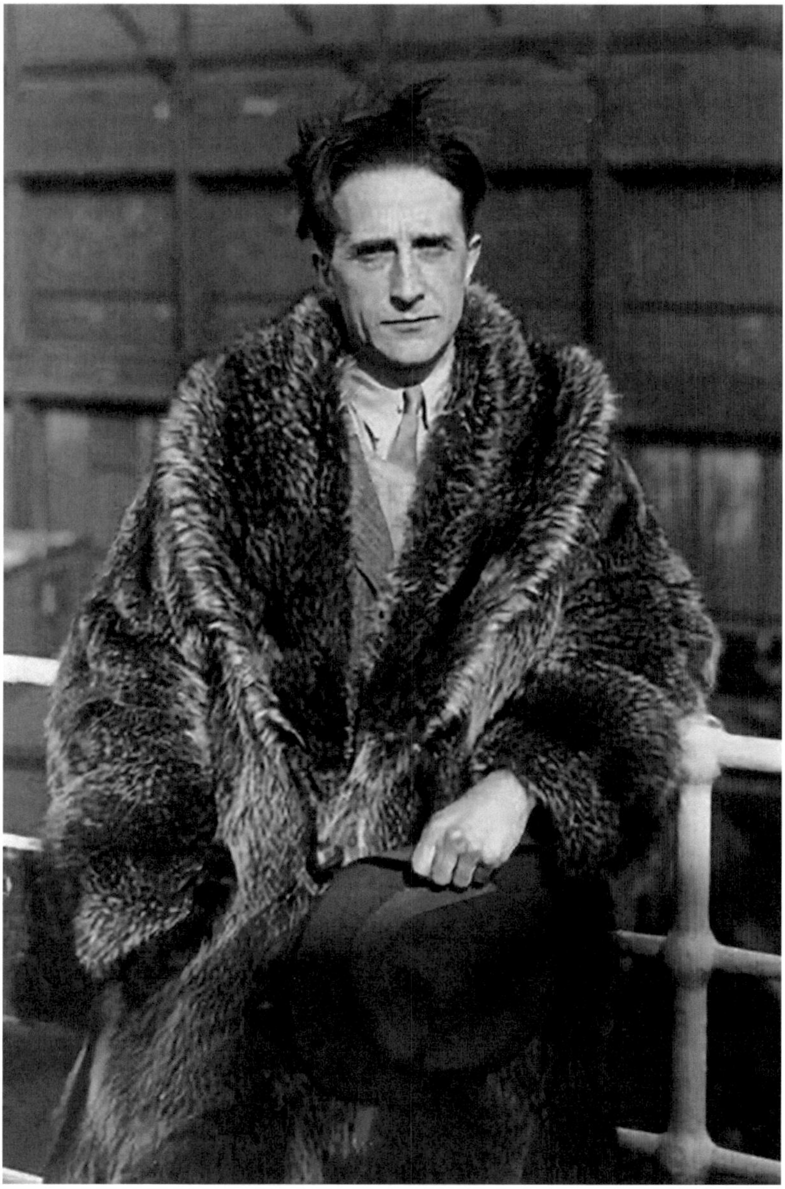

Figure P.4. Photo of Marcel Duchamp in raccoon coat at dock, about to depart New York, 1927. Photo by Bettmann. Courtesy of Francis Naumann.

Mina Loy looks for all the world like Venus in furs.[1]

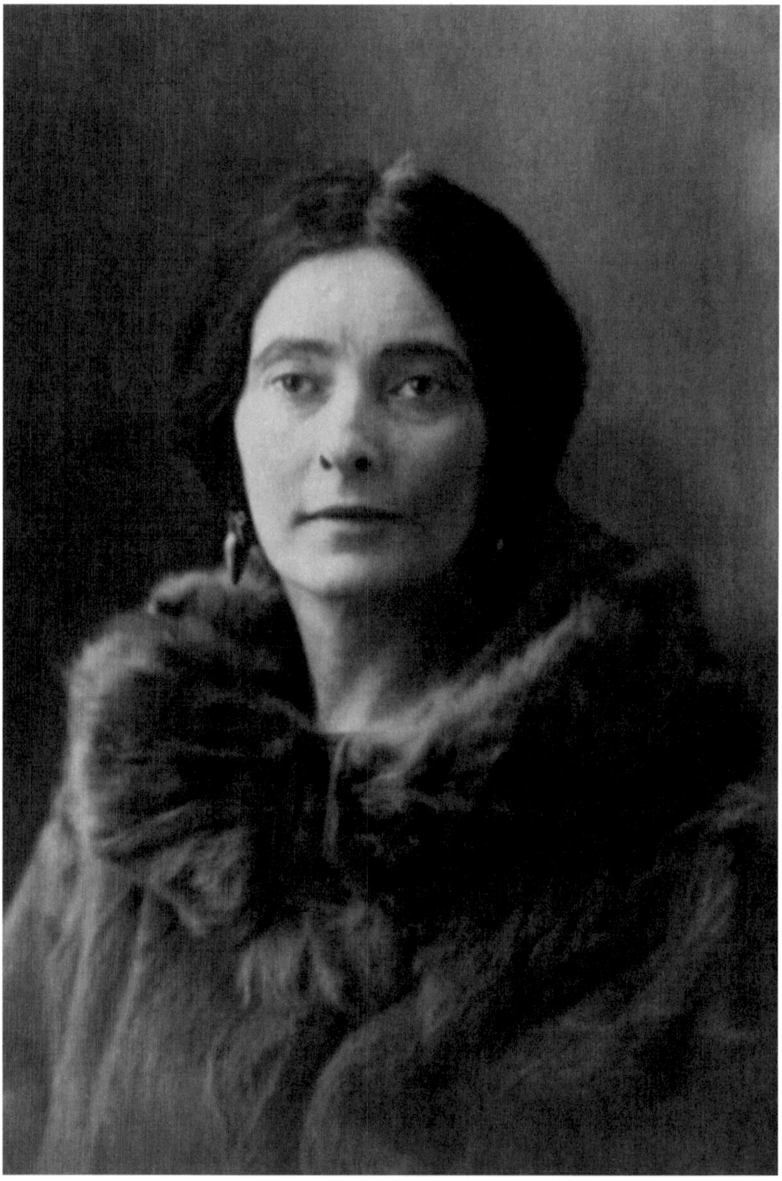

Figure P.5. Mina Loy, passport photo, circa 1916. Photographer unknown. Private Collection.

Although maps and photographs have been traditionally viewed as reliable, transparent, neutral reflections of "the world as it is," laid out objectively and scientifically on a two-dimensional grid, they are now more rightly understood as representations of obfuscations, agendas, and omissions that have an ideological underpinning. Maps and photographs are replete with power dynamics and politics. The seemingly innocent "group portrait" (Fig. P.3) presented here is such a case—a spatial story of power relations and social dynamics waiting to be unpacked. So too with the more intimate photograph of mother and daughter (Fig. P.1). One is a map of proximate relations between artists and writers who want to be seen together but don't know how to look together; the other is a map of desire and distance between a mother and daughter who don't know what to do with each other. Between these two photographs, taken less than a mile apart, there is daunting distance.

The geographies of Mina Loy's habitats are mappable, her addresses traceable. But no *Baedeker*, timetable, or passport can trace the topography of her dispositions or the itinerary of her self-eclipses, not to mention the ever-shifting and unpredictable *habillements* and ensembles of her mind. This book, for all its cartographic detail, recognizes that. By plotting Mina Loy's course, it reveals a geography of imagination and a search for station far beyond the schedules and maps suggested by biography and place. Mina Loy's work, literary and visual, is infused with the agony of displacement, the freedom of existential homelessness, and modern art's embrace of global identity and itinerancy, thus defining a new quest for independence as a form of resistance against boundary controls, nationalism, and neoliberalism. While inviting the reader to join Mina Loy on a time-traveling journey that anticipates our own globalized world of dislocation and mobility, *Travels with Mina Loy* does not deny that, in the end, Mina Loy's most extensive travels were into her own interior. Mina Loy traveled with Mina Loy.

Roger Conover
June 18, 2025

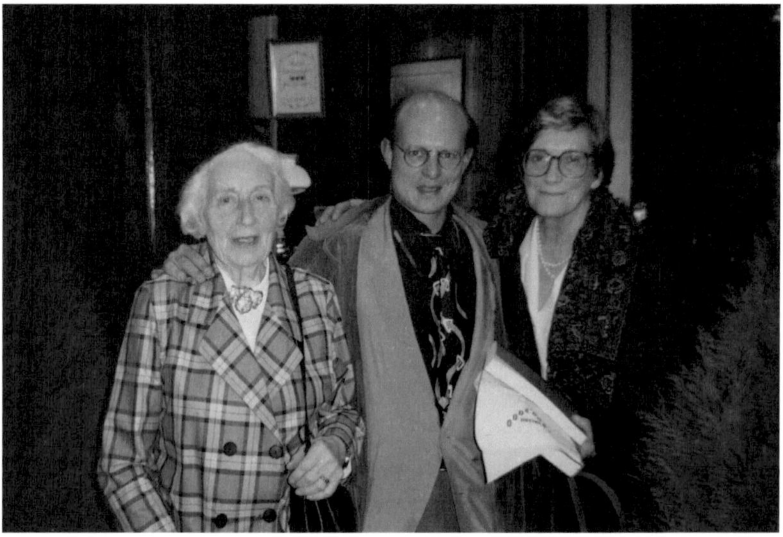

Figure P.6. Mina Loy's daughters Joella Haweis Bayer (L) and Fabienne Cravan Benedict (R) with Roger Conover at the *Arthur Cravan: Poète et Boxeur* exhibition, Galerie 1900–2000, Paris, 1992. Private collection.

Acknowledgments

No book is an island, entire of itself. As a companion to the scholarly website *Mina Loy: Navigating the Avant-Garde*, this multiauthored book is the outgrowth of a much wider collaboration among professors, students, scholars, collectors, archivists, librarians, technologists, administrators, grant program officers, and others who have contributed to our efforts to make Mina Loy more accessible to a broader audience.[2] Indeed, we relied on a large network of people to chart Mina Loy's artistic network, trace her perambulations across Europe and the Americas in the twentieth century, and represent them, if only partially, in both digital and print narratives.

Roger Conover, editor and executor of Mina Loy's literary estate, has supported our project from its inception. He made a bold leap of faith into our digital scholarship and opened his collections and home to us, sharing his knowledge and insights into all things Loy-related, past and present. Carolyn Burke, whose biography of Mina Loy served as a *Baedeker* to Loy's life, joined our venture into the digital realm and gave us permission to draw from her rich trove of Mina Loy papers. Nancy Kuhl at the Beinecke Library was an expert guide to the Mina Loy papers, and we are grateful for the Beinecke's digitization of these papers. Nancy Selleck was also with us from the earliest days of our collaboration, planting the essential seed for our feminist theorizing of the *en dehors garde* by suggesting the term and urging us to develop it. Andrew Rikard was an intrepid student innovator, supplying the mantra, "It's doable."

Although this companion book represents only a portion of the website and reflects significant changes in form, format, and content, it retains the thumbprints of the scholars who formed our advisory board: Sara Crangle, Irene Gammel, Alex Goody, Cristanne Miller, Tara Prescott, Shawna Ross, Stephen Ross, Mark Sample, and Whitney Trettien. Their innovative feminist and digital scholarly forays inform and inspire our own. We also drew upon the expertise, creativity, and original thinking of our technology and design team and the many undergraduate and graduate students who contributed to the development of the website. We are also grateful for the interest, support, and experimental creativity of a younger generation of Loy scholars, particularly Jennifer Ashby, Yasna Bozhkova, Diane Drouin, Jade French, Julia Heinemann, Juliette Utard, and Lottie Whalen, who have helped to realize Loy's vision to "make the world your salon" by developing an international digital Loy network through their 2023 conferences and websites.

Our technology and design team—Olivia Booker, Kristen Eshleman, Greg Lord, Jennifer Hall Mandula, Emily McGinn, Gesina Phillips, Sundi Richards, and Katie Wilkes—helped us take intellectual and creative risks and realize our vision. Research librarians Kristin Nielsen, Gesina Phillips, and Jayme Sponsel helped design and guide student research projects and the student-generated biographies for the website. Undergraduate and graduate students from Davidson College, Duquesne University, and University of Georgia at Athens brought new ideas, skills, and imagination to the table, and our work is invigorated by the energies of many students and conversations in our classes over the years. Those who contributed writings and projects to the website include: Matt Bell, Jillion Bennion, Claire Biggerstaff, Amy Bonnaffons, Nichole Brazelton, Mahalia Cooks, Matthew Days, Brett DiPuma, Courtney Druzak, Alexandra Edwards, Kenneth Estrada, Elise Foote, Meredith Foulke, Rochel Gasson, Sarah Gompper, Genevieve Guzmán, John Hadlock, Caitlyn Hunter, Jesse Jack, Jacqueline Kari, Annie Maisel, Taylor Maldonado, Casey Margerum, Erin McClenathan, Leah Mell, Jill Moliterno, Hannah Muczynski, Naira Oberoi, Jessica Riley, Lindsay Rufolo, Josie Rush, Anna Samuels, Molly Sharbaugh, Hannah Sommerlad, Severine Stier, and Maura Tangum.

We are grateful for funding and support from the National Endowment for the Humanities, particularly Jennifer Serventi (any views, findings, conclusions, or recommendations expressed in this book do not necessarily represent those of the NEH); Davidson College's Boswell Family Faculty Fellowship, Weinstein Summer Research Fellowship, Davidson Research Initiative, and Academic Affairs publication funding; Duquesne University's McAnulty College of Liberal Arts NEH Endowment and Hillman Endowment; the University of Georgia Libraries, English Department, Interdisciplinary Modernism(s) Research Cluster, Willson Center for Humanities and Arts, and Digital Humanities Lab. Our website was honored with the Garfinkel Prize for Digital Humanities, Honorable Mention, from the American Literature Association (2020); and the Modern Language Association Prize for Collaborative, Bibliographic, or Archival Scholarship (2022). We are also grateful to the Bowdoin College Museum of Art, with particular thanks to co-director Anne Goodyear and assistant registrar Theresa Choi, for supplying us with high-quality images of Loy's artwork and little magazine publications; for sharing research on the provenance of Loy's visual art; and for their support of our website and research.

As we explain in the Coda, transforming and remediating material from the website to book form was a much bigger challenge than we anticipated, and we owe our thanks to those who helped us bring this book to fruition: Sean Guynes, our editor at Lever Press; Michael Begnal and Owen Gregory, our copy editors; Mark Riley, Davidson College English departmental coordinator; Michael Allen, UGA Digital Lab; and the deans and English department chairs at Davidson, Duquesne, and University of Georgia who supported this project from 2015 until 2026, in both digital and print presentations. We extend our thanks to Lever Press for taking an innovative approach to academic publishing, and to Lisa Forrest, director of the library at Davidson College, for recognizing Lever's potential for sustaining humanities research in the digital age and partnering with them. We are grateful to Matt, Tom, Steve, and our families for their unwavering support, encouragement, and good humor throughout the process.

Above all, we are grateful for our friendship, which is at the heart of this collaboration and has deepened through the years of working together. At every step of the way, we have inspired each other to think and write better, bolstered each other's confidence in the face of doubts, and made the work of scholarship pleasurable and fun. In the face of personal struggles, health challenges, and family responsibilities, we fostered an ethos of care, flexibility, and understanding. It seems appropriate that our collaboration arose from a shared interest in Mina Loy, who forged her own network of female friends to sustain her artistic practice, and who modeled an en dehors garde ethos of curiosity, courage, and compassion.

List of Abbreviations

Insel	*Insel* (Black Sparrow Press, 1991)
LB23	*Lunar Baedecker* (Contact, 1923)
LBT58	*Lunar Baedeker & Time-Tables* (Jonathan Williams, 1958)
LLB82	*Last Lunar Baedeker* (Jargon, 1982)
LLB96	*Lost Lunar Baedeker* (Farrar, Straus & Giroux, 1996)
MLNAG	*Mina Loy: Navigating the Avant-Garde* (website, 2020)
MLSII	*Mina Loy: Strangeness Is Inevitable* (Princeton UP, 2023)
SE	*Stories and Essays of Mina Loy* (Dalkey Archive, 2011)

INTRODUCTION

Travels with Mina Loy

Suzanne W. Churchill, Linda A. Kinnahan,
and Susan Rosenbaum

1. OUT OF PLACE: MINA LOY AND THE AVANT-GARDE

Artist, writer, feminist, fashion designer, inventor, and entrepreneur, Mina Loy (1882–1966) traversed continents, artistic communities, media forms, and literary genres. She consorted with nearly every major twentieth-century avant-garde movement—including Futurism, Dada, and Surrealism—yet was wedded to none. She moved among the metropolitan hubs of modernism—London, Paris, Florence, New York, and Berlin—yet rarely felt at home. Her interest in avant-garde experiment was shaped by feminism, gender, and sexuality, leading her to self-consciously assume a position on the margins of avant-garde movements dominated by charismatic male leaders. Despite her peripheral status in the early twentieth-century avant-garde, Mina Loy exemplifies the interartistic experimentation that characterized these movements. Her innovative writing, typified by radically new uses of language, typography, and page space, appeared primarily in little magazines, garnering attention for its bold feminism and innovative forms. She wrote poetry, fiction, essays, plays, and found-conversation compilations. She painted in oils and watercolors and created constructions (or "refusées," as she called them) out of refuse she collected in city streets. She designed lampshades, hats, and corsets, and invented toys, household tools, and posture devices. As Sasha Colby points out, Loy was a multimedia artist before the term even existed: "retrospectively applied," the term "is appropriate to Loy, who was herself a multimedia producer of text, watercolors, montage, and *objets trouvés*" (Burke, *Becoming* 114).[1]

As a print and ebook companion to our previously published scholarly website, *Mina Loy: Navigating the Avant-Garde* (mina-loy.com), *Travels with Mina Loy* builds on the growing interest in Loy's multimedia work, offering a holistic handbook to her artistic and literary experiments across genres and media.[2] Our book companion aims not to reduce a complex career into a neat, chronological narrative, but to contextualize Loy's engagements with Italian Futurism, New York Dada, and transatlantic Surrealism in relation to the places she inhabited and the performances, exhibits, and audiences she engaged.[3] *Travels with Mina Loy* maps what Loy called a "long aesthetic itinerary" by grounding her artistic and literary forays in relation to geographic places, publication and performance platforms, and exhibition spaces (LLB82 300). Rather than offering a comprehensive tour of her career, we revisit familiar places from fresh vantage points, mapping the relations between place and aesthetics.

In simplest terms, this is a book about *place*, specifically the places that Loy inhabited for the most artistically productive periods of her life: Florence, New York City, and Paris. As the title suggests, *Travels with Mina Loy* is also about movement within and between places, migrations among artistic circles and people, and transit across arts. Mina Loy moved back and forth between Europe and America during her adult years, drawn to diverse places by personal desire, aesthetic aspiration, and economic opportunity or need. *Place* suggests crosscurrents of sociopolitical and economic spaces and contextualizes the ways in which components of identity, especially gender, race, class, and nationality, influence the navigation of social and geographic settings. *Place* insists on materiality and location as embodied experiences, with the body itself as "place" and "movement," as well as "performance" and "exhibit."

At the centers of artistic innovation, yet on the margins of avant-garde movements, Loy often found herself both "in-place" and "out-of-place." Indeed, being out of place, or no place, characterizes her reception until recently: as with many women and non-white artists, Loy was elided from historical and critical narratives of the early twentieth-century avant-garde, despite her active participation. During her lifetime, Loy's innovative art and writing earned critical acclaim and popular notoriety, to the extent that, shortly after she arrived from Europe to New York in late 1916, the *New York Evening Sun* hailed her as the epitome of the "modern woman," rhapsodizing that, "This woman is halfway through the door into tomorrow"—a metaphor that now seems like a harbinger of her future displacement ("Do You Strive"). Although she ignited a stir in her time, Mina Loy was soon forgotten in the annals of the historical avant-garde, a term that encompasses early twentieth-century, European, predominantly white, male-dominated art movements such as Futurism, Cubism, Dada, and Surrealism.

Take, for example, this archival photograph, unearthed and published on the cover of *The New York Times Style Magazine* in 2016, nearly

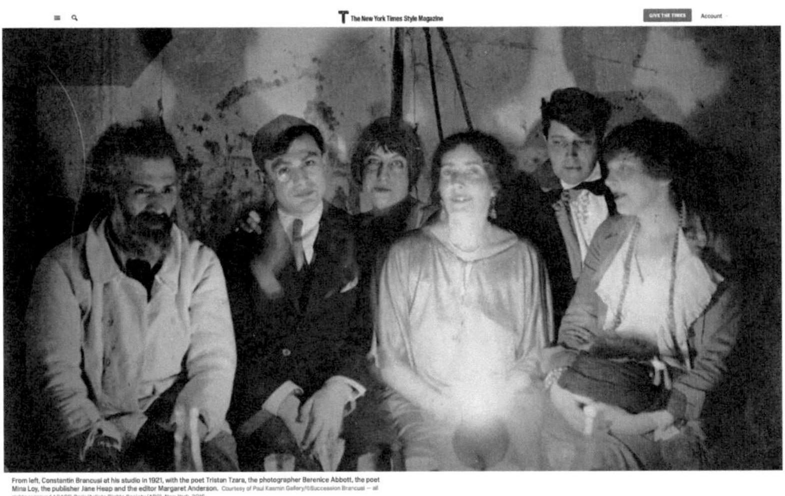

Figure 0.1. Artists in Constantin Brâncuși's studio in 1921. Cover illustration for James McAuley, "The Artists and Their Alley, in Postwar France," *The New York Times*, 22 Sept. 2016.

a century after the moment it records (McAuley, Fig. 0.1). The photograph depicts an avant-garde gathering in Constantin Brâncuşi's Paris studio in 1921 (from left to right: Brâncuşi, the poet Tristan Tzara, the photographer Berenice Abbott, Loy, publisher Jane Heap, and editor Margaret Anderson). As reproduced in *Style Magazine*, this iconic photograph typifies Mina Loy's position in the avant-garde. She is a central, illuminating presence, yet she is also a ghostly specter. Like the other women in the photo, she is listed only in the image caption but never mentioned or named in the article. In this way, Loy is representative of women in the historical avant-garde: although they played major parts as artists, writers, editors, critics, patrons, and publishers, women were relegated to supporting roles in avant-garde lore—posed in a photograph, mentioned in a caption, or deposited in a slim folder in the archive of a celebrated male associate.

In tandem with our website, *Travels* redresses a fault line between Mina Loy studies and theories of the avant-garde: whereas scholarship on Loy invariably mentions her avant-garde affiliations, histories of Futurism, Dada, and Surrealism rarely mention Loy. Centered on Loy but with broader implications, *Travels with Mina Loy* addresses this gap, offering our concept of the *en dehors garde* to adumbrate a wide lens for mapping early twentieth-century artistic innovation in ways that more capaciously accommodate the work of Loy and other women and marginalized artists. This term was suggested by Nancy Selleck, a scholar of early modern literature and culture, performance theory, theater history, and theater arts, who, appropriately, began her career as a professional ballet dancer. As used in ballet, *en dehors* describes a circular turn "toward the outside"; in relation to the avant-garde, it connotes how women and artists of color often came from the outside and circulated around the margins, working strategically to transform institutions and cultures that excluded them. Introduced on our website and discussed in greater detail below, the term *en dehors garde* thus represents a mode of theorizing commensurate with the artistic practices of Loy and other modernist women artists.

All of this leads to the place or status of Loy's work in literary and art history, which is complicated by the places where her work was published, exhibited, and collected (for a more detailed discussion of Loy's negotiation of the publishing, exhibition, and collection of her work, and how this shaped her archive, see the Coda). Loy published only two volumes in her lifetime, *Lunar Baedecker* [*sic*] (1923) and *Lunar Baedeker & Time-Tables* (1958), but her work in various genres and media appeared in Paris salons, transatlantic magazines, and galleries in London, Paris, Rome, and New York. Loy's unpublished writings, as well as her paintings, sculptures, assemblages, lampshades, and designs, comprised a larger body of work. Much of the uncollected material is held in Yale's Beinecke Library, while the visual art and some manuscripts reside with a number of private collectors.[4] The location of other work remains unknown.[5]

Loy's "place" in traditional scholarship moved from obscurity to exciting degrees of recognition beginning in the 1980s, as editions of Loy's work began to appear, and as feminists discovered and recovered the gender politics of her experimental poetics, especially tending to her early poems. Posthumous publications began with the 1982 publication of *Last Lunar Baedeker*, followed by the novel *Insel* (1991; 2014), *Lost Lunar Baedeker* (1996), *Stories and Essays of Mina Loy* (2011), and *Lost Writings: Two Novels by Mina Loy* (2024). By the 1990s, cultural studies approaches, along with greater access to and publication of work from the Loy archives, increasingly diversified readings of Loy amid broader reconsiderations of terms like "modernism" and "avant-garde," including more attention to the prose and late poetry. The 1996 publication of Carolyn Burke's biography, *Becoming Modern: The Life of Mina Loy*, contextualized the work of this elusive creator, appearing in the same year as a new edition of Loy's selected poems, *The Lost Lunar Baedeker*, edited by Roger Conover. These foundational works helped generate a surge of scholarship on Loy that continues unabated today, fueled by digital resources and archives including Andrew Pilsch's *Mina Loy Online* (2014), the Beinecke Library's digitization of the Mina Loy papers (2017), and our scholarly website, *Mina Loy: Navigating the Avant-Garde* (mina-loy.com, 2020), which emphasizes Loy's innovations across verbal and visual media and genres.

More recently, Loy's visual art has received long overdue critical attention, resulting in the organization of her first solo exhibition since 1959, *Mina Loy: Strangeness Is Inevitable*, held at the Bowdoin College Museum of Art in 2023 and the Arts Club of Chicago in 2024, accompanied by a catalog edited by curator Jennifer Gross. Gathering many previously unexhibited and unpublished works in one place, this exhibition provides an unprecedented opportunity to view Loy's visual art in a chronological arc; recognize recurrent themes, patterns, and aesthetics; and expose gaps in what has been preserved and is known about her career. Four of Loy's short plays were staged at Michigan State University in 2023 and the University of Maine at Farmington in 2024, giving contemporary audiences an opportunity to experience firsthand the continued relevance of her witty, ribald satires of gender and artistic genius. Additionally, two performances of Crystal Pantomime were staged by an experimental theater company in Chicago in 2024 as part of the programming for the exhibition.

These developments have brought Loy to new places and spaces—new digital environments, print articles and books, art galleries and catalogs, LPs, archives, and theaters—as her body of work motivates a lively, generative scholarly corpus. Indeed, reviewing the recent Chicago exhibition of Loy's art, Joan Rothfuss touches on her complicated relationship to place, noting her "refusal to be contained," while proclaiming that, "with this exhibition, she has finally arrived." The proliferation of Loy scholarship from the past twenty to thirty years that prepared for her late "arrival"—including monographs, articles, book chapters, dissertations, and reviews—indicates a remarkable interest in her literary and visual work, detailed in a retrospective "exhibit" of Loy scholarship found at the end of this book.[6]

II. "SUSPECT PLACES": LOCATING MINA LOY

Loy's long geographic and aesthetic itinerary offers important context for her artistic shifts on page and canvas, shifts that a phrase from her 1917 poem "Songs to Joannes," written between Italy and America, describes and portends, warning:

> These   are suspect places
>
> (LLB96 53)

While *Travels with Mina Loy* concentrates on Florence, New York, and Paris, there are "suspect places" outside of the parameters of place we observe, including Germany (where Loy studied in Munich as a young woman, returning to Berlin for the duration of 1923), Mexico (where she migrated with Arthur Cravan for the brief period of their marriage), Buenos Aires (where she joined friends while searching for Cravan after his disappearance), Austria (where she met Freud and drew his portrait in 1922), London (childhood home and location for the autobiographical, empire-critiquing long poem "Anglo-Mongrels and the Rose"), and Aspen, Colorado (where she lived from 1953 until her death in 1966). Concentrating our boundaries of place around Florence, New York, and Paris is neither arbitrary nor comprehensive but seeks to infuse each location as a place-bound encounter with the noisiest markers and makers of the historical avant-garde—and, in the process, to contemplate how Loy theorized and revised avant-garde ideas and practices through alternative feminist strategies we associate with the term *en dehors garde*. By charting Loy's approaches to these well-known sites of avant-garde modernism, we hope to encourage further study of overlooked experimental art and writing in these sites as well as in "suspect places" and regions beyond European and American capital cities.[7]

Our focus on travel, mapping, and place is thematic, formal, theoretical, and material. Tracing Loy's marginal positions (both chosen and enforced) in relation to recognized movements (Futurism, Dada, Surrealism), we reconfigure the roles of theory, performance, and exhibition for Loy as they developed in relation to the contexts of place. Interchanges in Loy's work between media—termed *intermediality*—are often tied to or shaped by encounters with specifics of place and the artistic energies she encountered there.[8] Loy's migrations across visual and verbal media and boundaries of genre offer another layer of mapping, as her aesthetic strategies were often infused with feminist proclivities shaped by specific place-based encounters with gender, race, and class. Her navigation of literal places influenced her approach to diverse aesthetic spaces, including the status of objects, the acts of collecting and observing, the understanding of audience, forms of performance and exhibition, and the heterodox constitution of the archive in relation to a migratory poetics.

Our attention to place, movement, and in-betweenness builds upon a scholarly interest in "location" that has emerged over the past two decades or more of modernist studies, while seeking to resist "accepting too quickly and uncritically the commonplace that modernism is a transnational or even supranational entity" and to "highlight the heretofore underexplored interrelations, affiliations and antitheses which emerge when we, in various senses, 'place' the work of modernist poets" in geographic spaces (Davis and Jenkins 4, 6). Joining a twenty-first-century turn toward "revealing literary works' involvement with and situatedness within the material cultures, societies and histories which produce them," our study explores Loy's work through "spatial and temporal crossroads [...] around which the activities and products of the literary imagination might be seen to arrange themselves" (McHale and Stevenson 5, 6). These crossroads, or "hotspots" as McHale and Stevenson call them, heat up further when factors such as gender, race, class, or nationality are brought into the frame, as "place" is never neutral. Cristanne Miller, noting in 2007 the growing critical attention to context and location, nonetheless identifies a lack of attention to "how cultural and national context affects women's writing with attention to poetry," demanding "that the local be understood in relation to gender and in comparison with other locations" (2). Inviting expanded attention to women's modernist poetry in this regard, she argues in her foundational study that "location significantly inflected modernist women's performances of subjectivity, gender, race, and religion in their texts and lives by making different subject categories available to them and enabling or preventing particular modes of expression" (2). In our study of Loy, "place" or location is marked by the coordinates of her varied engagements with the avant-garde movements active in those places, important to her work but by no means defining it. In this sense, *place* is mapped by contingent navigations of, resistances to, circulations around, and transformations of Futurism, Dada, and Surrealism.

As an accessible guidebook to Loy's work and career, *Travels* tropes on the structure and concept of the Baedeker travel guides popular in the nineteenth and early twentieth centuries, which helped stimulate modern tourism. The term "Baedeker" emerged in 1827, when German publisher Verlag Karl Baedeker began to publish travel guides for cities around the world, which included introductions, fold-out maps, travel routes, and information about important sights and destinations, all written by experts. Popularly called Baedekers, the guides became bestsellers and were translated into multiple languages. Indeed, "in Loy's lifetime the Baedeker guidebooks were not only an immensely popular cultural reference but also a modernist literary topos, referenced in works by modernist writers such as Henry James, E. M. Forster, and e. e. cummings" (Bozhkova 109). A world-traveler, Loy likely relied on Baedekers for practical advice and definitely drew upon them for imaginative inspiration, referencing them in her poetry and adopting the phrase "Lunar Baedeker"—guidebook to the moon—as the title of the two volumes of her writing published in her lifetime: *Lunar Baedecker* (1923) and *The Lunar Baedeker & Time-Tables* (1958). Significantly, the 1958 title registers movement across place *and* time by referencing a textual instrument—the timetable—mapping each. Posthumous collections of her work have used similar title phrases: *The Last Lunar Baedeker* (1982), and *The Lost Lunar Baedeker: Poems of Mina Loy* (1996).

Recent scholars have explored Loy's use of the Baedeker as a source, beginning with Tara Prescott's *Poetic Salvage* (2017). Tracing allusions in poems about Italy and France, Prescott concentrates on the guidebook in relation to Loy's poetic language use, arguing that while "authoritative guidebooks and dictionaries seek to fix the meanings of words, Loy is more interested in experimenting with the multiplicity of their meanings and the quality of their sounds" (21). Our website *Mina Loy: Navigating the Avant-Garde*, the digital companion and precursor to this book, centers ideas of navigation, place, and mapping to reconceptualize avant-garde practice and theory through Loy's interartistic experiments. The title and substance of the site's digital book (and a foundation for this study), *Mina Loy Baedeker: A Scholarly Guide for Digital Travelers* (https://mina-loy.com/chapters/), embraces multidimensional thinking about the notion of the Baedeker guide. Working in a similar vein, Yasna Bozhkova adopts the "central trope of the Baedeker guidebook" as an "important interpretive key" for reading Loy's work of the 1920s as charting a "constellation of modernist artists" (107). *Travels* builds upon the widespread interest in Loy's use of the Baedeker as source material for language, place details, and artistic networks to imagine new connections and mappings of her work, the "suspect places" she inhabited, the aesthetic innovations she advanced and absorbed, and the challenge her career presents to canonical theories of the avant-garde.

III. AVANT-GARDE THEORY AND ITS FEMINIST DISCONTENTS

Mina Loy's work falls under the broad umbrella of "modernism," a term that delineates a large field of modern, interartistic expression spanning from the 1890s to World War II, which includes but is not limited to the avant-garde. While modernists were dedicated to creating new forms of artistic expression, the avant-garde wanted not just to "make it new" but to explode past traditions: the avant-garde thus represents the experimental, confrontational, political edge of modernism. The term "avant-garde," derived from the "advance guard" of an army, emphasizes the militant, oppositional stance of the early twentieth-century art movements it came to describe. The *Oxford English Dictionary* (*OED*, second edition) defines "avant-garde" as:

> 1. The foremost part of an army; the vanguard or van.
> 2. The pioneers or innovators in any art in a particular period.
>
> 1910 *Daily Tel.* 1 July 14/6 The new men of mark in the *avant-garde*.

The *OED*'s recorded usage from 1910 of "avant-garde" in relation to the arts emphasizes masculine virility: the "new men of mark" were remarkable and visible because they stood at the forefront of culture. Implicitly white, educated, and able-bodied, they could make a mark by opposing cultural institutions because they had the authority and power to do so. Today, the term "avant-garde" is colloquially applied to anything new or experimental, especially in the arts. Scholars use the term "historical avant-garde" to refer to early twentieth-century, European, experimental art movements that opposed bourgeois values and tastes, and sought to challenge and shock audiences and to instigate violent revolutions and ruptures. The historical avant-garde embraced new technologies (such as photography, film, automobiles) and related features of modern life, including dynamism, speed, and simultaneity. They were often allied explicitly with radical political movements, employing confrontational tactics and experimental methods to disrupt art's traditional cultural role. The charismatic male leaders of these movements chronicled their exhibitions, publications, and performances, generating their own heroic histories and archives.

As Sarah Hayden observes, Loy did not merely overlap with these movements, "she actively intervened" upon them "as arch-theorist of avant-garde artist identity" (2). Laying the groundwork for the concept of the en dehors garde, Loy interrogates the "martialised" nature of what she terms the "avant guard" in a 1925 essay on Braque and Picasso, "Gate Crashers of Olympus," (SE 231). She observes of Picasso:

> Every new object to which he applied his disruptive aesthetic has had an extra crack knocked into it by his rabid opposers, i.e. disciples.
>
> For although modern warfare is not responsible for our revaluation of values, modern art which is the actual cause is martialised to the extent that he who steals a stunt from its originator, does so, for the redemption of the aforesaid art.
>
> (SE 230)

Picasso's "disruptive aesthetic" provocation was echoed and intensified by his "rabid opposers," who, Loy ironically suggests, became Picasso's "disciples" by copying his oppositional stance and martializing it. This "revolt" of the masculine avant-garde became a predictable "stunt" and was easily absorbed into the commercial logic that fueled the need for the "new," as Loy points out:

> This disjuncted guitar has in every 'avant guard' every year, in every land re-re-re-represented the imminent intellectual revolt for one quarter of a century.
>
> [...]
>
> Magazine slogan—
> Art is always 'new' to the uninitiate—
>
> (SE 231)

Loy suggests that this "martialised" stance does not generate real innovation or change but becomes replicated, recirculated, and "re-re-re-represented" under the false guise of the "new." Truly original "avant guard" art, she implies, does not violently oppose precedent in knee-jerk fashion, but constructively stimulates a "reevaluation of values" that it jealously seeks to "guard" (SE 231).

Although Loy could be forceful in articulating her revolutionary ideas—her 1914 "Feminist Manifesto" rejects "half-measure[s]" and calls for "Absolute Demolition" of tradition (LLB96 153)—she also recognized that transforming values and conventions need not entail strident opposition, violent rupture, or breakage, but might be achieved by strategies of renovation and rehabilitation. Her "Aphorisms on Futurism" (1914), written in the wake of the more militant Futurist manifestos of the early 1910s, calls for a *rehabilitation* of consciousness—a gradual expansion of the mind as it is stretched and reshaped by innovative art forms:

> CONSCIOUSNESS cannot spontaneously accept or reject new forms, as offered by creative genius; it is the new form, for however great a period of time it may remain a mere irritant—that moulds consciousness to the necessary amplitude for holding it.
>
> (LLB96 151)

By 1925, a veteran of varied avant-garde circles in Florence, Paris, and New York, Loy recasts "consciousness" through contexts of place and movement in an essay on "Modern Poetry." She theorizes that poetic innovation arises from the migrations of individuals and their languages and emerges in the places where they mix, claiming that the "new poetry of the English language has proceeded out of America" (LLB96 157). She proposes that the language heard "on the baser avenues of Manhattan" or in the street markets of First Avenue is an "English enriched and variegated with the grammatical structure and voice-inflection of many races, in novel alloy with the fundamental time-is-money idiom of the United States" (LLB96 158). "Alloy" of myriad cultures, nationalities, races, ethnicities, and languages, America nurtures a poetic dynamism shaped by ear and speech: America is a "country where the mind has to put on its verbal clothes at terrific speed," where "the ear [...] has listened to the greatest number of sounds," and where the new poet reckons with the expression of the "adolescent Slav who has speculated in a wholesale job-lot of mandarines and is trying to sell them in a retail market on First Avenue" (LLB96 159). This poetics of place—"the direct response of the poet's mind to the modern world of varieties in which he finds himself"

(LLB96 158)—demonstrates how America came to signify a democratic modernism for Loy and informed her theorizing of the avant-garde.

Loy's nascent theories of the "avant guard" would have little to no influence on subsequent academic formulations of the historical avant-garde, despite her canny critiques and discerning insights. Seminal theories—Clement Greenberg's "Avant-Garde and Kitsch" (1939), Renato Poggioli's *Theory of the Avant-Garde* (1968), and Peter Bürger's *Theory of the Avant-Garde* (1984)—respectively frame the avant-garde as a structural position of formal detachment, a psychological condition of alienation from mass culture, or a sociopolitical assault on bourgeois institutions aimed at restoring a connection between art and everyday life. The male leaders of avant-garde movements serve as models for these theories: just as the historical avant-garde marginalized women, the subsequent histories and theories based on these movements—including the exhibition of avant-garde art in museums from the late 1920s to the 1960s, and subsequent academic narratives about visual and literary modernism—largely erase the participation of women. As Griselda Pollock argues:

> the initial institutionalization of modernism not only failed to acknowledge the centrality of gender to both modernity and its modernisms; it actively fabricated a monogendered, selective narrative of modern art, even in the living presence of the women who defined their moment of modernity through their massive participation in all areas of culture. (795)

What results is a "heroic and exclusively masculine legend of the avant-garde" (Pollock 795).

More recently, feminist scholars have sought to clarify women's contributions, while articulating the importance of gender, sexuality, and race in the historical avant-garde, in studies such as Paola Sica's *Futurist Women* (2016), Naomi Sawelson-Gorse's *Women in Dada* (1998), and Whitney Chadwick's *Women Artists and the Surrealist Movement* (1985).[9] These reclamation projects join feminist critical and theoretical reevaluations (or rejections) of the avant-garde. Pollock, for example, reconceives the avant-garde as an assortment of "diverse and discontinuous avant-garde moments at which the defining collision of social and aesthetic radicalisms occurred" (796). Pollock's reformulation undermines the notion of the historical avant-garde as a singular entity, inviting us to instead think of it as shifting and provisional affiliations, made up of what James Martin Harding characterizes as "a variety of avant-garde communities, trajectories, or traditions where the sense of breaking new ground is always a relative variable subject to the context rather than categorical absolutes" (12). More recently, Sophie Seita focuses on "little magazines as media that capture and create provisional and heterogeneous communities," arguing "that artists on the periphery of an avant-garde group can revise our understanding of that group" (*Provisional Avant-Gardes* 2, 14). Shifting from militant models without rejecting avant-garde art's continuing capacity to shock, Seita offers the metaphor of "hospitality" for understanding the "complex interactions" that characterize magazine communities (3).

By emphasizing plurality, provisionality, and community, Pollock, Harding, and Seita expand the definition of the avant-garde to make room for women. But for Cathy Park Hong, the avant-garde is irredeemable. In "Delusions of Whiteness in the Avant-Garde" (2014), she rejects the term "avant-garde" altogether as representative of a fundamentally "racist tradition" and "white enterprise" that ignores "major swaths of innovators—namely poets from past African American literary movements—whose prodigious writings have vitalized the margins, challenged institutions, and introduced radical languages and forms that avant-gardists have usurped without proper acknowledgment." Hong has no interest in expanding the academic formation of the avant-garde to include artists of color: "Fuck the avant-garde," she concludes, "We must hew our own path."

Hewing a separate path is a dynamic mode of resistance to white power structures, but may repave avenues of containment and marginalization for non-white artists, without dislodging the value and prestige of the avant-garde moniker. Women artists on the outskirts of the historical avant-garde faced a similar predicament. As Harding observes: "performance in the margins can legitimately be characterized as a site of resistance against the compromises and acquiescences to the normative values that are demanded in the mainstream" (3); yet, marginality runs risks of obscurity and neglect: "However romantically or idealistically conceived, the margins are less a site of choice than of exile" (4). Loy explicitly addressed this predicament in many of her works that explore questions of witness, audience, exhibition, and display. She opted neither to pursue membership in Futurist, Dada, or Surrealist groups, nor to forge a separate path; instead, she moved from margins to center and back, occupying a liminal position both inside and outside the historical avant-garde.

IV. EN DEHORS GARDE: A NEW LENS

Inspired by Loy's practices and theories, *Travels with Mina Loy*, in tandem with our website, neither inserts nor disassociates Loy from seminal theories of the avant-garde; instead we propose a new, more flexible and capacious term for conceptualizing early twentieth-century artistic innovation: *en dehors garde*.[10] Taking a cue from ballet rather than warfare, we offer the term to describe the strategies of writers and artists whose mode of experimentation does not conform to the militant, oppositional stance associated with the historical avant-garde. In ballet, *en dehors* describes a directional movement: a dancer's leg moves away from the supporting leg where the weight is centered, reaching outward beyond the center:

> In dance, this term means outward. When turning, [...] this outward rotation is relative to the supporting (sometimes called standing) leg. The dancer is thought of as moving "outward" toward whichever leg is lifted in the turn or, in other words, "away" from the supporting leg.
>
> (Suzanne)

The en dehors movement also has a circular quality: the dancer's leg turns outward with an eye toward the center as a point of return. The circular motion does not follow a linear trajectory. It is also not hierarchical, having nothing to do with who is in front or behind, and requires significant core strength in the supporting leg to maintain equilibrium. In relation to the avant-garde, the term *en dehors garde* encompasses artists who circulated on the margins of centers of power and prestige, keeping an eye on avant-garde interventions even as they developed alternative practices to accommodate the insights and experiences of those excluded or objectified on the basis of gender, sexuality, race, ethnicity, class, disability, religion, or nationality.

Borrowing a term from the ballet to shed new light on Loy's intermedial artistic experimentation seems particularly apt, because, as Alex Goody observes, "dance plays a key role in the articulation of [Loy's] feminist aesthetics" ("Dance" 131). Although the Italian Futurists have long been credited as the catalyst that awakened Loy's artistic radicalism, in an undated letter to Carl Van Vechten, she credits Vaslav Nijinski dancing in the Ballet Russes as an equally important influence: "the things that have made me gasp were a few Picassos, Windham [*sic*] Lewis, Nijinski dancing—perfection is infrequent" (Loy to Van Vechten, image 121). Loy's interest in dance spanned her career, from early poems like "Sketch of a Man on a Platform" (1914), which depicts F. T. Marinetti as a ballet dancer; to her libretto for a ballet *Crystal Pantomime* (circa 1920s), which she revisits in her novel *Insel* (circa 1930s); to her poetic biography of the famed modern dancer Isadora Duncan, "Biography of A Songge Byrd"; and late poems such as "Stravinski's Flute" (circa 1950s). In all her writings about ballet and dance, Goody argues,

> Loy reads and writes dance as a woman writer concerned to articulate the specificity of women's experience. It is the particularity of embodied expression that interests Loy in dance, an expression which resists the abstractions of intellection and revalues perception that is based in, and returns to, the body as a site of meaning. ("Dance" 151)

Loy's concern with corporeality as a site of meaning "places her firmly in a tradition that seeks accurately to articulate women's lived bodily experience" (151); it also places her firmly in an en dehors garde tradition that is, by choice and necessity, attentive to the physical and material contexts of artmaking.

Inspired by Loy's interartistic interests and practices, the term *en dehors garde* offers an alternative vantage point on the historical avant-garde. Whereas "avant" means "before," implying that artists are in front of culture and ahead of their time, arranged in a spatiotemporal hierarchy, militant, and prepared for attack, "en dehors" means "toward the outside," implying that artists are turning away from the center or norm, moving in a circular motion, with an eye toward the center. Upon return, the center is transformed, adjusted, and reformed by the arc of the revolution. Rather than assuming a militant position at the forefront of culture, women, people of color, and queer or disabled artists rarely enjoyed the power, privilege, or authority derived from membership in the institutions of art, or even in the countercultural, avant-garde circles that challenged those institutions. Instead, they worked and moved strategically within and around the literary traditions and visual cultures that excluded or objectified them.

Introduced on our website and further developed here, the en dehors garde represents a mode of theorizing commensurate with Loy's artistic practices. Elastic, provisional, and contingent, her methods resisted the staticness of theory, as when she criticized D. H. Lawrence for converting to Freud and "dangerously damn[ing] his own creative flux with a theory" (SE 228). Like the term "intersectionality," en dehors garde is not a "grand theory," but a "lens" for bringing into view forms of artistic expression that are not visible in existing theories of the avant-garde.[11] This lens enables us to register experimental moves and strategies taken up by marginalized artists in particular settings, rather than trying to insert them retroactively into the theoretical frameworks that have elided them. To understand en dehors garde as a lens rather than a theory is to turn a noun into a verb: it is to transform theory into theorizing—a way of looking and investigating what might otherwise be overlooked. Rather than a modest, *feminine* hesitation to claim the status of Theory with a capital T, this move reflects a deliberate, *feminist* resistance to centralized authority in favor of ongoing, collaborative efforts to recover different spatialities for artistic and scholarly innovation.

Turning away from totalizing theories of the avant-garde, *Travels* maps the coordinates of Loy's career through the more contingent, flexible, and inclusive lens of the en dehors garde. As we discuss in subsequent chapters of *Travels*, Loy's en dehors garde stances and methods include but are not limited to:

- a different relationship to the audience or public from the celebrated avant-garde stance of bombastic aggression, in part because Loy didn't enjoy the same power, authority, and freedom as her white male contemporaries, and in part because she was more interested in art's amative and democratic potentials;

- a fluid relationship to high, popular, and commercial cultures: Loy borrowed whatever traditions assisted her in executing her witty critiques and investigations of systems of power and performance, and participated in commercial culture to make a living;
- an ambivalent stance of simultaneously participating in and critiquing artistic cultures, institutions, and conventions: Loy used a range of techniques and modes of irony and satire to acknowledge complicity and entanglement in the very discourses, processes, and systems she criticizes;
- an effort to both expose and erode divisions between opposed entities such as the public and private, the material and the spiritual, the bum and the saint, the universal and the personal, the hotly intimate and the coolly ironic;
- a predilection for circular artistic turns, revisiting ideas, techniques, and practices from her earlier artwork, as well as from earlier traditions, popular forms, new technologies of representation, and avant-garde movements, and repurposing them in new genres and contexts.

Viewing modernist art and literature through an en dehors garde lens allows us to recognize a diverse set of stances and methods adopted in response to dominant artistic and literary structures and conventions. Fully appreciating these alternative strategies requires repositioning creative work in its material, biographical, and historical contexts—the specific *places* in which artists operated. Our project attempts to widen our gaze to include the places and contexts that supported Mina Loy's experiments to initiate new histories of twentieth-century en dehors garde networks, many of which exist outside or on the margins of the historical avant-garde. As Susan Rosenbaum argues, we must broaden our lens to investigate the "infrastructure of experiment" and "networks" of support:

> If we regard experiment as a stance toward the work of writing, and as a method of generating that writing, literary history, particularly the history of the avant-garde, must be opened up and investigated anew. This involves not only the continuing recovery of forgotten and overlooked

> poets, but study of the infrastructure of experiment as it was being made, in anthologies, little magazines, middlebrow magazines such as *Vogue* and *Vanity Fair*, small press publications, poetry reading series, collaborations, gallery and exhibition catalogs, writing workshops, unpublished drafts, and letters. Women were actively involved in all of these pursuits, as poets, but also as visual artists, editors, publishers, translators, gallery directors, curators, and teachers. Widening our gaze to include the contexts that supported women's experiments opens up new histories of the twentieth century's social and artistic networks and institutions. ("'Do It Yourself'" 334)

Loy's participation in plays, little magazines, and gallery exhibits, for example, constitutes a form of social and artistic networking and infrastructure central to her lively interaction with a variety of artistic communities. We distinguish Loy's involvement in artistic networks from the related concept of collaboration. Although collaboration is central to the historical avant-garde, as well as to our own scholarly methods, Loy collaborated only occasionally with living artists or writers such as Clara Tice and Joseph Cornell, in the sense of materially working together to co-create an artwork (see chapter 4). She was devoted to the expression of her individual genius even as she understood that genius as part of a constellation or network of writers and artists with whom she interacted.[12] The cross-pollinating, network models that characterize Loy's artistic practices do not assume a one-way influence of the historical avant-garde upon her; rather, network models suggest that influence can flow in a number of directions.

In proposing the term *en dehors garde*, we are not trying to overrule existing theories of the avant-garde. Instead, we imagine that the en dehors garde might occupy the same stage as reigning theories of the avant-garde, but alter the choreography and bring new dancers and moves into view. Like the feminist avant-garde that Seita describes, the en dehors garde provides a framework for critiquing "previous, traditionally male-dominated avant-gardes by attending to what has been excluded and what must remain provisional" ("Politics" 165). From this perspective, "the allegedly anti-identity, theory-driven, hierarchical, and manifesto-heavy avant-garde is [...] only one among many other possible manifestations of 'avant-gardeness,' rather than the measure of all others" (165). What happens when we shift our perspective from centering the men of Futurism, Dada, and Surrealism, to looking at the avant-garde through the lens of Mina Loy and her "out-of-place" work?[13] Might we think of an *en dehors gardism* of place informing Loy's challenges to tradition, moving toward the "new" in social, political, artistic, and material ways?

V. A MAP OF THE BOOK

Inspired by Mina Loy's adventurous aesthetics, *Travels with Mina Loy* takes an unconventional approach to the scholarly book form. As in the companion website, we use clear, accessible language to chart Loy's career, orienting readers with an en dehors garde compass, ample illustrations, and exhibits that include a timeline of Loy's life, a map of her travels, and a survey of scholarship on her work. Whereas the website is designed for reading on a computer screen and invites visitors to choose their own itinerary, *Travels* offers a more streamlined, continuous narrative that can be accessed online, downloaded on an e-reader, or printed on demand. The book is tailored to readers who prefer a handheld print volume or tablet that they can read in an armchair or take with them if they travel to the places where Loy lived and worked. The ease and accessibility of online environments are changing reading practices, and we believe scholarly writing should respond in kind to meet the needs of a wider variety of readers. Accordingly, we have designed *Travels with Mina Loy* with readers' needs in mind, dividing long chapters into shorter sections with subtitles as signposts, and locating "exhibits" at the end of the book as reference points.

In chapter 1, "Navigating the Avant-Garde with Mina Loy," we revisit the sites of Italian Futurism, New York Dada, and Surrealism in Paris and New York through an en dehors garde lens, centering Loy in a narrative usually dominated by the charismatic male leaders of these movements. Designed for readers new to Loy and the historical avant-garde and those who want a brief refresher, the chapter provides a condensed biography of Loy entwined with short, Loy-centric discussions of Futurism, Dada, and Surrealism. Organized around the metropolitan centers that served as sites for these movements, the narrative overview lays a contextual foundation for the chapters that follow. Although the subsequent chapters proceed chronologically in charting Loy's en dehors garde turns toward Futurism, Dada, and Surrealism, their titles do not mention these movements because we do not want to repeat the effort to posthumously claim a place for women in the historical avant-garde. Instead, we shift the emphasis from the *avant-garde movements* to the *en dehors garde moves* Loy makes as she turns her attention to various geographic places and theatrical and artistic spaces.[14]

In chapter 2, "Loy's Italian Baedeker: Mapping a Feminist En Dehors Garde," Linda Kinnahan explores the importance of place to Loy's earliest poetry, written while living in Florence and during her association with Futurists. To enhance a sense of place for readers and invite imaginative (or real) visits to Loy's Italy, chapter 2 adopts a tour book style. Offering Baedeker-inspired directions alongside bits of information about Florence and its environs, the chapter mimics a travel guide in compiling a poetic Baedeker of Italian sites associated with Loy and often referenced by her. Exploring the poetry's Italian locations and offering visual guides and (usually walking) directions to various sites, Kinnahan explores how geographic, visual specificities inform Loy's emerging en dehors garde practice. Mapping geographies of gender, class, and nationality, this practice engages with and reimagines—rather than rejecting or destroying in Futurist fashion—surrounding elements of cultural pasts and poetic lineages that, for Loy, come to enable the modern innovations she developed in Italy.

In chapter 3, "Loy Takes the Stage: Playwriting and Publishing in New York Magazines," Suzanne Churchill reexamines Loy's migration from Italian Futurism to New York Dada, shifting the spotlight to her lesser-known plays and theatrical prose from the 1910s. New York-based little magazines provided a place for Loy to publish her unconventional writing: they offered a stage for her dramatic experiments and gave her access to broader audiences than her small circle of Florentine friends. Rather than viewing this transitional period as a shift in avant-garde allegiances, Churchill reframes it as a series of en dehors garde turns, in which Loy explores the artist's relationship to audience. Adopting playful, humorous approaches, Loy toys with the tactics and principles of Futurism and Dada in her plays and prose, evading affiliation with either group in her attempts to court new audiences and cultivate amicable relationships with the public. Beginning with Loy in Florence and moving with her to New York City, the chapter reviews her theatrical experiments, with subtitles signposting various performances in magazine spaces.

In chapter 4, "Loy and the Museum without Walls," Susan Rosenbaum explores Loy's engagement with Surrealism in Paris (1923–1936) and New York (1936–1953), examining the real and imagined spaces Loy navigated and created in the Surrealist movement's margins and shadows. This chapter emphasizes Loy's creation of alternative exhibition spaces and use of museum-inspired strategies of display as a crucial framework for her critical engagements with and adaptations of Surrealism, as well as a material means of displaying and preserving works marginalized by the avant-garde, as well as art galleries, museums, and publishers. The chapter tours these alternative exhibition spaces through an en dehors garde lens, using chapter sections and subtitles to signal entrance into a new site of exhibition or a new artifact on display. As chapter 4 builds Loy's "museum" of the en dehors garde, it illuminates her overlooked centrality to Surrealism's transatlantic history.

Travels with Mina Loy, along with its companion website, *Mina Loy: Navigating the Avant-Garde*, charts Mina Loy's formation of en dehors garde practices as she navigated the historical avant-garde. As we concluded our work on these projects, we came to recognize that our efforts to chronicle Mina Loy's literal and aesthetic travels, to place her in the context of her times while creating a more nuanced place for her in our aesthetic histories, would inevitably involve displacements and misplacements. Given the incomplete and fragmented nature of the Loy archive, Loy's "place" in our cultural histories is contingent and bound to change as new materials surface. In our Coda, we reflect on the importance of place to the collection, publication, and exhibition of Loy's work, to the history of her critical and scholarly reception, to the nature of women modernists' archives, and to the future of Loy studies. Placing Loy anew through scholarship, exhibits, and conversations is an ongoing process of travel and discovery requiring a fluid and changing cartography. Put more simply, the Coda addresses the questions: What happened to Mina Loy? And where do we place her now that so much of her writing and visual art can be accessed in print and online?

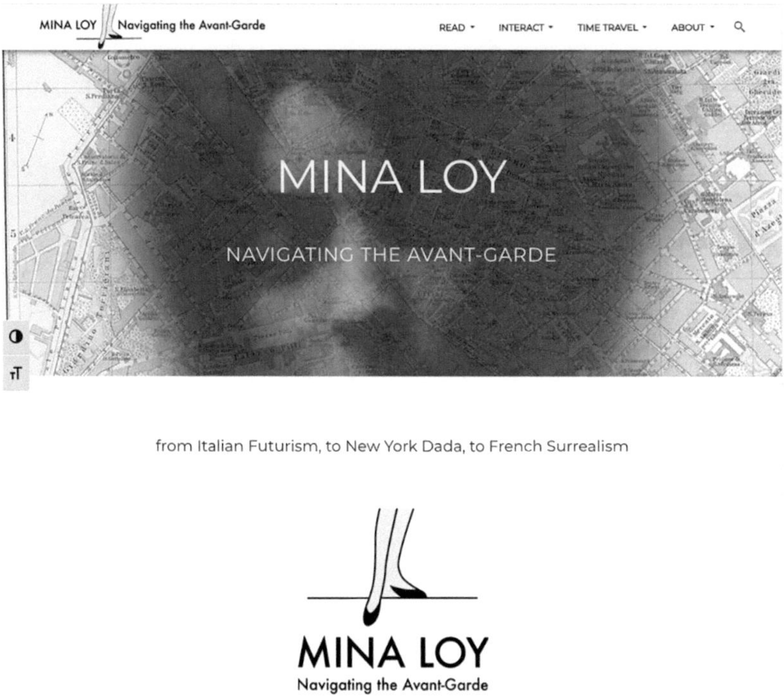

Figure 0.2. Home page screenshot. *Mina Loy: Navigating the Avant-Garde*, edited by Suzanne W. Churchill, Linda A. Kinnahan, and Susan Rosenbaum, University of Georgia, 2020. https://mina-loy.com/.

We also reflect on the process of creating this print and ebook companion to our website—a remediation that may seem like a counterintuitive retrenchment from a groundbreaking digital platform to a more traditional book form. Our website hosts a range of contributors that include students, scholars, artists, collectors, and tech designers, all working across different media and resourcing diverse materials—from archives, histories, and critical/theoretical studies to the inventive imagination. It also includes the scholarly "book" that inspires *Travels with Mina Loy*: our coauthored, born-digital *Mina Loy Baedeker: Scholarly Book for Digital Travelers*, which guides readers through her innovative work, migratory life, and en dehors garde networks (see Fig. 0.2). While the digital *Mina Loy Baedeker* mimics certain conventions of print media, such as organization by chapters, sustained analysis, and close readings, it actively engages the nonlinear and visually activated nature of a digital environment as it fully exploits the database structures and multimodal opportunities of a WordPress platform.

So why turn back to a more linear narrative form of book presentation? On a basic level, our motivation is to preserve the scholarship in the *Mina Loy Baedeker*, given the impermanence of digital forms, breaking of links, breakdown of functions, and difficulty of site maintenance in the face of rapidly advancing technologies. On another level, the process of moving from born-digital to book-form scholarship complicates questions often asked about the shift from print to digital scholarship, illuminating their differences while eroding the line between them. In preparing this book companion, we have had to figure out what affordances translate (or not) from website to book formats; how the narrative structure of a book revises the network and grid structures of a digital platform; and how digital environments and book formats shape different habits of thinking, writing, and reading. In the Coda we share insights about how the affordances of website design and book form shape the way we collect and exhibit Mina Loy to different audiences. To preserve some of the resources developed on our website beyond the *Mina Loy Baedeker*, and to aid our fellow travelers in Loy studies, we also curate two Exhibits: 1) "Mina Loy Bio, Map, and Timeline" offers a brief biography, visual map, and linear timeline of Loy's life and travels; and 2) "Collecting and Exhibiting Mina Loy: Timetable of Critical and Scholarly Reception and Creative Productions" provides a chronological tour of Loy scholarship, charting directions and destinations for further travel with Mina Loy.

CHAPTER ONE

NAVIGATING THE AVANT-GARDE WITH MINA LOY

Suzanne W. Churchill, Linda A. Kinnahan, and Susan Rosenbaum

Histories of Futurism, Dada, and Surrealism typically cast white, European men as the lead choreographers and principal dancers on the avant-garde stage. In this chapter, we shift our lens and alter the choreography to bring Mina Loy into view and accommodate her en dehors garde moves on the same stage as the historical avant-garde. The chapter offers an overview of Loy's navigation of Italian Futurism, New York Dada, and French and American Surrealism, recasting them as part of a larger array of contexts that shaped her wide-ranging, peripatetic career as she traveled around Europe and the Americas. Our aim is to provide a brief but foundational introduction to each movement and their relevance to Loy, which subsequent chapters build upon. This overview draws attention to the multifaceted ways Loy encountered, engaged with, and moved through artistic formations typically understood as the historical avant-garde, attending to Loy's experiences as representative of women's marginal status. Examining how Loy circulated between the margins and centers of avant-garde circles, we aim to provide an en dehors garde lens on interartistic practices, places, and histories, redirecting the focus from an authoritative (male) center to outward turns and liminal movements.

I. TOURING ITALY, TRAVELS WITH FUTURISM

While F. T. Marinetti, along with other artists and writers, began issuing manifestos in 1909 to engineer an aggressive Futurist avant-garde, Loy did not associate with this group until a few years later, although she was certainly aware of them and their prolific—and loud—publicizing.[1] The bellicose "Founding and Manifesto of Futurism," published on the front page of *Le Figaro* in 1909, blasted the Italian public, violently rejecting tradition, calling for the destruction of libraries and museums, glorifying war, and exalting speed and mechanization (in Rainey et al. 49–53). The manifesto "secured the attention of a global and general, non-art-world-specific audience" and "indelibly inscribed Marinetti into the role of visionary leader in the history of the movement" (Hayden, *Curious Disciplines* 19). The Futurists rejected "Italy's passéist (antiquated) cultural heritage" and cultivated "an aggressive iconoclasm seldom equaled in subsequent experimental literature" (White 22). Futurist art and aesthetics emphasized the movement's radical break with tradition and embrace of modern technologies of speed, war, and mechanization. The "Technical Manifesto of Futurist Literature" (1912) asserted the imperatives to "destroy syntax," "Abolish all punctuation," and "Destroy the 'I' in Literature" (Rainey et al. 119–25). Activating the space of the page and challenging distinctions between poetry and visual art, Futurists generated an "interdisciplinary ethos, one that encouraged cross-fertilization between media" (White 23).[2] While Loy's introduction to Florentine Futurism and her close relationships with leaders Filippo Tommaso Marinetti and Giovanni Papini are customarily considered to have "ignited her artistic aspirations," this origin story paints Loy as a blank slate, often omitting a decade or more of artistic and lived experience. By 1913, when Loy first personally associated with Futurists, she was prepared to critically engage, rather than merely learn from, their explosive aesthetics (Gross, "Truant" 32).[3]

Although Futurism's iconoclasm, interdisciplinary ethos, and "words-in-freedom" accorded with Loy's unorthodox, intermedial, and free-spirited artistic sensibility, by the time she met the Italian Futurists, she was well versed in modern art movements. In the years surrounding the century's turn, Loy studied art in London and Munich as a teenager, and by her early twenties in London with August John before entering the Académie Colarossi in Paris, just as coed life-drawing classes were allowed and restrictions barring women from art shows were overturned. She learned of post-Impressionism and Fauvism, and her first husband Stephen Haweis worked as a studio photographer for Auguste Rodin, capturing his innovations in modern sculpture.[4] Establishing herself as an artist, Loy first exhibited at the Salon d'Automne in 1904 (Gross, "Truant" 7), as well as in 1905, 1906, 1913, and 1923 (12). Building upon a decade of artistic study and practice, Loy's 1907 move to Florence initiated an extended contact with Italian culture, history, and society concurrent with her introduction to an Anglo-American community of writers and artists advancing ideas embraced as new and modern. She befriended Gertrude Stein and read her radical prose; admired Isadora Duncan's modern dance ideas; discussed Eastern spirituality at Mabel Dodge Luhan's Villa Curonia and at the salon of Isidore and Lili Braggiotti; deliberated modern theater with Irish poet-turned-theater director Herbert Trench; and explored socioeconomic concerns with the American George Herron, who espoused a progressive Social Gospel movement. In 1912, Loy traveled to London for a solo show of her paintings at the Carfax Gallery. While there, she attended Roger Fry's *Second Post-Impressionist Exhibition* at the Grafton Galleries, writing to Dodge Luhan about her interest in Wyndham Lewis (Gross, "Truant" 30).

Back in Florence, Loy eagerly received news about the 1913 Armory Show in New York and formed a new friendship with American artist Frances Simpson Stevens, who studied with Robert Henri and exhibited at the Armory, subsequently renting Haweis's studio when he left Florence in 1913. Loy welcomed Stevens into her home, agreeing to serve as the twenty-year old's chaperone while the younger woman continued her art training in Florence, and they joined in meeting Futurist painters and writers (Burke, *Becoming* 151). Together, they read the manifestos "as if they were news from the front" and associated with Giovanni Papini and various painters gathering at Giubbe Rosse café (Burke, *Becoming* 153). Loy would write to her wayward husband Haweis of her interest in Futurism as though sending a warning: "Do not fear I am not intellectual enough to become a futurist— But am intelligent enough to have given up everything else."[5] At the same time, in an undated letter to Carl Van Vechten likely from this period, she lists Futurism as one of many influences:

> the things that have made me gasp were a few Picassos, Windham [*sic*] Lewis, Nijinski dancing—perfection is infrequent. I *have* gasped too at a picture of Carr's & of course the shattering beauty [of] Marinetti's readings of Futurist poems and at the inebriation of early Papini in L'Uomo Finito & the sublime epics of the commonplace made by Arnold Bennet—& the eyes of a tuberculous beggar on the Via Tornabuoni—and a line I picked up of La Forgue's.[6]

Loy's poetic emergence in 1914 drew upon a city (and a decade of aesthetic experiences) quintessentially layered with historical, artistic, and social traditions, and energized by circuits of individuals challenging myriad traditions. She was well equipped to respond to Futurism in poetically sophisticated and socially aware ways.

At the same time, her correspondence with friends also expresses great interest in America's feminist movement, especially in letters to Dodge Luhan after her move across the Atlantic, and Van Vechten, who became her literary agent. In American poetry, she discerned a greater freedom about sexuality, especially in a figure like Whitman, that spoke to her own concerns as a woman and suggested the open-mindedness she hoped would meet her first published poems (1914) and greet her in New York two years later. Familiar with Italian and British feminism, Loy wrote her own "Feminist Manifesto" in 1914 and brought a range of feminist perspectives into the poetry she began writing.[7] The manifesto reflects Loy's dissatisfaction with conservative aspects of a modern woman's movement (especially the less radical elements of the suffrage movement) as well as a revised consideration of Futurism's denigrating discourse on "Woman," and an insistence on a woman's capacity to realize herself fully. Referencing Marinetti's "The Founding and Manifesto of Futurism" (1909), Rowan Harris reminds us that, for Futurists, "Woman was associated with all things condemned as 'passatista': sentimentality, nostalgia, pacifism, symbolist poetry, auratic art, psychology and nature [...]. A belligerent repudiation of Woman identified with resistance to modernity, was the bedrock of Futurism's power fantasies" (25). Tangling with masculine power, feminine complicity, and feminist perspectives, Loy's literary work complexly (re)considers Futurist ideas in relation to alternative discourses supplied by various voices of modernity, from feminisms to social movements, to philosophical and psychological thought.

By fall of 1913, Loy met Marinetti and, within a few months, exhibited artwork with the Futurists in Rome. She welcomed certain freedoms the movement preached, taking many ideas seriously and becoming personally involved with its two combative leaders, Marinetti and Papini. Nonetheless, Loy maintained a capacity to critique and question them, at times with a parodic humor and amusement. Her own sense of Futurism's limitations is suggested in a 1914 letter to Dodge Luhan, admitting her attraction but also marking her critical distance from Futurist ideas: "I am in the throes of conversion to Futurism—But I shall never convince myself—There is not hope in any system that 'combats le mal avec le mal'—& that is really Marinetti's philosophy—."[8] Loy's complex relationship with Futurism provides material for *Brontolivido*, a fragmented and unpublished prose recounting that straddles memoir, fiction, and satire through characters corresponding to herself (Sophie or Jemima), Stevens (Gloria), Marinetti (Bronty), and Papini (Johannes or Geronimo). Satirizing the performative masculinity of the "Flabbergasts" and their attitudes toward women, Loy does not spare herself from satire, much in the way various poems present "female figures caught up in Futurism" that "ironized their desire for Futurist recognition," although "the primary target of her satire was the posturing and anxious misogyny of the Futurists themselves" (Harris 27). Employing what Harris terms "feminine ventriloquy," Loy's fictionalized version of her own "throes of conversion" is rendered in terms both exuberant and self-mocking in her knowing sense of the dangers of self-extinction:

> She had got into the Flabbergast world where everything seemed to be worked by a piston--hiding away from herself in this man's jacket, she was caught in the machinery of his urgent identification with piston frenzy; a dropped consciousness of everything but Rush.[9]

As such passages build in satirical energy, Loy "undermines Futurist constructions of Woman by taking them on [...] oscillating between a professed vacuity and a formidable wit and superior disdain in deflating Bronty's hyperbole" (Harris 34).

In *Brontolivido*, Loy portrays the Marinetti character as a "Bombastic Superman," "so appallingly dynamic in his misogynist magnetism [...] gyrating on the pivot of his virility."[10] While subject to moments of infantilizing infatuation in his presence, the Jemima character nonetheless remains alert to the dangers of sexual or romantic possession as a form of feminine extinction--in women and men alike--that Futurism's machismo threatens. In a dialogue between Jemima and Bronty, the woman makes clear her awareness, speaking first:

> "[Y]ou know as well as I do that—you can never possess another human-being"
> "I know"
> "Then why in your reconstruction of the universe leave woman where you have kept
> her for centuries" [variant version: " ... leave woman out?"]
> "Woman" said the Martinet—is never going to change"
> "Then" said Jemima, ["]the side of you that responds to the feminine element is never going to develop—You're held down"!
> "We'll finish her off—[variant version: "The Flabbergast will finish her off"][11]

A delicious layer of irony permeates this exchange, arising from Jemima's penetrating diagnosis of fault lines in the Futurists' misogynistic logic: she reveals an intelligent awareness that Bronty lacks, even as he avows to "finish her off."

On December 12, 1913, Loy attended her first Futurist *serata,* or "evening," at the Teatro Verdi in Florence, an entertainment event initiated in Trieste in 1910, in which "art-making became a form of theater" (Hayden, *Curious Disciplines* 17). Orchestrated by Papini and Marinetti, the event attracted a crowd with a storm of publicity spread around the city via posters, fliers, and newspapers. During the *serata*, they railed insults and invectives at the audience, who reacted by hurling back jeers and rotten vegetables. Three days later, the Futurist newspaper, *Lacerba*, declared the event a triumph, claiming victory over a crowd of five thousand spectators, whose "overwhelming vulgarity, personal hates, posthumous resentments, drunken frenzy of being many against few, [and] raging stupidity" they had transformed into "a magnificent spectacle" (qtd. in Burke, *Becoming* 156; see Fig. 1.1).[12]

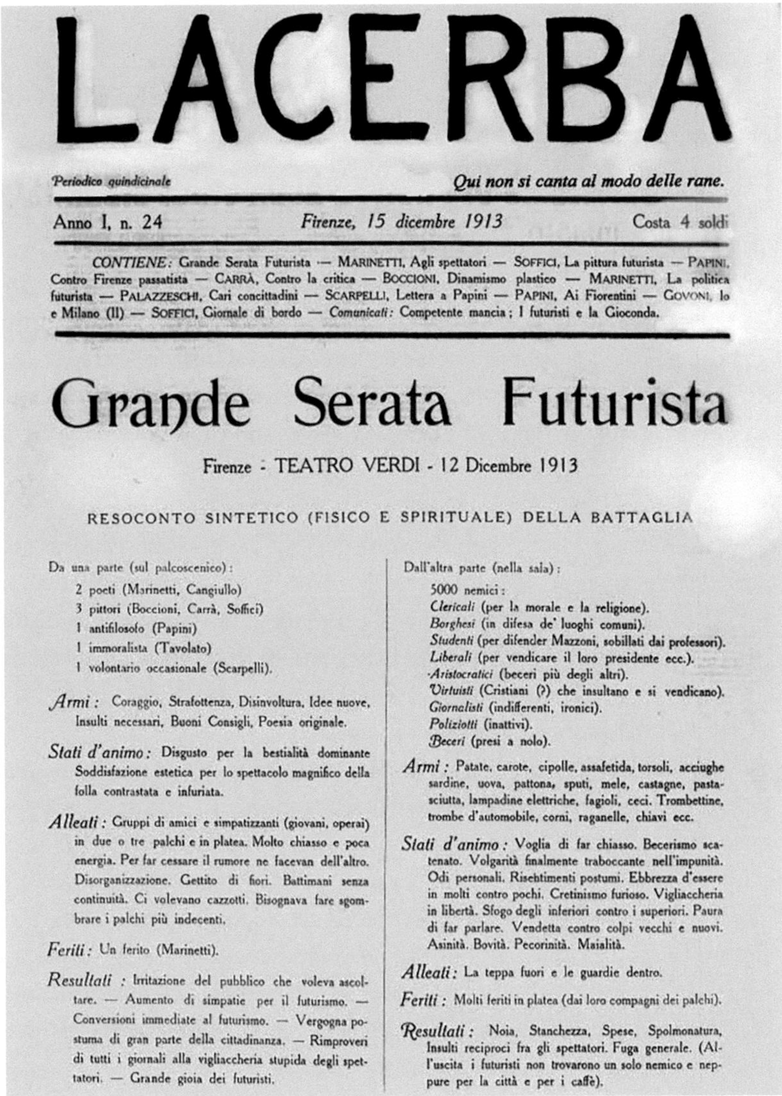

LACERBA

Periodico quindicinale *Qui non si canta al modo delle rane.*

Anno I, n. 24 *Firenze, 15 dicembre 1913* Costa 4 soldi

CONTIENE: Grande Serata Futurista — MARINETTI, Agli spettatori — SOFFICI, La pittura futurista — PAPINI, Contro Firenze passatista — CARRÀ, Contro la critica — BOCCIONI, Dinamismo plastico — MARINETTI, La politica futurista — PALAZZESCHI, Cari concittadini — SCARPELLI, Lettera a Papini — PAPINI, Ai Fiorentini — GOVONI, Io e Milano (II) — SOFFICI, Giornale di bordo — *Comunicati:* Competente mancia; I futuristi e la Gioconda.

Grande Serata Futurista

Firenze - TEATRO VERDI - 12 Dicembre 1913

RESOCONTO SINTETICO (FISICO E SPIRITUALE) DELLA BATTAGLIA

Da una parte (sul palcoscenico):
2 poeti (Marinetti, Cangiullo)
3 pittori (Boccioni, Carrà, Soffici)
1 antifilosofo (Papini)
1 immoralista (Tavolato)
1 volontario occasionale (Scarpelli).

Armi: Coraggio, Strafottenza, Disinvoltura, Idee nuove, Insulti necessari, Buoni Consigli, Poesia originale.

Stati d'animo: Disgusto per la bestialità dominante Soddisfazione estetica per lo spettacolo magnifico della folla contrastata e infuriata.

Alleati: Gruppi di amici e simpatizzanti (giovani, operai) in due o tre palchi e in platea. Molto chiasso e poca energia. Per far cessare il rumore ne facevan dell'altro. Disorganizzazione. Gettito di fiori. Battimani senza continuità. Ci volevano cazzotti. Bisognava fare sgombrare i palchi più indecenti.

Feriti: Un ferito (Marinetti).

Resultati: Irritazione del pubblico che voleva ascoltare. — Aumento di simpatie per il futurismo. — Conversioni immediate al futurismo. — Vergogna postuma di gran parte della cittadinanza. — Rimproveri di tutti i giornali alla vigliaccheria stupida degli spettatori. — Grande gioia dei futuristi.

Dall'altra parte (nella sala):
5000 nemici:
Clericali (per la morale e la religione).
Borghesi (in difesa de' luoghi comuni).
Studenti (per difender Mazzoni, sobillati dai professori).
Liberali (per vendicare il loro presidente ecc.).
Aristocratici (beceri più degli altri).
Virtuisti (Cristiani (?) che insultano e si vendicano).
Giornalisti (indifferenti, ironici).
Poliziotti (inattivi).
Beceri (presi a nolo).

Armi: Patate, carote, cipolle, assafetida, torsoli, acciughe sardine, uova, pattona, sputi, mele, castagne, pastasciutta, lampadine elettriche, fagioli, ceci. Trombettine, trombe d'automobile, corni, raganelle, chiavi ecc.

Stati d'animo: Voglia di far chiasso. Becerismo scatenato. Volgarità finalmente traboccante nell'impunità. Odi personali. Risentimenti postumi. Ebbrezza d'essere in molti contro pochi. Cretinismo furioso. Vigliaccheria in libertà. Sfogo degli inferiori contro i superiori. Paura di far parlare. Vendetta contro colpi vecchi e nuovi. Asinità. Bovità. Pecorinità. Maialità.

Alleati: La teppa fuori e le guardie dentro.

Feriti: Molti feriti in platea (dai loro compagni dei palchi).

Resultati: Noia, Stanchezza, Spese, Spolmonatura, Insulti reciproci fra gli spettatori. Fuga generale. (All'uscita i futuristi non trovarono un solo nemico e neppure per la città e per i caffè).

Figure 1.1. "Grande Serata Futurista," *Lacerba* (periodico quindicinale), Florence, Dec. 15, 1913, vol. 1, no. 24. pp. 281–96.

Loy comments on such Futurist performance from the satirical and critical distance of *Brontolivido*. After attending a *serata*, her alter ego Jemima is not convinced that the Futurists controlled the crowd, telling Brontolivido that he depends on the audience for his own identity and power. Her critique strikes a nerve, and he counters by forbidding her from attending any more Futurist *serate* or seeing her in public—another way to effectively "finish her off" ("Second Costa Visit," folder 8, image 5).

The verbal sparring in *Brontolivido* suggests Loy's own independence of mind regarding Futurism, demonstrating her attraction to satire--as in her poems--as a critical mode. While certainly stimulated by Italian Futurists and their animated Florentine stage between 1909 and 1915, Loy brought her own ideas and practices to the "canonical face of Futurist anima as trademarked by Marinetti" (Hayden, *Curious Disciplines* 15). She literally reimagined Marinetti's face, exhibiting three portraits of him and the painting *Dynamism of the Subconscious* (all lost) at the *First Free Exhibition of International Futurist Art* in Rome in 1914 (Ades 150). Loy's en dehors garde critique of Futurism drives multiple poetic and dramatic satires mocking the movement and its machismo, including "The Effectual Marriage," "Giovani Franchi," and "Man on a Platform," and several of her plays (see chapter 4). Although she adopts Futurist ideas and formal techniques in "Aphorisms on Futurism" (1914; see Fig. 1.2), the first Futurist Manifesto written in English, she supplants Futurist machismo with a more inclusive invitation to join in the effort to expand consciousness, calling for "rehabilitation" rather than destruction and supplanting "derision" with "respect" (LLB96 149, 152).

Even as they deliver criticisms of Futurism's explicit misogyny and arrogant machismo, Loy's intermedial responses to Futurism suggest how and why she, along with other feminist women, felt affinity with other aspects of the movement. Critics have tangled with this dynamic of critique and affinity. Harris notes that Loy's "poetic satires show that she was a formidable critic of the rabid and anxious misogyny of the Futurists"; however, it "is not possible [...] to understand Loy's formidable defence against the Futurist discourse on Woman without understanding her investment in it" (24). As Lucia Re observes:

> Critical interpreters of Italian Futurism, especially in the English-speaking world, have tended to be fascinated by its most violent and misogynistic

APHORISMS ON FUTURISM

DIE in the Past
Live in the Future.

THE velocity of velocities arrives in starting.

IN pressing the material to derive its essence, matter becomes deformed.

AND form hurtling against itself is thrown beyond the synopsis of vision.

THE straight line and the circle are the parents of design, form the basis of art; there is no limit to their coherent variability.

LOVE the hideous in order to find the sublime core of it.

OPEN your arms to the delapidated, to rehabilitate them.

YOU prefer to observe the past on which your eyes are already opened.

BUT the Future is only dark from outside.
Leap into it—and it EXPLODES with *Light.*

FORGET that you live in houses, that you may live in yourself—

FOR the smallest people live in the greatest houses.

BUT the smallest person, potentially, is as great as the Universe.

WHAT can you know of expansion, who limit yourselves to compromise?

HITHERTO the great man has achieved greatness by keeping the people small.

BUT in the Future, by inspiring the people to expand to their fullest capacity, the great man proportionately must be tremendous—a God.

LOVE of others is the appreciation of one's self.

MAY your egotism be so gigantic that you comprise mankind in your self-sympathy.

THE Future is limitless—the past a trail of insidious reactions.

LIFE is only limited by our prejudices. Destroy them, and you cease to be at the mercy of yourself.

TIME is the dispersion of intensiveness.

THE Futurist can live a thousand years in one poem.

13

Figure 1.2. Mina Loy, "Aphorisms on Futurism," *Camera Work*, no. 45, 1914, p. 13.

aspects, ignoring or dismissing its other sides and, in particular, the liberatory and empowering effect that its attack on bourgeois and traditional and moralist and repressive values had on a considerable number of women of various nationalities" (800).

According to Natalya Lusty, Marinetti actively recruited women: "In 1910, as part of his assiduous promotion of the Futurist movement across Europe, Marinetti read his manifesto at the London Lyceum Club for Women; included in the audience were many of London's most militant suffragettes" ("Sexing the Manifesto" 250). He even joined a 1912 suffragette march that culminated in a window-smashing campaign (250). But though Marinetti shared the suffragettes' "desire to eradicate the feminine ideal of the romantic woman," he was more attracted to "the anarchic energy of the suffragette's militancy" than committed to their political agenda (250–51). Loy's writing from this period, while encouraged by the Futurist discourse of freedom, nonetheless takes to task the foundations of "vilified femininity" undergirding its masculinized assumptions of individual freedom (Harris 25).

Loy's oft-quoted statement that she "woke up!" under the influence of the Futurists emphasizes her sense of their liberating impact, although by the time she met Marinetti and his cohorts, she had collected enough fuel to take that spark and forge a futuristic mindset and en dehors garde practice distinctly her own (Burke, *Becoming* 140). Loy's sense of newness was influenced *by* but also poetically located *in* the specifics of Florence and her place there, as shaped by class, race, nationality, and especially gender. Streets, churches, cafés, homes, and public spaces particular to this city offer lenses for viewing (observing) and *turning otherwise*, in poems rehabilitating traditional structures to move into the future. Observing her environs, Loy insisted on retaining the lyric "I" despised by Marinetti and identifying that "I" as a woman. The Florentine poems value the gendered subjectivity denigrated by Futurism, insisting on a voice decidedly female, and countering the bombast, sycophancy, and solipsism characterizing Futurist discourse (see chapter 2).[13]

The aesthetic principles derived from Loy's creative practice in these years realign Futurism's energies and consciousness with feminist critique and revision. Many of her early paintings and drawings resist

Futurism not only stylistically but also in their attentiveness to mothers and children, and even to breastfeeding. The material constraints of mothering also influenced her shift from painting to writing: with babies to feed and care for, pen and paper were much easier to access than an easel and paints. Loy's entrée into writing in the 1910s reflects her interest in American feminism, revealed in letters to Van Vechten and Dodge Luhan, and her awareness of Italian feminist discussions over the role and rights of women within the relatively new nation.[14] Rather than emphasizing aggression, speed, and conquest, Loy's Florence poems generate a socially aware dynamism attuned to class and gender through poetic forms that include visual techniques (rapid shifts, blank spaces, shifting margins, and abandoned punctuation) and lexical diversity (discourses of science, religion, natural observation, invented words, and word puns). Spinning outward from Futurism's center, Loy's poems realign its avant-garde discourse of battle and conquest, wonderfully enacted in "Sketch of a Man on a Platform" as the machismo of the "Man of absolute physical equilibrium," who "Has meddled in the more serious business / Of the battle-field" but is reduced in his "movements" to the "airy-fairy of the ballet" (LLB96 19). Referencing Marinetti's "recollections of his wartime experiences," the "bathetic juxtaposition" of war and ballet "registers a distinct imperviousness to Futurist rhetoric" (Hayden, *Curious Disciplines* 28). The displacement of war by ballet, while mocking, also happily foretells an en dehors garde strategy drawn from dance rather than battle.

Loy's Florentine en dehors garde writings center place and nation, not as jingoistic calls for war and action (à la Futurism) but as ideologically saturated sites to unpack old traditions of religion, gender, and class, and to promote a new formation through the act of critique. Being in-place and out-of-place at once—a British woman in Florence—makes Loy both an outsider to Italian nationalist discourse lacing Futurist proclamations and an insider to systems undergirding her native land's imperialism, so aptly taken up in the 1925 long poem "Anglo-Mongrels and the Rose."[15] Loy's thinking about nation and national identity in the Florence poems sets the stage for the later poem's more full-scale critique, as the early poems emphasize the role of the observer through adopting the distinctive perspective of the migrant, privileged by class and nationality, witnessing spectacles of social inequality. Moreover, an en dehors garde perspective shapes Loy's models and concepts of poetic and intellectual lineage; rather than abruptly casting off the past, Loy's nuanced gestures toward poetic self-placement mock a hypocritical retention of masculine authority attending avant-garde claims to break with the past. Loy's poems from this period map a feminist navigation of the tumultuous energies of modernity staged in this city famously enshrouded in history and tradition, as she encounters and performs "the new" *otherwise*—circling away from both the past and the futuristic avant-garde.

II. TAKING TURNS ON THE NEW YORK DADA STAGE

Just as Loy's first encounter with the Futurists has been romanticized as a sudden awakening, her move from Italy to New York has been mythologized as a flight from Futurism to Dada fueled by her feminist resistance to Futurist misogyny. But her relocation to New York was multifaceted, driven not only by her disaffection from Futurism, but also by more urgent personal and professional desires, namely: to make art, to make money, and to find love (see chapter 3). To support herself and her children as an artist, Loy needed to access receptive audiences for her innovative art and writing, and she believed she would find them in New York. By the time she emigrated to America in 1916, "New York, the capital of modernity, had acquired a mythic status," writes Carolyn Burke:

> More than a geographical place, it was the embodiment of the new, the site where the twentieth century was being unveiled and the frontier beyond which the future lay like terra incognita. New York soon acquired other meanings for [Loy]: as a vortex of energy, an urban parade, an artistic and intellectual community, and a refuge for those who, for diverse reasons, were the outcasts of Europe. (*Becoming* 212)

In Loy's imagination, New York was a place of freedom from prudish English social customs and Italian patriarchal constraints on women; it also promised distance and, she hoped, divorce from her controlling husband, Stephen Haweis. She anticipated that American audiences would be more receptive to her art, and the American commercial field would allow her to become financially independent. To a certain degree, she was right. According to Cristanne Miller, New York offered unprecedented opportunities for women writers to participate in "sizable, relatively stable literary communities," and the United States granted women more "access to education" and "control of property and personal finances" than any other country at the time (12). Perhaps most important for Loy, "American women did not sacrifice social respect by rejecting traditional roles" (13).

When Loy's ship sailed into New York Harbor on October 14, 1916, she thought the city looked like something she had only conceived in her imagination, describing it as "an architecture conceived in a child's dream," the skyscrapers soaring "with a glittering clamor of a myriad windows set like colored diamonds" (qtd. in Burke, *Becoming* 211). Loy's language conveys her romance with New York City as a place of opportunity, prosperity, and beauty. Her entrée proved swift and smooth: Frances Stevens met her at the pier, helped her secure a small apartment on West Fifty-Seventh Street, and took her to the evening gatherings at Louise and Walter Arensberg's duplex apartment at 33 West Sixty-Seventh Street, where Loy soon became a regular (Burke, *Becoming* 213–14). As Miller points out, "Loy enjoyed the potential for seamless integration into the mainstream population of every city she lived in: she was white, heterosexual, beautiful, a mother, femininely dressed, and (for the most part) identified as Christian" (161). She also spoke French and wrote outspoken poetry that was decidedly frank about sexual matters, qualities that endeared her to the Arensberg circle of French expatriates and American modernists.

Loy was welcomed into the coed coterie of proto-Dada artists who congregated at the Arensbergs' apartment, a rendezvous for Marcel Duchamp, Beatrice Wood, Carl Van Vechten, Donald Evans, Allen and Louise Norton, and others sympathetic to new and experimental art, including those associated with the little magazine *Others*—Alfred Kreymborg, Wallace Stevens, and William Carlos Williams were also frequent visitors. The fourteen-foot walls of the spacious duplex showcased the Arensbergs' modern art collection, including Henri Matisse's *Mlle Yvonne Landsberg*, Francis Picabia's *Physical Culture*, and Marcel Duchamp's *Nude Descending a Staircase*, while the fireplace was flanked by a sculpture by Constantin Brâncuși and an African figure. Parties at the Arenbergs' often lasted until morning, with midnight banquets of elegant hors d'oeuvres and desserts (Naumann 25–27). Stimulated and amused by the theatrical antics of this artistic salon, Loy incorporated the conversations, gestures, and performances she witnessed into her writings from this period, much of which she published in New York-based little magazines, including *Others*, *Rogue*, *The Blind Man*, and *The Dial*. Just as the Arensbergs' apartment provided a welcoming *place* to consort with like-minded artists, little magazines provided vital *places* for Loy's experiments to be received, recognized, and responded to, giving her the sense of connection with real audiences that she craved to validate her heterodox genius.

Dada was just emerging in New York at the time of Loy's arrival late in 1916. According to Francis Naumann, "a select group of artists in New York hear the term 'Dada' as early as November 1916, less than ten months after its invention by the Zurich group and even less than five months after the word first appeared in print" (192), though "a number of American artists had already embraced and employed the basic principles and ideologies that inspired their European colleagues" (10). Their principles and practices included a celebration of nonsense, chance, and childlike play; a subversion of tradition, propriety, and hierarchies; and an engagement with mass commercial culture and machine-made objects. Marcel Duchamp's pseudonymous submission of an overturned urinal, entitled *Fountain* and signed "R. Mutt," to the 1917 *Society of Independents Exhibition* has been mythologized as the epitome of Dada's challenge to the hallowed division between original art and manufactured objects. But as Ulrich Lehmann observes, "Dada's radicalism resided in much more than artful satire":

> Dada's founder Hans Arp had already dispelled the myth of subjective originality that was so dear to po-faced modernists in the West, by

declaring "Before Dada was there, there was Dada" and, indeed, a Zurich-based pharmaceutical company had promoted already in 1913 "Dada Hair Tonic and Lotion"; Francis Picabia had laid bare between 1913 and 1915 the mechanism of art world fashions by presenting in quick succession ironic collections of paintings that were tailored to Post-Impressionist or Cubist modes, and Kurt Schwitters used his professional work as typographer to deconstruct the boundaries between commercial imagery and ostensible "fine" art.

Roy Miki argues that Duchamp was a crucial generator and transmitter of Dadaist ideas from Europe to New York in the years prior to 1917 (37), while Steven Watson suggests that the catalyst of American Dada may have been an *Others* gathering in Grantwood in the fall of 1915, where Man Ray and Duchamp met for the first time (*Strange* 264–69). Although Loy was still in Italy during these early stirrings of Dada in America, her influence on its development was deeply felt and registered. Alfred Kreymborg and William Carlos Williams both mistakenly recall her participating in *Others*' Grantwood colony, even though she was still in Italy at the time (Churchill, *Little Magazine* 46). Even in her physical absence from New York, Loy's presence was manifest through her publications in little magazines, which channeled European sophistication, formal experimentation, and sexual daring. After she took residence in New York, Loy's influence was even more palpable: a regular at the Arensbergs' apartment, she was also a key player in the production of the proto-Dada magazine, *The Blind Man*, and collaborated with Man Ray on several portraits (see Fig. 1.3).

Loy developed an especially close and complex artistic kinship with Duchamp, who is often credited as the primary instigator and genius behind New York Dada. Although Carolyn Burke says Duchamp's "contrepetteries" (bilingual sexual puns) put Loy in an "awkward" position (*Becoming* 218), Roger Conover asserts that the two artists "had much in common besides a mattress" they shared with Beatrice Wood and two other revelers the night of the Blind Man's Ball, including "a distrust of doctrine and [...] distaste for bourgeois values" (Conover, "(Re)Introducing" 257). Marisa Januzzi contends that Duchamp was "the proximate irritant

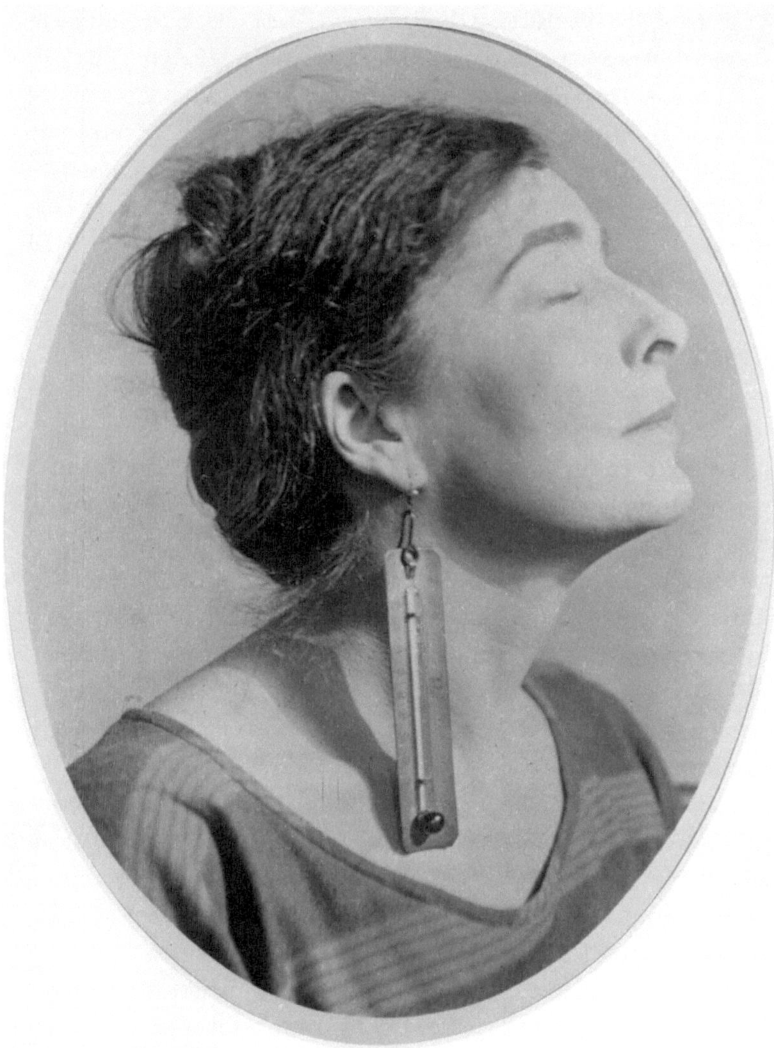

Figure 1.3. Photograph of Mina Loy by Man Ray, 1920.

for some of [Loy's] most creative and ultimately profound considerations of the verbal and visual terrain: the emergent mediascape in which Dada staked its claims" ("Dada" 596–97). Beyond their shared "interest in constructions and destructions of female virginity" (597), Loy must have recognized Duchamp's female alter ego, Rrose Sélavy, as a kindred spirit of her own pseudonymous masks: "Gina," "Imna," and "Ova," to name just a few. Man Ray's photograph of Rrose Sélavy (signed in 1920) bears a striking resemblance to a photo of Loy published in *The Little Review* in 1920 (Fig. 1.4), which, though unattributed, was likely taken by Man Ray.

Despite the formative roles of Loy and other women in Dada in both the United States and Europe, they remained marginal to the movement, eclipsed by charismatic male leaders and their fictional female alter egos. As Naomi Sawelson-Gorse explains, for all their dedication to rebellion, male Dadaists "maintained the status quo of the patriarchal socio-cultural judgments and codifications regarding gender of the late nineteenth-century bourgeois society in which they were born, and, in most instances, of Catholic upbringings" (xii). Women gained entry to the Dadaist constellation as "Dada's Mamas, a male artist's muse, sexual partner, sometimes even wife" (xii–xiii). This was unfortunately the case for Loy, who, if acknowledged in the annals of Dada, is cast as a hostess to the movement or caricatured as the trailing wife and wailing widow of Arthur Cravan, the celebrated boxer, Dada poet, and nephew of Oscar Wilde. Loy and Cravan met at the Blind Man's Ball in 1917 and fell in love.

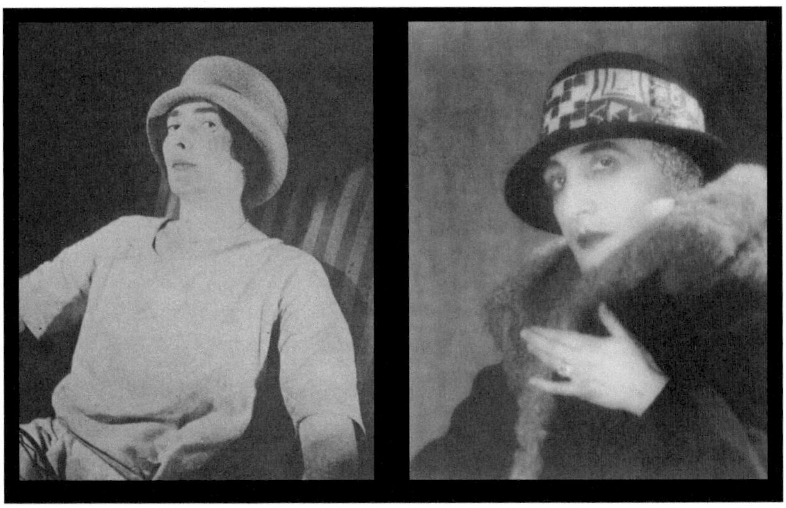

Figure 1.4. Mina Loy [L], *The Little Review*, vol. 7, no. 3, Sept.–Dec., 1920, p. 39; Rrose Sélavy (Marcel Duchamp) [R], photograph by Man Ray, 1923.

After securing a divorce from Haweis in 1917, Loy left the New York Dada scene in January 1918, traveling to Mexico City to marry Cravan, who had fled there to escape the draft. After he disappeared at sea en route to meet her in Buenos Aires, which they viewed as a safer haven, she searched for him in South America, eventually giving up and sailing back to England to give birth to their daughter in April 1919. Loy returned to New York in March 1920, remaining until the summer of 1921, when she returned to Europe to rejoin her children. During this period, she was far more preoccupied by her relationship with Cravan, his disappearance, the birth of their daughter, and her need to make a living than with the unruly antics of Dada.

While Loy focused on more urgent and practical concerns, Dada embraced her as a poster girl for the puckish movement: in the April 1921 issue of *New York Dada*, Man Ray and Marcel Duchamp announce a "coming-out party," a "grand socking cotillion" for the "Pug Debs" (pugilistic debutantes) at Madison Square Garden, casting Mina Loy in the role of hostess to the "pug" avant-garde (see Fig. 1.5). The announcement explains that Loy will introduce her male protégés—the Marsden

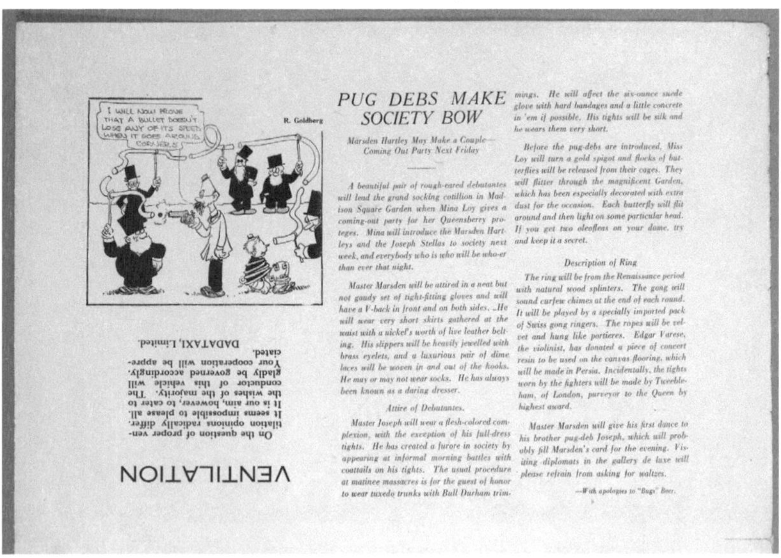

VENTILATION

On the question of proper ventilation opinions radically differ. It seems impossible to please all. It is our aim, however, to cater to the wishes of the majority. The conductor of this vehicle will gladly be governed accordingly. Your cooperation will be appreciated.

DADATAXI, Limited.

PUG DEBS MAKE SOCIETY BOW

Marsden Hartley May Make a Couple—Coming Out Party Next Friday

A beautiful pair of rough-eared debutantes will lead the grand socking cotillion in Madison Square Garden when Mina Loy gives a coming-out party for her Queensberry proteges. Mina will introduce the Marsden Hartleys and the Joseph Stellas to society next week, and everybody who is who will be who-er than ever that night.

Master Marsden will be attired in a neat but not gaudy set of tight-fitting gloves and will have a V-back in front and on both sides. He will wear very short skirts gathered at the waist with a nickel's worth of live leather belting. His slippers will be heavily jewelled with brass eyelets, and a luxurious pair of dime laces will be woven in and out of the hooks. He may or may not wear socks. He has always been known as a daring dresser.

Attire of Debutantes.

Master Joseph will wear a flesh-colored complexion, with the exception of his full-dress tights. He has created a furore in society by appearing at informal morning battles with coattails on his tights. The usual procedure at matinee massacres is for the guest of honor to wear tuxedo trunks with Bull Durham trimmings. He will affect the six-ounce suede glove with hard bandages and a little concrete in 'em if possible. His tights will be silk and he wears them very short.

Before the pug-debs are introduced, Miss Loy will turn a gold spigot and flocks of butterflies will be released from their cages. They will flitter through the magnificent Garden, which has been especially decorated with extra dust for the occasion. Each butterfly will flit around and then light on some particular head. If you get two oleofleas on your dome, try and keep it a secret.

Description of Ring

The ring will be from the Renaissance period with natural wood splinters. The gong will sound curfew chimes at the end of each round. It will be played by a specially imported pack of Swiss gong ringers. The ropes will be velvet and hung like portieres. Edgar Varese, the violinist, has donated a piece of concert resin to be used on the canvas flooring, which will be made in Persia. Incidentally, the tights worn by the fighters will be made by Tweebleham, of London, purveyor to the Queen by highest award.

Master Marsden will give his first dance to his brother pug-deb Joseph, which will probably fill Marsden's card for the evening. Visiting diplomats in the gallery de luxe will please refrain from asking for waltzes.

—With apologies to "Bugs" Baer.

Figure 1.5. "Pug Debs Make Society Bow," *New York Dada*, Apr. 1921.

Hartleys and Joseph Stellas—to society, adding glamour to the occasion by turning "a gold spigot" and releasing "flocks of exotic butterflies" ("Pug Debs").

Although relegated to a feminine role in this mock coming-out party, Loy had clearly gained the Dadaists' respect, perhaps due to her ability to spar creatively and romantically not only with the Dada icon Arthur Cravan, but also with the Futurist impresarios Marinetti and Papini. She was assigned a front-row seat at this Dadaist soirée, even if the role of "hostess" kept her out of the boxing ring. This ambivalent position—at once privileged and marginal—shaped Loy's en dehors garde response to the "pugilistic" avant-garde.

The New York Dada circle dispersed in 1921, around the time of Loy's second departure from New York. Duchamp and Man Ray returned to Paris, reuniting with Francis Picabia and Tristan Tzara in a vibrant Dada scene. But the Paris Dada group quickly splintered under the combined pressures of leadership struggles and anarchic energies, ending in a literal fistfight at a performance on July 6, 1923 (Rasula 196). This end was in keeping with the Dadaist embrace of boxing and boxers, and embodied the adversarial, pugilistic stance of the avant-garde. As the Dadaists mythologized Cravan and extended his legend, Loy became increasingly irked, especially by theories of Cravan's disappearance that suggested he sought to escape his marriage to her and implicitly cast her as the entrapping, pregnant wife (Burke, *Becoming* 284, 286, 301, 381). Wanting no part of these avant-garde escapades, Loy generated her own mythology. As Sandeep Parmar argues, Loy counters the mythologizing of Cravan by presenting her own "posthumous myth" of him in her unpublished autobiographical narrative, *Colossus*, likely begun in the early 1920s, where she portrays him not as proto-Dadaist but as the "father of modernity" (Parmar, "Mina Loy's 'Colossus'").

When Dada is viewed through an en dehors garde lens, Mina Loy's engagement with the movement appears not as a group affiliation (with the word's emphasis on brotherhood), but as a set of prods and practices that Loy took up and toyed with in her plays and prose of the mid-1910s, blending them with Futurist, popular, and traditional forms. Dada's humorous bent and playful spirit chimed with Loy's own eagerness to court audiences with her witty, innovative writings, and its resistance

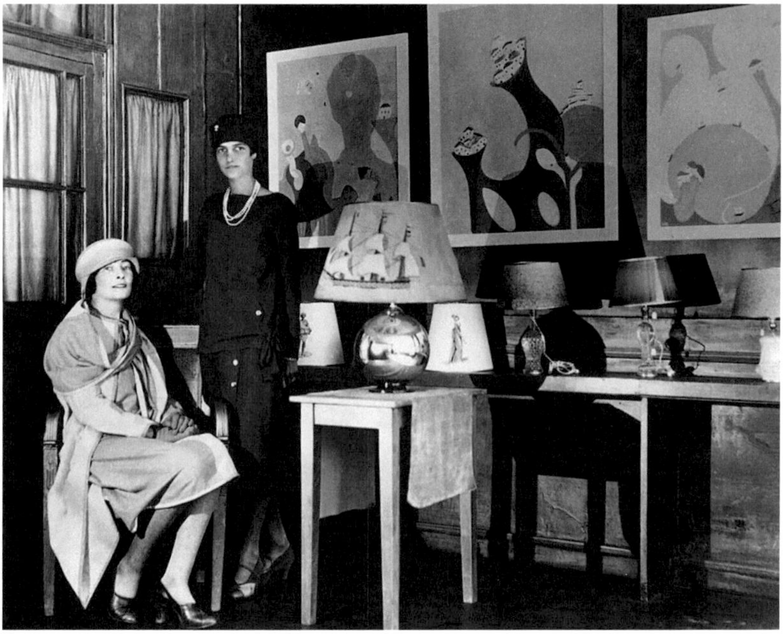

Figure 1.6. Mina Loy (seated) and Peggy Guggenheim (standing) in Loy's lamp shop, Laurence Vail paintings on wall, circa 1926.

to hierarchies accorded with her democratic leanings. Readers of *Rogue*, *Others*, *The Blind Man*, and *The Dial* proved to be her most appreciative audiences. Loy was less successful cultivating larger popular and commercial audiences in New York. Her relocation to Europe to reunite with her children and later open a lampshade shop (see Fig. 1.6) was less a shift in affiliation from Dada to Surrealism than another round of en dehors garde turns by a now forty-one-year-old, divorced, widowed, single mother in search of viable places where she could express herself as an artist, support her family financially, and exhibit her innovative artwork.

III. RETURNING TO PARIS AND NEW YORK: IN THE SHADOWS OF SURREALISM

Loy left New York Dada for Europe in Summer 1921: after extended stays in Florence and Berlin and a visit to Vienna where she met and drew

Sigmund Freud, Loy settled in Paris in spring 1923, where she would live until late 1936. Loy worked from 1931–1936 as the Paris agent for Julien Levy's New York gallery, a center for Surrealism in the United States. While French Surrealism had influenced American literary and artistic culture since the early 1920s, New York galleries like Levy's—aided by Parisian agents like Loy—played a pivotal role in the transatlantic movement of Surrealist art and ideas in the late 1920s and 1930s.[16] The literal relocation of many European Surrealists to New York during World War II led to dynamic exchanges with American artists, poets, galleries, and publishers, establishing Surrealism on firmer ground in American culture, and invigorating the postwar US avant-garde. Part of this larger migration, Loy made New York her home from late 1936 until 1953.[17] Loy's travels between Paris and New York invite a fresh look at this history from the perspective of an influential yet marginalized participant in the Surrealist scene. Although Loy played an important role in Surrealism's transatlantic career, she is missing from most Surrealist histories and exhibitions, and until recently, she was omitted from studies of women and Surrealism.[18]

In Paris, Loy witnessed the combative demise of Paris Dada and the equally provocative beginning of the Surrealist movement, inaugurated by the 1924 publication of poet André Breton's *Surrealist Manifesto*. Most figures involved in the French Surrealist movement had been involved in Paris Dada, and while the movements shared an anti-bourgeois stance and an interest in the anarchic energies of the irrational mind, Surrealism under the guidance of Breton would take a decidedly Freudian turn.[19] Surrealism, defined by Breton as "Psychic automatism in its pure state [...]. Dictated by thought, in the absence of any control exercised by reason, exempt from any aesthetic or moral concern" (*Manifestoes* 26), was devoted to expressing in conscious life the uncensored expression of unconscious thoughts, wishes, and desires. Like Freud, the Surrealists explored "the omnipotence of dream" and other forms of thought unconstrained by reason (*Manifestoes* 26), but whereas Freud sought a therapeutic outcome in the conscious recognition of unconscious wishes and desires, the Surrealists conversely sought in dreams a deepened perspective on and experience of the real: as Breton stated, "I believe in the future resolution of these two states, dream and reality, which are seemingly so contradictory, into a kind of absolute reality, a surreality, if one may so speak" (*Manifestoes* 14). Surrealists employed experimental methods and techniques to tap the unconscious and to convey the interpenetration of dream and reality, irrationality and reason, the unconscious and conscious mind (see Fig. 1.7).

Loy did not formally join the Surrealist movement in Paris, instead moving fluidly between a number of overlapping circles, described by Carolyn Burke as "a group comprised of British and American writers, their French counterparts, and assorted Dadaists or Surrealists" (*Becoming* 328). Loy's connections to the Futurists in Florence and Dadaists in New York, her status as widow of Dada idol Arthur Cravan, her reputation as an artist and poet, and her role as Paris agent for Julien Levy's New York gallery, facilitated her entry into Surrealist circles in Paris. With one foot in Surrealist circles and one outside, Loy's liminal, en dehors garde position reflected her aesthetic interest in the movement as well as her feminist skepticism and critical detachment. Loy was inspired by many elements of Surrealism: the Surrealists' explicit treatment of psychology, sexuality, and the irrational, unconscious, and mystical-spiritual dimensions of experience opened up a new means of exploring the relation between reality and dream, the material and the unseen forces structuring everyday life and the artistic imagination, which was a long-standing interest of Loy's. Yet even as she found aesthetic inspiration in Surrealist ideas and methods, Loy recognized the sexism of the movement, an uncomfortable echo of Futurist misogyny and the patriarchal ideology of Dada. As with Futurism in Florence and Dada in New York and Paris, most women remained on the margins of Surrealism's official ranks. Whitney Chadwick points out:

> Almost without exception, women artists viewed themselves as having functioned independently of Breton's inner circle and the shaping of Surrealist doctrine [...]. Their involvement was defined by personal relationships, networks of friends and lovers, not by active participation in an inner circle dominated by Breton's presence. (11, 55)[20]

Despite the misogyny of Breton and other Surrealist figures, women's participation and interest is crucial to the history of Surrealism and its en

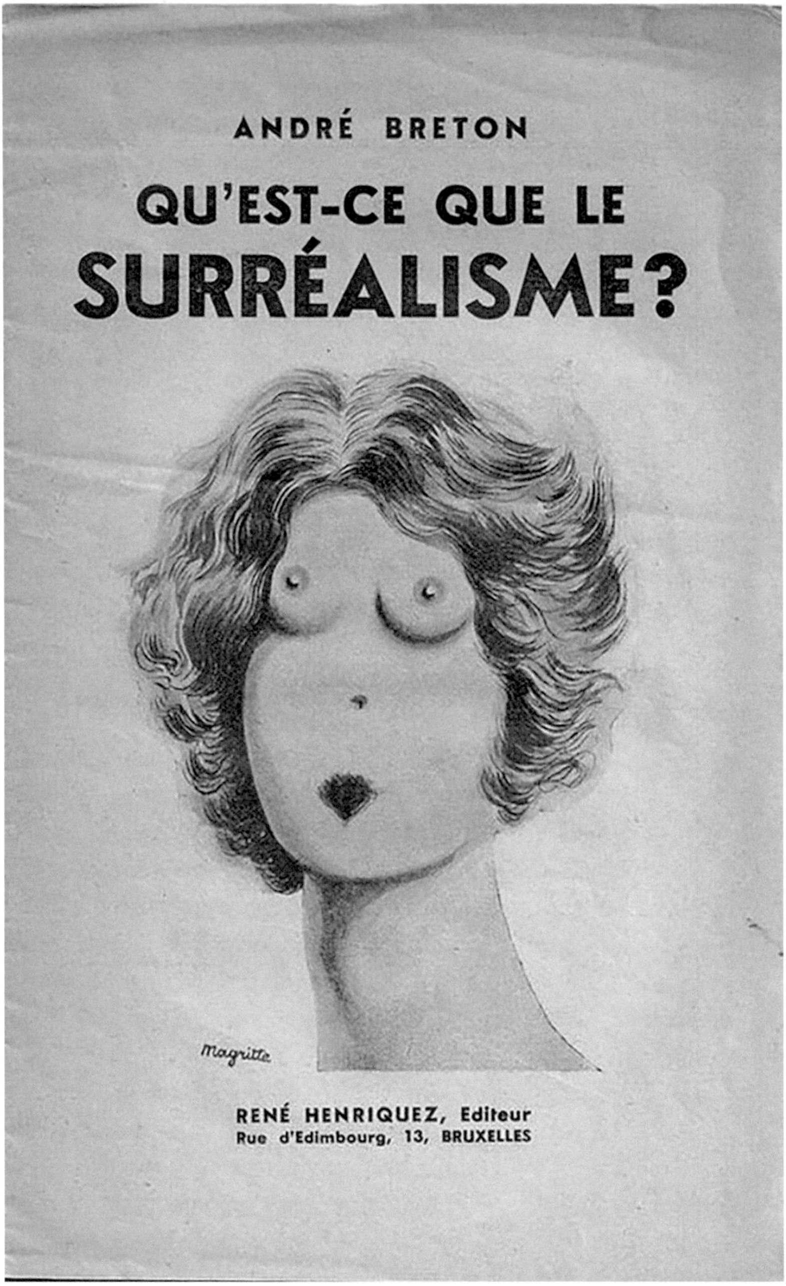

Figure 1.7. André Breton, *Qu'est-ce que le Surréalisme*, illustration by René Magritte, Paris: René Henriquez, 1934.

dehors garde spin-offs. Indeed, in 1931 Loy wrote to her daughter Joella and son-in-law Julien Levy that Surrealism was the only avant-garde movement that "could be wholly satisfactory" (qtd. in Fort and Arcq 34). As Penelope Rosemont argues, although the early Surrealist movement was male-dominated and many male Surrealists were not feminists, they were nevertheless "the irreconcilable enemies of feminism's enemies, and thus in many ways could be considered feminism's allies. They concentrated their attacks on the apparatus of patriarchal oppression: God, church, state, family, capital, fatherland, and the military" (xliv). Just as Futurism inspired a number of feminist suffragettes, Surrealism offered a "sympathetic milieu" to a

> group of women who dared to renounce the conventions of their upbringing, who attempted to find some consonance between their ideas and their lives, and who embarked on the difficult path to artistic maturity at a time when few role models existed for women in the visual arts and there was little encouragement for women to establish professional identities for themselves. (Chadwick 11, 9)

Working as an artist, writer, gallery agent, and curator, Loy was able to maintain a complex, en dehors garde position as both insider and outsider to Parisian Surrealism: she adapted aspects of Surrealist aesthetics into her art, designs, and writing, and played a pivotal role in the transatlantic movement of Surrealist art, even as she articulated her own critical, feminist slant on the movement and resisted explicit affiliation with it.

Loy was part of a broader effort to widen Surrealism's meaning: from the movement's outset, both Georges Ribemont-Dessaignes and René Crevel defined Surrealism as a revolutionary *spirit*, which they distinguished from its status as a *movement* controlled by Breton, a distinction that would prove important not only to disaffected French Surrealists but also to marginalized en dehors garde artists like Loy. Many women artists resisted any formal alliance with the movement, even as they participated in Surrealist exhibitions, contributed to Surrealist periodicals, and engaged with Surrealist ideas and techniques in their own work (Chadwick 10).[21] Surrealism's democratic ideal—what Breton called a dedication to a "perfect freedom" ("Surrealism" 22)—although inhibited by Breton's prejudices within the movement, was capacious enough that it enabled Loy and other marginalized artists to adapt and transform it. Surrealism's history in the twentieth century was one of increasing inclusiveness, as it traveled and influenced related movements in the United States, Latin America, the Caribbean, Africa, Egypt, and Japan, producing en dehors garde variants such as Feminist Surrealisms and Black Surrealisms.[22]

Surrealism provided Loy not only with new inspiration to explore the unconscious and mystical dimensions of experience, but offered an expanded "poetic" idiom for exploring the relations between poetry, visual art, fashion, and commercial design. Like Loy, and the Futurists and Dadaists who preceded them, the Surrealists adopted an intermedial approach to artmaking, but explicitly theorized this approach as a broadened understanding of poetry and the poetic. As Loy explored the relation between matter and spirit, the real and the "irreal" across her visual art, writing, and commercial designs, she engaged the Surrealists' broad, interdisciplinary understandings of poetry, and their use of "poetic" techniques of juxtaposition and hybrid mixture in their poetry, art, gallery installations, and exhibitions.

The distinct streets and economies of Paris and New York shaped Loy's literal and aesthetic navigations of Surrealism. In her poetry, essays, and autobiographical novel *Insel*, alongside her lamps, objects, paintings, and assemblages, Loy's experiments with verbal and visual media in Paris and New York were deeply informed by her material navigations of place. In both cities Loy found the materials for her art and designs in cast-off objects, as she picked through the flea markets of Paris and the trash heaps of the Bowery. Rare documentary film footage of Loy shopping at a Paris flea market demonstrates the importance of this urban collecting to her artistic practice (see Fig. 4.4). In Paris, Loy would transform particular locales through the dislocating light of her artisanal lampshades, and through the less tangible light of dream, the imagination, and the unconscious, rendered in her paintings, poems, and narratives of this time. When Loy moved from Paris to lower Manhattan, the economic deprivation and suffering of the homeless men and women living on the streets of the Bowery heightened her attention to the painful constrictions of the urban environment, resulting in poetry and collage constructions built from materials found on the urban streets that demonstrate what Linda Kinnahan terms "a form of urban documentary with inflections of Surrealist and Dadaist modes" (*Mina Loy, Twentieth-Century Photography* 124).

As Loy engaged and transformed Surrealism from its margins, she extended her interest in innovative sites of performance to include alternative sites and forms of exhibition and display. The history recorded in Loy's alternative exhibitions and analyzed in chapter 4 provides an important guide to the en dehors garde: Loy joined the Surrealists in their efforts to reimagine museum displays, but with a feminist twist. The Surrealists creatively defied the official museum's rational, didactic aims by creating exhibitions, galleries, and collections that transformed the museum into a stage for Surrealist-inspired ends, including the fusion of dream and reality, disorienting perspectives on the real, urban wandering, the pursuit of pleasure and desire, and the merging of art with everyday life (Kachur 79–81; Rosenbaum, "Brides" 1–2). In Paris and New York, Loy's alternative exhibition spaces were shaped by her need to make a living, her marginalization by and critique of the Surrealist movement, and her melding of her role as artist-poet with her roles as gallery agent, designer-inventor, and shopkeeper. In her writing, painting, collage constructions, and commercial designs created in both cities, Loy made use of available architectural spaces of exhibition (apartments, galleries, lamp shop, street) alongside "virtual" or "imaginary" spaces of exhibition (writing and artwork). In Loy's en dehors garde reimaginings of the museum, physical and architectural locations and virtual spaces often overlapped, resulting in a layered, dynamic understanding of exhibitionary space, through which Loy offered pointed commentary on the ways in which economic and social realities impinged on both the real and the surreal.

*

The three chapters that follow examine Loy's poetry, plays, prose, and art from the 1910s to the late 1950s, charting her navigations of Futurism, Dada, and Surrealism in greater detail while shifting the emphasis from these movements to the various places, stages, and exhibition spaces in which she conducted her en dehors garde experiments, ever in search of artistic liberty, personal fulfillment, and economic sustenance.

CHAPTER TWO

LOY'S ITALIAN BAEDEKER

Mapping a Feminist En Dehors Garde (1907–1916)

Linda A. Kinnahan

PREAMBLE: TOURING WITH THE EN DEHORS GARDE

> *Florence* (170 ft.), Italian *Firenze*, formerly *Fiorenza*, from the Latin *Florentia*, justly entitled "la bella", is situated in 43°46'N. latitude, and 11°21'E. longitude, on both banks of the *Arno*, an insignificant river except in rainy weather, in a charming valley of moderate width, picturesquely enclosed by the foothills of the Apennines on the N. and by the spurs of the *Monti di Chianti* [...] on the S.
>
> (Baedeker's Northern Italy 465–466)

> Firenze is Florence
> Some think it is a woman with flowers in her hair
> But NO   it is a city with stones on the streets
>
> —Mina Loy, "Giovanni Franchi" (LLB96 30)

Welcome to Mina Loy's Italy, a poetic tour inspired by her art and early poetry created in Florence, where she lived from 1907 through 1916. This period signals a pronounced interest in gender and class, especially in poems charting charged relations between modern energies and a still-present past illuminated within contexts of the Italian city's environs and figures. Florence itself becomes subject to an en dehors garde feminism expressed across these poems, as in Loy's telling refusal of the gendered language and imagery in popular Baedeker tour guides associating Florence with mythic feminine beauty. In the prefatory quotes above, the first from Karl Baedeker's 1906 *Italy: Handbook for Travelers, Northern Italy* and the second from Loy, the poet's reference to the city's name rejects Baedeker's traditional idealization of the feminine place and name of Florence, and she renders the "fairest flowers" of "la bella" as a "city with stones on the street."[1] Casting aside the mythic resonance of the city's name, she opts for the grounded materiality of woman's experience, an en dehors garde recognition of actual stones rather than imagined flowers.

The significance of place infusing Loy's poetic emergence draws upon diverse cultural pasts and presents surrounding her in Florence. As Laura Scuriatti remarks, "Florence was a space of complex cultural exchanges, where ideas about cosmopolitanism, national identity, and culture were discussed, and transnational projects implemented in parallel with specific versions of modernist and avant-garde experimentation" (*Mina Loy's Critical Modernism* 303). The streets, gardens, eateries, palaces, and churches in Loy's Italian poems signpost artistic, social, and gendered cartographies of Florence's early-century avant-garde, remapping the poet's development as en dehors garde innovation.

Loy-like, this chapter's remapping attends to but decenters the influence of Futurism that has dominated discussions of her early work, recontextualizing this innovative period in terms of place. In the experimental Italian poems, Loy creates a distinctive feminist poetics, positing the woman poet differently from the confrontational militarism of the avant-garde, so emphatically manifested by Florentine Futurism. Traveling geographies of gender, the poems assume the en dehors garde position; rather than the confrontational energy of conquest characterized by the Futurist avant-garde she encountered in Italy, the en dehors artist steps from and toward the outside, the margins, the peripheries to understand the lay of the land, not to conquer or relinquish it. Her own awareness of her en dehors position—coming from the outside as a British woman observing Italian places and people, creating herself as a visual artist and poet—informs her encounters with avant-garde formations in these Italian places.

Constituting her earliest poetic ventures, the Florentine poems suggest a poet marking a place for herself within an innovative circuit of new poetic techniques and practices, while also querying her place within or in relation to enabling forebears. Layering time and space, these poems approach poetic lineage through indirect, outward gestures that animate explorations of new and future-oriented poetic possibilities. Modifying the Futurist disdain for the past and calls to reject its influence while offering pointed critiques of tradition, Loy allows for the animation and refreshment of lineage rather than the totality of rejecting the past. In nuanced references to Italy's attraction to earlier British poets (Browning, Shelley, Milton), or to the city as home to innovative thinkers like Galileo, the Florentine poems inject a sub rosa inquiry into what lineage means in this modern century and how women's relative erasure from poetic tradition mitigates their relationship to authorizing lineages. Maintaining a distrust of authority, Loy's constructed lineal networks suggest temporal connections that challenge authority, working to rehabilitate the meaning of poetic lineage, particularly in throwing off aspects of cultural, political, and economic systems of male dominance infecting both conventional models of a poetic past and her materially informed poetic experiences in the present.

This chapter explores the importance of place and mapping to her emerging modernism in Italy (1907–1916). Comprising an imaginary Italian Baedeker, Loy's Florentine and Italy-inspired poems offer choreographies of place alternative to both literary and popular accounts of Italy, employing a modern feminist compass. Loy often used "maps and Baedekers" to "symbolize the quest that shaped her transits through the modernist landscape" and her "self-discovery" (Burke, *Becoming* vi–vii). Taken together, these poems comprise a Baedeker guide to her early en dehors garde steps.

A NOTE REGARDING THIS CHAPTER'S METHOD

Taking a cue from place references in Loy's poems, this chapter plays on the Baedeker genre through combining personal travel writing with research and textual analysis. Tracing Loy's Italy—her residences, homes of friends, gathering spots, galleries, landmarks, vacations, and views—I offer occasional directions that guide travelers to places relevant to Loy's Florence years; distinguished by shaded blocks of print, these directions most often reflect my own notes taken while exploring on foot and occasionally by other means, as well as research into places I have not personally visited. Throughout this chapter, I also quote excerpts from the 1906 Baedeker as guiding context for visiting these places while reading Loy's poems, in effect reading the 1906 Baedeker next to an imagined tour of Loy's Florence to capture the resonance and material presence of cultural pasts and presents by which she was surrounded. This approach purposefully deviates from a standard academic style to foreground a more experiential immersion within place—the textual place of the poems and the geographical places the poems reference—as a way of close reading texts and engaging scholarly conversations. Coupling the 1906 Baedeker guide with my own travel writing aims to encourage a materiality of place inspired by Loy's own mapping tendencies in poems composed as guidebooks to her feminist poetics.

Let us amble through the stony streets of Florence and the Italian locales that Loy visited. Let us consider the tour as an en dehors garde experiment, linking place to an emerging feminist poetics—

I. MAPPING FLORENCE: FIRST TOUR, VISITING LOY AT HOME

Villa Life in the Arcetri

With a Baedeker guidebook in hand, English-speaking arrivals in early twentieth-century Florence entered the city with a resource to its history, layout, and all manner of services. Information-rich pages and delicate pink foldout maps not only introduce the visitor to historic sites but also advise on daily, practical matters: navigating the city and region by electric or steam tramways, omnibuses, and cabs; finding Havana cigars or confectioners or cafés; locating the post office, telegraph office, and British consulates; visiting English-speaking churches, physicians, and chemists; or discovering the best baths, shops, booksellers, photographs, and photographic materials (significant, one would imagine, to Loy's photographer husband). Culturally, Baedeker pages offer recommendations for artists and teachers of music and Italian; for theaters, festivals, and the flower market.

Loy's poems signal that navigating the Italian city, as a British-speaking woman, was as much a matter of language as of physical orientation. In "Giovanni Franchi," the speaker's linguistic translations, necessitated by place, suggest the usefulness of an English-language tour book like the Baedeker for the English speaker in Italy (Prescott 20):

> We have read of
> Trattoria meaning eating-house
> Piazzas or squares (LLB96 30)

Loy's navigations of poetic language, as she moved between painting and writing in Florence, suggest how the concurrence of language shifts (from English to Italian) and geographic shifts (from England and France to Italy) provide critical context for her shifts and oscillations between media, from canvas to page, from visual modalities to verbal.

Upon first arriving at Florence's busy Stazione Centrale Santa Maria Novella, early twentieth-century English-speaking visitors consulted the Baedeker to find where to meet the "omnibuses" or a "cab," forewarned that "there is often a scarcity of conveyances" (Baedeker 457).[2] In the winter of 1907 with her husband Stephen Haweis, Loy might well have descended from their train to carefully unfold the pale pink Florence map inserted in the guidebook's copious chapter on the city (see Fig. 2.1). Tracing the route from the train station to their new home in Arcetri, in the hills south of the Arno, she might choose to cross the Ponte alla Carraia across the Arno River and take the Via dei Serragli to the Porta Romana, or perhaps traverse the Ponte Santa Trinita to the Via Maggio and, at the Pitti Palace, head west on the Via Romana to the Porta Romana. Whichever route was chosen, Loy and Haweis took a horse-drawn carriage to travel through town, southward across the Arno to a hill dotted with villas and splendid views high above the city, to arrive in the Arcetri area (Burke, *Becoming* 105–06). Their new home was a small villa called the Villino l'Ombrellino, complete with a small tower that Burke describes as its "distinguishing feature" and feeling a bit isolated from the bustle of the city, perched at no. 25 Via del Pian dei Giullari (now no. 50, with a second entrance at no. 54, formerly no. 23; see Fig. 5.2).[3] In her semi-autobiographical novel *Esau Penfold*, Loy describes the discomforts of the home inhabited by Esau (Haweis) and "little Ova" (Loy):

> Esau Penfold's house was a small cottage in this slum built without excavations on the damp earth
> for aesthetic economy the rough uneven inner walls were whitewashed – – – the damp crept up and blurred their virginity and in winter they wept from their surfaces.[4]

Pregnant with the child of her lover, Henri Joël Le Savoureux, the Parisian doctor who treated her for "neurasthenia after the death of Oda [her first child]" from meningitis, Loy had agreed to move to Florence to avoid scandal if Haweis consented to claim the child (Burke, *Becoming* 102). He demanded that they relocate from Paris to the Villino l'Ombrellino when a friend offered them her remaining lease, lasting until summer.[5] In Florence, they found an "Italian city with a strong English accent" and a well-populated Anglo-American community (Harold Acton, qtd. in Burke, *Becoming* 106).

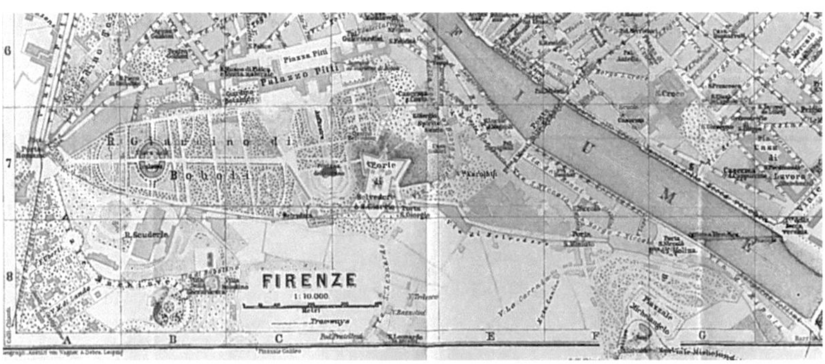

Figure 2.1. Map of Florence, Baedeker's *Italy: Handbook for Travelers, Northern Italy*, 1906.

To find Loy's first Florentine home, walk uphill on Costa San Giorgio in the Oltrarno area south of the river Arno (see directions in following section). Pass Galileo's home, Casa di Galileo Galilei, to arrive at Porta San Giorgio. Continue on to Via di San Leonardo to enter the Arcetri neighborhood, which will turn into the Via del Pian dei Giullari at a fork in the road (there is a bus stop nearby). Look for a red building with a tower, with the main entrance at no. 50 (formerly no. 25) and a second entrance at no. 54 (formerly no. 23).

In those first months, the new city felt isolating for the pregnant Loy. The couple—or sometimes just Stephen—sought acquaintances with other English residents. By spring of 1908, Haweis rented a studio on Costa San Giorgio in the Oltrarno section of the city. After the birth of daughter Joella, the family moved into a rented apartment in this area and subsequently purchased a home on Costa San Giorgio. From that point on, Loy increasingly found herself amid the jostling energies of avant-garde invaders—Futurist and otherwise—in Renaissance-laden Florence.

The Oltrarno/Across the Arno

Let us explore the charm and liveliness of living "across the Arno," where Loy lived on the Costa San Giorgio. By the early 1910s, the Oltrarno proved to be a fruitful space for Loy. A pleasant stroll from the Costa San Giorgio to the Centro, or city center, transported her to lively gatherings of artists and writers or led them to her studio. Tracing Loy's steps, your own tour—perhaps starting at the Duomo or the Giubbe Rosse, a café and gathering place for artists and writers at the time—descends quickly to the river Arno, where you may choose from multiple bridges to reach Florence's "left bank," as the Baedeker labels the district that made up "one-fourth" of the city Loy inhabited (536). Crossing the Ponte Santa Trinita lands you near the peaceful domed basilica of Santo Spirito, a Renaissance church begun in 1436. However, for the most direct route to the Costa San Giorgio, the hilly street where Loy and Haweis lived, amble across the Ponte Vecchio, which the 1906 Baedeker describes as a "quaint and picturesque" bridge, "flanked with shops, which have belonged to the goldsmiths since the 14th century" (537, 538). Stepping from the Ponte

Vecchio into the Oltrarno, enter streets of busy shops, cafés, and restaurants within a few hundred yards of the Pitti Palace and the entrance to the expansive Boboli Gardens.

To find Costa San Giorgio, you have two quick options after crossing the Ponte Vecchio into the Oltrarno area. For the first, turn left soon after the bridge, onto the Via de' Bardi, running parallel to the Arno. After a short block, a set of steps on the right takes you to Costa San Giorgio. Turn left at the top of the steps and climb the hilly street. Or, rather than taking the steps, start your climb up the Costa San Giorgio from its lowest origin point. Just after the Ponte Vecchio, cross directly over the Via de' Bardi and almost immediately enter the Piazza Santa Felicita on the left. The Costa San Giorgio begins at a narrow opening between two buildings in a far corner of the piazza.

On our tour of Loy's neighborhood, let us climb the hilly Costa San Giorgio, winding upward through the Oltrarno. On the same side of the Arno as the Arcetri area, but a steep descent from the hilltop Villino l'Ombrellino when coming toward the city and the river, Haweis's studio location likely helped prompt the couple's subsequent move to the same street later that summer to a rented apartment. In 1910, Loy and Haweis bought a home at no. 54 (now no. 60), midway up the hilly street, near the Chiesa di San Giorgio alla Costa, or Church of Saint George.[6] The couple purchased the home with the help of Loy's father (although, as was customary for the time, the house was in Haweis's name), following the births of daughter Joella and son Giles. The top floor, fronted by shuttered windows, was transformed into two studios (Burke, *Becoming* 118).

As you walk between rows of three-storied houses with shutters on windows flung open or closed tight, the close confines of the cobbled street continue to resonate with Loy's images from over a century ago. Street life provided material for her earliest poems; *how* these poems observe the people and activities on this street through the eyes and impressions of a female speaker configures and questions cultural authority, marking an emerging en dehors garde exploration of class, gender, and nationality. Such questions arise in two poems about the street, "The

Costa San Giorgio" and "Costa Magic," each part of the 1914 triptych titled "Italian Pictures" (which also includes "July in Vallombrosa," to be discussed in a later section).

In "The Costa San Giorgio" (first published in *The Trend*, November 1914), the speaker identifies herself as an outsider, one of the "English [who] make a tepid blot / On the messiness / Of the passionate Italian life-traffic / Throbbing the street" (LLB96 10). This stress on place, gender, and national identity refashions a Futurist influence through feminist means. The vitality and energy of the street, roiling with movement and sensory sensations, chimes with Futurist painting. Boccioni's *The Street Enters the House* (1912), for example, models the "dynamic sensation" valued by the Futurists, challenging "the limits of classical perspective by breaking the barrier between the woman's domestic space and the scene she sees from the balcony" (Burke, *Becoming* 153). Similarly evoking such sensation, the poem stages quick narrative vignettes. These snippets alternate with rapid collocations of fragments, blank spaces, synesthetic evocations, and geometries of light. A literal market and loud voices advertising "Oranges half-rotten" or "ICE CREAM" animates street commerce, as do the "hips of women [that] sway / Among the crawling children they produce." Markers of class make up the life-traffic, from references to women-as-producers to the rotten produce to the "consumptive / Left outside" with a broken chair; there is the "smell of small cooking" and "bandy legs" and shutters "clacking" (LLB96 10–12).

The poem's commerce with Futurism caught its first editor's notice, and that of subsequent critics, although Loy was hesitant (but practical) about the affiliation.[7] Publishing the poem in the November 1914 issue of *The Trend*, Carl Van Vechten introduced Loy as a poet "in sympathy with the Italian school of Futurists," who "has interested herself in the Italian Futurists, led by F. T. Marinetti, and for whom she has renounced the brush and taken up the pen" (ii, 101, qtd. in Burke, *Becoming* 17). In response, most likely, to Van Vechten's claim of Futurist affiliation, she signaled her ambivalent sense of being on the periphery, both within and without the Futurist movement: "I am so interested to find I am a sort of pseudo Futurist—but very good for advertising—couldn't I become an absolutist or something as I evolve?" (Loy, undated letter to Van Vechten, qtd. in Burke, *Becoming* 178). Willing to be associated with the Futurists in part as a commercial approach to attracting audiences, Loy's response suggests a classic en dehors garde position and strategy: on the margins of Futurism (a "pseudo") and eager to advertise her work.[8]

Not lost on Van Vechten, Loy's ambivalence toward this aggressive avant-gardism, particularly in relation to gender, manifests in the poem's prioritization of gender issues. Recalling a conversation at this time, he records that "Ducie Haweis" "gave sanction" to the opinion that Marinetti "loves noise and he loves war because it is noisy," and observed that she added "that the futurists also were violent against women" (Van Vechten 116). While slyly engaging techniques particular to Futurism, the poem suggests its rhetorical complicity with social, psychological, and physical violence toward women. The poem's women remain trapped in the social roles placed upon them, their bodies literally and metaphorically reduced: bodies of mothers are devoted to breeding; unmarried women have "little to do" but wait for "matrimonial beds"; the female "consumptive" is immobilized while others walk past her (LLB96 11, 10). "Bits of bodies" watch from windows, suggestively like the virgins or their keepers in "Virgins Plus Curtains Minus Dots," as the domestic space is prepared for the market goal of marriage, with matrimonial bedding and "china virgin" awaiting. Strikingly, anything endangering the market (people? things?) or that "might have contaminated intimacy," is thrown "OUT / Onto the middle of the street" (LLB96 11–12). Cultural authority, outside of traditional expectations, eludes the women in this poem. The church and masculine militarism blur, as they do on the actual street's conjunction of the church, Chiesa di San Giorgio alla Costa, and a military barracks just up the hill from Loy's home: "The church hits the barracks / Where / The greyness of marching men / Falls through the greyness of stone" (LLB96 10). The street grants a grim kind of agency to men within a market regulating gender. Items (and people) not fitting the market are abandoned.

As the speaker moves among the castoffs, she also notices her separateness. The street is no mere backdrop but a visual spatializing of economies of gender and class that the speaker can choose to join or shut out, suggesting how the act of witness complicates boundaries of voyeurism, othering, and engagement. The prose-poem "Summer Night in a Florentine Slum," written several years later and discussed below, amplifies this tension through allusions to British privilege that, once bared, are explicitly held in contradictory stance to the closeness the speaker feels to the women who speak to her from the street.

The companion street poem "Costa Magic," the third in the sequence of "Italian Pictures," complicates the observer's position by moving her more actively onto the streets, where currencies between male power, violence, and Futurist techniques play out in deadly fashion. The poem's referencing of Futurist painting, in its rapid shifts from word to word, often without connectives, produce a geometric fracturing of line, stanza, and page, enacting a feminist and verbal adaptation of Futurist visuals. At the time of writing this poem, Loy is also experimenting with Futurist painting techniques in paintings now lost.[9] Men prove particularly ominous amid these fractures and dynamisms. In the poem, a young neighbor girl, Cesira, takes ill after her father disapproves of her pending marriage. Male power, in the form of the father, the speaker's husband, and the doctor, circulates between house and street, figured as an "unnatural [...] bewitching" magic harming the girl, aligning veiled suggestions of incest alongside overt demonstrations of male power. Faced with this street drama, the speaker joins a feminine "we"—her neighbor, an aunt, the girl, and a "wise woman"—to try to help the girl, who becomes "my girl" to the speaker who enters a female "life-traffic" to combat, however futilely, the male street magic as the girl dies. The speaker moves from observer to engagement, joining the community of women forming to care for Cesira. This female community rises in response to the patriarch who looms over the street scene in disapproval of his daughter's plans to marry.

In their waiting and their trust in the wise woman's words about a magical tree's revelation, the community of women implicitly share the speaker's condemnation of the father's "unnatural" relation with his daughter, a "Bewitching" rife with erotic, incestuous suggestions:

> It is unnatural in a Father
> Bewitching a daughter
> Whose hair   down   covers her thighs (LLB96 14)

This final stanza issues from the countercultural perspective of women perceiving an "unnatural" system of masculine power crossing and linking all nodes of authority, from which they are excised, as the name "Cesira" (with links to "cut out") suggests.[10] The final line's white space, particularly in severing "hair" and "down" connotes private spaces on the body (hair *down there*), what Loy in the later "Love Songs" calls "suspect places."

Unlike in "The Costa San Giorgio," the female speaker—self-identified as a wife—is now on the street while the husband is at the window. She has moved from outsider to participant, described by Tara Prescott as a "closeness, either emotionally or physically" (19) and by Carolyn Burke as a moment in which the "distance between observer and subject could collapse in moments of sympathy when—as in Futurist painting—she places herself inside of the scene" (*Becoming* 199); thus, the poem compels a dual process of identification or sympathy and distance or critique that enables both participation and analysis. In relocating the observing woman from the window to the streets, the poem anticipates Loy's gaze upon the urban streets of New York in later Bowery poems of the 1940s and 1950s, suggesting her long-standing concern with the act of observation and complicated tensions between witnessing and voyeurism, or documentary and spectacle. We will again return to these issues most directly in reading "Summer Night in a Florentine Slum," written several years after "The Costa San Giorgio" and "Costa Magic."

Touring the Costa San Giorgio, recall women's street life rendered in Loy's poems as you continue your trek up the hill. Visit the lovely shop selling ceramics and fabric designs, all made by the resident artist Emma Draghi, who lives just steps from Loy's home, running her studio and shop on the first floor of her Costa house, no. 52. Admire the beautifully varied doors and wonder what life goes on behind shutters opening at different angles or latched shut. Imagine Loy's children running across this stony street.

As with "The Costa San Giorgio" and "Costa Magic," women populate Loy's earliest poems, set in homes, on streets, and in public areas. A quick gloss of several poems, to be expanded upon later, suggests a range of relationships between women and specific places. The characteristic closeness of homes depicted shows neighbors in regular and intimate contact with each other, including on the occasion of maternal labor. Widely considered the first poem about the physicality of childbirth, "Parturition" (published in *The Trend*, October 1914) places its "I" in a domestic space on a busy street that also becomes the "centre / Of a circle of pain" in which the "I" grows cosmic in force and self-creation—but also remains within the house and its feminized environs (LLB96 4). Shutters flung open, then as now, allow the outside world into the poem. Through the "open window," the male "voice" of a "fashionable portrait-painter" is heard as he runs "up-stairs to a woman's apartment," a not-so-oblique reference to the kinds of infidelities Loy suffered with Haweis (LLB96 5). Their son Giles was born on February 1, 1909, and a customary home birth would have placed the event in the initial apartment on Costa San Giorgio.[11] Whether based strictly in biography or not, the poem's final lines indicate the woman-centered rituals of birth on this street, in a domesticized space that men do not enter. The "Each woman-of-the-people" who is "Doing hushed service," while satirized as donning a "ludicrous little halo," is nonetheless present at the emergence of the speaker's absorption into "infinite Maternity" of "cosmic reproductivity," a female collective and space (LLB96 7).

Women also gather in "At the Door of the House" clustered around a tarot card reader, "Looking for the little love-tale / That never came true / At the door of the house," as the poem deromanticizes myths of love (LLB96 35). Doors on Costa San Giorgio, varied in their current beauty, signify gendered perspectives, passages, and tensions between mobility and enclosure in these early-century poems. "The Effectual Marriage" begins at a door: "The door was an absurd thing / Yet it was passable," and "Gina and Miovanni" "quotidienly [*sic*] pass through it":

> In the evening they looked out of their two windows
> Miovanni out of his library window
> Gina from the kitchen window (LLB96 36)

The poem divides space by gender, with Miovanni in the library, surrounded by knowledge, and Gina in the kitchen, surrounded by domestic tools of labor. Gina is yet another woman at the window, one marked femininely domestic in a poem that mockingly exposes the gender hierarchies presumed by the male Miovanni, a stand-in for the Futurist Giovanni Papini (as "Gina" is Mina). This poem's en dehors garde commentary on the male avant-garde neglects Futurist invocations to speed and aggression, finding in the Italian places of home and street a different energy that includes (while complicating) dynamic collectivity and self-knowledge among women.

After contemplating the Costa homes, stroll through the Boboli Gardens. Continue up the Costa San Giorgio to Forte di Belvedere. Look for an entrance to the gardens. Alternatively, especially if you do not want to hike up to the Forte, walk back down the Costa to Via de' Guicciardini and turn left toward the Pitti Palace, where you enter the gardens from behind the palace.

Likely the setting for the Public Garden of Loy's "The Black Virginity" and its cast of priests, old men, and young girls out for a walk, the Boboli Gardens is identified by the Baedeker as a favorite site for Sunday strolls:

> The Boboli Garden, at the back of the [Pitti] palace, extends in terraces up the hill. It [...] commands a succession of charming views of Florence with its palaces and churches [...]. The long walks, bordered with evergreens, and the terraces, adorned with vases and statues, attract crowds of pleasure-seekers on Sundays. (546)

In "The Black Virginity"—a commentary on sexuality, religion, and masculine power—an "I in lilac print" observes the crowd. The strollers include a parade of priests, seeming novitiates who emerge from their "hermetically-sealed dormitories," cloaked with "Fluted black silk" and a decidedly asexual authority. In their chastity, they dream "Not of me or you Sister Saraminta," surmises the speaker, who sardonically notes this male authority's dependence—since Eve—upon viewing woman as the origin of sin: "It is an old religion that put us in our places," for woman is made to be "Preposterously no less than the world flesh and devil." The "Baby Priests" stroll with others in the "Yew-closed" "green sward" of the park, alongside an "old man," busy "Eyeing a white muslin girl's school." Through its placement of characters, the poem draws "Parallel" lines between this suggestion of pedophiliac lechery and the Church's denigration of women, reversing the notion of woman as the origin of sin and indicting patriarchal systems (LLB96 42–43). Staging this scene in a "Public Garden" counterpoints the Biblical myth of the Garden of Eden as the site of Eve's transgression, suggesting its false justification for the "public" and private forms of masculine power enacted through and upon women's bodies.

Paths of Lineage: Elizabeth Barrett Browning and Galileo

> Once you descend from Costa San Giorgio, or before you climb it, consider a literary detour to Casa Guidi, the home of Elizabeth Barrett Browning, Loy's Victorian predecessor poet and expatriate. Casa Guidi is a short walk from the Ponte Vecchio, located on the Piazza San Felice (not be confused, as I initially was, with the Piazza Santa Felicita, found at the foot of Costa San Giorgio). When you cross Ponte Vecchio to enter the Oltrarno, continue straight onto Via de' Guicciardini as you step off the bridge. This street becomes the Piazza de' Pitti as you approach the Pitti Palace. The Piazza San Felice is at the south end of the Piazza de' Pitti, beyond the palace. Turn right, and Casa Guidi will be on your right.

The cultural past and places of Florence suggest paths of lineage for Loy, both imaginary and literal, that position her differently—especially as a woman—from the avant-garde's outright rejection of the past; indeed, Loy's Florence poems, while critical of the past, include moments that bridge but rehabilitate and complicate an inheritance that she, as a British woman in Italy, might assume or, alternatively, might unexpectedly claim. For Loy, modernizing rather than casting off enabling elements of the past, as the following discussions of Elizabeth Barrett Browning and Galileo explore, generates modern feminist perspectives on class, gender, and nationality.

Some fifty years before Loy resided in Florence, another British woman poet, Elizabeth Barrett Browning, lived not far from Loy's home, near the Boboli Gardens and Pitti Palace. Gazing upon Florentine streets from the windows of her home, she famously penned *Casa Guidi Windows*, a poem written in support of Italy's nineteenth-century nationalist revolutions. Imagine Loy strolling past the Casa Guidi, the home of Britain's famously Italianate Victorian poets, identified by a nineteenth-century plaque above the door. Perhaps Loy even sought out the home after reading about it and the poem in the Baedeker: "No. 9, Piazza San Felice, is the *Casa Guidi*, in which Robert and Elizabeth Barrett Browning lived from 1848 till the death of the latter in 1861 [...]. See her poem, 'Casa Guidi Windows'" (547). While her husband Stephen Haweis imagined they would become "another celebrated [British] couple" in Florence, striving to attain the social status of the Brownings, it seems more likely that Loy looked to Barrett Browning's revolutionary voice and perspective as sources for the modern woman poet to renovate (Burke, *Becoming* 107).

The "windows" of Barrett Browning's poetic title and actual house might well have intrigued Loy, whose Florence poems feature images of windows, doors, and shutters of the Oltrarno streets. Might Loy have heeded Baedeker's advice to read the older poet's book-length poem *Casa Guidi Windows*, in which a woman poet looks down from her windows onto the revolutionary streets of Florence? Both poets craft speakers who specify the position of a British woman gazing upon Italian streets and people of the Oltrarno; several of Loy's Italian poems feature a woman speaker gazing from a window or doorway. In the twentieth century, standing under Barrett Browning's windows, would Loy contemplate the poem's deliberate positioning of an English woman at the window of her Italian home in the mid-nineteenth century, looking onto the piazza at the tumult and energy of the street? Would such contemplation shape her own poetic attention to street energy, windows, and homes in Florence?

In the late 1840s and during the period she wrote the poem (published in 1851), Barrett Browning witnessed and supported the initial stages of the Risorgimento in Florence, the struggle to unify Italy finalized later in the century. *Casa Guidi Windows* witnesses the Italian people celebrating the struggle and is spoken by a female "I" watching from her window. Imagine Barrett Browning's speaker, viewing the lively street "'Neath Casa Guidi windows," in this house found "'Twixt church and [Pitti] palace of a Florence street" (1, 2). The female speaker, recalling "How we gazed / From Casa Guidi windows," describes the street scene below her, filled with Florentines, "bewailers for their Italy enchained" (Barrett Browning 33, 2). The poet's window position sets her apart but also links her, as British subject, with the Italian rebels and the populace, "With doors and windows quaintly multiplied, / And terrace-sweeps, and gazers upon all," as her view of the street expands into a vision of the Italian nation's rise (5).

The trope of the woman watching from the window that specifically connects Loy with *Casa Guidi Windows*, claims a cultural authority for women usually denied them. As depicted in Loy's "Virgins Plus Curtains Minus Dots" (1914), for example, young virgins suffer an imposed elision of authority. They "See the men pass" freely on the streets while they linger "behind curtains," kept in the domestic sphere as "Virgins for sale":

> Somebody who was never
> a virgin
> Has bolted the door
> Put curtains at our windows (LLB96 22)

Examining women's authority to observe and speak, Loy's Florence street poems often entangle gender positioning with other social contexts. "The Costa San Giorgio" (to be discussed more fully below), suggests (like Barrett Browning) both distance from and connection to the "passionate Italian life-traffic" on the street below the window, as observed by the English woman (11). She feels her difference while joining other observers "Variously leaning" from "the green shutters" to "Mingle eyes with the commotion," recalling Barrett Browning's depiction of private windows as portals to public and political life (12). For Loy, the gendered position of the observer is explicitly complicated by class and nationality.

This evocation of windows as linking while separating the private and the public, and by extension the observer and the observed, is further suggested in "Summer Night in a Florentine Slum," written in 1920 upon

Loy's return to Florence after years of absence.[12] Loy's first-person speaker, standing at her window, mingles and mixes her gaze with others on the street, much as Loy's earlier "The Costa San Giorgio" details neighbors leaning from windows, or as Barrett Browning imagines her comradery with the Italian people. In the prose piece, Loy's speaker observes:

> I leaned out of the window—looking at the summer-strewn street; late in heat—lit with lamps, and mixed my breath with the tired dust.
>
> The dust was hot, the dust was dry—it lay low, it travelled about; and among it, Latin families lay on the lousy stones, in what they could manage of an earthy abandon. (LLB82 81)

As did Barrett Browning, Loy's female speaker witnesses the Florentines' poverty, but instead of the earlier poet's praise of Italian patriotism as a route to justice, Loy's poem frames the scene as one of sexual aggression and women's mistreatment, which the speaker ultimately chooses to shut out. As Loy's piece ends, this speaker "drew in my head and pulled the English chintz curtains scattered with prevaricating rosebuds." With this move, which we will return to later when considering the piece again in the context of Loy's Madonna figures, the cultural authority of English privilege is both acknowledged and placed under subtle criticism as she finds herself under the gaze of a print of "Beardsley's Mademoiselle De Maupin [as she] drew on her gloves at me from the wall" (LLB82 83). This print alludes to a transgressive historical figure suggesting a lineage of women (including Barrett Browning) who challenge the cultural positioning of women that restrains or silences them, refusing to be the evasive or "prevaricating roses."

Let us place ourselves in this room and read this print together, extending the lineage of women we have been considering. The historical Julie d'Aubigny, Mademoiselle Maupin was a seventeenth-century woman notorious for tales of cross-dressing, sword mastery, and opera performances. Stories of Mademoiselle Maupin supplied the title and main character for Théophile Gautier's novel of sexual transgressions (1835) and Aubrey Beardsley's later illustrations, such as the one in the poem (1897). The print Loy references shows Mademoiselle Maupin in men's clothing, pulling on gloves and staring directly at the viewer, "at me," the speaker specifies. Loy might well have been intrigued by Maupin's cross-gendered performances and their replay in fiction and art; moreover, one can imagine Loy's bemused appreciation of the illustration's depiction of seventeenth-century men's fashion with its feminine decor and frill.

Much as the Beardsley print plays with gendered conventions, Barrett Browning anticipates a poetic cross-dressing in her preface to *Casa Guidi Windows*, claiming while seeming to coyly deny a political perspective usually reserved for men and issued from a feminine space, the home. While her preface claims to "witness" the events directly, she concedes that the critic might dismiss the act of witnessing "From a window"; in her preface, Barrett Browning strategically understands the gender coding of the domestic position and seeks to head off both dismissal and alarm that the poem might elicit by carefully reassuring the reader that the poem is merely a "simple story of personal impressions" (v). In muting the (clearly evident) sociopolitical project of the poem, these prefacing comments speak to Barrett Browning's negotiations of gendered authorship, which Loy confronts some six decades later, illustrating a politicized dimension of this literary lineage.

For Barrett Browning, lineage serves to help establish her speaker's position and her vocation as a woman poet. Her felt connection to the Italian cause leads her to inscribe within *Casa Guidi Windows* the importance of Italy and Florence to the British poetic tradition. In addressing Italy, Barrett Browning observes that "the cup of Milton's soul" was filled by "Your beauty and your glory," as Italy garners adulation in *Paradise Lost* (79). Milton's own poetic reference to Vallombrosa's mountain forests (not far from Florence) echoes through Barrett Browning's long homage to Italy, in which she also recounts a trip to Vallombrosa; whether intentionally or not, these homages eventually haunt Loy's 1914 "July in Vallombrosa" (to be discussed shortly). Chronologically standing between Loy and Milton, Barrett Browning praises how the earlier poet

> sang of Adam's paradise and smiled,
> Remembering Vallombrosa. Therefore is
> The place divine to English man and child--
> We all love Italy. (79)

Barrett Browning's poem, whether glorifying Vallombrosa or graphically depicting strife and hardship on Florence's streets, is insistently place-specific, mapping the city's environs with great attention to both historical sites and daily life. From this insistence on Italian places, further lineages branch out, beyond the literary.

Thematically, an emphasis on observation connects Loy, Barrett Browning, and the figure of Renaissance astronomer Galileo, drawn by the speaker in *Casa Guidi Windows* as she describes standing in the "Tuscan Bellosguardo [...] / Where Galileo stood at nights to take / The vision of the stars" (80–81). Loy's home on the Costa San Giorgio, located just up the hill from Barrett Browning's Casa Guidi, is also down the hill from one of Galileo's Florentine homes, at no. 13 Costa San Giorgio—positioned in between the homes of the scientist and poet.

On your tour, should you walk up Costa San Giorgio beyond Loy's home, you will come across the house, a tidy beige structure decorated with bold geometric frescoes. The house of Galileo sports a commemorative plaque and warrants an entry in the 1906 Baedeker. Moreover, should you seek out Loy's first Florentine home on Via Pian del Giullari in Arcetri, you will likely notice the white observatory dome marking Villa Galileo on the same road, where the scientist spent his final years in confinement after being condemned by the Church in 1633.

The proximity of Loy's city home to Galileo's, echoing the cross-temporal coincidence of their residences in Arcetri, might well have pleased the poet. Passing his home, perhaps she imagined the two of them as innovators sharing space across centuries, linked by their mutual distrust of convention and embrace of observational acuity and astronomy. Images of vision and technologies of vision, a ghostly graft of the modern moment upon the Renaissance—Loy's present upon Galileo's past—proliferate in her writing, like the characteristic insertions of scientific language into her literary productions. Links in time and space (same home, same street) map an imagined lineage in which Loy's poetic mapping of the real, material city overlays a celestial vision figured by the scientist as an en dehors garde "turning outwards."

A layered sense of place underlies Loy's "witness" to Florence (to use Barrett Browning's word) (v), as a traversal of poetry, space, and time, creating imaginary circuits across generations. Did Galileo's closeness, in place if not time, nurture her poetry's celestial imaginings and images? Did she remember Milton's praise for Vallombrosa, the mountain resort she visited from Florence (and likely saw the plaque to him there), or the other poets and artists who had earlier visited the Italian mountain top? Did Loy imagine Barrett Browning's window gazer as her own poems look upon the streets of Florence? Thinking about these previous figures emphasizes the interaction of vision and place that forms the "window" through which Loy views the Florentine streets, even as she departs from the particular lenses of her predecessors to respond to modern life.

These imagined intersections, however fanciful, locate Loy—as a British citizen in Florence—in a lineage informed by place and migratory traversals, a lineage that both informs and troubles her work. For example, Barrett Browning's imaginative evocations of "Florence wanderings" narrate an Italian history justifying the mid-nineteenth-century struggle for national identity (23). Loy's street (and geographic) wanderings explore a more gender- and class-focused set of identities, externally imposed and self-fashioned, brought into relief by the clashing collusion of national identities marking the British expatriate woman in Italy and complicating a comradery with her adopted country. The place-enhanced lineage traced here leads us to travel up the Costa San Giorgio and explore further the politics of gender, class, and nationality performed by Loy's transgressive female speakers observing the Florence streets.

II. MAPPING FLORENCE: SECOND TOUR, FRIENDS

The Villa Curonia

To visit the Villa Curonia, Loy could ascend hilly Costa San Giorgio and Arcetri roads by cab or foot. Walking the route allows for lovely views (and excellent exercise).

> If you want to journey by foot, prepare to hike (or, alternatively, hire a cab). If you are walking, a bit further up the

hill at the intersection of Costa San Giorgio and Via di San Leonardo, pass the "House of Galileo," which the Baedeker notes is at "No. 13 Via della Costa San Giorgio" (548). Traversing the Costa San Giorgio's southern end entails a rigorous uphill march to the Porta San Giorgio at the Forte di Belvedere San Giorgio.

Reaching the top of the street, you pass through the Porta San Giorgio. Beyond the porta, enter a walled street and stroll along the blessedly flat San Leonardo, traveling south of the Boboli Gardens and toward Arcetri, occasionally glimpsing the stunning Tuscan hills through gates or arches punctuating walled estates. Soon, you will cross a major road for the first time, passing a café but deferring temptation to advance southeast in the direction of Mabel Dodge's Villa Curonia. Curving left at the bottom of the hill onto the Via Suor Maria Celeste, follow to no. 13 and stand before a gated and walled estate, finding yourself denied any visual or physical access to the destination.

After moving into the city, Loy and Haweis continued to venture into the Arcetri hills, particularly once they met Mabel Dodge (later to become Dodge Luhan) and her second husband, Edwin Dodge, in 1910, when the American couple arrived in Florence and visited Haweis's studio.[13] Salons and gatherings at Dodge Luhan's Arcetri home, the Villa Curonia, were famously celebrated in Gertrude Stein's "Portrait of Mabel Dodge at the Villa Curonia," which Dodge printed up and distributed at the Armory Show in New York City, 1913. At these gatherings, Dodge Luhan introduced Loy to many modernist friends, including Stein, Carl Van Vechten, John Reed, and Alice B. Toklas. As we will explore shortly, Dodge Luhan and Loy vacationed together (along with Van Vechten and others) after Haweis left Florence. Their letters across the Atlantic during the 1910s, when Dodge Luhan temporarily returned to New York, included news of the feminist movement in America and Loy's response, a draft of her 1914 "Feminist Manifesto."

Let us travel the artistic and geographic pathways that take us to the Villa Curonia, Dodge Luhan's Florence home, following the directions heading this section. The Baedeker instructs us to venture out after noon:

> The heights surrounding Florence afford many charming views of the city and neighbourhood, and some of the edifices erected on them also deserve notice. The afternoon is the most favourable time for excursions, as the city and environs are often veiled in haze in the forenoon. (548).

On a May day, I attempted to trace Loy's steps on foot, walking uphill from her home at no. 54 (now no. 60) Costa San Giorgio, going beyond the street's intersection with Costa Scarpuccia and passing by Galileo's home.

Soon after passing Galileo's home, I passed through the Porta San Giorgio, part of the city's medieval walls, "adorned with frescoes of the 14th-century" and adjacent to an old fort. The Baedeker further informs that "Above the Boboli Garden rises the *Fortezza di Belvedere* ([...] now a barrack), constructed in 1590 by *Buontalenti* to protect the Pitti Palace" that lies below (548). Imagine Loy's passage through this gate, alluded to in "Italian Pictures." The "porta," "stained frescoe" [*sic*], and "barrack" appear in the middle poem, "The Costa San Giorgio": upon the gate, a bas-relief of St. George killing the dragon supplies the image of the "stained frescoe of the dragon-slayer" in her poem (LLB96 10). Above the arch of the medieval gate curves a fresco of the Madonna enthroned among saints, one of the many Virgin Mary images Loy would encounter on any daily walk.

Further flat terrain greets us after passing through the porta, as the uphill hike becomes a leisurely stroll past walled estates and stunning glimpses of the countryside below. If you take this walk, and then proceed down the Via Suor Maria Celeste, you will find that the Villa Curonia, privately owned by a family that tends its gardens, remains gated to the public, so you will not be able to enter the property but can see its approximate surroundings. Although I discovered that visitors cannot access or even view the private residence from the road, our coauthor Suzanne Churchill was later invited on a private tour of the estate by its current owner, who greeted her car at the top of the winding road to open the locked gate. The entrance to the villa opens into the gardens. The panoramic views of the Florentine countryside Loy would have enjoyed are now mostly blocked by tall, slender cedar trees. From the gardens, visitors may enter the villa on the ground floor into a long, wide, enclosed porch, opening to a larger gallery where Dodge Luhan hosted parties. Several rooms serve as spaces for installation art, continuing the experimental energy of Dodge Luhan's community.

After my own failed jaunt (or forced hike, more precisely) to see the Villa Curonia, I returned to the nearby café I had passed on the way. Sipping espresso, I speculated about the early 1910s, recalling images of the Villa Curonia from photographs in books and envisioning what those outer walls enclosed. Dodge Luhan and her expatriate community of Anglo-Americans fostered Loy's encounters with new ideas, artists, and writers. At Villa Curonia salons, Loy engaged in lively discussions about psychology, spirituality, occultism, and art. She met Alice B. Toklas and Gertrude Stein, read Stein's work (understanding it, Stein claimed, "without the commas") and shopped together for ceramic Madonna figures (a shared interest) in the Oltrarno neighborhood (Burke, *Becoming* 130–31).[14] A friendship ensued with Van Vechten, whom she came to consider her literary agent. He promoted her early writings as an editor of *The Trend* and was a fellow Greenwich Village habitué when Loy came to New York in 1916. Van Vechten's essayistic accounts of his extended prewar visit to the Villa Curonia in 1914, and a vacation with Loy and friends, appeared in issues of *Rogue* and also in his 1932 autobiography, *Sacred and Profane Memories*.

Dodge Luhan's own autobiography, *Intimate Memories*, reveals a rather conflicted regard for Loy, despite their friendship. The American's simultaneous attraction to and repulsion from Stephen Haweis complicates her relationship with "Ducie," as she called Loy. In a chapter devoted to Haweis, Dodge Luhan recalls his extramarital dalliances, including with Emily Sayre who reputedly committed suicide after his rejection, and concedes her own strange attraction, coexisting with a restless fear when alone with him. Employing metaphors of animals, reptiles, and insects, she describes Haweis as a decidedly "penguin type," "diminutive, black as a beetle, and very, very inky" (Dodge Luhan 338), with a "lizardy mouth" and "lips [...] shaped like a trowel" below "large, inky, oily dark eyes [that] would become fixed with the lids drooping over them" (342). Tellingly, she sculpted a penguin-like portrait of his image.

Dodge Luhan described Haweis and "Ducie" as a "strange couple together," dramatized by physical contrasts that resolved, nevertheless, into a strange similarity:

> His dark, inky eyes would have an oily glint in them and his long black hair that grew, like a page's, long and over his ears, used to grow damp and he would brush it back with his trembling lizardy hands [...]. She was beautiful, with dark hair parted and with a great knot on the nape of her white neck, a fair, fine skin with high cheekbones, and she was graceful.
>
> She looked like a painting by Augustus John. Her eyes were long and narrow of a nondescript color, something pale. There was something a little reptilian about her, too. Just as Stephen resembled a lizard or a little tortoise on end, so she made one think of serpents. (338)

Noting Loy's play with nomenclature, Dodge Luhan assumes Loy's pattern of changing names is intended to distance her from Haweis's surname and nickname for her: "Lilith her name might have been. But in reality it was Minna. Minna Levi. Then Minna Lowey. Then Minna Loy (after she finally divorced Stephen). He called her Ducie" (342).[15] Although Dodge Luhan spent a good deal of time with Loy and they corresponded once apart, her final summary of Loy sounds strangely cruel and cold, conveying a distanced aloofness from her friend:

> Ducie was very gifted in an unhappy, morbid way. She painted small, cynical pictures, picturesque and delicate, of ladies' tea-parties, or half-fantastic scenes from a fabulous world where her mind dwelt customarily in a perpetual half-tone, poetic and depressing. She was perfectly dissatisfied through some lack in herself. She seemed to grow dry as the years went on. It was not Stephen's fault, though perhaps he was difficult to live with after one outgrew the taste one had for him. (341)

Dodge Luhan admits her own duplicity as confidant to Loy while engaging an erotic dynamic with Haweis; according to Dodge Luhan, Haweis

> used to delve in magic things and knew a few little magical tricks [...]. He wanted power and he had some. There he was, married to Ducie Haweis,

> lovely as a Byzantine Madonna, taller than he by several inches; and there was Emily Sayre, who became infatuated with him [later committing suicide] [...] and I had too an interest in him. (338)

Dodge was aware that "Ducie hated him with a profound, convinced detestation which had been developed in intimacy. 'He is the kind that bites the hand that feeds him,' she told me once" (342). Although Loy did not feature her husband in her poems as directly as her Futurist companions, he appears in subtle ways, as suggested by the husband in "Costa Magic" who chants magical incantations suggestively contributing to a young woman's misery and death. In "Parturition," he likely provides the model for the deceitful husband, visiting a mistress while his wife gives birth; further, in Loy's play *The Sacred Prostitute*, he has a cameo role as "Tea Table Man."

Haweis's infidelity also surfaces subtly in "Lions' Jaws," likely written after Loy left Florence and, according to Conover, appearing to be her "final verse verdict on Futurist affairs" (LLB96 186). Parodying the Futurists as "the Flabbergasts," and implicating herself (as "Imna Oly") in their antics for a time, the poem mockingly recalls the major figures and the misogyny prompting what Conover calls their "sex war" (LLB96 188). While Haweis is not directly identified, "Mrs. Krar Standing Hail" stands in for his unfaithfulness and, perhaps, its roots in his shallow inability to understand Loy and her feminist modernity:

> As for Imna Oly
> I agree with Mrs. Krar Standing Hail
> She is not quite a lady. (LLB96 50)

Hail is a "stand-up jab for Stan Harding Krayl (a.k.a. Mrs. Garner Hale)," who numbered among Haweis's affairs and was a friend of Dodge's (Conover, LLB96 187). Dodge Luhan, while hinting that Krayl was also attracted to her, muses "It was perhaps not so strange that such women as Stan and the others fell so desperately in love with him. He must have had a strong element that they need." (338). Indeed, a complex social scene attended Dodge's gatherings.

The Braggiottis and the Scuola di Canto

Next on the tour featuring Loy's friends, let us visit the home of the Braggiottis, another of Loy's haunts during this period. Venture into the hills north of the city to find the Montughi area.

> From the city, follow the Via dei Cappucini until it becomes the Via di Santa Marta. Near the Chiesa dei Cappuccini at the end of the Via di Santa Marta (near the current Stibbert Museum) is the villa where the Braggiotti family resided from 1900 until 1918.

Their youngest daughter Gloria memorializes the villa in her autobiography:

> The villa my parents selected was in Montughi, on the outskirts of Florence, situated on one of the lovely hills overlooking the city. It was built of stucco, of a cheery vanilla color, with green blinds brightening all the windows. (Braggiotti 13)

The Braggiottis—an American wife and Italian husband with eight children—opened a music school at their villa, the Scuola di Canto. An active hub for guests and events, it hosted Saturday gatherings that "everyone in Florence knew about," which Loy attended with family and friends:

> The Saturday guests were a conglomeration of all types of people, nationalities, and ages, including the aristocratic families of Florence. There were also our American friends [...]. Musicians, artists, and writers visiting Florence were automatically informed of our musicales. Nobody waited for an invitation. Edward Johnson, Douglas Ainsley, Emma Eames, Muriel Draper, Paul Draper (aged seven), and Mabel Dodge were frequent visitors. (Braggiotti 63)

At the Braggiotti's villa, Loy met the Drapers, whom she would visit in London and during their Florence stays with Mabel Dodge Luhan (Burke, *Becoming* 125). Lili Braggiotti, the mother, embraced a clothing philosophy that rejected corsets and associated certain spiritual energies with different colors of clothing. Loy, noted for her distinctively creative, modern dress and fashion designs, was a likely fellow-traveler; indeed, the family's spiritual philosophy, mapped onto clothing and fashion, speaks to the importance Loy placed on clothing design. Raised by a respected London tailor, Sigmund Lowy, whose presence in her life seems to have offered a degree of support (albeit vexed) for her creative nature, Loy continued his interest in sartorial arts.[16] According to Burke, Haweis recalled that, in their time in Montparnasse, her innovative and modern dress patterns anticipated modern designers of a "new silhouette" for women in Paris, adapting reform movement clothing meant to be both functional and inexpensive by foregoing the corset for "natural lines" and fabric "draped softly" over the body (Burke, *Becoming* 90). An example of Loy's dress designs, sent to Van Vechten, will be further discussed in a later section.

Daughter Gloria recalls the proximity of the Braggiottis' villa to the Capuchin convent, next to the Chiesa dei Santi Francesco e Chiara, which still exists: "This tiny Catholic church was situated at the end of the dusty Via Santa Marta, about a half mile from our villa" (Braggiotti 31). Taken to church by their Italian nanny at times, the children came to know the *contadini* among their local neighbors:

> The Chiesa dei Cappuccini was built about the fifteenth century. It was a small and simple church, its parishioners consisting mainly of the *contadini*, servants and gardeners who worked in the villas and gardens in the Montughi section. (33)

The churchgoing was not a family affair, however, for, like Loy, the parents distrusted the confinements of orthodox Catholicism along with other conventions. They read aloud from "the Upanishads and the Bhagavad-Gita" (130), followed the vegetarianism of Hindu tradition, hosted regular concerts and performances, and held salons about spiritual matters. In 1912, Loy and Dodge Luhan attended weekly sessions with the Swami Paraman, who was staying with the expatriate Braggiotti family at their villa in these hills (Burke, *Becoming* 132).

The Braggiottis' philosophies of child-rearing and education included a belief in the child's unfettered freedom. Notorious for their refusal to wear clothes and freedom to roam the villa and surrounding fields, the children at times shocked their parents' friends. Gloria tells a story of British women coming for afternoon tea, finding the children running around the villa naked except for horns and tails made of sticks and leaves. Burke surmises that Loy was part of this group, the women slightly appalled by the children's inventive devils' tails made, as Gloria describes, "by sticking little branches into our 'fannies'" (Braggiotti 17). Whether Loy was among the shocked or not, her children often went to play with the Braggiottis, especially during weekly concerts the family attended.

The Braggiotti children attended the same English school with Joella and Giles, Miss Penrose's Academy, "an institution frequented by the children of foreign residents" (Burke, *Becoming* 276), which garners fond memories from Gloria Braggiotti:

> [Miss Penrose's school held] small, cosy classrooms, with tiny wooden chairs and desks, and the huge map of Europe nailed beside the blackboard, with each country tinted a different color. Italy, that lovable boot, was a shiny green, and ever since I have thought of it in that color. [...] Miss Penrose was a perfect schoolmistress because she truly loved her pupils. Her raspberry pink cheeks gave her the appearance of just having come in from a brisk walk on a cold day and of being very happy about it. Her slightly protruding teeth, which I have always associated with the English, enhanced her pleasant expression. Her teeth smiled even when she herself did not. Her graying hair was loosely rolled into a bun. [...] She never missed our Saturday musicales and when we returned from the seashore she always met us at the station. (127–28)

Indeed, Loy, having come to know the school mistress, entrusted Miss Penrose to keep her children when she left for New York in 1916 (Burke, *Becoming* 193).

III. FUTURIST FLORENCE/FUTURIST ROME

Florence as Futurist Canvas

Loy's encounters with artists and writers, from 1913 through her 1916 departure for New York, comprise our poetic tour of Futurist Florence, moving amid the city's geographies and the movement's stage-like manifestations.[17] We begin, appropriately, with Costa San Giorgio. Loy rented out Stephen Haweis's studio, upon his departure from Florence in 1913, to the young American artist Frances Simpson Stevens, arranging with her mother to "chaperone" the twenty-year-old, who had studied with Robert Henri and aimed to further her art studies. The women's adjacent studios energized each other's work and for a while brought together elements of Florence's avant-garde. Stevens, keen to meet the Futurists revolutionizing painting, sought out Carlo Carrà and Ardengo Soffici, who, along with Giovanni Papini, "began turning up at the Costa San Giorgio in hope of enlisting her in the movement" (Burke, *Becoming* 151). In *Brontolivido*, Loy's unpublished roman à clef, she describes Marinetti visiting to meet Stevens but turning his attention to Loy instead, a meeting Suzanne Churchill discusses in chapter 3 in relation to Loy's plays satirizing the movement and Marinetti.[18] Gordon Craig, theater set designer and editor of *The Mask* who hoped to start a modern school of theater, lived next door for a brief period, further enlivening the artistic circuit between Costa San Giorgio and the Centro's Futurist gathering spots. The year of Stevens's arrival, the two women likely attended the Futurist painting exhibit in November 1913, held at the Saletta Gonnelli, a covered courtyard at the Libreria Antiquaria Gonnelli, a bookshop frequented by Papini and D'Annunzio, located near the Duomo at Via Ricasoli, 6r (and still in business). This first showing of major Futurist artists in Florence received reviews in *Lacerba*, the Futurist little magazine.

Walking from the Costa to the Centro

Let us trace Loy's trips to meet fellow artists and writers in the city center, the Centro.

> Beginning at Loy's home (currently no. 61), descend Costa San Giorgio to its bottom point at Piazza Santa Felicita; enter the street and turn toward the Ponte Vecchio. Cross the bridge onto a main shopping street, Via Por Santa Maria, which takes you to the Piazza della Repubblica. During Loy's time, this square was known as the Piazza Vittorio Emanuele II,

home to two Futurist gathering spots. The Giubbe Rosse and Paszkowski's cafés sit on opposite corners of the piazza, near the arched opening of the piazza.

Built shortly before Loy's move to Florence, the Piazza Vittorio Emanuele II replaced ancient, medieval, and Renaissance structures torn down by the city to make way for the square's renovation as a celebration of Italy's new nationhood (see Fig. 2.2). The loss of older churches, towers, residences, and palaces earned the disdain of the 1906 Baedeker, scornful of modernization: the "uninteresting new PIAZZA VITTORIO EMANUELE [...] now forms the focus of the *Centro* and is especially animated in the evening" (532). During their early Florence years, Loy and Haweis visited the area to socialize with Gordon Craig, living then on the top floor of the old Palazzo Sassetti, directly behind the Piazza Vittorio Emanuele II. Haweis "contributed to Craig's cosmopolitan magazine *The Mask* as an illustrator" (Scuriatti, *Mina Loy's Critical Modernism* 307). Later moving briefly to Costa San Giorgio, Craig subsequently relocated to no. 4 Viuzzo di Gattaia, near the Piazzale Michelangelo, where he lived for seven years.

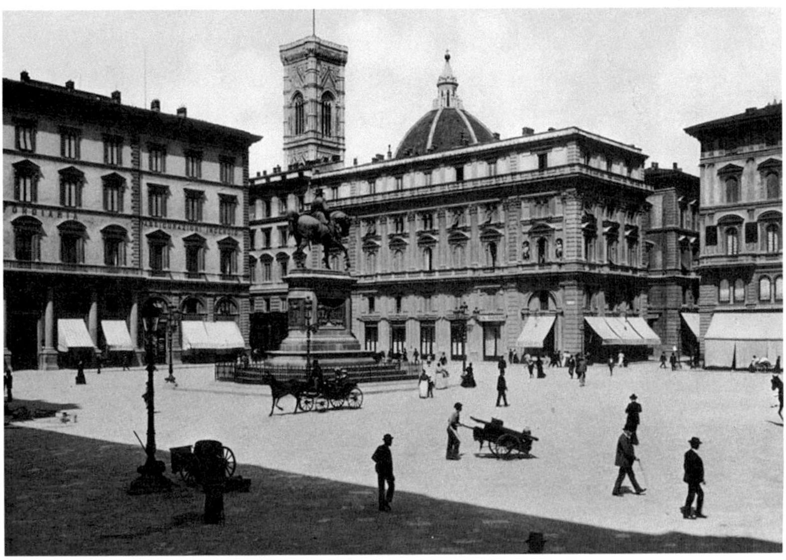

Figure 2.2. Piazza Vittorio Emanuele II, circa 1896, Florence, Italy.

Loy admired Isadora Duncan, the dancer and Craig's lover, although she was less fond of Craig. If she visited them on this hillside above the city, Loy might have taken the electric tramway No. 7 up the steep incline, as instructed by the Baedeker, where the extended views of Florence and the "villa-covered hills" are "charming" (549).

Heading off for Futurist evenings, Loy and Stevens walked down their stony street to cross the Ponte Vecchio to meet other artists and writers gathered in cafés just around the corner from the Duomo. *Lacerba* originated here, established by Giovanni Papini and Ardengo Soffici to report and extend the debates and animated discussions among Futurists at the Caffè Giubbe Rosse. Soffici's articles about the Caffè Giubbe Rosse mention conversations with Loy and Stevens (*Lacerba*, January 15, 1914, p. 30; in Burke, *Becoming* 153). Still in operation—and where you can order fabulous coffee, pastries, and thick Florentine grilled steaks—the Caffè Giubbe Rosse sports high vaulted ceilings and dark wood trim that transport visitors to an earlier time. The art and photograph-covered walls and Futurist-themed menu art celebrate the café's history as an incubator of modern art.

Directly across the piazza, find the literary gathering spot Caffè Paszkowski's, which merits mention in the satirical poem "Giovanni Franchi" (*Rogue*, vol. 2, no. 1, October 1916; composed May–July 1915). The poem parodies the homosocial circuits of adulation among Futurists, figuring a young aspirant (the fictional Franchi) whose worshipful relation with an older "philosopher," Giovanni Bapini (that is, Papini) verges on pederasty. Naively adolescent, with "sensitive down among his freckles" and suspect to patriotic propaganda for Italy's declaration of war, Giovanni Franchi's Futurism intertwines with the "patriotic souls of flags / Red white and green flags," a nationalism "filliping piazzas" or stirring up Italian public spaces. The "'National Idea' arrived on the Milan Express"—Marinetti's descent upon Florence from Milan and his clamor for war colors not only the red, white, and green flags of the relatively new nation but superficially tinges the dramatically authoritative rhetoric of the Futurists Papini and Marinetti. A parodied air of self-importance infuses the staging of Futurist spectacles, such as Giovanni Bapini's speeches issued through "monumental gums" that "importuned mobs." Rushing in and out of gatherings, the younger Giovanni strives to imitate this posture, unaware of its ridiculous emptiness, as he rushed "from Paszkowki's / Through plate-glass swingings / To look as busy bodily / As the philosopher's brain" (LLB96 28). The Futurist philosopher and his heir, intent upon a window display of profundity, are merely mental busybodies.

Asserting that "Futurism could only have been born in Italy, a country absolutely fixed on the past," the new movement heralded the call to "spit on the Altar of Art" through vigorous public debate and spectacle (Aldo Palazzeschi, qtd. in Burke, *Becoming* 152). In this sense, the Futurists transformed the Renaissance city of Florence into both canvas and stage for performing Futurism and its assault on the city's art traditions. As though matching their performative energy, Loy casts Futurism in decidedly theatrical ways, often in mimicry and satire in poems such as "Giovanni Franchi," recasting spectacle as pomposity born of masculine ego, which she also mocks in her plays and unfinished roman à clef *Brontolivido*. Furthering the performance of revolt and shock, Futurists took up the stage at the Teatro Verdi, on the Via Ghibellina. The corner building is fronted with arched door entrances and lovely iron scrollwork on the lamps and exterior brackets. Still a central performance site, the Teatro Verdi advertised a show for Elvis Costello when I strolled by in the spring of 2017. More than a hundred years earlier, on December 12, 1913, Loy attended the Futurist *serata*, a performance and "riot" in which the audience, provoked by the performers, threw rotten vegetables at the manifesto and poetry readers on stage to create a frantic explosion of Futurist energy (see chapter 3).

The Centro suggests the literal conjunctions Florence daily offered Loy, as a place of diverse cultural, historical, religious, and artistic energies. Around the corner from the edgy energies of Futurist cafés and the central, modern piazza, the Duomo's dome and tower rise high above the city. Like the Duomo, Catholicism's dominating presence encodes Loy's poetic Baedeker, mapping gender in poems including "Virgins Plus Curtains Minus Dots," "Babies in Hospital," "The Black Virginity," "The Beneficent Garland," "Involutions," and "The Prototype," and sitting ironically in conjunction with Futurism's ideas of gender, as the geography of Florence maps onto Loy's intersecting engagement with Futurism and Catholicism.

Roma and the *First Free Futurist International Exhibition*

Loy's only recorded exhibit with the Futurists took place in Rome at the Galleria Futurista di Giuseppe Sprovieri, at 125 Via del Tritone.

If you travel to this site, catch the train from Florence to Rome for an easy day trip. Once in Rome, stroll down the Via del Tritone, a busy car-filled street near the Piazza Barberini. Amid a looming sequence of nineteenth-century buildings, no. 125 sports lions' heads above formidably heavy doors.

Shortly after its establishment, the Galleria Sprovieri held the *First Free Futurist International Exhibition* in February and March of 1914. Loy contributed four paintings to the show, including three portraits of Marinetti and a painting titled *Dynamism of the Subconscious*. It is fascinating to contemplate how these visual works compare with her poetic portraits of Marinetti and other Futurists, but the paintings, alas, are now lost. Frances Simpson Stevens, the only American in the exhibit, showed eight paintings, including *Dynamism of a Market*, *Dynamism of Pistons*, and *Typographic Simultaneity*. Work by Marinetti and various Russian Futurists rounded out a show that Sprovieri hoped would shake the "provincialism of Italian art" (Burke, *Becoming* 166).

Traveling to the exhibit together and spending a few days in Rome, Loy and Marinetti began their trip at Florence's Stazione Centrale di Santa Maria Novella, the rail station near the church and piazza of the same name (the station was rebuilt in the 1930s just a slight distance from its original setting). Fearful that Stephen, then in New York, would discover her travel with another man, she nonetheless decided to "run the risk" rather than "stagnate in Florence" (Burke, *Becoming* 165). An account of the trip appears in *Brontolivido,* describing Brontolivido-as-Marinetti's energy in Futuristic terms: "the machinery of his urgent identification with motor-frenzy" evoked a modernity "where everything seemed to be worked by a piston."[19]

Such energy characterizes Loy's descriptions of Brontolivido's impromptu performances at the gallery, including manifesto-like speechifying. Rowan Harris usefully describes the fictionalized autobiography as "a kind of camp" reading of Futurism (labeled the Flabbergast movement, as in the poem "Lions' Jaws") in its presentation of "sex wars" as a "hyper-male and hyper-female" performativity of the main characters, Brontolivido (representing Marinetti) and Jemima or Sophia (interchangeable names representing Loy) (32–33). The spectacle of Bronty's "harangue of the embryo crowd" in responding to a "hideous article" by "Joannes" (which Burke identifies as alluding to Papini and his "latest diatribe in *Lacerba*, a bitter, almost hysterical call for the suppression of women") showcases Bronty's defense of "Women" as ironically reducing her to a capacity to serve male pleasure:[20]

> <u>Woman</u> he blazed is a <u>wonderful animal</u>—& when I print any part of her body I choose—It is in purist appreciation—I do not admit that I can write about a fondant which gives me some pleasure—& not about a vagina which gives me infinitely more—This is a beautiful word—it means what I say—It is a fact—& fact is divinity—it slights no one of you—for are you not all formed in the same way? ("Rome," box 1, folder 7, images 6–7).

Such boldness of language strongly affects Jemima, as Loy expresses what might have been her own reaction: "he had said one word—utterly unaffectedly—& it had broken down the barriers of her subconscious reactions in prudery, that divided self-truthfullness [*sic*] from self-expression" ("Rome," box 1, folder 7, image 7). Eager for ways to break through the restraints placed upon her sex and the capacity to speak of female experience, Loy would do so by critiquing and parodying (as in *Brontolivido*) the misogyny underlying Futurist proclamations about women and the female body, even while inspired by the Futurist assault on bourgeois moral conventions.

Despite their involvement with the Futurists, both Stevens and Loy have been erased from official histories of the movement, although recent scholars have recovered traces of their activity. Stevens's subsequent involvement with avant-garde circles in New York shows up in such publications as Alfred Stieglitz's *Camera Work* (where Loy's first publications appeared); moreover, in 1917 *Popular Science Monthly* published a full-length image of her in bohemian fashion, displaying a Futurist canvas cited as her "representation in line and color of the energy in motion in a great power-house. She calls it pictorial velocity."[21] That same year, amid a group of male artists representing the "art of the future"—including Albert Gleizes, S. MacDonald-Wright, Hugo Robus, Gene Crotti, and Marcel Duchamp—Stevens appears as the only woman in the pages of *Every Week*, a popular periodical running in America during the war years (see Fig. 2.3). The April 2, 1917 issue exhibits a gallery of artists and their work across the page. Diminutively titled "Miss Stevens," she is described as "fresh from a discreet New England boarding-school" but "plunged" by "fate" into Italy "just as the Futurists there published their fiery manifesto" and where she "allied herself with the revolutionists." In the photograph, evocatively centered on the page, she defiantly sports male garb (pants, a tie, a man's hat, riding boots, and crop) as she stands beside her large painting *Battle of Gorizia*, characterized by emphasis on movement and dynamism, her particular contribution to Futurism.[22] At the same time, *Every Week* frames Stevens's accomplishments with familiarly sexist assumptions—presenting her as an innocent ingénue swept up by "fate"—her inclusion evokes larger questions about women artists negotiating the sexism of even the most radical of avant-gardes.

These periodical pages offer glimmers of the en dehors garde (women artists remaining on the outskirts, coming from the outside) that, for Loy, coincided with the *First Free Futurist International Exhibition*. Her emerging poetry challenged conventions of gender by experimenting with topics deemed improper for women, bringing women's bodies and subjectivity into visibility through works such as "The Prototype," "Parturition," "Italian Pictures," "Three Moments in Paris," "Virgins Plus Curtains Minus Dots," "Songs to Joannes," and the unpublished "Feminist Manifesto." Loy's focus on an embodied female sexuality regards women's bodies as shaped by economic, religious, and social systems, restricting women from defining their own erotic, maternal, and bodily experience and knowledge; too often, men's voices—not unlike Brontolivido/Marinetti's bombastic appropriation of "vagina"—circumscribe their lives and bodies. Pushing back against the Futurist presumption that a man could either define or offer knowledge about women, Loy's en dehors garde approach addressed taboo topics, as a woman to other women, while also deploying

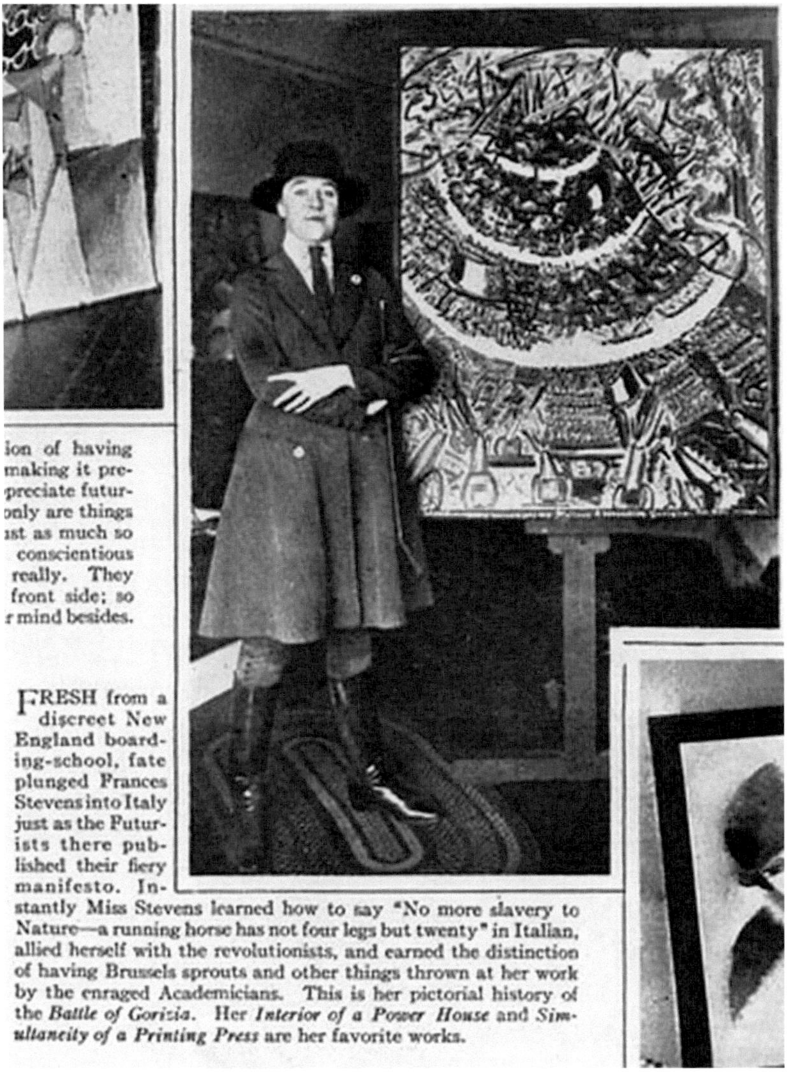

FRESH from a discreet New England boarding-school, fate plunged Frances Stevens into Italy just as the Futurists there published their fiery manifesto. Instantly Miss Stevens learned how to say "No more slavery to Nature—a running horse has not four legs but twenty" in Italian, allied herself with the revolutionists, and earned the distinction of having Brussels sprouts and other things thrown at her work by the enraged Academicians. This is her pictorial history of the *Battle of Gorizia*. Her *Interior of a Power House* and *Simultaneity of a Printing Press* are her favorite works.

Figure 2.3. Frances Simpson Stevens, center figure, "Sometimes We Dread the Future," photograph by Paul Thompson, *Every Week*, vol. 4, no. 14, Apr. 2, 1917.

a medical-scientific vocabulary (countering Marinetti in referencing the vagina) to reclaim knowledge of women's bodies from men and push back against Futurist misogyny. Writing to Van Vechten about "Parturition" in a letter of October 29, 1914, she declared, "I am glad to introduce my sex to the inner meaning of childbirth. The last illusion about my poor miscreated sex is gone" (qtd. in Conover, LLB96, 176–177).

Loy's "Futurist" Maps of Class and Gender

Loy's Futurist encounters fundamentally interacted with the experimental and feminist directions of her writing, as she both absorbed and resisted the movement's ideas and techniques. Adopting forms from Futurist models, "Aphorisms on Futurism" (*Camera Work*, January 1914) and the "Feminist Manifesto" (1914) test out favored Futurist genres, unconventional typography and spatial arrangement, and a language of dynamism, change, and shock. Poems like "Three Italian Pictures" or "Parturition" encourage sensations of rapid shifts, movement, and energy that Futurist painters developed through bright colors, fractured spaces, and geometric lines of force on their canvases. Loy's plays from this period prod the movement's sexism and attitudes toward audience, and the satires—"Sketch of a Man on a Platform," "Giovanni Franchi," "Café du Néant," "The Effectual Marriage," and "Lions' Jaws"—skewer Futurism's sexual politics while reworking its techniques (see chapter 3).

However, if we consider Futurism through Loy's en dehors garde lens, we see a class-conscious apprehension of the modern that contrasts with that avant-garde's disdain for the masses or the vision of the needy as weak and unworthy. Loy flips these attitudes on their head to critique Futurist hierarchies. Mapping Futurist-specific spaces in her poetry, Loy's references to location ironize overlapping social architectures of the city and the movement, mocking Futurism's claim to cast off convention. In "Giovanni Franchi," Loy draws on her familiarity with the Oltrarno, where she shopped and dined. The poem cuttingly counterpoints the class position of its young protagonist, "hooligan-faced and latin-born," with the aristocratic pose of the Futurist leader, satirically made to chime with monuments glorifying an aristocratic past ostensibly scorned in Futurist rhetoric. The haughty "Bapini" (again, a mocking play on Papini), claiming that "Everybody in Firenze knows me," shares physical attributes with the "stolid" Pitti Palace, the fifteenth-century palatial home housing the Medici family in the sixteenth century, followed by ruling families in Tuscany and, in the eighteenth century, used by Napoleon (LLB96 28, 29).

Establishing the poem's geography of class, the young "disciple" sits across from the grand Pitti Palace—the Palazzo—in the "Audaciously squatting" trattoria kept by his working-class "papa and mama," "watching the munchers supporting his parents" (LLB96 29). The "imposing palace" first built by a private citizen would become the "residence of the reigning sovereign" by 1550, continuing to be "that of the King of Italy when at Florence," the 1906 Baedeker informs its readers (538). As with the aristocratic posture adopted by Bapini, the Palazzo's "stolid" grandeur dwarfing the small shops and eateries across the street, architecturally disregards its proximity to the work-a-day establishment. Loy imagines the world existing beneath the Palace's gaze rendered invisible to the higher echelons claiming to be all-seeing but nonetheless oblivious:

> The Pitti Palace however stolid could hardly help noticing
> Being an aristocrat it went on looking
> ...
> The Pitti Palace has never been known to mention the trattoria
> Or mention Giovanni Franchi
> Sitting in it (LLB96 29)

Despite aristocratic efforts of the anthropomorphized palace to remain aloof, collisions and intersections of class and gender are all too evident on the street. Loy focuses on the discrepancy between the palace's history of grandeur and the working establishments and people around it. Certainly, the poem also echoes and ironizes the architectural attention to power and wealth found in the 1906 Baedeker's entry on the Palazzo Pitti (538–41). Moreover, the guide emphasizes the Pitti's art treasures over the course of three pages: "No collection in Italy can boast of such an array of masterpieces" (539). The poetic irony of Bapini's correspondence with the Pitti Palace mocks the Futurist disdain for the traditions and art of the museum as a pronounced hypocrisy.

As a book instructing foreigners how to interpret unfamiliar places and words, the Baedeker frames experience for the traveler. Analogously, in the poem, the male-to-male transmission of knowledge frames and sustains attitudes toward women. As the younger Giovanni "listened at the elder's lips," he learned of "earthquakes and women":

> Of women ----------------
> His manners were abominable
> He would kill a woman
> Quite inconspicuously it is true
> And neglect to attend her funeral
> I mean the older man (LLB96 30)

Loy's presentation of femaleness is part of this parody of Futurism. A slippage between the female references in the poem develops in relation to the street's environment and architecture, and the spatial dynamics of the poem's geography combine with strategic uses of visual spaces within the poem. The poem's early stanzas introduce a figure of "threewomen," a seeming composite of women or parts of a single woman. In a mindless devotion to the Futurist leader shared by the women and Franchi, the "threewomen" "Skipped parallel / To the progress / Of Giovanni Franchi." References to the "threewomen" morph into pronouns that connote different kinds of consciousness, becoming a singular "she" by mid-poem, ostensibly "to save time" (a "she" is shorter to read or say than the multisyllabic "threewomen") (LLB96 27, 29). The "she" visits the trattoria, where even the food suggests the brainwashing she (and Franchi) have fallen prey to:

> Trout   that might have been trained for circuses
> If minarets   grew in miniature whirlpools
> And mayonnaise   that helped her to forget
> That what is underneath   need never matter
>
> (LLB96 31)

Loy's blank spaces suggest something is always silenced and "underneath" in structures of power lived out by Bapini and the souls of masculine aristocracy marking the Florentine avant-garde. What is "underneath" also suggests the mark of woman's difference underneath her clothing that indeed matters, but is erased (made a blank space) by masculine authority. Recalling Marinetti's bold claim to the word "vagina" at the Rome Sprovieri exhibit, Loy here suggests that the Futurists had little actual regard for female genitalia or sexuality beyond serving their pleasure.[23]

At other points, an "I" speaks, suggestive of Loy. Adopting the first-person pronoun ("I" and then "we"), the poem slides between a speaker who is the "I" but also the "she" composite of the "threewomen," oscillating between keen critique of the Futurists but also her own willful obliviousness concerning the gender politics of this arrangement. The "she" is indicted for following (or perhaps just ignoring) the cultural gender script, while the "I" recognizes the cultural texts at play, including Bapini's bitter misogyny (evolving a vicious commentary on her intimate but failed relationship with Papini).

As in other poems, Loy's en dehors garde strategy implicates herself in the politics she challenges, recognizing and critiquing her simultaneous positions, both subject and object, singular and plural. As "threewomen," as "she," and as "I", this figure suggests Loy's position both outside of and entangled in the Futurist dynamics the poem parodies. Loy's positioning of the "I" in the poem inscribes an outside status so often adopted in other Florence poems, by virtue of her gender and her foreignness. One might read this positioning in her sly reference to the foreigner's travel guide, the Baedeker, when she writes (in first-person plural):

> We have read of
> Trattoria   meaning eating-house
> Piazzas   or squares
> The Pitti Palace   enormous
> And Paszkowski's   for beer
> All are in Firenze
> Firenze is Florence
> Some think it is a woman with flowers in her hair
> But NO   it is a city with stones on the streets (LLB96 30)[24]

The poem's critique of masculine misogyny, depicted so bitingly in the discourse on women issuing from the "elder's lips," also takes aim at the idealization of women (like Florence, or the goddess Flora, with flowers in her hair). The poem refuses the equation of "Firenze" with "a woman with flowers in her hair," insisting "it is a city with stones on the streets" (LLB96 30). This pernicious idealization, Loy recognizes, is like the trattoria's "mayonnaise," covering over what is underneath. The flowers conceal the hard stones trod by Futurism's royalty, just as their words of praise (remember Marinetti's ode to the vagina and insistence that "woman is a wonderful animal") ensure a woman's place is "underneath." Moreover, this refusal gains visual velocity through the big space following "NO" in the final line above, as blank spaces and the visual page become key strategies in Loy's poetic Baedeker that challenge both the 1906 touristic Baedeker and the Futurists' Florence. A dual consciousness of space—within the city and within the poem's visual page—builds a spatial dynamics of critique through both form and referential content.

IV. "FIRENZE IS FLORENCE / SOME THINK IT IS A WOMAN"

Loy gave birth twice in Florence, and her poetry keenly observes women's maternal roles and experiences. The poetic paths of Loy's Baedeker, pursuing feminist critiques and en dehors garde compositional strategies, explore new spaces in representing the maternal body. Following such pathways, amble through a handful of 1914 poems, including "The Effectual Marriage," "The Prototype," and "Parturition"; additionally, gaze on or imagine early paintings depicting maternity as both embodied and sacralized.

Florence hosts a cityscape gallery of maternal images. Amid the Italian Catholic atmosphere, Loy noticed women's material bodies residing in tension with the Virgin Mary, whose imagery marks almost every street. Traversing this Florentine iconography, the poems overlay a map of feminist observations upon the city's religious structures of gender. For Loy, Florence may be a woman but not the flower-bedecked or sanctified visions on offer. Let us see where her poetry takes us amid the Madonnas of Florence; in particular, let us pay attention on this tour to a place-bound commerce of the Madonna and a street that explores intersections of the sacred and profane.

Loy's Madonnas: Early Poems and Paintings

Reading Loy's Florence poems and traveling through her adopted city, we move among the carabinieri (militaristic police), the Ponte Vecchio, the Pitti Palace, the Duomo, the green shutters, the stony streets, the maternity hospital, Paszkowski's café, the trattoria, the "Public Garden" (probably the Boboli); we are joined by vendors, priests, nuns, tarot card readers, nurses, artists and poets, fathers, and children. And there are many women.

Maternal images appearing in the poems' streets and homes often frame the condition of poverty in relation to the body's needs and oppressions. At the same time, Loy's references to reproductivity envision women's empowerment and critique male attitudes that condescend to the maternal body or seek to possess its generative capacity. Satirically noting, for example, the Futurists' envy for woman's reproductive capacity alongside their expressive disdain for the sex, "Lions' Jaws" mocks "a manifesto / notifying women's wombs / of Man's immediate agamogenesis" (asexual reproduction that ironically does not require a male) (LLB96 47). Such commentary evokes Futurist works like *Mafarka the Futurist*, Marinetti's 1909 novel, in which he fantasizes about creating life without women: "it is entirely possible to create an immortal giant with unfailing wings, out of one's own flesh, without the collaboration and foul-smelling involvement of a woman's uterus!" ("Mafarka's Discourse" 38).

While satirically reacting to Marinetti's ideas, Loy's Florentine writings further suggest contemporaneous connections with Italian feminists who promoted "the idea of a female body which becomes creative through a sexuality which may lead to maternity without hindrance" (Scuriatti, "Transnational" 310). Feminist arguments in Italy, which Loy would have known, associated maternity with political activism and national identity, and ranged from a eugenics approach, to recognizing a woman's freedom to bear children outside of marriage, and to eliminating false oppositions of sexuality and motherhood (310). Loy's "Feminist Manifesto" likewise argues for ending such oppositions and understanding maternity as a right for all women, although with regrettable eugenicist overtones (see Fig. 2.4).[25]

Confronting the cultural primacy of the Madonna figure in configuring the maternal, Loy's Florence poems echo her familiar presence.

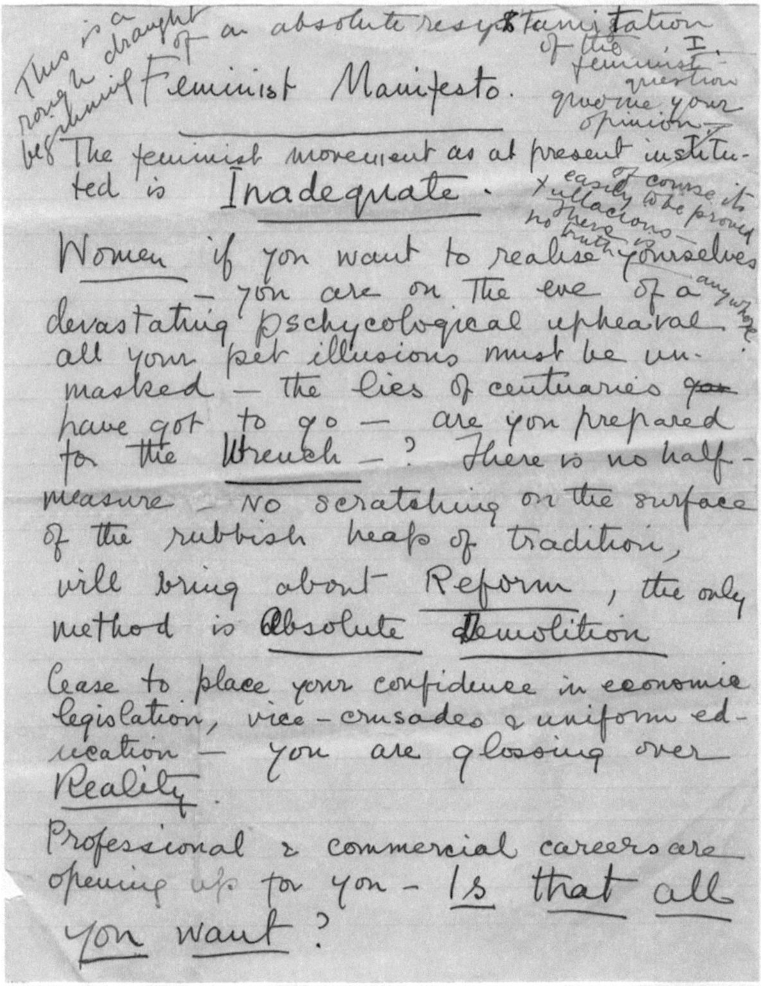

Feminist Manifesto.

The feminist movement as at present instituted is Inadequate.

Women if you want to realise yourselves — you are on the eve of a devastating pschycological upheaval — all your pet illusions must be unmasked — the lies of centuries have got to go — are you prepared for the Wrench —? There is no half-measure — NO scratching on the surface of the rubbish heap of tradition, will bring about Reform, the only method is Absolute Demolition

Cease to place your confidence in economic legislation, vice-crusades & uniform education — you are glossing over Reality.

Professional & commercial careers are opening up for you — Is that all you want?

Figure 2.4. Mina Loy, "Feminist Manifesto," holograph manuscript, YCAL MSS 196, Mabel Dodge Luhan papers, Beinecke Library, Yale University.

The Madonna is everywhere in Florence. Now as then, she appears in icons, bas-reliefs, statues, paintings, house decorations, and shrines that fill the streets. In Loy's poetry, the Madonna, even if not explicitly named, associatively emerges in scenes of maternal women and their broods of children; the graphic process of childbirth; the maternity hospital; the marketing of women by their fathers; the abuse of women by their husbands; and the poverty of women who must feed their children. Loy's images of mothers—whether swarmed by children on the street or giving birth in homes or downtrodden by poverty—insist on maternity as a bodily and often oppressed state. Most notably, "Parturition," converts this bodily state into a cosmic creative power resisting patriarchal oppression or definition.

"The Effectual Marriage" introduces and parodies gender ideologies enveloping the Madonna figure. Loy's sly mention of the Madonna blurs an image of Mary typical to Florentine homes and streets with the female figure in the poem, Gina, who is kept in her place (the kitchen) and denied her body, as though parodying the Virgin's disembodied purity: "Some say that happy women are immaterial" (LLB96 36). Foundational to Christian narratives, the Virgin's purity also offers protection. Familiar iconography of the Virgin protecting the faithful in the folds of her cloak or skirt finds its way into Loy's poem, perhaps mocking uses of the Madonna to enforce womanly meekness, a trait that Gina has learned equates to "being a female" (36). At the same time, the stanza devoted to the Madonna in this lengthy poem about gender power imbalances suggests that the disembodied Virgin Mary is a construct produced by the cowardice of men, who hide behind (and depend upon) this disempowered version of womanhood:

> Sundays   a warm light in the parlor
> From the gritty road   on the white wall
> anybody could see it
> Shimmered a composite effigy
> Madonna   crinolined   a man
> hidden beneath her hoop
> Ho for the blue and red of her
> The silent eyelids of her
> The shiny smile of her (LLB96 37)

Whether the viewpoint is looking from the parlor to an image of the Madonna on a roadside wall, or from the road looking into the parlor window, the view of the "composite effigy" includes a man hiding, the blank spaces of the lines punctuating his retreat behind the crinoline, beneath the hoop. As in other poems, white space reveals or makes visible something spatial that ordinary eyes cannot see. Sexual innuendo playfully suggests an erotic stimulation and a not-so-virginal Madonna. Indeed, this female "effigy" signals a sly knowledge and even, perhaps, an erotic power, in the "silent eyelids" and the "shiny smile" (37)—a patriarchal construct or "composite" of the blue-robed Madonna as obedient and spiritually blissful who, nonetheless, conveys a secret that exceeds her image. Much like Gina, or the "mad woman" who "inspired" this "narrative" (as the poem's postscript states) (39), the Madonna's secrets (her pleasure, her voice) threaten the male-dominated worlds of religion and family.

The Madonna figure carries a biographical weight, as associations between Loy and the Madonna appear in friends' memoirs. Gertrude Stein recalled a gift of a Black Madonna statuette from Loy's studio, after a visit there. Loy was herself referred to as a Beautiful Madonna and associated with the maternal sacrifice of Mary. Mabel Dodge Luhan judged her "lovely as a Byzantine Madonna" (338). The Madonna image shades Dodge Luhan's mention of the loss of Loy's first child, Oda Janet Haweis, born in Paris in May 1904 and dying of meningitis two days after turning one (Burke, *Becoming* 98). Dodge Luhan describes a painting done by Loy on the night her child died, titled *The Wooden Madonna* and bitterly satirizing the holy Madonna as a "foolish-looking mother holding her baby," oblivious to the maternal suffering around her:

> The night Ducie's little daughter died, she sat up all night and made the extraordinary tempera painting called "The Wooden Madonna" that I still have: the foolish-looking mother holding her baby, whose two small fingers are raised in an impotent blessing over the other anguished mother who, on her knees, curses them both with great, upraised, clenched fists, and her own baby sprawling dead with little arms and legs outstretched lifeless, like faded flower petals. (342)

This image of contrasting mothers, one divine and the other earthly, generates one of Loy's earliest poems, "The Prototype," demonstrating one of many correspondences between her visual art and poetry.

Indeed, Loy's long-standing artistic interest in images of mothers is revealed through exhibit records of painting titles and in surviving artwork, recently made accessible in the 2023 showing and catalog of her art, *Strangeness Is Inevitable,* edited by curator Jennifer R. Gross. *Women in Carriage* (circa 1907) shows a woman breastfeeding a baby (see Fig. 2.5).

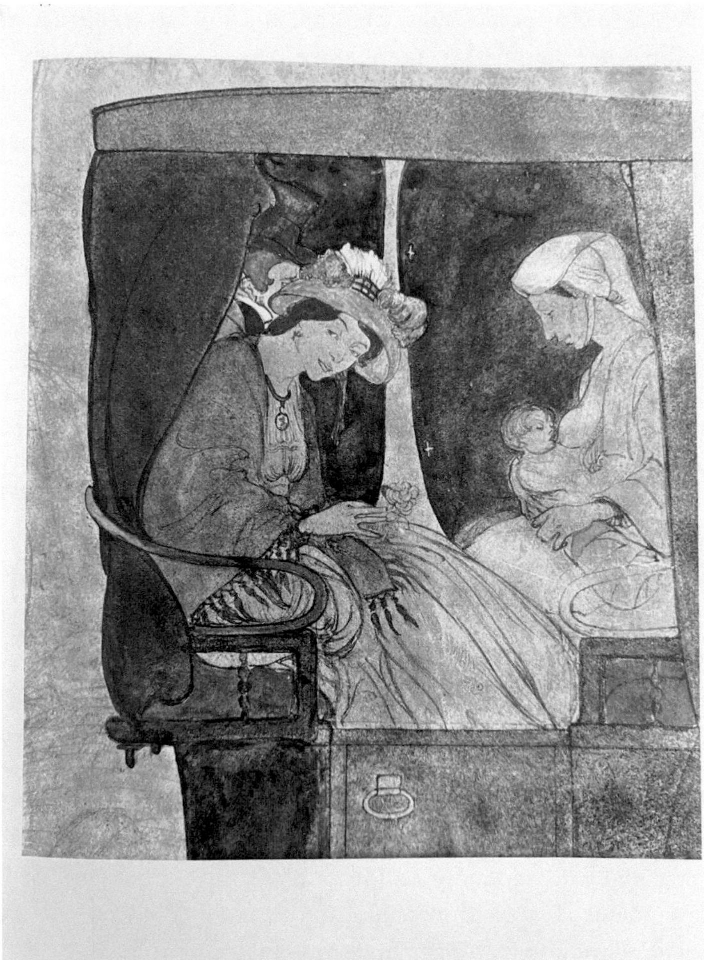

Figure 2.5. Mina Loy, *Women in Carriage*, circa 1907. Mixed media on paper, 8 × 8 in. (27.32 × 20.32 cm). From the collection of Jessica and John Gordon.

Her humble dress contrasts with the more fashionably attired, hatted figure opposite her (sitting beside a man in top hat, whose face is blocked by the woman's flowery headgear), whose outward gaze suggests Loy's face as the model (Gross, "Truant," 13).

The visual marks of class distinction suggested in this painting's attention to clothing interestingly correspond with a later untitled drawing, appearing in *Crapouillet* (circa 1915), following a classical triangular Madonna composition of mother and child to render a simply cloaked mother holding her infant and a female companion standing behind her (in Gross, "Truant," 19). The subject and style suggest models who populate her poems, such as the poorer Florentine women on her street.

During Oda Janet's short infancy, Loy painted a watercolor titled *The Mother* (now lost), suggesting an intriguing pairing with *The Wooden Madonna*. The titles contrast a material state of motherhood with an inanimate idealization, one being earthly, the other being divine but "wooden." *The Mother*, chosen for the 1904 Salon d'Automne along with six other watercolors, signals Loy's interest as a woman in representing maternity. As a pair of paintings on motherhood, they speak across that sad year of Loy's life as a new mother. Having likely seen *The Wooden Madonna* while visiting Dodge's villa in 1914, Carl Van Vechten wrote, "Was it only Mina Loy who dared protest sufficiently to paint her motherhood, with the dead child at her feet, upbraiding Mary?"[26]

Some twenty years later, the 1935 sculpture *Maternity* suggests her ongoing concern with this theme, reimagining the triangular composition of Madonna imagery through an image of an everyday woman, whose earthiness is captured through the chosen medium of clay (see Fig. 2.6).

Not surprisingly, given that Loy's turn to writing coincided with birthing and raising young children, maternity is featured in her earliest poems. "Parturition" and "The Prototype" center maternal bodies in relation to material conditions and claims of divinity. While "Parturition," the more-discussed of these two poems, radically insists

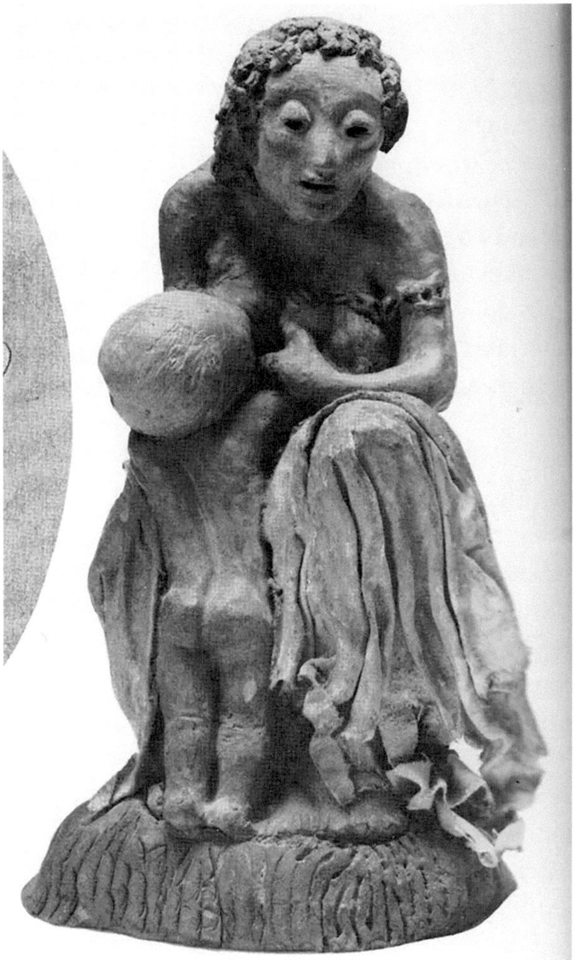

Figure 2.6. Mina Loy, *Maternity*, 1935 terracotta sculpture, now lost, documentary photograph (facsimile).

on the graphic, physical experience of labor while linking it to a cosmic creative power, "The Prototype" just as radically follows a different course, protesting the economics of the maternal body within socioreligious structures of power that oppress the material body through an idea of the feminine divine.

“Parturition”: Birth as Feminist En Dehors Garde

Most strikingly, “Parturition” asserts Loy’s feminist revision of the Madonna, situating maternity in the body that, while initially coerced by structures of social power, accesses a power particular to women through the process of labor. In contrast to Futurist ideas, “Parturition” links the birthing body and womb with an “infinite Maternity,” positing the maternal as a powerful site of “cosmic” intersections (LLB96 7). An “infinite Maternity,” absorbing the mother into “The was—is—ever—shall—be,” reimagines an embodied connection to divine maternity haunted by but resistant to the most heralded image of maternity in Catholic Italy, the Madonna.

Loy’s second and third children were born in Italy (after the death of Oda in Paris). She and Haweis moved in the hot summer to the cooler mountain resort of Bagni di Lucca to deliver Joella (July 20, 1907); Giles was born in wintry Florence about eighteen months later (February 1, 1909). Loy’s choice of the word “parturition” speaks to her Italian setting, evoking the painting genre of the Madonna del Parto, or “Our Lady in Parturition.” Appearing first in Rome (as a fresco in a ninth-century crypt) and early medieval Tuscany, this genre features the pregnant Mary calling attention to her womb, where God is made flesh, by pointing to her belly, cradling it, or resting her hand on it. Often she carries a book, symbolizing the Old Testament, and at times, as in the 1459 image by Piero della Francesca, the dress fabric opens to a contrasting slit down the center of her belly to further emphasize her body as vessel (see Fig. 2.7). The Madonna del Parto was venerated by pregnant women praying for safe deliveries.

Loy’s poem assumes this lineage while translating the iconic Madonna into an expansive cosmic energy absorbed by the laboring maternal body. Becoming the “centre / Of a circle of pain,” the poem’s “I” finds that “Pain is no stronger than the resisting force / Pain calls up in me / The struggle is equal” (LLB96 4). The graphic physicality of birth is pronounced—the “distorted mountain of agony” of contractions, the “delirium of night-hours” and the “gurgling of a crucified wild beast” attending the “foam on the stretched muscles of a mouth” (LLB96 5). Pain fosters a “Negation of myself as unit,” an emptying of preconceived and sanitized notions of birth and maternity. Images from nature yoke processes of life and

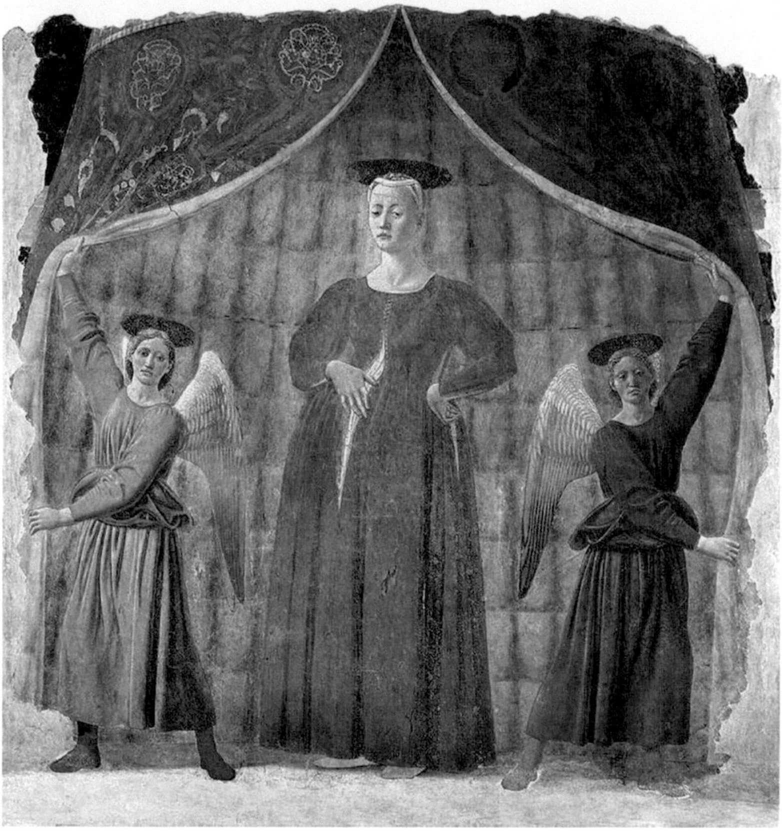

Figure 2.7. *Madonna del Parto*, Piero della Francesca, 1459.

death, underscoring the "infinite Maternity" and "cosmic reproductivity" the woman is "absorbed / into" (LLB96 7). The memory of a "dead white feather moth / Laying eggs" and the "Impression of a cat / With blind kittens / Among her legs" play across her mind as her body experiences parturition:

> A leap with nature
> Into the essence
> Of unpredicted Maternity
> Against my thigh
> Touch of infinitesimal motion

Scarcely perceptible
Undulation
Warmth moisture
Stir of incipient life
Precipitating into me
The contents of the universe (LLB96 6)

Like the Madonna of Michelangelo's late-life *Bandini Pietà*—situated in the Duomo in 1722 and showing Christ in Mary's arms, supported by Nicodemus and helped by Mary Magdalene—the maternal knowledge of the "undulation of living" collapses birth and death, so that in death one sees birth, and in birth one sees death. For Loy, this knowledge is not divinely obtained but arises from her "sub-conscious" and its worldly encounters:

Impression of small animal carcass
Covered with blue-bottles
--Epicurean--
And through the insects
Waves that same undulation of living
Death
Life
I am knowing
All about
Unfolding (LLB96 7)

"Parturition" ends with an image of women in church—"Each woman-of-the-people / Tip-toeing the red pile of the carpet / Doing hushed service"—a modest contrast to the speaker's claim to experiencing "infinite Maternity" and absorption into "cosmic reproductivity" (7). Nonetheless, the speaker is linked to this collectivity of women, just as she is linked to the birthing cat or the insect eggs, although she regrets the "ludicrous little halo" of submission they accept, "sublimely unaware" of a potential power that the "halo" could alternatively grant. The poem ends with a statement "heard in a church," that "--Man and woman God made them-- / Thank God" (8), a rather enigmatic turn to an institution that seems a foil for empowering women. We might read these lines as an insistence upon gender equality, a use of church language to denote men *and* women equally made by God, even as the church retains sexist hierarchies to the opposite effect. The blank space prior to the final "Thank God" suggests a moment's pause to absorb the radical interpretation of Biblical words, deflecting the standard hierarchy to which they are typically put. In en dehors garde fashion, the poem undercuts a central authority by replaying its words in alternative contexts and viewpoints, here from the perspective of the laboring woman whose body moves outward from biblically derived words to realize and recast them differently.

Perhaps Loy's most provocative statement on maternity appears in her 1914 "Feminist Manifesto," which calls on women to "demolish" the "division of women into two classes," the mistress and the mother (LLB96 154). Stressing marriage as an arrangement of commerce—one of the "trades"—she protests that women not "striking that advantageous bargain" by entering marriage are denied maternity. Instead, she argues "Every woman has a right to maternity," followed by a eugenicist-tainted (but not unfamiliar to Italian and American feminisms influencing her thought) declaration that "Every woman of superior intelligence should realize her race-responsibility, in producing children in adequate proportion to the unfit or degenerate members of her sex" (LLB96 155). In such statements, as critics have observed, Loy's early feminism overlooks social hierarchies that privilege her own position as a white British woman, a tension ambivalently unresolved in regard to class, race, and ethnicity even when she invokes her own Jewish heritage.[27]

Across both works, Loy's visual sense of the page (typographical play, visual spaces, unusual lineation) redirects Marinetti"s "words in freedom" and the favored Futurist form of the manifesto to orchestrate a feminist response to maternal images proffered by Church and avant-garde alike. The en dehors garde resonances of "Parturition" equate modernism's "birth of the new" with women's physical, intellectual, and creative agency and power.

Visiting the Duomo and the Cathedral of Santa Maria del Fiore

> Accessing the Piazza del Duomo from the Ponte Vecchio, stroll onto Via Por Santa Maria and continue onto Via Calimala. Turn right onto Via Calimaruzza, and then left onto Via dei Calzaiuoli. Or just follow the massive dome.

Searching out the socioeconomic and religious contexts attending a grimmer manifestation of maternity, Loy's Baedeker tour takes us next to the center of Florentine Catholicism, the Piazza del Duomo and its Cathedral of Santa Maria del Fiore. What Van Vechten termed Loy's "upbraiding" of Mary in her artwork motivates one of Loy's earliest poems, "The Prototype," composed in 1914. Setting the poem "In the Duomo, on Xmas eve" at a midnight mass of "1,000 candles," Loy presents two infant births: one is the worshipped Christ child, a "cold wax baby," "Perfect in pink-&-whiteness" with a "tinsel star / that rises on his forehead." The other is the "new-born Hungry One,"

> a horrible little
> baby—made of half warm flesh;
> flesh that is covered by sores—carried
> by a half-broken mother. (LLB96 221)

The cathedral's title, Santa Maria del Fiore, meaning St. Mary of the Flower, harkens to Loy's poetic dispute with the idea of Florence as a woman with flowers ("Giovanni Franchi"). Here, she gives us a more material image of Florentine womanhood.

The poem's placement in the Duomo suggests a space rich with Marian imagery that stands in stark contrast with the poverty of the "half-broken mother." The 1906 Baedeker describes the images of Mary particularly prominent above the portals to Il Duomo:

> Above the first door on the S. side is a Madonna of the 14th century. [...] in the lunette, the Madonna between two angels. [...] The admirable

bas-relief of the Madonna with the girdle, over the [N.] door, is ascribed to *Nanni di Banco* (1414). (479)

The octagonal "space beneath the dome" includes windows designed from Madonna images by artists such as Donatello (*Coronation of the Virgin*) and Paolo Uccello (*Adoration of the Magi*) (as would be expected in an Italian cathedral), and behind the high altar is "an unfinished group (Pietà) by *Michael Angelo* [*sic*] (late work)" (Baedeker 480). When you visit the Duomo, envision Loy entering its vast interior, gazing upon the high altar where Christological typology aligns the newborn Christ child with the corporeal suffering body from the cross. Such paired iconography customarily links the Madonna's innocence with her broken grief, the lamenting and distraught Mary of the *Florentine Pietà* (removed in 1993 to the Museo dell'Opera del Duomo) fulfilling the prophecy of the Adoration. Loy's poem inhabits that iconic connection between birth and death to reclaim the maternal as a site of justice rather than abstract divinity. In "The Prototype," the mother of the Florence streets experiences a child in pain and hunger, echoing the Mary holding her dead child rather than the idealized Virgin and the "perfect baby." The realization of Mary's grief as an aid to mothers displaces the idealized birth's distance, a turn toward Mary-in-pain that later suffuses Loy's World War II poem "Aid of the Madonna."

The speaker, a self-proclaimed "heretic," is the "only follower in Christ's foot-steps / among this crowd adoring a wax doll," for she alone worships "the poor / sore baby—the child of sex ignorance and poverty" (LLB96 221). Rather than praying to a "god," she prays to "humanity's social consciousness" for reproductive education and economic equity, calling for the adulation of Mary and Christ child to be translated from abstract worship to concrete help for the "half-broken mother," the earthly Madonna and her sick child. She invites a "New Gospel" to replace the idealized Virgin and child ("Throw away the wax-baby") with a church of social justice ("Use the churches as night-shelters").[28] In calling for a "New Gospel" to be preached, for the church to "do for that mother & that child in the light, what / the priests have tried to do in the dark" (LLB 222), Loy's poem suggests the influence of her friend George Herron, an American participant in the Villa Curonia's expatriate salons. Promoting the Social Gospel Movement, Herron advocated a Christianity of social justice, viewing poverty as the result of systemic forces rather than personal flaws (Burke, *Becoming* 275). As Keith Tuma notes, "Loy's Christ emerges [at this time] as a valued spokesperson for democratic and communal values, an optimistic voice [... that] begins to take on the shape of Herron's utopian socialism" (147).

At the same time, in "The Prototype" maternity emerges as a feminist claim to divinity-in-self, a rejection of the Church and society's parallel attitudes idealizing but denigrating women. The traditional Madonna image of virginal, disembodied motherhood finds resistance in the pronounced images of bodily, difficult maternity appearing in Loy's Florentine poems—as in "the hips of women [that] sway / Among the crawling children they produce" ("Italian Pictures" LLB96 10).

The Della Robbia: A Brief Jaunt on the Via de' Bardi

Take a riverside stroll down the Via de' Bardi, where Loy lived briefly at no. 27. Easily find the Via de' Bardi by crossing the Ponte Vecchio to the Oltrarno side and turning eastward. Via de' Bardi runs parallel to the river and just above its walls. Walking along the Via de' Bardi, with the Ponte Vecchio at your back, enjoy a view of the river and mountains rising outside the city. Just down the street, walking past the area of Loy's temporary abode, you will find a Florentine landmark—the church Santa Lucia dei Magnoli, adorned with a famous della Robbia.

Commerce and religion, the street and Madonna, converge on Loy's Florentine map at the site of the home she briefly rented on the Via de' Bardi, where she moved for a short period following Haweis's departure from Florence and as the war began in 1914. Having rented the Costa San Giorgio home to tenants while vacationing in Vallombrosa during that summer, Loy returned to the city without her children (who were left in the care of their nursemaid in the mountains as the war intensified) and moved into no. 27 Via de' Bardi (current house numbers have likely changed). The street, which flows parallel to the Arno's waters, hosts fascinating juxtapositions of literary lineage, romance, and Madonna iconography for Loy.

The 1906 Baedeker identifies two tourist destinations on the street: the della Robbia of Santa Lucia dei Magnoli, and the home that is the setting of George Eliot's *Romala*, a novel set in Renaissance Florence and including several historical Florentine figures from this era. Identified as a place of interest to English tourists, as it might have been to Loy, Eliot's home suggests yet another piece of a lineage connecting British literati and the city's cultural, political, and artistic culture. In Eliot's time, as in Loy's, the culture of the Madonna permeated the city. Both writers likely viewed the interior and exterior artwork of Santa Lucia dei Magnoli, an eleventh-century church restored several times in the following centuries.

On your street tour of the Via de' Bardi, visit the Santa Lucia dei Magnoli. As the 1906 Baedeker directs, walk a few blocks away from the Ponte Vecchio, where "rises the small church of Santa Lucia dei Magnoli," known for "containing a relief by the *Della Robbia* above the door, and an Annunciation by Jac. del Sellaio (1st altar on the left)" [*sic*] (548).

During the Renaissance, the period of Eliot's novel, a two-panel painting of the Annunciation—Mary receiving word of her impending and divine maternity—was commissioned for the church with the artist Jacopo del Sellaio (a student of Fra' Filippo Lippi and friend of Botticelli), as noted in the Baedeker's entry on the church. The lunette by Benedetto Buglioni, a student from the Renaissance workshop of the della Robbia, arches above the exterior doorway of the church, depicting Santa Lucia between two angels. This impressive example of the della Robbia devotional form exemplifies techniques for color-glazing terracotta developed by the fifteenth-century Florentine sculptor Luca della Robbia, most often to depict Mary and the Christ in distinctive shades of blue and white (although, as in this case, also depicting saints).

During the years of Loy's residence in Florence, the city's numerous della Robbia images were widely reproduced for sale, helping to sustain the profitable marketing of religious iconography in the city. Loy's response to the commodification of such idealizing processes surfaces in Burke's observation that,

> marveling at the number of certified "Della Robbia" Madonnas being shipped to America, she studied the pecking order among the dealers. Such persons conducted business by seeking to "fasten their right to exist upon the battered figurines of the Catholic past" (*Becoming* 124).[29]

In part, this suggests Loy's ongoing interest in commerce, given her own need to make a living at different times and through different avenues, such as fashion, lamp design, and myriad invention designs that she attempted to patent and sell (see chapter 4).

At the same time, her alertness to religion's commercial priorities and historical hoarding of wealth dovetails with her social concerns over inequality. Indeed, commerce of the Madonna and the street characterizes the intersection of sacred and profane in poems like "The Prototype" and "Virgins Plus Curtains Minus Dots" that evoke systems of commerce shaping profit and deprivation, power and injustice. As in "The Prototype," Loy's alertness to religious iconography as commerce highlights religion's economic motivations that consequently fuel systems of inequity. The poem denounces the idealization of the Virgin Mary as distracting attention from social and material realities—foregrounded in "The Costa San Giorgio" or "Costa Magic" or the prose piece "Summer Night in a Florence Slum"—that map the religio-economics of womanhood, virginity, and motherhood in her Italian poetic Baedeker.

V. ITALIAN RETREATS

Just as Loy's Florence poems call out to specific places in the city—and their geo-economies of gender and class—her art and poetry also draw upon the Italian retreats she frequented, especially in the hot summers. Her visits to the mountains and coasts of Italy help us trace her movements not just from city to country or seaside but also between artwork, writing, and financial scheming for survival, especially once Haweis left the family. In poems and paintings resonant with place specifics attentive to economics, and in her fashion designs and correspondence with friends while in Vallombrosa, Loy's travel to retreats embodies the lifelong boundary crossings of arts and commerce marking her en dehors garde ventures.

Seaside Retreats: Bagni di Lucca and the Coast of Forte dei Marmi

Should you travel to Florence, be forewarned that summer's heat and humidity present challenges. Loy's family found refuge in the mountains and sea to the west of the city. At the beginning of their Italian decade, Loy and Haweis awaited the birth of a child during such a summer. As Loy approached full term, the couple traveled westward to Bagni di Lucca, a mountain resort with natural baths just outside the medieval town of Lucca. Loy delivered Joella Synara Haweis on July 20, 1907. Both knew the child was the offspring from a union between Loy and her Parisian lover, Henry Joël Le Savoureux, the "French doctor who treated her for neurasthenia after the death of Oda"; indeed, the daughter's name Joella (from Joël) carries its paternal trace (Burke, *Becoming* 116). Their shared knowledge of Haweis's own dalliances prompted him to agree to claim the child as his own. Haweis's revenge for Loy's infidelity (ignoring his own) would include a demand for another baby to make up for the affair and manipulations of the funds contributed by Loy's father for their life in Italy (see Burke, *Becoming*). Baekdeker's *Northern Italy* (1906) beckons with enticing descriptions of Bagni di Lucca:

> From Lucca to the Bagni di Lucca, 15 M., railway in 1 hr. (fares 1fr. 80, 90 c.). [...] *Bagni di Lucca*, the terminus, is situated a little above the junction of the *Lima* and the Serchio.

> The Bagni di Lucca (season, May 1st to Sept. 15th), which were known as early as the 10th cent. under the name of the "Baths of Corsena," with springs containing salt and sulphur [...] consist of several different villages in the valley of the *Lima*. They are much frequented by English and American visitors.
>
> [...]
>
> The freedom from dust, glare, and excessive heat makes this a delightful summer-resort. [...]
>
> The valley of the Lima is cool and well-shaded, chiefly with chestnut-trees, affording pleasant walks. (448–449)

The history of British visitors flocking to this spot, as in Vallombrosa and Florence, boasts a litany of nineteenth-century British poets: Shelley, Byron, and the Brownings visited Bagni di Lucca, a connection appealing no doubt to Haweis's image of a "foreign poetic colony" they might join in Italy, fostered by "his mother's recollections of the Brownings, with their Victorian poeticizing about the Renaissance" (Burke, *Becoming* 107).

In years that followed, the seaside at Forte dei Marmi offered a place of healing for Loy and her children. Joella's poor health necessitated leaving Florence in the summer, so after Giles's birth the toddlers "spent two months in the mountains followed by two months at Forte dei Marmi" (Burke, *Becoming* 117). Loy's summers in Forte dei Marmi were flanked by children and their needs, although she entrusted the children's care to the nursemaid for stretches of time. However, when Loy herself suffered a period of illness in January 1913 (Burke suggests possible influenza and anxiety over the collapse of her marriage [141]), Forte dei Marmi offered a place of convalescence. Remembering this illness may have been the impetus for a reference to the seaside town in a postscript to her later poem "The Effectual Marriage" (1915), stating that "This narrative halted when I learned that the house which inspired it was the home of a mad woman. / — Forte dei Marmi" (LLB96 39). Transposing her illness in marriage onto her later relationship with Papini, satirized in the poem, connects the entrapment in gender roles crossing relationships and contributing, in Loy's poetic representation, to woman's illness. Nonetheless, in 1913, allowing herself to be cared for by her husband despite her fears about his plans to leave for Australia and his newest affair, Loy improved during the days on the coast. On her return to the coast after Haweis left Italy, the newly published poet drafted works that included her first long poem and satires like "The Effectual Marriage," bidding farewell to Futurism. Forte dei Marmi offered Loy space for healing and transitions, a liminal in-between where she could paint and write.

The seaside retreat was also a place of social stimulation for Loy. Her artwork from this period includes depictions of Forte dei Marmi that reflect beach gatherings and cultural attractions. Gloria Braggiotti, friend and schoolmate of Loy's children, recalls in her memoir that

> It was as chic for Florentines to spend their summers at Viareggio, Forte dei Marmi, or Levanto as it was for Parisians to go to Biarritz or Deauville. For years my parents spent every summer at one of these Italian resorts. (94)

A pair of Loy's seaside watercolors from these years pick up on the "chic" summer visitors of Forte dei Marmi while suggesting gender dynamics within the resort's settings.

Maison des Bains depicts the entrance to a boardwalk theater playing the popular *La Tosca* (see Fig. 2.8).[30] The painting signals Italian place and performance through the production's title. First a world-touring play starring Sarah Bernhardt and then restaged as the opera *Tosca* by Giacomo Puccini in 1900, the Rome-set story of ill-fated love and violence appealed to audiences, especially with Bernhardt—an adored celebrity—in the title role of the play. When writing the opera, which met with great success, Puccini lived in Torre del Lago, the town adjacent to Forte dei Marmi, until 1921, becoming friends with Gabriele D'Annunzio who lived nearby in the early years of the twentieth century. In staging a performance platform within a painting, as Suzanne Churchill discusses in chapter 3, the painting's figures "are themselves performers," "displaying Loy's keen interest in gender performativity."[31]

Such attention to performance and spectatorship structures the composition and subject matter of *The Beach* (see Fig. 2.9).[32] As a woman inside a vertically striped beach tent ostensibly changes from street clothes to beach wear (we see her booted feet sticking out beneath the tent), other

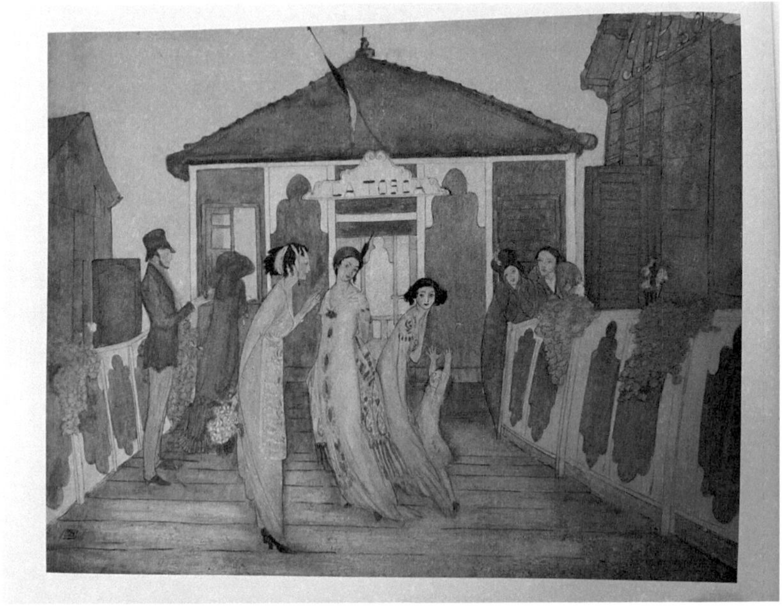

Figure 2.8. Mina Loy, *Maison des bains au Forte dei Marmi*, circa 1913. Gouache and ink with traces of graphite on paper mounted on cardboard, 13¾ × 17½ in. (34.93 × 44.45 cm).

women in their beach garb surround themselves with fashionable accessories, such as a beach hat propped beside an iron chair. Its curvy design resonates visually with the curved umbrellas and curly, draped hair to further signify the feminine curves of the covered bodies under the women's lovely beach robes. Intent on how they look, the women casually perform for each other and the viewer's eye. One, seated and wearing a filmy pink beach cover and tied hair cover (with curls escaping), holds a mirror but gazes in the direction of the tent. Another woman literally steps into a beach sandal, her bare leg (another curve) emerging with performative flair from her white beach robe as she drapes her (curved) long hair over one hand to dry it. She looks sidelong at the viewer.

Two pairs of children, girls and at least one boy, flank the central group of women. As they play in the sand, their part in this scene of gender performance includes their own dress—a little girl on the left wears a flouncy, lacy, white beach jumper and a hat with flower-like puffs,

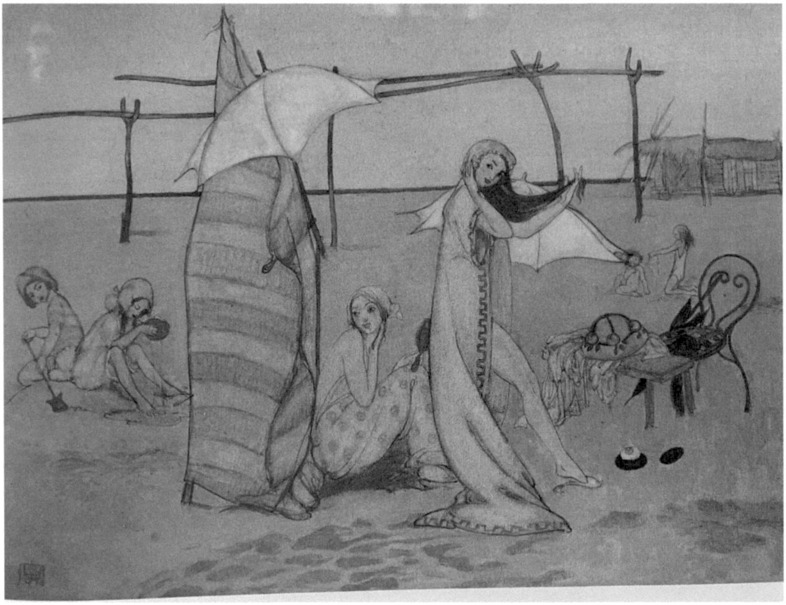

Figure 2.9. Mina Loy, *The Beach*, circa 1911. Watercolor and graphite, 20 × 25 in. (50.8 × 63.5 cm).

while the little boy has a striped shirt and front-brimmed hat. The pair of children in the right-hand background, which includes a sitting baby, seem oblivious in their play. Nonetheless, their presence suggests the generational transmission of gender codes in a socially sanctioned script of femininity that always includes children with women. Loy's painting registers her own time at the beach with her children, Joella and Giles, while its emphasis on performance suggests the subversive insights about gender flavoring her poetry of the period and her own self-presentations.

Years later, Loy's poetry returns to the coast in "The Mediterranean Sea," written in 1928 while living in Paris but picking up threads from her work in Italy, compiling in art and poetry a fabric of place that continues long after she leaves it. The final section of this chapter, a "post-tour" of sorts, considers two pieces written about Italy after she ceased to live there, poetically returning to Florence and the Mediterranean coast. First, however, let us continue our tour of Loy's Italian retreats as they appear in her Florentine poems.

Summer in the Mountains: Vallombrosa, 1914

Providing another retreat for family and writing, the mountains offered a cool weather alternative during summer months and, as international tensions built, a remove from encroaching political and military conflicts. In July 1914, as the Great War began and Florence felt increasingly tense and threatened, Loy traveled with her children and friends to the mountains outside of Florence, staying in Vallombrosa and Saltino and drafting the poem "July in Vallombrosa," noting the features of the place (see Fig. 2.10). The 1906 *Baedeker's Northern Italy* paints an enticing picture of Vallombrosa's monastery and national forest, with its long history of attracting English writers to relax, hike, and enjoy the views:

> VALLOMBROSA. A visit to this celebrated monastery is now easily accomplished in one day with the aid of the cable-railway from Sant' Ellero to Saltino; but in summer several days may be very pleasantly spent at Vallombrosa (rooms should be ordered in advance in July and August). The drive from Florence or Pontassieve [...] to Vallombrosa is charming.
> [...]
> The road steadily ascends, usually through woods, to *Vallombrosa* [...].
> [...]
> The convent of Vallombrosa (3140 ft.), situated in a shaded and sequestered spot on the N.W. slope of the Pratomagno chain, was founded in 1015 and suppressed in 1866. The present buildings, dating from 1637, have been occupied since 1870 by the *Reale Istituto Forestale*, the only advanced school of forestry in Italy. There are now only three monks here, who celebrate service in the church and attend to the meteorological observatory. (558–559)

The Paradisino, where Loy's friends would stay during their visit, also garners mention:

> *Il Paradisino* (3336 ft.), a small hermitage situated on a rock, ¼ hr. to the left above the monastery, is now an annexe to the Alb. della Foresta (see above; rooms not very comfortable). The platform in front commands an admirable Survey of the monastic buildings, and of the broad valley of the Arno as far as Florence, half of the cathedral-dome of which is visible behind a

> hill. The horizon is bounded by the Alpi Apuane (R. 21). — Another walk may be taken on the road leading from the hotel towards the N.E. along the mountain-slopes viâ *Villa del Lago* to the *Conusma Pass*. (559)

The entry on Il Paradisino includes directions for climbing hikes further "through dense pine forest" to a "crest of the ridge" and a commanding view of the Casentino Valley, the Arno, and Florence; even the "blue Mediterranean is sometimes visible in the extreme distance" (559).

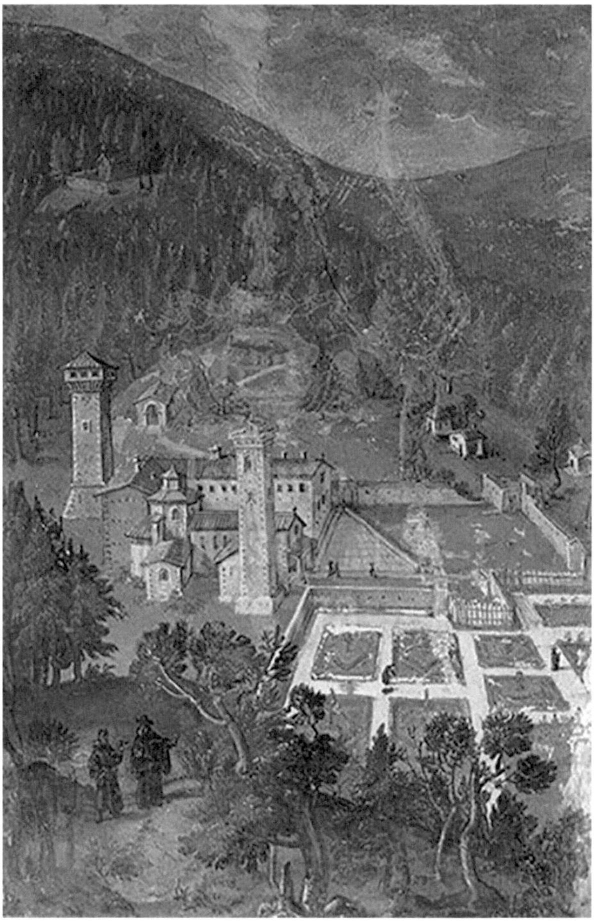

Figure 2.10. Vallombrosa Abbey, fresco detail, Giovanni Stradano, sixteenth-century.

If you travel to Vallombrosa and prefer not to drive, take an easy bus ride from Florence. In 1914, Loy traveled by train and cable-railcar, but now you can conveniently board the 343A bus for around six euros roundtrip at Florence's Stazione di Santa Maria Novella. Do be aware of limited time schedules for the trip, especially on the return. And be forewarned that businesses in Vallombrosa and Saltino are open primarily in the later summer months. In May, when I traveled there, the still-cool weather kept tourists and hospitality services at a minimum. From Florence, after several stops in small villages outside of the city, the bus climbs high up windy roads, where red poppies in late spring punctuate the dense green mountainside. The final stop, about forty-five minutes out of Florence, lands you in Saltino, just up the mountain road from Vallombrosa.

If you heed the Baedeker, you will know that July and August, rather than May, are prime months for visitors. That would have been the time of year that Loy traded the heat of Costa San Giorgio for the mountain air of Vallombrosa.

Climbing off the bus at Saltino, you will find a tiny cluster of buildings at the very top of the mountain and hope for the café perched beside the bus stop to be open, especially if you travel before high season. Wander the few roads, then walk a short distance down the mountain. To the left, observe stunning views; to the right, stroll through the tall firs of the national forest. Situated in the Reggello municipality, thirty kilometers from Florence in the Apennines, Vallombrosa became the first European national forest in 1867, renowned especially for its old-growth firs and beeches. Among the forest trails, you will likely spy hikers enjoying the dense forest's appeal. *Baedeker's Northern Italy* (1906) details several hikes, as this activity clearly held appeal during Loy's visits, too. Shortly, arrive at the gates of the old Benedictine monastery, where you will later catch the (only!) bus back to busy Florence.

In July and August of 1914, when Loy drafted "July in Vallombrosa," the first in the sequence of three "Italian Pictures," she traveled to the mountains with her children and friends—a group including Mable Dodge, Frances Stevens, Edith Dale, Neith Hapgood, and Carl Van Vechten—just as the war broke out. F. T. Marinetti would visit her in the mountains that summer (Burke, *Becoming* 171–74). Van Vechten's memoir recalls this somewhat tumultuous trip. Having arrived by train in Florence on July 31 to visit Edith Dale, living at the Villa Allegra, he caught a "glimpse of Ducie Haweis" and Neith Boyce Hapgood in a car upon leaving the station. Dale had made plans for them to join "Ducie" and others at Vallombrosa within a couple of days. On August 3, he awoke in Florence with "a dreadful sense of doom," feeling "everything seemed to be wrong with the world" upon learning from the papers that "the Germans had automatically declared war on France by entering Luxembourg," while the "Belgians and the Dutch were mobilizing" (Van Vechten 119). In these first days of war, and before Italy joined the fight against Germany, rumors of the cessation of mail, stoppage of Italian boats sailing from ports, a possible invasion of Florence by Hungary, and the severance of money's availability caused anxiety for the group of expatriates embarking upon the short trip to Vallombrosa. Boarding a train, with "Ducie [...] dressed in dull army blue," her children, friends, and two owls in cages, the group shared "a sense of doom" (Van Vechten 120–21). On the train, the group "smoked cigarettes in chains and were silent and irritable" (122).

Reading an issue of *The Trend*, the modernist little magazine (1911–1915) that Van Vechten subsequently helped edit, Loy did not notice the train stopping at Sant'Ellero, their initial destination in the journey. Sant'Ellero is described rather dismissively in the Baedeker as "an insignificant village with an old castle" (558). Only upon the train's movement from the station did Loy realize their mistake. Van Vechten recalls that "Ducie screamed, That's our station we've just passed? That's Sant' Ellero. It was too late" (122). Fearing they would have to take the train to its end point in Rome, "Ducie was extremely apologetic and stopped reading her magazine. After all, we had counted on her and she had failed us" (122).

Discovering they could get off the train at the next stop with a hotel, Arezzo, to pass the night and return to Sant'Ellero the next morning, the group elected to stay in the "exceedingly picturesque" town

(Van Vechten 124). There they encountered a fiesta celebrating the "completion of the façade of the cathedral in a festival which would endure a week," (123) initially making it difficult to find hotel rooms. Once settled, they strolled through the town, ate, and joined a crowd watching an "exhibition of moving-pictures" (124). The convergence of modernity (the war, the train, the new moving-picture technology) with the old (the cathedral, the charming town, the festival amid the opening days of Europe's new war) suggests a poignant point in time marking this journey. Traveling from Florence to Vallombrosa, they suspected the world would never be the same, Van Vechten tells us in hindsight.

Early the next morning, the group caught the train to Sant'Ellero, their destination for catching the "rack and pinion railway, with its superb views, up to Saltino" to then drive "through the pine forests to Vallombrosa" (Van Vechten 127). Consulting their Baedeker, they would find the innovative cable railway and the carriage-road thus described:

> The CABLE RAILWAY from S. Ellero to Saltino is 5 M. long with a maximum gradient of 22:100. The ascent takes about 1 hr.; fare 4, return-ticket 6 fr. — The train starts from the railway-station at S. Ellero and ascends through a grove of oaks, on the bank of the torrent *Vicano*, to the crest of one of the numerous spurs which the Pratomagno range throws out into the valley of the Arno. A striking view is disclosed; straight on, Saltino appears, above a steep slope. [...] Saltino (3140 ft.), finely situated on a barren promontory, commanding a splendid view.
>
> [...]
>
> The carriage-road leads through a dense grove of firs to (1¼ M.) *Vallombrosa*. The road which diverges to the right at the station and passes the *Scoglio del Saltino*, a projecting rock with a fine view of the Arno valley, is only a little longer. (558–559)

Upon arrival, the group stayed in rooms at Albergo del Paradisino, a former Benedictine monastery, just above the Vallombrosa abbey. Most of the monks were evicted in 1866 by the new Italian state, permitted to return only after World War II. The monastery and abbey still stand, and the grounds are open. Within a couple of days of arrival, Loy left the Paradisino to rent a cottage in nearby Saltino, where she and her children stayed with Frances Stevens. Settling into the cottage, Loy stocked up on sustainable food, "laying in stores of flour, beans, and oil," hoping to feed the whole group each night (her cook "scornfully rejected" the idea of cooking for everyone) (Van Vechten 132). Her cottage, built from prefabricated Swedish pieces, was a "small and unsightly red and buff house [...] entirely out of harmony with the landscape or the neighbouring cottages," Van Vechten notes disdainfully, but "it commanded a view of the magnificent plain below: even Florence was visible, gleaming in what appeared to be a shower of golden dust in the late afternoon light" (132).

Vallombrosa's Poetic Allure

While Loy moved to nearby Saltino, her friends remained that summer at the Paradisino. They were enchanted by legends of Milton's stay there and his reference to the Vallombrosa forest in *Paradise Lost*:

> Thick as Autumnal Leaves that strow the Brooks
> In *Vallombrosa*, where th' Etrurian shades
> High over-arch't imbow'r
>
> (Book 1, lines 302–04)

While Milton's visit remains debated, a plaque testifying to his presence is nevertheless installed on the grounds.

In Vallombrosa, like Florence, the sites of British writers who lived or visited there suggest how Loy experienced poetic lineage through Italian places, such as Barrett Browning's home, Casa Guidi. Considerations of place frame Loy's approach to matters of lineage in crafting a poetic identity and sense of the modern; in this regard, she differs subtly but significantly from the Futurists' blanket dismissal of past traditions, signaling instead a desire to locate herself in relation to—while modernly different from—the intersections of national identity, migration, and transit evident in the poetic lineages she references. Visiting Vallombrosa, Loy would be aware that a stream of British mid-nineteenth-century travelers to the area included poets and writers interested in the forest's natural beauty. William Wordsworth penned "At Vallombrosa" in direct reference to Milton, using his predecessor's lines as epigraph to his own poem, seeking the "leaves" of "Miltonian shades." Henry James, Mary Shelley, and Robert and Elizabeth Barrett Browning all write about Vallombrosa in travel writings and poems, creating a particularly British poetic claim traced to Milton.

Perhaps Loy knew also of the popular late-nineteenth-century British writer Adeline Sergeant, whose narrative *In Vallombrosa: A Sequence* (1897) opens with an inscription from Elizabeth Barrett Browning and is based upon a trip taken by the author with a female companion, describing travels from the city to the mountain air much like the one Loy would take some twenty years later. *In Vallombrosa* begins in ways that Loy's trip would echo:

> When she first came up from Florence to the heights of Vallombrosa for a breath of cool and bracing air, she found the delicate wind-flowers still in blossom and a few violets and primroses in the woods. The city had been gradually growing hot and oppressive during those last days of May, but while her carriage climbed the mountain roads she felt as though the seasons had been put back again and as if she had exchanged glaring summer for an early spring. There was even a touch of coldness in the deep shadow of the trees.
>
> She had disdained the little mountain railway and chosen to drive from Pontassieve, but the horses were barely strong enough for their work [...]. (1–2)
>
> The season had not begun, and none of the hotels near the monastery itself were open; even *Paradiso* [*sic*], up among the trees whose leaves still strew the brooks in Vallombrosa, where the cells of the hermits used to be, and where Milton, they say, was aforetime entertained—even *Paradiso* was closed against visitors; and she was obliged to leave her carriage at the monastery gates [...] and walk up to the higher ground near the little railway station at Saltino. (3–4)

Sergeant's narrative portends the geography and environment later traversed by Loy and inscribed into one of her earliest poems to be written and published, "July in Vallombrosa." Was she aware of joining a line of English writers to take this same journey, with pen in hand? Is her poem a rehabilitation or revision of the British expatriate line?

“July in Vallombrosa”: “there is always Nature”

In a September letter to Van Vechten that included several dress designs that she hoped he would shop around, Loy also referenced her summer’s writing and expressed “hope you got the manuscripts.”[33] Did the manuscripts include her three “Italian Pictures,” as seems likely, an enticing link between her ventures as fashion entrepreneur and poet? As editor of the October, November, and December issues of *The Trend*, Van Vechten published “Italian Pictures” in November 1914, within four months of their time together in Vallombrosa. His own time in both this wooded Italian retreat and a more bustling Florence would undoubtedly enhance his enthusiasm for the three-part poem. Perhaps he read drafts of “July in Vallombrosa” or the city-based poems from the sequence (“The Costa San Giorgio” and “Costa Magic”) while amid the giant trees and magnificent views, experiencing an ancient and sacred-like ethos that he describes:

> Centuries ago the monks planted these pines in straight rows and now the bare trunks rise to incredible heights before the branches spread, forming a canopy of green needles overhead, so that the effect is that of a natural cathedral. (Van Vechten 127–28)

The pines open “July in Vallombrosa,” which, not unlike works by earlier British authors writing about the forest, responds to the natural environment and its distinctive woodland. Barrett Browning, recounting a trip to Vallombrosa in *Casa Guidi Windows*, recalls how the “slow pinewoods ever climb and climb,” remarking how the English “all love Italy” (77, 79). Loy’s poem begins with a view of an “Old lady sitting still / Pine trees standing quite still” (LLB96 9). Yet the old lady is sick, waiting to die in a sanatorium-like environment. Nature is a site for commerce in the poem, enticing tourists seeking health, relaxation, or escape. Indeed, Vallombrosa became a health and tourist resort during the period of the Benedictine order’s absence (1866–1949) and the founding of the National Forestry reserve and school. The interplay of natural and sacred, manifested by the presence in the “cathedral” of trees of the monastery, abbey, and numerous shrines and chapels (many devoted to the eleventh-century founder San Giovanni Gualberto), appears in Loy’s poem as one of several dualisms. “July in Vallombrosa” opposes the British and American guests with Italian visitors, residents, or workers; counterpoints health with illness or death; and imbricates the "natural" with commerce and tourism.

In the poem, the "whispering" of "Sisters of mercy" under the pine trees surrounds the old lady. The nuns' whispers seek to "Oust the Dryad," producing a sterile "consecration of forest," a sacralization of the "uneventful" (9) that Tara Prescott also reads as an extinction of the "female tree spirit" (17), perhaps an ironic comment on the secular state's banishment of the monks from the monastery-turned-Paradisimo (a few were left to care for the abbey chapel and grounds). Just as the Church sought to banish the pagan, the state extinguished the monastery for the forest's caretaking—and its related commerce as tourist destination, literary pilgrimage, and health resort. The mountain's attraction to tourists seeking health cures or rest during illness bespeaks a trend beginning in the nineteenth century for what Loy's poem tags as a "respectable" British endorsement of "prolonged invalidism" (LLB96 9).

The English foreigners contrast with the "Wanton Italian matrons" who sit and sew "[a]round the hotel" and "Discuss the better business of bed-linen," suggestively savvy about the bedroom as a place for marketing women through marriage or otherwise (echoing similar references in "The Costa San Giorgio," discussed earlier) (LLB96 9). Other women appear in the poem as caretakers, a deadening duty. The Blue Nun, referencing an order in nearby Fiesole whose members traveled to care for the dying, follows the most "permissible [...] chastity" for women, conforming to a feminine duty linguistically reduced to a mere "hobby of collecting death-beds" (LLB96 9). Likewise diminished in her self-sacrificial duty, the daughter of the ailing old woman "has been spent / In chasing moments from one room to another," tending the "bronchitis-kettle" and losing "her last little lust [...] in a saucer of gruel" (LLB96 10).

The presence of tourists, whether seeking health or rest or respite from the noisier world, promotes commerce to support the "expensive upkeep" of a "Nature" portrayed to the public as pure and natural. While the commerce of tourism ensures "there is always Nature," it also ensures, rather sardonically, a supply of "loves" for the "head-waiters," the workers who seem the only passionate presence within the tourist scene (LLB96 10). In this rather dystopian view of the resort's economies, passion seems to serve and be restricted to men. Rather than passion or desire, the association of money with particularly Anglo-American tourism attends the image of the blankets the Blue Nun uses to wrap the body waiting upon the "ineffable moment / When Rigor Mortis / Divests [the body] of its innate impurity," for the blanket is "flannel and wool / Of superior quality from the Anglo-American" (LLB96 9). Prescott identifies "Anglo-American" as a store selling quality goods but also a clear reference to the nationalities of the guests (18).

In this early poem, among her first published pieces, Loy's "Anglo-American" designation, as distinct from the Italians she observes, is inscribed into the text. She is part of the non-Italian crowd, watching from the *outside*. That fall, she would return to Florence, to the rental at 27 Via de' Bardi, but leave the children in the mountain cottage with a nursemaid during the war's opening months. Living near Giovanni Papini on Via de' Bardi, she moved in and out of contact with him and with Futurism while her poetry explored the en dehors garde strategy of *coming from the outside* that "July in Vallombrosa" suggests in its acknowledged outsider's view of the scenes before her.

Loy's Figure of Fashion

The relationship between fashion and new forms of expression permeated the movements associated with Loy during her years in Paris, Florence, and New York. Embracing modern trends, she designed her own corsetless frocks suitable for Paris studio work and easy movement (Burke, *Becoming* 89). While in Florence, she encountered salons full of writers, artists, philosophers, and intellectuals whose new ideas resisted old fashions and traditions. Mabel Dodge Luhan famously donned Eastern garb, including a turban, under the influence of the swami visiting her villa. Other friends, like the Braggiottis, promoted progressive ideas about clothing. By the "winter of 1915–16, still in Florence and in the context of having to support herself and her children, she had started to decorate hats and clothes as the first step to entering the fashion business," and letters to Van Vechten, as discussed shortly, reference fashion design drawings as early as 1914 (Ades 149). Loy also "admired" the dancer Isadora Duncan and portrayed her "as the representative modern woman artist" (Burke, *Becoming* 111). The two women had met in 1908, when

Duncan was having an affair with Gordon Craig in Florence. By the time Loy arrived in New York in 1916, the same year that Duncan performed in the city, Loy would find *vers libre* or free verse described in terms of women's fashion and compared to the loosening of gender restrictions in politics, society, and the arts—especially in Duncan-inspired "modern dance" that replaced restrictive costumes with free-flowing materials, opted for bare feet instead of ballet shoes, and incorporated free movement rather than prescribed choreographies of style. The liberation of the female body in an expressive art of movement generated comparisons with a poetry freed from formal conventions and created by women.[34]

While in Vallombrosa, Van Vechten was struck by Loy's sense of fashion, along with her beauty. Remembering his meals and social gatherings with her and friends as they faced wartime shortages, he recalls the striking figure she presented, as "Twice a day, invariably, Ducie [...] visited the post-office to inquire for mail":

> She made an unforgettable figure with her grey-blue eyes, her patrician features, her waved black hair, parted in the centre. Tall and slender, her too large ankles were concealed by the tight hobble-skirts she wore. Her dresses, of soft dove-coloured shades, or brilliant lemon with magenta flowers, or pale green and blue, were extremely lovely. Strange, long earrings dangled from her artificial rosy ears: one amber pair imprisoned flies with extended wings. It is very easy to recall Ducie as she tramped along the dusty roads of Vallombrosa, enveloped in a brown cloak trimmed with variegated fur, scarcely able, thanks to her tight skirts, to move one smartly shod foot in front of the other. (Van Vechten 130)

Van Vechten stayed only a few days in Vallombrosa before finding passage back to New York and safety from the European conflict, departing from Naples with Dale and Hapgood on August 22. Despite his absence, Loy kept up their correspondence as he served as her literary agent and resource for other opportunities. A set of dress designs from 1914 (see Fig. 2.11), rendered in watercolor and ending up in Van Vechten's art collection, suggests ties between Futurist dictates on clothing and Loy's own designs as an expression of dissatisfaction with the avant-garde's collusion with gender norms. Her letters about fashion designs exemplify that

Loy's en dehors garde pursuits were consistently tied to material contexts in her need to make money, especially in wartime, and her ongoing willingness to engage in design ventures and commercial enterprises. On September 8, from Saltino, Loy wrote Van Vechten, sending a set of "eight fashion drawings," requesting that he give them to "someone," perhaps to the "Biggest dressmaker" in New York, who might then want to buy more from her portfolio of "hundreds" of fashion sketches.[35] Designing fashion while drafting and submitting her earliest poems to little magazines, Loy moved between different arts and economies, exploring design across media and expressive intent.

In this surviving watercolor of dress designs, we see her sense of design in the preference for "hobble-skirts," "soft dove-coloured shades" and a love of color (see Fig. 2.11).[36] While not established as the same "fashion drawings" accompanying the 1914 letter, the designs nonetheless evoke Van Vechten's description of Loy.[37]

The delicately painted dresses, each signed by Loy, suggest varied influences upon Loy's thinking about women's dress, while holding certain elements in common (such as narrowing at the ankles, like the Loy

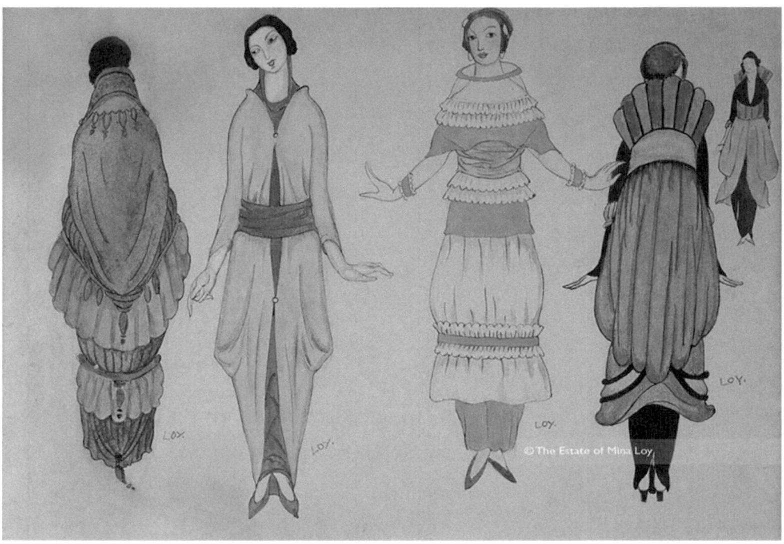

Figure 2.11. Mina Loy, *Fashion Designs*, circa 1915. Watercolor and gouache, 14 × 20½ in. (35.56 × 52.07 cm).

dress style Van Vechten described). While the designs convey sculptural dimensions, the dresses are loosely draped, captured at the waist by broad and soft bands of fabric that comfortably resist cinching. The second figure from the left evokes the freer and simpler clothing philosophy of the Arts and Crafts Movement. A light-blue garment sits open and unadorned at the neck, layered over a sienna gown that falls loosely below the knees, where gathers on either side create playful curves before narrowing to the ankles. The lines are simple but graceful, without tight or restrictive demands.

Layers of fringe, fabric, and pleats decorate the first dress on the left, viewed from the back as an enveloping cape or shawl that recalls details associated with Spanish, Middle Eastern, or eastern European dress.[38] These same design elements take on a more constructed nature in the somewhat futuristic, pre-Art Deco dress on the right-hand side of the painting, also illustrated from the back. The front view, the smallest image all the way to the right, shows a garment that appears to flow like a kimono, recalling the nineteenth-century and early twentieth-century inspiration of Japanese and Chinese art forms on European art and design, exemplified in the "loose smocks, Chinese pajamas" described among the *Others* crowd in New York in 1915 (Churchill, *The Little Magazine* 48).

In addition to these influences, the painting converses with Futurist ideas of fashion and clothing design circulating during this period, focusing on modern masculinity while subtly unsettled by the specter of women's fashion.[39] Fellow Florentine painter, Giacomo Balla, designed clothing and textiles in the early 1910s, while developing Futurist theories of fashion. In two manifestos—"The Anti-Neutral Suit" (1914) and "The Futurist Manifesto of Men's Clothing" (1914)—his theories of fashion emphasized simple lines, and loose fits to enable movement, and the elimination of decorous detail, combined with brightly colored fabrics, geometric designs, and asymmetry, or a "merry dazzle" from clothing that will "destroy all passéist clothings, and everything about them that is tight-fitting, colourless, funereal, decadent, boring and unhygienic" (Balla). His language of fashion espoused masculinist qualities of Futurism, lauding a fashion that is "Dynamic," "Aggressive," "Shocking," "Energetic," and "Violent." At the same time, he called for fashion to engage modern technologies through being "Illuminating," "Phosphorescent," and "Lit by electric lamps." Moreover, as Harris notes, Balla's 1914 manifestos ironically suggest that "women's fashions [in being colorful spectacles and needing to constantly be in a cycle of renewal and disposal and, therefore, always novel] *already were Futurist* [...]: he was haranguing men to dress more like women in order to achieve modernity" (31).

Loy's dress designs, like her poetry, acknowledge Futurism in some ways and move away from it in others. Her simplified lines, loose cuts (except around the ankles), and relative rejection of adornment accord with Balla and others, while she opts not to adopt his recommendations for asymmetry or bright colors or dynamically geometric designs, maintaining a cooler color palette and unpatterned fabrics. Loy's designs, in continuing the hobble skirts and adding some degree of ornamentation (such as the ruffles on one dress and raised, mounded series of pleats on the back of another), don't necessarily free the female body completely in ways that other modernist women like Isadora Duncan or Mabel Dodge Luhan urged; instead, Loy seems to develop her own style of fashion masquerade, sometimes exaggerating the objectification of the female body by heightening a sculptural and aesthetic sense of artifice. In this way, her designs forgo the more aggressive aspects of Futurist theories of fashion, while suggestively commenting upon them. Consider the pink and white dress just off-center, with its odd collar. The collar resembles a lamp shade, perhaps substituting her own interest in lighting design, which would constitute her Parisian business in the 1920s, for Balla's call for clothing lit "by electric lamps."

Fashion's role in gender performance, whether resisting or enforcing conventional ideas, encodes this watercolor's commerce with Futurism. Loy's attention to freeing while adorning the female body in modern fashion signals a rehabilitation of Futurist ideas for women. In 1920, the "Futurist Manifesto of Women's Fashion" by Volt (Vincenzo Fani) proclaimed that "Fashion is an art, like architecture and music."[40] Aligning the fashion designer and the modern writer, Volt urges that the "Futurist woman must have the same courage in donning the new styles of clothing as we did in declaiming our words-in-freedom," welcoming "gowns that trigger surprises and transformations, outfitted with springs, stingers, camera lenses, electric currents, reflectors." While Loy's designs in this painting predate Volt's manifesto, her efforts to connect commercial design, art, and writing as varied forms of creativity (and survival) testify to Volt's assertion that fashion *is* art.

Nonetheless, the ideas rehashed about women and their bodies would be drearily familiar to Loy. For Volt, the woman's body constitutes a site for exhibiting Futurist values, shaped by obsessions with modern machinery, warfare, and technology:

> *In woman we can idealize the most fascinating conquests of modern life.* And so we will have the machine-gun woman, the thanks-de-Somme woman [*sic*], the radio-telegraph antenna woman, the airplane woman, the submarine woman, the motorboat woman. We will transform the elegant lady into a real, living three-dimensional complex. There is no need to fear that in so doing the female silhouette will lose its capricious and provocative grace. The new forms will not hide but accentuate, develop, and exaggerate the gulfs and promontories of the female peninsula. [...] Upon the feminine profile we will graft the most aggressive lines and garish colors of our Futurist pictures. We will exalt the female flesh in a frenzy of spirals and triangles. We will succeed in sculpting the astral body of woman with the chisel of an exasperated geometry!

While claiming to liberate woman through design, making woman what Emily Braun terms a "principal agent of revolt, a 'walking synthesis' of the audacious, performance-oriented aesthetic of the Futurist universe" (37), Volt is careful to reassure the public that the desirable (to men) and sensual female body will still be wholly available (to men): "woman is still not the creator of her own image, but merely part of the fashion system to be reconfigured by the Futurists" (Enrico Crispolti, referenced in Braun 38).

Tweaking the technologically enhanced concept of the "radio woman,"and so on, combined with the "female silhouette," Loy's pink and white dress gives us a lampshade woman through an exaggerated femininity: the lampshade-like collar also resembles a display case on a dress that is almost excessively feminine in its pinks, whites, and ruffles, suggesting a playful reinterpretation of Futurist discourse on fashion. Just off the centerline of the painting, the model adopts a decidedly staged pose, confidently looking directly at us. She wears a pink and white dress bedecked with ruffles and an erect, transparent collar ringed in pink, suggesting a visual collision of Futurist design and feminine apparel. Like the "Feminist Manifesto" Loy penned in 1914, this image most provocatively brings "feminine fashion" into view and under critique, deploying customary tropes of feminized color (pink and white) and design (ruffles, bloomer-like skirt), put into unfamiliar alignment with a strangely untraditional collar, a loose green swag below the breasts, and an emphasis on dress-as-construction, as staging, as performance. Moreover, the collar can also be seen as a protective case, somewhat like a glass globe, highlighting and ironizing the need to protect virginity and preserve femininity. Viewed through an en dehors garde lens, the dress performs a satire of the idea of woman as beautiful object to be gazed upon, parodied through the direct stare of the model who seems to be taking ownership and control over the process of the gaze. The dress becomes a manifesto, Mina Loy-style, engaging with art and the marketplace.

As with the early poems and fashion sketches Loy sent from Vallombrosa, a confluence of artistic and monetary interests followed Loy throughout her career, partly as a matter of survival and partly as a sense of fruitful possibilities in the modern era's crosscurrents of commerce and aesthetics. While Loy remained interested in designing clothing through the 1940s, along with daughter Fabienne, her early fashion design evolves as a feminist collusion of pecuniary need with challenges to tradition that percolated within Florence, Futurist, and soon-to-be New York environs she inhabited in the 1910s.

Loy's en dehors garde involvement with fashion as a commercial enterprise threads through her business ventures of the 1920s. A few years after this Vallombrosa trip, living in New York, "Madame Mina Loy" marketed her fashion designs, seen in an ad for a dress and hats that appeared in a Pittsburgh newspaper in 1921, headlined "Would You Be 'Different?' Madame Loy Shows How" (see Fig. 2.12).

With drawings of a dress called "The Background for Stockings" and hats named "The Canoe" and "The Horse Ear," the ad reports from New York that "Madam Mina Loy is keeping busy these days creating for several houses here frocks and hats that should satisfy those who seek to be different." The designer's modern touch promises new paths for the fashion consumer: "Yes, if you want to be different, madame can

WOULD YOU BE 'DIFFERENT?' MADAME LOY SHOWS HOW.

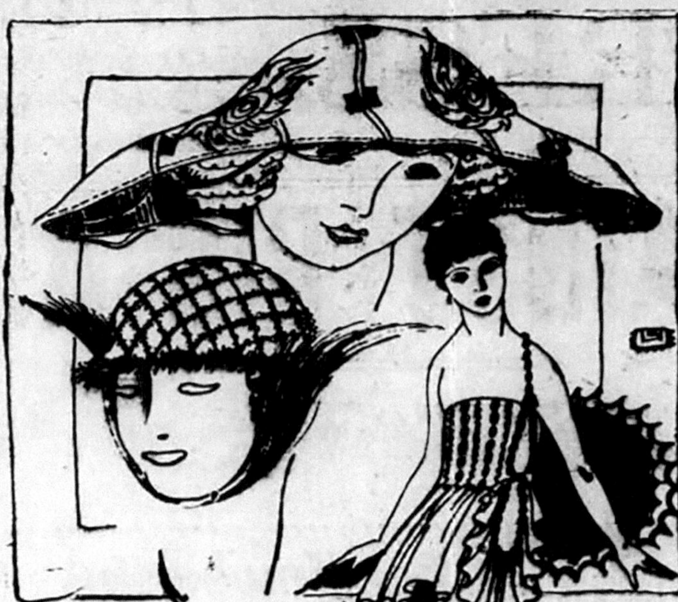

Three of Madame Loy's Creations as She Sketched them for THE PRESS. Above, "The Canoe"; Below, "The Background for Stockings;" at Left, "The Horse Ear."

By Newspaper Enterprise.

New York, April 2.—Styles for women generally may be turning toward the simple and severe, but if you prefer something more striking—

Well, Madam Mina Loy is keeping busy these days creating for several houses here frocks and hats that should satisfy the most ambitious of those who seek to be different.

Here is shown the design for a dress that Madame calls "a background for stockings."

It is of dove-gray taffeta—that is, the skirt from behind seems to be all that could be expected of it. The bodice and the underlining are of scarlet chiffon with a series of dots and stitchings in a cherry-colored twist. A panel at the side carries out the scheme in cherry-colored beads which run over the shoulder to the extreme right back. For additional description, see the sketch!

And the hats!

The "Canoe" is a rimless, crownless innovation. Oiled silk in light green with an underfacing of midnight blue pin-striped velvet. Tabs of this velvet are placed at intervals on the sunny side and ribbons of jade lace in and out over this canoe-like form.

Madame says her "Horse Ear Hat" is the very smartest. It's of cerise straw with a basketwork stitch in henna wool, and curving under the chin and ending in two ear-like sprays at either side of the head, the strap of real horsehair.

Then there's a satin gown with the directness of a bathing gown, and fur-trimmed, that is "stunning!" And a gown madam calls simple lines in a banded twill—black and gray. But here simplicity ends. Coming over the left should from center back is a half-sleeve half-capelike innovation in silver and dragon's-blood, with an edging of white fur. White fur catches it about the waist at the right and the fur descends from there almost to the hem.

Yes, if you want to be different, madame can point the way.

HOOVER HAS DEFINITE PLAN FOR RELIEF OF

Figure 2.12. "'Would You Be 'Different'? Madame Loy Shows How," *Pittsburgh Press*, Apr. 3, 1921.

point the way" ("Would You Be"). Always the entrepreneur supporting herself through fashion, lampshade, and other designs, Loy's sense of the modern intersected artistry with commerce, and imagination with survival.

Loy's interest in fashion continued through her life, graphic design, and writing. In Paris, she completed the 1925 long poem "Anglo-Mongrels and the Rose," autobiographically including the figure of her father, as Exodus, linking fashion-making to complexities of gender and art. In Paris, she lived near designer Elsa Schiaparelli's shop and referenced the designer in letters to her daughter Joella in New York in the early 1930s, hoping to get her youngest daughter Fabienne a job with her (Kinnahan, *Mina Loy* 103). As Susan Rosenbaum discusses, Loy's novel *Insel*, based on her 1930s interaction with Surrealism, alludes to using Schiaparelli's materials in her own readymade constructions (see chapter 4). In the 1940s, as Rosenbaum details, her fashion accessory designs found a buyer in Helena Rubenstein, who adopted a perfume bottle design. Both Loy and daughter Fabienne remained devoted followers of *Vogue* while living in New York in the 1930s and 40s. Indeed, Fabienne studied fashion design and hoped to work for the magazine. Loy's design sense extended beyond clothing, as her many experiments with lampshade design, toy design, and other "inventions" demonstrate.

Throughout her life, the exigencies of place—Florence, Paris, New York—had a shaping impact on Mina Loy's approach to finance (in her life and businesses) and her commentary on economic systems (in writing and art). Indeed, her late art assemblages, constructed in the 1940s and 50s in New York and Aspen, made of street debris and depicting the homeless and destitute, recycle economically disposable products to activate design and materials in critiquing forces that render humans disposable. Late poems including "Chiffon Velours," "Mass-Production on 14th Street," and "On Third Avenue" return to imagery of clothing and fashion in tracing a circuitry of consumption and poverty in mid-century capitalist America through figures of women who make and buy mass-produced clothing, figures whose clothing of remnants and scraps marks their destitution, and mannequins furthering the fashion's spectacle through design and clothing fashions.[41]

VI. FINAL TOURS AND POETIC RETURNS

A Return to Costa San Giorgio

In the spring of 1915, Loy left her rented flat on Via de' Bardi and returned home to Costa San Giorgio. Walking from her rented apartment on the Via de' Bardi to her old neighborhood, Loy would stroll past the Santa Lucia dei Magnoli's della Robbia and Annunciation, encountering stunning views of the Duomo as she mounted the hill on Costa Scarpuccia.

Should you want to trace Loy's imaginary path from her rented home to the Costa San Giorgio, follow the Via de' Bardi eastward (away from the Ponte Vecchio) and turn right onto the Costa Scarpuccia, near the Santa Lucia dei Magnoli. Pass a small shrine to Saint Francis of Assisi on the right and one to the Virgin Mary just before this turn. Follow the Costa Scarpuccia up the hill, appreciating the shady trees lining the street. Stop midway to catch a splendid view of the Duomo to your right. At the top of the hill, cross over the Costa San Giorgio to descend its lower part, walking toward the city (it will appear as the left street of a fork; the sharp left climbs upward on Costa San Giorgio). You will be facing a corner building with a bas-relief of the Madonna and Child above its door, and walking down the hill, you pass the Chiesa di San Giorgio, a medieval church that once housed Giotto's *Madonna di San Giorgio alla Costa* (1295–1300; removed at some point and attributed definitively to Giotto only in 1939).

On your tour, before leaving the Via de' Bardi, gaze upon the Arno and remember the river's illuminated backdrop for Loy's vexed geography of romance. This geography included frustrating relationships with Futurist leaders, Papini (who also lived on the Via de' Bardi) and Marinetti. Both figure in Loy's long collage poem "Songs to Joannes" (1917), a radical deromanticization of the lyric love poem. The male protagonist, most critics agree, is an amalgamation of Loy's romantic entanglements, combining Marinetti and Papini and haunted by other love experiences. Placing the demise of love and relationship near the Arno and suggesting the view from her temporary Via de' Bardi home, the poem's frustrated female speaker postulates, "We might have lived together / In the lights of the Arno" (LLB96 59), enumerating a series of romantic scenarios (unusual for Loy) that include playing "Hide and seek in love and cob-webs / And a lullaby on a tin-pan // And   talked till there were no more tongues / To talk with," before recounting their dawn awakening in contrastingly mechanized terms:

> Licking the Arno
> The little rosy
> Tongue of Dawn
> Interferes with our eyelashes
>
> — — — — — — — — —
> We twiddle to it
> Round and round
> Faster
> And turn into machines (LLB96 63)

Intermingling the image of the river with eroticized language of licking and tongue, these stanzas transform the sexual act into a mechanical image suggesting a temporary enthrallment to her Futurist lovers and mapping the complexities of modern desire onto Florence.

Loy began drafting this long poem in May 1915, upon returning to Forte dei Marmi with her children to escape the city heat. By this point, as opposed to her convalescent summer of 1913, she was seeking a divorce from her absent husband and found herself in a much different creative space as a poet appearing in exciting new magazines like *Camera Work*, *The Trend*, and *Rogue*. Writing "The Effectual Marriage" that summer at the shore, Loy furthers her goodbye to Futurism and its men with another satire, this time of her own relationship with Papini. Loy tags "The Effectual Marriage" with the place of its composition, after the sardonic postscript that "This narrative halted when I learned that the house which inspired it was the home of a mad woman. / — Forte dei Marmi" (LLB96 39).

Loy left Florence (sans children) for New York in 1916. There, she entered into new avant-garde circles that included Americans and

Europeans, meeting Marianne Moore, William Carlos Williams, Beatrice Wood, Marcel Duchamp, and—most enduringly—Arthur Cravan, the man she would marry and lose in a short span of time. When she returned to Italy in 1920, after these years of exuberance and tragedy, she re-encountered the streets of Florence as a widow and new mother. In Florence, the view from her windows beckons again in a short prose piece from that visit, but the perspective has grown more complex and ambiguous for this peripatetic expatriate, visiting Florence but never to live there again. Nonetheless, the imagery of Italy's places and people thread through later poems, looking back on the places she inhabited. This final "post-tour" will take us through Loy's "Summer Night in a Florentine Slum" (1920) and "The Mediterranean Sea" (1928) as they revisit and remap the transits of earlier poems.

"Variegated Madonnas": Loy's Return to Florence, 1920

The years between Loy's departure from Florence for New York in 1916 and her return to Florence in 1920 are crisscrossed with migratory travels, settling, and unsettling. From New York City, she and Arthur Cravan migrated to Mexico to marry. When he disappeared, she spent time searching for him in Chile and Buenos Aires, returning to New York before giving birth to their daughter Fabienne in England. With the new baby, Loy returned for a period to the Italian city to rejoin Joella and Giles.[42] During this reunion with her children and the city, in 1920, she wrote "Summer Night in a Florentine Slum."

By this point, Loy's place in "the new poetry movement"—as a poet regularly published in avant-garde little magazines, recognized by international circles of avant-garde writers, celebrated and scandalized as a "modern woman," and associated with Futurism and New York Dada—distinguishes this moment from her earlier Florentine residence and writing. A prose sketch of the street outside her window and a sequel to the 1914 "Italian Pictures," "Summer Night in a Florentine Slum" revisits the street view from her home. While our earlier discussion of this piece centered upon the figure of the woman at the window, let us first consider here the women on the street, where we re-encounter imagery of women-as-Madonnas, images of what Loy calls "variegated Madonnas," thus extending an important focus of her Florentine poems of the 1910s.

"Summer Night in a Florentine Slum" visually and audibly tours a "summer-strewn street" located near the shop-lined Ponte Vecchio. It is decidedly "inopulent," hotly mixing "tired dust" with arguments and intrigues. Looking out her window at the "Latin families," the speaker wearily sees them "lay on the lousy stones" of the street, "in what they could manage of an earthy abandon" (LLB82 81). Interrupting this uncomfortable leisure, raucous conflicts between the sexes, threats of violence and predation, and images of deformity twist the "passionate messiness" noted in the earlier "The Costa San Giorgio" into something foreboding, lurking, uncontainable.

Among the noise and activity are "variegated Madonnas scooping the air for a last gasp of a mother's love and hairpins," adding to the referential litany of Madonna figures in Loy's Florence poems and explicitly, if ironically, linking the Mary figure and the embodied, oppressed women surrounding the speaker's residence. The unorthodox "Madonnas" observed by the speaker include the "hair-strewn fury" of a "woman at home with four children" who is "big again" and—with a "gesture" that is "purest operatic"—accusing her husband "of being unfaithful" (LLB82 81). This "maddened woman" waits for her husband in the street all day, and only at dusk has she "slunk away to the imminent maternity hospital" (LLB82 83). A second mother and her husband, "friends of mine" who live in poverty, come to the window:

> Sophia came up to the window, with her husband, and a large wicker perambulator some goddess had showered philanthropically upon her [...] so babies fell about in it, on the wooden bottom.
>
> Sophia was lovely and ran like a spider, curls and skirts behind her [...] very beautiful indeed. (LLB82 82)

For a brief moment, the speaker steps into the standard choreography of the maternal-as-Madonna only to change it, granting agency and empathy to the women. The images of the Virgin Mary blur with the actual mothers described as the "variegated Madonnas" populating the Florentine streets, catalyzing a point of momentary connection for the speaker. Then, rather suddenly, the narrative shifts as she withdraws her gaze and any contact with the Italian street by closing her curtains. The poem's immersive view of the street couples with this final, strong gesture of separation and retreat.

Loy's complex mapping of Florentine Madonnas in her poems includes, in this piece, the speaker's felt connection with the women on the street—women framed in relation to the maternal body—and illuminates a vexed awareness of her complicity with British attitudes of superiority, emerging in the piece as self-critique, even as her middle-class status would have been looked down upon by British upper class in England. Presenting her retreat into social privilege as a betrayal of the mistreated and marginal figures on the street, the closing of the curtains also speaks to her own elision (from authority, from self-determination) circumscribed by a gender she shares with the women on the street. Such a tension with the street she stands above and observes is both condescending and empathetic, a severance that is also a connection by virtue of the self-critique signaled in the final lines imagining the disapproving gaze of the rebelliously cross-dressing figure in the British print hanging on the wall, who seems to question the speaker's retreat into English privilege and an aestheticizing viewpoint (as discussed earlier).

This tension suggests Loy's discomfort with avant-garde tactics promoting a heightened sensibility for the artist. Instead of Futurist haughtiness or Dada parody, Loy's en dehors garde viewpoint complexly communicates her refusal to exempt herself, as artist, from social prejudices that shape her capacity to perceive and represent others around her or to conceal her complicity with avant-garde positions even as she critiques them. The Madonna constitutes a ground for such choreography, upon which Loy builds felt connections of maternity and womanhood yet steps aside to witness socially oppressive conditions of gender and class that the Madonna image—and Loy herself—are shown to complicitly uphold. The Italian poems map intertwining circuits of witness and complicity, of critique and participation, of poet and Madonna.

Loy's "Mediterranean Sea": "the rouse and hush of drowsing foam"

In "Songs to Joannes," Loy places love's demise between Italian waters, the River Arno and the Mediterranean Sea, suggesting an underlying geography of loss:

> We might have lived together
> In the lights of the Arno (LLB96 59)
>
> […]
>
> The moon is cold
> Joannes
> Where the Mediterranean -- -- -- -- -- (LLB96 67)

The series of long dashes following the reference to the sea suggests a broken love's loss of potential, of what might have been in this place now lit by cold moons.

Poetically, Loy returns to the Mediterranean a decade later. In our final tour, let us visit "The Mediterranean Sea," a poem written years after she moved from Italy but threaded through with the places of retreat so important to her and her family, encapsulating many of the place-oriented associations we have thus far traveled. Living in Paris, Loy wrote "The Mediterranean Sea" in 1928, suggesting how the Florentine years imprinted an Italian sense of place upon her modernist emergence and lineage. The poem enfolds geographical points with an aura of their history, while suggesting the "volcanic privacies" that the landscape hosted for her own life in Italy (LLB96 101). In 1928, looking back upon her near-decade in Italy, she would see a geography of loss and vibrancy, a "monstrous sapphire" (LLB96 101) of a jewel that, like the Mediterranean Sea she metaphorizes, could both overwhelm and infuse her.

For Loy, the Romantic era's Shelley resonated with Italy's intertwined history of tragedy and richness. She writes:

> From the green incline
> of vengence [*sic*]
> the Vesuvian vine

drips lucently
Lacrimae Christi
to drift   imperceptibly
with the lost sob of Shelley (LLB96 101)

These lines layer ancient history of Vesuvius as both a deadly force, destroying most famously the town of Pompeii in little time, and a fertile giver of life, as the lava-enriched soils on the slopes produce a grape for the celebrated Neapolitan wine, Lacrimae Christi. The wine most equivalent to that drunk by the ancient Romans, the name means "Christ's tears," derived from the legend that the savior wept tears over the fall of Lucifer; from the spot on the ground where the tears fell, grapes grew. Ancient Rome and Christian Rome join in this wine of lament and celebration.

Loy connects the wine and Christ's tears to the poet Shelley. Mary and Percy Shelley lived in Florence in 1818, on the Via Valfonda near the railway station in a house that stood until its destruction in World War I (currently, a plaque identifies its location). Their three-year-old son William would die the following year and be buried in Rome's Protestant Cemetery, joined some hundred yards away in 1822 by Shelley's interred ashes after he drowned off the Gulf of Spezia in the Ligurian Sea, an arm of the Mediterranean Sea on the northwest coast of Italy. Shelley's "lost sob" echoes Christ's tears, invoking his loss of a child as well as his own death.

Just as the tears "drift   imperceptibly" from Christ to wine to Shelley to sea, Shelley's body would drift at sea before washing up on the Ligurian shore. His friends cremated him on the beach of Viareggio, just south of Forte dei Marmi. Shelley's drowned and cremated body lingers in the image of "aqueous ashes / of the tinselled sands" that ends the poem, ashes and water conjoined in the liminal space of the coastal sands (LLB96 102). Perhaps Loy visited the monument to Shelley the Baedeker describes in Viareggio's Piazza Principe Amedeo, a bronze bust by Urbano Lucchesi on a pedestal "encircled by intertwined branches of oak and olive" and inscribed with words of tribute to the poet "drowned in this sea, consumed by fire on this shore," bequeathing his poetry to "every generation" in "its struggles, its tears, and its redemption" (Baedeker 122). Written a few years after son Giles's death in Bermuda, where he was taken by his father without Loy's permission, "The Mediterranean Sea" folds Loy's own "sobs," perchance, into Shelley's and the sea. The sea, "il mare" in Italian and "la mer" in French aurally chimes with "mère," or "mother" in the French that Loy would be speaking and hearing in her daily life in Paris.

Reference to the conjunction of the sea and marble locates the poem in relation to Forte dei Marmi, described by the Baedeker as a "little seaside resort surrounded by pine-woods, with a quay for shipping marble" (121). There, the Apuan Alps seem to descend directly into the sea, a visual feature that Loy's poem captures in imagery combining maternity and the labor of making. For centuries, the marble quarried nearby shipped from the seaside resort. In Loy's time, blocks of marble, especially from nearby Carrara, stood perpetually stacked for shipment at the pier. Known since Roman times for its marble, Carrara supplied materials used in the Pantheon, the tower of Pisa, and many churches, monuments, and sculptures. The mountains, as seen from Forte dei Marmi, hold expanses of white appearing to be snow but actually are marble.

An excursion to Carrara, easily accomplished in Loy's time from Forte Dei Marmi, might well include "a visit to the quarries [...] best made early in the morning when the weather is warm," as the 1906 Baedeker instructs; the view of the quarries gained from hiking up mountain paths would reveal "expanses of dazzling white débris (*raveneti*)" below (120). Reading the Baedeker's rather detailed entry on Carrara, Loy might have been struck by the attention given to the marble workers, including their wages and working hours, in the entry on Carrara. It is

> a pleasant little town with 21,000 inhab., most of whom gain their livelihood by working the marble.
>
> [...]
>
> The Marble Quarries (*Cave*) of Carrara enjoy a worldwide fame. The deposits of marble occur throughout almost the whole of the *Apuan Alps* [and have been mined since Roman times]. [...] The industry now grows steadily; in 1901 about 204,000 tons of rough blocks were exported, besides 164,000 tons of sawn blocks and 29,700 tons of otherwise worked blocks. [...] The quarrymen, who receive 1–3 fr. per day, work from 8 to 4 in winter, in summer from 5 to 3. (120)

How might this backdrop of Italian labor inform the Italian land and seascape Loy imagines? Loy's final stanza visualizes the alps as they descend into the sea, while emphasizing the working labor by which the "dazzling white" marble is "Hewn":

> Hewn in the Apuane [*sic*]
> Carrara stands
> as marble sentinel
> beyond the blazing rust
> of branches
> roofing amphibian babies
>
> as they rise
>
> from the Ligurian gullies
> Their polished thighs
> armoured with aqueous ashes
> of the tinselled sands. (LLB96 101–02)

The language of protective militarism ("sentinel," "armoured") accords with Loy's stress on the Italian name for the Alpi Apuane, spelled Apuan in English but granted the Italian "e" by Loy. Might she have read in the Baedeker that the "name of the *Alpi Apuane* is derived from the warlike tribe of the *Apuani*, subdued by the Romans in 180 B.C.," enfolding that name history into the image of a "sentinel" of marble in these distinctive mountains, their "boldly shaped peaks" standing "in vivid contrast to the flat rounded summits" of the nearby Apennines (123)? The "spears" of "the mistral" that open the poem (LLB96 101), moreover, suggest a rejuvenating energy in this force, for the mistral is the renewing wind that clears both dust and atmospheric clouds to bring sunny and clear air to the Mediterranean coast.

In the poem's image of the mountains, this protective and renewing sentinel emerges as an agency of labor, the marble "hewn" by workers. Carrara, the marble capital of the world, set where the Alpi Apuane descend into the Mediterranean Sea, produced the marble preferred by Michelangelo and Bernini. Loy encodes their lineage into the poem with the mere mention of this marble but places—as does Baedeker's 1906 guide—the work of the quarrymen into this lineage. By the end of the nineteenth century, Carrara was a center of anarchism in Italy, especially among quarry workers organizing labor.

Loy's diction and imagery merge physical labor with maternal labor: the sentinel mountains, "as they rise" from the sea, are "roofing amphibian babies" within that sea. The ambivalent grammar of "as they rise"—the "they" referencing both mountains and babies—figures the liminal meeting space of mountain and sea as the liminal stance of the maternal. A space both sentinel and fertile, the "polished thighs" of marble receive "the rouse and hush of drowsing foam" (LLB96 102, 101), recollecting the imagery of birth scandalously voiced in her poem "Parturition" more than a decade earlier. The 1928 poem's ostensibly descriptive picture of the Mediterranean coast charts a map of labor—physical, economic, poetic, reproductive—upon the coastline, guiding us to a revisionary maternal space of strength, endurance, and "hewn" or creative shelter.

The poem's language and imagery anticipate later artwork, suggesting how Loy returns to various themes, images, and places throughout her career, albeit in different media. The 1933 series of oil paintings, *Drift of Chaos*, includes *The Sentinels*, featuring a hooded figure standing in a tumultuously churning sea of wave-like amorphous shapes suggesting metamorphosizing human bodies. The figure's outstretched arms seem to ward against dark, unrecognizable forces, protective and towering over the emerging suggestions of incipient life or form—perhaps "amphibian babies" imagined under the sentinel's protection in "The Mediterranean Sea," but taking on a darker cast by the early 1930s amid Europe's drift toward chaos.[43] Almost two decades later, the image of "amphibian babies" is echoed by a "late cut-paper assemblage" from 1950, *Untitled (The Drifting Tower)*, which shows a baby tethered by a cord to a white tower, seeming to swim through surrounding ocean waves (see Fig. 2.13).[44]

The white tower evokes the earlier imagery, in poem and painting, of a "marble sentinel," constituting an inter-arts correspondence between motifs of maternity and protection that cross time periods in Loy's various forms of artistic expression.

Crafting a modern en dehors garde poetics during and through her Italian years, Loy's place-infused poetic expression evolves as a mix of social, economic, aesthetic, and religious geographies, allowing her to

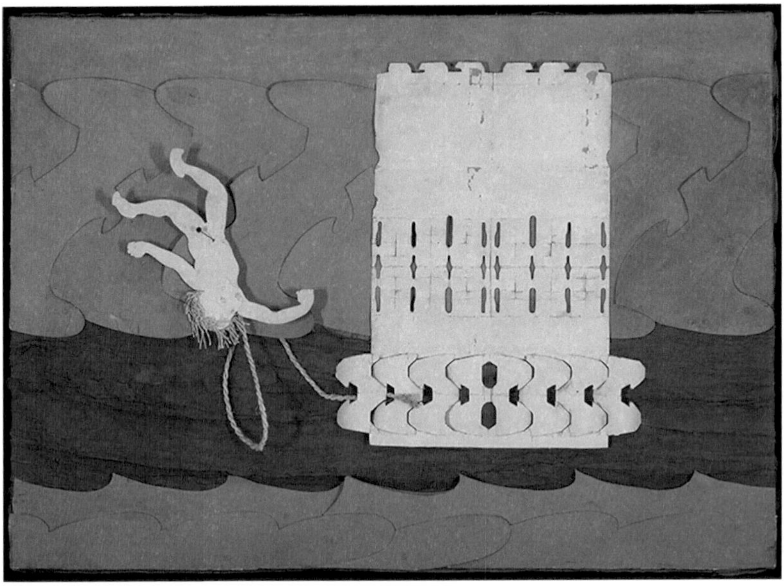

Figure 2.13. Untitled *(The Drifting Tower)*, circa 1950. Cut-paper and mixed media collage on canvas, by Mina Loy. 28¾ × 39 in. (73.03 × 99.06 cm).

find a "place" as an artist and writer within a "place" of colliding energies. Rebellion and rejuvenation go hand in hand in these early poems, as the poet's evolving understanding of the "new" locates her moment and self in relation to the "old," rehabilitating what works for her, wrestling with lineages of poetry, motherhood, and exploration—both cosmic and material. In mapping Florence, Loy's poetic Baedeker maps a poetic self-attuned to new possibilities among the old.

A final point on the map of our tour takes us back to Costa San Giorgio, near Loy's home and studio, where the artist Emma Draghi makes and sells her ceramics, fabric art, and knitted wares (see Fig. 2.14). Working across several media, combining artistic aspiration with commercial need, she is grounded in this place. She tells me her family has been in the current no. 52 since the 1920s. Loy rented the current no. 54 next door (numbered as 48 at the time and seen in Fig. 2.14), and the home she and Haweis bought (now no. 60) is steps away. Before departing Florence for good in 1922, would Loy have overlapped, just barely, with Draghi's Costa

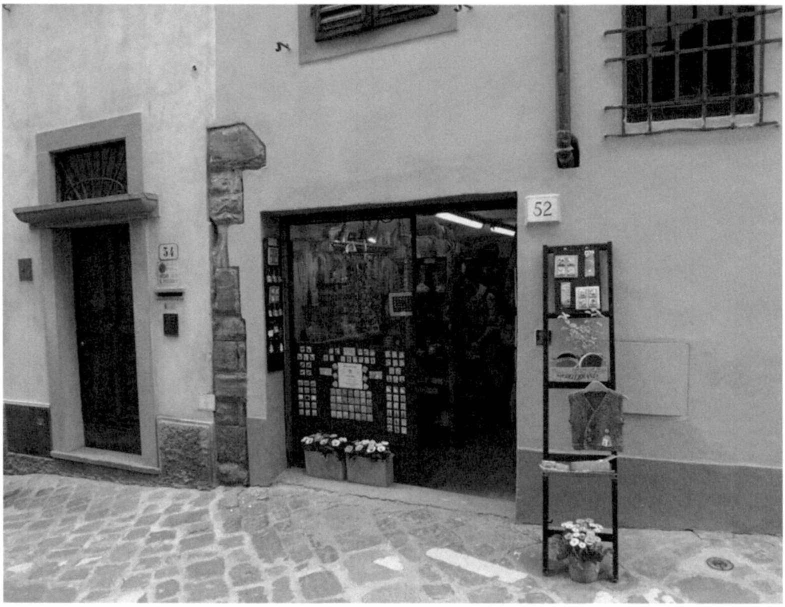

Figure 2.14. Artist's shop at no. 52 Costa San Giorgio. Photograph by Linda Kinnahan.

ancestors, possibly sharing the space of this street or, at least, the spirit of it? As another artist's creativity now imbues this first-floor studio, one wonders what traces of Loy abound, what lineages and vectors continue to map this Italian space.

CHAPTER THREE

LOY TAKES THE STAGE

Playwriting and Publishing in New York Magazines (1914–1921)

Suzanne W. Churchill

I. COURTING AN AUDIENCE

Mina Loy "woke up!" under the electrifying influence of the Italian Futurists, so the story goes, but she was repelled by their misogyny—the infamous "contempt for woman" declared in the "The Founding and Manifesto of Futurism" (Burke, *Becoming* 178–79; Marinetti, "The Founding" 50). Frustrated by the limits of her love affairs with F. T. Marinetti and Giovanni Papini, Loy packed her bags, left her children in Italy with a nanny, and sailed to New York in 1916, where she was hailed as "the modern woman" and embraced by the New York Dada cohort that congregated at the apartment of the warm, welcoming, and wealthy art collectors, Walter and Louise Arensberg.[1] In their sophisticated, playful, transnational salon, Loy found herself as attracted to Marcel Duchamp, Beatrice Wood, and Dada as she had been to Marinetti, Papini, and Futurism—and when she met Dada icon Arthur Cravan, much more so.

Loy's involvement with the Italian Futurists has become a touchstone of Loy studies, essential to her avant-garde mythos, but her migration from Italian Futurism to New York Dada was actually more complicated than this story admits. Loy never fully affiliated with any avant-garde group, and her move to New York was less a flight from Futurism than a quest for artistic and personal fulfillment motivated by multiple, overlapping desires: to make money, access an audience, and find love. She desperately needed an income to create art freed from her family's tight purse strings, telling Carl Van Vechten, her confidant and literary agent in New York, that she was "in a fix" and wanted "to come over to New York & do commercial drawings, advertisements or Vogue covers or anything. Do you think I could earn over there?"[2] In summer 1916, she wrote of her decision to sail to New York, saying, "I have only one idea in my mind—make money—and can turn my hand to anything that comes along & do it quickly" (Loy/CVV 42). Loy also craved recognition of her genius by sympathetic readers, repeatedly asking Van Vechten what people thought of the pieces she sent him: "Did nobody love them?" (Loy/CVV 5). She imagined the American public as a more receptive audience for her work: "I am longing to get one [of my things] in print in your nice civilized country" (Loy/CVV 65). After a series of disappointing affairs, she also longed for a companionate lover, lamenting, "Oh Carlo, do you think there is a man in America one could love?" (Loy/CVV 1).

Loy's critique of Futurists was also multifaceted: it was not just about their misogyny, though that was certainly part of it.[3] She also resisted their arrogant, domineering attitudes toward audiences, whether they were orchestrating a public spectacle on stage or manipulating their acolytes and lovers in more private settings. Whereas the Futurists claimed autonomy and superiority over their spectators, Loy understood the relationship between artist and audience to be mutual, reciprocal, and reversible—an interpersonal exchange that plays out in both private and public settings, on both intimate and grand scales.

To scrutinize the relationship between artists and audiences, Loy turned to theater, writing four experimental plays between 1914 and 1920.[4] Although none of them were produced in her lifetime, three were published in New York-based magazines. Ribald, funny, and provocative, the wartime plays turn their attention from European battlefields to artistic and sexual skirmishes. Loy puts private performances on the public stage for analysis, appealing to the audience to appreciate her satirical insights into the "sex war" and its entanglement in the art economy.[5] In all four plays, men are the spectacle—we look at them and they perform for us—while women serve as audiences, directors, and procurers. The comical micro-dramas, *Collision* and *Cittàbapini*, combine Futurist and popular techniques to explore the male artist's relationship to the public. The more risqué *The Sacred Prostitute* burlesques Futurist performance as a new arena in an age-old sex war. *The Pamperers* satirizes the entire avant-garde industry, portraying a Dada-esque artist/collector of found objects who gets co-opted by consumer culture.[6] In the midst of this playwriting stint, Loy produced a series of proto-Dada prose experiments in *The Blind Man* that continue her investigation of artistic performance and audience reception. Theatrical and highly conscious of an audience, these prose pieces explicitly address the relationship between the artist and the public. This chapter puts the spotlight on Loy's early plays and prose experiments to reframe her migration from Italian Futurism to New York Dada as a series of related en dehors garde turns toward audiences, rather than a shift in avant-garde affiliations.[7] I examine these works in their little magazine contexts to shed light on the en dehors garde strategies Loy uses to take the stage and appeal to audiences.

The theatrical experiments Loy conducted during her first sojourn in New York in the 1910s are important because they show her practicing a different kind of avant-gardism from her male contemporaries—an en dehors gardism that entails neither contempt for audiences nor naive claims of artistic autonomy. As Elisabeth Frost and Jessica Burstein argue, Loy's avant-garde practice is characterized less by revolution and rupture than by a strategic engagement with tradition. According to Frost, "Loy's poetic practice reveals attitudes toward language that, compared to Marinetti's, are considerably more attuned to the intransigence of social custom and the elusiveness of revolution" (30). Burstein sets up a similar contrast between the historical avant-garde's insistence on a violent break with the past and Loy's reinventions of conventions and traditions: "As radical as Loy was in her prosody, she was less interested in breaking with tradition" than with reinventing the traditional, domestic, and banal, as well as rehabilitating the outcast, devalued, and marginalized (155). Loy's plays combine Futurist and Dada techniques with traditional and popular forms to court audiences rather than condescend to them, staging scenes in which spectators join artist-cum-celebrities in dramas that amuse and absorb them all. Her prose experiments adopt a jovial, playful approach to the audience, simultaneously indulging and critiquing the Dada ethos of leveling hierarchies between the Artist and the Public. Loy's early plays and prose experiments seek to engage the public's interest without pandering to their tastes, aiming to lead rather than feed the public appetite for art. Turning toward audiences, these en dehors garde writings engage with and respond to Futurism and Dada, even as they ironically evade affiliation with either group.

II. TURNING TO PLAYWRITING

Although Loy's plays have been overshadowed by her more celebrated poems and manifestos of the same period, they were just as important to her, if not more so. "I will try & send you some more poems that will suit," she wrote to Carl Van Vechten in the mid-1910s, "But my whole attention for the moment runs to the impossible play I am so much enjoying writing" (Loy/CVV 65). A sense of drama and theatrical tropes likewise infused her poems, paintings, and romans à clef during this period, but the plays offered her a larger stage for investigating gender performativity, social roles, and power dynamics. Whereas her poetry can be cerebral and introspective, the plays resist psychological depth in order to scrutinize surfaces, spectacles, and social patterns. Loy was not merely interested in looking inward to solve her own problems: she wanted to examine the big picture, understand her position in a larger social and economic system, and engage a wider audience. Playwriting allowed her to explore her personal predicament on a public stage, transforming and generalizing her experiences into art. The plays script scenes in which male characters parade and preen, while female characters frequently vie for center stage, only to be displaced to the margins, absorbed into the upholstery, or trapped in cycles of self-negation.

Loy's plays have received little critical attention, partly because they have been difficult to access and partly because, well, they are just difficult.[8] The strange, disjunctive, metatheatrical comedies defy conventions of realism. Sarah Bay-Cheng classifies them as "poetic dramas," a term that highlights Loy's attention to words as sounds, objects, and props, but may arouse misleading expectations of introspection and "deeper meaning" in plays that actually emphasize the surface of language, characters, props, and scenery.[9] What words *mean* in these comedies may be less important than what they *do*. Loy's poetic dramas do not seek to orient theater toward lyric introspection, but rather to heighten audience participation in a physical encounter with language.

Recently, theater practitioners have begun to realize the dramatic potential of Loy's plays.[10] In December 2023, Alison Dobbins collaborated with an interdisciplinary team of performing artists and scholars to stage *Mina Loy, Futurist, Feminist, Fabulist: The Poetic Dramas of Mina Loy* at Michigan State University's Broad Art Museum and the University of Michigan-Flint. Melissa C. Thompson, who directed and acted in the Michigan production, also directed a student production of *The Sacred Prostitute and Other Plays* at the University of Maine at Farmington, in April 2024. These experimental productions aimed to maximize the plays' potential for registers of humor ranging from the slapstick to the satirical, taking cues from the physical comedy of Charlie Chaplin, the conversational wit of Oscar Wilde, and the social satire of Greta Gerwig's *Barbie* movie. According to Dobbins,

> The humor and satire of the plays really came through once staged—much more so than when the plays were read on the page. We also discovered that Loy's plays cannot be performed using commonly accepted modern realism styles of acting. The conceptual characters in *Sacred Prostitute*, for instance, communicate a very different story if played as real humans, rather than the idea of Love, the idea of Futurism. The humor dies if these plays are presented in a way that strives for authenticity of circumstance or realistic emotion. (Dobbins, email to Churchill, Mar. 14, 2025)

To break down the fourth wall and encourage audience interaction, the Michigan productions were staged in a museum café and a black box theater. Dobbins and her team exploited costumes, music, sound effects, and environmental design as sources of humor. The actors animated long-winded speeches with gestures, poses, and physical movements, using clowning techniques to elicit laughter and recognition. The plays struck a chord with contemporary audiences, who said that the characters and their performances felt "very current—and the fact that the stereotypes of men were written a hundred years ago was both eye-opening and depressing" (Dobbins, email to Churchill, Mar. 14, 2025).[11]

Loy began thinking about theater, performance, and audience in the early 1910s while living in Florence. She gained insights into theatrical techniques by observing the Italian Futurists perform on stage before large crowds, as well as in smaller settings—in salons where they boasted to and bullied their disciples, and boudoirs where they coaxed and seduced their lovers. According to Christine Poggi, the Futurists imagined their public audience through the topos of *la folla*, or crowd, which they conflated with masses and understood "to be 'feminine' in its malleability, its incapacity to reason, its susceptibility to flattery and hysteria, and its secret desire to be seduced and dominated" ("Folla/Follia" 711). In his "Dynamic and Synoptic Declamation," Marinetti boasted of his "experience of the femininity of crowds and weakness of their collective virginity in the course of forcing futurist free verse upon them," characterizing his approach as both a cerebral rape and an erotic seduction:

> I have amused myself with seducing and moving them better and more reliably than all the other declaimers of Europe, insinuating into their obtuse brains the most astonishing images, caressing them with the most refined vocal sensations, with velvety softnesses and brutalities until, mastered by my look or entranced by my smile, they feel a feminine need to applaud something they neither understand nor love. ("Dynamic" 220)

Here, Marinetti opposes his masculine dominance to the feminine submissiveness of the crowd, casting himself as superior and autonomous. This approach did not sit well with Loy, and not just because of its sexism. She saw the folly in the Futurist fascination with *la folla*. After attending a *serata* at the Teatro Verdi in 1913—a spectacle in which the Futurists declaimed their artistic and nationalist agendas in militant, aggressive rhetoric—she reflected on the event and her ensuing exchanges with Marinetti in her roman à clef *Brontolivido*, using the semi-fictional genre to gain critical distance on her ambivalent response to Futurist performance.[12]

Although Burke treats *Brontolivido* as memoir, Rowan Harris views it as "some of Loy's earliest experimental writing," in which she deploys "forms of irony, ventriloquy and indeterminacy in her effort to mediate both a defence against and an investment in Futurist rhetoric" (31). Loy's ambivalent response to Futurist rhetoric is palpable in a scene in which Loy's fictional alter ego (alternately called Jemima or Sophia) encounters the Flabbergast leader Brontolivido and is unsettled by her attraction to his repulsive machismo: "He was so appallingly dynamic in his misogynist magnetism—the room was vibrating with his emanations—gyrating on the pivot of his virility" (*Brontolivido*, "Second Costa Visit" 1). Jemima/Sophia regains self-control by mocking Brontolivido, telling him he does not "exist outside a crowd; & even there you are a spurious entity, drawing 'something' out of an audience to give back to them in your superb pretentiousness as yourself" (*Brontolivido*, "Second Costa Visit" 1). Far from being autonomous and all-controlling, Loy discerned, the Futurists depended on audiences for the power and energy they transmitted, just as Jemima feeds on Brontolivido's "appalling dynamism" to fuel her own critical response.

As Loy analyzed the Futurists' poses and gestures on stage and in more private settings, she became acutely aware of the performative nature of intimate relationships, perceiving that every social interaction, even between two lovers, involved an audience. She began thinking of her interactions with the Futurists as a kind of theater, sketching out scenes from her own life in *Brontolivido*. One particularly theatrical fragment depicts her first encounter with Marinetti, when his Futurist disciples escort him to meet the young American artist Frances Simpson Stevens, whom Loy was chaperoning. Brontolivido (Marinetti) rewrites the script, choosing to ignore his intended conquest Gloria (Frances) and instead direct his attention to Sophia (Mina), orchestrating a "coup de theatre for the benefit of his comrades" (Burke, *Becoming* 154):

> The leader of the flabbergasts [Marinetti] took Sophia's [Mina's] hand, cutting her through for a slow minute with his eyes and begged her to 'give herself' to him. Skillfully manipulating a sensation among his disciples—Gloria [Frances] being the woman he had been invited to admire—he would have renounced Venus to hold his movement together. (*Brontolivido*, "Gloria" 1)

The "leader of the flabbergasts" deploys the male gaze like a weapon, using it both to seduce women and to "manipulate" his male "disciples." Loy anticipates Eve Sedgwick's theory of male homosocial desire, cannily pointing to the ways Brontolivido uses women to strengthen the bonds between the men in his movement. Loy makes male homosocial bonding explicit when she describes him shouting "as if his dictatorship depended on attaching the other men to him with chains of his female conquests" (*Brontolivido*, "Gloria" 2). Sophia provides a rapt audience for Brontolivido's performances, urging him on by saying: "You're much more fun when you are theatrical" (*Brontolivido*, "First Costa" 28). But she also plays an active role in their exchanges: she spars with him in "verbal combat," and, when he kisses her, revels in "watching a spectacle she had never seen acted just that way before. There was something of a Sicilian heel-tapping in his rapid insistence" (*Brontolivido*, "First Costa" 27). In these ways, Loy's alter ego exercises an active, female gaze and objectifies Bronty's performance of masculinity. Never one to exempt herself from her ironic critiques, Loy subjects women's role-playing to equal scrutiny: when Sophia and Bronty have sex for the first time, she observes that "Women in those days could be relied upon to play their part. Sophia had once been told that men were horrified if a woman did not react. She knew enough to emit little gasps" (*Brontolivido*, "Rome" 1).

The roman à clef form, along with her poems and paintings of this period, which Linda Kinnahan discusses in chapter 2, gave Loy a canvas for an up-close and personal investigation of gender performativity. But Loy wanted more than a two-dimensional plane: she wanted to see the scenes enacted, crowing to Van Vechten about the satisfaction she got from enlisting Marinetti to read the part of "Futurism" in one of her dialogues, while she took the role of "love" (Loy/CVV 45). Writing and reading aloud scenes from her roman à clef led Loy to playwriting, a genre that allowed her to step back and analyze Futurist performance from a greater distance, while also investigating the artist's relation to public and private audiences on a three-dimensional stage.

As she scrutinized performances in her life and art, Loy engaged in probing discussions about modern theater with the expatriate community in Florence, which included Herbert Trench, an Irish poet, playwright, and former director of the Haymarket Theatre. She reported to Van Vechten:

> Trench is writing a tremendous play—& the theory at the back of it which is all he has imparted to me so far—is so deep—I wonder where the public is to come from—The Futurist Theatre is very poor by the way—there is little being evolved here. (Loy/CVV 104).

From the start, Loy was thinking about the audience for modern theater, wondering "where the public is to come from." Her assessment of the moribund state of theater in Italy was a double dig targeting not only the Futurists but also Gordon Craig, an English stage designer who was a neighbor and close friend of Stephen Haweis. The two men avidly discussed the "theater of the future" and collaborated on illustrations of set designs for publication in Craig's magazine, *The Mask* (Burke, *Becoming* 110–11). According to Burke, Loy disliked Craig and "found his relations with [his lover, the modern dancer] Isadora Duncan far more interesting than his plans to modernize the theater" (111). Nevertheless, she would have had a hard time resisting *The Mask*, given how desperate she was for news of the art world beyond Florence. *The Mask* gave her access to "Magazine Reviews" of *Camera Work*, *The English Review*, *The Century*, and other periodicals; discussions of the latest developments in European theater; histories of folk drama and puppetry; and a translation of Marinetti's 1914 manifesto "Futurism and the Theatre." Did Loy also discuss playwriting with Gertrude Stein during her summer residencies in Florence? Stein began composing "conversation plays" or "parlor plays" in 1913, around the same time that Loy began experimenting with her own conversational dramas.[13] Loy would likely have learned about American developments in modern theater from Neith Boyce and Hutchins Hapgood, resident representatives of the Provincetown Players. Did they tell her about how playwrights Rachel Crothers and Susan Glaspbell were using realist techniques to expose gender inequality and women's oppression? Crother's 1911 play *He and She*, a battle of the sexes between husband-and-wife artists, became a Broadway hit in 1920, and Glaspell's *Trifles*, a one-act play about rural wives subverting patriarchal authority, was performed by the Provincetown Players in 1916. If Loy's satire of the sex war, *The Sacred Prostitute*, was not directly influenced by these early feminist dramas, it partakes of the same zeitgeist.

Loy may also have attended open-air theater productions in the summers between 1909 and 1915, while staying at the seaside town of Forte dei Marmi with her children. One of her seaside gouache paintings (circa 1913) depicts what appears to be an entrance to a performance of *La Tosca* (see chapter 2, Fig. 2.8). On the reverse, Loy has written "Maison des bains a Forti dei Marmi," suggesting the scene could be an entrance to a private bathhouse. Whether the painting depicts an entrance to a bathhouse or theater, however, the scene has a stagy, theatrical feel. The people lining up to enter *La Tosca* are themselves performers. Dressed in elegant costumes, they pose on the boardwalk, observed by curious onlookers on the sidelines. *Maison des Bains* depicts the theater of life, displaying Loy's keen interest in both theater and gender performance.

III. LITTLE MAGAZINES AS PERFORMANCE SPACES

Loy's multimodal investigation of gender performativity, performance, and audience coincided with the period in which she first appeared in print, debuting in *Camera Work* in 1914 with "Aphorisms on Futurism," and then having her poems appear in *The Trend*, *Rogue*, and *Others*. These little magazines relieved her sense of isolation in Italy and provided access to American audiences. *Collision* and *Cittàbapini* were published under the title *Two Plays* in *Rogue* (June 15, 1915), *Cittàbapini* reappeared in *Rogue* in December 1916, and *The Pamperers* appeared in *The Dial* (July 1920). Loy tried to secure a magazine venue for *The Sacred Prostitute* in the mid-Teens, but was unsuccessful, possibly because of the play's provocative title and racy subject matter.[14] She also tried her hand at acting, costarring with William Carlos Williams as "Wife" and "Husband" in Alfred Kreymborg's *Lima Beans*, a one-act play produced by the Provincetown Players in December 1916.[15] Loy may have been attracted to the project not only because of her loyalty to Kreymborg, who published her "Love Songs" in the debut issue of *Others*, but also because of the Provincetown

Playhouse's openness to feminist experiment and collaborative approach to audiences. The following spring, she continued her investigation of the artist's relationship to the audience by publishing three performative prose pieces in *The Blind Man*: "In...Formation"; "Pas de Commentaires! Louis M. Eilshemius"; and "O Marcel - - - otherwise I Also Have Been to Louise's."

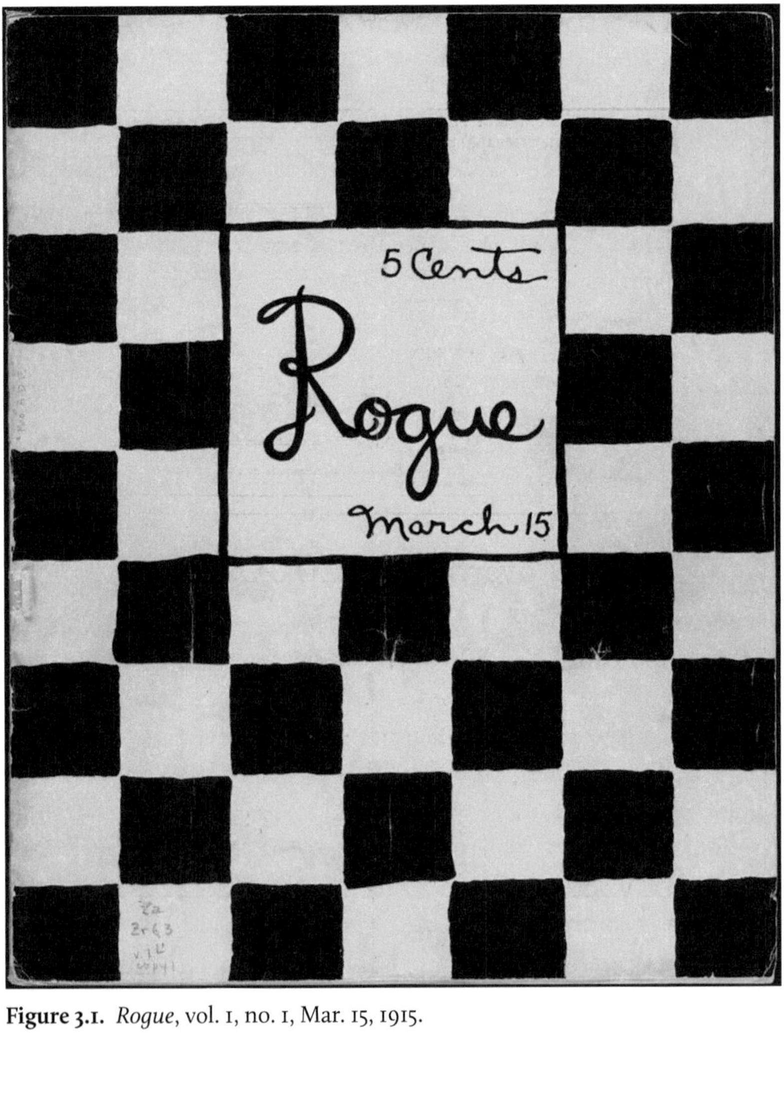

Figure 3.1. *Rogue*, vol. 1, no. 1, Mar. 15, 1915.

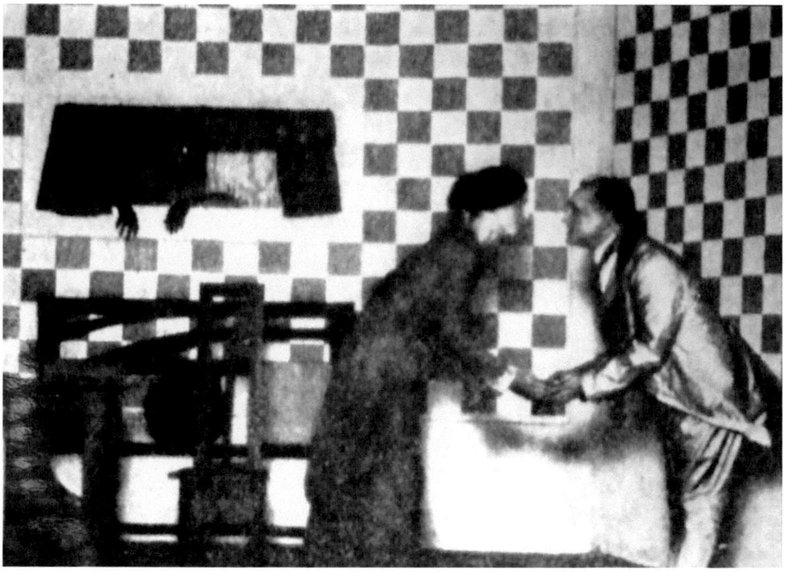

Figure 3.2. Loy and Williams in the Provincetown Players production of *Lima Beans* (1916). Carolyn Burke Collection on Mina Loy and Lee Miller, Yale Collection of American Literature, Beinecke Rare Book and Manuscript Library.

Little magazines supplied both stages and receptive audiences for Loy's unconventional writing: they provided *places* for her en dehors garde experiments. These small, noncommercial venues for unconventional ideas and forms functioned as experimental performance spaces, more akin to theaters than books. As I have argued elsewhere, "Little magazines are intimate and social: they bring together an ensemble of writers into a small space, staging a performance for a familiar audience of like-minded people, who read each issue during the same limited time period" (Churchill, "The Lying Game" 179). The same artists and aesthetics transfer from one magazine to another, ensuring an understanding, appreciative audience for literary, artistic, and dramatic experiments. The aesthetic and social interconnections between little magazines and theaters can be seen in the striking resemblance between the checkerboard cover of *Rogue* and the checkerboard set of *Lima Beans*, designed by *Others* contributors Marguerite and William Zorach, based on screens by *Mask* editor Gordon Craig (Kreymborg 243, Figs. 3.1 and 3.2). Kreymborg and Walter Arensberg were avid chess players, and the game of chess was a popular pastime among the New York Dada set that congregated in the Arensberg salon. Loy's publications in *Rogue*—the decadent, irreverent, "cigarette of literature" whose title and fashion commentary playfully mimic *Vogue*—introduced her to a coterie audience of avant-garde artists, wealthy patrons, and Greenwich Village bohemians who were open to experiment and receptive to gamesmanship, irony, and play. Aiming for a larger audience, *The Blind Man* was a self-proclaimed forum for interpreting modern art to the public, which extended Loy a wider platform for performing Dada prose experiments. *The Dial* elevated her to a more sophisticated and serious international stage when it published *The Pamperers*, introduced by art critic Henry McBride, to launch a new "Modern Forms" section "devoted to exposition and consideration of the less traditional types of art" (McBride 61).

Loy's interest in playwriting rose in conjunction with her growing desire to move from Florence to New York. To Loy, New York symbolized modernity, economic opportunity, and artistic and social freedoms (see chapter 1). She anticipated joining a social circle of like-minded, convention-defying artists who wrote for and read the same little magazines, providing both entertainment and audiences for each other. New York was, therefore, a place tied in Loy's imagination to the little magazines that provided a stage for her innovative work. As a locus of modern fashion and commercial culture, the city also provided a gateway to a broader culture of consumers who read *Vogue* and *Vanity Fair* and shopped in department stores such as Wanamaker and Macy's, where Loy's lampshades would be sold in the 1920s (see chapter 4). In typical en dehors garde fashion, Loy embraced both avant-garde coteries and middle-class consumer culture, courting a wide audience to read, view—and purchase—her work.

IV. PARODYING FUTURIST PERFORMANCE

****

Collision & Cittàbapini

****

Loy's *Two Plays* restage Futurist public spectacles in miniature, recalibrating the Futurist artist's antagonistic approach to audience into a more playful, collaborative relationship. As published in *Rogue* (June 15, 1915), the *Two Plays—Collision* and *Cittàbapini* [Bapini's City]—together take up only a page and a half (see Figs. 3.3 and 3.4). Each can be read or performed in less than five minutes, though making sense of them could take considerably longer. With little dialogue and stage directions that dominate, the plays read more like narrative descriptions of dramatic action than actual scripts. As Julie Schmid observes, "*Two Plays* exemplifies Futurist theatre in their use of lighting and kinetic scenery," as well as their deployment of disjunctive, telegraphic language (3).

The micro-drama *Collision* puts the Futurists' big ideas to the test, taking their performative rhetoric and transforming it into an actual dramatic performance. "Man" is the sole character, enacting the Futurist dream of autonomy. After being shut in a large, vacant hall, Man proclaims that isolation and emptiness are necessary precursors for creation, interpellating himself as an artist or godlike figure. He presses a button, and the hall erupts in a cataclysm of noises, lights, convulsions, and explosions. As the chaos intensifies, Man relaxes and announces that the vibrations have reached the intensity required for individual self-actualization. The vibrations accelerate until he stiffens, unites with his mechanized surroundings, and silence ensues. After a brief pause, a tremor arises to restart the cycle, initiating a "secondary inception."

In depicting a man merging with his mechanized environment to achieve a creative apotheosis, *Collision* anticipates with uncanny precision the aesthetic program Marinetti would promote a year later in his 1916 manifesto, "Dynamic and Synoptic Declamation." Calling for a "warlike, mechanical declamation of his poetry," Marinetti directs "the performer [...] to dress anonymously, dehumanize his voice and face, metallize or electrify his voice, and in all ways imitate motors and their rhythms, until ultimately, he has 'disappeared'" (Poggi, "Dreams" 39), or, as Marinetti puts it—"our literary *I* or ego consumes and obliterates itself in the grand cosmic vibration" ("Dynamic" 220). This sounds a lot like *Collision*, when Man declares his readiness for autonomous creation: "At last—vibration is intensified to the requisite ratio—for every latent conscious and sub-conscious impulse to respond to automatically." Just as Marinetti's performer "obliterates itself in the grand cosmic vibration," in Loy's stage directions, Man "attain[s] unison" with his dynamic, mechanized environment. I am not suggesting that Marinetti plagiarized Loy's

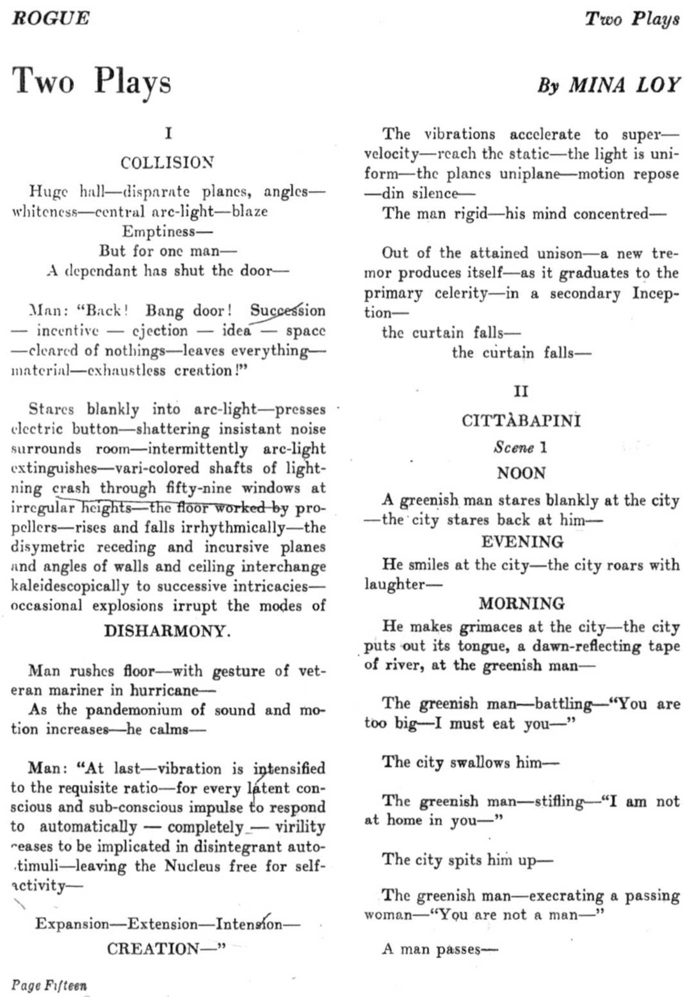

ROGUE — Two Plays

Two Plays

By MINA LOY

I

COLLISION

Huge hall—disparate planes, angles—whiteness—central arc-light—blaze
Emptiness—
But for one man—
A dependant has shut the door—

Man: "Back! Bang door! Succession — incentive — ejection — idea — space —cleared of nothings—leaves everything—material—exhaustless creation!"

Stares blankly into arc-light—presses electric button—shattering insistant noise surrounds room—intermittently arc-light extinguishes—vari-colored shafts of lightning crash through fifty-nine windows at irregular heights—the floor worked by propellers—rises and falls irrhythmically—the disymetric receding and incursive planes and angles of walls and ceiling interchange kaleidescopically to successive intricacies—occasional explosions irrupt the modes of
DISHARMONY.

Man rushes floor—with gesture of veteran mariner in hurricane—
As the pandemonium of sound and motion increases—he calms—

Man: "At last—vibration is intensified to the requisite ratio—for every latent conscious and sub-conscious impulse to respond to automatically — completely — virility ceases to be implicated in disintegrant auto-stimuli—leaving the Nucleus free for self-activity—

Expansion—Extension—Intension—
CREATION—"

The vibrations accelerate to super—velocity—reach the static—the light is uniform—the planes uniplane—motion repose—din silence—
The man rigid—his mind concentred—

Out of the attained unison—a new tremor produces itself—as it graduates to the primary celerity—in a secondary Inception—
the curtain falls—
the curtain falls—

II

CITTÀBAPINI

Scene 1

NOON

A greenish man stares blankly at the city—the city stares back at him—

EVENING

He smiles at the city—the city roars with laughter—

MORNING

He makes grimaces at the city—the city puts out its tongue, a dawn-reflecting tape of river, at the greenish man—

The greenish man—battling—"You are too big—I must eat you—"

The city swallows him—

The greenish man—stifling—"I am not at home in you—"

The city spits him up—

The greenish man—execrating a passing woman—"You are not a man—"

A man passes—

Page Fifteen

Figure 3.3. Mina Loy, *Two Plays* [*Collision* and *Cittàbapini*], *Rogue*, vol.1, no. 6, June 15, 1915, p. 15.

ROGUE *Two Plays*

The greenish man—"Horrific resemblance to myself—I am not—unless—disparate to the neighbors—I am—to prove myself unique—"

The greenish man climbs to mountains vertex—to meditate on differentiation—prior to conclusion—

The mountain shakes him off—

The greenish man—rolls down into the city again—

The curtain falls in the mud—

Scene 2

The city is fast asleep—

The greenish man—wide-awake—

The greenish man—with a stylograph and a bouquet of manuscript—is spreading himself over the city—feverishly—"Now I shall never see anything but myself—"

He drops a tear into the river—

The river washes him away—

He smiles into the sun—

The sun receives the greenish man—
And burns the city up—
The curtain does not fall

February 28, 1915, Firenze.

ROGUE

The Cigarette of Literature

Rogue Trusts Everyone But Himself

ROGUE SELLS THE TRUTH AND THE UNTRUTH FOR
5 Cents $1.00 a Year

Enclosed is a Dollar for one year's subscription to *Rogue*—or my PROMISE to PAY *at my convenience!*
Underline the Dollar or the Promise.

*Name*__________

Town or City __________

State (if necessary)__________

Address ROGUE, 149 West 35th Street, New York City

Page Sixteen

Figure 3.4. Mina Loy, *Two Plays* [*Collision* and *Cittàbapini*], *Rogue*, vol.1, no. 6, June 15, 1915, p. 16.

play, but rather, that *Collision* reflects her attentive listening to his grandiose Futurist rhetoric and her inquisitive desire to test his abstract ideas in a more concrete setting.

One could easily interpret *Collision* as an expression of unbridled enthusiasm for Futurist ideals, but Loy's en dehors garde experiments are always alloyed, mixing curiosity and zeal with ironic critique. Even as Man declares his creative autonomy, the preponderance of stage directions emphasizes his dependence on material contexts. To achieve "emptiness," he must be shut in a "huge hall" by "a dependent," the architecture of the space dwarfs him, and mechanical propellers control his rhythmic movements. The play culminates not in his apotheosis, but with the stage direction, "The curtain falls," emphasizing the theatrical nature of the spectacle, which depends on both a physical theater and a human audience. In *Rogue* magazine, "the curtain falls" is printed twice, possibly signaling the cyclical nature of the creative process.[16] But the repetition is more likely a printer's error, since in Loy's typed manuscript, "the curtain falls" only once, and in a letter thanking Van Vechten for a copy of the *Rogue*, Loy quips, "we've had nearly enough of 'then the curtain fell'" (Loy/CV 27).

Loy's early writings interrogate not only Futurist claims of autonomy, but also their fantasy of male-generated, non-biological reproduction—a concept Loy mocks in her poem "Lions' Jaws" as "burst in a manifesto / notifying women's wombs / of Man's immediate agamogenesis" (LLB96 47).[17] The script of *Collision*—with its emphasis on contractions, expansions, and rhythmic vibrations—echoes "Parturition," a poem about childbirth that she published in *The Trend* in October 1914, less than a year before *Two Plays* appeared in *Rogue* (Bacon et al.). A comparison of the language of "Parturition" and *Collision* shows Loy investigating biological procreation and artistic creation in similar terms, albeit assigning them different values. The contractions and dilations of childbirth in the poem resemble the rhythmic "Expansion-Extension-Intension" that leads to "CREATION" in the play. Like Man in *Collision*, the speaker in "Parturition" finds herself alone in a confined space, her body subject to vibrations beyond her control:

> In my congested cosmos of agony
> From which there is no escape

On infinitely prolonged nerve-vibrations
Or in contraction
To the pin-point nucleus of being (LLB96 4)

As in *Collision*, where Man disintegrates "leaving the Nucleus free for self-activity," Loy uses scientific discourse to describe a dissolution of ego in "Parturition":

the ego succeeds in unifying the positive and negative poles of sensation
Uniting the opposing and resisting forces
In lascivious revelation

Relaxation
Negation of myself as a unit (LLB96 6)

Self-negation serves as the precursor to (pro)creation in both works. In *Collision*, Man unites with automated mechanisms to merge with "a new tremor," while the speaker in "Parturition" becomes "Identical / With infinite Maternity" and is "absorbed" into "cosmic reproductivity" (LLB96 7). But Loy distinguishes maternal reproduction from mechanized creative production by its animal physicality ("I am that cat") and divine power ("Thank God") (LLB96 7–8). Whereas "Parturition" depicts the cosmic "Unfolding" of childbirth, *Collision* dramatizes a Futurist fantasy of autonomous mechanized creation that results not in *conception*, but a mere "secondary *Inception*" (emphasis added). Read in dialogue with "Parturition," *Collision* appears to be less an enthusiastic dramatization of Futurist aesthetic ideals than a way of concretizing them in a stage set and inviting audiences to scrutinize their power and limitations.

Whereas *Collision* stages a mock Futurist spectacle, *Cittàbapini* is a cartoonish skit that pokes fun at the male ego and patriarchal authority, deploying physical comedy and slapstick humor to elicit laughter from the audience.[18] With actors and settings cast in antagonistic, gendered relationships, the play can be interpreted as a comical skirmish in the sex war (Bacon et al.). The first scene depicts an accelerated, twenty-four-hour game of copycat between "a greenish man" and "the city." The city provides a mise-en-scène audience for his antics, serving as a feminized urban crowd or "folla" for his follies. At noon, the man stares at the city, which stares back; in the evening, he smiles, and the city laughs back; in the morning, he mocks the city, and the city swallows him and spits him back out, like a giant whale or maternal monster. He then berates a female passerby, saying, "You are not a man," and scowls at a passing man, grumbling about his "Horrific resemblance to myself." Turning his back on his fellow citizens (and audience), he climbs a mountain, which shakes him off, sending him rolling back down into the gaping maw of the city. The mountain, a personification of nature that acts in cahoots with the city, is implicitly gendered female, since for the male Futurist, "nature is understood as the locus of the feminine and maternal" (Poggi, "Dreams" 24). The stage direction "The curtain falls in the mud" makes a parodic allusion to Marinetti's "Founding and Manifesto of Futurism," where a high-speed, pre-dawn drive culminates with him crashing his car into a muddy "maternal ditch" (Marinetti, "Founding" 50). In Scene 2, the greenish man, wielding a pen and manuscript, attempts to write himself across the sleeping city and thereby assert his power and authority over his feminized audience—the slumbering "folla." But once again his ambitions are dashed: he is washed away by the river and subsumed by the sun, which "receives" him and burns up the city. "The curtain does not fall" this time, implying that natural elements have subsumed human creations.

In both plays, Loy uses parody to amuse audiences by ridiculing the performative attitudes and behaviors of Futurist men through condensed, exaggerated mimicry. In *Collision*, the Man who aligns himself with machinery resembles Marinetti, whereas the title *Cittàbapini* (City of Bapini) and "greenish man" point to the frog-faced Papini, the self-proclaimed ugliest man in Italy (Bacon et al.). In both plays, the joke is on Futurist Man, an artist manqué who expresses contempt for the public and performs for his own satisfaction and self-aggrandizement. In *Collision*, Man bangs the door shut to isolate himself in an act of "CREATION" that actually produces nothing and is eclipsed by a mechanical curtain drop. In *Cittàbapini*, Man taunts the city, execrates fellow citizens, and declares, "I am not—unless—disparate to the neighbors—I am—to prove myself unique—," yet is swallowed by his surroundings. While Futurist Man achieves an artistic apotheosis, he proves to be neither autonomous nor supreme. He is ultimately subsumed by elemental forces greater than himself and outside his control, whether mechanical (*Collision*) or natural (*Cittàbapini*). The Futurist artist is exposed as the object rather than the orchestrator of the creative process.

In these experimental micro-plays, Loy develops an eclectic, en dehors garde method that blends elements of Futurist theater with popular forms of entertainment in ways that still delight audiences: theatergoers at the 2024 Michigan production pronounced them "thrilling and bizarre" (Dobbins, email to Churchill, May 8, 2025). Although inspired by Futurist discourse, the animated sets, simple plots, and clownish caricatures in *Two Plays* also suggest the influence of the popular traditions of cinematograph and puppetry.

Cinematograph, an early form of film and animation, was first developed in the 1890s, and by the 1910s had become a popular form of entertainment in European cities including Florence. Loy and her Florentine expatriate cohort were avid cinemagoers: Gordon Craig says he goes "very often to a Variety Theatre and to the Cinematograph" in a 1914 essay "On Futurismo and the Theatre" in *The Mask* (195), and Van Vechten reports stopping with Loy and several other expatriates to watch an "exhibition of moving-pictures" in the Italian town of Arezzo en route to Vallombrosa in July 1914 (124). Loy's lifelong interest in cinema would extend to her later filmic engagements with Surrealism (which Susan Rosenbaum illuminates in chapter 4). Were the animated buildings and personified planets in *Two Plays* inspired by early cinematograph films that similarly defy the laws of physics, toy with perspective, and deploy cosmic tropes? In George Méliès's *Le voyage dans la lune* (1902), live actors climb into a torpedo-shaped spaceship, which is launched into the sky, where it strikes a cartoon moon face in the eye.[19] Robert W. Paul's *The '?' Motorist* (1906) uses similar visual tricks, combining live actors and animations, as well as mechanical and natural elements, to depict a car motoring down a road, driving up the vertical facade of a building, and ascending into the heavens.[20]

Loy may have been thinking about such "magical" effects when she wrote the seemingly impossible stage directions for *Two Plays*. *Collision* calls for "shafts of light [to] crash through fifty-nine windows" and "the floor [to be] worked by propellers." These are difficult effects to achieve in a small, low-budget experimental theater, but might more easily be accomplished through cinematographic animation.[21] The Man could merge with his mechanized surroundings, much as the driver of the car gets swept up into the heavens in *The '?' Motorist*. Similar special effects could be used to animate the city in *Cittàbapini*, allowing the city to laugh, swallow, and spit out the greenish man. He could ascend the mountain, much as the car speeds up the side of a building in *The '?' Motorist*, and a dramatic shift in perspective could enable him to write with a "stylograph" across the face of the city. At the end of the play, the greenish man could "drop a tear into the river" and be washed away and then "received" by the sun using animation techniques similar to those used when the spaceship pierces the eye of the moon in *La Voyage dans la Lune*, releasing drops of blood or tears.

The cartoonish violence in *Cittàbapini* also harkens to puppet theater, which Loy was exposed to from an early age. Growing up in London, she saw Punch and Judy shows, which she references in her autobiographical long poem "Anglo-Mongrels and the Rose" (Kinnahan, "Economics" 257). As an adult living in Italy, she had ready access to the folk tradition of Italian puppetry, which was staged in the streets of Florence. Puppetry was also embraced by avant-garde theater and dance practitioners in the early twentieth century, taking center stage in works such as the Ballet Russes 1911 production of *Petrushka* and the interlinked dances "Le Pantin et la Mort" (The Puppet and Death) and "Les Pantins Dansent" (The Puppets Dance), choreographed in 1917 by Valentine de Saint-Point, author of the 1912 "Manifesto of the Futurist Woman" (Girdwood 271–72). Alfred Kreymborg published a collection of *Puppet Plays*, with a preface by Gordon Craig, in 1923. As Megan Girdwood argues, Loy, too, got caught up in the avant-garde mania for marionettes, using puppets as vessels for exploring the human body, mechanized automation, and spectacle in poems such as "Sketch of a Man on a Platform," which appeared in the April 1 1915 issue of *Rogue*, just three months before *Two Plays*. Written in the context of Loy's flirtation with Futurism, the poem's title conjures a Futurist man standing on a train station platform, ready to leap on a high-speed locomotive (LLB96 19). But the platform could just as easily be the stage for a puppet show, as Loy likens the man to a dancing marionette whose body is "easiest to lift from the ground" and whose movements "Savor of the airy-fairy of the ballet" (LLB96 19). As Roger Conover wryly observes, "The pseudo-man on the platform flexing his male fallacies with untroubled superiority bears all the signs of a mock Marinetti. [Loy] pulls the strings; Marinetti is reduced to an amusing spectacle—Marinetti as marionette" (LLB96 181).

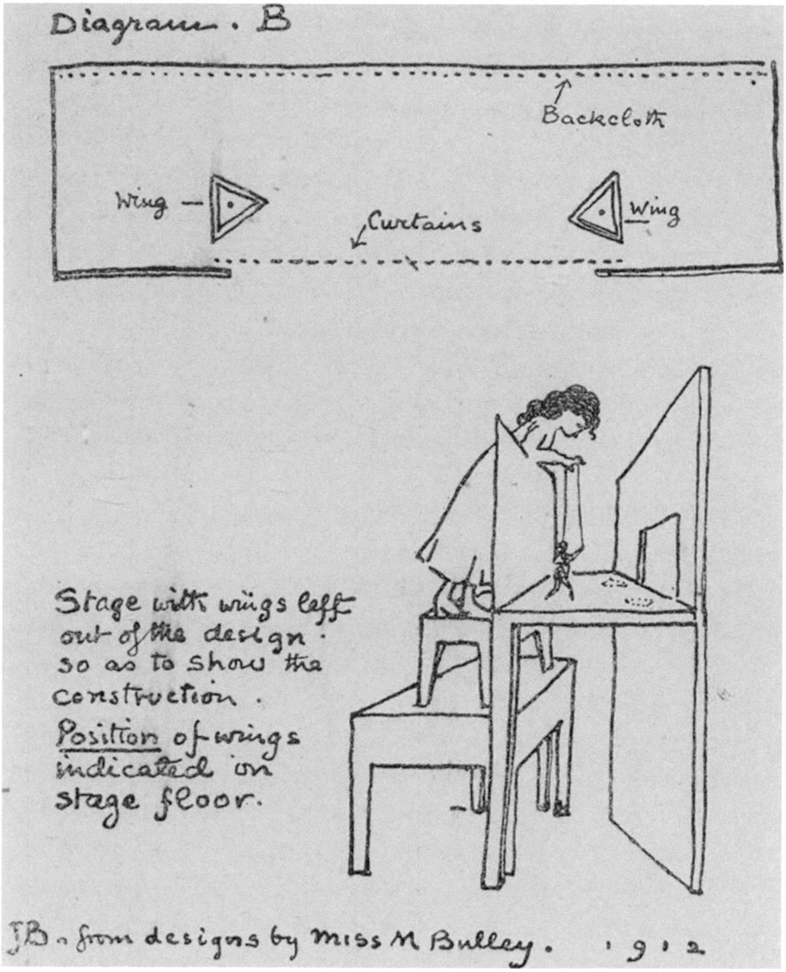

Figure 3.5. J. B. [John Bull], Diagram B., from designs by Miss M. Bulley (1912). *The Mask*, vol. 5, no. 3, Jan. 1913, p. 243.

Loy's interest in the marionette may have been piqued by reading *The Mask*, a platform Gordon Craig used to promote puppetry as a vital resource for modern theater. From April 1912 to January 1914—the span when Loy became interested in theater and playwriting—Craig ran a ten-installment English translation of Yorick's "History of Puppets," originally written in the 1880s by P. Ferrigni, drama critic of the Florentine *Nazione*, under the pen name "Yorick" ("Some Notes" 301). The chapters most likely to arouse Loy's interest, on English and Italian puppetry, appeared in issues that also featured discussions of Futurist theater, a topic she would have found irresistible. The first chapter, "Some Notes on Ancient Puppets," appeared along with an article on "The Futurists" that promised to explain their polarizing effects on audiences (Craig, "The Futurists" 277). The January 1914 special issue on Futurist theater included Yorick's chapter on "Puppets in England," along with an English translation of Marinetti's manifesto on "Futurism and the Theatre," and essays on Futurist theater by John Semar and Craig. Loy would have also been enticed by John Bull's diagrams for the construction of puppets and puppet stages in the first installment of "Puppets in Italy" (January 1913, Fig. 3.5).

It is likely that Loy not only read about such puppet shows, but saw them performed in the streets of Florence. In the July 1913 installment on "Puppets in Italy," Yorick supplies "A Few Statistics" to demonstrate their enduring popularity, reporting "more than four hundred Marionetti 'edifizi,' large and small, on Italian soil" and more than forty-thousand "burattini" (hand puppets) in the 1880s (27). Roving companies staged puppet shows in public plazas and theaters across the country, including in Florence (27–28). This popular tradition may have inspired Loy to apply similar techniques to her plays to amuse her own audiences. The simple, comical plot of *Cittàbapini*, with its crude, violent caricatures, recalls Italian puppet shows and could be staged in a small puppet theater with "marionetti" or "burattini." Small scuffles could break out between the greenish man and his fellow city dwellers. The city buildings and sun could come to life as violent, voracious puppets that devour, spit out, and sweep up the human puppets.

Both Loy and Craig were particularly enchanted by marionettes. The October 1912 issue of *The Mask*, "dedicated principally to the Marionette," exalts "the majesty of the marionettes" in terms that Loy reserves for the artist/genius, asserting that "these wonderful little beings" have "in them something of the divine" and "live with the life of the immortal gods" (Semar 95). Craig proclaims that the "wires which stretch from Divinity to the soul of the Poet are wires which might command [the marionette]" (Craig, "Gentlemen" 97)—language that echoes in Loy's boast in "Songs to Joannes": "I know the Wire-Puller intimately" (LLB96 55). Craig also highlights puppetry practices that resemble Loy's own predilection for pseudonyms and sympathy for outcasts, noting that the marionette "has many disguises and he impersonates known heroes and despised persons equally well" ("Gentlemen" 96). A few pages later, Anatole France explains the venerable origins of the humble puppet in contexts that would undoubtedly appeal to Loy's fascination with virgins, Madonnas, and even lampshades:

> The marionette is august: it issues from the sanctuary. The marionette or *mariole* was originally a little virgin Mary, a pious image. [...] In old Spain, in the ardent land of the Madonnas dressed in beautiful gowns similar to lamp-shades of gold and pearls, the marionettes acted mysteries and represented the drama of the Passion. (France 100)

With her fascination with the Madonna figures that appear in her poems of this period (which Linda Kinnahan examines in chapter 2), Loy would have certainly recognized their sisterhood with the marionette. The subsequent item in the marionette issue—an excerpt from Arthur Symons's "Apology for Puppets"—would have tapped into Loy's interests in theater, dance, and comedy, and accorded with her desires to amuse and elevate (rather than denigrate) audiences. After seeing "a ballet, a farce, and the fragment of an opera performed by the marionettes at the Costanzi Theatre in Rome," Symons declares the marionette an unrivaled communicator between artist and audience, or as he puts it, the "perfect medium between the meaning of a piece, as the author conceived it, and that other meaning which it derives from our reception of it" (103).[22]

Given her affinities with the ideas expounded in the marionette issue of *The Mask*, it is hard to imagine that Loy did not devour the magazine, store it away, and draw upon it, consciously or unconsciously, when she began writing and acting in plays.[23] A diagram that follows Gordon Craig's instructions for the design of a marionette stage seems like a perfect illustration of her en dehors garde approach to playwriting. Like the female

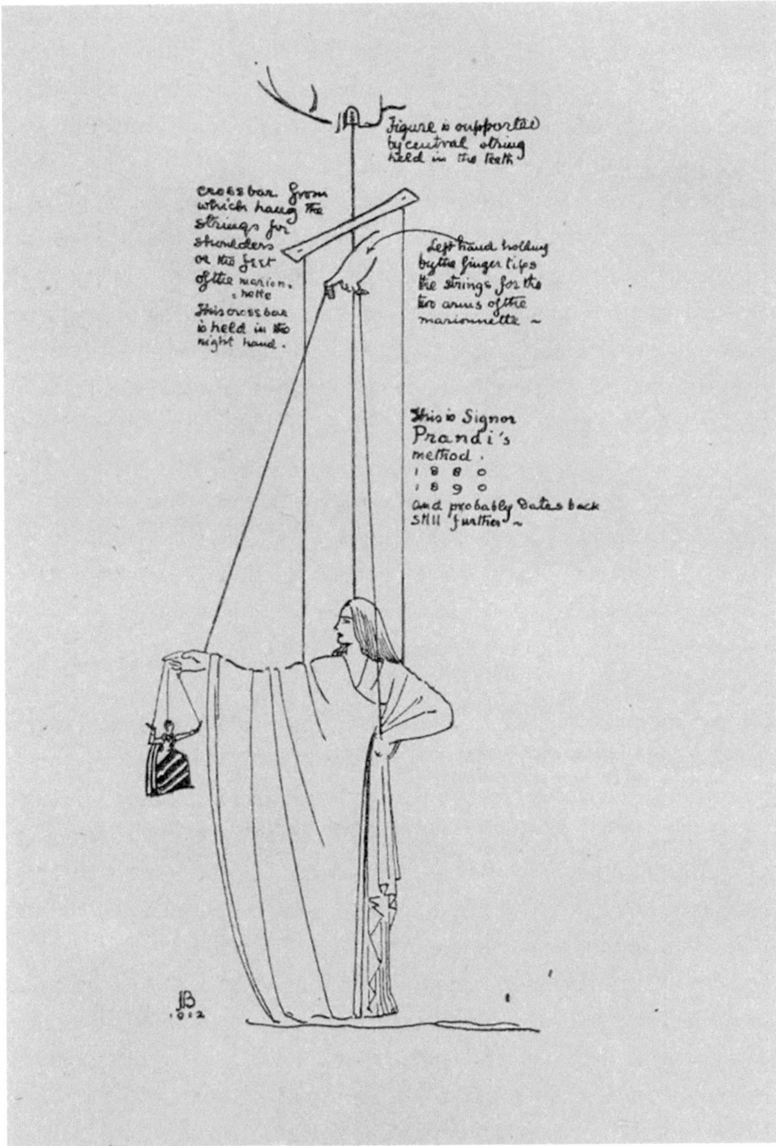

Figure 3.6. J. B. [John Bull]. "This is Signor Prandi's method." *The Mask*, vol. 5, no. 2, Oct. 1912, p. 153.

marionette dangling a smaller one from her hand, Loy manipulates her characters like puppets, even as she recognizes that she too is strung up by wires in a larger system of pre-scripted performances (Fig. 3.6).

As we will see in *The Sacred Prostitute* and *The Pamperers*, Loy directs her female characters to strike poses of classical elegance, beauty, and power, even as she adorns them in gowns whose folds blend with the curtains and materialize their difficulty extricating themselves from what she calls "the social fabric" (SE 162). Her interest in women's fashion is also evident in her poems and drawings of this period, discussed by Kinnahan in chapter 2. Loy enjoyed her own stint dressing up and playing the role of a puppet when she costarred in Alfred Kreymborg's 1916 puppet play *Lima Beans*. Kreymborg conducted rehearsals with a baton and directed the actors to perform like marionettes; Loy was game, appreciating the irony of playing the role of "Wife" as if she were a puppet controlled by a wire-puller (Burke, *Becoming* 221).

Whereas Futurist theatrical techniques aim to alienate and defamiliarize an audience, cinematograph and puppetry seek to amaze, entertain, and amuse. By combining Futurist techniques with elements of cinematograph and puppetry in *Two Plays*, Loy attempts to convert an alienating theatrical experience into a jovial, collaborative relationship between artist and audience. Parody is an inside joke that relies on mutual understanding and recognition; it is a collaborative form. Loy thought of the "Rogue people" as kindred spirits who would provide a sympathetic audience for her plays, telling Van Vechten, "I long for news of what all the Rogue people & so on are doing" (Loy/CVV 104). Readers of *Rogue*—a sophisticated coterie of avant-garde enthusiasts—would have been receptive to the parody. As Jessica Burstein argues:

> the magazine is so much a series of inside jokes [...] and so thick with contradiction, emendation, and self-referentiality that it demands being read, not just "cover to cover" as one of the advertisements suggests, but from one issue to the next (163–64).

Rogue's coterie audience would have read Loy's "Sketch of a Man on a Platform" in the April issue and discerned the outline of Marinetti, a "Man of absolute physical equilibrium," whose "force," "movements," and hostility to the public bear striking resemblance to the Man in *Collision*. They could be relied on to detect an allusion to Papini in the title *Cittàbapini*, be amused when "Giovanni Bapini" reappears on the *Rogue* stage in 1916 in Loy's poem "Giovanni Franchi," and delighted when the play *Cittàbapini* returns for an encore later that year.

The positioning of *Two Plays* above an invitation to subscribe to *Rogue* suggests a mutual kinship between author and readers (Fig. 3.7).

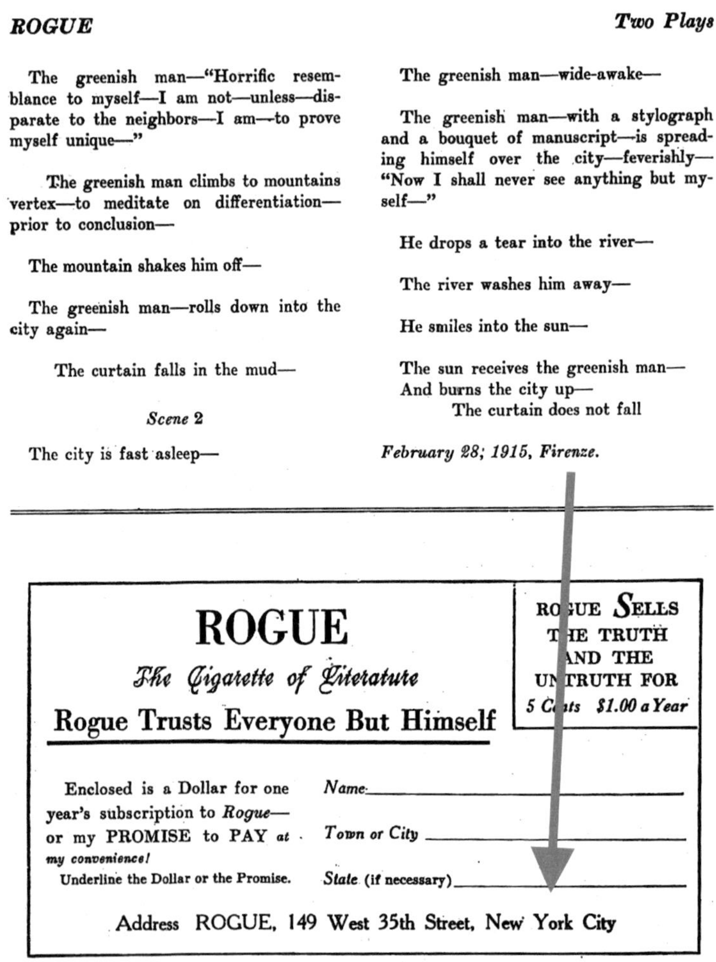

ROGUE ***Two Plays***

The greenish man—"Horrific resemblance to myself—I am not—unless—disparate to the neighbors—I am—to prove myself unique—"

The greenish man climbs to mountains vertex—to meditate on differentiation—prior to conclusion—

The mountain shakes him off—

The greenish man—rolls down into the city again—

The curtain falls in the mud—

Scene 2

The city is fast asleep—

The greenish man—wide-awake—

The greenish man—with a stylograph and a bouquet of manuscript—is spreading himself over the city—feverishly—"Now I shall never see anything but myself—"

He drops a tear into the river—

The river washes him away—

He smiles into the sun—

The sun receives the greenish man—
And burns the city up—
The curtain does not fall

February 28; 1915, Firenze.

Figure 3.7. Advertisement to subscribe, *Rogue*, June 15, 1915, p. 16.

The editors assumed Loy's plays would induce readers to subscribe by stimulating their appetite for experimental writing from abroad. The italicized date and place of composition—"*February 28; 1915, Firenze*"—highlights Loy's position as a representative and translator of the European avant-garde. The time/space coordinates also link her modern cosmopolitanism to the project of the magazine, which provides its own parallel coordinates, 149 West Thirty-Fifth Street, New York City, in the subscription ad beneath. The subscriber is given blanks to fill in "Name," "Town or City," and "State (if necessary)," the implication being that *Rogue* readers should come from a metropolis large enough to need no further explanation. Thus, author, magazine, and reader, no matter how far-flung, are brought together within an intimate, cosmopolitan community of people "in the know."

In *Two Plays*, Loy adopts an eclectic, en dehors garde approach to theater, combining avant-garde techniques, popular forms, personal references, and inside jokes, in order to entertain her audience with parodies of Futurist performance. It seems apt that the plays were published in a little magazine that parodied *Vogue*, while nevertheless positioning itself on the "cutting edge" of modern life and fashion. As published in *Rogue*, Loy's plays position an amicable audience at a critical distance from Futurist performance that allows them to enjoy the spectacles, even as they laugh at the antics of the arrogant male artists. The male characters think that they have orchestrated the spectacles, but Loy's clever staging shows us that they are the puppets rather than the directors of the performances.

V. FERRETING OUT THE INNARDS OF THE SEX WAR

****

The Sacred Prostitute

****

Loy began writing *The Sacred Prostitute* in 1914 while living in Florence, as a burlesque of her affairs with the Futurists. She continued to revise it well into 1915, experimenting with different forms (play, review, conversational review) and titles ("Conversational Sex - Love Review," "The Prostituted Paradox") for the play. Loy describes her motivations in an unusually long, self-revealing 1915 letter to Van Vechten, which begins with discussion of her ongoing revisions to *The Sacred Prostitute* and concludes with a description of a new project she calls "Possessions," which Harris identifies as an alternate title for *Brontolivido* (Harris 32n38):

> So I am writing a book now called "Possessions" which is wonderful—I do really think it has something of genius in it—It is trying to ferret out the innards of the "Sex War"—as manifested in the passionately intense frictional attraction—between Genius & Woman. It is absolutely personal & entirely impersonal—It tries to analyze moods—newly—it never gets away from fact—& is tremendously imaginative—brutally impartial & never unkind—pathetically dramatic & very funny. Everything to quote myself 'just is & there it is.' But oh poor me it's all about sex—& the artistic creative faculty—but the issues of course are something entirely transcending sex—I have tried to analyse—or give the impression on a "seeking neutrality" of sexual intercourse—there is just one short bit—which I think is magnificent—But it's something bigger than the thing as one is accustomed to accept it— (Loy/CVV 86–87)

Loy's discussion of "Possessions" sheds light on *The Sacred Prostitute*, a play that likewise tries to "ferret out the innards of the 'Sex War'" by staging a "passionately intense frictional attraction" between "Genius" (Futurism) and "Woman" (Love). Her use of allegory makes the play "absolutely personal & entirely impersonal," grounding the story in fact while allowing for imaginative expansion. She restages scenes from her roman à clef, converting her characters into archetypes, adding new scenes, and heightening the humor and artifice. *The Sacred Prostitute* is "all about sex—& the artistic creative faculty," yet also gets at "something bigger," addressing issues "entirely transcending sex." These "bigger" issues include investigating how gender performances play out in both intimate and public exchanges, and figuring out ways to dramatize these patterns in ways that are "very funny," "brutally impartial & never unkind" to her characters or her audience.

Writing the play preoccupied Loy: she mentions it in more than a dozen surviving letters to Van Vechten and Mable Dodge Luhan, which circle between her work-in-progress, troubled romantic relationships, and shifting attitudes toward World War I. Early in the writing process, Loy used her American friends as a test audience and attempted to pique their interest in *The Sacred Prostitute*, telling Dodge Luhan:

> I am writing—what at first seemed to be going to be a play—& is now a conversational review. Love the sacred prostitute strayed into the world brothel. If the idea interests you—I will send you a copy—it's quite long already, though only half finished—the futurist love scene is very amusing-& the "prominent" suffrage leader is too. (Loy/MDL 39)

In December 1914, she gave Van Vechten a preview, writing, "I am going to send you—a part of the Love-Sex Review—'The Sacred Prostitute'" (Loy/CVV 57). She followed up with a teaser installment and inducement to read it: "I am longing to hear what you think of my last things—I read the S. Prostitute to Mrs. Clapp [Maud Caroline Ede, wife of Frederick Mortimer Clapp]—& she is wild about it—says it's brilliant—& must be published" (Loy/CVV 97). These letters reflect Loy's pressing need to find a sympathetic audience for her play.

As she developed the manuscript, Loy's confidence fluctuated. At first, she boasted of its artful simplicity, asking Van Vechten:

> did you not get the bundle of the Conversational Sex-Love Review—I sent you or did they make so little impression—I am just going to send you the whole lot—& please give me your fullest attention—it's so simple as to hide some of its subtlety— (Loy/CVV 69)

But then she had second thoughts early in 1915, worrying that the script was too transparently personal:

> I should have like to have got your opinion of the Sacred Prostitute—as I found it very heavy—after the first unconscious enthusiasm of writing it—the second part is better—But very recognisable—I don't know if I want it to be read—I may send it to you for your eyes only—But I haven't decided what I think about it. (Loy CVV 11–12)[24]

Although in this letter Loy expresses doubts about publishing the play, by September 1915 she presses Vechten to share it widely, asking, "Is anything going to happen to the Sacred Prostitute? [...] —did you get the corrections [...] & does anyone like it? It's so encouraging to hear as there isn't a soul here to talk those things with" (Loy/CVV 31). After further revisions, she grants him consent to publish it: "I have tried to make the first part of S. Pros. less long winded—& will send you a copy—you can shew it to anyone you like—or publish it" (Loy/CVV 82). She sets aside her fears of moral condemnation and affirms her boldness and originality in dramatizing a prostitute's inner life: "English men write about prostitutes—& it's found daring—But we all <u>know</u> there are prostitutes—but nobody <u>tries</u> to find out how or rather express—what they react to things" (Loy/CVV 84).

After Loy completed "the second part of the Sacred Prostitute—who has now become the Prostituted Paradox—" she offered a more ambivalent assessment of the play, as if trying to convince herself of its value:

> the incursion of Futurism still amuses me immensely—but the rest leaves me cold—so it is difficult to judge—as at first I thought it all amusing—I like too—Don Juan [...] "who chased their silly souls into the corners of their propitious mouths"— & I like "Youth"—& his whatever is called Nature in the country—it's all in their wet looking [...] eyes—also I adore the end of Love saying—"when my stories were ended—You said they were not true—" I think Futurism & Love is very good most of the time—(Loy/CVV 40)

In this exchange, Loy recognizes the artist's need for an audience, admitting that "it is difficult to judge" the play's artistic merits on her own. As she revised the play, possibly eliminating "Youth" and Love's concluding lines, Loy kept her audience in mind, recognizing that they might find the play difficult to comprehend: "The first scene is irrational—intentionally—people may miss the significance of each point being negated by the next—But it's most important—the psychological portent [...] is big—& new—" (Loy/CVV 40). Despite her doubts, she was convinced that the play's insights were important and trusted the public to grasp its "psychological portent." She designed *The Sacred Prostitute* to amuse, cajole, and enlighten her audience by providing new insights into age-old problems. Her collaborative approach to the audience is evident in a dedication she proposed for the play, "To Those Who Are No Better Off —," which implies that she is caught in the same predicament.

In *The Sacred Prostitute*, Loy turns her laser-like satirical eye from Futurist public performances to intimate relationships, exposing gender as a performance, love as a game that women cannot win, and the "sex war" as a commercial trap from which no one—not even the Futurist genius—can escape.[25] The title, *The Sacred Prostitute*, collapses the division between virgin and whore, distilling an idea from Loy's "Feminist Manifesto":

> The first illusion it is to your interest to demolish is the
> division of women into two classes   the mistress,
> & the mother (LLB96 154)

In Loy's view, the sacred and profane are both entangled in a sexual economy in which women exchange virginity for financial security and male protection. In *The Sacred Prostitute*, Loy casts Futurism and Love as allegorical figures to analyze her relationships with Marinetti and Papini from an intimate perspective and, on a grand scale, investigate whether Woman and Genius can transcend the gender inequalities of the heterosexual economy to form mutual, loving partnerships. The plot of the play, if it can be said to have one, is set in motion by a group of men lambasting modern womanhood, which sets the scene for a competition between Futurism and Don Juan for male supremacy, with Love as the female lead and conquest. Futurism attempts to seduce and dominate Love in an ensuing sex war that degenerates into a farcical boxing match. The match ends in something of a draw, as the Procuress and Directors of the World Brothel appear on stage to expose the commercial agenda underlying the riotous show.

Although *The Sacred Prostitute* comically satirizes the "sex war," it also seriously examines spectacle, staging three plays within the play: the Procuress and Directors of the World Brothel (Nature, Reality, Purity, and Joy) observe Futurism and Loy, who watch the amateur production, "Man and Woman" (Bacon et al.). The metatheatrical comedy looks at looking, making a spectacle in order to scrutinize the making of a spectacle. Loy upstages male Futurist performance, spotlighting his gestures, poses, and ruses before various audiences. In the process, the play exposes gender as performance—one that comes with a prefabricated script and is highly dependent on an audience. As in *Two Plays*, Loy deploys an eclectic, en dehors garde method, courting an audience by combining Futurist themes and techniques with popular and traditional forms. In *The Sacred Prostitute*, she also incorporates inside jokes that reference Futurist writings, including the Futurist fantasy of male procreation (agamogenesis), identification with the machine, and proposal to put glue on theatergoers' seats. Loy heightens the humor with elements of burlesque and variety theater. The play comprises a series of comical skits, held loosely together by common themes and stock characters, combined in absurd, surprising ways.

Even as she invokes Futurist ideas and popular theatrical forms, Loy draws on an allegorical tradition that harkens back to medieval and early Tudor morality plays and Renaissance masques. Allegory is a narrative and dramatic form in which the story plays out simultaneously on two levels: the literal and the symbolic. Characters, plots, and settings "are contrived to make coherent sense on the 'literal,' or primary, level of signification, and at the same time to signify a second, correlated order of agents, concepts of events" (Abrams 4). Derived from the Greek "to speak otherwise," allegory allows Loy to write from an "other" perspective—to look beyond her personal predicament with the Futurists and see the bigger picture of the ongoing "sex war." She stages scenes with characters who resemble herself and her Futurist cohorts, but who also represent symbolic concepts such as Don Juan, Futurism, Love, Nature, the Procuress of the World, and World-Flesh-and-Devil. The minor character Tea Table Man is, on one level, her husband Stephen Haweis, whom she described as having a "parasitic orientation towards dillitante [*sic*] tea-tables" (Loy/MDL 16).[26] Yet his allegorical name allows him to simultaneously represent a social climbing masculine type. In making *The Sacred Prostitute* operate on two levels, Loy anticipates T. S. Eliot's theory of poetic drama: "what distinguishes poetic drama from prosaic drama is a kind of doubleness in the action, as if it took place on two planes at once" (Eliot, "John Marston" 172).

The Sacred Prostitute has the potential to be a cheeky burlesque of sexual relations, produced with the kind of smart, campy meta-humor that animates Greta Gerwig's award-winning blockbuster 2023 film *Barbie*. Like Gerwig's Barbies and Kens, Loy's characters are exaggerated types, some even interchangeable, and without a defined setting the action could take place anywhere at any time. One way to highlight the theatricality of the characters' poses and maximize audience participation would be to stage the play in a café or plaza, where the line between players and audience members could blur, exposing their mutual investment in the gender performances and heterosexual economy that fuel the entertainment industry. The play opens with what Janet Lyon calls "a rogue's gallery of *male* types" (an assortment of Ken dolls) discussing "the problem of love" and debating strategies for seducing women (395). Loy's choice to begin *in medias res* implies that the misogynist discourse is timeless and ubiquitous—unbounded by history or geography. Indeed, the debate constitutes both the setting and characters, appearing at the top of the manuscript, where we would expect to find a set description and cast of characters.

Though the debate's themes may be timeless, as Harris points out, its rhetoric betrays an "anxiety about modern reality, specifically about the emergence of new feminine identities" (29). Nowhere is this anxiety more apparent than in the lead male character, Futurism (Artist Ken), who arrives on the scene "with a loud report," determined to stir things up, demonstrate some new moves, and display his dominance and virility. Futurism enthralls his male audience by conjuring an illusion of the future with his bare hands (*The Sacred Prostitute* 193).[27] "A prophet has come among us!" the Men exclaim in unison (195). Eager to preserve the heterosexual economy from this eruption of homosocial desire, the Procuress (Weird Barbie) exclaims, "My word—the women ought to see this" (196). She summons the Women (Barbies) onto the stage, and Futurism promptly "lascivates" them with his eyes, leaving them begging to sign their names in his autograph album, "a tome labelled 'Women I have had'" (196).[28]

Watching from the sidelines, Dolores (Sad Barbie) dryly observes that Futurism has "successfully plumbed the feminine shallows" (197). She presents Futurism with a greater challenge, introducing him to a character with a "hermaphroditic aspect—it calls itself Love" (197). For Loy, H.D., and other Imagist poets, the hermaphrodite was a figure of fascination, signifying somatic ambiguity, erotic power, and personal transformation (see Susan Rosenbaum's discussion of Loy's art-object *Lobster Boy* in chapter 4), but in *The Sacred Prostitute*, patriarchal logic puts the kibosh on the hermaphrodite's transcendence of the gender division. The Men look at Love dispassionately and declare "it's hardly seductive," while Futurism reacts violently: "he drags off Love's roseate hood, dislodging a shower of golden curls" (197). After exposing Love as a woman (Stereotypical Barbie), he "declaims Futurist attack on love—most drastic" (197). When Love runs away, he drags her back by the hair, showing the Men how he "just take[s] them off like this—tic-tac" (198). Loy's slapstick treatment of domestic violence presents a challenge for contemporary productions, which have responded with efforts to make "the ludicrous demands of Futurism more obvious and highlight Loy's delicious parody of toxic masculinity" (Dobbins, email to Churchill, Mar. 20, 2025). The Michigan productions enacted the violence with exaggerated and stylized movements, while the Maine production flipped the genders of the actors playing the roles:

> Director Dr. Melissa Thompson theorized that swapping the gender of the actors playing the roles of Futurism and Love would help the audience see the characters as concepts and the boxing rounds as metaphor—rather than the characters as humans and the boxing as relationship violence. [...] This allowed the verbal jousts in the boxing match metaphor to land with more impact without replicating bystander guilt or the stereotype of the helpless female. (Dobbins, email to Churchill, Mar. 20, 2025).

Loy's script prepares for such interpretations by suggesting the comic violence of a Punch and Judy puppet show, and indeed, like *Two Plays*, *The Sacred Prostitute* could be staged with puppets in a marionette theater. When the characters are played as archetypes, the audience is invited to see the violence as heightened artifice designed to expose a real social problem.

Loy's script emphasizes the theatricality of Futurism's verbal and physical abuse of Love, which he admits is performative. Janet Lyon explains: "For the benefit of his male audience, 'Futurism' manhandles Love, but when his audience leaves (not wanting to witness another man's triumphs)," he grows gentle and apologizes, saying, "Excuse me, I hope I didn't hurt you. I have to do that for the sake of my reputation" (Lyon 395; *Sacred Prostitute* 198). Futurism's confession exposes masculinity as a homosocial performance, in which men dominate women to impress other men, and heterosexual romance operates in service of "bromance." Even after the other characters leave the stage so that Futurism and Love can exchange private intimacies, Loy makes it clear that they are still play-acting in the "game of love"—a "game of advantages" that women cannot win because, as Love points out, "it's not fair play" (203). Futurism's private display of tenderness proves merely to be the flip side of toxic masculinity—a "toxic fragility" deployed to manipulate women by piquing their desires for emotional intimacy (Bacon et al.). After an exchange of verbal sparring and seductive sallies, Futurism declares "check-mate" and stuffs Love into his pocket (204).

In both public and in private, Futurism—exemplifying masculine performance—attempts to delude, outwit, seduce, and triumph over an audience he presumes to be feminine, inferior, and pliable. Loy orients performance in a different way in her play, trusting her audience to recognize the parody. Staging is key to her en dehors garde critique of Futurism. The scene in which Futurism stuffs Love into his pocket offers a case in point. At first glance, it seems impossible to stage, but clever designs for costumes and set could conjure the theatrical illusions Loy calls for. Stage directions indicate that Love is wearing "a formless roseate garment" (199), and her gown could have a detachable scarf that Futurism pulls off as he picks her up. He could stuff the scarf into his breast pocket as the actress slips away behind a curtain. If the stage had a roseate curtain for the backdrop from which Love first emerged, the set would make visible the way in which women serve as audiences for male performance and are indistinguishable from the domestic spaces that define their roles and delimit their orbits.[29] As Nancy Selleck astutely observes, this beat is an important allegorical moment in the play, because it literalizes female objectification.[30] When Love is put in a man's pocket, like a wallet, she is reduced to a commodity that can be exchanged in a male-dominated economy. "What have you done with her?" the men ask Futurism, who "absent-mindedly" replies, "Oh, everything—and nothing," signifying her sexual availability and devaluation (204). Although Loy cannot evade female objectification, she can analyze it, put it on view for the audience to scrutinize, and expose an underlying truth about gender inequality. In this way, she unveils the workings of a system that inflates male power by commodifying and marginalizing women.

Just after this beat, Loy stages a play within the play, alerting her own audience to attend to the metatheatrical meanings. The Procuress reappears to announce, "We are just going to have some amateur theatricals—if you care to stop?" (204). Futurism, carried away with his own theatrics, does not get the joke and keeps performing. The Procuress ignores him, introducing a play called "Man and Woman." Stage directions indicate: "The audience sit circle-wise on the outskirts of the hall to watch the performance" (204). We do not get to see the theatricals, however, because the next page of the manuscript indicates: "Seven pages of manuscript missing." This omission may be a deliberately ironic, metatheatrical move on Loy's part, because at this crucial turn, the actors are transformed into an audience, and Futurism and Don Juan's reactions to "Man and Woman" become the spectacle we watch.[31] Loy's play-within-a-play calls to mind Charlie Chaplin's 1915 film *A Night at the Show*.[32] Chaplin plays two characters, the highbrow Mr. Pest and the lowbrow Mr. Rowdy, and their antics as audience members become the "show" cinemagoers watch. In a scene in which Mr. Pest tussles with another man for the hands of a beautiful blonde woman seated between them, the two men resemble Don Juan and Futurism comically competing with each other while another show goes on in front of them. Chaplin triangulates the camera among highbrow theatergoers in the dress circle, lowbrow audience members in the balcony, and scenes from the Orientalist show they are supposed to be watching. In contrast, in *The Sacred Prostitute* Loy limits our attention to the highbrow characters watching the amateur theatricals. Apparently, she is more interested in satirizing the antics of the male avant-garde than in poking fun at audiences.

Bored by a performance that doesn't include them, Futurism and Don Juan plot to convince Nature (ironically summoned as "Mammy!") to destroy women and allow men to self-propagate—an obvious parody of the Futurist fantasy of male agamogenesis (205). When Nature rejects their proposal, Futurism suggests that they turn their backs on her and "identify ourselves with machinery!" (206). But because Don Juan feels stronger comparing himself to women than to machines, he asks to "hear some more about the latest amorous strategics," so that he can learn new tactics for the sex war (207). Futurism agrees to perform, and stage directions indicate that he deploys a masculine sleight of hand and male gaze to conjure Love back on stage: "with an off-hand gesture he draws Love out of his pocket, scattering the newspapers, shakes Love out and stands her on the floor in front of him, taking her measure with a masterful eye as she pulls herself together" (207). In this beat, Loy objectifies the male objectification of women, turning the process into a spectacle for audiences to laugh at and critique. As Futurism literally sizes Love up to enhance his own power, Loy invites the audience to recognize and critique his performative moves. To heighten the spectacle, Futurism announces, "This is the sex war," and conscripts Love into the role of his costar in a boxing match: "Come along—you must pretend, anyway," he tells her, "Somebody's probably looking" (207–08).

A recurrent theme in Loy's writing, boxing here serves as a metaphor for the pugilistic stance of the masculine avant-garde in relation to both women and audiences. Loy felt a strong attraction to the hypermasculine figure of the boxer/genius; within a year of writing *The Sacred Prostitute* she met and fell in love with Dada poet and champion boxer, Arthur Cravan. Nevertheless, in typical en dehors garde fashion, she weds her passionate attraction to hypermasculinity with ironic critique. The campy boxing match comically exposes gender as a performance, staged for the audience's entertainment. Like the previous scene of gender-based violence, this scene explicitly calls for staging that highlights the artifice of the spectacle. The couple don cartoonish, heart-shaped, red boxing gloves and begin sparring.[33] The match plays out in three farcical rounds, with tactics shifting in each. Round one is a violent conquest, in which Futurism battles Love and wins a kiss, returning it with a punch and a caress. Round two enacts a romantic seduction, in which Futurism lures Love into a hypnotic state, until she snaps to her senses and remembers his misogyny. Round three stages a sexual awakening, in which Futurism excites Love's primal instincts and she becomes animalistic and territorial, driven by violent jealousy to protect her future offspring. Loy uses exaggerated body language for comic effect in the boxing match, which calls to mind a Punch and Judy puppet show. Although Love begs Futurism to "fight me with new weapons—I do want to be amused" (210), the boxing match comes to an abrupt halt when the players realize that the "latest amorous strategics" are nothing but an "elementary old-fashioned fool's game" (207, 214): the match is just another round of the same primitive battle of the sexes that has gone on for centuries. By directing the players to perform stock "strategics" that end in a draw, however, Loy's play wittily restages predictable moves in ways that enable the audience to recognize and laugh at the patterns.

Laughter is a great leveling device, but in *The Sacred Prostitute* it exposes rather than dismantles hierarchies of power. In an ironic epilogue that reveals the entire spectacle to be a mass commercial scheme, the Procuress reappears on stage, accompanied by the Directors of the World Brothel: Nature, Reality, Purity, and Joy. Loy remixes allegorical characters from medieval morality plays in her en dehors garde drama in order to unveil the old-fashioned ideas animating even the most avant-garde performances. As the Procuress and her accomplices discuss "balancing accounts" in relation to "supply" and "demand," we discover that they have orchestrated the spectacle, and their goal is neither to solve the problem of love nor end the sex war, but to ensure a sold-out crowd for the long-running show. Reality, "a composite person called World-Flesh-and-Devil," gets the final line, promising to "gloss over" the "mess" and "keep the surface glittering" (214–15). Loy's epilogue exposes the producers' complicity in the capitalist economy of sex, implicating herself, as author of the play, in the enterprise.

The Sacred Prostitute collapses the difference between virgin (Love) and prostitute (Procuress), showing how they both propel the same sexual economy. Dolores acts as a commercial agent or go-between, further eroding the dichotomy between the sacred and profane. Loy's en dehors garde method neither exempts herself from the critiques of romance and commerce nor mocks an uncomprehending audience. Instead, she aligns herself simultaneously with the savvy but world-weary Dolores who arranges the match, the fatuous Love who falls for Futurism, and the cunning Procuress who produces the show. Wittily staging, restaging, and upstaging gender roles, *The Sacred Prostitute* dramatizes how an en dehors garde artist may occupy multiple positions, assume different strategic poses, and be intimately and emotionally entangled in the sexual economies she critiques. The play's conclusion reveals that commercial interests control the game of love and even the most free-thinking, avant-garde artists cannot break out of the plot. Nevertheless, Loy stages the entire enterprise in order to analyze it, get a purchase on it, and enlighten her audience about their shared predicament. She does not objectify her audiences as in Futurist theater, but gives them agency and respects their intelligence, trusting them to enjoy the entertainment and appreciate its ironic critique of the heterosexual economy. Rather than attacking the audience for their naiveté and conventional tastes, Loy lets them in on the joke and shows how impossible it is to get out of it.

VI. PLAYING WITH DADA

****

The Blind Man

****

In the midst of her playwriting stint, Loy moved from Florence to New York City, motivated in no small part by her desire to connect with a sympathetic audience for her work. New York gave her entrée to a central gathering place for the writers and artists who wrote for, edited, and read *Rogue* and *Others*: the Arensbergs' salon. Loy found the Arensberg circle sympathetic to her own ironic and playful artistic disposition. "An instantaneous affection was fashionable," she recalled of the group; "One heard little less than exhortations to love" (qtd. in Burke, *Becoming* 219). But rather than joining the amorous intercourse, Loy observed the theatricals from a distance: "I watched the men cooing the assertively 'modern' women into the nests of their astringent lusts, to crush them 'tomorrow' in the contracting pupils of their observant eyes" (219). Loy viewed the free-loving New York set as a "marionette theatre" in which "interchangeable actors and audiences played into each other's hands" (219).

Loy's eagerness to engage and amuse the public naturally inclined her to collaborate with Henri-Pierre Roché, Beatrice Wood, and other members of the Arensberg circle to produce *The Blind Man*, a venture that enabled her to continue her investigation of the artist's relationship to audiences (Fig. 3.8). The magazine was issued in two installments to coincide with the first *Exhibition of Independent Artists* in New York in April 1917, a democratic, "no jury" event that promised to display any artist's work for a six-dollar membership and entry fee—no credentials necessary. But when an overturned porcelain urinal titled *Fountain* was submitted under the name R. Mutt (purportedly Marcel Duchamp's pseudonym), the hanging committee rejected the piece, generating a furor that has become one of the most celebrated chapters in American art history. Although Duchamp's role in the controversy has been well-documented,

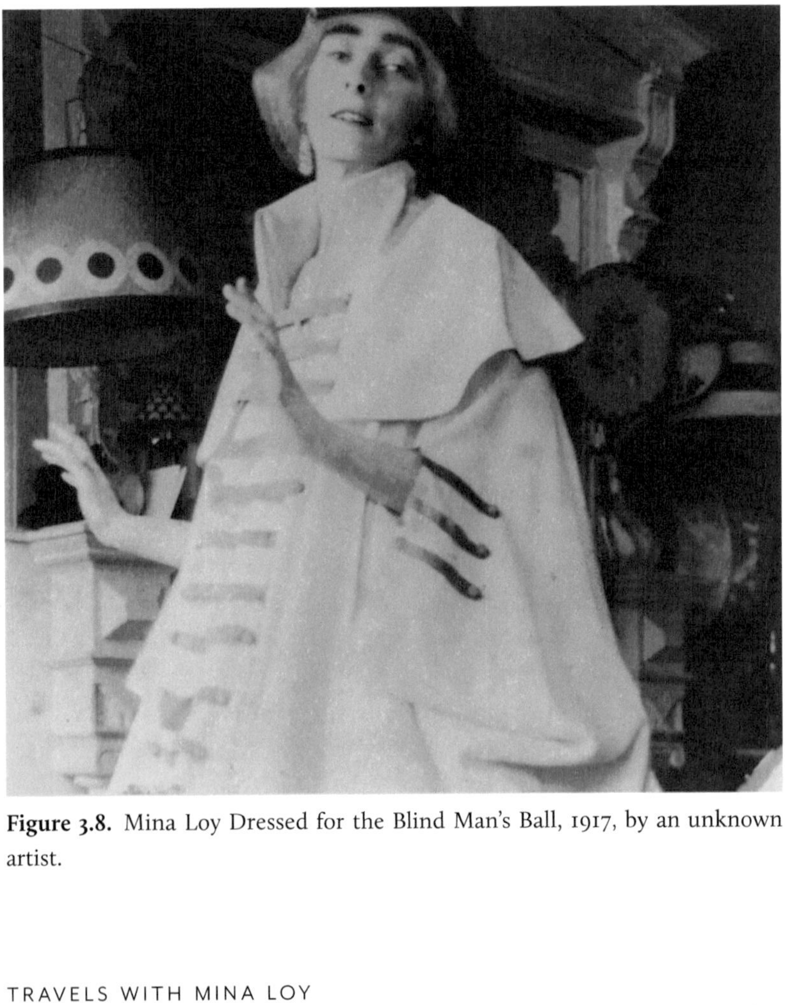

Figure 3.8. Mina Loy Dressed for the Blind Man's Ball, 1917, by an unknown artist.

Loy's participation has received considerably less attention, even though she was a coconspirator in the New York Dada provocations that allowed *Fountain* to make history.

"At every stage in its production, from artistic creation and submission to democratic editorial policy and printing," Sarah Hayden observes, "the *Blind Man* positioned itself in a tripartite, egalitarian dialogue between 'The Artist and The Public'" (*Curious Disciplines* 91). The first issue of the magazine vaunts its commitment to educating audiences for modern art in a proto-Dada manifesto by Henri-Pierre Roché that proclaims the magazine to "be the link between the pictures and the public—and even between the painters themselves" (4). *The Blind Man* aims to entertain, amuse, and activate the American art-loving public, or as Roché puts it, "He will give to lovers of art the pleasure of thinking aloud and hearing others do likewise" (4). Roché praises the Independents' exhibition for extending "equal opportunity" to all; for representing all schools "from the most conservative to the most radical"; and for encouraging the American public "to think for itself, and no longer accept, mechanically, the art reputations made abroad" (3). By thinking for itself, the American public will cease to be mindless consumers of foreign art imports. *The Blind Man*'s editorial procedure will be equally democratic—a "referendum" in which readers are invited to submit questions and responses (4). The manifesto encourages reader participation by proposing a series of "Questions" ("Which is the work you prefer in the Exhibition? And why?), "Guesses" ("What will be the total number of visitors?"), and "Suggestions" ("Write about the Indeps [...]. A dramatic story of less than one hundred words") (4–5). It is as if *The Blind Man* were a museum guide or children's theater production, and indeed Roché likens the magazine's inclinations to a "little theatre" movement:

> Russia needed a political revolution. America needs an artistic one.
> Your "little theatre" movement has come.
> "291" and "The Soil" have come. (6)

Magazines, in this metaphor, are theaters of revolution, designed to overturn hierarchies of knowledge in the art world and rouse the public to unleash childlike, uninhibited responses to art. In this spirit, Loy's contributions to *The Blind Man* are performative, theatrical, and conscious of an audience, even as they explicitly raise and address questions concerning the artists' relationship with the public.

* Act I *

In…Formation

Echoing the audience-friendly ethos of Roché's manifesto, Loy's "In…Formation" is a comical sketch that highlights its own theatricality (Fig. 3.9). The essay, often referred to as "The Artist and the Public," was written as Loy's play *The Pamperers* "gestated" (Crangle, *Nethered Regions* 201), and can thus be seen as a continuation of her investigation of artistic performance and audience responses. *The Artist* and *The Public* are capitalized and italicized, as if they were the main characters in an allegorical play, and Loy casts them in an amicable relationship that is more akin to Dada's jocularity than to Futurism's scorn. Indeed "In…Formation" can be read as a playful endorsement of Dada's leveling of hierarchies, delight in "childish and puerile humor," and embrace of a "regression toward childhood" (Hayden, *Curious Disciplines* 67–68). The elliptical title subverts the business of giving "information," implying that education enforces conformity by aligning people and ideas "in…formation": that is, in rigid, hierarchical structures. Loy defends the public against the prejudicial influences of schooling: "I do not suppose the Independents 'will educate the public'," she writes, "the only trouble with the public is education" (7). If the public would remove their academic "spectacles," they might recover a "wholesome," innocent, childlike vision. Uncorrupted by training, the Public, Loy insists, will be innately sympathetic to new and irreverent art: "*The Public* likes to be jolly; *The Artist* is jolly and quite irresponsible. Art is *The Divine Joke*, and any *Public*, and any *Artist* can see a nice, easy, simple joke, such as the sun" (7). Loy's joke is absurd. It makes no sense. It makes nonsense—which is nice, simple, jolly, and quintessentially Dada.

Yet in a characteristically en dehors garde move, Loy undercuts her proto-Dada dissertation with an ironically ambivalent conclusion. Highlighting the hypocrisy of her stance as a writer instructing the public to reject education, Loy concludes by assuming the pose of an irritated

THE BLIND MAN 7

hind a picture marked Schmidt. I came to a doorway, and the doorway became obstructed with large canvases with heavy gold frames. I began to move them and I felt my back breaking, and each time I looked for the name of the artist I saw Schmidt. It made me so mad I took the whole pack, which I had with such difficulty moved, lightly on my head and began running. I ran in and on and over walls. Once I jumped into a picture and sat still, looking like a Chinese god while men passed. I am worth $800 dollars, I thought and I laughed. And I was a piece of soap with nails in my back stuck on a canvas. A big flood came and swamped all the first floor, and the canvases began whirling on the ground . . . blue arms and green legs floated past, and I said to myself: those are the art-critics.

As I was a piece of soap, I, too, must melt, so I flung up my arms wide and I was on a high, high pedestal, looking deep down onto the destruction, and some tiny black man was climbing up to save himself, and as he reached my wing I bellowed, "Who are you," and he answered, "I am—but the rush of the waters drowned his voice, and I woke up.

B. W.

In . . . Formation

I do not suppose the Independents "will educate the public"—the only trouble with the public is education.

The Artist is uneducated, is seeing IT for the first time; he can never see the same thing twice.

Education is the putting of spectacles on wholesome eyes. The public does not naturally care about these spectacles, the cause of its quarrels with art. *The Public* likes to be jolly; *The Artist* is jolly and quite irresponsible. Art is *The Divine Joke,* and any *Public,* and any *Artist* can see a nice, easy, simple joke, such as the sun; but only artists and serious critics can look at a grayish stickiness on smooth canvas.

Education in recognizing something that has been seen before demands an art that is only acknowledgable by way of diluted comparisons . . . . it is significant that the demand is half-hearted.

"Let us forget," is the cry of the educator; "the democratically simple beginnings of an art,"—so that we may talk of those things that have only middle and no end, and together wallow in gray stickiness.

The Public knows better than this, knowing such values as the under-inner curve of women's footgear, one factor of the art of our epoch . . . it is unconcerned with curved Faun's legs and maline twirled scarves of artistic imagining; or with allegories of Life with thorn-skewered eyes . . . it knew before the Futurists that Life is a jolly noise and a rush and sequence of ample reactions.

The Artist then says to *The Public,* "Poor pal; what has happened to you? . . . We were born so similar—and *now* look!" But the Public will not look; that is, look at *The Artist*—it has unnaturally acquired prejudice.

So *The Public* and *The Artist* can meet at every point except the—for *The Artist*—vital one, that of pure uneducated *seeing.* They like the same drinks, can fight in the same trenches, pretend to the same women; but never see the same thing *ONCE.*

You might, at least, keep quiet while I am talking.

MINA LOY.

Published by Henri Pierre Roché

Figure 3.9. Mina Loy, "In...Formation," *The Blind Man*, no. 1, 1917, p. 7.

lecturer, scolding, "You might, at least, keep quiet while I am talking" (7). The abrupt remark is a double-edged sword, cutting at both her own didacticism and her audience's inattention. The direct address to "you" is a performative gesture that invokes a public space and an audience, implying that Loy is talking directly to people who are physically present but childishly distracted. Reframed as a public talk, Loy's essay exposes the limitations of Dada's leveling ethos. When the audience is freed from hierarchies of knowledge and respect for authority, they refuse to listen. Rather than producing a jovial, collaborative relationship between the Artist and the Public, the Artist's talk is drowned out by the Public's chatter. The title of the talk —"In...Formation"— acquires new meaning, signaling the breakdown of information and hinting at the chaos that might result if the anarchic, proto-Dada tenets of *The Blind Man*'s manifesto were actually fulfilled.

* Act II *

Pas de Commentaires! Louis M. Eilshemius

Loy conducts two more performative experiments in the second issue of *The Blind Man*. The first, "Pas de Commentaires! Louis M. Eilshemius," picks up where "In...Formation" leaves off, contemplating what happens if Dada's leveling principles are taken to their extreme (Fig. 3.10). Hayden describes "Pas de Commentaires!" as "a prose-text to test the definition-demolitions effected by New York Dada"; if the boundaries "between art and non-art are dissolved," anyone can be declared a genius—even Louis Eilshemius (102). A poet-painter of minimal talent and maximum self-regard, Eilshemius was impishly championed by Duchamp, who gave the "best in show" award to Eishemius's contribution to the first Independents' Exhibition: a painting, titled *Supplication*, of a nude woman in the wilds, her arms outstretched, breasts splayed, back awkwardly arched, and legs bent in a way that could scarcely support her ample figure (Hayden, *Curious Disciplines* 93). Hayden argues that critics have overlooked the "facetious tone" and "tactical deployment of irony" in Loy's extravagant praise of Eilshemius, miscasting her as Duchamp's ardent ally and Dada's loyal devoted disciple (92). Instead, she argues that "Pas de Commentaires!" should be understood as "a conceptual duet by Loy and Duchamp: a mischievous mediation on quality performed by a woman unafraid to perform her own critique of the potential consequences of the Duchampian denigration of art" (98).

THE BLIND MAN 11

Pas De Commentaires! Louis M. Eilshemius.

"Soul....Soul! Your artists haven't got it; for them things are just chair, or table, or stables. Was it Aristotle who said, 'A picture is a silent poem?' — — — — —

"But you are not seeing my pictures **now**... What is a minute, an hour? Ruskin, (have you ever heard of Ruskin?) found it necessary to look at a picture for a steady week.

"I have two thousand pictures—how long do you suppose it would take an **ordinary** artist to paint this one?" asked Louis Eilshemius pointing to 'Maidenhood Confronted By Death'— —. This is the first time she has seen death; observe the effect—**Horror**—! that's quite new—the stormy sky enforces the idea; see how it bursts,—death, that's it, a burst!" We computed that it would take perhaps three weeks to paint such a picture—. "Well it takes me just two hours! I always paint on cardboard, that's new! You can't get such quality on canvas." Wandering round the bountifully endowed studio we found such variety of subject and treatment, as to give us some idea of the scope of this artist's mind. As Rousseau of the French spirit painted in France, does Eilshemius of the American spirit paint in America, with the childlike self-faith of a Blake.

His conceptions are traditional of the simple soul unhampered by a traditional mode of representation. Eilshemius paints women dancing, moonlight and the devil, and it is significant after looking him straight in his unspoiled eye, that his princes of darkness are repeatedly the best tempered, most unsophisticated young devils imaginable, and that his nearest approach to evil is in the symbol of the horn.

Eilshemius has not evolved, he has just grown to scatter seeds hap-hazard but at will to blossom in the amazing variations of his pictures, which, outside every academic or unacademic school, untouched by theory or "ism," survive as the unique art form that has never been exploited by a dealer, **never** been **in fashion!**

His is so virginally the way a picture must be painted by one unsullied by any preconception of how pictures are painted, so direct a presentation of his cerebral vision, that between his idea and the setting forth of his idea, the question of method never intrudes.

The complicated mechanism that obtains in other artists a prolonged psychological engineering of a work of art, is waived; his pictures, if one may say so, are instantaneous photographs of his mind at any given moment of inspiration.

"I am very broad-minded," said Eilshemius, "I like everything that is nice, everything," smiling benignly, "that is **nice** you understand. I can paint anything, anywhere, beautiful pictures on your hat or your dress, if you like! — And I only use five colours, any particular five colours? Certainly not. I'm not one of your hocus-pocus painters who have to have certain colours, certain palettes, certain — — —. I paint with my imagination, look at this! Victis—you know what victory is? Pressing the other fellow down!"

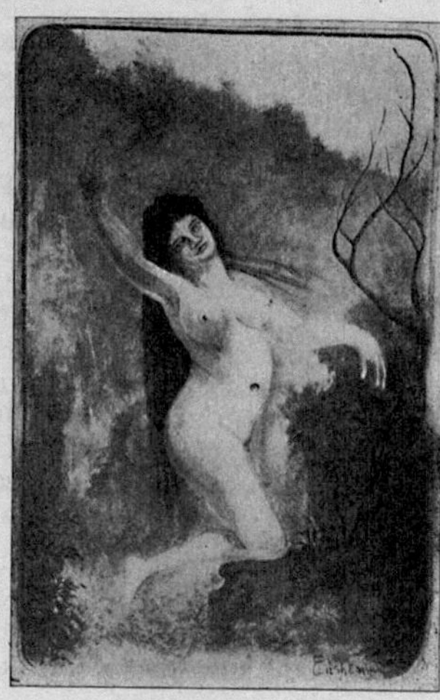

"SUPPLICATION"

Three fine nudes in an evening sky, each with a different coloured ribbon; the one on top, is the one on top! "See that one there on the right he's dying; you notice that on his face."

Hopefully inspired by the granite simplicity of the painter's speech I asked him if he ever wrote—"Don't you know who I am—" he gasped?

"Louis M. Eilshemius, M. A. Supreme Protean Marvel of the Ages. The Peer of all who create Painting, Literature and Music."

As I am used to do in reading I found by intuition the finest passages while skimming the volumes handed to me:

"How most are sore misled by pope and priest
To think that God hath arms and feet and eyes—"

"And my weird soul hath felt
The whiffs that waved from forth my heart."

Figure 3.10. Mina Loy, "Pas de Commentaires! Louis M. Eilshemius," *The Blind Man*, no. 2, May 1917, p. 11.

Loy's title tips off her a tongue-in-cheek tone: "Pas de Commentaires!" translates to "no comment," signaling in French innuendo that her critique of Eilshemius is implicit, as in any good satire. But the title also implicates Loy in the satire through paralipsis—the rhetorical device of emphasizing by professing not to say what you are actually saying (for example, "I won't even mention your poor hygiene"). Loy's title pokes fun at her own hypocrisy in proceeding to comment on Eilshemius's art after saying she will withhold comments. Loy may well have thought Eilshemius was a charlatan: his crude, extravagant paintings sentimentalize and eroticize female bodies in ways Loy should have found objectionable, and his brazen overestimation of his own genius is laughable. But she may also have been attracted to his childlike narcissism, much as Mrs. Jones is attracted to the young artist in Loy's 1937 novel *Insel*, which she based on her relationship with the German surrealist Richard Oelze (see chapter 4). Even if Loy objected to Eilshemius's paintings, she may have admired his insouciance, his willful disregard of good taste, and his willingness to paint clichés on cardboard, using methods and media more sophisticated artists and audiences would renounce. Throughout her career, from her 1914 call in "Aphorisms on Futurism" to "LOVE the hideous in order to find the sublime core of it" and "OPEN your arms to the dilapidated," to her 1940s refusés depicting socially marginalized men in the Bowery and made of debris she collected in the streets, Loy found beauty and value in the outcast and debased (LLB96 149). Loy may be satirizing Eilshemius's tasteless vulgarity, while also entertaining notes of genuine appreciation for his artistic chutzpah and empathy for his outsider status.

As in "In...Formation," Loy closes "Pas de Commentaires!" with an ambiguous remark that reframes the preceding argument, whether it is taken literally or facetiously: "Anyhow, Duchamp meditating the leveling of all values, witnesses the elimination of Sophistication" (12). With this abrupt remark, Loy shifts the perspective from looking at Eilshemius, to looking at Duchamp witnessing the consequences of demolishing the line between good and bad art. "Pas de Commentaires!" works at multiple levels, explicitly celebrating an outsider artist in keeping with New York Dada's ideals, implicitly critiquing Eilshimius's tactless and technically deficient art, and obliquely directing readers' attention to a broader debate about artistic value. With Duchamp as witness, readers must judge for themselves. Loy's essay "testifies to her readiness to join in the Dada revolt, to problematize and pulverize the givens of the art world; but, conversely, it also signals her resistance to accelerating the devaluation of value promised by its negative, anti-art project" (*Curious Disciplines* 103). It is both a celebration and critique of genius, whether he takes the form of Eilshemius or Duchamp—a way of playing with New York Dada that simultaneously indulges and resists its ethos, while activating readers to draw their own conclusions.

Loy's ambivalent stance reflects her mixed feelings about New York Dada, which extends to the primitivist, racialized discourse that pervades *The Blind Man*. From Roché's comparison of the exhibition to a "virgin forest, full of surprises and dangers" (3); to Beatrice Wood's "Dream of a Picture Hanger," in which she imagines herself as a soap on a high pedestal, "looking deep down onto the destruction," where "some tiny black man" tries to climb up and "save himself," but is drowned out by "the rush of waters" (7); to Louise Norton's "Buddha of the Bathroom," a defense of *Fountain* which begins with a meditation of the evolution of "the monkey race" (5), *The Blind Man* is riddled with primitivist tropes. When Loy writes that "Eilshemius has not evolved," she dips into primitivist rhetoric even as she ironizes it, snidely adding the convoluted claim: "His is so virginally the way a picture must be painted by one unsullied by any preconception of how pictures are painted" (11). Given Loy's satirical critique of virginity in *The Sacred Prostitute*, "Feminist Manifesto," and her poems of this era, it is hard to take seriously her claim that Eilshemius's "virginal" method enriches his art. Although she extols childlike ways of seeing in both "Pas de Commentaires!" and "In...Formation," Loy was unconvinced by the avant-garde's embrace of childlike regression as a form of primitivism—a way of going "native" or playing "savage." Skeptical of the European formulation of savagery, she soon came "to look on the word <u>savage</u> as a synonym for 'European imbecility' in applying it" (Loy/MDL 13–14).[34] Nevertheless, her exuberant contributions to *The Blind Man* do not rise above or step outside the avant-garde's racialized discourse; rather, as Susan Rosenbaum discusses in greater detail in chapter 4, Loy takes an en dehors garde approach, deploying racialized discourse in order to analyze its power and ramifications.

* Act III *

O Marcel – – – otherwise I Also Have Been to Louise's

Loy's other contribution to *The Blind Man* 2, "O Marcel – – – otherwise I Also Have Been to Louise's," likewise both indulges in and critiques the ethos and antics of New York Dada, but in a form that, at first glance, may seem more like an esoteric investigation with language than a way of courting an audience (Fig. 3.11). The piece is a fractured transcript of conversational snippets from a soirée, presumably the Blind Man's Ball on Friday, May 25, 1917, which is advertised inside the cover of the magazine. The magazine issue is dated May 1917, however, so the ball would have already had to have taken place for Loy to have transcribed conversations, which would suggest that the full-page ad for the ball is intended not as an invitation to buy tickets but to arouse readers' interest in an event that has already happened (so much for audience participation).

Loy's gossipy compilation entices readers with flagrant name-dropping and intriguing innuendos. In addition to foregrounding "Marcel" [Duchamp] and "Louise" [Norton] in the title, the piece mentions "Mina" [Loy], "Clara" [Tice], "Carlo" [William Carlos Williams?], and [Charles] "Demuth," all members of Arensberg's exclusive salon (14–15). The chief allure of "O Marcel – – – otherwise I Also Have Been to Louise's" is the chance to eavesdrop on an exclusive event—as if "otherwise" you also have been to the ball. But if the goal is to figure out what went on, once you gain entrée to the scene, you discover that very little happens. "Marcel"—if the transcript records his utterances—demands a bottle (three times), gives paper to "Mina" (three times), gossips about a "salting lady" (three times), and orders a tongue sandwich (five times). The repeated references to "salting" and "tongues" may pique your interest, but they are unlikely to satisfy your appetite for knowledge.[35] To add to the frustration, the names that are sprinkled through the composition do not seem to stick to anybody or clarify personalities. Someone remarks, "You speak like Carlo, well when he wants to imitate" (15). If someone is speaking like Carlo when he is imitating someone else, then identity is not authentic, but merely a copy of a copy in a chain of reproduction that does not lead to an original. Indeed, the compilation concludes with someone quoting someone else, saying, "what shall I say. Ti li li

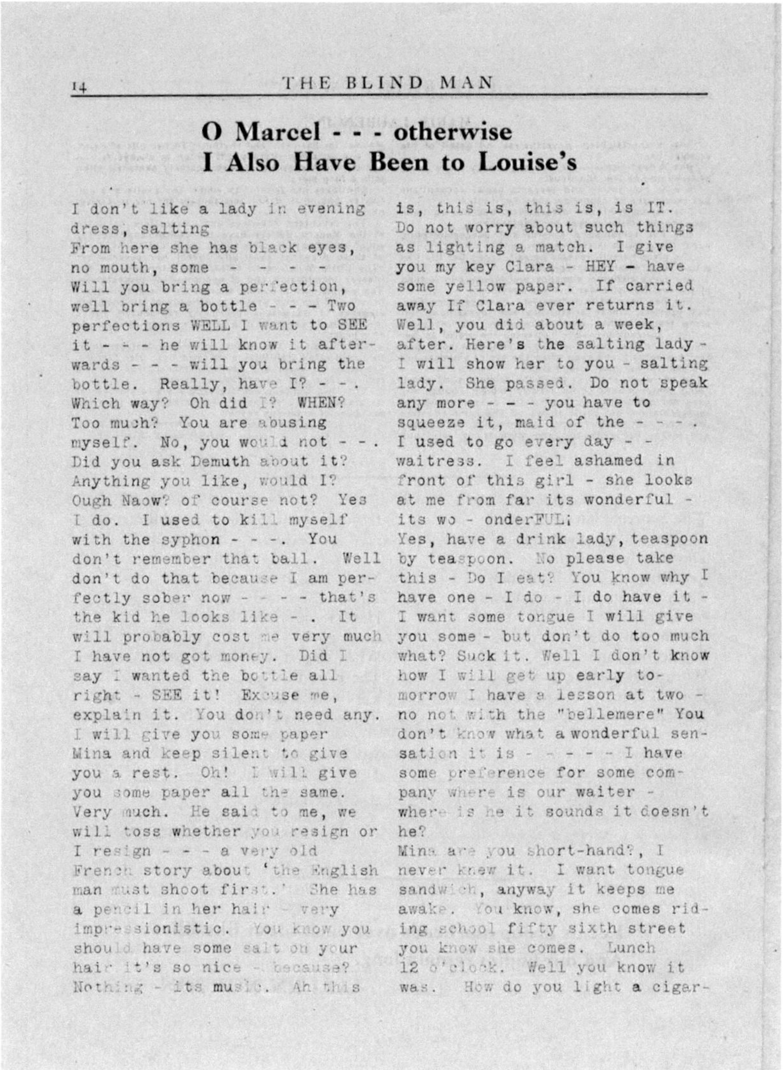

14 THE BLIND MAN

O Marcel - - - otherwise I Also Have Been to Louise's

I don't like a lady in evening dress, salting From here she has black eyes, no mouth, some - - - - Will you bring a perfection, well bring a bottle - - - Two perfections WELL I want to SEE it - - - he will know it afterwards - - - will you bring the bottle. Really, have I? - - . Which way? Oh did I? WHEN? Too much? You are abusing myself. No, you would not - - . Did you ask Demuth about it? Anything you like, would I? Ough Naow? of course not? Yes I do. I used to kill myself with the syphon - - -. You don't remember that ball. Well don't do that because I am perfectly sober now - - - - that's the kid he looks like - . It will probably cost me very much I have not got money. Did I say I wanted the bottle all right - SEE it! Excuse me, explain it. You don't need any. I will give you some paper Mina and keep silent to give you a rest. Oh! I will give you some paper all the same. Very much. He said to me, we will toss whether you resign or I resign - - - a very old French story about 'the English man must shoot first.' She has a pencil in her hair - very impressionistic. You know you should have some salt on your hair it's so nice - because? Nothing - its music. Ah this is, this is, this is, is IT. Do not worry about such things as lighting a match. I give you my key Clara - HEY - have some yellow paper. If carried away If Clara ever returns it. Well, you did about a week, after. Here's the salting lady - I will show her to you - salting lady. She passed. Do not speak any more - - - you have to squeeze it, maid of the - - - . I used to go every day - - waitress. I feel ashamed in front of this girl - she looks at me from far its wonderful - its wo - onderFUL; Yes, have a drink lady, teaspoon by teaspoon. No please take this - Do I eat? You know why I have one - I do - I do have it - I want some tongue I will give you some - but don't do too much what? Suck it. Well I don't know how I will get up early tomorrow I have a lesson at two - no not with the "bellemere" You don't know what a wonderful sensation it is - - - - - I have some preference for some company where is our waiter - where is he it sounds it doesn't he? Mina are you short-hand?, I never knew it. I want tongue sandwich, anyway it keeps me awake. You know, she comes riding school fifty sixth street you know she comes. Lunch 12 o'clock. Well you know it was. How do you light a cigar-

Figure 3.11. Mina Loy, "O Marcel – – – otherwise I Also Have Been to Louise's," *The Blind Man*, no. 2, May 1917, p. 14.

laere—she said—all right!" (15). How do we make sense of this nonsense, which seems like quintessential Dada play, staged purely for amusement? Loy's prose experiment presents several interpretative possibilities, each geared toward a different audience.

Perhaps it is a private, insiders' joke for the Arensberg circle, whose members could have the fun of decoding the cryptic utterances. Interpreted as self-referential linguistic play, the avant-garde is talking to itself about itself, aggrandizing its own activities through both explicit and coded self-references. The giant letters "P • B • T," which appear on the cover of *The Blind Man* 2 reinforce this interpretation, as they refer cryptically to magazine's instigators, Pierre Roché, Beatrice Wood, and "Totor," Roché's nickname for Duchamp (Watson, *Strange* 318). Stephen Voyce argues that Loy's "reference to Duchamp in the title ["Oh Marcel"] makes it likely that he is the one speaking (at least for most of the text)" (641), but the profusion of names, polyglot nature of the transcript, and party setting suggest that the disparate utterances come from various drunken revelers. If the text is, as Hayden suggests, a collage of voices "embedded with knowing winks and nods to a coterie cognoscenti" (*Curious Disciplines* 108), readers outside the circle would remain in the dark—"blind" to the insiders' joke.

But perhaps the joke is on the insiders, geared toward a public audience that is skeptical of the avant-garde's self-indulgent antics. Such an interpretation is plausible, given Loy's tendency to implicate herself in her satires. Cryptic as it may be, Loy's fractured transcript exposes the antics of the avant-garde to public scrutiny, much in the way her plays do. In this way, the transcript may be interpreted as a satire of the New York avant-garde—a "portrait of the debauched debutantes of the Blind Man's Ball" (*Curious Disciplines* 104). Loy may be "pointing out the hollowness of fashionable life," as Burke argues she does in *The Pamperers*, which begins with a similar collection of "tag ends of overheard conversation" (*Becoming* 222–23). Or, as Hayden suggests, Loy may be staging "an audacious, calculated irritation of public opinion, an affront to what was, as Burke reminds us, 'a country at war'" (*Curious Disciplines* 103).

Yet if it's just a joke on the avant-garde, why the unconventional form? Loy seems to be conducting a serious artistic experiment to generate a new American art form, attempting to document modern life as it happens. Understood as a "slice of life" in the New York avant-garde, Loy's experiment fulfills the program for art outlined by Frank Crowninshield a few pages earlier in *The Blind Man*: a truly native American art,

Crowninshield argues, "must very closely embody the spirit of our time, however morbid, however hurried, however disorganized, however nerve-racking that time may be" (10). Loy's "O Marcel" is a record of its time—a hurried, disorganized transcript of the New York avant-garde in the spring of 1917. Cristanne Miller describes the transcript as "narrative collage" (72), and Voyce says that Loy uses the collage form "to construct mobile constellations of bodies and objects, consciously emphasizing exchange, movement, and transition" (642–44). But Marjorie Perloff dissents, arguing that "Loy was not a collagiste":

> She does not paste together disparate verbal fragments, letting their spatial juxtapositions create a complex network of meanings. Rather, hers is a temporal mode, a satiric narrative, however broken and self-interrupting, in which structures of voice and address take precedence over [...] the Image. (144)

In "O Marcel," patterns of "voice and address take precedence" over any concrete visual scene. The transcript emphasizes sound patterns, accents, and pronunciations, and patterns in the cacophony suggest a preoccupation with accent and conversation: "You are Pennsylvania I am Boston. Do you want some cigarettes – – Did you put the pronunciation" (15). Loy seems interested in recording the process by which verbal utterances both constitute personal identity and dissolve it in a performative mix of postures, poses, and pronunciations. Loy explores similar questions about language and identity in *The Sacred Prostitute* and *The Pamperers*, as well as in her 1925 essay "Modern Poetry," which describes modern poetry as emerging from the rhythm and sounds of American vernacular, or as she puts it, "English enriched and variegated with the grammatical structure and voice-inflection of many races, in novel alloy with the fundamental time-is-money idiom of the United States, discovered by the newspaper cartoonists" (LLB96 158). Language here forms not just individual personalities, but a collective, national identity.

Loy's experiment may be interpreted as the verbal equivalent of a photograph—what we might call a "sonograph," or sound writing. The signature line, "Compiled by Mina Loy," suggests that Loy has not written these remarks, but simply found them, recorded them, and placed them in a new context (Fig. 3.12).[36] The typeface used for the piece resembles a typewriter or telegram—modern, mechanical forms for recording and communicating information quickly. The "typewriter" font highlights the sonograph's mechanical character and presents a vivid contrast to the printer's typeface used in the rest of the magazine. In these ways, "O Marcel" is analogous to a readymade or, more precisely, to the readymade that is the centerpiece and focal point of *The Blind Man* issue 2: R. Mutt's *Fountain*.[37] Like the urinal overturned, signed with a pseudonym, submitted as a work of art, photographed by Alfred Stieglitz, and reprinted on page four of *Blind Man* 2, Loy's "O Marcel" calls into question the authenticity of the work of art as well as the authority of the artist, who is no longer a god-like creator, but a human collector, or merely a mechanical compiler. The compiler turns over her composition to the audience to interpret, investing them with the power of conferring meaning and value on the artwork. Yet even as the verb "compiled by" "denies authorial responsibility," Hayden argues, the proper noun "Mina Loy" "makes a claim for the recognition of the compiler" (*Curious Disciplines* 106). Loy's experimental form is characteristically ambivalent, undercutting its own claims to dissolve artistic identity by acknowledging the theatrical experiment as an act of artistic hubris.

"Is he serious or is he joking?" anxious art-lovers ask in response to the provocation of R. Mutt's *Fountain*. To which Louise Norton replies in defense of the work, "Perhaps he is both! Is it not possible?" (6). The same could be said of Loy's contributions to *The Blind Man*, which may be any or all these things: an insiders' joke, a joke on the insiders, a serious artistic experiment, and a challenge to the aesthetic, moral, and commercial conventions that govern the art world. "It puts it rather up to you," Norton says (6). In turning her unconventional work over to the public to interpret, divesting the author's name of originality and ownership, and acknowledging her own role in the performance, Loy plays with New York Dada on *The Blind Man*'s stage, even as she choreographs her own en dehors garde moves. Loy's sonograph proves to be another way to give her art over to an audience, trusting their inquisitiveness and inviting them to play along.

THE BLIND MAN 15

ette - how do you light a match Did you, well it is not dangerous at all - Did you got it? Are you an American representative - I am sorry. You are Pennsylvania I am Boston. Do you want some cigarettes - - Did you put the pronunciation. Waiter! tongue sandwiches. Do you want hot milk. Two perfections she doesn't want anything - you got it? She can't write it down anyway - through the flag oh some cigarettes - waiter I want some cigarettes for Mina - this is a wonderful tune Ti lis li laera Mina I give you two dollars, it means to me two dollars - Ti li li laera - - it is twice I need to shave now. Demuth you must be careful of your key she keeps it about a week every key she gets she keeps. You speak like Carlo, well when he wants to imitate - well have a drink! You know those two girls are crazy about that man, they mustn't, you must get him out. I will have a tongue sandwich - you must suck it - - - Censorship! Don't let your flag get wet - - is that Billy Sunday. One should have had an additional star Billy Sunday - There's always a sky in heaven! - - - that is too low. My ancestor is tall people. Don't write, he is going to leave you for a minute. Sandwiches - Oh I forgot to telephone - what shall I say. Ti li li laere - she said - all right!

Compiled by Mina Loy

---

291 Fifth Ave., New York
April 13, 1917.

My dear Blind Man:

You invite comment, suggestions. As I understand the Independent Society its chief function is the desire to smash antiquated academic ideas. This first exhibition is a concrete move in that direction. Wouldn't it be advisable next year during the exhibition, to withhold the names of the makers of all work shown. The names, if on the canvases, or on the pieces of sculpture, etc., exhibited could be readily hidden. The catalogue should contain, in place of the names of artists, simply numbers, with titles if desired. On the last day of the Exhibition the names of the exhibitors could be made public. That is each number would be publicly identified. A list of the identified numbers could also be sent to the purchasers of catalogues. To no one, outside of the committee itself, should any names be divulged during the exhibition. Not even to those wishing to purchase. In thus freeing the exhibition of the traditions and superstitions of names the Society would not be playing into the hands of dealers and critics, nor even into the hands of the artists themselves. For the latter are influenced by names quite as much as are public and critics, not to speak of the dealers who are only interested in names. Thus each bit of work would stand on its own merits. As a reality. The public would be purchasing its own reality and not a commercialized and inflated name. Thus the Society would be dealing a blow to the academy of commercializing names. The public might gradually see for itself.

Furthermore I would suggest that in next year's catalogue addresses of dealers should be confined to the advertising pages. The Independent Exhibition should be run for one thing only: The independence of the work itself. The Society has made a definite move in the right direction, so why not follow it up with still more definiteness.

NO JURY—NO PRIZES—NO COMMERCIAL TRICKS.

Alfred Stieglitz.

Figure 3.12. Mina Loy, "O Marcel – – – otherwise I Also Have Been to Louise's," *The Blind Man*, no. 2, May 1917, p. 15.

Alas, the American public did not get *The Blind Man*'s jokes. The irreverent little magazine "failed to provoke a scandal," perhaps because no one read it, or because "a country at war could not tolerate such insouciance" (Burke, *Becoming* 246). Years later, in 1945, when Loy granted permission to reprint "O Marcel" in an issue of *View* dedicated to Marcel Duchamp, she offered an explanatory note that resolves some of the sonograph's ambiguity:[38]

> THIS was written at the Ball where I saved Marcel. With his robe afloat, the symmetry of his bronze hair rising from his beautiful profile, wavering as a flame, he was—actually—climbing a paper festoon hung from the top of the dome to the musicians' gallery.
>
> To clarify his "subconscious" In Memoriam of that era—when my notes in "The Blind Boy" caused, in New York, a bewildering uproar as to the base immorality of the modernists—I mention: Marcel let fall his "favor"—a miniature American flag—into his champagne.
>
> MINA LOY (51)

Loy's note confirms that "O Marcel" was an experiment in recording modern life as it happened at the Blind Man's Ball in 1917. Describing Marcel's "robe afloat," "bronze hair [...] wavering as a flame," and gymnastic movements, the note supplies the visual context so conspicuously absent from the sonograph. By clarifying the context, however, the note undoes some of the sonograph's ambiguity, wresting interpretive authority away from readers and restoring it to the author's name. Although in 1917 Loy placed more trust in her audience's receptiveness, the 1945 note suggests a marked shift in attitude from geniality to disdain, retrospectively aligning Loy with Duchamp and "the modernists" in opposition to a "bewildered," bourgeois American public. Marcel's nonchalant gesture of dropping "a miniature American flag" into the champagne is a flagrant defiance of compulsory American wartime patriotism.[39] It is also an indulgence in theatrical play, an activity Loy embraced in 1917, using *The Blind Man* as a stage for en dehors garde turns toward an American public she hoped would be receptive to her theatrical experiments.

VII. SATIRIZING THE AVANT-GARDE

****

The Pamperers

****

While Loy's prose contributions to *The Blind Man* adopt and test Dada ideals to playfully arouse American audiences' interest in modern art, *The Pamperers* steps back to put the relationship between the Artist and the Public on stage for serious satirical analysis. In her fourth play, Loy puts the spotlight on the relationship between the avant-garde "genius" and the public—the consumers and collectors of avant-garde art who also serve as the target audience for its provocations. The action—to the extent that action occurs outside conversation—takes place in a sophisticated literary salon, hosted by Diana, who introduces Houseless Loony, a leading genius of the Vitalist movement to the "Picked People" gathered there. The script is dominated by Loony's Vitalist declamations, as the mesmerizing Diana maneuvers among the roles of muse, seductress, and ultimately, impresario and business manager (Gilmore 289). "Diana the heroine is the Last Word in Modern woman," *The New York Sun* declared in a 1917 profile of Mina Loy ("Do You Strive" 10). In *The Pamperers*, Diana gets the last word, telling Loony, who has submitted to her stratagems, not "I do," but "you'll *DO*."

The Pamperers depicts the avant-garde artist's relationship to the audience as one of cooptation and interdependence rather than domination. Combining elements of Futurism and Dada and anticipating Surrealism's interest in hypnotic, dreamlike states and subconscious transformations (see chapter 4), *The Pamperers* satirizes the avant-garde by exposing its collusion with bourgeois commercial culture. As Jeffrey Twitchell-Waas observes, the play is "directed broadly at an avant-garde that allows itself to be patronized, sanitized, and co-opted by the very class it set out to undermine" (113). Siobhán Scarry, who directed a 2010 staged reading of *The Pamperers*, emphasizes its metatextual dimensions: "the textual form of the poetic drama is always self-consciously evident, even in performance" (1). Loy's metatextual emphasis on language requires more audience participation, as Scarry explains: "Loy enacts a constant staging and restaging of language [...]. She never lets the audience, or the readers for that matter, experience language as a transparent medium—it is always present" (1), and always performative. *The Pamperers* erodes the lines between artmakers (geniuses), collectors (patrons and hostesses), and consumers (audiences), all of whom are players in the same linguistic and commercial enterprise. But rather than ridiculing bourgeoise audiences, Loy uses satire to invite them in on the joke.

The male lead, Loony, is an avant-garde artist who, like Duchamp, creates art from found objects—Loony has a penchant for collecting cigar butts. In the course of the play, Loony

> is seduced and allows himself to be seduced into complete bourgeois co-optation. The play takes place in a salon, presided over by Diana, who is not averse to using her feminine wiles to enact this transformation of the loony into a bourgeois puppet." (Scarry 1)

Hailed as a genius and displaying an ego that rivals Marinetti's and Eilshemius's combined, Loony spouts grandiose ideas that sometimes echo Loy's own ideals of artistic freedom and consciousness expansion, but tend to dissolve in vapid abstractions and self-aggrandizing jargon. Like Loy, Diana participates in the avant-garde theatrics even as she scrutinizes them to offer an ironic counterpoint. She thus serves as a stand-in for Loy's en dehors garde position as both insider and outsider of the avant-garde. It would be convenient to read *The Pamperers* as the culmination of Loy's playwriting project, a satire of the avant-garde industry composed after her affairs with Futurism and dalliance with Dada, when she had tired of both movements and moved on to new en dehors garde pursuits. But as always with Loy, things are more complicated.

Although she did not complete the play until 1919, Loy began writing it as early as 1915, reporting to Van Vechten:

> I wrote a play called 'The Pamperers'—which is simultaneously a parody of the "Genius"—& the society that takes him up—it's a good deal longer than the ones in Rogue—the hero is a man who picks up cigar ends. (Loy/CVV 105)

What is striking about this letter is that Loy either absorbed or anticipated Duchamp's notion of the readymades at least a year before she met him in New York in 1916. Duchamp created his first readymade, *Bicycle Wheel*, in 1913, following up in 1915 with *In Advance of a Broken Arm*, works she may have read about in Mabel Dodge Luhan's letters or article on the 1913 Armory Show in New York (Burke, *Becoming* 145–46). Loy may also have drawn her ideas from other found-object precedents, such as Picasso's *Still Life with Chair Caning* (1912), a collage that incorporates a piece of chair caning, or Degas's application of a piece of tutu onto his *Little Dancer of Fourteen Years* (1881). Whatever the sources for her parody of avant-garde genius, Loy was sharply attentive to the ways in which both Cubist collage and Dada readymades subvert traditional measures of artistic value and authorial originality. She also ironically points to men's domination of the avant-garde by making Loony collect discarded cigar butts—the ultimate symbol of masculine power and leisure.

In summer 1916, as she was planning her move to New York, Loy wrote to Van Vechten about her aims for *The Pamperers*, expressing her frustration with Futurist theater and the movement in general:

> I wrote a play—a good deal longer than the ones in Rogue—called 'The Pamperers'—which I must finish—I think it would do well for the Bandbox Theatre. I shall do some more. The Futurist Theatre is very bad here. They have theories & no genius to carry them out—the words in liberty are in a putrid condition—things are really funny. The intellectuals & geniuses have all left the movement—& Marinetti has raked up some imbeciles to carry it on. Result— [...] the imbeciles—have finished up Futurism. (Loy/CVV 44–45)

This letter indicates that Loy had distanced herself from Futurism and its "imbecile" acolytes well before moving to New York. Her disparagement of Futurist theater in particular reflects her desire to get beyond theory and put things that are "really funny" before live audiences. Rather than seeking magazine publication, Loy aspired for a real stage and audience at the Bandbox Theater on East Fifty-Seventh Street near Third Avenue in New York, which she likely heard about from Hutchins Hapgood and Neith Boyce. Built in 1912 and closed in 1926, The Bandbox was amenable to avant-garde theater, providing the playhouse for the Washington Square Players' 1915 season, which began with four experimental one-act plays ("Bandbox").

Once she arrived in New York in 1916, Loy used *The Pamperers* to impress the public and woo an audience for the play, discussing it in a 1917 *New York Sun* interview: "she has seen so many movements rise and fall that she has decided to initiate one herself [...]. The play is called 'The Pamperers.' It satirizes the Vitalists and the unvital sort and everybody," the article reports, suggesting that no one escapes the satire ("Do You Strive" 10). Loy also expressed unbridled enthusiasm for her new city of residence, saying, "No one who has not lived in New York has lived in the Modern World" ("Do You Strive").

Alison Dobbins describes *The Pamperers* as Loy's "least playlike" drama, as well as the most difficult to stage because it involves so much talk and so little action.[40] Given Loy's conviction that Futurist theater had become too abstract and theoretical, the opening of *The Pamperers* is especially puzzling. As in her other plays, Loy "breaks down the barriers between dialogue, scenery, and stage direction" (Schmid 4), but in *The Pamperers*, she also blends characters and audience into the textual mix. The cast of characters and setting resemble a Futurist words-in-freedom poem more than they evoke a physical context, but they also prefigure Loy's interest in Surrealism (Fig. 3.13). The two-column arrangement of the cast of characters blurs the line between verbal and visual art. Loy arranges adjectives and nouns irregularly, inviting us to read spatially and generate different permutations: is the Obvious Invisible, or are People Invisible, Obvious and Picked? Is Loony Houseless or are Obvious People Loony? The subsequent paragraph comprises a montage of mismatched, oxymoronic objects and descriptors, ranging from "Porcelain breath," to "Gilded crimson," "Tailored muscles," and "Ooze." The players merge with objects in the salon setting: "Picked people melted by a distinguished method among the upholstery." Harkening to Loy's sonograph in *The Blind Man*, the play's opening lines are a montage of "Tag Ends of Overheard Conversation," beginning with the metatheatrical observation, "The social fabric is a curtain" (162), implying that social behaviors disguise authentic motives and feelings, even as they provide costumes and frame stages for people

THE PAMPERERS

BY MINA LOY

Invisible Obvious
Picked People
Houseless Loony

Porcelain breath — Sèvres bow — Gilded crimson — Curved flutings — Brocade — Tailored muscles — Whipped cream — Blue spirals — Salved lips — Salon — Debussy — Azaleas — Ancestors — Armorial complacencies — Ooze

Picked people melted by a distinguished method among the upholstery.

TAG ENDS OF OVERHEARD CONVERSATION

The social fabric is a curtain . . . and that warm garnet fold-shadow there, for souls hide and seek. . . .

Figure 3.13. Mina Loy, *The Pamperers*. *The Dial*, vol. 69, no. 1, July 1920, p. 65.

to perform their identities. Whereas an ongoing conversation establishes the setting in *The Sacred Prostitute*, here, the bits of conversation actually constitute the set.[41]

All social discourse, *The Pamperers* suggests, is performative, as the characters literally materialize out of the fabric settings and fashionable talk that set the scene. Loy's interest in women's fashion and self-fashioning spans her career. A similar effect can be seen in her drawing of dress designs from this period: female figures model colorful, column-like dresses, embellished with draperies, tassels, and scalloped valances that emphasize the connections between fashion, architecture, and upholstery (see chapter 1; Fig. 2.11). Loy likewise figures women as furnishings in her circa 1935 painting *Surreal Scene* (see chapter 4, Fig. 4.1). Whereas her paintings allowed Loy to visualize connections between women's bodies, fashions, and upholstery, her plays weave an additional connection between fashion, performance, and discourse. As Susan Gilmore points out, "talk, or gossip, introduces us to Loy's heroine" (285–86);

indeed, the stars emerge from the celebrity gossip about them, their roles not so much performed for admiring audiences, but produced by those audiences. We learn about Loony, the genius who collects cigar butts, and Diana, the hostess who collects geniuses, long before they appear on the stage, as "Somebody" gossips about them with "Somebody Else" (*Pamperers* 162–64).[42] The identity of the genius is thus bestowed on him by his audience and molded by their discourse.

Loy makes it clear from the outset that public tastes and appetites determine an artist's value in the art market. When the genius-finder Ossy tells Diana about his latest avant-garde discovery, their conversation makes the work of the culture industry explicit:

> OSSY: Di...if you half guessed what I've caught in the stables, you'd throw futurism to...
> DIANA: Don't mean...that I'm out of fashion again
> OSSY: Since 1 P.M....dispensing entirely with the middleman, we now have the genius served directly to the consumer
> DIANA: Let us consume... (167–68)

High culture is exposed as commercial culture, as art collectors feed consumers' appetites for the latest fare. When Loony is served up to Diana, her interactions with him humorously highlight the gendered logic that governs the avant-garde and limits women's participation to pre-scripted roles. Diana first assumes the role of "backlit muse" (Gilmore 288), attempting to dazzle Loony with gemstones and seduce him with feminine wiles and felicitous wordplay:

> I am the elusion [*sic*] that cooed to you adolescent isolation, crystallized in the experience of your manhood. [...] I know the moment to press the grape to thy lip...put ice on your head; for I am the woman who understands. (169)

Loy's neologism "elusion" fuses the words "elision" (deletion), "elude" (escape), "illusion" (fantasy), and "effusion" (gush) in a quintessential expression of feminine beauty, self-fashioning, and self-abnegation. But Loony proves impervious to Diana's feminine charms and refuses to take her with him to "the Grand," because, he claims, she would have no place in the "Fraternity," where she would be "slighted," "criticised," and "considered soft." Here, the avant-garde is exposed as a male field, closed off to women (171–72).[43]

Although men dominate and control the boundaries of the art world, Loy makes it clear that the "genius" is not an autonomous creator, but requires recognition from an audience to affirm his greatness. After Loony denies Diana direct access to the realm of genius, he escorts her to the window to see "The Grand," effectively conscripting her to join the audience for his artistic performance. From this vista, he declaims a Futuristic free-verse poem that exalts his own creative prowess and scorns his audience's narrow bourgeois sensibilities. In the midst of his declamation, he taunts: "what have you to find / Where can you pick things up?" (175). At this point, Loy inserts this stage direction: "Diana indicating an ash tray, he reverently pockets half a manilla" (175). The stage direction is significant because it points to Diana's keen-eyed perception. She is, it appears, a more adroit collector of cigar butts than he. Yet, though we see Diana's genius, Loony remains oblivious to any but his own.

Diana, prohibited by her gender from joining Loony on the Grand as an artistic genius, continues to try to win him over, resorting to a role that is readily available to her: "precocious trump" (178). When her striptease fails to arouse him from his drowsy slumber, she summons her male assistants, commanding them to take Loony to the bathroom and dress him in a new costume. When he returns from "The Immersion," he proves amenable to her will, and she instructs him on the proper decorum for a genius:

> Stand up—Sir—and dress your soul for dinner. Throw out your chest [...] Those tirades about the Grand are *the* thing...dock them up a bit...muddle people up more...But when you're not holding forth you must be like us... you (*hypnotically*) *are* like us... (180)[44]

At the end of the play, Diana succeeds in transforming the avant-garde artist into a commercial product and luring him into the business of selling himself to gullible consumers. The mysterious off-stage immersion shifts the power dynamic, stripping the male artist of agency (and clothing) and transforming him into a puppet controlled by a female profiteer. It is possible to read *The Pamperers* as a satire of male Futurist performance, in which a wily woman beats a male genius at his own game. Janet Lyon offers this interpretation, arguing that the play "suggests that some women are equipped to be better Futurists than men. [...] In Loy's play, the woman is the artist, while (male) 'geniuses' are merely the found objects (the cigar-butts, as it were) with which artists like Diana work" (397). But Diana has no more mastery of the system than Loony: she must operate within the female roles available to her. As Loy makes explicit in her "Feminist Manifesto," both men and women are victims of patriarchal gender roles. Rather than achieving access to "the Grand"—that seemingly limitless realm of artistic creation—Diana, too, remains trapped in a grand commercial scheme to sell the latest art to consumers who are dazzled by anything new.

Through the character of Diana, Loy implicates herself in her satire of the avant-garde. As Sarah Hayden argues:

> By parodying the means by which artists are mediated and manipulated by third parties, "The Pamperers" both reflects on the commodification of Loy's own artist persona and bears witness to a tendency [...] for the author to admit (and encode in her writings) complicity with the objects of her critique. (8)

Loy does not position herself above her audience or outside her critique. This recognition of complicity is a characteristic en dehors garde move: Loy is both outside and inside the logic she critiques, both a producer and audience for the dramatic performances she stages.

As in *Two Plays* and *The Sacred Prostitute*, Loy adopts an eclectic method, combining avant-garde and popular forms, addressing serious questions with comically absurd effects, and producing an original, disconcerting blend. The play could easily become boring and talky if its opportunities for humorous caricatures and physical comedy are not fully exploited to elicit laughter from the audience. Some of the play's greatest comic potential arises from the occasional, odd stage directions, such as "Diana's chameleon rattles her emeralds" or "Picked People evaporate"

(167, 177). Loy seem to anticipate elements of Surrealism, offering directions that could come straight out of a Dalí painting:

> *(Diana turns off the light, sits on the pekinese which sinking still deeper into cushions notices nothing; and meditates in a fussy silence on the dial of a luminous watch.)*
> *(Two intimate friends sidle into the conservatory)* (165)

The friends have a conversation that reads like a montage, interrupted when Somebody says:

> Diana dear, you might tell us where you *were*...while we were so patiently watching you?
> *(Diana's chameleon rattles her emeralds.)* (167)

It is as if Diana has fallen into a dreamlike state and is rattled awake by a chameleon who exists only in a dream.[45]

The most baffling stage direction comes just after Loony mentions his pub companions, "God Gives" and "the Devil to pay," who prove to be "one and the same" (170). At this point, Loy directs:

> *(The room fills rapidly with the Loony's curiosity, the "taken for granted" advances to audience gravenly noticeable.)* (170)

Loy's syntax is strange, but "'taken for granted' advances" seems to describe Loony's posture and gestures toward the audience. Presumably, he takes their attention for granted, and his advances to them are "gravenly noticeable" because he carves himself out as an object of their worship, resenting and accosting them when they do not comply. In calling for the room to be filled with Looney's curiosity, Loy seems to be anticipating surrealist film techniques that move from external reality to internal states of mind, reversing the process to connect Loony's internal state of mind to his outward "advance" toward the audience he depends on.

Loy blends such strange, surrealistic stage directions with familiar elements of burlesque, like the repeated striptease, first performed by Diana and later by Loony. In this way, *The Pamperers* both challenges the audience with intellectual provocations and indulges us with erotic spectacles. But even as she arouses and indulges sexual appetites, Loy defies the conventional gender script, which limits women to what Loy describes in her "Feminist Manifesto" as a choice between "Parasitism, & Prostitution—or Negation" (LLB96 154). Loy attempts to outwit these gender conventions in *The Pamperers*. Her heroine Diana tries out the roles of model, seductress, and prostitute, ultimately becoming a procuress or impresario who, though she cannot escape the sexualized economy of the art world, can at least profit from it. In this way, Loy's en dehors garde play choreographs a series of strategic moves, showing how a female artist can work from the margins in an effort to gain greater insight and purchase on central, defining norms.

The publication of *The Pamperers* in *The Dial*, in the company of Arthur Rimbaud, James Joyce, Ford Madox Ford, André Derain, and Babette Deutsch, elevated Loy as a representative, spokesperson, and interpreter of the international avant-garde for an audience of educated, open-minded readers. Selected by the editors to inaugurate a new "Modern Forms" section of the magazine, *The Pamperers* represents the quintessential avant-garde form. Although Hayden argues that Loy's "processual theorizing" of the avant-garde "barely registered in the instant of their production and partial publication" (*Curious Disciplines* 4–5), the positioning of *The Pamperers* in *The Dial*, like the publication of *Cittàbapini* in two separate installments of *Rogue*, suggests that little magazine editors and readers were not only cognizant of Loy's power as avant-garde interpreter, but also hungry for her sharp wit and perceptive insights.

In his foreword to "Modern Forms," art critic Henry McBride does not mention *The Pamperers*, but he discusses the very problem that the play addresses: how to assess the meaning and value of new, experimental art. McBride addresses the question of how to distinguish authentic new art from frauds and hoaxes. Situating Arensberg's "exclusively modern" studio as the hub of the New York avant-garde, McBride offers "Marcel's latest"—a hermetically sealed vial of air from Paris—as a case in point. McBride contrasts his enlightened understanding of Duchamp's readymade to the befuddled reactions of a "friend" with conventional, bourgeois tastes. Whereas the friend deems Duchamp's so-called "art" incomprehensible and highly suspicious, McBride finds it "pleasant and droll": "Perhaps I instantly saw that the joke did not apply to me so much as to my educated friend," he explains, "That's the advantage in not being a bourgeois yourself" (62). Unlike Loy, who exposes her complicity in the systems she satirizes, McBride exempts himself from critique by positioning himself outside the bourgeoisie in a superior class of avant-garde artists and audiences. Ironically, even as McBride emphasizes his and his readers' distinction from the bourgeois, however, he addresses them as would-be art collectors, offering advice about how to become more sophisticated consumers of art: "My own recommendation [...] is—to know a 'modern' artist" (63). He thus trains readers to become consumers in the capitalist economy of avant-garde art that *The Pamperers* proceeds to satirize.

Although McBride's attitude toward bourgeois audiences is more dismissive than Loy's, his "Foreword" may not actually be at cross-purposes with her play. After all, both attempt to generate interest in avant-garde art. *The Pamperers* does not aim to warn us out of a phony art market, but to get us in on the joke and to make us recognize that we are all in on the scam—artists, wealthy collectors, and bourgeois audiences alike ("you must be like us...you [*hypnotically*] are like us..."). In this way, Loy trusts that her audience—unlike the trend-chasing art consumers in *The Pamperers*—will be cunning enough to recognize the scam, even if they, like her, cannot extricate themselves from the market.

VIII. IN...CONCLUSION

The American public was not as "jolly" as she had hoped, as she explained to Mabel Dodge Luhan: "I have not been able to get along in the commercial field in New York because I cannot understand their distinctions between one nothingness and another" (qtd. in Burke, *Becoming* 304). Expressing her frustration with the disintegration of public value judgments, Loy refers to the commercial field in ways that evoke a Dada playground, which, as Francis Picabia described it:

> smells of nothing, nothing, nothing.
> It is like your hopes: nothing.
> Like your paradise: nothing. (qtd. in Hartley 250)

Dada's nihilistic celebration of "nothing" did not interest Loy and could not satisfy her material and physical needs. "More absorbed in efforts to earn a living [...] than in her friends' antics," Loy turned away from New York Dada (Burke, *Becoming* 301). She and Cravan left the United States for Mexico late in 1917 so that he could avoid the draft. They wed in Mexico and, when she became pregnant, decided to decamp to Buenos Aires, Argentina, where Cravan might have better luck evading the secret police. Their love affair ended tragically when he disappeared at sea en route to meet Loy there. She traveled alone to Valparaiso, Chile, and on to Buenos Aires in fall 1918. In March 1919, she sailed from Argentina to London, where she gave birth to Jemima Fabienne Cravan Lloyd. She took the infant to Europe to meet Cravan's family and see her other children, Giles and Joella. In March 1920, she sailed back to New York for a year before returning to Europe to pursue more lucrative outlets for her art (*Becoming* 301, 303). Despite her disenchantment with New York, Loy expressed nostalgic affection for her time there, summing up her experience in a 1920 letter to Mabel Dodge Luhan:

> There comes a time when one ceases to be able to Breathe in New York—when it turns its emptiness inside out on your head—& you go—but I was very happy there—it is the only spot I have ever had to say a thank you to. (Loy/MDL 16)

While Loy moved on, Francis Picabia and Tristan Tzara continued to champion Dada, "join[ing] forces to make Dada an international phenomenon," and working especially hard to promote it in New York newspapers (Naumann 198). Although they "succeeded in generating precisely the publicity they sought" (Naumann 198), by the time they nominated Loy to their roster of presidents on the cover of the 1920 *Bulletin Dada*, she was already moving on to other pursuits.

Although Loy's plays and experimental prose failed to generate the public interest Loy hoped for, these theatrical experiments, examined within the context of little magazines in which they appeared, provide a record of her evolving understanding of the artist's relationship to an audience. In *Collision* and *Cittàbapini*, the Futurist artist turns his back on his audience to achieve an artistic apotheosis: characters merge with kinetic settings to become part of a larger creative process, which is staged for the audience's amusement. But in *The Sacred Prostitute* and *The Pamperers*, there is no turning away from an audience and no way out of the performance. Loy attempts to write her way out of prefabricated scripts, but the plays ironically reveal that men and women, artists and audiences, are all caught up in the same game: though they may be dealt different hands, they play by the same gendered rules. Loy exposes both love and art as part of a heterosexual economy—a culture industry intent on perpetuating itself and preventing even the most forward-thinking geniuses from rewriting the script. In her contributions to *The Blind Man*, Loy turns from intimate sexual relationships to the relationship between the Artist and the Public, seeking more amorous, egalitarian intercourse, even as she recognizes the difficulty and risks of leveling hierarchies. She plays with Dada, but recognizes that it, too, may be a losing game. Nevertheless, for Loy—and for her audiences—there is pleasure in the play, and critical insights to be gained from it.

Shifting attention away from Loy's more celebrated poems and manifestos to her Futurist-inflected plays and proto-Dada prose allows us to reframe her engagement with avant-garde *movements* as en dehors garde *moves*, rather than allegiances to any groups or schools. Deeply tied to material and social contexts and interpersonal relationships, Loy's en dehors garde moves are akin to what Sophie Seita describes, using Loy's terminology, as "proto-forms": creative experiments enacted within specific collaborative communities and little-magazine contexts (*Provisional* 3).[46] Loy's early plays and experimental prose invite us to view her migration from Italian Futurism to New York Dada not as a linear progression, but as a series of en dehors garde turns that bring about revolution in the sense of turning ideas over and over again in a variety of forms and media, re-forming and rehabilitating them, without ever reaching a resolution. When she returned to New York in 1920, Loy continued to experiment with performative genres in an effort to excite the public interest in art, dashing off a note to Van Vechten describing her latest en dehors designs for a ballet:[47]

I am sending you Fantasy Street [...] —don't you think it would be wonderful as a ballet—in a review—or even in Opera—Do they have the Opera Ballet here? I know the public would adore it if it was properly done & I can design it in a way that would make em sorry they had to go on being alive after it was all over— (Loy/CVV 106–08)

CHAPTER FOUR

LOY AND THE MUSEUM WITHOUT WALLS

(Paris 1923–1936, New York 1936–1953)

Susan Rosenbaum

I. SETTING THE SURREAL SCENE

This chapter turns to Mina Loy's engagements with and critical transformations of Surrealist ideas and techniques, as she encountered the Surrealist movement in Paris (1923–1936) and the Surrealist scene in New York (1936–1953). As described in chapter 1, Mina Loy's transatlantic travels coincided with and shaped the history of Surrealism in significant ways. Loy's career alongside Paris Surrealism and its New York offshoots in the 1920s and early 1930s, followed by her return to New York and connections to European artists in exile and American experimental artists, embodied the larger trajectory of the Surrealist avant-garde during these decades. Loy's en dehors garde response to Surrealism is an important yet understudied part of this history, aided by her development of alternative exhibition spaces to display and preserve her work created on the Surrealist movement's margins.

Loy's understanding of Surrealism was shaped by her navigation of the streets and economies of Paris and New York. Encountering Surrealism as a writer, artist, and as a designer who struggled to make a living, Loy traveled the Paris flea markets and walked the streets of New York's Bowery with both aesthetics and economics in mind: she turned cast-off objects and discarded materials into lamps, lampshades, inventions, and collage constructions. In Paris, Loy would transform particular locales through the dislocating light of her artisanal lamps, and through the less tangible "light" of dream, the imagination, and the unconscious. When Loy moved from Paris to Lower Manhattan, the suffering of the homeless men and women living on the streets of the Bowery, amplified by her own poverty, shifted her lens to the material constrictions of the urban environment and to recasting the Surrealist "marvelous" in a documentary light (Kinnahan, *Mina Loy, Twentieth-Century Photography* 124). As Loy explored the relation between matter and spirit, the conscious mind and unconscious inspiration, the real and the "irreal" across her visual art, writing, and commercial designs, she drew inspiration from Surrealist poetics, in particular the Surrealists' broad, interdisciplinary understandings of "poetry," and their uses of techniques of juxtaposition and hybrid mixture in their artwork and innovative installations and exhibitions.

How to reach a public with her commercial designs, writing, and art remained a pressing concern for Mina Loy in both Paris and New York, a matter both of economic survival and of pursuing her experimental ideals. Loy shared with the Surrealists the broader avant-garde aim of merging art and everyday life:[1] as she had pointed out in her essay "In...Formation" in *The Blind Man* (1917), "The only trouble with the public is education," which she described as "the putting of spectacles on wholesome eyes" ("In...Formation"). Encouraging the public to remove these old spectacles, Loy proclaimed in her 1921 manifesto "International Psycho-Democracy" "'Live life at first hand.' / *Make the World your Salon*" (MLSII 44).[2] The Surrealists sought to integrate art into everyday life by defying the official museum's rational, educational mission (the "putting of spectacles on wholesome eyes"), creating installations, galleries, and collections that transformed the museum into a stage ("salon") for Surrealist-inspired ends, including the fusion of dream and reality, disorienting perspectives on the real, urban wandering, the pursuit of pleasure and desire, and the merging of art with ordinary objects and locales.[3] Loy's engagement with the Futurist and Dadaist movements through experimental drama and little magazine "performance" would extend under the influence of Surrealism to alternative sites and forms of exhibition and display, an aim she articulated in a 1924 essay on Gertrude Stein, whose experimental path guided her own navigation of Surrealism in Paris:

> The pragmatic value of modernism lies in its tremendous recognition of the compensation due to the spirit of democracy. Modernism is a prophet crying in the wilderness of stabilized nature that humanity is wasting its aesthetic time. For there is a considerable extension of time between the visits to the picture gallery, the museum, the library. It asks "what is happening to your aesthetic consciousness during the long intervals?"
>
> The Flux of life is pouring its aesthetic aspect into your eyes, your ears—and you ignore it because you are looking for your canons of beauty in some sort of frame or glass case of tradition. Modernism says: Why not each one of us, scholar or bricklayer, pleasurably realize all that is impressing itself upon our subconscious, the thousand odds and ends which make up your sensory every day life. (LLB82 297–298)

In her work created in dialogue with Stein and Surrealism, Loy would seek to capture the "flux of life" in the "long intervals" and in "every day" places outside of the "picture gallery, the museum, the library," an aim particularly important for women artists whose work was marginalized by the avant-garde, and rarely featured in museums and libraries.

As discussed in chapter 1, women participated in Surrealist exhibitions and publications, but they remained on the margins of Surrealism's official ranks. Loy is a case in point: she played an important role in Surrealism's development but is missing from most Surrealist histories and exhibitions, and until recently she was omitted from studies of women and Surrealism. Yet Loy's participation is crucial to the history of Surrealism and its en dehors garde transformations. Working as an artist, writer, designer, and Paris agent for Julien Levy's New York gallery, Loy maintained a complex, en dehors garde position as both insider and outsider to the Surrealist movement in Paris: she incorporated Surrealist aesthetics into her work, even as she articulated her own critical, feminist slant on the movement and resisted explicit affiliation with it.

Although Loy was inspired by many elements of Surrealism, she was no fan of André Breton,[4] Surrealism's founder and de facto leader, dubbed the "pope" for his careful policing of the movement, including his habit of publicly breaking with or expelling those who disagreed with his ideas.[5] Breton's sexism and homophobia were well known, and Loy would pointedly criticize Breton and the Surrealist treatment of women in her work of the 1920s and 1930s. Similarly, while Loy had met Freud in Vienna in 1922 and acknowledged his importance, her feminist views on sexuality put her at odds with Freudian thought, and from the 1920s onwards she would explicitly criticize Freud's understanding of the unconscious and eros, and the Surrealists' applications of these concepts.[6]

Yet Surrealism's democratic ideals, although inhibited by Breton's prejudices within the movement proper, inspired Loy and other women artists to adapt and transform Surrealist ideas and methods. Through feminist adaptations like Loy's, Surrealism became something new, what Rachel Blau DuPlessis has termed a "fair realism" after the Surrealist-inspired poet Barbara Guest (*Blue Studios* 9, 180, 183). Loy embedded feminist commentary into similar changes in nomenclature, coining her own terms for her adaptations of the unconscious, Surrealism, and the surreal: she refers to the "subconscious" ("Parturition," LLB96 7), "subconsciousness" ("Aphorisms on Futurism," LLB96 152), "subconscious archives" ("O Hell," LLB96 71), "subvisual resources / in the uncolor of the unknown" ("Ephemerid," LB82 117), the "irreal" (*Insel* 109), "galleries of the increate" (*Insel* 125), and "sub-realism" ("Phenomenon in American Art," LB82 300). Notably, Loy often swapped out "un-" (not) and "sur-" (over or above) for "sub-" (under or below), suggesting a below-the-surface excavation of visible places and creation of liminal spaces through her artistic gaze.

Loy's en dehors garde position navigating Surrealism in Paris—as participant and skeptic, artist and agent, collector and curator, spectator and spectacle—is exemplified by her painting *Surreal Scene* (circa 1935) (see Fig. 4.1). The composition depicts a nude female figure or mannequin, surrounded by tableaux which present female bodies in various states of objectification, entrapment, or transformation, signifying the gendered conventions, scenarios, and gazes that women in Surrealist circles

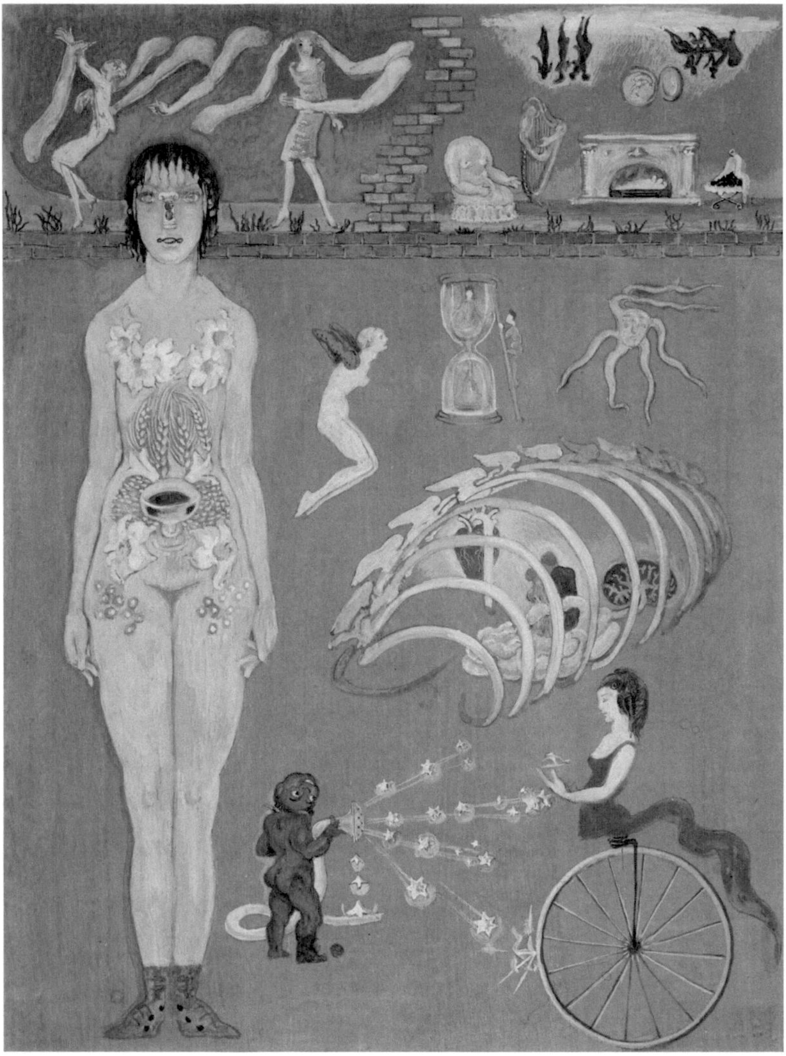

Figure 4.1. Mina Loy, Untitled (*Surreal Scene*), circa 1935. Private collection, photography by Jay York.

navigated. The style of the painting resembles Florine Stettheimer's *The Cathedrals of Broadway* (1929), but Stettheimer's various scenes unfold in a particular landscape. *Surreal Scene*'s spatial design—small scenes arranged against an abstract, peach background, creating spatial juxtapositions that invite the spectator to generate poetic connections between its constituent parts—indicates how Surrealism provided Loy with a poetic idiom for portraying the fluid relations between poetry, visual art, fashion, and commercial design. Critics now understand Loy's work as intermedial, an approach to artmaking that the Surrealists shared with the Futurist and Dadaist avant-gardes, but which the Surrealists explicitly tied to their broad, interdisciplinary understanding of poetry and the "poetic," with juxtaposition and hybrid mixtures of media their favored poetic techniques.

In *Surreal Scene*, Loy critically reappraises Surrealist art and ideals through her feminist curation and re-vision. Although relegated to the margins of Surrealism, women's *figurative* role was central to the movement: representations of women, erotic desire, and the female body provided the material for much male Surrealist work. Just as Loy critically mapped the scenes of Futurist Florence in her poetry, and satirized the bombast of Futurist and Dadaist rhetoric in her plays and prose experiments, *Surreal Scene* exhibits and provides ironic commentary on the aesthetic preoccupations of the Surrealist movement, as it extended into domestic, public, aesthetic, and psychological terrain. For instance, in the center of the painting Loy depicts a kneeling woman (or angel) with clipped or folded insect-like wings, adjacent to a woman trapped in an hourglass or bell jar with an attendant climbing a ladder. Both scenes suggest the place of women in Surrealism: Breton idealized women as muse, as romantic ideal, and as a childlike medium to irrational or unconscious states, and conversely as "sorceress, erotic object, and femme fatale" (Chadwick 12), figurations of women that Loy depicts as limiting and entrapping. In another scene, Loy depicts a large ribcage, possibly that of a whale, containing a heart, liver, and entrails. An embracing male and female couple are coiled in intestinal links. Here Loy subjects metaphors of love and romance (the "heart") to a withering critique, by literally depicting the heart's bodily origin. The placement of the couple implies that the seat of love is not the heart but the digestive tract, a juxtaposition that recalls the "pig cupid" of "Songs to Joannes." Loy supplies a satirical X-ray vision, going inside the body to find not unconscious dreams, wishes, and erotic desires, but anatomical ribs and organs, a pointed rejoinder to Freud and to the gendered romantic ideals of the Surrealists.

In this painting, Loy embeds feminist commentary in her treatment of female figures as the material, muse, and "scene" of male Surrealist art. Just as Loy objected to the idealized conflation of Florence with "woman" as discussed in chapter 2, in *Surreal Scene* she alludes to the Surrealists' conflation of Paris with an idealized woman (as in Breton's novel *Nadja*), but points out the pitfalls of such idealizations.[7] For example, in the upper left-hand corner of *Surreal Scene*, Loy depicts women walking in public as objects of sexual pursuit, a scene she divides with layered bricks from a depiction of a living room, to suggest the movement from domestic to public space and the gendered limits that structure each space. However, Loy turns the tables by objectifying the men who pursue these women, depicting them as nothing more than disembodied arms. Detached from the body, the arms become, in Surrealist fashion, strange creatures: by painting varied sexualized actions of the arms, Loy denaturalizes the grasping, encircling, touching motions to which women become habituated in the city streets, objectifying the male libido rather than the feminine object of male desire.[8]

In her depiction of the large female figure or mannequin on the left side of the painting, Loy positions Surrealist art, Classical myth, and fashion as related cultural forms that "dress" and alter—through sexual and gendered tropes—how we view the female body. Jennifer Gross suggests that Loy's painting of the large female figure may be a version of and commentary on the Surrealist "exquisite corpse" (*cadavre exquis*), the collaborative "game" that divided the human body into sections, each part supplied by a different artist, which resulted in a Frankensteinian figure, composed of the juxtaposition and hybrid mixture of unrelated images.[9] The female figure wears lace-up boots: the incongruity of the image lies in the fact that her feet are the only part of the body that are conventionally clothed. If we regard the female figure as a mannequin, Loy may invite viewers to think about fashion—and shoes in particular—as a language through which the female body is compartmentalized, objectified, and fetishized.[10] In place of the female figure's nose, Loy paints a superimposed shape that suggests a headless Greek statue or Dalí-esque telephone decorated with disembodied eyeballs, and in place of lips Loy paints a tied red ribbon, signifying the silencing of women in Surrealism. The figure's hair is coiled in rivulets on each side of her face that resemble streams of blood, a possible allusion to Jean Cocteau's 1930 film *Blood of a Poet* (and Loy's role as poet). While this iconography alludes to Surrealist representations, Loy's depiction of the woman's torso with flowers, wheat, and a chalice of wine, overlaying the location of breast, ovaries, and uterus, alludes to the Biblical and mythological conventions of depicting the female body through symbols of fertility. Through her use of this varied iconography, Loy implies that ostensibly "new" Surrealist figurations, just like Biblical and mythological representations, reinforce inherited gender roles and stereotypes.[11]

Even as she casts a keen critical eye on women's bodies as the material and scene of Surrealist art, Loy's painting stakes out her role as a dynamic participant in and chronicler of the "Surreal Scene." In its collection, display, and pointed juxtaposition of varied scenes and tropes of Surrealist art and artistic production, *Surreal Scene* serves as an independent artwork and as an unconventional exhibition, one that illuminates from the movement's shadows the gendered places and practices sustaining Surrealist art. Formally exhibited for the first time in 2023, this painting insists on its own status as an unconventional, en dehors garde exhibit. Acting on her own call to "pleasurably realize all that is impressing itself upon our subconscious" outside of the "frame or glass case of tradition," Loy's painting challenges the "canons of beauty" cemented by the "picture gallery, the museum, the library" (LLB82 297–98), as well as the gendered ideals enshrined in the avant-garde's experimental exhibits.

Surreal Scene exemplifies Loy's creation of alternative exhibition spaces as a crucial framework for her interventions in and commentaries on Surrealism, as well as a material means of displaying, preserving, and commenting on her artwork marginalized by the avant-garde. To illuminate the importance of these liminal exhibitionary spaces to Loy's navigation of Surrealism in Paris and New York, I discuss the importance of Surrealist poetics to Loy's intermedial work, focusing on her use of techniques of juxtaposition and hybrid mixture. Building on Loy's adaptation of Surrealist poetics, I tour the en dehors garde exhibits and poetic collections that Loy created in dialogue with Surrealism in Paris and New York, indicating entry into and analysis of a new space of exhibition or artifact on display through section breaks and titles. Through this tour of Loy's engagement with Surrealism, a transatlantic history of the en dehors garde unfolds.

II. SURREALIST POETICS

Mina Loy's creative output during the Paris years continued to develop the intermedial nature of her artistry evident from the outset of her career navigating Italian Futurism and New York Dada. If we consider Loy's published and unpublished poetry, essays, stories, and autobiographical fiction, alongside her lamps, objects, and paintings, the Paris years 1921–1936 are notable for her experimentation with and across verbal and visual media, in conversation with Surrealist poetics.[12] Loy responded to the possibilities and limitations of "The word" (LLB82 297–98) and of paint, clay, fabric, and found objects as an artist and designer capable of working adeptly with many kinds of media: like the Surrealists, she was interested in expanding an understanding of poetry and in experimenting with new mixtures and understandings of hybridity.

Surrealism originated as a poetic movement, and one of its enduring legacies was to expand the understanding of "poetry." As articulated by Breton in his writing of the 1920s and 1930s, Surrealism was devoted to expressing in conscious life the workings of the unconscious mind, taking inspiration from Freud's interest in "the omnipotence of dream" and other forms of thought unconstrained by reason (*Manifestoes* 26). Breton's interest in automatism—the uncensored expression of unconscious thoughts, wishes, desires—exemplified the Surrealist search for an imagination freed from "a state of slavery" (4) induced by the "absolute rationalism" and "reign of logic" in twentieth-century culture (9). Breton abandoned Freud's therapeutic quest for the conscious recognition of unconscious wishes, instead seeking "the future resolution of these two states, dream and reality, which are seemingly so contradictory, into a kind of absolute reality, a surreality, if one may so speak" (14). Breton called the activity of revealing the interpenetration of dream and reality "poetry," and thus the *poetic act* was as central to film, photography, and painting as it was to poems proper. With his roots in Dada, Breton did not limit poetic creation to a particular genre, but understood poetry *as a way of knowing*, its value located in its capacity to realize a surreality. Building on Lautréamont's statement that poetry should be made by all, Breton promoted a democratic understanding of poetry, stating that he wanted "to put [poetry] within reach of everyone" (37).[13]

The incongruity between the unconscious and conscious states of mind served as the central poetic principle of Surrealist art (regardless of media), and was conveyed through the juxtaposition of discordant elements, often meant to shock the reader or viewer into exploring new understandings of the relation between dream and reality. Dadaists had developed the technique of juxtaposition through collage and photomontage, with Max Ernst a key figure whose collages bridged Dada and Surrealism. Breton explained the principle of juxtaposition through Pierre Reverdy's definition of the image:

> The image is a pure creation of the mind. It cannot be born from a comparison but from a juxtaposition of two more or less distant realities. The more the relationship between the two juxtaposed realities is distant and true, the stronger the image will be—the greater its emotional power and poetic reality." (*Manifestoes* 20)

Reverdy and the Surrealists took inspiration from Lautréamont's celebrated comparison of beauty to "the chance meeting upon a dissecting table of a sewing-machine with an umbrella," which Max Ernst paraphrased as "the fortuitous encounter upon a non-suitable plane of two mutually distant realities" (8).

To generate these unlikely juxtapositions and to facilitate unconscious expression, many Surrealists employed methods such as automatic writing and painting, collaborative games including the exquisite corpse, and other chance operations. Ernst adapted collage to Surrealist ends, and devised new techniques, including frottage and fumage. Man Ray brought the unconscious to vivid life by altering the conventional realist modes of film and photography. Influenced by Surrealist photography, Salvador Dalí contrasted dreamlike content with precise detail in his paintings, as in *The Persistence of Memory* (1931), which hung in Loy's apartment before shipment to New York. The unlikely juxtapositions that centered the Surrealist image were furthered by mixtures of media and by collaborations between artists and writers, resulting in Ernst's and Paul Éluard's collaborative books, Man Ray's film-poem *L'Etoile de Mer*, Breton's poem-object, and Sonia Delaunay's dress-poem, among other hybrid works.[14]

Like the Surrealists, Loy experimented with techniques of juxtaposition to generate and explore new hybrid mixtures. As Cristanne Miller and Linda Kinnahan point out, however, Loy's use of radical juxtaposition and hybrid mixture in early poems such as "Songs to Joannes" (1915–17) anticipated the use of such techniques by the Surrealists, and reflected the influence of Cubism, Futurism, and Dada; similarly, Loy's experiments with juxtaposition in the 1920s and 30s unfolded in dialogue with the concept of the "Surrealist image" but were never solely indebted to it.[15]

Loy addressed the Surrealist image in a comment about Arthur Cravan that illuminates her own approach. She wrote,

> Talking of Cravan—nothing would have enraged him more than to be appropriated by the Surrealists—But there is no denying that they 'have raisons' somehow or other—La Bête Noir reprinted one thing of his the other day and I noticed at once how extraordinarily it anticipated Surrealism. Only the approach was entirely different. C. got the most bizarre antitheses through the mere expression of his direct reactions as a simple living entity—he had no theories—except the conviction of his superiority over the rest of mankind. I remember discussing Freud with him—thinking him (F) then a great man. Cravan said no—They have showed me.[16]

In Loy's estimation, Cravan's "bizarre antitheses" resulted from a creative sensibility responding to modern life, not from applying the grand "Theory" of the Surrealist image or the Freudian unconscious.

Like Cravan, Loy was guided by a conviction of her "superiority over the rest of mankind" as demonstrated by her poem "Apology of Genius" (LLB96 77–78); her preference for theorizing as a flexible response to particular circumstances rather than applying a prescribed theory; and her criticisms of the Surrealist movement: she, too, "anticipated Surrealism" in her use of "bizarre antitheses," but her "approach was entirely different." Loy did not dispute the powerful role of the unconscious, but felt that Freud limited the unconscious with his theories; Loy was more interested in the unconscious as the realm of artistic creation than as the repository of repressed wishes and desires.[17] As she commented in "Modern Poetry" (1925), "I believe that the quality of genius must be largely unconscious"

(LLB96 160). She emphasized this point in her essay "Conversion," subtitled "Critique / of D. H. Lawrence / Psycho-Analysis / & the inconscious [*sic*]" (SE 375), written in the 1920s in response to Lawrence's *Women in Love* (1920).[18] Distinguishing her aims from those of the Catholic Church and Freud, Loy writes, "The aim of the artist is to miss the Absolute — the only possible creative gesture — whereas the mystic impulse is to embrace a 'ready-made' in the way of absolutes / And the Absolute of this new mechanised mysticism of the Psycho-Analyst is the Unconscious" (SE 228). Linking the Catholic God to the Freudian unconscious as "ready-made" absolutes, Loy implies that such concepts and the belief systems they engender are received mechanically. In "Aphorisms on Futurism" (1914) Loy referred to the "mechanical re-actions of the subconsciousness, that rubbish heap of race-tradition—" (LLB96 152), suggesting that the critical, conscious mind must mediate this unconscious "rubbish heap." Whereas artists like Duchamp and Loy transform the readymade object or idea, Loy implies that Catholic and psychoanalytic converts accept an already defined "absolute," shutting down spiritual and intellectual inquiry. Loy accuses Lawrence as a convert to Freud of "dangerously damn[ing] his own creative flux with a theory" (SE 228), an accusation she had also lodged at the Surrealists in her discussion of Cravan's proto-"Surrealist" imagery.

In contrast, Loy would seek to unleash those forces elemental to creative flux (including the unconscious) through "bizarre antitheses," and she would look to Gertrude Stein as an important influence in this regard. Although Loy and Stein had been friends since meeting in 1911 in Florence, Loy mounted a careful study and public defense of Stein's writing while living in Paris, publishing essays in 1924 and 1927 which simultaneously illuminated her own poetics.[19] As Marisa Januzzi convincingly argues, during the mid-1920s Loy's aesthetic "resulted from her resistance to the canonization of Dada and the dawning of Surrealism with a theoretical return to Stein" ("Dada through" 602).[20] For Loy, Stein's democratic mode of experiment was paramount: "The pragmatic value of modernism lies in its tremendous recognition of the compensation due to the spirit of democracy. [...] Gertrude Stein has given us the Word, in and for itself" (LLB82 297–98). Loy was dismayed that Stein's democratic experiment had not struck a deeper chord, arguing in 1927 that

> She has prodigiously dismantled the raw materials of style, and radically swept clean the literary arena, making new performances possible. Which has given rare courage to countless young people.
>
> In America, many an author has gained renown by following one of the paths opened up by Stein's experiments. But Gertrude herself has been systematically undervalued in her own country, where for years now people have been crying out for a few properly American pioneers.
>
> Well, here she is, the all-American pioneer! (SE 233)[21]

Alongside Stein, Loy would experiment with techniques also used by the Surrealists, but adapt them to her own ends.[22] In a concise poem published as an epigraph to her 1924 *transatlantic review* essay, Loy pronounced Stein the "Curie / of the laboratory / of vocabulary," using analogies to scientific experiment to convey Stein's linguistic invention:

> she crushed
> the tonnage
> of consciousness
> congealed to phrases
> to extract
> a radium of the word. (LLB96 94; 203)

Gertrude Stein's use of juxtaposition initiated a new apprehension of the materiality of words and tenderized (rendered pliable) their reference to everyday objects and experiences, an aim that Loy and many subsequent critics would connect to Cubism. As Loy noted, "It has become the custom to say of her that she has done with words what Picasso has done with form. There is certainly in her words an interpenetration of dimensions analogous to Cubism" (LLB82 291). In loosening the relation between words and things, Stein created abstract verbal pieces that, like Cubist portraits and still lifes, enabled multiple perspectives on an object, inviting the subjective, possibly unconscious associations and interpretive connections of the reader.

While Loy acknowledged the importance of Cubism to Stein's use of verbal juxtaposition, in her discussion of "A Sweet Tail (Gypsies)" from Stein's *Geography and Plays*, Loy reveals how Stein's Cubism also shaped Stein's engagement with Surrealism. Loy closely examines Stein's phrase: "And really all the chance is in deriding cocoanuts real cocoanuts with strawberry tunes and little ice cakes with feeding feathers and peculiar relations of nothing which is more blessed than replies" (LLB82 293). Loy comments:

> In "feeding feathers" the omission of the woman between her feeding and her feathers results in an unaccustomed juxtaposition of words by associating a subject with a verb which does not in fact belong to it, but which visually, is instantaneously connected. This process of disintegration and reintegration, this intercepted cinema of suggestion urges the reactions of the reader until the theme assumes an unparallelled [*sic*] clarity of aspect. (LLB82 293)

Loy points out that through unconventional verbal juxtaposition in the phrase "feeding feathers" Stein disrupts conventional referential meaning, but creates a suggestive "cinematic" visual image that invites "her associations and your own" (LLB82 298). Loy argues, "Like all modern art, this art of Gertrude Stein makes a demand for a creative audience, by providing a stimulus, which [...] leaves us unlimited latitude for personal response" (LLB82 297). More pointedly, Stein's juxtapositions invite a personal response that includes the input of the subconscious mind: "when Gertrude Stein leaves Grammatical lacunae among her depictions [...] the mind trips up and falls through into the subconscious source of associated ideas" (LLB82 298).

This imagery of tripping and falling into the subconscious alludes to Lewis Carroll's tale *Alice's Adventures in Wonderland* (1865), a connection Loy develops: Stein uses verbal juxtaposition to conflate subject and object, achieving challenges to human perspective and a "refutation of logic" that is "parallel to Alice in the Looking Glass," a text that Loy would explicitly connect to Surrealism's "'Alicism' world of topsy-turvy logic" in her 1950 essay on Joseph Cornell (LLB82 301). Loy demonstrates this hybrid perspective of both subject and object in a prose passage featuring a lizard on a human hand: "To interpret her description of the lizard you have to place yourself in the position of both Gertrude Stein and the lizard at once (LB82 295)."[23] Loy adds:

> She has taken on the consciousness or rather the unconsciousness of the lizard in the inexplicable predicament of its transportation. [...] She is turning the lizard outside in, its specular aspect fuses with its motor impulses and now she represents the palm of the hand to you as a land surveyor might a prospect. (LLB82 295)

Through this shift between the human and lizard perspective, Stein unsettles the relation between "subject" and "object," an aim evident in Loy's earlier poetry and plays, and in the work of many Cubist as well as Surrealist artists. Loy signals the connection to Surrealism when she comments, "Compare this lizard episode with an example of a dream animated by the projection of the intellect into the intimacy of the inanimate" (LLB82 296), which is an apt description of a technique favored by the Surrealists in their films, paintings, and objects, and which was also deployed by Loy in her poem "The Ceiling" (1930). Stein's destabilization of the distinction between subject and object unsettles perspective, but also challenges a Freudian lens: "The greatest incertitude while reading Gertrude Stein is the indecision as to whether you are psychoanalyzing her, or she, you" (LLB82 296).

The poem "The Ceiling", unpublished during Loy's lifetime, reflects the influence of both Stein and Surrealism in its themes, techniques, and imagery. While the poems of Loy's first collection *Lunar Baedecker* [*sic*] (1923) mapped the constellation of feminist, Futurist, and modernist artists and ideas important to Loy in the 1910s and early 1920s, the poems that Loy wrote from the mid-1920s through 1936 in Paris have not received attention as a coherent body of work, largely due to the fact that Loy did not publish them as a distinct collection. Rather, Loy published some poems from this time in magazines and anthologies,[24] while others remained unpublished until Roger Conover's posthumous collections *The Last Lunar Baedeker* (1982) and *The Lost Lunar Baedeker* (1996).[25] If we widen our en dehors garde lens to include not only poetry publications but also Loy's lamps, her paintings and objects, her unpublished poems and autobiographical fiction, her essays and stories, the Paris era assumes a far different character—one of experiment, exploration, and self-definition across a number of genres and media, in dialogue with Surrealist poetics.

"The Ceiling" exemplifies this intermedial understanding of poetics. A fragment of a typed draft states: "MINA LOY / 9 Rue St Romain Paris 6 / August 26 1930," indicating that Loy wrote the poem in her Paris apartment in the year she sold her lamp shop, and turned her attention to her writing and painting.[26]

THE CEILING

Afloat in oval of unclosing eye

white-washed shadow-drifts
of indoor dawn
film idle clouds — —

a Cinema-Nirvana
shifts
palid [*sic*] ideograms
the epitaphs of dreams

upon a white slab slanted.

Visual echoes
in blanched rows

— — — the dissolved, derouted
traffic of slumber.

An arid air-flower
adrowse in the etiolate pasture
of our
arousing.

As droning day
dilates
in early light
[a] the spectral acre

[As] Under
the sunless artifice
of this four cornered sky

lingering flies
convolve their slim-winged circles.

Here in "The Ceiling" Loy juxtaposes sleep and waking, dream and reality, night and day, subject and object to explore the liminal state between dreaming and waking that for Breton and the Surrealists epitomized the surreal. Dawn signifies that liminal state when the light of day encroaches and the conscious mind begins to awaken but the remnants of dream and night remain. The speaker appears to be lying on her back in bed, slowly becoming conscious of the ceiling above as she awakens, but through juxtaposition and imagery Loy transforms this everyday domestic scene into the site of the surreal.

Loy describes this liminal state as a kind of "Cinema-Nirvana" with perception tuned both internally and externally. Thus, from the start of the poem Loy conflates eye and ceiling, perceiving subject and external object: the opening line "Afloat in oval of unclosing eye" may refer either to the ceiling that floats above an eye staring up at it from a horizontal position in bed, or to the "epitaphs of dreams," internal images that float in or remain visible to the mind's inner eye. Similarly, the opening imagery—"white-washed shadow-drifts / of indoor dawn / film idle clouds"—may describe either the actual play of dawn's light on the ceiling, or the remnants of internal dream imagery, Loy evoking in this way the conflation of external and internal perception. The word "Nirvana" in a Buddhist context alludes to a state of transcendence of self, desire, and suffering, a spiritual state that Loy suggests is made possible by this moment between sleep and waking, perceiving self and external reality.

The ceiling's "white slab slanted" serves as a blank screen for the surreal "film" created through the mixture of real shadows and the remnants of the dream, a visual projection that Loy progressively describes as "palid ideograms," "epitaphs of dreams," "visual echoes / in blanched rows" and as "the dissolved, derouted / traffic of slumber." This last phrase suggests that as the dreams of slumber shift into the liminal state between sleeping and waking, the visual sharpness of the dream dissolves. Already the sleeper begins to see "visual echoes / in blanched rows," the elusive, colorful dream giving way to the "blanched rows" of the waking mind, which asserts rational order and in exchange loses the color and vividness of the dream.[27] Loy's language of "epitaph" and "slab" connotes the death of the dream, inaccessible to the waking subject, while "visual echoes" and "ideogram," a term made famous by Ezra Pound, suggest that recollected dreams take a form that is both visual and verbal, the act of trying to capture or remember the dream akin to inscribing language upon an ephemeral film.

In the following stanza, Loy juxtaposes night and daylight, natural growth and aridity, to convey the increasing distance of the dream from the waking sleeper: "An arid air-flower / adrowse in the etiolate pasture / of our / arousing." "Etiolate" refers to the action of bleaching a green plant by isolating it from sunlight, affecting its growth. Loy inverts this logic, likening the dream to a dry or barren flower adversely affected by the appearance of light and consciousness, since night is what sustains the life of the flower-dream. The appearance of "droning day" "dilates / in early light / the spectral acre": these lines create an image of the light spreading to and illuminating the rectangular edges of the ceiling, but the word "dilates" also connotes an opening eye or camera aperture, so may also refer to the subject's "oval" eye or to the creation of a film capturing dawn's arrival.

As the subject moves from a state that balances internal dream and external perception towards full consciousness, she begins to perceive the ceiling not as a screen on which float figments of dream mixed with real shadow, but as a "spectral acre," a quantifiable space haunted by the dream, and as day arrives, this space becomes a "four cornered sky" under "sunless artifice." The rectangular shape of the ceiling asserts itself with the complete opening of the eye, implying a return of full consciousness and the assertion of reason. The clouds and pastures that had appeared to the eye in its liminal state between dream and waking at the start of the poem have transformed into "sunless artifice," perhaps connoting an electric light, and the conscious recognition of the unreality of these dream images. All that remains of the dream are "lingering flies" that "convolve their slim-winged circles."

If we consider the ceiling not only as a film screen but also as a figure for the blank page on which the poet writes the poem, "Ceiling at Dawn" reflects on the fertile creativity of the state between dream and waking, word and image: the poem only ends when day begins and the rational, conscious mind takes over. Loy does not employ tropes of writing but instead uses figures that conjoin word and image: rows of visual echoes (suggesting lines on the page), ideograms (which are both verbal and visual signs), and circles (evoking letters) drawn by lingering flies. In this way Loy self-reflexively engages the visual-verbal mixtures at the center of Surrealist poetics, and locates such mixtures as the product of the poet's attempt to verbally capture the elusive visual dream, to mediate the visions of the unconscious mind. In an undated manuscript titled "Dream Analysis," Loy similarly recounts a dream through allusions to shapes, lines, and letters, dwelling on transformations of images into writing.[28] Although Loy would depart from and criticize Freud and Surrealism in significant ways, notably rejecting pure "automatism" for the mediating role of the conscious mind, "Ceiling at Dawn" indicates that she shared Stein's and the Surrealists' belief in the primacy of the unconscious mind in poetic creation (Rosenbaum, "Exquisite Corpse" 282–84).

Similarly, in her focus on the eye as a projector for internal and external vision and her conflation of the perceiving subject's oval eye and the oval of the ceiling, Loy adapts a favored technique from Surrealist film: the close-up of the eye or manipulations of the eye as a means of signaling the inadequacies of realist vision and the shift to the vision of film and dream. Some famous instances of this practice include the scene in Buñuel and Dalí's *Un Chien Andalou* (1929) when a razor cuts into a woman's eyeball, and the final scene in Man Ray's *Emak Bakia* (1926) when we see a woman's open eyes, only to realize as she opens her eyes that we had been gazing at false eyes painted on her eyelids. Loy's portrayal of two eyeballs on the structure replacing the female figure's nose in *Surreal Scene* (see Fig. 4.1) also signals this disruption of realist vision. "The Ceiling"'s transformation of an everyday domestic setting through allusions to Surrealist film, destabilization of the distinction between subject and object, and juxtaposition of imagery of natural and artificial light, echoes the effects of Loy's lampshades, and anticipates several scenes in her autobiographical novel *Insel*, also set in her Paris apartment.

As “The Ceiling” demonstrates, Loy often juxtaposed opposed entities (dream and waking, night and day) to generate new liminal spaces that merged material realities (a bedroom, the working day) with the immaterial nature of dream and imagination, resulting in a poetics in dialogue with Surrealism. In her Paris-era work, Loy’s use of juxtaposition invites a dialectical action of mind resistant to accepted oppositions, a practice that resonates with Breton’s well-known comment in his “Second Manifesto of Surrealism” (1930):

> Everything tends to make us believe that there exists a certain point of the mind at which life and death, the real and the imagined, past and future, the communicable and the incommunicable, high and low, cease to be perceived as contradictions. Now search as one may one will never find any other motivating force in the activities of the Surrealists than the hope of finding and fixing this point. (*André Breton: Selections* 152–53)

Although Loy’s juxtapositions in “The Ceiling” invite comparison to the Surrealist image in bringing together “Two more or less distant realities,” Loy often embedded feminist critique and ironic commentary into her uses of juxtaposition and generation of liminal spaces.

In Paris, Loy used a feminist-inflected practice of juxtaposition to comment on the gendered and racial histories and assumptions that influenced the Surrealist scene. In this practice of juxtaposition Loy, drew inspiration not only from Stein but from the democratic juxtapositions of American jazz, which emerged from African American history and experience, and the contact between African, European, and American musical forms. Thus, from its start in New Orleans, jazz embodied and gave voice to cultural mixture and to the promises and limitations of democracy, in particular the African American struggle for freedom and civil rights. In works of the 1920s and early 1930s—including the painting *Surreal Scene* (circa 1935), the essay “Modern Poetry” (*Charm*, April 1925), and the poems “Crab-Angel” (LB 1923), “Lady Laura” (circa 1927; *Pagany*, Summer 1931), and “The Widow’s Jazz” (circa 1927; *Pagany*, Spring 1931)—Loy positioned American jazz as the key cultural form that embodied new mixtures emerging from juxtaposed entities, providing a revisionary history of Surrealism’s roots.

Loy's essay "Modern Poetry" (1925) clearly articulates the influence of American jazz on her own practice of juxtaposition at this time.[29] Connecting the new rhythms of free verse to the rhythmic freedoms of jazz, Loy finds a shared commitment to new forms of "movement" (like jazz dance) that enact individual responses to "contemporary life" (LLB96 157): "on the baser avenues of Manhattan every voice *swings* to the triple rhythm of its race, its citizenship and its personality" (LLB96 159; emphasis added). Loy describes this American vernacular—what she calls in "The Widow's Jazz" (LLB96 96) an "unerring esperanto" (alluding to the international language developed in the late nineteenth century that sought to bridge diverse language users)—as forged by juxtapositions, "English enriched and variegated with the grammatical structure and voice-inflection of many races, in novel alloy with the fundamental time-is-money idiom of the United States" (LLB96 158). The modern forms that put this "esperanto" in motion—poetry and jazz—give voice not to a theory of the Surrealist image, but to the "living" juxtapositions of the "melting-pot":

> You may think it impossible to conjure up the relationship of expression between the high browest modern poets and an adolescent Slav who has speculated in a wholesale job-lot of mandarines and is trying to sell them in a retail market on First Avenue. But it lies simply in this: both have had to become adapted to a country where the mind has to put on its verbal clothes at terrific speed. (LLB96 159)[30]

In her works of the 1920s and 30s that engage jazz, Loy connects jazz to visual and verbal amalgams that move beyond the Surrealist image in coupling not just distant but opposed entities: "abbess-prostitute" (LLB96 98), "Jazz-Mass" (LLB96 98), "Crab-Angel" (LLB96 85), "brute-angels" (LLB96 96). These verbal juxtapositions emphasize connection and division, by joining opposed words with a dash: Loy places words that connote the physical body, sexuality, and bohemian culture adjacent to words that connote the soul, organized religion, and the angelic or divine, creating a friction that invites awkward movement between poles. In this way the effort to overcome the opposition and the impediment to doing so both remain visible, a strategy Loy explored in her earlier play *The Sacred Prostitute* (see chapter 3) and which she would later explore in Bowery poems such as "Hot Cross Bum" (LLB96 133–44). The hybrid mixtures that Loy generated through such juxtaposition are often "grotesque" in the art-historical meaning of the term, referring to combinations of the human and the bestial, although Loy, like the avant-garde, often extended the grotesque to encompass combinations of the human and the mechanical, or the human and everyday objects. In Loy's painting *Surreal Scene* (Fig. 4.1), for instance, the kneeling woman with folded insect wings and the figure that is half-woman and half-bicycle wheel, exemplify grotesque hybrids. In her poems, Loy describes the distinct, often awkward movements of these "grotesque" hybrid performers unfolding to jazz music: as the circus performer Crab-Angel falls, "The jeering jangling / jazz / crashes to silence" (LLB96 87), while Lady Laura, likened to a mixture of human and swan, "proceeds recedingly" through the Montparnasse bar Zelli's, an "abbess-prostitute" who "presides / Jazz-Mass" (LLB96 98).

In the painting *Surreal Scene* (circa 1935) and the poem "The Widow's Jazz" (1927), which Loy performed at Natalie Barney's Paris salon, Loy's use of juxtaposition emphasizes the role of race in the Parisian avant-garde, jazz functioning as a key site of Loy's engagement with racial difference.[31] In Paris, the Surrealists embraced American jazz as an art form that they felt embodied the forces—the unconscious, primal sexuality, and spontaneous, "natural" expression—necessary to challenge the "reign of logic" in European culture.[32] Although the Surrealist movement opposed European imperialism and colonialism as part of its revolutionary poetics,[33] the Surrealist reception of jazz was shaped by negrophilia and a history of European primitivism based on stereotypes of non-white races as exotic and primitive others.[34] As Petrine Archer-Straw argues, in the 1920s negrophilia "reinforced negative stereotypes of blacks, especially in respect to primitivism," a representational practice "created to be oppositional to or to complement the Western rational 'I'" in its emphasis on sexuality, savagery, and deviance (10–11).[35] Nancy Cunard's 1934 anthology *Negro*, which published a number of essays by the European Surrealists, explored connections between jazz and Surrealism in ways that celebrated jazz and affirmed the rights of a global Black citizenry, while simultaneously employing racial stereotypes of the primitive other.[36] Loy's depictions of jazz similarly affirm the artistry of African American musicians, but were at once shaped by and critical of the avant-garde's primitivism.

Loy's juxtapositions in *Surreal Scene* and "The Widow's Jazz" emphasize entrenched racial divisions. The dark-skinned girl holding a horn-like instrument is the only non-white figure in *Surreal Scene*, while "The Widow's Jazz" begins with a body/soul division marked by race: "The white flesh quakes to the negro soul" (LLB96 95). Signaling the long history of Black entertainers subjected to the racialized and often racist assumptions of a white audience, Loy's use of juxtaposition offers a critical window onto this dynamic, while simultaneously extending it through use of primitivist stereotypes. In "The Widow's Jazz," Loy acknowledges the white audience's appetite for primitivism and the Black musicians' intentional playing to that appetite, as she describes "the lethargic ecstasy of steps / backing into primeval goal" and "impish musics" who "crumble the ecstatic loaf / before a swooning flock of doves" (LLB96 95–96). Here Loy represents primitivism as a sophisticated performance designed to meet a white audience's stereotype of jazz as "primeval." Loy draws on and challenges primitivist motifs in her description of the jazz musicians as "black brute-angels / in their human gloves / [who] bellow through a monstrous growth of metal trunks" (LLB96 96). In these lines, Loy likens metal instruments—saxophones or trumpets—to facial growths or bodily appendages akin to elephant trunks, with the adjective "monstrous" depicting the musicians and their instruments as a "grotesque" synthesis of human and animal, the organic and the mechanical. However, the juxtaposition "black brute-angels" challenges an understanding of jazz as "primitive" by suggesting that jazz bridges the brute and the angel, the bodily and divine. The musicians' "human gloves" embody this mix, connoting the divine hand and origins of art, but also the boxing glove and physical struggle for survival.

Even as Loy's juxtaposition challenges primitivist stereotypes, she echoes stereotypes of the primitive other as a "monstrous," less than human "black brute." Similarly, Loy's use of Black vernacular depends on racial stereotypes ("White man quit his actin' wise / colored folk hab de moon in dere eyes" (LLB96 95), extending minstrelsy's racist history of blackface performance. While Loy's goal in using jazz-inspired juxtapositions was to illuminate and overcome oppositions between Black performers and white audiences, to generate "a synthesis / of racial caress" (LLB96 96), her echoing of racist stereotypes also worked to confirm rather than bridge that divide. As Archer-Straw argues:

> In the case of 1920s Paris we are faced with a doubling act: whites act out what they think is black, based on stereotypes. The difference between the negro's and the negrophile's acting is that one is about material survival, while the other is about the survival of art, poetry, and fantasy. (105)

Loy employs juxtapositions that echo the imagery of "The Widow's Jazz" in the painting *Surreal Scene*, likely composed after the poem, illuminating the importance of jazz both to Surrealism and to Loy's critical curation of it (Fig. 4.1). Loy depicts a small, dark-skinned girl naked except for one red boot, with an upside-down head, holding a snaking trunk-like horn that emits white stars and doves, adjacent to a figure composed of a bicycle wheel attached to a white woman's head and torso. The girl's musical horn combines animal and mechanical qualities: the horn's head resembles a showerhead with holes for water, while its tail suggests an elephant trunk or a snake tail, a mixture echoed by the bicycle woman's green dress which ends in a similar snakelike tail. This depiction of the girl's snaking trunk-like instrument closely echoes Loy's description of jazz instruments as a "monstrous growth of metal trunks" and as a "tangle of pale snakes" in "The Widow's Jazz" (LLB96 96, 95), and may allude to Joseph Cornell's cover for Julien Levy's *Surrealism* anthology, which depicts a boy blowing the letters spelling "Surrealism" out of a horn-like instrument (see Fig. 4.10). The girl's upside-down head aligns her with the upside-down figures that appear to hang from the ceiling in the upper right-hand corner of the painting, an inversion of perspective that concretely depicts the Surrealists' radical overturning of rational perspective and effort to represent the surreal, a perspectival shift that Loy labeled "topsy-turvy" (LLB82 301).

The girl holding a horn can be interpreted as a figure signifying the influence of American jazz on the Surrealist scene, but more specifically, Loy's topsy-turvy figure may allude to Josephine Baker, whose jazz-inspired dance performances captivated Parisian audiences including the Surrealist avant-garde.[37] While Loy invests the "topsy-turvy" girl in *Surreal Scene* with an impish agency that sparks the implied action of the painting, her depiction of the girl—with pigtails and no clothes except one shoe—echoes racist images of the "pickaninny," a figure made famous by the character of Topsy in Harriet Beecher Stowe's *Uncle Tom's Cabin* (1852).[38] Baker began her career as "Topsy Anna" in *The Chocolate Dandies* (1924), a role "straight out of the racist minstrel tradition: she was a ragamuffin in blackface wearing bright cotton smocks and clown shoes" (Dalton and Gates 911). In Loy's painting, the hose-like horn the girl holds appears to emit musical stars, while white doves below the horn latch on to cloud-like puffs; this echo of the imagery of "The Widow's Jazz" positions Baker as one of the "impish musics" who perform primitivism, who knowingly "crumble the ecstatic loaf / before a swooning flock of doves." More pointedly, in Paris Baker mobilized and critiqued minstrel and primitivist stereotypes in *La Revue nègre* (1925) through slyly humorous hybrid mixtures that may have influenced Loy's practice of hybrid juxtaposition in the late 1920s and 30s. For instance, in the opening of *La Revue nègre*, a "Mississippi River Boat Scene," Baker was dressed as a "picaninny," but by performing exaggerated bodily expressions, movements, and sounds "appeared to be part animal [...] and part human," confounding the audience (Dalton and Gates 911). Baker's "danse sauvage" which ended *La Revue nègre*, began with a male dancer carrying Baker upside down onto the stage, and then turning her right side up, in a literal topsy-turvy inversion of perspective.[39] Hybrid mixtures and inversions of perspective were two important tools in Baker's performative arsenal, contributing to her satirical remaking of racist stereotypes and roles from the traditions of American minstrelsy and European primitivism.[40]

Loy's representation of the topsy-turvy girl challenges even as it reinforces racial stereotypes. Loy's depiction not only emphasizes the girl's self-conscious performance for a white audience, but suggests that her performance—including directing the musical horn of jazz from between her legs like an artificial phallus, perhaps an allusion to Josephine Baker's banana skirt in *Danse des bananes*[41]—propels the perspectival experiments of the entire *Surreal Scene*.[42] For instance, the spatial juxtaposition of the girl and other figures invites connection, distinction, and figurative "sparks": the "musical" stars from her horn land on and propel the adjacent bicycle wheel, and the bicycle-woman has caught one star which she holds in her hands. In this way, Loy offers a feminist, en dehors garde revision of Surrealism's origin story, framing the juxtapositions of perspective attributed to the Surrealists as emerging from American jazz. Loy underscores this revisionist lens through her depiction of the chubby, childlike figure as a Black, female version of the impish male putto or cherub from Renaissance and Baroque painting, a figure that typically mediates the human and the divine. In Loy's *Surreal Scene*, American jazz assumes this quasi-divine role.

Loy's perspective on the figure, depicting her from the back rather than front, challenges her sexual objectification: just as with the white naked mannequin on the painting's left, also wearing only boots, Loy avoids representing the figure's breasts or genitals.[43] However, Loy depicts the girl with breast-like buttocks, which may serve as an echo of the putto; another topsy-turvy bodily inversion (exhibiting the figure's breasts on or as her rear); or an allusion through Baker, called the "Black Venus" (*la Vénus noire*), to Sarah Baartman, who was exhibited as the "Hottentot Venus" in early nineteenth-century Europe. In this way Loy's depiction exemplifies how even the most modern Parisian stage was shaped by sexual and racial objectification endemic to the longer history of European colonialism and ethnographic display.[44]

On one hand, Loy's representation of female bodies in *Surreal Scene* explicitly draws attention to their treatment by the masculine avant-garde. In this context, Loy's depiction of the topsy-turvy girl uses the theatrical stage of primitivist performance to both cite and subvert a white audience's sexual and racial stereotypes. However, even as Loy draws out the potential of juxtaposition and inversions of perspective to challenge stereotypes, her recognizable use of the pickaninny stereotype with its racist history, reinforces racial and sexual hierarchies. Although both Baker and Loy were artists who used grotesque hybrids and satirical subversion to challenge the racial and sexual assumptions of the Parisian avant-garde, Loy's use of racial stereotypes as a white artist-observer not subject to anti-Black racism signified differently than Baker's performances, which stemmed from Baker's position as both a critic of racial primitivism and minstrelsy, and an artist who was subject to its demeaning stereotypes.[45] In an urban cultural scene defined by a diverse mix of genders, races, classes, and nations, yet still subject to persistent hierarchies of power and access, Loy's liminal spaces and hybrid creations were shaped by her particular navigation of these material contexts, even as she sought to imagine new forms and understandings.

III. "I'M NOT THE MUSEUM": EN DEHORS GARDE SPACES OF EXHIBITION (1923–1936)

Exhibit 1
"Lunar Baedeker" and Duchamp's *Large Glass*

The statement "I'm not the museum" appears in Loy's loosely autobiographical narrative *Insel* in which Loy reflects on her role as Julien Levy's Paris gallery agent as well as her own aspirations as a writer, designer, and painter engaging Surrealism. After angering the artist Insel by offering pointed, feminist commentary on his painting *Die Irma* intended for the Levy Gallery, Loy's avatar Mrs. Jones quips, "What does my opinion matter? *I'm* not the museum" (133), distinguishing her perspective and power from that of the gallery-museum network she served.

"I'm not the museum" reflected a broader en dehors garde transformation of publication, display, and exhibition. Mina Loy and other women artists used their position on the margins of both the museum and the avant-garde as an impetus to reimagine both, and in doing so, to comment variously on institutions of memory, the practices of Surrealist display, and gendered modes of looking. As they reimagined the museum, these women approached it not simply as a physical space for exhibition, but also considered it as an arbiter of cultural value, an archive or repository of cultural memory, a script for viewing modern art, an epistemology, and a malleable, hybrid form of collection and display (Rosenbaum, "Brides" 3–4). For writers and artists who lacked access to exhibiting in physical museums and galleries, curation through forms of print and visual media (the gallery catalog, the fashion magazine and little magazine, the gallery film, archival photographs, poetic collections, fiction) resulted in new, hybrid spaces of exhibition, that often extended and transformed physical gallery spaces. For Loy, architectural spaces of exhibition in Paris and New York included her Paris lamp shop; the Julien Levy Gallery, Martha Jackson Gallery, and Bodley Gallery; and, less publicly, her private apartments in Paris and New York. Forms of print and visual media that functioned as non-architectural, virtual spaces of exhibition for her imaginative creations included little magazines, museological paintings and collages, documentary photographs of her paintings and collections, her loosely autobiographical novel *Insel*, and her poetic collections.

Anticipating André Malraux's concept of the *musée imaginaire* or "museum without walls," these "virtual museums" asserted the importance of portable, imaginatively realized collections as alternatives to and extensions of traditional architectural museum sites. Print and visual media collections enabled modernist women to display and sell their work outside of the gallery-museum network, to advance their own aesthetic aims (often in critical dialogue with the masculine avant-garde), and as Melanie Micir has demonstrated, to ensure an archival legacy despite marginalization by official museums and publishing houses.[46] As Jessica Burstein argues, Loy often used one media form to comment on her designs created in a different medium (190); this intermedial commentary also served as a form of self-curation and archival preservation, particularly in the case of Loy's artworks that were not physically exhibited. Just as Loy's poem "The Ceiling" transformed her Paris apartment into a liminal space poised between night and day, waking and dream, material reality and artistic imagination, Loy often used virtual collections to comment on, extend, or transform architectural sites of exhibition, including buildings and streets, resulting in a layered, dynamic understanding of exhibitionary "space," through which Loy offered pointed commentary on the ways in which economic and social realities impinged on the surreal.

The poem "Lunar Baedeker" (1923) is an important example of Loy's reimagining of the museum, and poetic collection, as a liminal space. The year 1923 marked Loy's move to Paris, her initial contact with the Surrealist movement, and the publication of her first collection of poems, *Lunar Baedecker* (Contact Press, 1923). Divided into two sections, Poems 1921–1922 and Poems 1914–1915, the collection provided an aesthetic, historical, and geographical itinerary of the artists, places, and works of modernism that had mattered most to Loy on her journey.[47] As the titular poem, "Lunar Baedeker" serves as a Baedeker guide to the collection's aims more generally: it not only looks back at the path Loy had navigated, but anticipates the growing importance of the unreal and surreal to Loy's work of the later 1920s and 1930s. In turn, Loy's treatment of eros and the museum in this poem provides an important guide to her first poetic collection as an "imaginary museum," and to the en dehors garde collections Loy would create in its wake; in this sense the poem "Lunar Baedeker" serves not only as the culmination of Loy's journeys from 1914 to 1922, but as a map to new territory.

Loy characterizes her lunar landscape through the absence of desire, or "Eros obsolete" (LLB96 82). The problem of eros—and of female sexual desire specifically—interested Loy, alongside a number of women artists, throughout her career, and preceded her engagement with Surrealism.[48] She shared this interest in eros with Marcel Duchamp: Loy's friendship and artistic connection with Duchamp began in 1916 in New York's Arensberg circle, and would continue through the late 1950s when he helped arrange a 1959 exhibition of her "constructions" built from discarded materials found in the Bowery (Burke, *Becoming* 214–18, 433–35). Like Loy, Duchamp cultivated an engaged but ironic distance from a number of avant-garde movements over the course of his career, but Loy's feminism provided an additional layer of irony, one that she would direct at Duchamp. Duchamp's appearance in Man Ray photos from the early 1920s as Rrose Selavy (a pun on his proclamation "Eros, c'est la vie") indicated that like Loy, he considered gender and eros ready to be remade. Although Duchamp and the male avant-garde remained largely preoccupied with the masculine experience of eros, Duchamp's treatment of the "bride" in *The Bride Stripped Bare by Her Bachelors, Even*, known as *The Large Glass*, which Loy had visited in New York as early as 1917 (Burke, *Becoming* 228), inspired a number of women artists (Rosenbaum, "Brides").[49]

A large glass display for his earlier readymades, Duchamp's *Large Glass* is an unconventional museum without walls, that critically engages and transforms the context in which it is placed (see Fig. 4.2). A way of "breaking the frame" of conventional exhibitions, women's en dehors garde museums often took inspiration from *The Large Glass*'s display of previous readymades, its citations of diverse media such as film and photography, its "wedding" of verbal and visual elements, its portability, and its "window" on to variable surroundings.

Split into two halves horizontally, the *Glass* set in motion a spatialized "plot" involving heterosexual desire and a frustrated romance, with the abstract Bride in the top half of the *Glass*, separated from her prospective mates, the Bachelors, in the bottom half. Duchamp's Bride, positioned within but also resistant to the plot of heterosexual desire and feminized spectacle, could be written over by women who were redefining gender roles in their own works and lives; as Dalia Judovitz emphasizes, the abstract and mechanical qualities of Duchamp's Bride and Bachelor

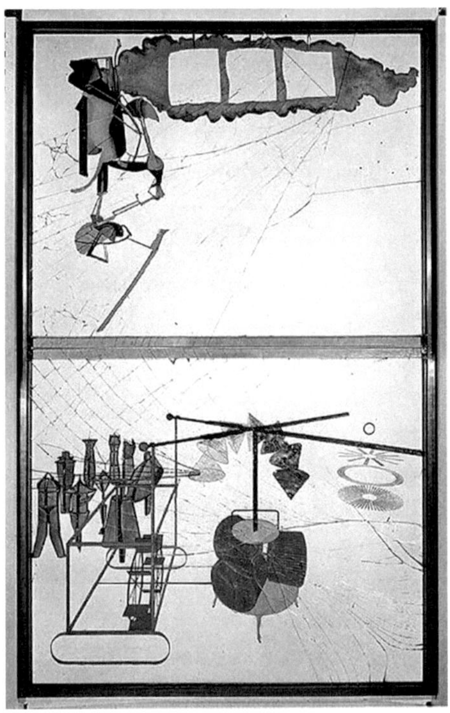

Figure 4.2. Marcel Duchamp, *The Bride Stripped Bare by Her Bachelors, Even* (*The Large Glass*), 1912–1923.

allow them to "defy traditional gender qualifications" (*Unpacking* 71). In turn, *The Large Glass*'s function as a form of display and its creation of an active role for the spectator proved generative to Loy and other women who were interested in establishing new models of producing, displaying, and consuming experimental art.[50]

The poem "Lunar Baedeker," like Duchamp's *Large Glass*, explicitly engages histories of museums and display, while offering itself as a lunar lens onto the real places and environments (cities, museums, streets, artworks) that Loy navigated. Approaching the poem as in dialogue with and a verbal lens on to Duchamp's *Large Glass* clarifies how Loy's depiction of a landscape defined by "eros obsolete" critically engages the masculine avant-garde's treatment of women, while opening up new understandings. "Lunar Baedeker" describes an otherworldly city:

> A silver Lucifer
> serves
> cocaine in cornucopia
>
> To some somnambulists
> of adolescent thighs
> draped
> in satirical draperies
>
> Peris in livery
> prepare
> Lethe
> for posthumous parvenues (LLB96 81)

Inspired by Baedeker's guidebooks, Loy's poetic map guides the reader through an "irreal" city (LLB96 134)—which she variously depicts as a city on the moon, a city of the dead, a city viewed only in black and white as if recorded by photographs or film—whose urban scenes reflect, distorted and transformed through lunar light, New York, Florence, Berlin, and Paris ("Peris"). Loy's geography of the moon is both fantastical and real, tied to the cities she navigated and to her imaginative vision; this geographical and imaginative dislocation allowed her to critically engage the avant-garde's gendered scenes and its outworn erotic tropes, while breaking new aesthetic ground. Loy's use of visual poetics, as in her Florence poems, contribute to her poetic mapping, with the visual design, layout, and typography of the poem figuring the landscape of the moon (see chapter 2).

Just as Man Ray's *Dust Breeding* (1920), a photographic close-up of dust on a section of Duchamp's *The Large Glass* (see Fig. 4.3), transforms the glass into a strange new landscape, Loy's "Lunar Baedeker" transforms the abstract elements of Duchamp's *Glass* into the surface of the moon:

> Cyclones
> of ecstatic dust
> and ashes whirl
> crusaders
> from hallucinatory citadels
> of shattered glass
> into evacuate craters (LLB96 82)

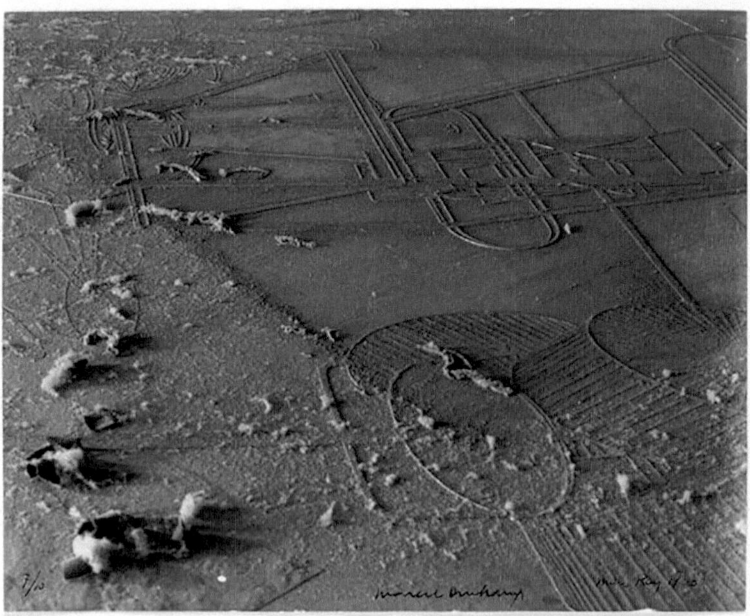

Figure 4.3. May Ray, *Dust Breeding*, 1920.

Loy's imagery of "ecstatic dust" and "shattered glass" alludes to both the Man Ray photo and Duchamp's *Large Glass*, while the Biblical allusion to ashes signifies the absence of mortal life, echoed by her depiction of the moon as a "Necropolis" (LLB96 82). In *The Large Glass*, Duchamp's bachelors experience a frustrated desire for the bride, but Loy's landscape is completely drained of eros and the colors that conventionally signify sex, passion, and fertility: the red-light district becomes the "eye-white sky-light / white-light district / of lunar lusts" (LLB96 81). Rendering her lunar landscape in photographic tones of black and white, Loy's language may allude to Man Ray's photo and the ways in which film, photography, and photomechanical reproduction mediate and delay sexual desire, a central theme of *The Large Glass*.[51]

However, Loy's allusions to *The Large Glass* and *Dust Breeding* as lunar landscapes drained of eros pointedly comment on the lack of understanding of female desire in the works of the masculine avant-garde, a longstanding theme of her writing. Man Ray's 1920 photographic portrait of Loy wearing a darkroom thermometer earring rendered that lack of understanding personal.[52] At the end of her "Feminist Manifesto" (1914) Loy stated,

> Another great illusion that woman must use all her introspective clear-sightedness & unbiassed bravery to destroy—for the sake of her <u>self respect</u> is the impurity of sex the realisation in defiance of superstition that there is <u>nothing impure in sex</u>—except in the mental attitude to it—will constitute an incalculable & wider social regeneration than it is possible for our generation to imagine. (LLB96 156)

Although Freud had provided a rationale for the modernists to challenge sexual taboos, Loy found that Freud and the male modernists were operating under a number of illusions that prevented them from acknowledging women's real sexual desires and experiences. In *Insel*, Loy's protagonist Mrs. Jones claimed to have "superseded Freud" (166). Loy would later argue in "History of Religion and Eros" that

> Freud is unnecessary to the future. His utile achievement lay in his solution of the problem, "To mention or not to mention." By making it, aided

> by the scientific aegis – – – fashionably polite to mention. Clearing a way out for inhibition." (SE 252)[53]

Although Freud had helped to lift sexual inhibitions, Loy found his understanding of eros "blind": "that terrain, exploited by his followers, is become an infinitely extensible maze of introversion in search of Eros – – – the little man who isn't *there* – – – –" (SE 252). In naming Freudian eros "The little man who isn't *there*," Loy be*littles* the search for an eros defined by men, a search that preoccupied Surrealists such as Breton.[54] Loy would turn from Freud to Havelock Ellis and other sexologists for a fuller understanding of female sexuality; Loy preferred Ellis's realism to Freud's theories and male modernists' illusions, which she dismantled in her essay "Library of the Sphinx."[55] As Loy would ask in "Faun Fare," composed after her move to New York, "for is not / Eros / forever overall / a male?" (LLB96 128).

Similarly, in Loy's 1923 "Lunar Baedeker," women's presence is restricted to outmoded, clichéd depictions of desirable women as imagined by and represented in the European tradition:

> in the oxidized Orient
>
> Onyx-eyed Odalisques
> and ornithologists
> observe
> the flight
> of Eros obsolete (LLB96 82)

Notably, Eros has vacated the scene. Loy's "odalisques" from the "oxidized Orient"— referring to female slaves or concubines in a Turkish harem—connote the worn-out or "oxidized" Orientalism of a European tradition that had long conflated female sexual allure with racialized others, a tradition that shaped modernism, notably in Matisse's paintings of odalisques (1917–1930). Onyx, a silicate mineral characterized by black and white bands, develops the imagery of glass ("onyx-eyed odalisques") and may refer to the black and white color of women's eyes, or, may refer to an artistic rendering in which onyx stones take the place of eyes, reinforcing the odalisque's status as a sexual ornament. As in the painting *Surreal Scene* (see Fig. 4.1), Loy's poem surveys a landscape in which women's representations hinge on their objectification, subservience, or entrapment to the male gaze and male desire. However, the odalisques and ornithologists are able to "observe" the absence of eros, Loy emphasizing the importance of this word by setting it on its own line. Observation opens up new possibilities for understanding and representation.

Female eros had been "fossilized" in visual and literary history, and Loy's description of the lunar landscape as dead and infertile culminates in her depiction of it as a museum:

> And "Immortality"
> mildews...
> in the museums of the moon
> "Nocturnal cyclops"
> "Crystal concubine"
> — — — — — — — —
> Pocked with personification
> the fossil virgin of the skies
> waxes and wanes— — — — (LLB96 82)

The poem concludes with Loy's representation of the outworn clichés of the feminized moon as rendered in the masculine poetic and artistic tradition: either "concubine" or "fossil virgin," conventional representations of the moon canonized in Western art and literature are tied to outmoded gender roles and binaries (mistress/mother, whore/virgin) that deny and erase female eros. But by capitalizing and placing "Immortality" in quotation marks, Loy challenges the permanence of these canons: treating the word "Immortality" like the title of a painting or artifact hanging on museum walls, Loy signals that ironically, judgments of a work's permanence are contingent upon the architectural museum's *claims* to the permanence of its collections. Works deemed "immortal" by the museum, however, are subject to history, nature (mildew), and change. In the same manner, Loy places clichéd personifications of the moon—"Nocturnal cyclops" and "Crystal concubine"—in quotation marks, on their own lines, to indicate the outmoded depictions of the moon one encounters hanging in museums and galleries, whether of the dominant culture or the avant-garde. “Crystal concubine” may refer to Duchamp’s Bride, trapped in glass as she is trapped by the masculine depiction of women and eros. However, Loy’s long line of em dashes, and the em dashes which conclude the poem, visually open up space in the lunar landscape that signifies an absence, but also a palpable location where new language and new thinking about female desire might emerge: a pathway to new understandings.

Loy’s “Lunar Baedeker” casts Western culture’s museums in a new light: the light of her critical, satiric intelligence, intent on demolishing the old clichés persistently defining the artistic landscape, alongside the transformative light of “lunar” dislocation, which creates a liminal landscape, a lunar map superimposed on actual places, to show the possibility of new vision, and new understanding. Like Duchamp’s *Large Glass* which provides an abstract window onto the particular environment in which it is placed, Loy’s poem provides a transformed window onto the real places and environments (cities, museums, streets, avant-garde scenes) Loy navigated.[56] Loy’s word coinages in the poem embody this practice, as in her description of “Stellectric signs / ‘Wing shows on Starway’ / ‘Zodiac carrousel’” (LLB96 81).[57] Loy merges words in a manner that combines their sounds and connotations, as in “Stellectric” as a combination of “stellar” (star) and “electric,” and “Starway” as a combination of “star” and “Broadway”: these new words convey an image of a lunar-lit transformation of the signs, theaters, and entertainment on New York’s Broadway. Altering “readymade” words, Loy’s coinages open up new vistas.

Duchamp’s *Large Glass* displays abstract depictions of a bride, bachelors, and other readymades, suggesting that received notions of gender and eros can be remade, alongside exhibitionary spaces. Loy revisits this territory, yet through her lunar lens illuminates a further feminist, en dehors garde zone beyond that imagined by Duchamp and the masculine avant-garde. Loy’s collections of the 1930s would extend and explore this en dehors garde territory through her lamp shop and novel *Insel*, while her New York work would revisit it in poems and three-dimensional “constructions” created with an altered documentary lens.

Exhibit 2
Mina Loy's Lamp Shop and Lamps

Loy's interest in illumination, poetic and metaphorical, would take material form in her lamp designs and Paris lamp shop. Her interest in lamp design was long-standing; as an artist and poet who needed to make a living, Loy began making and selling lampshades in New York in 1917, and she exhibited a painting (now lost) titled *Making Lampshades*, at the Society of Independent Artists exhibition (Burke, *Becoming* 224, 227, 340). As Linda Kinnahan argues in chapter 2, one of Loy's Futurist dress designs resembles a lamp, and in Paris, lamps would take on particular meaning in the context of Surrealism. Ilene Susan Fort connects the pink background in Loy's painting *Surreal Scene* to Louis Aragon's 1924 poem "Une vague de rêves," which states:

> There is a surrealist light: at the time of day when towns burst into flame
> it is the light that falls on the salmon pink display of silk stockings. [...]
> There is a surrealist light in the eyes of every woman. (Fort and Arcq 34)

That "surrealist light" would become literal for Loy, who in 1926 applied herself to creating functional yet beautiful lamps that could transform their everyday surroundings.

Carolyn Burke refers to Loy's New York lampshade business as "moderately successful" (*Becoming* 340), and in 1926 Loy decided to return to making lampshades, after trying her hand in 1925 at making objects titled "Jaded Blossoms" that "crossed the traditional still life with Cubist collage" (338–39). Peggy Guggenheim and Laurence Vail took these objects to New York where they were sold at Belmaison Gallery in the Wanamaker Department store, Macy's Department Store Gallery, and Cargoes Gallery.[58] Alert throughout her career to productive intersections between art, fashion, commerce, and unconventional gallery spaces, Peggy Guggenheim helped to finance Loy's lampshade shop.

Along with Loy, a number of avant-garde artists pursued intersections between Surrealism, fashion, and design, and the playful wit evident in Surrealist objects exhibited at galleries and museums extended to objects intended for the consumer market, including clothing, hats, jewelry, and objects for the home (Chadwick 118). For instance, Meret Oppenheim and Leonor Fini created Surrealist objects but also made objects and jewelry for Surrealist designer Elsa Schiaparelli (Chadwick 122); Fini designed the famous Mae West-inspired bottle for the perfume Shocking (1936), named after Schiaparelli's signature color Shocking Pink.[59] In 1940 following her move to New York, Loy sold a jewelry bottle design to Helena Rubinstein which she called Pipes of Pan, made from recycled glass containers for cigarettes, renamed Syrinx by the company (Burke, *Becoming* 301). Loy wrote a poem that she hoped, like an advertisement, could help "launch the Syrinx bottle."[60] The permeable boundary between lyric and advertisement, poem and perfume, indicates that Loy did not position the lyric (the most idealized of poetic genres) outside of the marketplace, even as she commented critically on the fashion industry, class, and economics.[61] As an en dehors garde artist, Loy often honed aesthetic designs to economic ends: her clever reuse of the glass cigarette containers, considered by most as trash, is a twist on the found object that echoed her reuse of bottles as lamp bases, and anticipated her use of trash found on the street as the material for her Bowery assemblages.

Loy's lampshade shop was located in a wealthy shopping district at 52 rue de Colisée, a street connecting the Champs-Elysées and rue du Faubourg-Saint-Honoré (see Fig. 1.6).[62] The shop opened in September 1926 and was so successful that Loy hired assistants and opened a workshop in Montparnasse (Burke, *Becoming* 342–44, 365). Guggenheim initially used the shop to display (in addition to Loy's lamps) lingerie, slippers, and her husband Laurence Vail's paintings (341–42). Tristan Tzara wrote the catalog introduction for the exhibition of Vail's paintings (342): that the lampshade shop also served as the "Galeries Mina Loy" was in keeping with the overlap between art and commerce in both Guggenheim's and Loy's careers and in their engagement with the exhibitionary "scenes" of Surrealism.

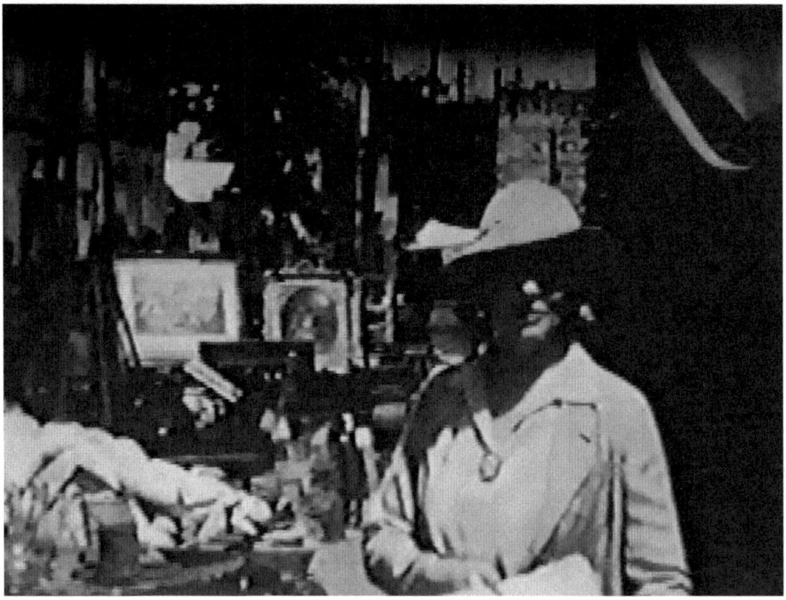

Figure 4.4. Film still of Loy at Marché aux Puces, 1932. Film made by Julien Levy.

Loy designed the lamps herself, using antique bottles she found in the Paris flea markets as lamp bases, and creating the lampshades by hand from a variety of opaque and translucent papers including cellophane, and from synthetic materials including rhodoid and Crystal Lux (Burke, *Becoming* 340–42). In her lamp designs Loy engaged the *objet trouvé* or found object, a particular kind of Surrealist object defined by André Breton in "Equation de l'objet trouvé" (1934) and in a passage from *Mad Love* (1937) centered on the Paris flea markets; however, Loy was less an idle flaneuse strolling through the flea market waiting for unconscious desire to strike her, than a glaneuse or "gleaner," who merged aesthetic style and economic necessity (see Fig. 4.4).[63]

Loy's feminist commentary on the Surrealist found object emerges in an episode from her autobiographical novel *Insel*, in which the artist Insel comments on a lampshade designed by Mrs. Jones (based on Loy) that "It would surely be of the greatest interest to Freud" (166). Mrs. Jones replies:

> The still life that intrigued him was a pattern of a 'detail' to be strewn about the surface of clear lamp shades. Through equidistant holes

> punched in a crystalline square, I had carefully urged in extension, a still celluloid coil of the color that Schiaparelli has since called *shocking* pink. Made to be worn round pigeon's ankles for identification, I had picked it up in the Bon Marché.
>
> Out of this harmless even pretty object an ignorant bully had constructed for me, according to his own conceptions, a libido threaded with some viciousness impossible to construe.
>
> I was astounded. (*Insel* 166–67)

Mrs. Jones is incensed that Insel blithely echoes Freud's limited understanding of female eros, while ignoring the innovative thrift and economic necessity legible in the repurposing of pigeon's ankle celluloid as part of the lampshade design.[64] Loy's reference to Schiaparelli's "shocking pink" aligns the lamps with Schiaparelli's merging of Surrealist design and fashion, while indicating that Mrs. Jones preceded Schiaparelli in her use of this color.

Carolyn Burke describes the lamps as a "streamlined version of Art Nouveau" (*Becoming* 365), but Loy also engaged Dada and Surrealist aesthetics in her designs, particularly if we consider the lamp bases and other elements (such as the "shocking pink" celluloid coil) as found objects, and the lamps as poetic conduits capable of transforming domestic interiors into aquatic or celestial environments through the generation of shadows and silhouettes.[65] Loy's lampshade designs were inspired by the oceans, celestial maps, and the natural world: those inspired by the sea included a sailing ship, waves, and a fish, while her illuminated celestial and world globes and star sconces "seemed to have materialized from the pages of *Lunar Baedecker*" (Burke, *Becoming* 343). Loy's water plant, water lily, calla lilies and swan lamps created a vision of a pastoral garden pond inside the home, a good example of the kind of liminal landscape that Loy explored in "The Ceiling" and "Lunar Baedeker," transforming familiar spaces through a dislocating light.

One critic admired the "lampshades whose fairylike shadows transform the decor and domesticate dreams" (Burke, *Becoming* 343), while an *Arts and Decoration* magazine writer commented in 1927 on Loy's "red fish" lampshade: "The effect of this lamp shade [...] is as though the fish were swimming through the water in an aquarium, very clever and

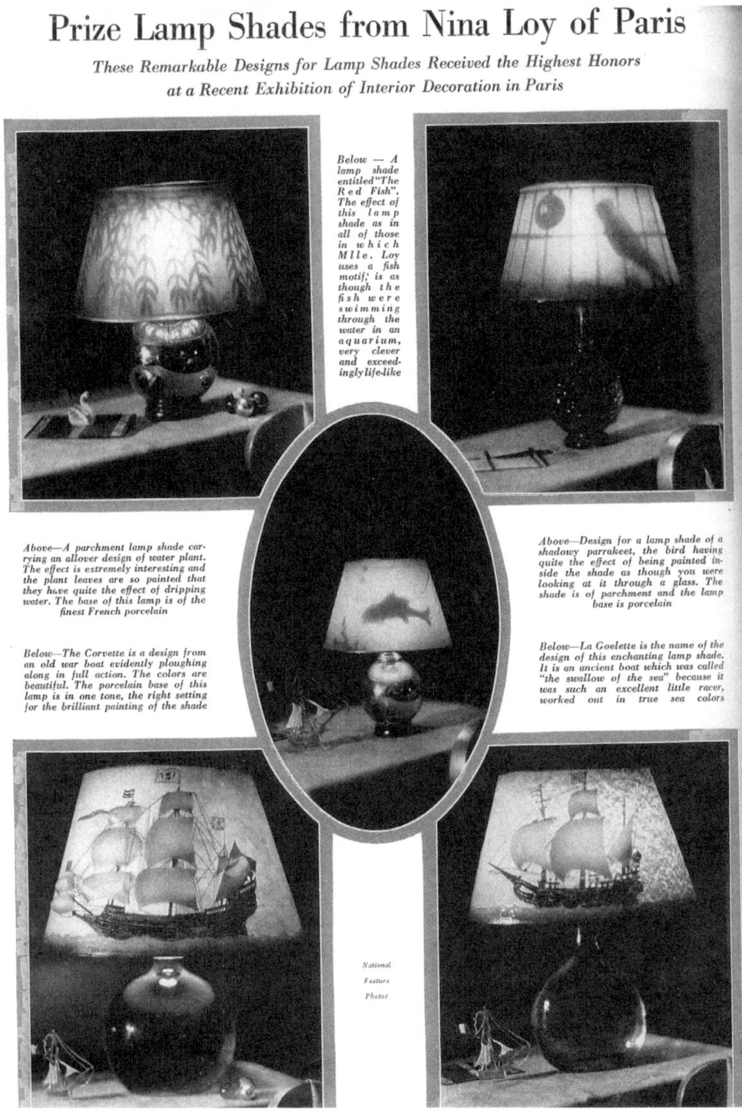

Prize Lamp Shades from Nina Loy of Paris

These Remarkable Designs for Lamp Shades Received the Highest Honors at a Recent Exhibition of Interior Decoration in Paris

Below — A lamp shade entitled "The Red Fish". The effect of this lamp shade as in all of those in which Mlle. Loy uses a fish motif,' is as though the fish were swimming through the water in an aquarium, very clever and exceedingly life-like

Above—A parchment lamp shade carrying an allover design of water plant. The effect is extremely interesting and the plant leaves are so painted that they have quite the effect of dripping water. The base of this lamp is of the finest French porcelain

Above—Design for a lamp shade of a shadowy parrakeet, the bird having quite the effect of being painted inside the shade as though you were looking at it through a glass. The shade is of parchment and the lamp base is porcelain

Below—The Corvette is a design from an old war boat evidently ploughing along in full action. The colors are beautiful. The porcelain base of this lamp is in one tone, the right setting for the brilliant painting of the shade

Below—La Goelette is the name of the design of this enchanting lamp shade. It is an ancient boat which was called "the swallow of the sea" because it was such an excellent little racer, worked out in true sea colors

National Feature Photos

Figure 4.5. *Arts and Decoration* magazine, July 1927, p. 56.

exceedingly life-like." Loy described the power of light to transform an apartment interior into just such an "irreal aquarium" in her novel *Insel*:

> The world of the Lutetia had materialized. An infiltration of half-light softly bursting the dark, a thin cascade, the ferns dripping into a green

> gloom. Here, where dawn and noon and midnight were all so dim and Insel lay sensitive to clarity as a creature of the deep sea; the closely shuttered studio with its row of glass doors was a real replica of the irreal 'aquarium'. (109)

Indeed the "ferns dripping into a green gloom" describe well one of Loy's lampshades featured in *Arts and Decoration* magazine (see Fig. 4.5). In her poem "The Ceiling" Loy established the power of "half-light softly bursting the dark" to generate the liminal space in between day and night, waking and sleeping, rational thought and dream vision. Loy's *Drift of Chaos* paintings, created in the 1930s, also portray "ferns dripping into a green gloom" and creatures of "the deep sea" (MLSII 106-09). Loy explored the importance of light to the generation of liminal landscapes not only through her physical lamp designs, but also in "metaphorical lamps"—paintings, poems, and fictions created in Paris—demonstrating the overlap between Loy's commercial designs and her more experimental art.

Exhibit 3
Loy's Paris Apartment: Home, Studio, Art Gallery

Loy approached her 9 rue Saint-Romain apartment (where she lived with her daughter Fabienne from 1929 to 1936) as a domestic living space but also as a space of creation and display, a studio and self-curated gallery: she painted many of her Surrealist-influenced works of the early 1930s there, including *Surreal Scene* (see Fig. 4.1), wrote "The Ceiling" and other poems, and drafts of *Insel*. In this apartment Loy also read drafts of Djuna Barnes's *Nightwood* which likely influenced *Insel* (Burke, *Becoming* 368). Economic thrift and domestic duties influenced Loy's transformation of her apartment into a studio-gallery space; unlike many of her male counterparts in the avant-garde, she had neither the time nor money for a separate studio. Yet many of Loy's avant-garde acquaintances—the Arensbergs, Katherine Dreier, Peggy Guggenheim, André Breton—similarly transformed their homes into domestic galleries (Rosenbaum, "Brides" 8–9). In her writing and artwork of this time, Loy attends to this layering of space and function.

In addition to housing her own art materials and artwork, Loy's Paris apartment served as a transient gallery for works awaiting shipment to Julien Levy's gallery in New York. In Summer 1931, Levy bought Dalí's *The Persistence of Memory* and stored it in Loy's apartment prior to shipping; the painting was shown in the Levy Gallery's first Surrealism exhibition (January 1932) and "stole the show" (Burke, *Becoming* 385; "Loy-alism" 69, 72).[66] The painting *Expectation* (1935–1936) by the artist Richard Oelze (who inspired Loy's novel *Insel*) also hung in Loy's apartment before transport to Levy's gallery in fall 1936 and on to the Museum of Modern Art's permanent collection in 1940 (Burke, *Becoming* 385; "Loy-alism" 72). Levy included both *The Persistence of Memory* and *Expectation* in his print collection *Surrealism* (1936, plates 52 and 58), but did not include work by Loy. Yet Loy hung these works alongside her own objects and art in her apartment, a curatorial, juxtapositional practice that she extended into textual and painterly spaces, with pointed commentary.

Loy's biographer Carolyn Burke suggests that Loy not only put great care into the design of her 9 rue Saint-Romain apartment, but that it also influenced the design of her lampshade shop and the "artistic spirit" of Julien Levy's New York gallery ("Loy-alism" 67) (see Fig. 4.6). Burke describes Loy's apartment thus:

> A poetic mélange of flea market finds, decorative schemes devised to hide flaws, and idiosyncratic art gallery composed of Mina's paintings, Fabi's drawings, and photographs of Cravan, it also featured Mina's collection of antique bottles, Fabi's bird cages as room dividers, and silver paper in floral patterns pasted over cracks in the plaster. ("Loy-alism" 67)

Julien Levy similarly described the apartment's design as "by Loy out of the Marché aux Puces" (qtd. in Burke, "Loy-alism" 69), alluding to Loy's ability to transform the material she found in the flea market. Burke

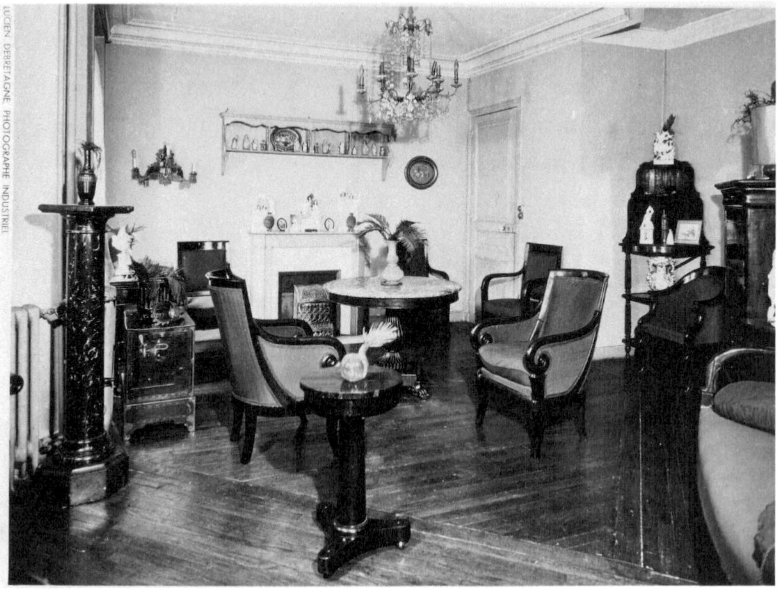

LUCIEN DEBRETAGNE PHOTOGRAPHIE INDUSTRIEL

Figure 4.6. Mina Loy, 9 rue Saint-Romain apartment.

documents Loy's careful curation of the display of objects in her apartment, noting that:

> [Joseph] Cornell kept in his files, possibly for future use, a photograph of the mantelpiece in Mina's rue St.-Romain apartment labeled 'Paris, 1920s.' It showed, in evocative juxtaposition, an owl statue, a harlequin figure, several old-fashioned toys, a figurine in a long robe, and a tiny Madonna in a bird cage. (*Becoming* 407)

This photo (photographer unknown, but possibly Julien Levy) has been preserved in Cornell's papers in the Archives of American Art (see Fig. 4.7).

Loy had clearly transformed a mantelpiece in her apartment into a small installation that anticipated the juxtaposition of found objects in Cornell's boxes. The photograph creates a box-like frame, and the spatial position and relation of objects invites poetic connections and distinctions. For instance, the female figurine's central position, with left arm extended and open hand, echoed by the harlequin's left arm, implies her creative function or figuring of the artist. The position of her head in

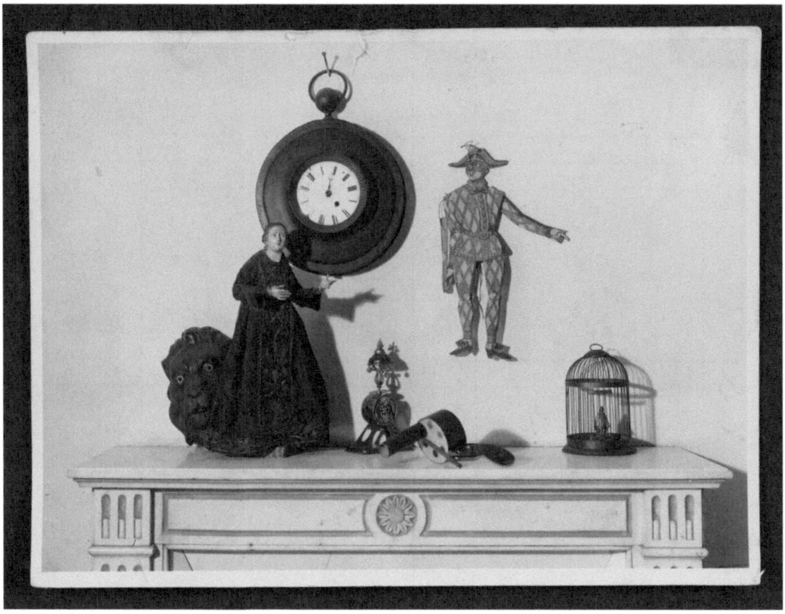

Figure 4.7. Mantelpiece in Mina Loy's 9 rue St.-Romain apartment.

front of a clock with a lion's head peeking out from behind her skirts, may signify the artist's creative powers and her uses of time as media. The objects allude to Loy's art and designs: the lion's head recalls her Florentine poem "Lions' Jaws," the caged Madonna echoes Loy's use of this figure in her Florentine poetry and art, while the viewfinder connotes the mediated vision important to her art. The harlequin was a central figure in Picasso's cubist painting but also alludes to Loy's interest in dress design, collage, and creating new objects out of found scraps.

Loy's careful arrangement of objects is also evident in the photo of her rue Saint-Romain apartment sitting room (see Fig. 4.6) and in the handwritten lists she maintained of her bottle collection, which carefully document the location of every bottle in her apartment, several visible in the photo.[67] The photo of her apartment interior also documents a number of objects with feathery appendages (presumably lost), and Loy likely created her Surrealist object *Lobster Boy*, recorded only in a photograph (see Fig. 4.9), in this apartment as well. Although little is known about Loy's solicitation of these photographs, their careful documentation of her artwork and her apartment as a curated "gallery" space provides a crucial archival record and a virtual form of display.[68]

Exhibit 4
Loy's Paris Apartment Gallery and Surrealist Objects: *Lobster Boy*

Loy not only engaged the Surrealist "found object" in her lamp designs, but made a number of objects in the 1930s, now lost but documented and preserved in the photographs taken in her Paris apartment. Loy also presents several incarnations of the Surrealist object in her painting *Surreal Scene* and in her novel *Insel*, which illuminate her thoughts about the Surrealists' use of this form.

Interest in the Surrealist object grew in the 1930s. As Chadwick argues, "Capturing the images of the dream in reality, crystallizing the objects of desire and affirming the magic link between the unconscious and the real world, the Surrealist object became the perfect meeting point of Surrealist theory and practice" (118). Chadwick notes that "Surrealist objects by male artists often have an explicitly erotic content (Bellmer's Dolls, Duchamp's *Please Touch*), disturb by means of violent juxtapositions (Man Ray's *Gift*, Dominguez's *Conversion of Energy*), or combine both functions (Dominguez's *Arrival of the Belle Epoque*)" (118). As Kinnahan argues, "visual and literary Surrealism centralized the image of the female body as a terrain for violence, borne of desire and anxiety and manifest through myriad images of women's bodies penetrated, bound, mutilated, gagged, or ominously manipulated" (*Mina Loy, Twentieth-Century Photography* 89).

In *Surreal Scene*, Loy provides feminist commentary on the male Surrealists' objectification of women through her depiction of an armchair in the shape of a headless white female body, and a harp with arms strumming its strings (see Fig. 4.1).[69] The chair conflates women with domestic comfort and sexual availability, as the woman-chair is literally a mindless thing positioned to physically receive others. Similarly, the headless harp has arms that are plucking strings, providing music for others in the room. In this way Loy comments on woman's function as a decorative, sexualized, secondary object and muse in Surrealist art and design. As Suzanne Churchill points out in chapter 3, in Loy's set design for her play *The Pamperers*, Loy described "picked people melted by a distinguished method among the upholstery" and commented, "The social fabric is a curtain." In a similar "set" in the painting, Loy also suggests that arrangements of people and furniture reflect how class and gender shape the social fabric: Loy's woman-chair reveals woman's material presence yet intellectual absence in the Surrealist scene.

Women artists also made Surrealist objects in the 1930s, which often commented on sexual objectification and explored facets of the object resonant with gendered experience.[70] For instance, Meret Oppenheim's fur-lined teacup became virtually synonymous with the MoMA's 1937 *Fantastic Art, Dada, and Surrealism* exhibition; the MoMA was dubbed by *Harper's Magazine* the "fur-lined museum" (Genauer 129). Critical of how Surrealists objectified and fetishized the female body in their objects, Loy also created an object of her own: although the object has been lost, a photograph of it displayed in Loy's apartment remains, contributing to the importance of photography as a virtual form of display and archival record (see Fig. 4.9). Loy's *Lobster Boy* object, although its precise date of composition is unknown, was likely created in Paris prior to her move to New York in late 1936, and reflects her interest in human-animal hybrids and in crustaceans of various kinds in her Paris-era work.

Loy's object consists of a youth likely sculpted out of clay, with an actual lobster tail in place of legs and lobster claws in place of arms, set in a small glass bell jar. The glass bell jar is not simply a container for the lobster boy, but is also a display case which evokes a water-filled aquarium in which the creature swims. Loy evokes the transformation of her apartment into an "irreal aquarium" in *Insel*, and sought to create similar effects with her lamps and paintings, transforming interior rooms into aquatic environments through the play of light and shadow.[71] Similarly, in 1925 Loy painted a fresco of mermaids and lobster-human hybrids on her bedroom wall at Peggy Guggenheim's villa in Prasmousquier (Burke,

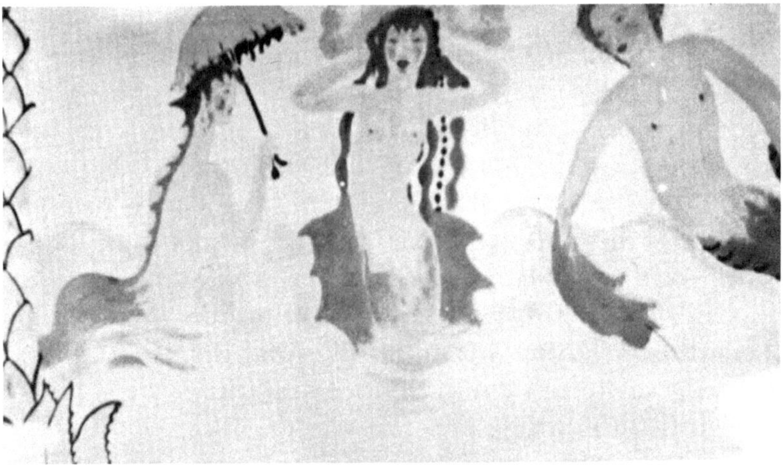

Figure 4.8. Wall painting by Mina Loy, Peggy Guggenheim's villa, Prasmousquier, 1925.

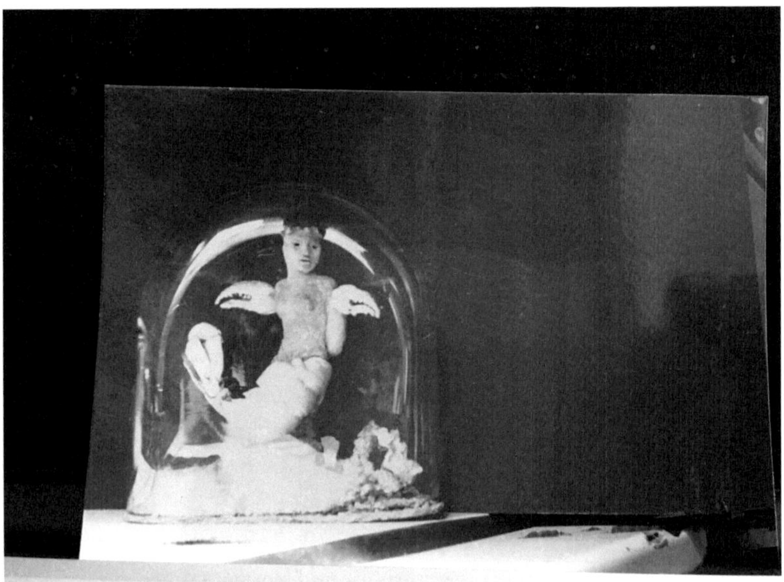

Figure 4.9. Mina Loy, *Lobster Boy* object, n.d.

Becoming 334–35) (see Fig. 4.8). Guggenheim wrote, "Mina painted a fresco in her bedroom. She conceived lobsters and mermaids with sunshades tied to their tails" (Guggenheim, *Out of This Century* 78). In the fresco, the mermaids appear to be female and the lobster figure's gender is unclear, but it could be a model for or version of Loy's *Lobster Boy*. Although titled "Lobster boy" on the back of the photograph, the sculpted figure in the bell jar clearly has breasts (see Fig. 4.9). Loy's *Lobster Boy*, like the figure on the right-hand side of the Guggenheim fresco, appears to be Loy's crustacean twist on the mermaid: the "lobster boy" has a lobster tail and claws, but a human head and torso.

Loy's *Lobster Boy* object with breasts suggests a hermaphroditic mixture of a lobster boy and female mermaid. The figure's ambiguous or hybrid gender, coupled with its conjoining of human and crustacean forms, suggests new physical configurations of sex and gender. Although Loy's *Lobster Boy* object cannot be precisely dated, her work as Dalí's agent (including temporary storage and exhibition of *The Persistence of Memory* in her apartment) suggests Loy's pointed response to Dalí's use of the lobster. Dalí's lobsters began to appear in his work in 1934, most famously in *Aphrodisiac Telephone* (1936), on the dress he designed with Schiaparelli (1937), and in his *Dream of Venus* pavilion at the 1939 World's Fair, which featured nude mannequins with lobsters in place of bathing suits. Spectators entered Dalí's pavilion through the legs of a woman, the "very womb of Venus" (Kachur 133), and similar to Loy's depiction of her Paris apartment as an "irreal aquarium," the interior resembled an underwater scene, including tanks with female mannequins and swimming, bare-breasted female mermaids (Kachur 137, 140; Kinnahan, *Mina Loy, Twentieth-Century Photography* 105). In George Platt Lynes's 1939 Surrealist photo of Dalí posed behind a female mannequin at the *Dream of Venus* pavilion, Dalí's placement of the lobster suggests the addition of male genitalia to the woman's torso, challenging the assignment of sex and gender, while the prominent lobster claws may signify the castrating potential of female sexuality. Lucy Flint points out that in male Surrealist art, "The female, seen in horror and longing as both victim and victimizer of male sexuality, is often a crustacean or insectlike form" ("Alberto Giacometti").

While Dalí employed the lobster motif to simultaneously challenge conventions of gender and to provoke anxiety about male control and female sexuality, Loy's *Lobster Boy* object conjoins human and crustacean to generate a true hybrid. As discussed above as an adaptation of Surrealist poetics, Loy explored human-animal ("grotesque") hybrids in *Surreal Scene* and in her Paris-era poems to challenge entrenched gendered and racial divisions. Human-animal hybrids such as *Lobster Boy*, alongside Loy's depiction of hybrid creatures in her 1930s paintings—snail-people, moon-angels, an oyster woman, a butterfly woman—interrogated firm lines of sexual identity and expanded the realm of the natural. Chadwick points out that in many Surrealist paintings by women, hybrid human-animals function as "symbolic intermediaries between the unconscious and the natural world [...] they replace [...] the image of woman as the mediating link between man and the 'marvelous'" (79). Loy's *Lobster Boy* object shares qualities with her paintings and poems from the 1920s and early 30s, indicating the varied forms in which Loy explored her ideas about hybridity at this time. Through these hybrid mixtures Loy generates the potential for a new definition of the human, but with a *female* difference.[72]

While *Lobster Boy* may critically engage Surrealism, Loy's interest in sexual hybridity and androgyny was longstanding: her earlier paintings had often portrayed androgynous figures (for example, *La Maison en Papier*, 1906; *L'Amour dorloté par les belles dames*, 1913) (MLSII 17, 15). In the 1910s, hermaphroditism was explored by poets who (like Loy) were associated with the little magazine *Others*, including Frances Gregg ("Hermaphrodites," November 1915) and Alice Groff ("Hermaphrodite-Us," January 1916).[73] H.D.'s "Hermes of the Ways" appeared in *Poetry* in 1913 and she also published in *Others*. In Loy's April 1925 essay "Modern Poetry," published in *Charm* magazine, Loy cited H.D. as "an interesting example of my claims for the American poet who engages with an older culture," adding that H.D. "has written at least two perfect poems: one about a swan" (LLB96 160).

Alongside H.D., Loy explored modern renditions of Classical myth. The head of the *Lobster Boy*, with its hollow eyes, suggests the head of a Greek or Roman statue. The figure appears to have a garland around his forehead, possibly an allusion to the laurel crown worn by Apollo and given to Greek poets and warriors. In her 1923 poem "Marble," published in a prospectus for the *transatlantic review*, Loy wrote:

> Greece has thrown   white shadows
> sown
> their eyeballs with oblivion
>
> A flock of stone
> Gods
> perched upon pedestals (LLB96 93)

In merging human and lobster in this statue-like figure, Loy was likely generating her own en dehors garde rendition of Classical myth, joining artists such as H.D. whose poetic adaptations of the hybridity and metamorphoses central to Greek myth were shaped by her modern, nonbinary understanding of sex and gender. Loy would similarly transform Classical myth, specifically the birth of Venus, in her Paris-era paintings *Oyster Woman* and *Venus* (MLSII 107, 126).

Exhibit 5
Transatlantic Spaces and Exhibits: The Julien Levy Gallery

In 1931, Loy began to serve as the Paris agent for the innovative Julien Levy Gallery (1931–1949), which not only held the first Surrealist exhibition in New York in January 1932, but throughout the 1930s and 1940s served as the premier American gallery for Surrealist work of all kinds.[74] With Julien and Edgar Levy's financial help, Loy was able to buy out Peggy Guggenheim's share of her lampshade shop in 1928, and sold it in 1930, permitting more time for her writing and art. Levy opened his New York gallery in November 1931 and arranged for Loy to become his Paris representative (Burke, *Becoming* 377). As the agent in Paris who arranged the purchase and transportation of Surrealist art to Levy's Gallery from 1931–36, Loy was a central figure in European Surrealism's transatlantic career and reception in the United States.[75]

Mina Loy not only worked as an agent for the Levy Gallery, but exhibited her paintings at the New York gallery in January–February 1933 (a solo show) and in 1937 (a group exhibition). Although she was located in Paris, Loy's exhibition shown in New York reflected the ways in which Surrealist exhibits could travel and navigate physical and virtual spaces distinct from their origins and creators, creating a layering of geographical, architectural, and virtual places. As if capturing the ways in which exhibitions could reference many places simultaneously and create new, liminal, en dehors garde spaces, Loy's paintings for the 1933 exhibition explored the celestial subjects of her poem "Lunar Baedeker": moons, comet, dawn, light, stars. A number depict hybrid creatures—snails with human faces, angel heads with wings—what Burke calls "primordial shapes in the act of becoming" on a "blue-gray base of mixed sand, gesso, and plaster [Loy] called 'fresco vero'" ("Loy-alism" 70–71).[76]

Although the Museum of Modern Art's 1936–7 *Fantastic Art, Dada, Surrealism* exhibition brought Surrealism to wide public prominence in the United States, Levy's gallery had provided the blueprint and some of the art for the exhibition.[77] James Thrall Soby said that Levy "was as close to being an official Surrealist himself as one could come without signing one of André Breton's guidelines to the Surrealist faith" (Schaffner, "Alchemy" 23). Levy admired Loy's lampshade shop-gallery, and in his own gallery he would sell books, magazines, and "his own photo objects, trompe-l'oeil wastebaskets and lampshades" (23). The gallery was as much a salon as a shop and exhibition space, where European and American artists could meet. As Philip Johnson commented "We give credit to [Levy] for establishing a home for Surrealism in America" (Schaffner and Jacobs 172).

In its innovative layout (the gallery had curved white walls), its inclusion of books and periodicals, and its exhibitions of painting, film, photography, ballet, cartoons, and theater, Levy's gallery had much in common with Surrealist-curated galleries and exhibitions (Schaffner, "Alchemy" 21, 33). As Ingrid Schaffner notes, "Pictures hanging on those walls took on a cinematic sequencing, directed by the dealer" (21).[78] Understanding the power of cinema to transform space, as evidenced by

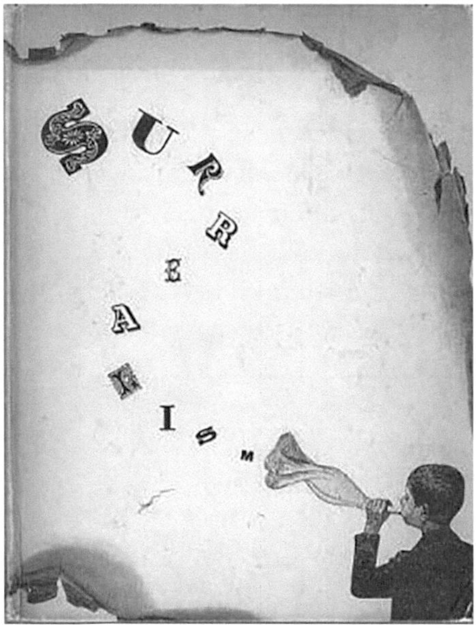

Figure 4.10. Joseph Cornell, cover of *Surrealism*, edited by Julien Levy, Black Sun Press, 1936.

her poem "The Ceiling," Loy influenced Levy's gallery as a physical space that could be altered and transformed into a dreamlike, psychological space through the projection of film. After viewing Luis Buñuel's *L'Age d'Ôr* in 1932 with Julien Levy and Lee Miller, Loy encouraged and helped to arrange the film's premiere in New York (Burke, *Becoming* 378–79; Schaffner, "Alchemy" 37). Levy screened films at his gallery by Buñuel and Dalí, Léger, Disney, Cocteau, Duchamp, Man Ray, and Joseph Cornell.[79]

Loy's influence is also evident in Levy's book *Surrealism* (published in 1936 by Caresse Crosby's Black Sun Press) as a textual exhibition of Surrealism that illuminates and extends the aims of Levy's physical gallery. Levy's book demonstrates his American adaptation of Surrealism, underscored by the cover, a Joseph Cornell collage of a small boy trumpeting the word "Surrealism," a collage that was shown in the gallery's 1932 Surrealist exhibition (see Fig. 4.10). In contrast to Breton, Levy avoided defining Surrealism as a movement, emphasizing that:

> unlike so many other 'isms' surrealism is evidently not a deadend, it is not static, but is a dynamic and expansive *point of view*. Just as surrealism

> could invite the genius of Picasso so it may still invite the new generation of poets and painters. (*Surrealism* 27; italics added)

Levy's perspective on Surrealism as a dynamic lens echoed that of Loy, Crevel, and others, and would influence American artists interested in adapting Surrealist ideas and techniques without formally joining the Surrealist movement. Prior to her physical relocation to New York, Loy had made her presence felt through Levy's gallery.

Exhibit 6
A "Gallery of the Increate": *Insel* as Textual Gallery and Archive

Loy's dealings on behalf of the Levy Gallery with the German surrealist painter Richard Oelze in 1935–36 would inspire her loosely autobiographical novel *Insel*, which chronicles the relationship between Mrs. Jones, a character modeled on Loy's role as Levy's Paris agent, and Insel, based on Oelze.[80] *Insel* as a cryptic, highly allusive text can be read in many ways, but in its ties to Loy's art career, it serves as an experimental, textual gallery in which she critically curated Insel's (Oelze's) art, while providing poetic glimpses of her lamp designs, her 1930s paintings and objects, and her rue Saint-Romain apartment, her carefully curated domestic gallery that (as noted earlier) included at one point Oelze's painting *Expectation* (1935–36) (Burke, *Becoming* 385; "Loy-alism" 72).[81] Several scenes from the novel take place in Mrs. Jones's Paris apartment, which resembles Loy's, suggesting how Loy's writing transforms her rue Saint-Romain apartment from a literal gallery space into a textual gallery space, creating a layered exhibitionary venue as much psychological and imaginary as visible and architectural.

In *Insel*, Loy animates the scene of Surrealist art's reception by a female spectator to create a critical, feminist twist on Surrealist exhibitionary practices. More pointedly, Loy's treatment of her fictional protagonist

Mrs. Jones, based on her own experience as Levy's agent, allowed her to explore the difficulty of being slotted into the category of spectator, collector, or "patroness" rather than painter or writer, and to subtly merge these often oppositional roles. Like Loy, Mrs. Jones is an artist and writer who arranges not only to serve as the artist's agent, but also to write his biography (32). She meets Insel on the "unexplored frontiers of consciousness" (159) and finds him to be a "congenital surrealist" (63) who "had no need to portray. His pictures grew, out of him, seeding through the inter-atomic spaces in his digital substance to urge tenacious roots into a plane surface" (103). Insel possesses a "conjurative power of projecting images" (53) but Jones learns that "he suffered [...] from the incredible handicap of only being able to *mature* in the imagination of another. His empty obsession somehow taking form in obsessing the furnished mind of a spectator" (156). Mrs. Jones must also supply the literal furnishings for Insel's art: while she sometimes feels that Insel "has found a short cut to consummation in defiance of the concrete. That he is filling the galleries of the increate" (125), at other times she sees him in her role as gallery agent as a blocked artist whom she must urge to finish work for New York. In Mrs. Jones words, her job is "feeding a cagey genius in the hope of production" (74).

To elicit that production, Mrs. Jones allows the destitute Insel to stay in her apartment, and undertakes housework that distracts her from her own art, a situation that sheds light on Loy's dual role as gallery agent and artist. She comments that "the effort to concentrate on something in which one takes no interest [...] is the major degradation of women" (39). In preparation for Insel's stay, Jones stuffs her own "scribbles" into a "corpse-like sack" which she locks in a room (40), an allusion to Man Ray's *Enigma of Isidore Ducasse* (1920), a sewing machine wrapped and tied up in an army blanket. Loy transforms Man Ray's homage to Lautréamont's famous description of beauty as "the chance meeting on a dissecting table of a sewing machine and an umbrella" through the gendered economic realities that shaped women's engagement with Surrealism: Mrs. Jones sews to support herself, and in this instance stitches her own art into a sack to make room for Insel's.

As a collector and spectator of Insel's projected images, Mrs. Jones not only allows Insel to "mature in [her] imagination," but in writing down her diverse encounters with him and his art, creates her own visionary gallery of Surrealism, rendering spectatorship an artistic, transformative, and feminist act. The novel offers itself as a hybrid exhibition, one that draws on Oelze's Surrealist ideals and techniques while subjecting them to feminist critique, gothic humor, and an American popular culture keen for Dalí-style "extravagant [...] publicities" (27). Loy often employs popular, commercial contexts of display in her portrayals of Insel, as a means of undercutting his spiritual, ascetic pretensions: Mrs. Jones describes Insel as an exhibit in a wax museum, as the walking-dead star of a horror film, as an actor "playing" Kafka to eke out his meager living, and as a Broadway showman. As the novel unfolds, Jones rather than Insel proves to be the master of Surrealism's "magical" techniques in her Surrealist descriptions of Insel and Paris, even as she skeptically debunks his "black magic" as showmanship, trickery, and the possible effect of morphine addiction.[82]

Mrs. Jones's visit to Insel's studio exemplifies her feminist curation of Insel's Surrealist art.[83] Insel shows Jones his painting *Die Irma*, which resembles Oelze's *Frieda*, a work inspired by a character in Kafka's unfinished novel *The Castle* (see Fig. 4.11).[84] Mrs. Jones implies that *Die Irma* is Insel: her eyes are "flat disks of smoked mirror" that reflect her "creator" (131), and she has "male hands that hardly made a pair" (132). Mrs. Jones records the scene thus:

> "Die Irma," he repeated lovingly to introduce her to me, and the magnetic bond uniting her painted body to his emaciated stature—as if she were of an ectoplasm proceeding from him—was so apparent one felt as if one were surprising an insane liaison at almost too intimate a moment. (131)

Mrs. Jones raises up the sexual subtext to Insel's painting when she observes, "He hung over Die Irma like a tall insect and outside the window in the rotten rose of an asphyxiated sunset the skeleton phallus of the Eiffel Tower reared in the distance as slim as himself" (132). Creating her own surrealist painting in this description, Mrs. Jones reveals the phallic aggression expressed by Insel towards his female muse and echoed by the culture through its revered symbols. Mrs. Jones objects to Insel's use of the female form as a thinly veiled medium for his own narcissistic preoccupations; *Die Irma* is mere "material" for Insel's self-expression, the

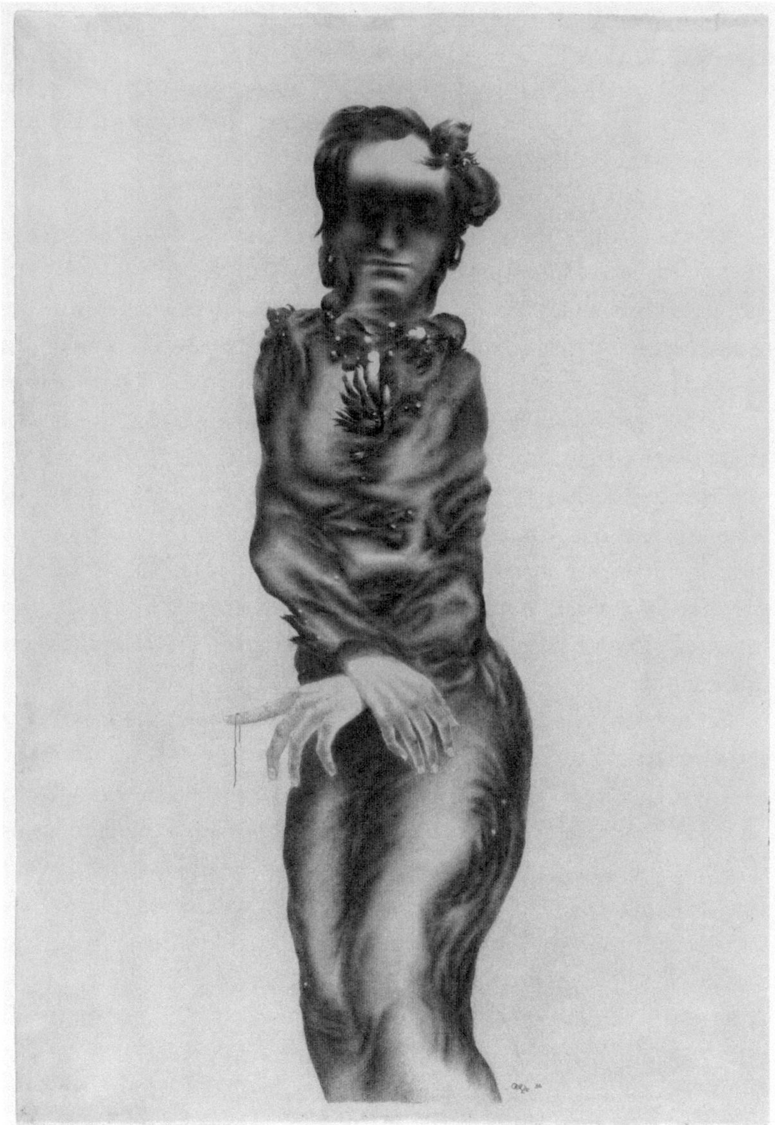

Figure 4.11. Richard Oelze, *Frieda*, 1936. Conté crayon on paper, 24⅞ × 17¼ in. (63.2 × 43.8 cm).

"bride" a projection of the "bachelor," just as Insel feeds parasitically off of female prostitutes and patrons. She comments, "You have formed her of pus. Her body has already melted," adding, "I don't care for it" (132–33). It is when Insel grows angry and threatens to destroy the painting that she quips ironically, "What does my opinion matter? *I'm* not the museum" (133).

By articulating the sexual subtext of Insel's portrait, Mrs. Jones refuses *Die Irma*'s role as a silent, pliable female muse. This refusal is echoed in the plot when Mrs. Jones objects to Oelze's exploitation of Black prostitutes (88–90), and criticizes his "maniac sadism" expressed in the "pounding tread of the infuriated male" (136). As Mrs. Jones refuses the role of muse or "bride," Insel behaves like an "alienated husband" (167) and tries to strangle her, to force her to play the part he has assigned her: to "give in—obsessed by my beauty—having no hope—endlessly resigned" (158). Insel is impotent as both a man and artist, Mrs. Jones implies, and thus vampirically draws his power from the female form; when Insel comments that "*Die Irma* is wet," implying that he has just finished the painting, Mrs. Jones fully intends the double meaning in her reply: "She isn't, she's bone dry. I felt her" (133–34).

Economically bound to the role of agent and spectator, Jones merges these roles with those of creator and curator of her own *textual* collection. Loy comments on the novel's curatorial composition through Mrs. Jones: although Mrs. Jones risked a paralyzing "disintegration" and "dematerialization" akin to that of Insel (150–51), by the novel's end she "had reached the stage [...] for creation, when all that one has *collected* rolls out with the facility of the *song of a bird*" (177; italics added). In contrast, Insel remains blocked and fragmented, and risks remaining uncollected: in her visit to Insel's studio to see *Die Irma*, Mrs. Jones advises Insel to "pull yourself together [...] you've got to finish this for the museum" (134).

Oelze claimed in a letter to Alfred Barr, director of the MoMA, that he had destroyed the painting Frieda, but a charcoal sketch (1936)—likely mailed by Loy—was included in Barr's 1937 *Fantastic Art, Dada, Surrealism* exhibition, along with Oelze's painting *Daily Torments* (1934).[85] Burke notes that when Oelze moved to Switzerland in October 1936, his paintings were shipped to Julien Levy; Oelze returned to Germany in 1938 where he served in the war, was imprisoned, and released in 1945

("Loy-alism" 74, 79). The Oelze works that were exhibited as part of the 1936–7 *Fantastic Art, Dada, Surrealism* exhibition, an exhibition crucial to the history of Surrealism in the United States, remain in the Museum of Modern Art collection.

While Oelze's paintings were exhibited at MoMA and are housed in its permanent collection, Loy's work was until recently effectively erased from the history of Surrealism. The novel *Insel* transforms Mrs. Jones's "I'm not the museum" into a badge of honor, a sign of her creation of independent en dehors garde work shaped by progressive attitudes on feminism, gender, and sexuality, that critically absorbs but is not obligated to Surrealism; yet Loy's self-curated collection exists in ironic tension with official archives, museums, and publishing houses. Despite attempts to interest James Laughlin in publishing *Insel* in 1938 and again in the 1950s and early 1960s, Loy's novel would remain unpublished until Elizabeth Arnold's 1991 edition.[86] Many of Loy's paintings from the Paris era were largely unknown until the 2023 exhibition at the Bowdoin Art Museum, despite her efforts to collect and exhibit them; Jennifer Gross records Loy's efforts through Duchamp and friends in England to try to exhibit and sell her work there in the early 1930s ("Truant," MLSII 81). Nevertheless, Loy attempted to "include" and curate these works in *Insel*, writing them into history and into her personal archive.[87] Just as Loy hung Oelze's paintings in her apartment alongside her own works, in *Insel* she would also "exhibit" works that had been sold (lamps) or overlooked (paintings) alongside her textual "framing" of Oelze's art.

For example, photos taken by Maurice Poplin housed with Carolyn Burke's papers at the Beinecke (labeled "Julien Levy Gallery 1933"), document a sequence of sixteen paintings, not exhibited in Loy's 1933 exhibition at the Levy Gallery, but carefully numbered and titled by Loy, suggesting a planned exhibition. Loy may have shown or sent the Poplin photos to Julien Levy as possible paintings to include in the 1933 exhibition, or they may have been part of a planned second exhibition at the Levy Gallery that never came to fruition.[88] While much about these unexhibited paintings remains unknown, *Insel* offers some clues, particularly to the *Drift of Chaos* series. In one scene, Insel spots "some photographs of paintings lying on the table" in Mrs. Jones's apartment, and asks her,

"Whose pictures are these? [...] Who could have done these?" adding, "You are an extraordinarily gifted woman." Mrs. Jones responds:

> "Those" are my "last exhibition" cancelled the moment the dealer set eyes on them [...] I felt, if I were to go back, begin a universe all over again, forget all form I am familiar with, evoking a chaos from which I could draw forth incipient form, that at last the female brain might achieve an act of creation. (37)

Mrs. Jones adds, "I did not know this as yet, but the man seated before me holding a photo in his somewhat invalid hand had done this very thing—visualized the mists of chaos curdling into shape. But with a *male difference*" (*Insel* 37).

Loy may refer in this passage to the set of Poplin photos of her paintings. Moreover, in a number of scenes in the novel, Loy appears to describe some of the *Drift of Chaos* paintings depicted in the photographs. For instance, in one passage Loy evokes the painting *Drift of Chaos IV: Oyster Woman* (photographed by Poplin), satirizing erotic ideals of women underpinning classical mythology and Surrealist art (see Fig. 4.12). In this scene, Loy transforms Mrs. Jones's apartment into an "irreal aquarium" and the sleeping Insel into "a creature of the deep sea" through her description of the "half-light softly bursting the dark" (109), a description, as discussed above, alluding to her lamp designs. As Loy describes Mrs. Jones, her language becomes painterly:

> Because I found the place somewhat chilly when sunless—I had thrown a great white blanket over my thin dress. [...] Fairly inflexible—it curved around me loosely, encaving me—its stiff corner trailing off like a sail.
>
> I sat on the edge of the couch at the feet of that rigid flotsam—in a huge white shell. [...] Somehow, unable to dissolve into mist, and thus too dense to enter a mirage, the nearest I could conform to the arid aquatic was in becoming crustacean. (109–110)

Loy's description of Mrs. Jones resonates with the imagery of her undated (circa 1930s) *Drift of Chaos IV (Oyster Woman)* painting, and both text and painting allude to Botticelli's *Birth of Venus*, which Loy had likely

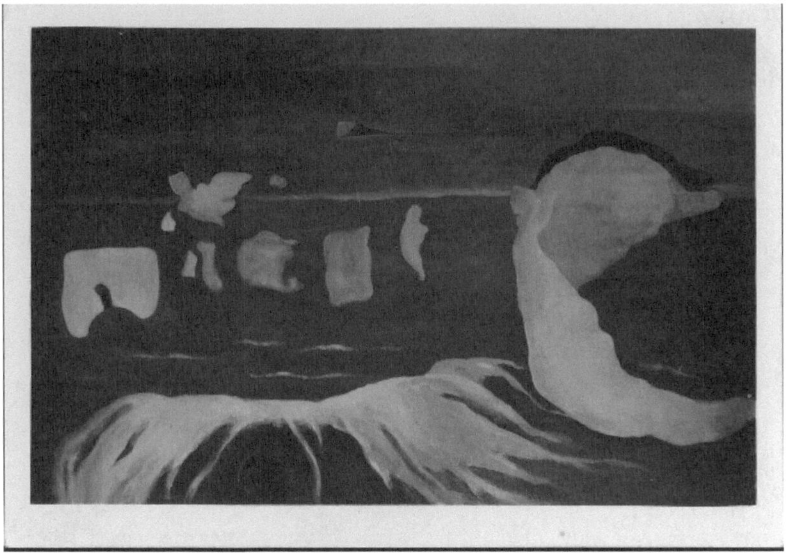

Figure 4.12. Mina Loy, *Drift of Chaos IV, Oyster Woman*.

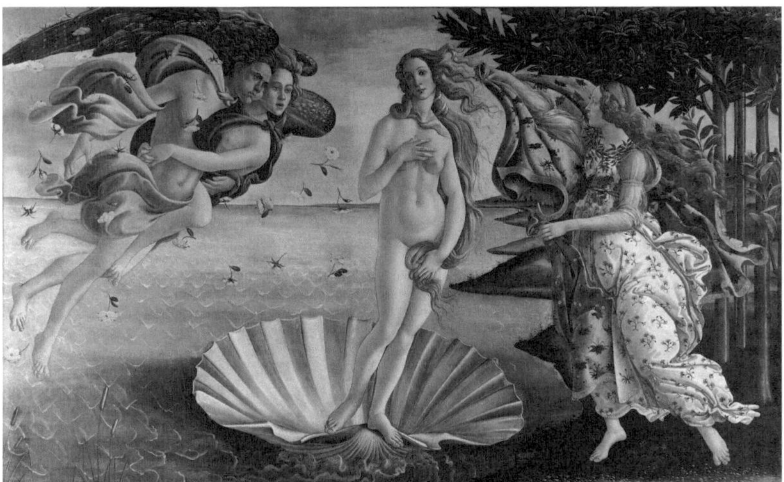

Figure 4.13. Sandro Botticelli, *The Birth of Venus* (1483–85).

viewed in the Uffizi Gallery in Florence (see Figs. 4.12 and 4.13).[89] Venus, the Roman goddess of erotic love, took her shape from sea foam. Loy's painting depicts a woman whose body has been replaced by a white shell, which appears to trail behind her like a sail, echoing her description of Mrs. Jones sitting in a "huge white shell." Floating above the shell, where Botticelli's Venus resides, are white fragments that do not cohere. Mrs. Jones' attempt to "birth" a Surrealist Venus fails: she cannot leave behind her human body to "dissolve into mist," and "becoming crustacean" is all she can do to conform to the "arid aquatic."

The "arid aquatic" refers to Mrs. Jones' apartment transformed by light projected through her artful lampshade into an "irreal aquarium," but figuratively, "arid aquatic" may refer to the cultural "sea" that generated Venus and the erotic ideals of women underpinning both Classical mythology and Surrealism, including works such as Dalí's *Dream of Venus* pavilion (1939). With the word "arid" Loy subjects these ideals to her corrosive irony, as she did in depicting *Die Irma* as "bone dry," and eros as "obsolete" in the fossilized landscape of "Lunar Baedeker." "Becoming crustacean" may reference Loy's *Lobster Boy* object (circa 1930s), her feminist response to Dalí and Surrealist hybridity.

As a self-curated textual gallery and archive, *Insel* extends and comments on Loy's material archive, shining a figurative "lamp" on her overlooked artwork while offering a critical engagement with Surrealist art and the museum-gallery network she served. The importance of Loy's having saved the Poplin photos and the drafts of her novel *Insel* for posterity is clear, yet neither "exhibition" reached a public during Loy's lifetime despite her concerted efforts. Both the novel and the unexhibited paintings constituted semi-visible, en dehors garde collections, and constitute Loy's most sustained engagement with Surrealist themes and techniques. Loy, not Oelze, presents us with a gallery of the "increate" (*Insel* 125), which in its very marginality to the Surrealist movement and its bid to posterity through exhibitions and publications, advances the claim that avant-garde ideals were most powerfully realized on these en dehors garde margins, in "museums without walls."[90] An approach to *Insel* as textual gallery or "imaginary museum" reveals the layered, dynamic understanding of exhibitions Loy developed in Paris, demonstrating that her visual art and designs need to be read alongside and in conversation with *Insel* and her other writing of the era, and explored as dislocating lenses onto the material spaces in which she created, curated, and exhibited her art.

IV. NEW YORK'S SURREAL SCENE (1936–1953): "LUNAR BAEDEKER," REDUX

When Hitler curtailed the citizenship and rights of Jews through the passage of the Nuremberg Laws (September 1935) and reoccupied the Rhineland in spring 1936, Julien and Joella Levy became increasingly concerned about Mina Loy and her daughter Fabienne, given Loy's partial Jewish heritage. In December 1935, Loy sent Fabienne to New York to live with Joella and Julien (Burke, *Becoming* 386), and followed herself in late 1936. She would live in New York until 1953, when she moved to join Joella and Fabienne and their families in Aspen, Colorado. Loy would remain in Aspen until her death in 1966.

Although Loy had served as the Levy Gallery's Paris agent, when she arrived in New York in 1936 she found that the gallery didn't need her help, a change in role that was exacerbated by Julien's and Joella's separation in 1938. Despite her earlier time in New York (1916–17, 1920–21), Loy felt (in her words) like "just another refugee" who had found herself "in a strange country" (Burke, *Becoming* 387, 389): fifty-four years old and dependent on her daughters' financial help and care, Loy's youthful days in Greenwich village were a distant memory.

But Loy was not alone in making this journey: many artists and writers associated with the European avant-garde relocated to New York during World War Two.[91] A transatlantic Surrealist scene flourished at Julien Levy's and Peggy Guggenheim's galleries, and before long, a number of small galleries and little magazines dedicated to the work of the Surrealists in exile had emerged. While Surrealism had exerted a powerful influence on American literary and artistic culture since the early 1920s, through little magazine publications, exhibitions, and Levy's Surrealist-centered gallery, the presence of many European Surrealists in New York during World War Two energized the American avant-garde, as poets and artists absorbed and adapted Surrealism.

Mina Loy's continued engagement with the avant-garde while living in New York is an important yet neglected part of this history. Scholars have emphasized Loy's poverty, loneliness, and alienation in New York in the 1940s and early 1950s, and at times have used Loy's biography to support a reading of her late work as an epitaph to or commentary on the failure of an earlier European avant-garde moment and the failure of her own career. But this era was a vital one for Loy, involving an active working through of ideas and techniques that she had absorbed from the Futurists in Florence and from Dada and Surrealism in New York and Paris. Just as Futurism shaped her work well beyond her time in Florence, Loy's critical transformations of Dada and Surrealism did not end with her move to New York in 1936, as she revisited earlier avant-garde ideas and methods to navigate moving forward. In each stage of her career Loy continued to experiment and innovate: navigating her years in New York (1937–53) challenges conventional histories of the avant-garde and invites us to come up with fuller, more complex accounts of women's en dehors garde contributions to this history.

Despite her reclusiveness, Loy remained connected to other important artists, poets, and gallery owners in New York in the 1940s and 1950s, resulting in the Bodley Gallery exhibition of her "constructions" in 1959 and in the publication of her second poetic collection, *Lunar Baedeker & Time-Tables* by Jonathan Williams's Jargon Press in 1958. These two events echoed and amplified the verbal-visual, interdisciplinary aesthetics of Loy's late work. While living in New York, Loy published in Charles Henri Ford's Surrealist-oriented magazine *View* in 1942 and 1945, helped Breton publish Arther Cravan's previously unpublished "Notes" in *VVV* (no. 1, June 1942; no. 2–3, March 1943), and published new poems in *Accent*, *New Directions*, *Partisan Review*, and *Between Worlds* (Burke, *Becoming* 401–02; Januzzi, "Bibliography" 524–26). Loy also established or maintained important relationships with figures who, like Loy, were involved in the reception and transformation of Surrealism in the United States, including Joseph Cornell, Clarence John Laughlin, Julien Levy, Berenice Abbott, Frances Steloff, Charles Henri Ford, James Laughlin, Kenneth Rexroth, Marcel Duchamp, Peggy Guggenheim, Djuna Barnes, David Mann, Gilbert Neiman, Kenneth Rexroth, Henry Miller, and Jonathan Williams, among others (Burke, *Becoming* 359–424; Conover LLB96 207–18; Januzzi, "Bibliography"). In New York, Loy was marginalized but not forgotten: she had begun to establish the reputation and forge the relationships that would result in a small but influential group of admirers and her growing importance to a postwar, transatlantic avant-garde.

In Paris, Loy had developed a feminist perspective on Surrealist artwork and the Surrealist movement through her paintings, lamps, objects, poetry, and autobiographical fiction. Her critical framing of Surrealism in works such as *Surreal Scene* and *Insel* countered Surrealism's dominant narratives, gendered tropes, and claims to urban space, using the dislocating light of the moon, dreams, and the subconscious superimposed on the rationally mapped city to illuminate liminal spaces and alternative exhibitions omitted alike from the Paris Baedeker and from the galleries, cafés, and studios frequented by the avant-garde. In New York, Loy extended her interest in the "museum without walls" while she deepened her criticism of those who "are looking for [their] canons of beauty in some sort of frame or glass case of tradition" (LLB82 297–98). Through rapport with the American artist Joseph Cornell, Loy developed her interest in the Surrealist found object and Surrealist poetics, shaped by Lower Manhattan's geography and the realities of the homeless men and women Loy encountered there. Rejecting the "museums of the moon" and the official Baedeker guides that curated a narrow slice of art and culture, she instead embraced the "flux of life" (LLB82 297–98) in the streets, exploring an altered, increasingly documentary vision of everyday people and scenes and inviting critical reflection on how a culture's "canons of beauty" are formed.

Exhibit 7
"On Third Avenue" (1942) and "Lunar Baedeker" (1923)

In conversation with the "poetic baedekers" she had created by navigating Futurist aesthetics and the streets of Florence (see chapter 2), Loy's late work suggests an ongoing engagement with her previous avant-garde affiliations, even as she navigated a new urban setting. More specifically, since the Baedeker served as a key motif for Loy's geographical and aesthetic travels in both Paris and New York, it's possible to chart how Loy's 1936 move to New York transformed her engagement with Surrealist aesthetics through her return to and recasting of her 1923 poem "Lunar Baedeker." While Loy's 1923 poem mapped her en dehors garde imagination, the poetic ability to critically filter and transform the real, her 1942 poem "On Third Avenue" revisits and revises the themes and urban imagery of "Lunar Baedeker," providing a measure of the aesthetic and personal distance Loy had traveled from Paris to New York. "Lunar Baedeker" uses the moon to displace, distort, and critically transform Loy's experience of European cities including Paris, New York, Berlin (and their avant-gardes); in contrast, her New York Baedekers such as "On Third Avenue" are located precisely and concretely in Lower Manhattan, employing a documentary lens to locate moments of the unreal and surreal erupting from ordinary life.[92]

Loy would grapple with themes of anonymity, invisibility, and marginality in her 1940s and 1950s poems, assemblages, and collages. Relevant to her own status as an aging female artist, these themes would allow her to explore her urban environment and the contradictions of American democracy in new and compelling ways. Loy became a US citizen in 1946, and due to this formal identification with the United States, she perhaps felt the ideals and pitfalls of American democracy all the more keenly. The poet who had praised Stein for her democratic experiments as an "all-American pioneer," and who had aligned free verse with American democratic experiment in her April 1925 essay "Modern Poetry," would in later decades consider those who were marginalized or expendable in democracy, building poems and artwork from the refuse of postwar American culture.

"On Third Avenue" begins with a statement in quotations: "'You should have disappeared years ago'—" The speaker is not identified, and neither is the "you," but several possibilities emerge as the poem unfolds:

> so disappear
> on Third Avenue
> to share the heedless incognito
>
> of shuffling shadow-bodies
> animate with frustration (LLB96 109)

The moral judgment implied in the quoted phrase "*should have* disappeared" suggests that the "you" persists against all expectation, and despite the disapproval of the first line's speaker. The poem's speaker, possibly distinct from the speaker of the first quoted line, responds: "so disappear." The "you," then, may variously refer to the poet, to one of the many "shuffling shadow-bodies" on Third Avenue, to one of the faceless urban crowd, or given the poem's subsequent imagery, to one of the impoverished, homeless men and women in Lower Manhattan who would take center stage in "Hot Cross Bum" and "Chiffon Velours."

Loy typed and handwrote many drafts of this poem, which are housed in the Beinecke Library's Mina Loy collection. These drafts deserve careful study, with an early draft of the poem titled "Gloria Populi" revealing that the "you" may refer to the poet herself (see Fig. 4.14).

The draft begins:

> Refuse mould
> of offspring
> "you should have disappeared years ago"
> For the alleviation of the Beloved
>
> I disappear—
> Amid shuffling shadow bodies
> Animate with frustration,
> unto death

This draft suggests that the source of the opening quoted line is the poet's disapproving offspring, and that the "you" is the poet, who responds, "I disappear— / Amid shuffling shadow bodies." While this draft reveals a personal conflict in the poem's opening lines, tellingly Loy later revised the opening lines to obfuscate the quotation's source as her "offspring" and the "you" as herself.

Changing "I disappear" to "so disappear" in later drafts allows the "you" to refer both to the poet and to any of the nameless "shadow-bodies" on Third Avenue.[93] In turn, this change permits readers to imagine many possible speakers for the opening quoted line: the speaker could be Loy's children; Loy herself (perhaps articulating a fear of how others perceive

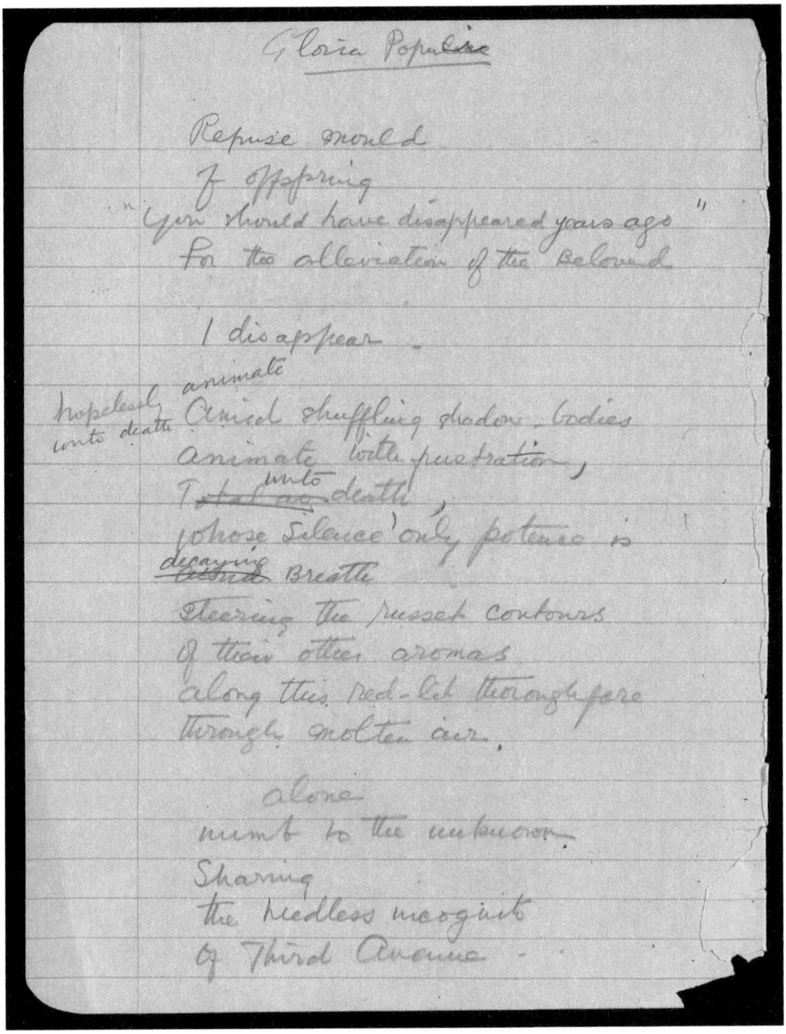

Figure 4.14. Draft page, "On Third Avenue," 1942.

her, as a relic of an older modernist moment); any surprised or disapproving spectator; the disapproving voice of American society that judges the homeless for their failure to meet ideals of success, productivity, and progress; and so forth. Loy's choice to change the line from "I disappear" to "so disappear" as she revised the poem signals that she moved outwards from the particulars of her own situation in order to enter and explore society's "refused" population. This change also transforms a condition suffered into an imperative command, empowering the speaker even as it points to her lack of visibility.

If we read "On Third Avenue" as a self-reflexive investigation of a poetics grounded in an actual versus a lunar street, the poem constitutes Loy's answer to the opening judgment—"you should have disappeared years ago"—by enacting a new kind of poetry that emerges when the poet disappears to share "the heedless incognito // of shuffling shadow-bodies" (LLB96 109). In sharing the "heedless incognito" of Lower Manhattan's street population in this and other poems, Loy's poetic speakers explore the trials of everyday survival in the city, as well as moments of what Breton called the Surrealist "marvellous," as experienced by its poorest residents. Rather than use the lunar landscape to dislocate and transfigure the real, as in "Lunar Baedeker," in "On Third Avenue" Loy locates what poet Elizabeth Bishop would call a "surrealism of everyday life" in urban streets rendered with documentary precision (*Poems, Prose* 860–61).

Loy described the city in the 1923 "Lunar Baedeker" as a "Necropolis" from the ancient Greek "city of the dead, cemetery" (OED). As such, it comes into focus through visible absences, by the signs of what was once present ("eros obsolete"), a city as seen in "a flock of dreams," or dark negatives held up to the light. As discussed above, "Lunar Baedeker" provides an imagined, poetic "tour" of the moon, while alluding to and transforming actual cities Loy had navigated, including New York and Paris: the poem creates its own Baedeker, at once an ironic guide to human pretensions to knowledge and immortality embodied by the "museums of the moon" and the guidebooks that curate its cultural treasures, and a map to new, feminist ways of seeing this landscape.

Loy conducts a similar tour in "On Third Avenue," but bodies are not absent but all too present, "animate with frustration," vessels of suffering and decay. Rather than moving through the "eye-white sky-light / white-light district / of lunar lusts" lit by "Stellectric signs" (LLB96 81), these shadow-bodies move "through the monstrous air / of this red-lit thoroughfare," while

> Here and there
> saturnine

neon-signs
set afire
a feature
on their hueless overcast
of down-cast countenances. (LLB96 109)

This dark landscape lit by a fiery neon red connotes not the "red-light district" but the agonies of hell.

While "Lunar Baedeker" invokes dreams and cocaine as agents of vision, and harnesses natural and celestial sources of illumination ("Lucifer" the morning star; "infusoria," microscopic organisms found in decaying organic matter; "Stellectric signs"), "On Third Avenue" limits itself to human sight and the man-made illumination of "neon signs." This is what Walter Benjamin in his discussion of Surrealism termed "profane illumination," a "materialistic, anthropological inspiration," which he contrasted to "religious ecstasies or the ecstasies of drugs" (*Reflections* 179). Although the "shadow-bodies" are materially present, they seem to literally "disappear" into their dark environment, hovering on the edge of visibility. Unable or unwilling to meet the eyes of others, the impoverished figures remain faceless, abstract rather than particularized, a "feature" visible only "here and there" as the neon catches it. Or as Benjamin stated, "no face is surrealistic in the same degree as the true face of a city" (*Reflections* 182), and Loy's poem allows us to glimpse that face.

Loy uses the language of art (sculpture and cinema) in her depiction of these figures: even as they refuse to meet the speaker's eyes, they invite the poet's transformative vision:

For their ornateness
Time, the contortive tailor,
on and off,
clowned with sweat-sculptured cloth,
to press
upon the irreparable dummies
an eerie undress
of mummies
half unwound. (LLB96 109–10)

Likening the vagrants to tailors' dummies, Loy reflects with irony on how time and sweat resulting from the effort to live on the urban street, "sculpt" the clothing of the homeless, an effect she would echo in the sculpted fabric she used to depict the bodies of the homeless in assemblages such as "Communal Cot" (1949). Susan Dunn suggests that the poem depicts the "salvages of the garment industry" in Lower Manhattan, and alludes to its sweatshops ("Fashion Victims"). This sculpture is an "art" not just found in but fashioned by living in the street. The final image of mummies half unwound evokes a gothic scene from a horror film, the undead "shuffling" down the streets of Lower Manhattan and literally disappearing as they fall apart.[94]

Loy explicitly divides the poem into two halves, numbering the first and second sections. While the first section of the poem depicts the liminal state that results from the injunction "so disappear," the second section reflects on what can be seen and gained through the speaker's "disappearance" into the shadow-bodies of Third Avenue. The speaker twice begins, "Such are the compensations of poverty, / to see——-" and as Linda Kinnahan argues, the descriptions of the urban scenes that follow this refrain are akin to photographic snapshots (*Mina Loy, Twentieth-Century Photography* 141), arrested moments in the dynamic, changing "museum" of the street. Loy's speaker finds aesthetic value in objects and scenes which are human, mutable, and fleeting, the antithesis of the "museums of the moon":

> Like an electric fungus
> sprung from its own effulgence
> of intercircled jewellery
> reflected on the pavement,
>
> like a reliquary sedan-chair,
> out of a legend, dumped there,
>
> before a ten-cent Cinema,
>
> a sugar-coated box-office
> enjail a Goddess

aglitter, in her runt of a tower,
with ritual claustrophobia. (LLB96 110)

Loy describes a cinema box office in a series of similes that transform it into an "electric fungus / spring from its own effulgence," into a "reliquary sedan-chair, / out of a legend," and finally, into a tower that imprisons a goddess, the cinema attendant. Through these similes, superimposed upon the actual box office, Loy draws attention to the incongruity of the gritty street and its realism juxtaposed with the "sugar-coated box-office" and the "ten-cent" fantasies it peddles. The box office, like the poem, mediates reality and unreality.[95]

In contrast to escapist cinema, however, Loy's mini-surrealist film constructed from this sequence of juxtaposed images allows the street to generate its own cinema, redolent with irony, an unfolding space for chance visions:

Such are compensations of poverty,
to see——

Transient in the dust,
the brilliancy
of a trolley
loaded with luminous busts;

lovely in anonymity
they vanish
with the mirage
of their passage. (LLB96 110)

The "luminous busts" connote the grandeur and memorializing function of the museum, yet they are located anomalously in a trolley, the mystery of this juxtaposition left unexplained. Tara Prescott suggests that Loy may describe the literal movement of busts in a trolley, or more abstractly, "The upper halves of commuters, seen through trolley windows" on the Third Avenue El train (182, 203). The beauty of this scene lies not only in the juxtaposition of busts and trolley but in their movement and subsequent vanishing, emphasized by the haunting half-rhyme of "mirage" and "passage." The word "mirage" embodies the effect of the trolley's appearance and disappearance; a "mirage" refers to a visual illusion generated by atmospheric conditions. At stake in the mirage is the Surrealist relationship between the real and the unreal, everyday life and art: attuned to found juxtapositions, the poet becomes a conduit for the Surrealist "marvellous," discovered on the city sidewalks.

In poems such as "Ephemerid" (LLB96 116–18), Loy is critical of her own tendency to transform the ordinary, factual events of the street into the unreal or fantastical, and many of her poems from this time probe the ethics of the poet's use of her found images, subjects, and materials. As Kinnahan argues, these ethical questions were central to the "Surrealist documentary" project that compelled Loy and photographers including Berenice Abbott, a friend of Loy's from her time in Greenwich Village and Paris.[96] Kinnahan emphasizes that Loy's engagement with Surrealist documentary is a vitally important feature of her 1940s and early 1950s New York poetry and art, richly read alongside the photographs of Berenice Abbott, Clarence John Laughlin, and others:

> A cluster of Loy's late poems, written primarily during the 1940s and early 1950s while living in New York and focusing on the Bowery streets, fall outside of the oppositions between social art and experimental art, weaving together a form of urban documentary with inflections of Surrealist and Dadaist modes. [...] In their attention to social issues of modern poverty, Loy's Bowery poems stand in interesting parallel and relation to the "documentary impulse" of the 1930s and its reliance upon the camera as a visual tool of social responsibility—a role for the camera that brought its own history to the documentary 1930s. (*Mina Loy, Twentieth-Century Photography* 124)

Adapting Surrealist techniques through a documentary lens, Loy would reveal and ironize the features of postwar society that rendered democratic freedoms questionable; for instance, in an ethical adaptation of the Surrealist image, Loy would juxtapose "penury / with dream" ("Ephemerid" LLB96 118). Loy's documentary turn would also alter the materials she used in her poetry and art; while Loy had frequented the Paris flea markets, purchasing cast-off items to use for her lamps, objects, and other designs, in New York, she would use trash she picked up while walking the streets for her "constructions."

At mid-century, the Bowery neighborhood appeared to Loy to be distinctly separated from the rest of the city, as a trash-like "container" for the city's "refused" population. Like an ironic showman or tourist guide, Loy opens a "curtain" on her (1950) poetic tour of the Bowery, "Hot Cross Bum," with a nod to the area's rich nineteenth-century theatrical history, and to its subsequent "celebrated degeneration" (Federal Writers Project 119):

> Beyond a hell-vermilion
> curtain of neon
> lies the Bowery (LLB96 133)

The Federal Writers Project *New York City Guide* (1939) described the Bowery as "fixed [...] forever in the Nation's consciousness as a place of unspeakable corruption":

> The Bowery today is chiefly given over to pawnshops, restaurant equipment houses, beer saloons, and miscellaneous small retail shops. Here flophouses offer a bug-infested bed in an unventilated pigeonhole for twenty-five cents a night, restaurants serve ham and eggs for ten cents, and students in barber "colleges" cut hair for fifteen cents. Thousands of the nation's unemployed drift to this section and may be seen sleeping in all-night restaurants, in doorways, and on loading platforms, furtively begging, or waiting with hopeless faces for some bread line or free lodging house to open. No agency, at present (1939), provides adequate food, shelter, and clothing for these wanderers. Missions furnish food and lodging for a few, and try by sermon and song to touch the souls of the down-and-outers and the sympathies of generous tourists. (120)[97]

As a place where the homeless and unemployed congregated, the Bowery had become not only the city's "trash can" but a perverse tourist site or exhibition, a fact Loy acknowledges in "Hot Cross Bum":

> for your loafing
> is the fashion

conditional compassion:
appreciation
of your publicity value
to the Bowery (LLB96 137)

Excavating the forces that shape the Bowery and the predicament of the homeless, Loy's late work challenges the "conditional compassion" of the tourist's gaze and probes the "bums'" status as unwitting "actors" in a public spectacle.

Trash—and its removal—served as a central metaphor and literal material for Mina Loy's Bowery Baedekers (poetry and visual art), as a passage from "Hot Cross Bum" makes clear:

Collecting refuse more profuse than man
the City's circulatory
sanitary apostles
a-leap to ash-cans
apply their profane ritual
to offal

Dust to dust

Even a putrescent Galaxy
could not be left where it lay
to disgust

Scrapped are remains
empty cans remain. (LLB96 142–43)

In their function as receptacles that separate ephemeral trash from the built environment, empty "ash-cans" are inverted, street analogs of "Lunar Baedeker"'s "museums of the moon": while the museum confers value, significance, and even "immortality," displaying and preserving artworks deemed worthy, empty ash cans embody the cultural effort to erase what threatens society's dominant functions and values. "Lunar Baedeker"'s "ecstatic dust / and ashes" become an all-too-human, too-mortal ("dust to dust") "putrescent Galaxy" that generates "disgust."[98] With a nod to Duchamp's 1917 *Fountain* (urinal), and to her Futurist aphorisms in which she depicted the "mechanical re-actions of the subconsciousness" as "that rubbish heap of race-tradition—" (LLB96 152), Loy draws attention to "ash-cans" as mechanically routing the "circulatory" *processes* of moral and aesthetic hygiene she witnessed on the streets of Lower Manhattan. Loy depicts the ash cans as metaphorical "sanitary apostles," "cleansing" the city of bodily "offal" (awful) by enclosing their digestive function and the city's "remains." Embedding critical commentary in her framing of these found, street "readymades," Loy maps in her Bowery poetry and artwork an alternative role and space for art, that of the en dehors garde. Notably "en dehors" can refer to "outside" as in "en plein air," connoting those who lived outside on the street (see Fig. 4.15).

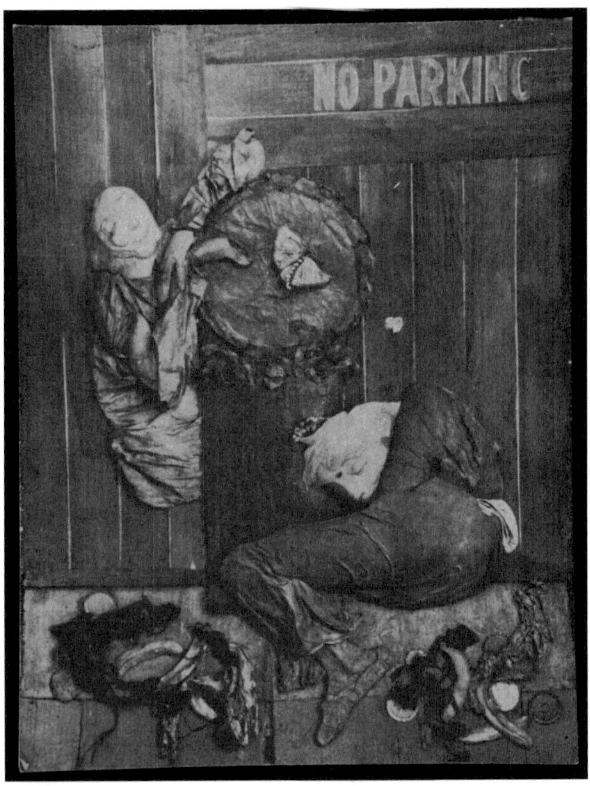

Figure 4.15. Mina Loy, *No Parking*. Cover of exhibition announcement, Mina Loy "Constructions," Bodley Gallery, 14–25 Apr. 1959.

While living in Lower Manhattan, Loy created a remarkable series of constructions inspired by the homeless men and women she encountered on the Bowery, assembled from the trash she collected, developing what Kinnahan calls a "personal aesthetics of scavenging" (*Mina Loy, Twentieth-Century Photography 134*) that embedded commentary in the reuse of refuse. Burke suggests a critical engagement with the avant-garde (specifically Picasso, Duchamp, and Cornell) at work in Loy's choice to use actual trash and other found material to create these assemblages, observing that "Mina brought to her shabby materials an acute sense of the cost involved for those who searched the garbage cans: rather than posing as outsiders, as the avant-garde had done, they actually lived at the bottom of the heap" (*Becoming* 420). Loy called the series of assemblages she made "Refusées," which Burke describes as a "punning blend of *refuse*, *Refusés*, and *refugees*, which summed up her long itinerary from West Hampstead to the Bowery" (420). Amy Elkins has discovered and published Berenice Abbott's photographs of a number of Loy's constructions as they were displayed in her Stanton Street apartment, including three previously unseen; as in Paris, Loy treated her New York apartment as a studio-gallery, with Abbott's photos the only surviving documentation of several works and Loy's curation of them.[99]

Sensitive to the experience of poverty, anonymity, and neglect, Loy was able to bring to the en dehors garde position of "outsiderdom" a lived sense of "the cost involved." While anonymity was not simply Loy's choice at this time, in its guise Loy deepened and transformed her experimental project in "Lunar Baedeker" (1923) by adapting it to the Bowery, reflecting on the suffering and resilience of those who live outside "the museums of the moon." More pointedly, "On Third Avenue" brings to fruition the democratic understanding of modernism that Loy had first articulated in Paris in her 1924 appreciation of Gertrude Stein and which she would develop in conversation with Joseph Cornell during her years in New York.

Exhibit 8
Sidewalk Surrealism: Mina Loy and Joseph Cornell

Loy's artistic friendship with "American surrealist" Joseph Cornell provides an important context for her adaptation of Surrealist poetics in New York. Loy and Cornell shared a method influenced by Surrealism but tempered by Christian Science and a skepticism of Surrealism's "black magic." Both used Surrealist techniques centered on collage, juxtaposition, and the interplay between word and image, verbal and visual media. Both located artistic and spiritual meaning in found objects, particularly the neglected or overlooked materials of everyday life. Both were interested in the constellations and in the "museums of the moons," and shared the struggle to express the reality of the "evanescent" through material means. These aesthetic affinities converged in Cornell's museum-like boxes and Loy's interest in "museums without walls," affinities that sustained both artists during the 1940s and 1950s, even as Loy's method and materials diverged from Cornell's due to her ethical, documentary aims. Their ongoing artistic exchanges indicated how an intermedial method based in curation and collage could merge into collaboration, centered on a sequential, layered response of what Loy called "superimposed viewpoints" (LLB82 302).[100]

Thanks to Julien Levy as intermediary, Loy and Cornell had established an aesthetic affinity and collaborative exchange long before they met in person in New York in 1943. Like Loy and Julien Levy, Cornell was a practitioner of Christian Science, which cemented his friendship with Loy. Julien Levy was a literal transatlantic conduit between Loy and Cornell: in 1932 Levy toured the Paris flea markets with Loy, and when he returned to New York, he gave Cornell the antique puzzle boxes and watch parts he had found, which Cornell transformed into small objects and boxes featured in the Levy Gallery (Burke, *Becoming* 379). Levy was likely the person who took and possibly gave Cornell the photograph of Loy's "installation" of found objects atop her Paris apartment mantelpiece. Continuing the transatlantic collaborative exchange, in the 1930s Cornell made two boxes in homage to Loy and Levy. In 1935–36, Cornell sent Loy in Paris a small box (now lost), which she described in *Insel*, and which (according to the semi-autobiographical text) she apparently gave to Richard Oelze before moving to New York:

> "Here," I hailed the will-o'-the-wisp, "after all I will give you the little box." This box he desired, it was black, was a small object by the American surrealist, Joseph Cornell, the delicious head of a girl in slumber afloat with a night light flame on the surface of water in a tumbler, of bits cut from early *Ladies' Journals* (technically in pupilage to Max Ernst) in loveliness, unique in Surrealism—the tidal lines of engraving cooled its static peace. Under the glass lid a slim silver slipper and a silver ball and one of witch's blue came raining down on the gray somnolence when one lifted it up.
>
> I should have preferred to keep it myself had I not suddenly realized she belonged in those idle hands to which the unreal Insel intermittently returned. (*Insel* [1991] 168–69)

Cornell's "little box," sent to Paris and likely given by Loy to Oelze, signified an "American" twist on Surrealism that Loy admired ("in loveliness, unique in Surrealism"). As Loy's narrative *Insel* provided a "textual box" or curatorial frame for Cornell's collaged box, her paintings, created in her Paris apartment and exhibited at the Levy Gallery in 1933, inspired a second box created by Cornell.

Levy exhibited Cornell's work in solo shows and group exhibitions in his gallery from 1932 to 1943. As a gallery regular, Cornell saw Loy's 1933 painting exhibition, and on November 21, 1946, he wrote Loy about the "indelible impressions the sky-blue of your painting left mingled with my canvassing experiences in strange out of the way parts of Long Island and Brooklyn" (qtd. in Burke, *Becoming* 405). His comment indicates that he understood the travel beyond the walls of the gallery that her paintings invited, as he made sense of them "in strange out of the way parts" of the city. Inspired by Loy's poetry and by seeing Loy's sky-blue paintings, Cornell created a second box collage (see Fig. 4.16). *Portrait of Mina Loy* contains a Man Ray photo of Loy in a top hat, inscribed on the back with the phrase "imperious jewelry of the universe," a line from Loy's poem "Apology of Genius," which Levy included as an epigraph to Loy's 1933 Levy Gallery exhibition catalog (Burke, "Loy-alism" 76). Tara Prescott notes that "Cornell assembled several layers of materials, including blue stained glass, a mask cut from a plate illustrating

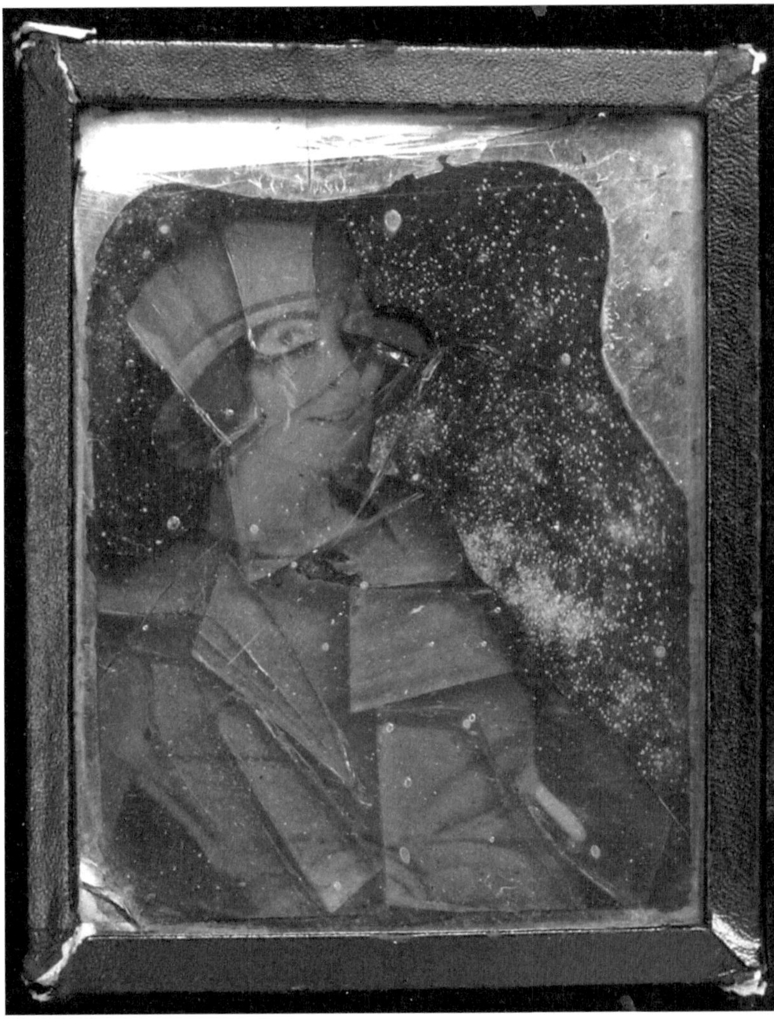

Figure 4.16. Joseph Cornell, *Portrait of Mina Loy*: Box with Man Ray photograph of Mina Loy.

nebulae, glass shards, and a gelatin silver print, to create an homage to Loy and her poetry" (107). In this box, Cornell presents Loy as both muse and poet; as Prescott observes, the glass shards that cover the Man Ray photo of Loy can be moved around, and thus they "fracture the image of Loy's face in a myriad of unsettling, intriguing ways, befitting a poet who constantly challenged and redefined her shifting identities" (107). As a result, "The photographs of this piece of art that exist today are all exceptionally different" (107): in the photo included here, the shard of glass placed over Loy's right eye at once frames her eye but also suggests her transformative vision as a poet.

The movable shards of glass in the Loy box also indicate the dynamic connection between curation, collage, and collaboration, a recurrent theme in the exchanges between Loy and Cornell. As Kinnahan writes, "The portrait's use of a photographic portrait already in existence and produced by a different artist underscores the reproducibility of the photographic image, while insisting upon the artist's vision through performing a collaboration between Man Ray and Cornell" (*Mina Loy, Twentieth-Century Photography* 34). Prescott argues that "Cornell may have been the first of Loy's artist friends to put into practice the same collage techniques that she used and apply them to a work dedicated to her" (107). In *Insel*, Loy curated and added a verbal frame or layer to Cornell's sleeping-girl box. Cornell's art became a muse for and element of Loy's textual museum, just as Loy's image, art, and poetry became a muse for and element of Cornell's box-museum. If Loy functioned in a conventional gendered manner as a kind of "beautiful muse" for Cornell's collage boxes, he also recognized Loy as an artist in his tributes to her paintings and poems, suggesting the permeability of the roles of artist, curator, muse, and audience in their ongoing epistolary dialogue, which as discussed in the introduction, can be considered as a form of sequential collaboration.[101] Loy's and Cornell's ongoing, layered responses to one another's work cemented an artistic affinity defined by a shared interest in collage, intermedial poetics, and museums without walls.

Cornell's understanding of his box-like constructions of collaged elements and found objects as "museums" indicated that he shared Loy's and Duchamp's interest in experimenting with the concept of the museum, even as he exhibited in official venues including the Museum of Modern Art in New York (Rosenbaum, "Elizabeth Bishop" 64–68). Cornell's *Soap Bubble Set* (1936; Fig. 4.17), his first "box" of juxtaposed texts and objects—included by Levy in *Surrealism* and by Alfred Barr, Jr., in MoMA's *Fantastic Art, Dada, Surrealism* exhibition (1936–7)—seems to

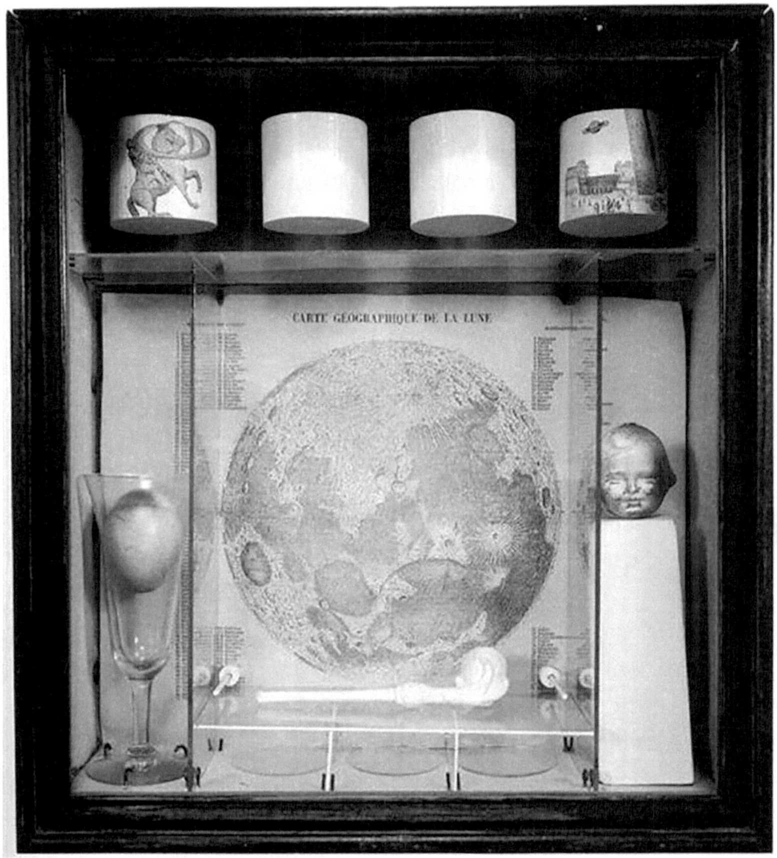

Figure 4.17. Joseph Cornell, Untitled (*Soap Bubble Set*), 1936.

realize through its arrangement of objects Loy's landscape in her 1923 poem "Lunar Baedeker," and even features a "Carte Géographique de la Lune." Cornell's box, like Loy's poem, reflects on and makes room for a "flock of dreams" that emerges from imaginative dislocation and transformation, outside of the "museums of the moon."[102] Just as Loy's poem can be seen as a verbal lens on Duchamp's *Large Glass*, so Cornell's *Soap Bubble Set* can be understood as a realization of Loy's poetic museum in a different medium. Cornell described his method in "Portrait of Ondine" in 1940 as "image-making akin to poetry" (qtd. in Hartigan 75, 83) and understood his arrangement of found texts, images, and objects in his boxes as a form of "poetics" (Hauptman 91) consistent with Surrealist poetics: his boxes can be regarded as poetic structures containing juxtaposed verbal and visual elements that must be brought into poetic relation through the imaginative vision of the spectator.

This 1930s transatlantic artistic and epistolary exchange set the stage for a close artistic friendship when Loy moved to New York, what Loy biographer Burke describes as Loy's "most fulfilling relationship" (*Becoming* 408).[103] Both Loy and Cornell would explore alternatives to the official museums of modernism in their collections and assemblages built from materials found in New York in the 1940s and early 1950s, and their dialogue allowed them to articulate their thoughts about a similar aesthetic vision adapted from Surrealism and indebted to collage.

For instance, on November 21, 1946, Cornell wrote a long letter to Loy about a "lesson in INSPIRATION" (Burke, *Becoming* 408), worth quoting at length. He had noticed the "enseigne" on the side of a smoked-fish delivery truck, depicting "a still life of the various stock—fat pieces of meat surmounted by whole fishes in colours that make one think it might at one time have been a bright decalcomania." He added, "Viewed close up the background sky-blue betrayed beneath the black lettering of a former, less picturesque version of trade-mark, the effect shabby and uninspired like the afternoon."

With a flash of inspiration, Cornell quickly recalled that he had "glimpsed it in MOTION exactly two years ago for the first time on a beautifully clear shining day on a ride on my bicycle" and "That little still life is still traveling in 'chambers of imagery'"; he was moved to discover that "it is possible to see 'lightning strike in the same place' more than once" (in Burke, *Becoming* 408). He added,

> all of the above seems sometimes so evanescent and nebulous that I have never even mentioned the trifle to anyone. But terms like "evanescent" and "nebulous" are defeatist, are they not, to those who like ourselves are tortured most of the time by their reality? I have generally paid a pretty high price for the above kind of experience, however silly this might sound to some. But way down deep these things can be unconscious, although sturdy, weapons against discouragement. And though my attempt at

> communication sometimes seems as shabby as the paint on the "enseigne" I can still rejoice that a glorious "light" once illuminated it for me in "colours" never to fade.[104]

The chance encounter with the faded, peeling decalcomania revealing the lettering of an earlier trademark underneath, and its summoning of the memory of an earlier encounter with this "still life," seemed to Cornell to crystallize the kind of layered, doubled vision that he hoped to express in his objects and collages: a visible, everyday, even "shabby" reality (the enseigne) is given significance by invisible forces, whether memory, chance, or a spiritual "light." Loy had explored this kind of layered vision in her 1923 poem "Lunar Baedeker," and Cornell's poetic letter about an ordinary delivery truck becoming the vehicle of the marvelous ("in colours never to fade") resonated with the kinds of vision Loy was exploring in poems such as "On Third Avenue."

Both artists shared the struggle to express the reality of the "evanescent" in their adaptations of Surrealist techniques, but differed in their materials and ethical stance. In recognition of the similarity of their method but difference in materials, Cornell ends a July 3, 1951, letter to Loy, "Enclosed—a 'hot cross bum' item."[105] In the late 1940s, Loy was writing the long poem "Hot Cross Bum" (published in 1950 in James Laughlin's *New Directions*) and working on her Bowery constructions. However, as Burke argues:

> Though Cornell's assemblages had inspired her to evoke the spirit in bric-a-brac, by using junk rather than the scraps of European culture he favored, she was dethroning the idea of art's *belle matière*—unseating an art whose status relied on its superiority to humbler forms of expression. (*Becoming* 420)

Loy foregrounded her humble materials, not allowing them to simply become figure or metaphor, emphasizing a sense of the "lived costs" for those who had to survive in the streets (Burke, *Becoming* 420). Whereas Cornell's "romantic" museums often featured historical materials and explored the theme of nostalgia, Loy rejected a romantic lens on the trash she picked up in the streets as material for her assemblages, providing documentary, ethical attention to her materials.

This distinction in material and ethical stance may help to explain the fact that Cornell did not admire Loy's assemblage constructions as much as he did her 1933 paintings. After Loy moved to Aspen in 1953, and Julien Levy and Marcel Duchamp began the work of collecting the assemblages that Loy had left behind in New York, Loy wrote Cornell (September 26, 1955), thanking him for an "object card" that he had sent her, and commented:

> I heard you were displeased with my trion pictures—which however some people appreciated deeply—one man said he's seen the God in them. Now you know this is Mina Loy writing you—do give me news of you—had many exhibitions?

She signed the letter, "Longing for news of you artist."[106] In her mention of God, Loy clarifies that her attention to the bodiliness and material challenges of survival nevertheless enabled glimpses of a spiritual world. Asserting the authority of her name (and, implicitly, of her genius) by stating "Now you know this is Mina Loy writing you," Loy at once corrects Cornell's response and invites the next letter, with hope that the reciprocal exchange would continue.

Exhibit 9
"Phenomenon in American Art": Cornell's *Aviary* Exhibition and Loy's "Property of Pigeons"

The connections and distinctions between Loy's and Cornell's artistic materials, methods, and "museums" would come into focus for Loy in December 1949 when Cornell invited her to his *Aviary* exhibition at the Egan Gallery (December 7, 1949–January 7, 1950). As each artist developed their understanding of poetic museums, the figure of the bird, a common trope for the lyric poet, would play a central role. In the *Aviary* installation of twenty-six boxes featuring birds, Cornell would begin to explore a new kind of abstraction in his art, one that struck Loy as poetic and spiritual. She was inspired to write a prose appreciation of the exhibition, the first since her essays on Gertrude Stein (Burke, *Becoming* 418); like the Stein essays, the Cornell essay would illuminate Loy's methods. The finished essay, "Phenomenon in American Art," is dated November 25, 1950, and although she did not publish it, Loy sent it to Cornell (on November 27, 1950) who replied (dated two days later) "how overwhelmed I am with the piece, with the winged words" (in Burke, *Becoming* 419).

Cornell's *Aviary* exhibition featured a variety of boxes resembling "bird houses or cages," with most boxes containing a

> white-painted habitat for a paper cockatoo or parrot [...] From one box to the next, the birds variously perch amid a stack of drawers, eye themselves in broken bits of mirror, or listen, bemused, to actual musical boxes hidden behind a wallpaper of old travel posters. (Solomon 186)

Cornell arranged the boxes in the Egan Gallery on perches of differing heights, such that the gallery came to "resemble a bird shop" (Solomon 192). Each box is akin to a bird "habitat," Cornell probing the connection between box, cage, and museum (see Fig. 4.18).

In "Phenomenon in American Art," Loy clarifies the importance of Surrealism to Cornell's art, and to her own.[107] As with her earlier essays on Stein, Loy's occasion is the momentous but unrecognized step forward taken by Cornell: "Something insufficiently heeded has occurred in American Art. / The creations of Joseph Cornell" (LLB82 300). To measure the importance of Cornell's *Aviary* boxes, Loy jumps back in time to an equally momentous aesthetic event, her memory of seeing Brâncuşi's *Golden Bird* at Mariette Mills's home: "A metallic mould of static soaring whose reflections of boughs within Parisian skies beyond her windows gave to solidity an hallucinatory transparence. / Is not the aerial content of a bird partly of the sky?" (LLB82 300). Brâncuşi's *Bird*, like Loy's lamps, merged conventionally opposed spaces and entities—in this case, Parisian skies with an interior room, solidity with transparence. This

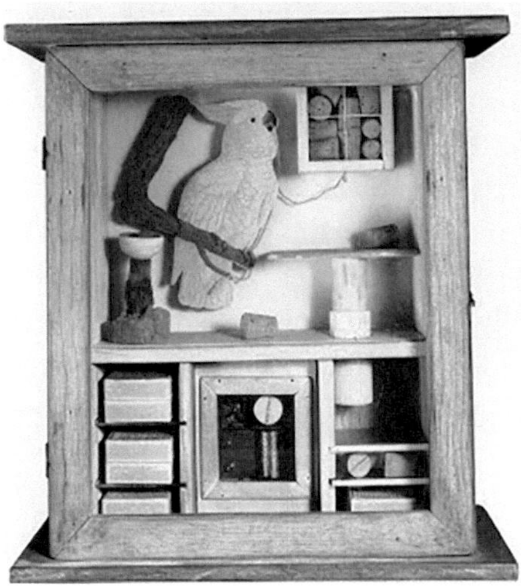

Figure 4.18. Joseph Cornell, Untitled (*Cockatoo with Corks*), 1948.

sculpture, or possibly Brâncuşi's photo of the sculpture first printed in *The Little Review*, inspired Loy's poem "Brancusi's Golden Bird," initially published in *The Dial* (November 1922) alongside Brâncuşi's photo of the sculpture.[108] Loy connects Brâncuşi and Cornell through their uses of abstraction:

> It is a long aesthetic itinerary from Brancusi's *Golden Bird* to Cornell's *Aviary*. The first is the purest abstraction I have ever seen; the latter the purest enticement of the abstract into the objective, even as cubism marks an itinerary of return to composite form, something which cubists predicted would never again preoccupy the artist. Gertrude Stein explained the air of cubism to me as "deconstruction preparatory to complete reconstruction of the objective." I do not know if anyone considers this reconstruction process yet accomplished. (LLB82 300)

In this brief trajectory through the history of modernist art, Loy suggests that Brâncuşi's pure abstraction, routed through cubist de- and reconstruction of the object, has led to Cornell's "reconstruction" of the object through abstraction.

Breton commented in the catalog to the opening exhibition of Peggy Guggenheim's Art of this Century Gallery that "Cornell has devised an experiment which completely overturns the conventional use of the object" (qtd. in Guggenheim, *Art* 26). Loy considers Cornell's "reconstruction" of the object in the context of the Surrealist movement: "So often l'École declines to petty larceny, the disciple to a pickpocket who picks merely the lining, missing the aesthetic specie." Her example is followers of Picasso: "How many signs of ennui would have been spared if only Picasso could have copyrighted the Picassian" (LLB82 300).[109] Yet Cornell, she implies, was not an obedient Surrealist disciple:

> Surrealism was the latest movement to produce a novelty for intellectual concern. Although ethically hindered by its ingenuity of Evil, it was sufficiently valid to take part in that series of ocular surprises propelling the history of art. Its theoretic contrivance for somersaulting reasons into an "Alicism" world of topsy-turvy logic greatly entertained me [but] my conclusive reaction to much of it was "Black Magic." From black to white magic in one movement. For almost as though it had been better described as sub-realism, Cornell, while theoretically adhering to surrealist formula, raised it above reality, achieved an incipience of sublime solidified. (LLB82 300–01)

Instead of merging reality with the unconscious "depths" repressed by civilized society—unlicensed sexuality, anger, irrational violence—with their connotation of "black magic," Cornell in his *Aviary* boxes looks to the skies, to "white magic" and to the realm of spiritual longing.[110] The romantic Sublime as that which overwhelms the human capacity of rational understanding here takes on the connotations of the divine, or what Loy calls in her essay "the Kingdom of Heaven."[111] Loy observes that Cornell "achieved an incipience of sublime solidified," bringing together mundane reality not with repressed "depths" but with the spiritual "heights," necessitating a new term that indicates this opposed goal by replacing sur- with sub- in "sub-realism." Cornell and Loy in their "white magic" depart in particular from the dissident Surrealists associated with Bataille and the journal *Documents*, who had split from Breton in 1929 to pursue a less idealized, gothic version of Surrealism, embracing a "sinister love of darkness and monstrous taste for the obscene" including the occult and sadism (Archer-Straw 143).

While emphasizing Cornell's departure from Surrealism's "black magic," Loy demonstrates Surrealism's importance to Cornell's method:

> When Max Ernst masterpieced a wonderworld he brought in a new-view by cutting and rearranging dead engravers' illustrations. A contemporary brain wielding a prior brain is a more potent implement than a paint brush. This appropriation of others' handiwork is not pilfering, but lifting out of the past another's sight tinged with family likeness—aspects added to the original by the altered observation of modern eyes. Thus the birds in the Aviary, had not to be made by Cornell, they were elected by Cornell, located by Cornell. (LLB82 301)[112]

Loy points out that "Surrealism recognized such effigies of superimposed viewpoints as partial creation, with the imperative to conceive unprecedented ambient for their entire recreation" (LLB82 302). Here Loy effectively restates Ernst's definition of the Surrealist image, "the fortuitous encounter upon a non-suitable plane of two mutually distant realities" ("Inspiration to Order" 80). For Cornell, this "unprecedented ambient" is "simplicity—bits of white wood restrained to retain the entity of weedling, of branching, of foliage, consolatory shade" (LLB82 302). For Loy's late poems and assemblages, the ambient is equally simple and striking, but also particular and ethically specific: the city sidewalk. For both Loy and Cornell, the "unprecedented ambient" extended to their creation of alternative exhibitions, in spaces outside of the museum, gallery, library.

In her approach to Cornell's use of "superimposed viewpoints," Loy suggests a kind of palimpsestic, doubled vision much like the kind Cornell described in his letter about the smoked-fish delivery truck. This method suggests a number of connections to Loy and the avant-garde. First and foremost, Loy's description of a method of "superimposed viewpoints" alludes to Cubist collage. Adding in the element of time, the "altered observation of modern eyes," a constellation is also formed between past and present. Walter Benjamin's definition of the constellation or dialectical image in his *Arcades Project*, similarly built out of juxtaposed fragments of the past and present, was a key to his method, and constellations as historical, conceptual, and imaginative mappings had long interested Loy.[113] The "lifting out of the past another's sight tinged with family likeness—aspects added to the original by the altered observation of modern eyes" also encompasses works created in collaborative dialogue with Duchamp's *Large Glass*, works that offer a new lens onto or new framing of an older artwork or environment, as in the lunar light ("altered observation") cast onto the *Glass* ("another's sight") by Loy's poem "Lunar Baedeker." Such works offer a curatorial twist on collage (offering a new "frame" onto another work or environment) and, in Futurist fashion, extend a "museum without walls" into new landscapes, media, and dimensions, as exemplified by Loy's verbal lens onto Duchamp's *Glass*. Finally, Loy sees Futurist aesthetics as a key to Cornell's *Aviary*: Cornell doesn't simply connect past to the present but instead "has brought about a crisis: Art's first intimation of a new potency [...] to encompass the future" (LLB82 302). Cornell's boxes imagine "the consummate arrival of flight," solidifying the trajectory from Brâncuşi's *Bird* with its Futurist qualities.

More pointedly, Loy argues that both Brâncuşi's bird and Cornell's *Aviary* boxes encompass the future through materials that capture and reflect light, transforming their environment, and joining the material and the immaterial world. The *Golden Bird*'s "metallic mould" permits its "reflection of boughs within Parisian skies" allowing it to merge "solidity" with "transparence." Similarly, Loy locates Cornell's efforts to give material dimension to spirit (the "crystal clue to virtues") in his use of mirrors,

> mirrors so poised to reflect only the anomalous depths of their own brightness in a blackness nevertheless outdistancing diamonds—a hocus-pocus at play with dimension, a depthless surface absorbing all distance, inviolate to what they reflect, outlasting all passing, instantaneously returning to the potential emptiness of their status quo. [...]
>
> The Holy Ghost alit in cloisters with mirrors and meek architecture. Songsters of silence pause before cabinets of Elysian apothecaries whose drawers store only such supreme alleviations as Elixirs of Life, Panaceas of peace. (LLB82 302)

Deborah Solomon sees the role of the mirrors as Cornell's means of including the spectator in his art. Discussing his 1942 box featuring a palace with a mirror backdrop, she writes:

> As we see our face reflected in the box's mirrors, a Renaissance building is brought into the present and made to seem part of that modern cityscape in which passersby glimpse their reflection in shop windows a thousand times a day, and in which every urban voyager is also a voyeur. (141)

Mirrors include the current environment just as *The Large Glass* provided a window onto its surroundings, glass figuring inviting and anticipating "aspects added to the original by the altered observation of modern eyes" (LLB82 301).

Continuing the sequential collaborative circuit initiated while Loy was in Paris and Cornell in New York, Loy adds a verbal frame (or "collage layer") to Cornell's *Aviary* boxes through the altered observation of modern eyes. Reflecting on this long transatlantic aesthetic itinerary, Loy revisits the Cornell box she had first described in *Insel* and given to Oelze:

> Songsters of silence pause before cabinets of Elysian apothecaries whose drawers store only such supreme alleviations as Elixirs of Life, Panaceas of Peace.
>
> Or [...] the delicious head of a girl in slumber afloat with a night light flame on the surface of the water in a tumbler. Under the glass lid a silver slipper and one of witch's blue. (LLB82 302)

Bringing this lost, absent box into an essay on a current New York exhibition, Loy adds a less visible, yet dimensional curation that reflects her en dehors garde journey and perspective. Ekphrasis comes up short in encompassing Loy's intermedial art: her essay is narrowly ekphrastic, but can be more precisely understood through curation, collage, and collaboration. Loy concludes, "So long I have sought a sentence to reproduce the sublimity of Cornell's objects. Without success. Still, we can take the sublime for granted. After all, it is a sensation. Visitors to this exhibition might gasp on confrontation" (LLB82 302).[114] Loy may ruefully signal the failure of words versus images to convey the sublime; however, Loy's verbal response to Cornell's *Aviary* exhibition, positioned as part of an ongoing verbal-visual sequential collage indebted to Surrealist poetics, suggests a more reciprocal understanding of the relation between artist and muse, word and image. Her verbal response to *Aviary* can be considered a "superimposed viewpoint" with "aspects added to the original by the altered observation of modern eyes," a "partial" because collaborative "creation."[115]

"Property of Pigeons": Loy's Sidewalk Surrealism

While Loy admired Cornell's *Aviary* boxes, the difference in their approach to "museums without walls" would surface in her creation of a poetic structure for a very different kind of bird, the pigeon, in its urban habitat. In taking the pigeon as her subject, Loy responded to Cornell's romantic treatment of birds as feminized muses in his *Aviary* boxes.[116] For Loy, both the feminized bird and the aviary were long-standing subjects that preceded her friendship with Cornell: Loy's autobiographical manuscript *The Child and the Parent* (published in 2024 as *Lost Writings: Two Novels*, edited by Kelsey) begins "with the metaphor of a bird alighting as a symbol of the soul's appearance in the world" (Burke, *Becoming* 354), and contains a chapter titled "Ladies in an Aviary" that depicts Victorian women as birds trapped in their cages. The Madonna in a birdcage was a central element of Loy's arrangement of objects above the fireplace in her Paris apartment, a photograph of which was sent to Cornell. Loy's long poem "Biography of Songge Byrde" (1952), written after Loy saw the *Aviary* exhibition, was occasioned by the life of Isadora Duncan, who was also a favorite of Cornell's; in this poem Loy engages the "songge byrde" both as an artist and as a female muse, in conversation with Cornell's treatment of birds as feminized muses. Beyond Cornell's use of the aviary, Loy likely saw Man Ray's photo of a birdcage placed over the head of a gagged female mannequin in the 1938 *International Exhibition of Surrealism*.[117] While Cornell didn't gag his birds, he caged them; Loy's pigeons were notably uncaged.

While the metaphors of bird and aviary were familiar ones to Loy, her experience of "disappearing" into the shuffling shadow-bodies of Lower Manhattan would profoundly alter her perspective on both. This shift in perspective is evident in her poem "Property of Pigeons," which takes the humble pigeon as subject, and the urban sidewalk as environment, cement replacing Cornell's bits of white wood in his *Aviary* boxes as "unprecedented ambient." The bird has a long history as a figure for the lyric poem and poet, and in her focus on the pigeon Loy fixes her poetic gaze on the prosaic sidewalk, to encompass the documentary reality of urban life for those struggling to survive, imbuing pavement, a stark "ambient," with ethical meaning.[118] Moving outward from her interest in the aesthetic margins to engage the experience of those literally living outdoors, Loy circled back to her 1920s statements—"Make the World your Salon" (1921) and "The Flux of life is pouring its aesthetic aspect into your eyes, your ears—and you ignore it because you are looking for your canons of beauty in some sort of frame or glass case of tradition" (1925)—with a new perspective.

Perspective is central to Loy's poem. Pigeons, looked down upon by many city dwellers as scavengers and carriers of dirt and disease, are part of everyday life in the city, omnipresent yet noticed only when they become a nuisance. In this regard they are much like the "shuffling shadow-bodies" of the homeless that Loy chronicled in the city, eking out an existence in an inhospitable world. As the 1939 Federal Writers' Project's *New York City Guide* commented of the Bowery, "Here flophouses offer a bug-infested bed in an unventilated pigeonhole for twenty-five cents a night" (120). Loy would take such comparisons seriously. For both pigeons and the homeless population, survival entailed finding a "pigeonhole" in a concrete environment: in several of her late collages, Loy depicts homeless men either asleep on the sidewalk or literally trapped beneath the sidewalk, employing perspective to demonstrate how they are looked down upon and walked over not just figuratively but literally. In "Property of Pigeons" Loy does not depict the pigeons as a simple allegorical figure for the homeless; rather she undertakes a similar shift in perspective that requires a decentering of the human, a shift that Cornell would also explore in his films centered on pigeons.[119]

The precise composition date of "Property of Pigeons" is unknown. However, Loy includes the poem in a list typed on August 21, 1944, so a date of composition in the early 1940s is likely. Along with a number of other poems from this era, the poem was published by Gilbert Neiman in *Between Worlds* (1961).[120] The poem has strong affinities with Cornell's boxes, his 1949 *Aviary* exhibition, and his pigeon films. Cornell began making his bird boxes in 1939 with *Fortune Telling Parrot*, followed by a parakeet box in 1941, and a series of owl boxes in the mid-1940s, prior to the parrot-centered boxes exhibited at the Egan Gallery (Solomon 186). It's possible that Loy's "Property of Pigeons" poem influenced Cornell's late 1940s *Aviary* boxes, or his 1950s films featuring pigeons. Cornell featured pigeons in two films he made with Rudy Burckhardt, the painter, photographer, and experimental filmmaker: *The Aviary* (1955) and *Nymphlight* (1957). Like "Property of Pigeons" these films allow an altered perspective on the city and its human inhabitants to emerge through a focus on the pigeon's habits and habitat, and at carefully chosen moments take up the pigeons' point of view.[121] Whether or not the poem influenced Cornell, Loy's curatorial attention to the pigeons and their ephemeral habitats explicitly engages birds, aviaries, and Cornell's boxes, while her choice of a sidewalk ambient and treatment of perspective reflects her ethical commentary.[122]

The speaker's careful observations of the pigeons' actions in the city structure the poem: "Pigeons doze, / or rouse"; "Pigeons arise, / alight"; "Pigeons make irritant, alluring / music"; "Pigeons disappear"; "Pigeons [...] / appear to reappear [...] to peer" (LLB96 120). As the speaker describes the pigeon's habits and habitat, she emphasizes the limits of human sight and knowledge, which cannot account for the mysterious ability of pigeons to survive in the city.

Loy begins the poem with two stanzas (Italian for room) reminiscent of Cornell's bird boxes, establishing an analogy between the visual, spatial design of her poem and the pigeons' environment:

> Pigeons doze,
> or rouse
> their striped crescendos
> of grey rainbow
>
> a living frieze on the shallow
> sill of a factory window. (LLB96 120)

The factory window establishes the Cornell-like frame or box in this scene, against which the pigeons make "a living frieze" (defined as "a broad horizontal band of sculpted or painted decoration, especially on a wall near the ceiling"). Loy aestheticizes the pigeons with this language, even as she draws attention to the aesthetic incongruity of a *moving* frieze and the backdrop of the factory exterior. Conventionally friezes are found indoors, yet Loy's stanzas evoke and challenge the ideals of privacy and containment that we associate with domestic interiors. The line break and enjambment between "shallow / sill" form an edge akin to the shallow sill: as we read up to and over the line break, we experience a spatial analogy for the window sill, whose shallowness is reinforced by the narrow two-line stanza or "frieze."

In contrast to the exotic birds housed in Cornell's aviary boxes, the shallow window "box" in Loy's poem is external, open to the elements, and provides a temporary shelter. A lack of property and private space defines the pigeons' existence, accentuated by their shelter on the edifice of a factory, where the production of goods helps to fuel the human economy. The subsequent stanzas form a similar "box":

> Pigeons arise,
> alight
> on vertical bases
> of civic brick
>
> whitened with avalanches
> of their innocent excrements
> as if an angel had been sick (LLB96 120)

In this "whitened" scene reminiscent of the white, abstract background that Cornell would use in many of his *Aviary* boxes, Loy pointedly ties the color white to pigeon excrement, commonly viewed as a nuisance but here termed "innocent" and angelic. As Prescott points out, Loy's language transforms the pigeons standing on whitened brick into "tiny feathered sculptures" (184), a kind of marble statuary one might expect to encounter in a museum or civic building. In this unexpected juxtaposition of excrement and innocence, Loy makes visible and challenges understandings of waste as what must be expelled to make cultural and moral "cleanliness" possible, a challenge akin to her treatment of the trash cans in "Hot Cross Bum."

Pigeons and their excrement bring into focus human economies, but pigeon economies are more difficult to ascertain; Loy comments that excrement is "all that is shown to us / of bird-economies, / financeless, / inobvious as the disposal / of their corpses" (LLB96 120). Throughout the poem Loy uses the anthropomorphizing language of economy and finance ironically, to emphasize the limits of the human perspective on and knowledge of the pigeons ("all that is shown to us"): the human observer knows nothing of the death of pigeons or the disposal of their corpses.

Loy also uses the diction of private property, domestic economy, and marriage—those pillars of life taken for granted by the middle class—to highlight how pigeons creatively survive outside houses and other spaces of protection, preservation, and cultural value:

> Too and fro, frowardly they live
> burnishing each other's
> gorgeous halters
> in the feathery drive
>
> of preliminaries
> to their marriages.
>
> Pigeons disappear,
> their claws, a coral landing-gear,
> dive for the altar-stair
> to their privacies—
>
> a slice of concrete
> fallen on a cornice
> leading into darkness;
> the slit adjacence of houses
>
> where the caressive dusts,
> the residue of furnaces
> upholster the gossamer
> festoons of intestate spiders
> for nuptial furniture (LLB96 121)

The allusions to marriage, altars, upholstery, and nuptial furniture generate irony through the disparity between these middle-class foundations and the daily existence of pigeons, whose "property" is that "slice" of the urban landscape that is nominally public, where they are barely tolerated, yet in which they survive. The pigeons manage to create a "private" space out of the gap between human houses,[123] which Loy gives visual as well as textual form in a box-like stanza:

> a slice of concrete
> fallen on a cornice
> leading into darkness;
> the slit adjacence of houses (LLB96 121)

Loy's poem reveals to human observers the ingenuity of the pigeons who make do in the urban margins of human culture, transforming these shadowed places into the material of pigeon life, permitting the reproduction and survival of the species. In contrast to Cornell's box-like habitats, Loy's pigeons invent temporary shelters out of shadows, gaps, adjacencies, the liminal spaces of those who are "en dehors." The poem concludes by emphasizing the limits of what the human eye can see and know:

> Pigeons through some conjurous procedure
>
> appear to reappear
> upon the altar-stair
> at startling instants
> in the immature
> torsos of their giant infants;
>
> timid and unflown
> stark of plume
> naive in nativity
> to peer into a vast transparency. (LLB96 121)

As with other "inobvious" features of pigeon life, the appearance of large pigeon infants to the human observer seems "startling" or sudden, a species of "conjury"—inexplicable because unobserved. Echoing her description of "Brancusi's Golden Bird" as "unplumed" (LLB96 79), Loy's infant pigeons are also "stark of plume"; while Brâncuşi's abstract sculpture captured "the nucleus of flight" (LLB96 79), the pigeons are pre-flight, "timid and unflown."

The speaker's close observation of the pigeons and what cannot be seen or known results in a new vision and understanding of the bird, one with spiritual connotations. "Nativity" connotes the birth of Jesus Christ, and can refer to the artistic representations of Christ's birth. Powell argues that "Loy's pigeons are figures for the holy spirit" (16) and Burke sees them as "the intertwining of body and soul" (*Becoming* 417); both critics suggest that the poem alludes to the Sermon on the Mount:

> Therefore I tell you, do not worry about your life, what you will eat or drink; or about your body, what you will wear. Is not life more than food, and the body more than clothes? Look at the birds of the air; they do not sow or reap or store away in barns, and yet your heavenly Father feeds them. Are you not much more valuable than they? (Matthew 6:25–26, New International Version)

Maeera Shreiber argues that "Departing from that mystical tradition which endeavors to look into the secret life of things, Loy claims that all things have a life that remains necessarily secret" (474); she adds, "Loy's visionary poems are located in the small spaces between what can and cannot be known" (475), an apt description of the en dehors garde and of Loy's Surrealist-influenced "museums without walls." Whether or not one sees the birds as figures for the spirit, through the pigeons Loy's speaker seems to acquire an understanding of a new kind of vision beyond that of the material eye. To peer means to look carefully or with difficulty, and Loy's punning, rhyming language—disappear, appear to reappear, to peer, transparency (a pun on "parents see")—positions the young pigeons' sight as beyond the visual knowledge of the human speaker.

"Vast transparency" is an abstraction, an undemarcated space that is penetrable by vision (transparent), and connotes a kind of window (echoing the factory window at the start of the poem, and perhaps alluding to Duchamp's *Large Glass*), but it is a window that lacks an edifice or frieze: this abstract opening points to the possibilities but also to the limits of human vision and knowledge, allowing one to imagine how or what the young birds might see as they first climb the stairs up to the city street, but also to confront the unknowability of this view. Loy signals a similar unknowable view with her em dashes at the end of "Lunar Baedeker" (1923), and the speaker who attempts to understand what the birds see, confronts this limit. Loy's statement about Brâncuşi and Cornell—"The first is the purest abstraction I have ever seen; the latter the purest enticement of the abstract into the objective"—applies to the conclusion of her poem, which can be read as a belated, altered response to Brâncuşi's *Golden Bird* and to Cornell's *Aviaries*.

Loy explored the shift in perspective central to "Property of Pigeons" in a number of her constructions created in New York and Aspen. Loy uses the vertical presentation of the bum's horizontal position (lying on the sidewalk) to invite viewers to see this figure with fresh eyes, much as she does with her pigeons. For example, *Prospector 2* (1959) changes depending on one's perspective (see Fig. 5.1). Loy depicts a bum buried under sidewalk pavement, with only his hands and head emerging. If the work is placed on a floor or tabletop and viewed horizontally, the bum would appear to be imprisoned under the cement, equivalent to garbage to be trod on, or emerging from it like one of Loy's incipient forms. However, if the work is hung on a wall and viewed vertically, the bum appears to be hanging, transcending rather than trapped in the body, a Christ-like figure akin to the figure in Loy's construction *Christ on a Clothesline* (MLSII 133, 174). Loy uses the vertical presentation of the bum's horizontal position (lying on the sidewalk) or what she called "topsy-turvy" shifts in perspective to invite an ethical extension of perspective and reflection on the relation between matter and spirit.[124]

In Paris, Loy used juxtaposition and perspectival shifts to create hybrid forms and liminal places between self and other, dream and reality, interior and exterior, night and day, enabling nuanced, feminist commentary on the Surrealist avant-garde. In her New York work, Loy would bring Stein's democratic, "American" experiments to fruition: Surrealist juxtapositions of perspective grounded in the actual landscapes of Lower Manhattan illuminate the possibilities and costs of democracy, and of the human spirit confronted by material limits, of the body and the external environment. One such limit that Loy experienced in Paris and New York was the marginalization of her work as a woman artist, designer, and writer: extending her interest in Surrealist poetics to novel forms of collection and display, Loy created alternative "museums without walls," charting new possibilities for aesthetic experiment and its histories. Her late art and writing extended this practice to the literal street: taking the cement sidewalk as environment, Loy assembled "exhibitions" built from ephemeral moments, unhoused people, and discarded materials overlooked by official guidebooks. Through her material and aesthetic navigations of Paris and New York, Loy created a museum of the en dehors garde—less visible but no less visionary than those of the Surrealists—and curated a place for her work.

CODA

COLLECTING MINA LOY

Archives and Archival Mediations (Exhibitions, Publications, Scholarship, Art)

Suzanne W. Churchill, Linda A. Kinnahan, and Susan Rosenbaum

I. PLACING AND MISPLACING MINA LOY: *PROSPECTOR 2*

After rescuing Loy's Bowery artwork in 1990 from a locker where it had been stored since 1959, Roger Conover recalls "one epiphanic moment after another as I unwrapped an astonishing collection of paintings and assemblages." One of these was *Prospector 2* (1959), a large assemblage of crushed tin cans and other debris arranged on cardboard, with delicately painted paper cutouts of the face and hands of a man pasted in the top left corner (Fig. 5.1).[1] Conover writes that when he first saw the piece and its 1957 companion, *Prospector 1*,

> I assumed the tin and copper plates and cans floating in loose gravity before the hands of a beatific bum looking back at us with contented consolation from a cardboard-fashioned face (modeled after Duchamp?)

> had been constructed in the Bowery. But when the two *Prospector* pieces were sent to the Williamstown Art Conservation Center for evaluation and stabilization in preparation for the exhibition at Bowdoin College Museum of Art in 2023, it suddenly became clear that these pieces had not been made in the Bowery, but in Aspen, Colorado. When the framing and backing material was removed, the place and date of composition were revealed in bold marker, in her own hand: "Mina Loy, Aspen, 1959." Mina Loy carried her downbeat aesthetics and recycling practice from the streets of Lower Manhattan to a former mountain mining town (then in the process of becoming a ski-resort) in Colorado. But whereas she once considered herself a collector of trash, she now credited herself with depositing it, as if in defiance of her daughters' wish for her to leave her "garbage art" behind. Alongside the date and signature on the backs of her *Prospector* pieces, she proudly scrawled the words "I'm a Litterbug." (Introduction, "Mina Loy, *Prospector 2* [1959]")

Through its forms and motifs, as well as its circuitous provenance, *Prospector 2* is a meditation on the materiality of place and larger questions of displacement, not only of the "bums" and homeless persons depicted in many of these works, but of en dehors garde artists like Loy, and the fragmented, scattered nature of their archives and tenuous toehold in cultural histories and institutions.

As Conover points out, Loy's "beatific bum" resembles Marcel Duchamp, Loy's fellow traveler in the avant-garde, whose career path intersected with Loy's in many times and places but led to very different ends: he became a celebrated icon of the historical avant-garde; she fell into relative obscurity. Is *Prospector 2* an oblique portrait of Duchamp, commenting on his hallowed status in the avant-garde? Is the artwork's tone one of reverence, irony—or both? Loy's play with perspective adds to the ambiguity. By positioning the figure's hands and face emerging from the concrete sidewalk, Loy may reflect on how the humble materials of the urban streets can be resurrected into art, particularly if the work is hung vertically. As discussed in chapter 4, Loy may use the vertical Christlike presentation of the bum's horizontal position (lying on a sidewalk) to invite viewers to view this figure dynamically, to shift restlessly between pity and reverence, and thus to consider their own ethical perspective.

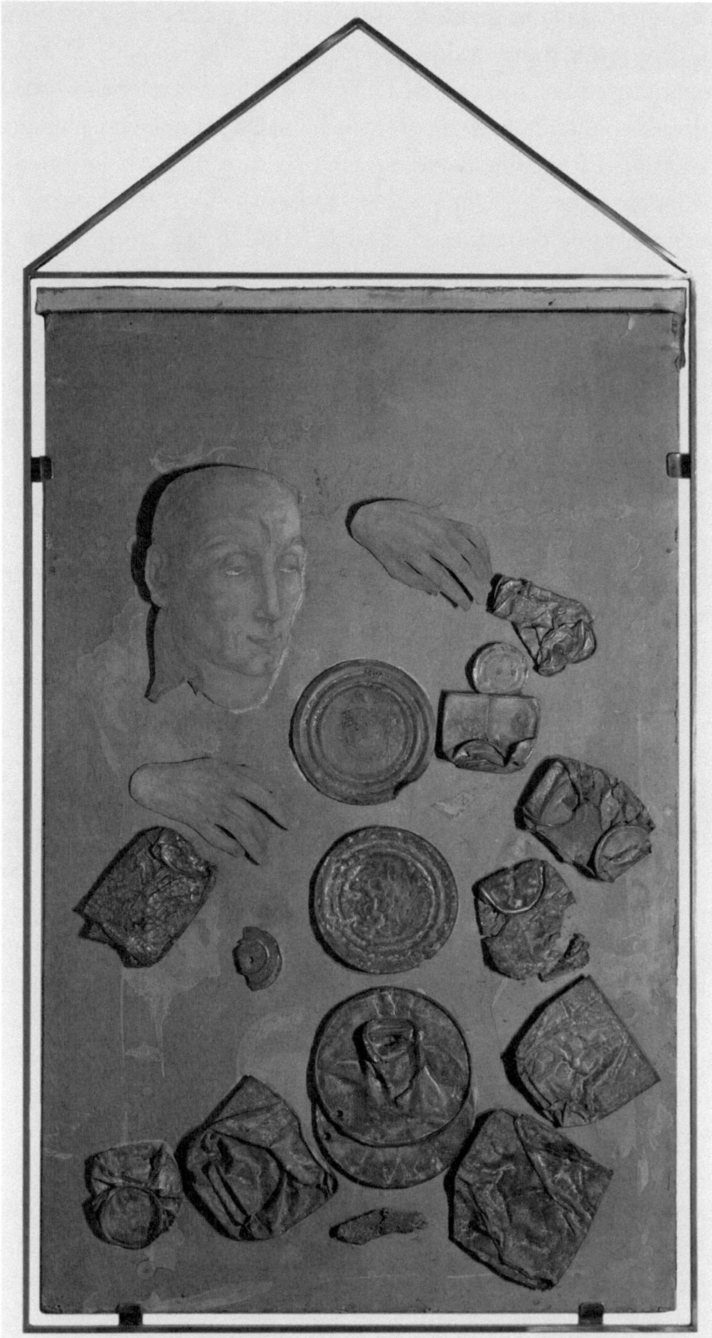

Figure 5.1. Mina Loy, *Prospector 2*, 1959.

The battered plates that Loy has suspended resemble old, well-used coins, a currency so worn down that its "face" (value, place of origin, iconography, and so on) cannot be read. The plates raise the issue of literal and economic sustenance for the homeless, and the broader question of value. Is the bum, like the trash that surrounds him, disposable in the larger American economy? How does the gaze and hand of the artist confer value upon these materials found in the street? These are questions initiated by Duchamp in the 1910s with his readymades, and further explored by avant-garde artists ranging from Pablo Picasso to Joseph Cornell. Loy, however, brings an en dehors garde lens and adds a distinctly human element to the found-object assemblages she called "refusées," as her materials and technique consider the social disposability of the outcast.

The milky blue wash in *Prospector 2*—splotches of paint that splash down from the figure's blue collar and around the composition—suggests clothing and takes the shape of a human body. The body, evoked through a faint wash or flimsy fabric, all too easily disintegrates into the scattered debris. In this way, the blue wash evokes the body's fragility and vulnerability. But Loy's construction, as if taking up the charge she issued forty years earlier in her "Aphorisms on Futurism" (1914), also calls viewers to "OPEN your arms to the dilapidated, to rehabilitate them" (LLB96 149). Just as the figure opens his hands to embrace the refuse on the street, so Loy's refusées invite viewers to recognize the beauty, fragility, and humanity of the outcast, rejected, and reviled. Loy employs drawing and painting techniques that mark the human representation as lovingly created, while the arranged objects are defiant in both their found quality and their artistic transformation. Similarly, the formal qualities prompt a recognition of the figure's humanity amid, but distinct from, strewn trash. Loy's insistence upon material trash as art reenvisions a sense of the cast-off, both human and nonhuman, and the transformative potential of both objects and people.

Prospector 2 raises questions about the relations between the human and nonhuman, refuse and art, the material and the spiritual, which it refuses to answer. But its provenance alerts us to other mysteries, reminding us how little we know about Loy's time and artmaking process in Aspen, which was itself an important site of late modernist architecture and art.[2] As we bring *Travels with Mina Loy* to a close, having considered Loy's time in Italy, New York, and Paris, we face all that remains to be learned about Loy's art and travels. Given the scattered nature of Loy's archive, the fragmentary evidence accompanying her surviving art and writing, and the incomplete histories of her life in Aspen and many other places, we have come to realize that "placing" Loy is an ongoing process, and, like her peripatetic life and career, involves a fluid, changing narrative. New discoveries and materials continue to appear, suggesting the contingency of "placing" Loy definitively and the importance of collaborative sharing among Loy's scholars and readers. In an exciting discovery, the Loy painting *Lady Reading*—a previously unknown work that appears to date from her time in Florence—surfaced following reviews of the Bowdoin exhibit (see cover illustration and Fig. 7.1). Indeed, even as our manuscript was being copyedited, we received new information about the exact address of l'Ombrellino, Loy's first Florence home (see chapter 2). We have placed a photograph of the entrance to this villa here to signal that our Coda is as much a closing of this book as an opening of the door to new Loy scholarship and discoveries (see Fig. 5.2).

Travel, place, and the ephemerality of placement serve as a useful means not only of approaching Loy's geographically dynamic career but also for understanding the history of her cultural and historical placement through publication, exhibition, archival collection, and critical and scholarly reception. In the case of *Prospector 2* just discussed, Roger Conover recently discovered—working from Loy's handwriting on the verso revealed during restoration and other contextual evidence—that the titles of *Propector 1* and *Prospector 2* are reversed in the Bowdoin exhibit catalogue and the date for the former should be 1957, not 1959.[3] Recovering an accurate history of *Prospector 2* involved travel as well: the assemblage moved from Aspen to Julien Levy's storage unit in Connecticut, then to Roger Conover's Maine home where it hung for years. For purposes of the 2023 solo exhibit, it was shipped to Bowdoin College Museum of Art, then to the Williamstown Art Conservation Center for restorations, before returning to Bowdoin for the first retrospective exhibition of Loy's visual art, *Strangeness Is Inevitable*. It then traveled with the exhibit to the Chicago Arts League and finally back to

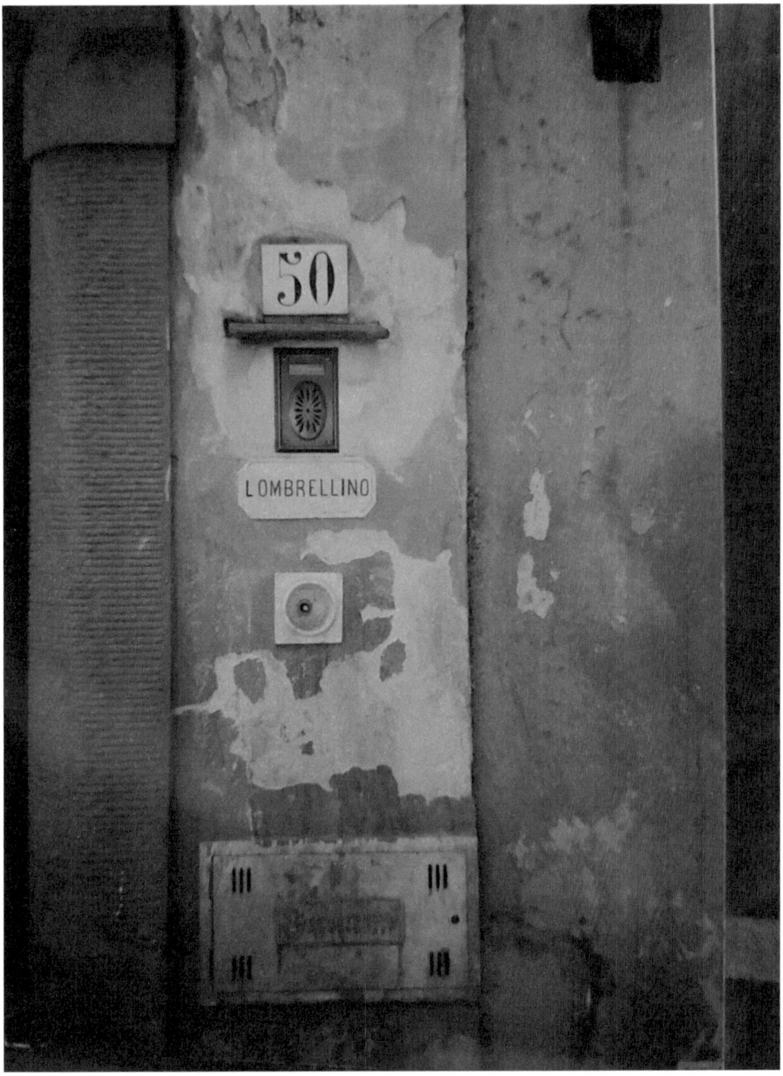

Figure 5.2. The current door number and house name at the entrance of Loy's first Florentine residence, Villino l'Ombrellino, formerly no. 25 Via del Pian dei Giullari in Arcetri, Florence. Houses have been renumbered since Loy's residence, and this entrance is currently no. 50. Photograph by Antonella Francini.

Conover's home in Maine. Traveling also across media and aesthetics, *Prospector 2*'s multimedia construction includes elements of Futurism, Dada, and Surrealism, embodying and reflecting on Loy's long career in and travels alongside the historical avant-garde. And as her rueful allusion to Duchamp as bum indicates, Loy was thinking, too, in her assemblages and late Bowery poems, about her posthumous "remains": the possibility that her en dehors garde work would be thrown out like the trash, in contrast to Duchamp's, or would remain in the shadows of work by her more recognized peers. Yet she also had faith in the enduring power of her art, telling Joseph Cornell that her "destiny was ravelled up somehow with the lunar globe."[4]

Loy's unstable place, both "inside" and "outside" the historical avant-garde and larger modernist canon, reflects her lifelong concern with outcasts. In a 1915 letter to Carl Vechten, written as she planned her move from Florence to New York, Loy worries about her own potential status as an "outcast":

> Haweis wrote to a friend—saying my work was so "offensive"—that in future where-ever I go I can only associate with outcasts—& therefore it is useless for me to have my freedom. Now my dear I've got a beautiful daughter—I can't outcast—what shall I do reassure me.[5]

Loy's maternal responsibilities make her fearful of social rejection and exile, though she would come to embrace the "outcast," both in herself and others. A quarter-century later, Loy channeled the charge of being outcast into the damning voice which opens "On Third Avenue": "'You should have disappeared years ago'—" (LLB96 109). She responded "so disappear," illuminating the institutions that marginalized her work alongside the defiant challenge to make a new kind of art. For Loy, to "disappear" signaled a loss of culturally sanctioned power but also permitted a different kind of agency, an artistic freedom to experiment without care for the world's judgment. Disappearance—at once imposed by age and circumstance, but also embraced through personal inclination—resonated with Mina Loy's en dehors garde travels on the margins of the avant-garde, which profoundly influenced the publication, exhibition, and archival collection of her work.

II. EN DEHORS GARDE PLACEMENTS: LOY'S NAVIGATION OF PUBLICATION AND EXHIBITION

Travels with Mina Loy, in tandem with our scholarly website (mina-loy.com), demonstrates Loy's ambivalence about and tenuous relation to codified avant-garde movements and established public channels of recognition. Although Loy privately felt certain of her artistic genius and wanted her art to reach the public, her critical engagement with the avant-garde, coupled with her skepticism of mainstream art museums and literary institutions, presented obstacles to publishing her writing, performing her plays, exhibiting her art, and finding backers to help produce her commercial designs. Her choice to publish her poems in little magazines, her "performance" of experimental plays in print, her display of her visual art in ephemeral exhibitions and small avant-garde galleries, and her creation of improvised "museums without walls" (see Malraux) in her apartments, lamp shop, and unpublished novel, reflect en dehors garde stances on the margins of the historical avant-garde, which was already situated on the margins of the wider culture. Underlining the difficult relationship between creating art and disseminating it to the wider public, Loy's publications and exhibitions constitute only a fraction of her artistic output, much of which is now lost or scattered across library archives and private collections.

Loy avidly sought public outlets for her work in the 1910s and early 1920s (corresponding to her Florence, New York, and Paris years), pursuing publication of her writing and display of her art in little magazines, theaters, salons, art galleries, and department stores. Those efforts, coupled with the 1923 publication of *Lunar Baedecker* [*sic*], established her reputation as a writer and visual artist. Her solo exhibition at the Levy Gallery in 1933 solidified her reputation as a visual artist. Scholars have concluded that Loy withdrew from public view after her return to New York.[6] Cristanne Miller suggests that "Loy's passivity about her later publishing may be a sign of her general lack of perceived agency in the infrastructures of modernism" (180), and Sara Crangle similarly argues that,

> as "modernism" became an aesthetic construct, Loy did not become part of its canon, a fate she shared with many of her female peers. [...]

> As explanations for her waning popularity, critics point to Loy's reclusiveness, as well as her disinterest in self-promotion and publishing in her later years. However, it should be borne in mind that Loy was only ever well known within avant-garde circles, and even there, she often remained on the periphery. ("Introduction" ix)

Both scholars imply that Loy's reclusiveness may have been a result rather than a cause of her marginalization: although Loy remained on the periphery throughout her career, her desire to publish and exhibit the work she created in Paris, New York, and Aspen did not diminish. Her efforts to secure publication and exhibition were often unsuccessful, however, and her letters record her frustration.[7] Conover and others have noted that Loy grouped her late New York poems—mingling urban scenes of destitution and war themes—under the title "Compensations of Poverty" and "probably hoped to publish them as a book" (LLB96 207).

Throughout her career, as she sought to circulate her work to the public, Loy relied on the help or collaboration of friends, editors, publishers, and gallery directors, many of them men, even as her work was deeply individual, critical of organized art institutions, and scornful of male privilege. Loy's editors and biographers (chiefly Marisa Januzzi, Carolyn Burke, Roger Conover, and Sara Crangle) in their careful tracing of Loy's exhibitions, publications, and critical reception, have demonstrated that Loy's connections to particular circles (the *Others* group, the New York Dada circle, the *Little Review* community, Natalie Barney's salon, the Julien Levy Gallery) were her bridges to the public. Loy depended on friends in these circles to help place her writing and arrange showings of her visual art. At the start of Loy's career in Florence, Mabel Dodge and Carl Van Vechten placed Loy's poetry in little magazines, while in later years, Djuna Barnes, Peggy Guggenheim, and Julien Levy assumed this "agent's function" (Conover, LLB82 xxx). Loy's friendship with William Carlos Williams and Robert McAlmon resulted in the publication of her first poetry collection, *Lunar Baedecker* with Contact Press, an offshoot of their little magazine *Contact*. During her Paris residency, her connection to her son-in-law Julien Levy resulted in her job as gallery agent and the exhibition of her paintings at the Levy Gallery in 1933.

When she returned to New York in 1936, Loy was no longer tied directly to a particular little magazine or artistic circle that could help her navigate a route to the public. Her key relationship to Julien Levy and his gallery, although more tenuous than in Paris, proved to be critical at this juncture; in the 1940s and 1950s Loy was in frequent contact with Levy, pressing him to arrange an exhibition for her Bowery constructions. Levy continued to help place Loy's poetry and to mediate her connection to publishers and art galleries, while old and new friends recognized the value of her Bowery poems and constructions.[8] In addition to Julien Levy, a handful of these friends—Djuna Barnes, Berenice Abbott, Joseph Cornell, and Marcel Duchamp—stepped in to help publish and exhibit her work, as did a younger generation of writers, editors, artists, gallery directors, and bookstore proprietors, including Kenneth Rexroth, Gilbert Neiman, Henry Miller, Jonathan Williams, William Copley, Frances Steloff, and David Mann. At this time Loy published work in Charles Henri Ford's *View* (1942 and 1945), helped Breton publish Arthur Cravan's previously unpublished "Notes" in *VVV* (no. 1, June 1942; no. 2–3, March 1943), and published new poems in *Accent*, *New Directions*, *Partisan Review*, and *Between Worlds* (Burke, *Becoming* 401–02; Januzzi, "Bibliography" 524–26).

Thus, in the middle decades of the twentieth century, as she continued to write and make art, Mina Loy remained marginalized but not forgotten: while she suffered neglect, she also received significant moments of recognition. The intersecting efforts of old friends and recent admirers resulted in two related events in the late 1950s that ensured Loy's public reception and continuing relevance to the avant-garde: the publication of her second collection of poetry, *Lunar Baedeker & Time-Tables* by Jargon Press in 1958, and the exhibition of Loy's collage constructions at David Mann's Bodley Gallery in 1959. Though she may not have generated the same stir she aroused in the 1910s, Loy's influential advocates, who perceived the value of her late poetry and constructions, ensured their publication and exhibition.

Loy's peripatetic life and career along with the ephemerality of many of her designs, have rendered any collection of the elusive "Mina Loy" necessarily fragmentary and incomplete. Yet as her work came back into the public eye in the late 1950s, Loy's two "collections"—a book of poems and an exhibition of her constructions, which in Loy's understanding were parts of a poetic whole—invited a rethinking of what public collections do. Troubling the line between word and image, visibility and disappearance, experimental art and democracy, Loy's late work challenged her audience to leave behind the well-trodden path through the museum—the "frame or glass case of tradition" (LLB82 297–98)—to navigate the overlooked poetry of the urban streets, a "museum without walls." In her en dehors garde work, amplified and preserved through the Bodley gallery exhibition and Jargon Press poetry collection, Loy secured an audience and a place for her work.

In a twist typical of Loy's career, the constructions that did not sell at the Bodley Gallery disappeared from public view for decades. They were placed in Julien and Jean Levy's barn in Connecticut until damage to the structure prompted their removal to a storage locker.[9] The unsold constructions remained in this storage locker for almost forty years, until they were rediscovered by Conover. Conover, along with Loy's biographer Burke, took up the task begun by Mabel Dodge Luhan and Carl Van Vechten, Gilbert Neiman, Jonathan Williams, Julien Levy and Marcel Duchamp, of collecting, editing, publishing, and chronicling the works of a poet-artist who both desired and resisted making her work public, or rather, who wanted to reach the public on her own terms, even while dependent on others to help secure an audience.

III. HOUSEHUNTING: LOY'S EARLY COLLECTORS AND THEIR LEGACY

Loy moved often, but preserved letters, manuscripts, drafts, drawings, sketches, designs, inventions, portraits, family photos, and photos of lamps and artwork. She presumably kept much of this material in her home, and later in life, in the homes of her daughters Joella Haweis Bayer and Fabienne Benedict. This material now anchors what most think of as the "Mina Loy Archive," housed in the Beinecke Rare Book and Manuscript Library at Yale. The materials were donated by Joella Bayer in 1974 and 1975, with additional materials donated by Jonathan Bayer, Loy's grandson, in 2009.[10] Although the Beinecke contains the bulk of Loy's papers, her archive, like her life, requires a map, exceeding the boundaries of one institution. Even within the Beinecke we find Loy's writing not only in the Mina Loy papers, but also in the papers of Burke, Van Vechten, Stein, and Dodge Luhan. Beyond the Beinecke library, her letters can be found in a number of archives, including the Julien Levy collection at the Philadelphia Museum of Art, and the Djuna Barnes collection at the University of Maryland.[11] Her visual art and some manuscripts reside with a number of private collectors, while many are lost.

Despite the dispersed nature of the archive, we know quite a bit about Mina Loy, and have access to much of her writing and visual art, thanks to Conover's foundational work as Loy's editor, art collector, and literary executor, and to Burke's collection, biography, and research materials on Loy, the latter now housed at the Beinecke. The importance of these two figures, who in the 1970s began retracing Mina Loy's footsteps, tracking down and speaking with her family and friends, locating uncollected manuscripts, designs, inventions, and artwork, cannot be overstated. Much archival scholarship and further biographies, editions, publications, and most recently the Bowdoin exhibition, have been made possible by their foundational efforts (see Exhibit 2).

Burke's and Conover's efforts to collect, publish, and archive the works of Loy have comprised a task deeply shaped by Loy's understanding of the fluid nature of the stage, museum, library, and archive. Both Burke and Conover recognize the fine line Loy walked between her experimental ideals and the reality of cultural marginalization—between the democratic ambition of merging art and everyday life, and the danger of becoming part of the debris of the past. In his 1982 introduction to *The Last Lunar Baedeker*, Conover points out that most readers assume that Loy's editors and archivists are hunting down and publishing "fugitive material" in order to "return a forgotten poet to her 'rightful place'"; he counters that, "Such notions are romantic. And they derive from a canonical mode that was foreign to Mina Loy's way of thinking" (LLB82 xv).

In other words, the irony of inserting Loy into a canon she criticized is clear; instead, in collecting Loy's work, we can track how she transformed canonical structures of value and preservation. In fact, home-galleries and househunting emerge as an important component of both Conover's and Burke's archival engagements with Loy, reflecting how both followed in the footsteps of Loy's poetic Baedeker. Suzanne Zelazo describes Conover's home-gallery in Maine:

> Equal parts avant-garde library, contemporary art gallery, artist's studio, weight room, and subaltern spa, the Gesamtkunstwerk that is Conover's home is bio-rhythmically attuned to the art and energy of Loy and Cravan. [...] Conover's living and working space has enabled Loy's visual and literary work to interpenetrate, but also to shift organically with the surroundings. ("Roger Conover")

In her essay "Mina Loy & *Househunting*, or Biography as Restoration," Burke recounts how she came to acquire this assemblage and her efforts to have the fragile work restored, concluding:

> In some ways, *Househunting* is also an emblem of my peregrinations as a biographer, [...] and more generally, of my life as what we might call a serial expatriate. Like Loy, I have often moved house and country, and at times, been in fear or in thrall to the idea of being "unhoused." Haven't we all dreamed our own "househunting" dreams—domestic, vocational, artistic, spiritual—the contradictions of which still challenge us some one hundred years after Loy wrote in her 1914 [Futurist] Manifesto, "Forget that you live in houses that you may live in yourselves."

Conover's and Burke's foundational archives, inspired by Loy's travels and her domestic galleries, have shaped Loy's archival legacy, including the creation of digital archives. The Loy papers housed in the Beinecke Library were digitized in 2017 under the direction of Nancy Kuhl, curator of poetry, expanding access and changing the meanings of the archive in significant ways. An act of preservation for the fragile materials, this digital archive is also a sign of Loy's cultural value. While the Loy papers reside within the Beinecke's walls, in providing digital windows to the archival materials for readers around the globe, the Beinecke has in this partial sense realized Loy's democratic ideal of an archive without walls.

As Loy's material archive expands through further discovery and publication projects, digital access to Loy's archive, put in careful dialogue with the material artifacts contained in physical libraries and archives, will hopefully expand as well. Expansion of Loy's archive has fueled new scholarship and is transforming understandings of Loy's art, writing, and importance to modernism. This scholarship, which we tour in an exhibit following this Coda, also serves as a mode of collecting and exhibiting Mina Loy. Scholars select artifacts from Loy's archive and published work, and embed it in narrative interpretations that reframe the meaning and value of her work for academic audiences. Our website, *Mina Loy: Navigating the Avant-Garde*, is an archival mediation and meditation, offering digital scholarship and exhibits that aim to make Loy's published and unpublished work more accessible to broader audiences, inviting a closer, more informed engagement with her career, writing, and visual art.

The 2023–24 retrospective exhibition *Mina Loy: Strangeness Is Inevitable*, held at the Bowdoin College Art Museum and the Arts Club of Chicago, has likewise extended Loy's archive to wider audiences. The exhibit and catalog, curated by Jennifer Gross, collect art and archival materials from private collections to publicly show, for the first time, the chronology of Loy's long artistic career. The Bowdoin College Art Museum has expanded the reach of its physical exhibition not only through its physical catalog but through its comprehensive digital exhibition (including selected works, illustrated exhibition labels, gallery talks, and installation views), making Loy's visual art available to those who cannot attend the exhibit or access the catalog. The Arts Club of Chicago also includes installation images and a video of select proceedings from the exhibit on their website. This new visibility prompts one reviewer to posit that the show "implicitly asks why Loy has been so overlooked in comparison with her notable compatriots. The exhibition answers without needless justifications and excuses, instead presenting its case with a strong display of the artist's work" (Gilbert). Another reviewer attributes Loy's relative invisibility as an artist to the difficulty in categorizing her work: "Perhaps the main reason we don't know much about Loy today is due to the artist's refusal to conform to a set method, material, movement, or style" (Ford). Loy's refusal to adhere to any particular medium, movement, or style has proven to be a generative force: in recent performative mediations of the archive, artists have taken up Loy's work as a source of inspiration (see chapter 3 for discussion of theater productions, and Exhibit 2 for a list of creative productions in theater, music, and art).

IV. ARCHIVAL MEDIATIONS: EXHIBITING LOY IN DIGITAL AND MATERIAL FORMATS

Bowdoin College's physical and digital exhibitions of *Mina Loy: Strangeness Is Inevitable* underscore a lesson we learned as we completed research for our website, *Mina Loy: Navigating the Avant-Garde*: the necessity of working in the material archive alongside the digital. The digital archive allows users to see Loy's work up close, but it may distance them from the materiality of the objects, what Natalie Zemon Davis describes as "the marginal notations missed by the camera, the signatures cut off, the paper not available to the touch, the bindings unseen" (xvi). Digital archives can unwittingly promote a fantasy of comprehensive coverage, particularly fictive in the case of Loy's archive, centered in the Beinecke but also located in many other places. We conceived of our website as a scholarly Baedeker for the archive writ large—a travel guide that helps users navigate both the digital and the material archive, with attention to their overlaps and gaps. This book companion furthers that goal, offering a supplementary, portable guidebook—accessible on Lever Press's online platform and as an ebook, PDF, or print codex—that distills our arguments from the website's "Mina Loy Baedeker: Scholarly Book for Digital Travelers,"[12] offering a narrative rather than non-linear reading experience (Fig. 5.3).

We have wrestled with the surprisingly difficult task of remediating our website into book form, as our link-activated, visually animated, nonlinear, database-structured web chapters are revised, rethought, and reformatted for comprehensibility and intellectual engagement in book form. Different technologies demand different scholarly approaches and methods responsive to quite distinct reading habits. The affordances of the website platform opened new possibilities for scholarly production and dissemination, including but not limited to:

- Collaboration and co-writing
- Diversity of contributions and contributors

- Resisting hierarchy between faculty, students, librarians, designers
- Design as feminist critical act and mode of exploring and generating ideas
- Creative forms of scholarship (postcards, galleries, games, social maps, story-maps, etc.)
- Richly contextualized and interlinked reading environments
- Less-linear storytelling
- Visual and verbal hyperlinks (inviting different paths of exploration and modes of reading)
- Image saturation along with visual reading and analysis
- Interactivity
- Connecting with wider audiences, including non-specialist readers
- Free sharing and open access.

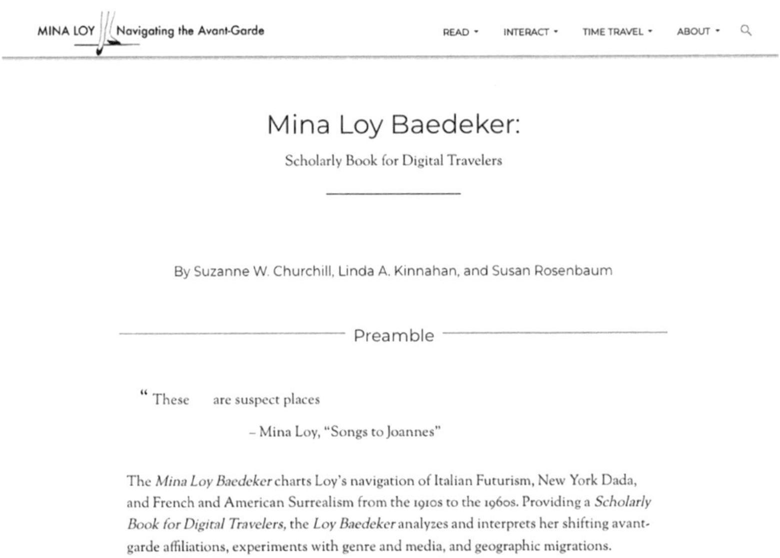

Figure 5.3. Landing page. "Mina Loy Baedeker: Scholarly Book for Digital Travelers," *Mina Loy: Navigating the Avant-Garde*, edited by Suzanne W. Churchill, Linda A. Kinnahan, and Susan Rosenbaum. University of Georgia, 2020.

The digital platform enabled networked scholarship: in homing in on any one facet of Loy's travels and art, it was possible to contextualize place and history through links to related resources, documents, and photos, as well as to connect Loy's particular aesthetic strategies across time through simple links to other chapters. Similarly, in connecting Loy's aesthetics to a broader avant-garde and en dehors garde, the internet provided a host of contextual materials that were easy to reference and cite. The work of contextualization, in other words, was greatly enhanced on a scholarly website.

This interlinked connectivity in turn affected the shape of the arguments we produced. In contrast to the traditional print model of the literary scholarly essay, which begins with a focused thesis, demonstrates and develops that thesis with evidence, and concludes by emphasizing the new understanding to scholarship that emerges, our born-digital writing took the form of a series of interlinked "exhibits" or "tours" of Loy's work. We were able to trace her peripatetic movements and follow the digressive tangents of her art, without being locked into a linear narrative. Readers likewise did not have to read linearly: they could come to any chapter or section of a chapter, and move horizontally, backward or forward in time, selecting topics from a Pinterest-style grid or interactive carousel.

What we initially thought would be a simple matter of piecing together a collection of short born-digital "posts" into a continuous book chapter proved to require extensive editing, rethinking, and rewriting. In a digital environment, each post had to be self-contained to allow users to approach it from different navigation paths and search engines, even as the posts existed in larger collections called "chapters." But when reassembled for chapters in book form, these digital posts seemed rambling and repetitive. The rhizomatic, networked structures of narrative and argumentation that undergird web design required a more coherent, linear story or argument for book publication. Revising all of this material into book form required pulling together a great deal of material, both what we had written, and the broader contexts of networked links. We had to omit a great deal and choose the strongest "throughlines" to provide a coherent framework for decades of Loy's wildly varying artistic production and life experiences. Academic readers of scholarly books expect a clear, focused throughline, as monographs are designed to be read linearly. Of course, the conversion to linear narrative risks oversimplifying or distorting Loy's varied art and career. We worried that the circular turns we observed in her work would be lost or compromised in the book format, although we have done our best to signal them.

Committed to scholarly collaboration in our work on the web project, we have continued but modified how such collaboration—as a feminist practice in its nonhierarchical dynamics and processes of assemblage—remains critical to *Travels with Mina Loy*. Our collaborative writing process changed, as we each sought to clarify throughlines for our respective parts of the book. Rather than working in tandem and interlinking short posts, we returned to more traditional processes of writing, revising, and commenting on each other's completed work. The shift from website to book form also diminished our focus on feminist design. Even though books have important design elements, they do not come into play in the drafting of the manuscript, but are considerations addressed after the text has been written and revised, and are constrained by publishing costs. In contrast, with born-digital writing, the text constantly changes in relation to the layout of the web page: form and content develop in synergistic relationship to one another, each modifying to amplify the meaning and effects of the other.

In creating the website, we enjoyed a sense of exploration and discovery—of not knowing what the outcome would or should be. (There was also a fair amount of getting lost, frustrated, and overwhelmed by uncooperative new technologies.) Our foray into born-digital scholarship made us think and work in new ways; enabled broader collaborations among scholars, students, technologists and audiences; and allowed more readers to interact with our work in their own ways. Yet the website is less stable and permanent than a book, and less capable of sustaining a long, in-depth argument, or providing the satisfactions of such an endeavor. When it comes to reading, we still prefer the book form. Although the existence of PDFs and ebooks erodes the distinction between print and digital formats, the book form is immersive in a different way from a media-rich website: a book enables sustained concentration, calls for imaginative collaboration from readers, and rewards investment in a continuous, coherent narrative. It allows readers to find and recognize patterns and allows for a deeper—if more curated and controlled—understanding of Mina Loy's life and work.

The process of remediating our "Mina Loy Baedeker: Scholarly Book for Digital Travelers" leads us to affirm and assert the continued value and viability of the book in the digital age while recognizing that the affordances of a website—its ease of access and media-rich environments—require the scholarly book to respond in kind and attend to readers' needs much in the way websites must respond to their users. In her poetry, plays, essays, and mixed-media collage "constructions," Mina Loy exploits page layout, stage design, and visual effects to deliver unconventional and disruptive insights about gender, sexuality, identity, and the physical body. Loy's multimedia work serves as the occasion for us to reflect on the continued relevance of books in the digital age and to argue that the print codex remains an essential handheld device, designed for readers who yearn for the physical properties of paper, the heft and weight of a volume, the visual comfort of the printed page. At the same time, Lever Press's Fulcrum platform, ebook, and PDF versions provide greater ease of access, portability, and searchability than a physical book. Just as Mina Loy refused to choose a single medium, group, or platform, so our readers no longer have to choose, but can travel with her online, in an ebook, or in a print companion.

EXHIBIT 1

MINA LOY BIO, MAP, AND TIMELINE

I. A BRIEF ITINERARY OF MINA LOY'S LIFE AND CAREER

Mapping the coordinates of Loy's career is no small challenge, as her life was characterized by travel and migration within and across Europe and the Americas.[1] Born in London in 1882, Mina Gertrude Lowy was the firstborn child of an English Protestant mother and a Hungarian Jewish father. She was raised with two sisters in a Victorian household that aspired to middle-class respectability. Imaginative and precocious, Mina was prone to inventing colorful stories and drawings—and disinclined to proper feminine decorum. She was sent to art school: first in London, then Munich, then Paris. By age twenty-one, she had begun a lifelong migration between places, countries, continents, and cultures.

In Paris, where she resided as an art student from 1903 until 1906, Loy met fellow artist Stephen Haweis, who was attracted to her beauty and intelligence. Though her feelings toward him were deeply ambivalent, she married him in 1903 out of necessity: their daughter, Oda Janet, was born in 1904, five months after the wedding. That same year, Loy exhibited six watercolors at the prestigious Salon d'Automne under the self-styled name and signature, "Mina Loy."[2] But just as her artistic career took off, her personal life crashed. Oda died of meningitis in 1905,

Loy's marriage to Haweis deteriorated, and she succumbed to grief and depression. When she became pregnant by the doctor who treated her for neurasthenia, Haweis agreed to claim paternity if Loy moved with him to Italy. Divorce was financially impossible, socially unacceptable, and legally prohibitive, so Loy complied, and the couple moved to Florence in 1907. Her father contributed to their finances, allowing them to later purchase a home at no. 54 Costa San Giorgio (now renumbered by the city as no. 60).

While in Italy, Loy gave birth to daughter Joella in 1907 and, with Haweis, to son Giles in 1909, the same year she began her lifelong interest in Christian Science. As her marriage disintegrated, she developed sustaining friendships with expatriates Mabel Dodge Luhan, Gertrude Stein, Carl Van Vechten, and her ward and artistic protégée, Frances Simpson Stevens, who introduced her to the Italian Futurists in 1913, soon after Haweis left Florence for good. In 1914, Loy became involved in love affairs with F. T. Marinetti and Giovanni Papini. She exhibited works (now lost) in the *First Free Futurist International Exhibition* in Rome and embarked on a literary career, publishing poems, plays, and essays in various American and European little magazines, starting with *Camera Work* and *The Trend*. In 1915, "inflamed by the pro-war sentiment around her" in Florence, Loy briefly worked for the Italian Red Cross as a nurse in a surgical hospital (Burke, *Becoming* 187).

The years 1916–1923 were the most peripatetic in Loy's migratory life. In the autumn of 1916, she left her children with their Italian nursemaid and sailed to New York, arriving in October and determined to reinvent herself as an artist. In New York, Loy found compatriots in often overlapping artistic and literary circles associated with the modernist poetry magazine *Others* and Louise and Walter Conrad Arensberg's salon—where she associated with William Carlos Williams, Alfred Kreymborg, and Marianne Moore, among others—and a proto-Dada avant-garde circle that included Marcel Duchamp, Man Ray, Beatrice Webb, and the great love of her life, Arthur Cravan—a boxer, Dada poet, and nephew of Oscar Wilde. Loy managed to secure a divorce from Haweis in 1917, and in January 1918 she and Cravan sailed to Mexico City so that he could escape the draft, and they married there. Loy became pregnant, and they set off for Argentina on separate boats. Cravan never made it: his sailboat disappeared off the coast of Mexico, and he was never heard from again. Loy searched for him in Valparaiso, Chile, and Buenos Aires, Argentina, without luck, and finally sailed to Surrey, England, in March 1919 to give birth to their daughter, Fabienne in April. After taking the baby to Europe to see her other children and meet Cravan's family, Loy sailed alone to New York in March 1920. She returned to Florence in summer 1921, visiting Paris that summer and again in November 1921 (Burke, *Becoming* 307, 310). While Loy was traveling, Haweis passed through Florence and took their twelve-year-old son Giles to live in the Caribbean (304). In Spring 1922, Loy traveled to Vienna, where she met and drew Freud, and then moved to Berlin.

In Spring 1923, Loy published her first collection of poems, *Lunar Baedecker* [*sic*], and settled in Paris, where she would remain until 1936. In these years, she grieved the loss of her son Giles, who died of cancer in Bermuda in 1923 (Burke, *Becoming* 327); raised her daughters Joella and Fabienne; opened a lampshade shop featuring her lamp designs, funded by Peggy Guggenheim; and celebrated Joella's marriage to Julien Levy. Loy moved fluidly between a number of overlapping circles in Paris, described by Burke as "a group comprised of British and American writers, their French counterparts, and assorted Dadaists or Surrealists" (328). She created objects and paintings, wrote poetry and fiction, and worked as the Paris agent for Julien Levy's photography and Surrealist gallery in New York, where she had a solo exhibit in 1933. As Levy's agent Loy met the Surrealist painter Richard Oelze, and drew upon their relationship for *Insel*, a semi-autobiographical novel about the Surrealist scene.

Concerned about rising anti-Semitic hostilities in Europe in the 1930s and vulnerable because of her Jewish background, Loy left Paris for New York in 1936. There she established new friendships with figures including Joseph Cornell, and renewed ties with old friends Djuna Barnes, Berenice Abbott, Duchamp, and many of the European Surrealists in exile during World War Two. Her move to New York coincided with a growing sense of national identity as an American, and she became an American citizen in 1946. Moving to the Bowery in 1949, she lived in a communal household, writing poems about the destitute inhabitants of lower Manhattan and creating assemblages from refuse and found objects.

In 1953, Loy moved to Aspen, Colorado, to be near her daughters. She continued to create assemblages, combining materials like old cans, lids, and neon signs, prefiguring pop-art's fascination with popular culture and advertising. Jonathan Williams published a second collection of Loy's poems, *Lunar Baedeker & Time-Tables* (1958), and Marcel Duchamp and Julien Levy organized a 1959 exhibition of Loy's Bowery constructions at David Mann's Bodley Gallery. In the year before her death, Paul Blackburn recorded an interview with Loy in which she read a number of her poems.[3] She died of pneumonia at the age of eighty-three, on September 25, 1966, in Aspen, her grave marked by a circular stone in the Aspen Grove Cemetery.

II. MAP OF MINA LOY'S MIGRATIONS

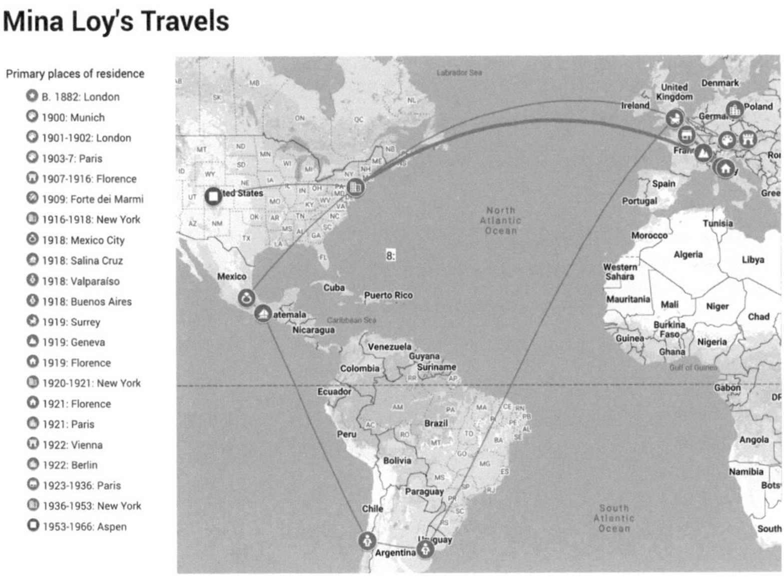

Figure 6.1. Map of Mina Loy's travels around Europe and the Americas.

III. TIMELINE OF MINA LOY'S LIFE

1882 Mina Gertrude Lowy born in **London**.

1897 Attends St. John's Wood Art School in **London**.

1900 Travels to **Munich** and enrolls in the Society of Female Artists' School.

1901–02 Attends art school in **London** taught by August John.

1903 Travels to **Paris** and enrolls at Académie Colarossi, where she meets Stephen Haweis; Loy and Haweis marry on the last day of the year.

1904 Oda Janet Haweis born in **Paris**; Loy exhibits six watercolors at Salon d'Automne under the name Mina Loy.

1905 Oda dies of meningitis. In mourning, Loy paints *The Wooden Madonna*, which she later gave to Mabel Dodge (now lost).

1906 Affair with doctor Henry Joël Le Savoureaux and subsequent pregnancy; Loy elected member of Salon d'Automne.

1907 Moves to **Florence**, Villino Ombrellino in Arcetri area; Joella Sinara Haweis born, July 7, in Bagni di Lucca.

1908 Moves with family to rented apartment on Costa San Giorgio, in the Oltrarno section of **Florence** (address unknown).

1909 John Stephen Giles Musgrove Haweis born, February 1. Loy adopts Christian Science. After Giles's birth, Loy takes the children to the mountains in Vallambrosa or the Carreras (May–June) and to the seaside resort of **Forte dei Marmi** (July–August).

1910 With Haweis, Loy buys home at no. 54 Costa San Giorgio (now renumbered as no. 60). Meets Mabel Dodge Luhan.

1911 Meets Gertrude Stein and Alice B. Toklas.

1912 One-woman show at Carfax Gallery in **London**.

1913 In January, Loy suffers from possible influenza and anxiety over the collapse of marriage; in the summer, Haweis cares for her in **Forte dei Marmi** on western coast of Italy; later in the year, he leaves for Australia. Frances Simpson Stevens rents a studio from Loy, and they become friends, engaging with Futurist artists and writers, including Giovanni Papini and F. T. Marinetti. In November, Loy and Stevens attend the first major showing of Futurist paintings in **Florence**, at the Saletta Gonnelli. In December, Loy attends a Futurist *serata* (performance) at the Teatro Verdi in Florence.

1914 *Lacerba* publishes article on the Futurists and their meeting place, the Giubbe Rosse Café, and mentions Loy and Stevens (January 15). Loy paints portraits of Marinetti and exhibits works (now lost) at the *First Free Futurist International Exhibition* at the Galleria Sprovieri in Rome (February–March). Loy embarks on love affairs with Marinetti and Papini. Debuts "Aphorisms on Futurism" in *Camera Work*. Vacations in **Vallombrosa** with Dodge, Carl Van Vechten, family, and others as war breaks out (July–August). Marinetti visits Vallombrosa. Van Vechten publishes Loy's "Italian Pictures" in *The Trend* in November, introducing her as a "Futurist." Loy returns to **Florence** in the fall, living temporarily at no. 27 Via de' Bardi while her house is rented; Papini lives down the street. Loy begins writing plays and drafts "Feminist Manifesto" and sends it to Mabel Dodge in New York.

1915 Loy relocates to no. 52 Costa San Giorgio in the spring, until she can move back into her home at no. 54. Spends summer in the seaside town of **Forte dei Marmi** with her children. "Love Songs" appears in the first issue of *Others* (July), and "Two Plays" appears in *Rogue* (August 1). Volunteers for the Italian Red Cross as a nurse in a surgical hospital in **Rome**.

1916 Sails to **New York** and arrives on October 14. Introduced by Frances Simpson Stevens who now lives in New York City, Loy meets Duchamp, Kreymborg, and Williams, and other members of the overlapping Arensberg and *Others* circles. In December, she costars in Provincetown Players' production of *Lima Beans*.

1917 *New York Sun* publishes a feature on Loy as the "modern woman." Loy meets Arthur Cravan at the April opening of the Independents' Exhibition; divorces Haweis in September. *Songs to Joannes* published as a special issue of *Others*, and Loy contributes four prose pieces to *The Blind Man*.

1918 Loy and Cravan travel to **Mexico** to avoid draft; get married in January. Loy travels to **Valparaiso, Chile**, and on to **Buenos Aires** in fall 1918. Cravan disappears.

1919 Returns to Surrey, **London**, in March; Jemima Fabienne Cravan Lloyd born in April; travels to **Geneva** to meet with Cravan's family and then **Florence** to see Giles and Joella.

1920 Returns to **New York** in March. Meets Djuna Barnes. *The Pamperers* is published in *The Dial* (July).

1921 Haweis returns to Florence and takes Giles to the Caribbean. In summer 1921 Loy returns to **Florence** and visits **Paris** that summer and again in November 1921.

1922 Loy travels to **Vienna** in the spring, meets Freud, and moves to **Berlin**.

1923 Returns to **Paris**; *Lunar Baedecker* [*sic*] published by Contact; Giles dies in Bermuda.

1925 Peggy Guggenheim organizes exhibits of Loy's *Jade Blossoms* in America (Cubist still-life picture-collages). The works are exhibited and sold at Wanamaker department store's Belmaison gallery, Macy's Gallery, and Cargoes Gallery.

1926 Loy opens a lampshade shop at 52 rue de Colisée, **Paris** in September.

1927 Joella marries Julian Levy.

1928 Edgar Levy loans Mina Loy the money to buy the lampshade shop from Peggy Guggenheim.

1929 Loy puts the lampshade shop up for sale in the fall.

1930 Loy sells the lampshade shop in March.

1931 Levy opens gallery in New York in January at 602 Madison Avenue; Loy becomes adviser and purchasing agent in **Paris**.

1933 Levy exhibits Loy's paintings in New York gallery (January–February); meets Richard Oelze in **Paris**.

1935 Loy sends Fabienne to New York to live with Joella and Julien in December.

1936 Loy moves to **New York**.

1940 Lives on Lexington Avenue, near Fifty-Eighth Street, in Midtown East, **New York City**.

1941 Moves to East Thirteenth Street, near Union Square, close to Third Avenue, which turns into the Bowery.

1942–45	Publishes in Charles Henri Ford's *View* and helps Breton publish Cravan's previously unpublished Notes in *VVV* (no. 1, June 1942; nos. 2–3, March 1943), and published new poems in *Accent*, *New Directions*, *Partisan Review*, and *Between Worlds*.
1943	Begins friendship and correspondence with Joseph Cornell.
1944–48	Moves in with daughter Fabienne and her new husband Hans Fraenkel on East Sixty-Sixth Street.
1946	Loy becomes an American citizen.
1948	Moves to a communal house on Second Street, bordering the Village and the Bowery.
1949	Loy moves with the communal household a few blocks to 5 Staunton Avenue on the Lower East Side. Visits Cornell's *Aviary* exhibit at the Egan Gallery.
1950	Loy finishes her essay "Phenomenon in American Art" and sends it to Cornell in November.
1953	Loy moves to **Aspen, Colorado**.
1958	*Lunar Baedeker & Time-Tables* published by Jargon Press.
1959	Loy's "constructions" exhibited at Bodley Gallery.
1966	Loy dies in **Aspen**.
1982	Roger L. Conover publishes *The Last Lunar Baedeker*.

This timeline includes only select publications that are most relevant to works discussed in this book. For a chronological, comprehensive list of her publications, see Januzzi's "Bibliography."

EXHIBIT 2

COLLECTING AND EXHIBITING MINA LOY

Timetable of Critical and Scholarly Reception and Creative Productions

Though elusive and, until recently, not broadly accessible, Mina Loy's body of work has motivated a lively, generative scholarly corpus. Indeed, over the past twenty to thirty years, a proliferation of Loy scholarship, including monographs, articles, book chapters, dissertations, and reviews, constitutes a remarkable revival of interest in her literary work. Interdisciplinary attention to her art, designs, and theatrical compositions currently energizes our understanding of her cross-media career, and access to much of her surviving art has been fundamentally enhanced through a solo exhibit (1993–94) and its accompanying catalog; attention from art historians; and a scholarly website devoted to her work across media. Feminist scholarship, cultural studies approaches, formalist readings, critical race theory, materialist theory, performance theory, genre theory, art history contexts, archival studies, geohistories, economic theory—all and more have enhanced the varied and growing body of scholarship that has brought Loy from relative obscurity to pronounced visibility.[1]

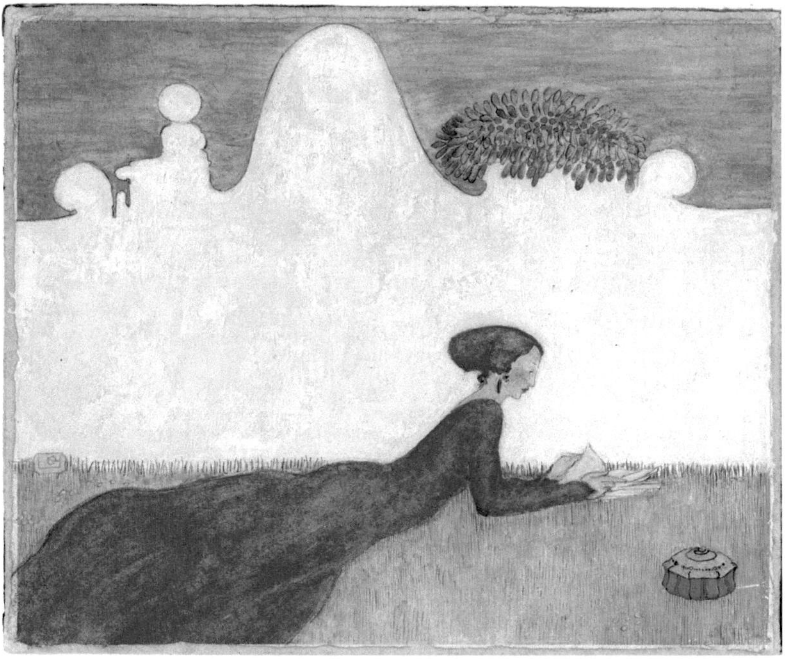

Figure 7.1. Mina Loy, *Lady Reading*. Private collection.

One might mark 1996 as a turning point in Loy scholarship, when access to her life and work greatly expanded because of two publications: Carolyn Burke's biography and Roger Conover's (second) edited collection of Loy's poetry. Burke's *Becoming Modern: The Life of Mina Loy*, a comprehensive biography, draws upon extensive archival research and develops crucial connections between Loy's life, art, and poetry. The biography coincided with the publication of Conover's new collection of Loy's poetry, *The Lost Lunar Baedeker*, with comprehensive notes. Together, these important 1996 publications helped generate a rapid uptick in scholarship, contributing to a revisionist expansion of modernism that came to be known, by the late 1990s, as the "new modernist studies" (Mao and Walkowitz 737). The scholarship produced in the thirty years since these two publications, we are happy to report, wholly belies Helen Vendler's dour review of them, echoing the disregard accruing through New Critical versions of modernism: Loy's "poems do not add up, in my view, to a major body of work." "Major," however, as Loy scholars have argued for years, is a term weighted by sociocritical assumptions that are now, we trust, disproved.

A primary impetus to Loy scholarship has been the publication of more of that "body of work," as well as the exhibit and reproduction of her artwork and the expansion of access to the archives. Her prose work, so little published during her lifetime, has interested scholars in the archives and increasingly been brought into print. Publication of Loy's 1930s semi-autobiographical novel *Insel*, based in circles of Surrealist art in Paris, called attention to her various semi-autobiographical drafts and fragments by the 1990s (1990, ed. Elizabeth Arnold; 2014, ed. Arnold and Sarah Hayden).[2] Further, Sara Crangle's edited collection, *Stories and Essays of Mina Loy* (2011), significantly added to Loy's prose work in print (previously scant). And, even more recently, *Lost Writings: Two Novels* by Mina Loy (2024), edited by Karla Kelsey, brings connected texts begun in the 1930s and written over two decades into print, *The Child and the Parent* and *Islands in the Air*; and Alison Dobbins collaborated with Loy scholars to publish Loy's early plays as an open-access book titled *Futurism, Feminism, and the Right to "Genius": Mina Loy's* The Sacred Prostitute *and Other Plays* (2025).

The digitization of primary holdings of Loy's papers at the Beinecke Rare Book and Manuscript Library at Yale University in 2017 includes further unpublished prose and poetry in varying stages of completion, as well as visual artifacts like designs and sketches. The Carolyn Burke Collection on Mina Loy and Lee Miller, which includes Burke's research files for biographies of both women, are now housed at the Yale's Beinecke Rare Book and Manuscript Library, expanding the archival holdings already located there but not yet available online.

Loy's critical presence was slight in the years leading up to Burke's 1996 biography and the selected poems, but she never disappeared completely, in large part thanks to Conover's first edition of Loy's poems, *The Last Lunar Baedeker* (1982), and to individual voices calling for her work to be recognized. Certainly, in the years of her greatest visibility as a poet, Ezra Pound and T. S. Eliot had paid homage to her work (Pound, "Others" and Eliot, "Observations", both 1918); by the late 1920s and after, she appears in memoirs by other central figures of American modernism like Carl Van Vechten, Alfred Kreymborg, and Mable Dodge Luhan. The art dealer and her son-in-law Julien Levy detailed her 1930s Parisian associations with artists in his *Memoir of an Art Gallery* (1977), and various poets—Kenneth Rexroth, Yvor Winters, Basil Bunting, Denise Levertov, William Carlos Williams among them—penned tributes to her in the 1940s and 1950s. Within a few years following her second and final book, a smattering of articles appeared, challenging the reasons for Loy's obscurity or neglect (Larry Krantz, Kenneth Fields, Jonathan Williams, Samuel French Morse). The emergence of feminist literary criticism in the 1970s, motivating recoveries of forgotten women writers and revised literary histories, furthered and deepened Loy's reclamation. In 1980, an entry on Loy by Burke appeared for the first time in the *Dictionary of Literary Biography*, and that same year, Virginia Kouidis's 1980 critical biography, *Mina Loy, American Modernist Poet*, made a claim for Loy's centrality in modernist poetry. Focusing primarily on poetry of the 1910s and 1920s, Kouidis stresses the intersections of female selfhood and modernist innovation while providing contexts of biography and publication history. Shortly thereafter, Conover's first collection of Loy's poems, *The Last Lunar Baedeker*, appeared with Jonathan Williams's Jargon Society press and was issued the following year in Britain by Carcanet Press in 1983.

Readers began to pay attention to this lost modernist, aided by feminist networks and projects of recovering forgotten women writers. For example, Burke shared news of Loy in short pieces appearing in *HOW(ever)*, a 1980s journal of women's innovative writing that made the recovery of women modernists critical for its challenge to sexist traditions in publishing, writing, and reception. Fuller critical essays by Burke appeared in the 1980s, focused on Loy and joining a feminist insistence on decentering modernism's central male figures and bringing women from the margins into literary histories. William Drake's survey of women modernist poets, *The First Wave: Women Poets in America, 1915–1945* (1987), places Loy in the context of diverse poetic practices by women writing in the 1910s, from Sara Teasdale to Lola Ridge. And, differing from the dominant focus on Loy's poetry of the Teens and early Twenties, Melita Schaum's 1986 essay was the first to trace Loy's life and poetics through the "automythography" of Loy's 1925 long poem, "Anglo-Mongrels and the Rose."

Through the 1990s, scholars increasingly explored Loy's ideological, formal, and gendered challenges to male-centered formations of modernist poetics. Linda Kinnahan's study of the intersecting histories of modernism and feminism, *Poetics of the Feminine: Literary Tradition and Authority in William Carlos Williams, Mina Loy, Denise Levertov, and Kathleen Fraser* (1994), positions Loy in relation to American first-wave feminism. In 1998, Maeera Shreiber and Keith Tuma edited the first collection of essays on Loy, appearing in the National Poetry Foundation's "Man/Woman and Poet" series as *Mina Loy, Woman and Poet*. Wide-ranging topics highlight Loy's connection to Futurism, fashion, and Christian Science and explore concepts of devotional poetics and female subjectivity within her work. Clusters of essays on "Love Songs to Joannes" and "Anglo-Mongrels and the Rose" pay particularly concentrated attention to her innovations with the long poem and the love lyric and her feminist revisions of genre and poetic subject matter. Short pieces by contemporary poets collectively speak to Loy's significance in a lineage enabling innovative poetics, especially for women. The *Woman and Poet* collection includes an annotated bibliography by Marisa Alexandra Januzzi, the first to compile and annotate Loy's published work (including artwork in reproduction and posthumously published pieces) alongside a comprehensive listing and annotation of critical work on Loy, done between 1914 and 1996.[3]

More critical interest in Loy's 1925 long poem, "Anglo-Mongrels and the Rose" developed further through works such as Tuma's analysis of Christianity, Christian Science, mysticism, and theological discourse in her poems (in *Fishing by Obstinate Isles: Modern and Postmodern British Poetry and American Readers*, 1998); Susan Stanford Friedman's explorations of the long poem (in *Dwelling in Possibility: Women Poets and Critics on Poetry*, edited by Yopie Prins and Maeera Shreiber, 1997); and Elisabeth Frost's extended reading of the poem's exploration of language and female consciousness as part of an American feminist avant-garde (in *The Feminist Avant-Garde in American Poetry*, 2003). Rachel Blau DuPlessis's analysis of the poem in *Genders, Races, and Religious Cultures in Modern American Poetry, 1908–1934* (2001) stimulated and joined a trend of discussions of her Jewishness, as DuPlessis expanded paradigms of modernism that have excluded gender and race to argue for poetry's articulation of social debates over "new" identities, reading Loy within tensions and anxieties attending modernity's identity formations of the New Woman and the New Jew.

Reflecting Loy's wide range of interests and areas of practice, the marked interdisciplinarity of twenty-first-century scholarship reads Loy in relation to science, economics, book and magazine history, visual culture, religion, material culture, and more. DuPlessis's book marks a trend toward cultural studies approaches to Loy, while Suzanne Churchill's 2006 study of publication history, *The Little Magazine* Others *and the Renovation of Modern American Poetry* (2006), situates Loy's early poetic development in the context of the little magazines that provided her space for poetic experimentation and allowed her unconventional writing to be recognized as poetry. Similarly situating Loy in the places she inhabited, Cristanne Miller's *Cultures of Modernism: Marianne Moore, Mina Loy, and Else Lasker-Schüler* (2007) asserts the constitutive importance of the cosmopolitan locations of New York and Berlin to Loy's (and the other poets') experiences of subjectivity, gender, race, and religion, particularly through discourses and patterns of diverse immigration, racial, ethnic, and religious identities and languages.

Technology and science offer another vector with Loy's work by the 2000s. Loy is central to Alex Goody's (re)mapping of the modernist moment as generated through forces of technology, Jewishness, the body, consumerism, and war. Goody argues in *Modernist Articulations: A Cultural Study of Djuna Barnes, Mina Loy, and Gertrude Stein* (2007) and in a subsequent essay on "Anglo-Mongrels" (2011) for a materialistically feminist modernism responding through the maternal body to modernity's oppressive, patriarchal forces. Lara Vetter, in *Modernist Writings and Religio-Scientific Discourse: H.D., Loy, and Toomer* (2010), situates Loy in relation to other writers to argue a "religio-scientific discourse" underlying representations of the body. Vetter maps Loy's sustained interest in Christian Science, Eastern religion, and Judaism, in relation to scientific discourses of electromagnetism and evolutionary biology. Other techno-scientific contexts motivate Tim Armstrong's treatment of technology, mechanical systems, the body, and self-constructed female agency in Loy's 1919 pamphlet, "Auto-Facial Construction" in *Modernism, Technology, and the Body: A Cultural Study* (1998). Jessica Burstein's *Cold*

Modernism: Literature, Fashion, Art (2012) includes a chapter that moves between Loy's early writings and her inventions and designs, paying particular attention to concepts of the body that develop over her career as artist, designer, entrepreneur, and writer, and taking part in what Burstein theorizes as a "cold modernism" concerned with exteriors rather than internalized subjectivities.

The pronounced move into the archives and discussions of archival theory informing twenty-first-century literary studies further expands our apprehension of Loy's writing across genres. As with Crangle's 2011 edition of stories and prose, scholars have brought more attention to Loy's prose. Sandeep Parmar, in *Reading Mina Loy's Autobiographies: Myth of the Modern Woman* (2013), offers the first sustained reading of Loy's published and unpublished autobiographical works, constructing a chronology of these writings and seeking to counter the mythmaking tendency she judges as problematic in feminist readings of Loy as a "new woman."

These works exemplify how new directions in modernist studies have shaped approaches to Loy but also the ways in which enhanced understandings of Loy's life and works inform how we might rethink modernism and the avant-garde. *The Salt Companion to Mina Loy* (2010), edited by Rachel Potter and Suzanne Hobson, seeks to acknowledge the "proliferation of [...] different Loys" due to changing directions and approaches in modernist studies. The *Salt Companion* draws upon "British-based scholarship" in discussions of prose, poetry, and drama, and in bringing emphasis to the later work balanced with new readings of the early work.

A turn to the digital humanities reveals further projects inspired by Loy, exploring how digital technology brings new reading practices to her avant-garde experimentalism and intermediality. Our interactive website *Mina Loy: Navigating the Avant-Garde* (mina-loy.com) explores the digital environment as a space of collaboration, interdisciplinarity, and immersive scholarship (2020). On the site, the "Mina Loy Baedeker: Scholarly Book for Digital Travelers" (mina-loy.com/chapters/) contextualizes and interprets Loy's relationship to the avant-garde, offering contextualized readings of her poetry, prose, letters, artwork, designs, and related artifacts. This digital space invites "user-directed" inquiry, allowing users to chart their own course through Loy's career and to interact with archival materials, artwork, maps, and other artifacts.

The digital environment enables innovative engagement with Loy's writing, design, and art. In 2014, Andrew Pilsch launched *Mina Loy Online*, a digital collection of Loy's Futurist works, formatted to preserve line breaks and spacing. A recent special issue of *Feminist Modernist Studies*, "Feminist Modernist Digital Humanities," includes two essays on Loy. Margarat Konkol's "Prototyping Mina Loy's Alphabet" considers the "interpretive and methodological implications of using 3D printing technologies to prototype the archival diagrams of a proposed but never constructed plastic segmental alphabet letter kit" (294). Our article, "Feminist Designs: Modernist Digital Humanities and *Mina Loy: Navigating the Avant-Garde*," considers how "design is fundamental to feminist digital humanities studies" (Churchill et al., "Feminist Designs" 243). Further exploring digital approaches to archival materials, our "Digital Baedeker: A Feminist Experiment with Mina Loy's Archive," appears in *Poets and Archives* (2019).

Interdisciplinary attention to visual and performing arts—Loy's paintings, designs, theatrical compositions, and interest in modern dance—currently energizes our understanding of her cross-media career, as has new access to much of her surviving visual art. Until recently, a critical lacuna about Loy as a visual artist persisted due to scarce or difficult access resulting from the loss of so much of Loy's visual art, the dispersal of known pieces among private collections, and the limited amount of artwork reproduced in publication. A primary goal of our website involves tracing and analyzing visual and verbal connections across Loy's work. With the support of Roger Conover and generous access to his foundational collection of Loy's art, the website includes discussions and reproductions of numerous art pieces. Essays on this site include Burke's narrative of pursuing Loy's late assemblage *Househunting*; Suzanne Zelazo's piece on Conover's house and collection of art and books; and Conover's account of the recovery of her 1959 assemblage, *Prospector 2*. Moreover, story-maps and images enabled by this project's digital environment (often developed by students) and our own "Digital Baedeker" speak to vital dimensions of Loy's work as an artist.

New availability of Loy's art, such as the discovery by Amy E. Elkins of "lost" photographs by Berenice Abbott of Loy's late assemblages (held at the Ryerson Gallery) richly includes among its reproduced images a set of previously unpublished works by Loy (2019). While attracting the interest of literary critics for years, Loy's artwork has begun to gain the attention of art historians and institutions to further recognize Loy's career as an artist and develop fruitful cross-disciplinary study. Adding to art historical perspectives on Loy is Mary Ann Caws's recent biography, *Mina Loy: Apology of Genius* (2022), with its generous inclusion of some fifty-four illustrations, many of artwork previously unpublished.

And it is the art itself that so many of us have wanted to see! Promising to have a major impact on Loy studies going forward, the 2023 exhibition *Mina Loy: Strangeness Is Inevitable* brought together the largest collection of her work seen together and constituted her first show since 1933 (Levy Gallery) and 1959 (Bodley Gallery).[4] The accompanying catalog, bearing the same title and edited by curator Jennifer Gross, includes essays by art historians (Gross, Anne Collins Goodyear, and Dawn Ades), a poet (Ann Lauterbach), and Loy's major collector and literary executor, Roger Conover (also a poet and critic).

Significantly, a profusion of critical monographs devoted to Loy have appeared in the short period of time since 2017, signaling the accumulated interest in this once-forgotten modernist with new approaches and contexts for reading her work. Much of this work is especially attentive to avant-garde formations and cultures. Tara Prescott's *Poetic Salvage: Reading Mina Loy* (2017) serves as a directed guide through Loy's (especially early) poetry, excavating previously underexplored sources for Loy's writing, such as the Baedeker travel guidebooks, Parisian sites like the Cabaret du Néant, and a range of little magazines publishing her work. Linda A. Kinnahan's *Mina Loy, 20th-Century Photography, and Contemporary Women Poets* (2017) charts the relationship between the rise of photography and Loy's poetry, with particular attention to developments in Surrealism, documentary photography, and photojournalism in the 1930s and 1940s. Sarah Hayden's *Curious Disciplines: Mina Loy and Avant-Garde Artisthood* (2018) foregrounds Loy's involvement with the twentieth-century avant-garde art movements (Futurism, Dada, Surrealism, "degenerate art"), arguing for Loy's intervention, critique, and participation in efforts to construct new notions of art and theories of artistic identity. Laura Scuriatti's *Mina Loy's Critical Modernism* (2019) brings much needed readings of the Italian cultural and literary sources informing Loy's Florence period and explores her relations with a global modernism. Yasna Bozhkova's *Between Worlds: Mina Loy's Aesthetic Itineraries* (2022) analyzes the intermedial, inter-arts development of Loy's work, particularly in relation to her various geographic and aesthetic migrations. And recently, the two-volume study by Sara Crangle, *An Anatomy of Mina Loy: Nethered Regions* and *Elevated Realms* (2024), comprehensively analyzes Loy's published and unpublished writing to examine a feminist relation to body and soul.

Promising a vigorous future and growing community, Loy scholarship is currently generating exciting forms that are truly international, interdisciplinary, and intermedial—like Loy herself. Significantly, the current field is refreshingly energized by younger generations of scholars and writers. Marking the centennial of Loy's first book *Lunar Baedecker* [*sic*] (1923), two international symposia, organized by and including a new generation of emerging international scholars, focused on new directions, materials, and connections. Each gathering embraced interdisciplinary, multimedia, and innovative formats, using digital means to inclusively reach a broad audience: *Mina Loy and Her Networks* (held in-person in Paris and digitally, September 2023) and *"All about / Unfolding": Mapping Mina Loy Studies* (digital symposium, August 2023).[5] These symposia both energized a lively, expansive sense of community that promises to grow even stronger as new and existing scholars, artists, and readers encounter Loy by realizing her admonition to "Make the world your salon."[6]

Responding to Loy's call, scholars and practitioners across the arts have begun to explore modes of performance as strategy and form in her literary, visual, and dramatic works. Recently, the performance space of the theater has opened up for Loy with experimental productions of her plays, which illuminate aspects of the poetic dramas that are less palpable in print: their resistance to introspection, the use of costume as a source of humor and social commentary; the importance of noise and sound effects; and the deployment of physical comedy along with verbal sparring (see chapter 3). Loy admired modern dancers Isadora Duncan and Vaslav Nijinsky, suggesting aesthetic links to this art form that critics

Alex Goody and Megan Girdwood explore, and her prose ballet *Crystal Pantomime* has inspired recent adaptations. Loy's work has also inspired scholarly and creative explorations of its musical dimensions, including Susan Rosenbaum's examination of Loy's jazz aesthetics (see chapter 4), Andrew Michael Roberts's focus on jazz and rhythm in Loy's poetry, and Conover's discussion of references to Loy in popular music by Busterwolf, Thurston Moore, and Billy Corgan,[7] to which one can add the Pittsburgh-based band Short Fictions, led by Sam Treber, who learned about Loy in a college English class. Indeed, Loy's literary and visual works have influenced a wide variety of original creative projects, ranging from an off-Broadway play, to dance performances, art exhibits, and musical productions. The lists below include all the exhibits, performances, and productions known to us, which, if recent interest in Mina Loy is any indication, will surely grow.

I. CHRONOLOGY OF EXHIBITS INCLUDING LOY'S ARTWORK[8]

- 1904, exhibits six watercolors at the Salon d'Automne in Paris, as Mina Loy, including *The Mother*
- Spring 1905, two watercolors at the Salon des Beaux-Arts
- Fall 1905, four drawings, portraits of women at Salon d'Automne
- Spring 1906, Burke suggests that Loy has work in the Salon des Beaux-Arts but does not specify (*Becoming* 100)
- Fall 1906, Loy exhibits watercolors in Salon d'Automne described by the *Gazette des Beaux-Arts* as "uncommon watercolors where Guys, Rops and Beardsley are combined, [showing] us ambiguous ephebes whose nudity is caressed by ladies dressed in the furbelows of 1855," including *L'amour dorloté par les belles dames* (Burke, *Becoming* 100) (color plate, Gross 15); invited to become a member of *sociétaire*, the Salon d'Automne society (Gross 16)
- 1912, one-woman show, Carfax Gallery, London, includes *Maison en Papier*, *Ladies at Tea*, *Japanese Toys*, *Voyageurs*, *Bridge at Dinan* (all lost except first) (Gross 30)
- 1913, Salon d'Automne (*The Sewing Machine* [oil]; *Le Cirque Hagenback à Florence*, *La Petit carnival*, *La Grotte de Cythere* [drawings]) (Burke, *Becoming* 151, Gross 30)

- 1914, exhibits two works at the Friday Club (Vanessa Bell) in London (*Woman's Head* and *Maria con Bruno*) (Burke, *Becoming* 159)
- 1914, *First Free Futurist International Exhibition*, Sprovieri Gallery, Rome, contributed three portraits of Marinetti and the painting *Dynamism of the Subconscious*, all lost (Burke, *Becoming* 166)
- 1915, Loy included in a group exhibition at the Architectural League of New York
- 1917, *Society of Independent Artists* exhibition, New York, including Loy's painting *Making Lampshades*, now lost (Burke, *Becoming* 227)
- 1921, shows drawings from Italy at Belmaison Gallery, New York (Gross 46)
- 1923, exhibited one painting, *Marchands de New York*, at Salon d'Automne (Burke, *Becoming* 338)
- 1925, Peggy Guggenheim arranges exhibits of Loy's pressed flower "arrangements," titled *Jaded Blossoms*, in New York galleries and department stores such as Macy's and Namm Gallery in Brooklyn; and the Cargoes Gallery (Gross 56)
- 1925, Exhibit of Loy's portrait drawings of friends such as Stein, Brâncuşi, and Marinetti, arranged by Guggenheim at the Little Gallery at the Mattatuck Historical Society, Waterbury, Connecticut (Gross 57)
- 1925, with Guggenheim's backing, Loy opens a lamp shop in Paris, Galeries Mina Loy on the rue du Colissé, exhibiting and selling her lamp and lampshade creations; shop closes in 1930
- 1933 (January 24–February 14), Loy's painting *Faces* (later titled *Stars*) exhibited in Chick Austin's *Exhibition of Literature and Poetry in Painting since 1850* at the Wadsworth Atheneum (arranged by Levy) (Gross 70)
- January–February 1933, solo show at the Levy Gallery, NY, *Paintings by Mina Loy*
- 1959, Bodley Gallery exhibit of Bowery assemblages, what Loy called her "Refusées" (works left in her Stanton Street apartment when she departed for Aspen in 1953, under care of friends Alex Bossom and Stevie Ferris), arranged by Marcel Duchamp, Julien Levy, and David Mann
- 1959, Frances Steloff exhibits *No Parking* in her Gotham Book Mart's Window, alongside Loy's 1958 book, *Lunar Baedeker & Time-Tables*. (Burke, *Becoming* 436)

- 2005, McCullen Museum of Art, Boston College, *Accommodations of Desire: Surrealist Works on Paper Collected by Julien Levy*, includes Loy's painting *Surreal Scene*
- 2006, *Daughters of Dada*, Francis M. Naumann Fine Art, New York, June 8–July 28, exhibits several paintings and assemblages; review in *The New York Times* (July 6) includes a photo of *Christ on a Clothesline*; a review in *The Sun* (July 20) includes a photo of *Communal Cot*; the website for the show displays several images of Loy's work: *Teasing a Butterfly* (painting); *Portrait of Man Ray* (pencil)[9]
- 2012, *In Wonderland: The Surrealist Adventures of Women Artists in Mexico and the United States*, LACMA, included Loy's *Surreal Scene*
- 2019, *The New York Dada and Arensberg Circle of Artists*, Francis M. Naumann Fine Art, New York, included *Communal Cot* (1949) and pencil self-portrait (1905)
- 2022, Venice Biennale, *59th International Art Exhibition*, curated by Cecilia Alemani, included Loy's assemblage *Househunting* (circa 1950)
- 2023, *Mina Loy: Strangeness Is Inevitable*, solo retrospective, Bowdoin College Museum of Art
- 2024, *Mina Loy: Strangeness Is Inevitable*, solo retrospective, Chicago Art League
- 2024, Mina Loy's mixed media assemblage *Househunting* exhibited as part of the *Judy Chicago Herstory* exhibition at the New Museum (New York), displayed in *The City of Ladies* exhibition, which was part of the Herstory exhibition.

II. CHRONOLOGY OF THEATRICAL PRODUCTIONS OF LOY'S PLAYS

- 2010, *The Pamperers*, staged reading at the Open Space Gallery, Victoria BC (Canada), directed by Siobhán Scarry
- 2023, *Mina Loy's Feminist Futurist Dramas*, Michigan State University, a production of Loy's early plays involving a team of interdisciplinary artists, professional actors, and scholars led by Alison Dobbins; directed by Melissa C. Thompson[10]

- 2024, *The Sacred Prostitute and Other Plays by Mina Loy*, University of Maine at Farmington, student performance directed by Melissa C. Thompson
- 2024, two performances of Loy's prose ballet, *Crystal Pantomime*, staged by the experimental theater company, Every house has a door, in conjunction with the Chicago Arts Club exhibit of *Mina Loy: Strangeness Is Inevitable*.

III. ORIGINAL CREATIVE PROJECTS AND PRODUCTIONS INSPIRED BY LOY

A. Visual Art and Exhibits

- 2007, Ulrike Müller, *Curiosity (Drawings)*, a series deriving titles from lines of Loy's poem "Lunar Baedeker" (1923), which for the artist "evokes particular otherworldly qualities of light, temperature, and scenery" (interview with Steel Stillman); included in *"What 'F' Word" (for Feminism)* at Cynthia Broan Gallery, New York
- 2018–2022, Kim Rae, *Aging beyond Modernism: The Modernism Project*, oil portraits of aging modernist women writers and artists (developing project), includes portrait of an aged Loy; 2018, exhibit at Triangle Gallery at Sinclair College, Dayton, Ohio; 2019, Back Room Gallery, Delray Beach, Florida; 2022, Kennedy Heights Art Center, Cincinnati
- 2020, Mary Montgomery Lee, *Househunting*, inspired by Loy's assemblage of that name and exhibit digitally, *Mina Loy, Navigating the Avant-Garde, Post(cards): En Dehors Garde Flash Mob*; included in her unpublished *Dada, Stitch, and Story*, a multimedia series on Dada using found materials and collage, included in the Brooklyn Art Library Sketchbook Project
- 2025, Cheremoya Gallery, Los Angeles, *Islands in the Air* (July 9–August 16, 2025), group exhibition organized around Loy's recently published novel *Islands in the Air* (ed. Karla Kelsey, 2024).

B. Music and Dance Productions[11]

- 1994, *Argentum*, billed in the program as "a suite for silver flutes and percussion (mostly silver), inspired by silver, and silver related poems," presented *Silver Lucifer*, a musical interpretation of Mina Loy's "Lunar Baedeker," at the Cleveland Museum of Art in December, 1994

- 1998, *Mina and Colossus* (a new musical) written by Ron Nyren with music by Sam David and directed by John Neville-Andrews, presented at the Video Studio, Media Union at the University of Minnesota School of Music
- 1999, *The Sacred Prostitute and Other Tales from the Home of a Mad Woman*, staged at the Rarig Center Xperimental Theatre at the University of Minnesota in November, directed by Anja Klock
- 1999, *Gina & Miovanni*, a dance performance, performed at Cankarjev Dom Cultural Center in Ljubljana, Slovenia, by the dance company En-Knap, choreographed by Maja Delak
- 2005, The song "Mina Loy: M.O.H." appears on the first solo album by Smashing Pumpkins' frontman Billy Corgan, *The Future Embrace*, and is performed by Corgan on *The Late Show with David Letterman* (June 20)
- 2007, *Mina*, an off-broadway play written by Leslie Lee and performed at La Mama E.T.C. Theater
- 2011, Thurston Moore of Sonic Youth releases "Mina Loy" on his solo album *Demolished Thoughts*, with *Rolling Stone* naming it one of the "Best 25 Songs of the Year"
- 2019, rock band Short Fictions, led by Sam Treber, releases "Property of Pigeons," drawing on Loy's poem, on the album *Fates Worse Than Death*
- 2024, Busterwolf performed his 2016 track "Mina Loy" during closing events for *Mina Loy: Strangeness Is Inevitable*, Bowdoin College (January 22, 2024).

Notes

PREFACE

1 The German novella *Venus in Furs* (*Venus im Pelz*, 1870) by Leopold von Sacher-Masoch bears reading with Mina Loy's "Feminist Manifesto" (1914) and her relationship with Filippo Tommaso Marinetti in mind.

ACKNOWLEDGMENTS

2 https://mina-loy.com/

INTRODUCTION

1 For fuller discussions of Loy's biography, see Burke, *Becoming*; Caws, *Mina Loy: Apology of Genius*; Kouidis, *Mina Loy: American Modernist Poet.*

2 For a fuller history of the website project, see Churchill et al., "Digital Baedeker."

3 Specifically, *Travels with Mina Loy* recasts our born-digital book *Mina Loy Baedeker: A Scholarly Guide for Digital Travelers* that appears on our scholarly website (https://mina-loy.com/chapters/). While some of the content is similar, much has been revised, and the network and database structures of the website have been remediated here into the linear narrative and argument characteristic of the book format.

4 According to the Beinecke Library, "The Mina Loy Papers were donated to the Beinecke Rare Book and Manuscript Library by Loy's daughter, Joella Haweis Bayer, in 1974 and 1975. Additional materials were donated by Mina

Loy's grandson, Jonathan Bayer, in 2009" ("Mina Loy Papers: Collection Overview").

5 Carolyn Burke's biography and the recent Bowdoin catalog of Loy's visual art make tantalizing references to many works of visual art that have been lost.

6 See Exhibit 2: Collecting and Exhibiting Mina Loy: Timetable of Critical and Scholarly Reception and Creative Productions.

7 See Exhibit 1: Mina Loy Bio, Map, and Timeline.

8 The term *intermediality* has usefully entered discussions of Loy. See, for example, work by Scuriatti, Bozhkova, Hayden, and Gross, as well as our website, *Mina Loy: Navigating the Avant Garde*.

9 See also: Bentivoglio and Zoccoli, *Women Artists of Italian Futurism*; Kamenish, *Mamas of Dada*; Rosemont, *Surrealist Women*; and Caws et al., *Surrealism and Women*.

10 In first proposing a new feminist theory of the en dehors garde on our website *Mina Loy: Navigating the Avant-Garde*, we also sought to generate theory in a new way, activating theory-making through a collaborative method enabled by digital tools and platforms. Typically, theory is written by a lone scholar and delivered in a coherent, linear argument. We instead orchestrated a digital flash mob and invited artists, writers, and Loy readers to submit "post(card)" submissions online, offering their theoretical formulations of the en dehors garde in whatever medium or format they chose.

11 Kimberlé Crenshaw coined the term "intersectionality" in 1989 to expose how interlocking systems of power affect marginalized individuals via intersections of gender, race, class, and other identity categories that are not detectable when each factor is considered in isolation. In recent interviews, Crenshaw defines intersectionality as "a prism to bring to light dynamics within discrimination law that weren't being appreciated by the courts" (qtd. in Coaston); she insists that it is not a "grand theory" but a "lens through which you can see where power comes and collides, where it interlocks and intersects" ("Kimberlé Crenshaw on Intersectionality"). See also Crenshaw, "Mapping the Margins."

12 In contrast, Scuriatti and Bozhkova approach ekphrasis and dialogic relations between Loy, creative movements, artwork, and artists as forms of "collaboration" or "constellation." Scuriatti argues for the dialogic process—understood as a "modality of being that is based in interaction and dialogue" with "the works of others"—as a form of "collaboration"; Bozhkova draws upon Loy's own language of "constellation" as a "conceptual model for an aesthetic encounter between artists" (7) or "modernist communities" and

"disparate aesthetics" with which Loy creates "dialectical tensions and complex dialogues" (8). Bozhkova focuses chiefly on Loy's ekphrastic poems to demonstrate this dialectic engagement. Drawing on the work of Elizabeth Bergmann-Loizeaux, we regard Loy's dialectic engagements as chiefly a form of ekphrastic response to and dialogue with *previously created* artworks and past artists, as distinguished from "collaborations" which involve "an exchange between poet and artist in which there is some contact and discussion between the collaborators (whether it be face-to-face or not) and in which at least one of the partners creates in response to the other's work (whether it be on the same page or not)" (Bergmann-Loizeaux 137). Although Loy did not create hybrid works with other living artists, her sequential epistolary exchange with a living artist (such as Cornell) serves as a literary form of social-artistic networking, and can be usefully approached as a form of *sequential* collaboration or collage, as discussed in chapter 4. See Bergmann-Loizeaux's cogent overview of ekphrasis and collaboration in her book *Twentieth-Century Poetry and the Visual Arts*.

13 For discussions of decentering the historic avant-garde, see for example Bäckström and Hjartarson, *Decentering the Avant-Garde*; Benson and Forgács, *Between Worlds*.

14 *Travels with Mina Loy* draws upon both print and digital archives of Loy's art and writings. Each chapter makes note of which collections it uses and how it cites them.

CHAPTER ONE

1 See Hayden, *Curious Disciplines*, 16–17. Hayden reads Loy's Florentine poems as "witnesses to her engagement with, digestion of, and ultimate rejection of Futurist conceptions of artistic identity" (25). We want to suggest, moreover, a view of Loy that decenters Futurism with her own en dehors garde movements, rather than to proffer a direct connection to the movement (as Hayden substantively explores).

2 On the Futurists' visual poetics, see Bohn, *Modern Visual Poetry* and *Reading Visual Poetry*; Webster.

3 Hayden notes that, while Loy "repeatedly attested to the movement's ignition of her literary career, the degree to which her poetic is indebted to a specifically Futurist model remains a contentious issue" (25).

4 Burke notes that Haweis's photography garnered attention and "the firm of Haweis and Coles produced over two hundred photographs of Rodin's work" in 1903 and 1904, including Haweis's portrait of Rodin, which received

critical praise along with other photographs he showed at the time (*Becoming* 91). Loy often modeled for him.

5 Loy to Stephen Haweis, 27 Mar. 1914, Mabel Dodge Luhan papers, YCAL MSS 196.

6 Loy to Van Vechten, undated, Carl Van Vechten papers, YCAL MSS 1050, images 121–122.

7 See Scuriatti, *Mina Loy's Critical Modernism*, for an excellent history and analysis of Italian feminism following the formation of the Italian nation and into the early twentieth century, especially concerning debates about women's rights and the relation of maternity and national identity, as important contexts for Loy's feminist expressions.

8 Loy to Dodge Luhan, Feb. 1914, Mabel Dodge Luhan papers, YCAL MSS 196, image 8.

9 "First Costa Visit," box 1, folder 2, YCAL MSS 6, series 1, image 17. This chapter makes use of the Beinecke Library's digital collection, in which *Brontolivido* is found in YCAL MSS 6, series 1. The manuscript is divided into sections titled by Loy, which reside in different folders. Subsequent quotations from *Brontolivido* parenthetically reference the titled subsection, folder number, and digital image number. Relevant URLs can be found in the works cited list.

10 "Second Costa Visit," box 1, folder 8, image 1.

11 "First Costa Visit," box 1, folder 2, image 5, (variant) image 25. Harris notes that Loy refers to this manuscript as "Possessions" in letters to Van Vechten, gesturing toward the "campy" treatment of "sex wars" underscored by a satirical analysis of romantic possession, as both submitted to and resisted.

12 "Grande Serata Futurista," *Lacerba* (periodico quindicinale), Florence, 15 Dec. 1913, vol. 1, no. 24. pp. 281–96.

13 See Marinetti, "Technical Manifesto."

14 Scuriatti offers valuable overviews of Italian feminist discussions, especially regarding the place of women within the relatively new nation, and how they might have helped shape Loy's feminist perspectives. See "Transnational" and *Mina Loy's Critical Modernism*.

15 The entire sequence of "Anglo-Mongrels and the Rose" is included in LLB82. During Loy's lifetime, portions were published in *The Little Review* (1923), the *Contact Collection of Contemporary Writers* (1925), and *Lunar Baedeker & Time-Tables* (1958).

16 On Surrealism in American little magazines, see Dickran Tashjian, *Boatload of Madmen*; Rosenbaum, "Exquisite Corpse" .

17 On the Surrealists in New York during World War II, see in particular the studies by Martica Sawin, Dickran Tashjian, Jed Perl, and Sandra Zalman.

18 An important exception here is Ilene Susan Fort and Tere Arcq's *In Wonderland*, which includes a full-page reproduction of Mina Loy's painting *Surreal Scene* (1930), as well as a brief biography and treatment of her engagement with Surrealism. In addition, both Sarah Hayden in *Curious Disciplines*, and Linda Kinnahan in *Mina Loy, Twentieth-Century Photography, and Contemporary Women Poets*, offer in-depth analyses of Loy's relation to the Surrealist movement and her critical adaptations of Surrealism. More recently, the essays on Loy's visual art by Jennifer R. Gross, Ann Lauterbach, Dawn Ades, and Roger Conover engage Loy's debts to Surrealism (MLSII), while Sara Crangle discusses Loy and Bataille (*Elevated Realms* 43–51).

19 Figures involved in the Paris Surrealist movement who had been involved in Dada include Tristan Tzara and Francis Picabia, as well as the poets Breton, Philippe Soupault, and Louis Aragon, who together edited the journal *Littérature* (Rasula 169–75).

20 Chadwick further notes, "Their photographs are missing from formal Surrealist group portraits taken as late as 1934, but they appear frequently in informal snapshots of group activities" (9). On women and Surrealism, see in particular Allmer; Chadwick; Caws et al.; Conley; Fort and Arcq; Lusty, *Surrealism, Feminism, Psychoanalysis*; Hubert; P. Rosemont; Watz. See also the recent studies of individual women artists and their relationship to Surrealism, including Claude Cahun, Leonora Carrington, Meret Oppenheim, and Grace Pailthorpe.

21 Some women strongly identified as Surrealist, but others like Loy refused to do so, often owing to the movement's treatment of women, and ambivalence about affiliations with male-dominated avant-garde movements more generally (Chadwick 66). If we take a perspective broader than that of Bretonian Surrealism's official roster and histories, then, from the 1920s forward we can track many women who were "associated with Surrealism" (Chadwick 10).

22 See Rosemont and Kelley, *Black, Brown, & Beige*; for a summary of this history and the scholarship, see Rosenbaum, "Surrealist Histories," MLNAG.

CHAPTER TWO

1 Tara Prescott, discussing textual links between Loy's poetry and the Baedeker guide, speculates that Loy, in reading the Baedeker, "hears Flora, the Roman goddess of spring and flowers, embedded in 'Florence'"; subsequently, as in this quote from "Giovanni Franchi," she demythologizes this association for the tourist in her poem-as-guidebook (21).

2 All subsequent quotations reference this thirteenth edition (Karl Baedeker, *Italy: Handbook for Travelers, Northern Italy*, 1906), which includes a substantial entry on Florence and information about other places in the region that Loy references or visits.

3 Antonella Francini generously shared the exact location of Loy's first home in Florence, derived from her research in the State Archives in Florence. She also identified for us the passages in *Esau Penfold* that describe this first home (email to Kinnahan, June 22, 2025), which Carolyn Burke also draws upon in *Becoming Modern* (105–106). The website *Mina Loy: Navigating the Avant-Garde* mistakenly locates this home at the similarly named Villa dell'Ombrellino, which is in Bellosguardo in the hills southwest of the city. We are grateful to Francini for calling our attention to this error.

4 *Esau Penfold*, Mina Loy papers, YCAL MSS 6, box 1, folder 24, image 1.

5 Francini further notes that "Between the years 1900 and at least until 1923 this Villino was owned by Ms. Marianna Vanni, the person who may have loaned it to Stephen. It was later sold to a certain Carlo Eyre. I am told by the archivists that this Carlo Eyre may have lived in the Villino also at the beginning of the century, and perhaps he was the one to sublet it to Mina and Stephen" (email to Kinnahan, June 22, 2025, drawing upon State Archives of Florence).

6 Florence has subsequently renumbered houses on the street, and Loy's home is now no. 60 according to Carolyn Burke, Loy's biographer, who stayed in the home at one point in her research. Antonella Francini's research in the State Archives of Florence and Loy's letters reveal that Loy's rented apartments on the Costa San Giorgio were located at no. 45 (now no. 77) and no. 48 (now no. 54).

7 See chapter 1 on Loy and Futurism. Also see Hayden, *Curious Disciplines*; Scuriatti, "Transnational" and *Mina Loy's Critical Modernism*; Burke, *Becoming*; Schmid; Re; Lusty, "Sexing the Manifesto"; Stauder.

8 Hayden notes, for example, that "her alignment with the movement endowed her with a marketable public profile" that "Aphorisms on Futurism" exploits (*Curious Disciplines* 38).

9 Loy contributed four paintings to the *First Free Futurist International Exhibition* in February and March of 1914, including three portraits of Marinetti and a painting titled a *Dynamism of the Subconscious*. See Section III: Futurist Florence/Futurist Rome in this chapter.

10 The etymology of the girl's name suggests this excision, or being cut out of power: "Cesira is of Latin origin and it is used mainly in Italian. The name Cesira means 'she who was cut out of the womb, she with a head of hair, blue-grey color.' It is derived from *caedere* meaning 'to cut, to excise';

caesaries 'head of hair'; *caesius* 'blue-grey color.' From the Roman nickname. Cesira is the feminine version of the English *Caesar*" ("Cesira - Meaning of Cesira," *BabyNamesPedia*, https://www.babynamespedia.com/meaning/Cesira, accessed 9 June 2025).

11 Burke suggests that the poem references Haweis's infidelity while Loy gave birth to Oda in Paris (*Becoming* 95).

12 "Summer Night in a Florentine Slum" was first published in Contact 1 (December 1920), pp. 6–7. It is republished in LLB82; all subsequent references are to this publication.

13 In 1923, Dodge married Tony Luhan, thereafter using the name Mabel Dodge Luhan, including for her memoir herein referenced. While Loy knew her initially as Mabel Dodge in Florence, the full name she chose upon marrying Luhan will be used throughout.

14 Burke references a 1911 letter from Loy to Stein (Dec. 2, 1911), Gertrude Stein papers, Beinecke Collection of American Literature.

15 "Ducie" is an alternatively spelled version of "Dusie," the nickname she derived as a student in Munich and that continued with Haweis (see Burke, *Becoming* 62; Hayden, *Curious Disciplines* 229). See Churchill, "Loy's Signature Style" for examples of her handwritten names and a discussion of her changing nomenclature.

16 She would place Lowy in a central role as the immigrant Jewish figure of Exodus in her later long poem "Anglo-Mongrels and the Rose."

17 For further context, see chapter 1, "Touring Italy, Travels with Futurism."

18 Rowan Harris notes that the unpublished novel *Brontolivido* is called "Possessions" in Loy's correspondence with Van Vechten (Mina Loy Papers, YCAL MSS 6, folders 1–6) and should be read as evidence of early experimental writing by Loy rather than a transparent autobiography (32).

19 "First Costa Visit" box 1, folder 2, YCAL MSS 6, series 1, image 17 (qtd. in Burke, *Becoming* 165). This chapter makes use of the Beinecke Library's digital collection in which *Brontolivido* is found in YCAL MSS 6, series 1. The manuscript is divided into sections titled by Loy, which reside in different folders. Subsequent quotations from *Brontolivido* parenthetically reference the titled subsection, folder number, and digital image number.

20 Drafts of "Rome" exist in two boxes, each containing the same language for this quotation: box 8, folder 195, image 2; and box 1, folder 7, image 5 (qtd. in Burke, *Becoming* 166).

21 "Power-House" 538.

22 "Sometimes We Dread the Future" 14, with photographs by Paul Thompson. *Every Week* was published from 1915 to 1918, with a subscription reaching

600,000 readers. The digital archives, accessed through the University of Nebraska-Lincoln, are described as "a rich cultural resource for those interested in the World War I home front, popular fiction, advertising, and constructions of race and gender during this period" (http://everyweek.unl.edu/).

23 See Harris and Scuriatti (*Mina Loy's Critical Modernism*) for interesting discussions of sexuality, as viewed respectively by Loy and by the Futurists, within contexts of contemporaneous theories advanced variously, for example, by Otto Weininger or by Italian feminism.

24 Prescott identifies "echoes" of the Baedeker guide in the "language of these lines," establishing connections between the popular travel guides—which would define "trattoria" and "piazza" for British inhabitants like Loy—with Loy's work (21).

25 Mabel Dodge Luhan papers, YCAL MSS 196, series 2, box 62, folder 1658, images 1–7. Loy's writing continues an extensive interest in female anatomy, theorizing women's creativity and intellect at various points in relation to the womb and the potential for reproduction. See her chapter "The Outraged Womb" in *The Parent and the Child* (in *Lost Writings*, ed. Kelsey) and Crangle's "'Upon Bossed Bellies': Loy and the Accursed Muse" in *Nethered Regions: An Anatomy of Mina Loy*.

26 "Nightingale and Peacock," *Rogue*, May 1915; later reprinted in *Sacred and Profane Memories*, 91.

27 Historically contextualizing Loy's manifesto in relation to Italian feminism, Laura Scuriatti argues that maternity "is seen as a right in the 'Feminist Manifesto,' and as a contribution to the betterment of the race, whereas it is equated with creation in 'Parturition'" (*Mina Loy's Critical Modernism* 308).

28 Issuing such calls, "The Prototype" prefigures Loy's Bowery poems of the 1940s and 1950s, especially "Hot Cross Bum."

29 Burke quotes from "The colonial lady artist," a section among the fragments of Loy's unpublished prose narrative *Esau Penfold*.

30 The title is written on the back of the painting, now in Roger Conover's collection. Although the title translates as "Bath Houses," the subject matter of the painting clearly depicts signage of a play title and individuals dressed for a theater outing.

31 See also Churchill's story-map at *Mina Loy: Navigating the Avant-Garde*, "Mina Loy, 'Maison des Bains a Forte dei Marmi'" (https://mina-loy.com/art-exhibits/maison-des-bains-a-forte-dei-marmi/).

32 See also Kinnahan's story-map at *Mina Loy: Navigating the Avant-Garde*, "Mina Loy, 'The Beach'" (https://mina-loy.com/art-exhibits/storymap-of-the-beach/).

33 Carl Van Vechten papers, YCAL MSS 1050, series 1, box 76, folder 1082–83, image 62, letter Sept. 8, 1914. Loy signs the letter "Dusie" rather than the spelling adopted by Van Vechten and Mabel Dodge. At other times, she signs "Doosie," and around 1915 starts signing "Mina." See Churchill, "Loy's Signature Style."

34 A case in point involves the first issue of the little magazine *Others*, appearing in 1915. Featuring Loy's "Love Songs," it prompted controversy about the poem's sexualized content and disjunctive, spatially active form. One critic of *vers libre*, writing a 1915 article on modern free verse for *The New York Call*, titled it "This Summer's Style in Poetry, or the Elimination of Corsets in Versifying," likening the abandonment of restrictive female fashions to the elimination of poetic conventions (Julius 3). That summer, the *New York Tribune* furthered the comparison with modern dance and women's liberation, producing a story headlined "Free-Footed Verse Is Danced in Ridgefield, N.J. Get What Meaning You Can Out of the Futurist Verse [...] It's as Esoteric as Gertrude Stein Herself" (Johns 7). Visiting the artists' colony where Alfred Kreymborg developed *Others*, the reporter Margaret Johns noted the "early prominence taken in it [the free verse movement] by women" (7). Equating women's suffrage and "free-footed verse," as Burke observes, suggests that the "unfettered movement" of a dancer like Isadora Duncan (who danced in New York in 1916) "lay behind the metaphor of 'free-footed verse': the image of bare feet, liberated from stiff shoes and dated choreographies," like the radical female dancer and her free-flowing costumes, "recurred whenever people discussed the new movement" (Burke, "The New Poetry" 45–46).

35 Carl Van Vechten papers, YCAL MSS 1050, series 1, box 76, folder 1082–1083, images 59–60, letter Sept. 8, 1914.

36 See also Kinnahan's story-map at *Mina Loy: Navigating the Avant-Garde*, "Mina Loy, Fashion Designs" (https://mina-loy.com/art-exhibits/mina-loy-fashion-designs-c-1914/).

37 Moreover, the painting (now in Roger Conover's collection) was once in Van Vechten's possession, a provenance secured by a label on the back of the painting stating "From the Collection of Carl Van Vechten." Perhaps these designs, each signed by Loy, inspired his vivid memories of Loy's own self-fashioning, more than a decade after their sojourn to Vallombrosa.

38 See chapter 3, where Suzanne Churchill notes the dresses' resemblance to curtains and upholstery, a connection Loy makes explicit in the theatrical set of *The Pamperers*.

39 Eight separate Futurist manifestos on fashion were published between the 1910s and the 1930s.

40 Most Futurist fashion manifestos focused on men's clothing.

41 See Kinnahan, *Mina Loy, Twentieth-Century Photography* for a more in-depth discussion of these late poems and issues. Also see the digital story-map, "Mina Loy, Fashion Designs" found on our website, *Mina Loy: Navigating the Avant-Garde* (https://mina-loy.com/art-exhibits/mina-loy-fashion-designs-c-1914/).

42 Loy revisited New York for a period in 1920–1921, returning to Europe after Haweis took their son Giles to his Caribbean home without her knowledge or permission. She would not see her son again. Giles died of cancer in 1923, at the age of fourteen.

43 Photographs of the *Drift of Chaos* series, attributed to Maurice Poplin, are housed at the Yale Beinecke Rare Book and Manuscript Library, Carolyn Burke papers (YCAL MSS 778, Box 9) (https://collections.library.yale.edu/catalog/11140354). A digital scan of *The Sentinels* (image 27 in the archive) is available at https://collections.library.yale.edu/iiif/2/11174898/110,0,1483,1390/1483,1390/0/default.jpg.

44 Reproduced in Gross, *Mina Loy: Strangeness Is Inevitable* (2023), the image shows the baby seeming to fall headfirst into the ocean (97). However, according to Anne Goodyear, the museum director, line drawings discovered on the painting during restoration indicate that the figure, a cut-out paper pinned to the painting, was intended to be positioned horizontally (as though swimming) rather than vertically (as though tumbling headfirst).

CHAPTER THREE

1 Loy was upheld as the icon of the "modern woman" in the article "Do You Strive to Capture the Symbols of Your Reactions? If Not You Are Quite Old Fashioned," *New York Evening Sun*, Feb. 13, 1917 (10).

2 Loy, undated letter to Carl Van Vechten, Carl Van Vechten papers, series 1, box 76, folder 1082–1083, image 94, https://collections.library.yale.edu/catalog/2043789. This chapter makes use of the Beinecke Digital Collections, which currently group all Loy's letters to a given correspondent in a single folder of digital images, often out of chronological order. To make it easier to locate the exact letter, I will hereafter refer to the Beinecke Digital Collection of Loy's letters to Carl Van Vechten parenthetically as Loy/CVV followed by the image number.

3 Recent scholars have identified additional facets of Loy's critique of Futurism: Jessica Burstein observes that Loy diverged from the Futurists in her thinking about originality and habits of affiliation (155–156). Sarah Hayden argues that Loy developed alternative views of artistic identity and

"used the transatlantic loudspeaker thus granted her, in *Rogue*, *Camera Work*, and *Others*, to launch a complex critique of the [Futurist] movement—not for its problematic politics but for the flaws and fractures that trouble its template of avant-garde artisthood" (*Curious Disciplines* 58).

4 Although Sara Crangle classifies *Crystal Pantomime* as a drama (in Crangle's *Stories and Essay of Mina Loy*), as Alex Goody points out, the undated work is "actually a libretto for a ballet that Loy probably began in the early 1920s" ("The Dance" 138). This chapter limits its focus to Loy's en dehors garde turns toward audiences in the 1910s, which coincide with her move to New York City.

5 Loy uses the term "sex war" in undated letters to Mabel Dodge Luhan and Van Vechten, circa 1914–1915, as when she describes her affairs with the Futurists as "my utter defeat in the sex war" (Loy to Luhan, n.d., image 32 in the Mabel Dodge Luhan papers, series 1, box 24, folder 664–665, https://collections.library.yale.edu/catalog/10000282). Hereafter I will refer to this collection of Loy's letters to Mabel Dodge Luhan as Loy/MDL followed by the image number.

6 Manuscripts of these plays are available in the Beinecke Library's digital collection of Mina Loy papers: Poems and Plays [contains *Collision* and *Cittàbapini*] (YCAL MSS 1050, series 2, box 188, folder 2508, images 42– 47, https://collections.library.yale.edu/catalog/2112213); *The Sacred Prostitute* (YCAL MSS 6, series 1, box 6, folder 176, https://collections.library.yale.edu/catalog/12154402); *The Pamperers* (YCAL MSS 6, series 1, box 6, folder 169, https://collections.library.yale.edu/catalog/11859518). *The Sacred Prostitute* and *The Pamperers* are collected in *Stories and Essays of Mina Loy*, ed. Sara Crangle. All four plays are available in the open-source edited collection, *Futurism, Feminism, and the Right to "Genius": Mina Loy's* The Sacred Prostitute *and Other Plays*, ed. Alison Dobbins.

7 I am immeasurably grateful to Nancy Selleck for her dramatic expertise and generative ideas. Our conversations catalyzed my thinking about Loy's plays, and her insights percolate in this chapter. Grateful appreciation also goes to Vivien Dietz, Suzanne Guasco, Annie Merrill, Anne Wills, Gabriel Ford, Ann Fox, Randy Ingram, Ben Mangrum, Naomi Watson, and Cate Goodin for their ideas and questions on various digital and print incarnations of this chapter.

8 Siobhán Scarry, who directed a staged reading of *The Sacred Prostitute* in 2010, describes them as "plays that draw attention to themselves as literary creations that are never subsumed into the apparent reality of the play" ("Introduction"). The few scholars who discuss the plays emphasize their importance to Loy's feminist critique of Futurism. Julie Schmid contends that they "constitute one of the only feminist responses to and reworkings of the futurist dramatic aesthetic," and "continue her critique of futurism and

women's place in the movement" (1, 3). Janet Lyon interprets them as satires of Futurist sexual politics and assertions of an alternative, maternal model of artistic genius (397).

9 Bay-Cheng explains that "poetic drama balances the theatrical engagement of the audience against the audience's ability to see through the physical performance to the structure of language underneath" (21). Asserting that "the concept of audience participation and collective engagement was once the essential aim of poetic drama," Bay-Cheng cites Loy's friend and contemporary Alfred Kreymborg, who wrote: "If there ever was a common art—an art in which authors, interpreter, and audience meet at the same performance—it is the drama, and especially the poetic drama" (qtd. in Bay-Cheng 26).

10 Mina Loy's *The Sacred Prostitute and Other Tales from the Home of a Mad Woman* was staged at the Rarig Center Xperimental Theatre at the University of Minnesota on Nov. 11–13, 1999, directed by Anja Klock. Loy's prose ballet *Crystal Pantomime* has also generated interest for its theatrical potential. In 2010, it was produced by the Poetry Project at St. Mark's Church in New York City, and in 2024, in conjunction with the *Strangeness Is Inevitable* exhibition of Loy's artwork, the Arts Club of Chicago invited the theatrical company Every house has a door to offer two performances of a new work anchored by a reading of *Crystal Pantomime* (https://www.everyhousehasadoor.org/performances/upcoming/crystal-pantomime).

11 To inspire and assist future productions of Loy's plays, Dobbins and her team published *Futurism, Feminism, and the Right to "Genius"*, an open-access educational resource that includes annotated scripts and video recordings of the Michigan and Maine productions.

12 This chapter references the manuscript of *Brontolivido* in the Beinecke Library's digital collection, YCAL MSS 6, series 1, https://archives.yale.edu/repositories/11/archival_objects/674898. The manuscript is divided into sections titled by Loy, which reside in separate digital folders. Subsequent quotations from *Brontolivido* parenthetically reference the section title followed by the digital image number.

13 In *The Autobiography of Alice B. Toklas*, Stein describes the friendship she struck up with Mina Loy during her summers in Florence in the early Teens, observing that Loy "equally interested was able to understand without the commas. She has always been able to understand" (*Selected Writings* 124). Not two paragraphs later, the narrative notes, "It was during this winter that Gertrude Stein began to write plays" (125). The temporal and narrative proximity of Stein talking with Loy and writing plays suggests the possibility that they may have influenced each other's forays into playwriting. An excerpt "From

a Play by Gertrude Stein" was reprinted in *Camera Work* no. 45 (June 1914), pp. 17–18, in the same issue as Loy's "Aphorisms on Futurism" (pp. 13–14), so we can assume that Loy read at least a sample of Stein's early plays. Certainly, Adam Frank's descriptive term for Stein's early "parlor plays" could equally be applied to Loy's poetic dramas of the same era, which share Stein's interest in conversation, intimacy, performativity, and scenes of everyday domestic and social life: "'Parlor play' improves on [Jane Palatini Bowers's term 'conversation play'] by retaining the connotations of speech (parler) but specifying an intimate, shared, psychically charged domestic space. Parlor, I suggest, foregrounds the performativity of setting and the compositional continuities between scenes of writing and other scenes of Stein's everyday life with Alice Toklas and their salon associates in Paris." Indeed, *The Pamperers* could be staged as a dramatization of Stein's famous salon, with the character of Diana a composite figure of Stein, Mabel Dodge, and Loy herself.

14 *The Sacred Prostitute* was not published until 2011, when it was collected in *Stories and Essays of Mina Loy* and graphically illustrated in *Triple Canopy*. While working on *The Sacred Prostitute*, Loy wrote to Van Vechten, saying, "I am going on with my play—which would not be printed in any magazine—it's too absolutely pure" (27 Via de' Bardi, Dec. 27, 1914, Loy/CVV 1). Characteristically, she uses the word "pure" to refer to her bold, explicit handling of sexual themes and defiance of conventional Christian morality.

15 Loy enjoyed acting enough to audition in December 1920 for the role of Esther, a "drab" spinster, in Laurence Vail's play *What D'You Want*. The play was staged by the Provincetown Players in early 1921, but Loy sailed for Europe before it finished its run (Burke, *Becoming* 296–297).

16 Schmid interprets the repetition as deliberate, arguing: "these stage directions indicate that the process is about to begin again, and at the end of the play the repetition of 'the curtain falls—the curtain falls,' subverts the conventional dramatic action of closure or resolution: what occurs isn't a singular process but, rather, a repetitive cycle of which the play records a mere fragment" (4).

17 The Futurist fantasy of male asexual reproduction is the driving theme of Marinetti's 1909 novel *Mafarka the Futurist*, whose eponymous hero's project "is to bypass the vulva and impregnate the ovary that is the male spirit" (Spackman 89–90), or in Mafarka's terms, "to create an immortal giant with unfailing wings, out of one's own flesh, without the collaboration and foul-smelling involvement of a woman's uterus!" ("Mafarka's Discourse" 38). Although Loy may have shared the Futurists' interest in generating new forms and engendering a more evolved human race, as Maren Linett argues,

she "clearly rejected Futurism's exclusion of women's bodies from the project" ("All Winged" 1166). Her critique finds expression in *Collision*, as well as "Parturition" and "Lion's Jaws."

18 In the 2024 production of the plays at Michigan State University, Brett Beaudry used clowning techniques to play the part of "the greenish man" and find the physical comedy in the script (Dobbins, email to Churchill, Mar. 14, 2025).

19 *Le voyage dans la lune* may be accessed online at the Internet Archive: https://archive.org/details/Levoyagedanslalune.

20 *The '?' Motorist* may be accessed online at BFI Player: https://player.bfi.org.uk/free/film/watch-the-motorist-1906-online.

21 For a production that makes use of digital animation tools, see Leah Mell's 3D animation of *Collision*.

22 Symons's explanation for the marionette's widespread appeal chimes with Loy's own aesthetic sensibility and aims for her poetic dramas: "The appeal in what seems to you these childish manoeuvres is to a finer, because to a more intimately poetic, sense of things than the merely rationalistic appeal of very modern plays. If at times we laugh, it is with wonder at seeing humanity so gay, heroic and untiring. There is the romantic suggestion of magic in this beauty" (103). In her plays and experimental writings of the mid-Teens, Loy similarly deploys "childish manoeuvres" to amuse audiences, yet is equally drawn to what she describes in her ballet *Crystal Pantomime* as "impression[s] of ethereal beauty" (SE 152).

23 This special issue may also have influenced the composition of "Biography of a Songge Byrd" (1952), Loy's unpublished tribute to Gordon Craig's lover, the modern dancer Isadora Duncan, which mentions marionettes: Loy states "and for another thing / of the love that did spring / up between John Silence / conceiver of Opera Houses / for Marionettes voices // and Songge Byrd / who, upon seeing him, / loosened her girdle / without a word" (4).

24 Loy continues to hound Van Vechten for feedback. After sending him the second half, she mails a letter on May 17, 1915, asking, "Did your kind friend ever get my roll of m.s.s.? With the latter half of the Prostitute Paradox (latest title)?" (Loy/CVV 20–21). She hopes her "things haven't got lost—& that [she will] soon get [his] opinion of them" (Loy/CVV 23). Frustrated with his silence, she writes another letter (circa fall 1915) complaining, "I have not had a word from you for months—only magazines— [...] I permitted you to publish anything you like—& I sent you all the trimmings & corrections of the Sacred Prostitute" (Loy/CVV 27).

25 See Sarah Crangle for a reading of *The Sacred Prostitute* as "the drama that is Loy's most overt, sustained riposte to the unexamined contradictions at the heart of the modernist affective economies that traffic in maintaining the subjugated uncertainty that is 'Woman!?!... .'" (*Nethered Regions*, 186).

26 Amy Feinstein quotes this letter in "Goy Interrupted," an essay that examines Loy's use of allegory in her unfinished 1930s novel *Goy Israels*.

27 From here on, I cite *The Sacred Prostitute* as published in the Crangle-edited *Stories and Essays of Mina Loy* (2011).

28 Crangle argues that Loy parodies Marinetti's best-selling *How to Seduce a Woman* (1917) (*Nethered Regions* 18).

29 Loy revisits the idea of women as domestic furnishings in her painting *Surreal Scene*, which Susan Rosenbaum discusses in detail in chapter 4.

30 Nancy Selleck shared this insight with me in one of our many conversations about the plays and this chapter.

31 Given that Loy's letters to Van Vechten refer to characters and lines absent in the surviving manuscript, it is possible that pages of the manuscript genuinely went missing.

32 View this film at *Public Domain Movies*, starting at 9:12: https://publicdomainmovie.net/movie/charlie-chaplins-a-night-in-the-show-1915.

33 "If the individual human heart is estimated to be the size of its owner's fist," Sara Crangle observes, "these hearts are cartoonishly outsized, satirically disproportionate symbols of what is really lacking in heteronormative intimacy" (*Elevated Realms* 6).

34 This complicated statement should be read in context, not to excuse Loy from harboring racist, primitivist, or orientalist ideas, but to show her willingness to question them. While traveling to Chile on a ship carrying "<u>Hundreds</u> of Jap[anese] rice pickers—sent out on contract—to Peru," Loy was struck by the fact that, even in the "horrible hole" they were subjected to, they were "so civilized—that the whites in the 1st and 2nd class appeared like malformed indecencies" in comparison. Yet even as Loy rejects European white supremacy, she proceeds to offer an Orientalist theory about the innate "relationship between their souls & bodies & clothes and customs that transcends anything we can shew over here" (Loy/MDL 13–14).

35 The mysterious "salting lady" may be a coded reference to "salt cellar"—in French, "marchand du sel," a transposition of "Marcel Duchamp" that became the title of Duchamp's collected writings and was playfully translated into English as "salt seller." If intended, this multilingual pun on Duchamp's name only multiplies the play on names to dizzying extremes.

36 Loy would later revise the role of the artist and elevate it to greater spiritual significance in her discussion of Joseph Cornell, insisting that "the birds in the Aviary, had not to be made by Cornell, they were elected by Cornell, located by Cornell" (LLB82 301).

37 Significantly, Duchamp also used his signature to undermine the authenticity of the artist as creator of the readymade. For example, he inscribed a snow shovel, "In Advance of a Broken Arm / From Marcel Duchamp." As Michael R. Taylor argues, "the idea of the piece being 'from' rather than 'by' the artist was important, since the French 'de' did not carry his intended meaning, which was to lose the concept of art as a manual, handcrafted enterprise" (206–207).

38 This issue of *View* may be accessed online in the Duchamp Archive: https://www.duchamparchives.org/pma/archive/component/MDR_B014_F006_001/. Erin McClenathan offers a close reading of the issue at *MLNAG*.

39 As Taylor points out, the date of this flippant dunking of the American flag is significant, coming on the heels of the US entry into World War I: "On April 6, 1917, exactly four days before the opening of the *Society of Independent Artists Exhibition*, the United States declared war on Germany" (210). American nationalism rose to a fever pitch, and as an English-born woman with French and Italian cultural ties, Loy may have felt especially alienated from the American public.

40 According to Dobbins, long-winded speeches make *The Pamperers* challenging to perform. Using physical movements to reframe what the words meant and exaggerating the satire, the actors played Loony as creative with an insatiable desire for public recognition, and Diana as a stodgy British matron trying to be sexy (Dobbins, personal conversation with Churchill, Jan. 15, 2024).

41 In the 2023 production at Michigan State University, the actors held fans and used "fan language" to highlight the way fashionable talk blends into the costumes and setting (Dobbins, personal conversation with Churchill, Jan. 15, 2024).

42 Hereafter I will refer to *The Pamperers* as it appears in the Crangle-edited *Stories and Essays of Mina Loy*, pp. 162–187.

43 In her final stanza of 1944 poem "Property of Pigeons," the pigeons "peer into a vast transparency" (LB96 121), suggesting that Loy remains interested in what the human eye can see and know, and what it may be prohibited from seeing; see Susan Rosenbaum's analysis of this poem in chapter 4.

44 See Crangle for a discussion of the ellipses ("...") that, she argues, "take center stage" in *The Pamperers* (*Nethered Regions*, 191–195).

45 In chapter 4, Susan Rosenbaum references this stage direction in her analysis of Loy's response to Gertrude Stein's *A Sweet Tail (Gypsies)*, arguing that "Stein's Cubism shaped [Loy's] engagement with Surrealism." Rosenbaum points to Loy's discussion of a passage in Stein's work concerning a lizard on a human hand. The similarities between Diana's chameleon and Stein's lizard raises the tantalizing possibility that Stein may be a model for the character of Diana, and indeed *The Pamperers* shares theatrical techniques and concerns with Stein's "parlor plays" of the same era (see Frank, "The Expansion of Setting"). Diana may also be a composite figure, an amalgamation of Gertrude Stein, Mabel Dodge Luhan, and Mina Loy—analogous to the "threewomen" figure who appears in Loy's poem "Giovanni Franchi" (see chapter 2).

46 Seita writes: "My concept of avant-garde 'proto-forms' conceives of avant-gardes as provisional networks of affiliation rather than rigidly demarcated groups, where *proto-* suggests provisionality and heterogeneity, while *forms* stresses media, genres, and groups" (*Provisional* 3).

47 Alex Goody conjectures that Loy is referring to *Crystal Pantomime* in this letter ("Dance" 138).

CHAPTER FOUR

1 See Michael Sheringham, *Everyday Life*.

2 Loy published this manifesto in *The Little Review*, Autumn 1921; a facsimile is reprinted in MLSII 44.

3 See Lewis Kachur, *Displaying the Marvelous*; Susan Rosenbaum, "Brides Stripped Bare."

4 Julien Levy asked Loy to keep in touch with Breton, who wanted to publish Cravan's surviving manuscripts (Burke, *Becoming* 380); Breton published them with Loy's permission in *VVV* (no. 1, June 1942; no. 2–3 March 1943). Loy presents an unflattering portrait of Breton as "Moto" in her quasi-autobiographical novel *Insel*: "It's funny how people who get mixed up with black magic do suddenly look like death's heads—they will grin and there is nothing but a skull peering at you, at once it's all over—but you remember" (*Insel* 1991, 21). Loy addressed Surrealism's "black magic" in her essay on Joseph Cornell's Aviary exhibition, "Phenomenon in American Art," discussed later in this chapter.

5 Breton expelled René Crevel and Louis Aragon: in Crevel's case for his homosexuality; and in Aragon's for political differences regarding Surrealism's

communist commitments (see Maurice Nadeau, *History* 154–65, 175–82, 191–98; J. H. Matthews, *Introduction* 154). Ribemont-Dessaignes commented in *The Little Review* in 1926, "They don't agree any more about Surrealism than they used to about Dadaism. The same thick swamp subsists. Who is surrealist, who is not? They know it only at the Central Office—where everybody is it" (41).

6 The first translation of Freud into English was *Studies in Hysteria*, translated by A. A. Brill and published in 1909; see G. G. Meynell, "Freud Translated." Freud's *Five Lectures on Psychoanalysis*, delivered at Clark University in Worcester, Massachusetts, in 1909, were published in 1910 in English. Loy had read Freud as early as 1910, possibly in the original German (Burke, *Becoming* 119). She used Freudian language in her early poems and manifestos, and Freudian psychoanalysis was the "topic of choice" during Loy's years (1916–1917) as part of the Arensberg circle in New York (Burke, *Becoming* 214). She met Freud in Vienna in spring 1922, prior to moving to Paris; Freud read Loy's stories while she drew his portrait, and he pronounced her story "Hush Money" "analytic" (Burke, *Becoming* 312–13).

7 Breton aligns Nadja with the Surrealist potentials of Paris itself—she embodies the city's chance encounters, irrational energies, anarchic freedoms, and uninhibited sexuality. His gendered idealizations and denigrations of Nadja irked Loy, as demonstrated by her novel *Insel*; Elizabeth Arnold proposes that *Insel* "can be read not only as an experiment in surrealist narrative, but as a satire on the whole surrealist endeavor," with Breton's *Nadja* as its chief object ("Afterword," *Insel* [1991] 186). Loy reverses *Nadja*'s plot, with Insel serving as male muse for Mrs. Jones's "willful descent into a forbidden psychology" (Arnold, *Insel* 99; see also Miller, *Late Modernism*; Bronstein, "Caustic Critique").

8 In Freudian thought, a fetish involves the "transference of the libido from the whole object of affection to a part, a symbol, an article of clothing" (Schaffner and Jacobs 116), as in women's shoes in Surrealist art. In the disembodied arms Loy objectifies the male libido, providing a critique of the Freudian fetish as it appeared in the work of male Surrealists.

9 See Gross, "Truant," MLSII 78. Sarah Hayden argues that in her novel *Insel* Loy creates the character based on the Surrealist artist Richard Oelze as "the literalized embodiment of the Surrealist *cadavre exquis*" (*Curious Disciplines* 153) and as "the site upon which Surrealism happens" (147), suggesting the connections between Loy's methods in both painting and novel.

10 Shoes were a privileged fetish in the works of both Dada and Surrealism, but were also appropriated by designers such as Meret Oppenheim and Sonia Delaunay for their art and fashion. A similar pair of woman's shoes appear on

a disembodied female leg in *New York Dada* (1921), and in Umbo's 1928 photo of a mannequin's disembodied legs (Schaffner and Jacobs 120), while a female mannequin's legs with shoes are made to "dance" in Léger's *Ballet Mécanique* (1924). As Linda Kinnahan discusses in chapter 2, Loy critically responded to the "Futurist Manifesto of Women's Fashion" by Volt (Vincenzo Fali), which promised to graft Futurist lines, shapes, and colors onto the female form, with her own dress designs: "Loy's attention to freeing while adorning the female body in modern fashion signals a rehabilitation of Futurist ideas for women." *Surreal Scene* suggests a similar, critical response to the Surrealists' stances on and uses of women's fashion.

11 See Yasna Bozhkova's astute discussion of Loy's intertextual poetics, and specifically "her technique of condensing a multiplicity of oblique allusions into enigmatic fragments" (*Between Worlds* 22). Often Loy condenses images, allusions, and aesthetics "in tension with one another" (*Between Worlds* 279); this demonstrates "the subtle ways in which, with her characteristic irony, her work confronts the most revolutionary avant-garde aesthetic projects with the spectral memory of artistic tradition" (8, 71). See also Kinnahan's discussion of Loy's layered depictions of the Madonna in chapter 2.

12 If we consider only the number of published poems, compared to the number of poems Loy wrote from the 1910s through the early 1920s, and from 1937 through the early 1950s in New York, the Paris era does not appear to be a prolific one. But this focus on poetry publications is misleading: Loy's duties creating lamps and running her lampshade shop absorbed her time and energy from 1926 to 1929, and after the 1930 sale of the shop, she wrote *Insel*, constructed Surrealist objects, and created paintings, some exhibited in 1933 at the Levy Gallery.

13 Breton noted "The freedom [Surrealism] possesses is a perfect freedom in the sense that it recognizes no limitations exterior to itself. As it was said on the cover of the first issue of *La Révolution Surrealiste*, 'it will be necessary to draw up a new declaration of the Rights of Man'" ("Surrealism" 22). Decentering the romantic notion of the artist as an autonomous originator, the Surrealists instead regarded the poet as a "modest recording instrument" who conveyed the expression of the unconscious (Breton, *Manifestoes* 28). Poetry was the means of a dialectical resolution of opposed states, the first step toward a broader social, political, and economic revolution. As Tzara put it, "Life and poetry were henceforth a single indivisible expression of man in quest of a vital imperative" (qtd. in Motherwell 406).

14 Collaboration facilitated the Surrealist image and practices of collage and frottage. Breton argued in his "Surrealist Manifesto" that "The forms of

Surrealist language adapt themselves best to dialogue. Here, two thoughts confront each other" (*Manifestoes* 34), and he described *Les Champs Magnétiques* (The Magnetic Fields), his collaboration with Philippe Soupault, as "The first purely Surrealist work," a "dialogue [...] freeing both interlocutors from any obligations of politeness" (*Manifestoes* 35). Similarly, Max Ernst in *Beyond Painting,* argued, "When the thoughts of two or more authors were systematically fused into a single work (otherwise called collaboration) this fusion could be considered as akin to collage" (qtd. in Lydenberg 279).

15 Cristanne Miller argues that Loy's interest in verbal juxtaposition preceded Surrealism and her Paris-era poems (7–8). As Kinnahan argues, "Loy's poetry moved in directions later identified or compatible with Surrealism, not unlike many avant-garde writers of the 1910s, pushing boundaries of rationality and convention" (*Mina Loy, Twentieth-Century Photography* 75).

16 Carolyn Burke Collection on Mina Loy and Lee Miller, Yale Collection of American Literature, Beinecke Rare Book and Manuscript Library, YCAL MSS 778, box 1.

17 For a sustained discussion of Loy's critical engagement with Freudian thought, see Sara Crangle's two-volume work, *An Anatomy of Mina Loy: Nethered Regions* and *Elevated Realms*. Crangle argues that "it is specifically Freud's fragmented theory of the psyche, alongside psychoanalytic misogyny, that prompt Loy's resistance to Freud," a resistance that "inflects her entire oeuvre and is emergent in her earliest writings" (*Nethered* 79). More specifically, Crangle argues that "Loy actively resists Freud's defining anatomisation of the psyche. Instead, she twins her significant understanding of psychoanalysis with occult discourses that promote harmony, that unite self and universe as Freud does not" (*Nethered* 56). While Freud's empirical claims for psychoanalysis as a science hinged on "actively distinguishing psychoanalysis from its occult lineage," Loy recognized its roots in "mesmerism, followed by spiritualism and telepathy"; in banishing this occult lineage, Freud presented "wish fulfilment" or "magical thinking" as science, resulting in what Loy termed a "mechanized mysticism" (*Nethered* 56). In turn, Crangle argues that Loy's feminist critique of Freud's "representation of women's sexuality and reproduction" is evident as early as "Pazzarella" (circa 1914–16): Loy "challenges Freud's inability to generate a psychology that sustainedly, impartially articulates an independent female consciousness" (*Nethered* 56–57). A number of earlier studies also engage Loy's critique of Freud; in particular, Andrew Gaedtke reads Loy's *Insel* as an ethical critique and transformation of the Freudian psychoanalytic case study (see his "From Transmissions").

18 Crangle notes that Lawrence's *Women in Love*, referred to in the essay, was published in 1920 (SE 376). My hunch is that the essay was written in the early 1920s after Loy met Freud (1922) and read *Women in Love*. Suzanne Hobson dates the essay between the mid-1920s and 30s ("Mina Loy's 'Conversion'" 249). Hobson's insightful essay discusses "Conversion" at length, as a means of illuminating the "profane religion" of Loy's poetry (248). Loy establishes an analogy between the Catholic Church and Freudian analysis: "The obsessions prescribed by the Holy Church of Rome, are re-edited by the Psychoanalyst. / The Fathers and Freud successively established confessionals for neurotics, and it will not be long before they are fitted with domestic appliances" (SE 227). Catholic and psychoanalytic confession both invite the revelation of repressed or proscribed sexual actions and desires, with the aim of moral regulation on the part of the Church, and therapeutic recognition on the part of Freud. Although divided by a secular gulf, both "The Fathers and Freud," Catholicism and psychoanalysis, operate with rigid, patriarchal understandings of femininity and maternity. Just as Loy connects Freud to the Church fathers, she connects the Freudian "Eternal Mother" to the Virgin Mary, noting that "In psycho-analytic literature, at least, we are offered no escape from the post-natal womb of the Eternal Mother / And the Eternal Mother devours her literary kittens—invariably" (SE 227).

19 The first two essays appeared in the September and October 1924 issues of the *transatlantic review*, as a defense of Stein, possibly in response to Kenneth Burke's review of Stein's *Geography and Plays* in the April 1923 issue of *The Dial* (Januzzi, "Bibliography" 522–23). Loy also delivered an essay on Stein in French in 1927 at Natalie Barney's salon, and Barney published the essay in *L'Aventure de l'Esprit* (1929); Martin Crowley translated the 1927 essay for the 2011 publication of *Stories and Essays of Mina Loy* (SE 380).

20 More pointedly, Januzzi argues that Loy's essays on Stein "suggest that Stein was the all-important transatlantic bridge, that she indicated a way by which Loy could bring her avant-garde aesthetics to bear in an idiom Loy tropes [...] as feminist and democratic" ("Dada Through" 603). Cristanne Miller argues that in Loy's 1920s poems, she "steps away from the conflicted freedoms of an explicitly sexual politics to map what is problematic in both embodiment and language as modes of intimacy and communication" (119). Stein had provided a provisional map: "Ordinary language, [Loy] implies through her poems, is inadequate, but the poet's disjunctions, juxtapositions, multilingual puns, and grammatical wrenching function less to relay information or feeling than to approach the Stein-like crushed consciousness that releases a pure 'radium of the word'" (120).

21 Loy quickly modified this conflation of Stein and America: "our obliging pioneer has reduced the English language to a foreign language even for Anglo-Americans" (SE 234). Isabelle Alfandary suggests that we should approach "Stein as a deterritorialized writer rather than an expat writer" and suggests that Stein's salon "isn't only a Parisian location but [...] a space in which English, major language par excellence, can become minor and a-grammatical" (Posman and Schultz 13–14).

22 See Ery Shin, *Gertrude Stein's Surrealist Years*. Shin discusses Stein's interest in and overlaps with Surrealist themes and methods; like Loy, Stein never identified as Surrealist, but socialized in Surrealist circles in Paris and developed her experimentation alongside and in conversation with Surrealist poetics.

23 In chapter 3, Suzanne Churchill discusses the chameleon that is part of Diana's costume in Loy's play *The Pamperers*, which anticipates elements of Surrealism.

24 Several poems from the long sequence "Anglo-Mongrels and the Rose" appeared in *The Little Review* (1923–24), and the entire sequence was published in the *Contact Collection of Contemporary Writers* (1925); "Marble" appeared in a 1923 prospectus for Ford Madox Ford's *transatlantic review* (LLB96 202); "Gertrude Stein" was included as an epigraph to Loy's 1924 essays on Stein in *transatlantic review* (202–03); the essay "Modern Poetry" was published in *Charm* magazine (April 1925); and "The Widow's Jazz" and "Lady Laura in Bohemia," both written in or by 1927, appeared respectively in *Pagany*, vol. 2, no. 2 (Spring 1931) and vol. 2, no. 3 (Summer 1931) (LLB96 203–05).

25 Poems that Conover definitively dates to the Paris era include "Jules Pascin" (June 1930), as well as "Nancy Cunard" and "The Mediterranean Sea" (both from the late 1920s) (LLB96 205–07). In addition, the poem "The Ceiling" (titled "Ceiling at Dawn" in LLB82) was included in *The Last Lunar Baedeker* (1982) and is dated August 26, 1930, in a Beinecke draft.

26 The Loy archive at the Beinecke Library includes three handwritten and two complete typed drafts of the poem, with Loy's corrections. A fragment of a third typed draft states: "MINA LOY / 9 Rue St Romain Paris 6 / August 26 1930," indicating that Loy was working on the poem in 1930. I consider the two typed drafts labeled by the Beinecke as 1.[2] and 1.[6] to be the latest drafts, and they differ slightly. L6 types out the handwritten addition in L2 of "four" in "four cornered sky," which indicates L6 may be the later draft. I have used the text of 1.[6], indicating Loy's hand-penciled corrections in parentheses. L2 differs in line 8, where Loy has crossed out "the" for "and" in the line "The epitaphs of dreams." Both typescripts differ from the version published in *The Last Lunar Baedeker* (242) in that the line "Traffic of

slumber" in both typescripts ends with a period, not an em dash as printed in LLB82, and both are titled in capital letters "THE CEILING," rather than "Ceiling at Dawn," which both LLB and the Beinecke use to title the poem (Loy does not use this title for any draft) ("The Ceiling," Mina Loy papers, Yale Collection of American Literature, Beinecke Rare Book and Manuscript Library, https://collections.library.yale.edu/catalog/11699205).

27 Or as Freud would argue, the latent content of the dream gives way to its manifest content, that which the sleeper recalls upon waking. See *Interpretation*.

28 "Dream Analysis," n.d., Mina Loy papers, Yale Collection of American Literature, Beinecke Rare Book and Manuscript Library, YCAL MSS 6, box 6, folder 183, image 113.

29 Loy locates the "vitality" of the new in both "American jazz and American poetry," calling modern poetry "pictured song" and elaborating that "modern poetry, like music, has received a fresh impetus from contemporary life; they have both gained in precipitance of movement. The structure of all poetry is the *movement* that an active individuality makes in expressing itself. Poetic rhythm [...] is the chart of a temperament" (LLB96 157; emphasis added).

30 Cristanne Miller summarizes well the discussion of what critics including Marjorie Perloff, Elisabeth Frost, and Marisa Januzzi have termed Loy's "mongrel" aesthetic, involving mixtures of "linguistic registers" and racial, ethnic, and national idioms (163).

31 Roger Conover notes that Loy wrote "The Widow's Jazz" in 1927 and published it in *Pagany*, vol. 2, no. 2, Spring 1931. Recognizing jazz as a musical and dramatic form, on May 6, 1927, Loy performed this "just completed" poem at Natalie Barney's Academie des Femmes, and Barney later described the reading in her *L'Aventures de l'Esprit* (1927). See Conover, "Notes on the Text," LLB96 203–04.

32 On the history of American jazz in Paris and the French Surrealists' embrace of jazz, see Thabiti Asukile, "J. A. Rogers' 'Jazz at Home'," 26–28.

33 While many Surrealists reinforced racist stereotypes of the primitive other, the Surrealist movement opposed imperialism and colonialism, and Surrealism was unique among the historical avant-gardes in its appeal to and critical transformation by artists and writers marginalized due to race. As Franklin Rosemont and Robin D. G. Kelley point out in *Black, Brown & Beige*, although people of color have been excluded from histories of Surrealism, writers and visual artists of color from the Caribbean, the United States, Mexico, South America, Africa, Egypt, and Japan participated in Surrealist activities and contributed art and writing to Surrealist books and journals, exhibitions, and anthologies, positioning Surrealism as "The

only major modern cultural movement of European origin in which men and women of African descent have long participated as equals, and in considerable numbers" (6). Jean-Claude Michel writes that the Surrealists "held the belief that poetry was a kind of magical and primitive weapon capable of changing the world as well as mankind's way of life" (3); as such, poetry became "eminently revolutionary" and for Black Surrealists, helping to generate "the vision of a New World order" (2). Kelley and Rosemont emphasize Surrealism's anti-colonialist stance, and note the Surrealist support for "The revolt of And el-Krim and the Rif tribespeople of Morocco in the summer of 1925" (9). Michael Richardson notes that the Surrealists opposed the 1931 Colonial Exhibition in Paris, creating a counter-exhibition dubbed "The Truth about the Colonies," and they published an anti-colonialist tract "Murderous Humanitarianism" in Nancy Cunard's 1934 *Negro: An Anthology*, which was also signed by two writers from Martinique, Jules Monnerot and Pierre Yoyotte (4). As Brent Edwards argues, the connection between Parisian Surrealism and the development of Négritude is complicated, as these intellectual traditions mark a "complex field of influence and debate, in which surrealism is only one term, and a hotly contested one at that" (193). In early 1930s Paris, a dialogue between Francophone Caribbean writers and Surrealism was initiated that would shape the development of Surrealism in the coming decades, helping to shift its center away from Europe and contributing to Afro-Surrealism (Eburne).

34 As Petrine Archer-Straw writes, negrophilia "means a love for black culture. In the 1920s, the term was used positively by the Parisian avant-garde to affirm their defiant love of the negro [...] the word was meant to be provocative and challenging to bourgeois values" (9). Archer-Straw chronicles how "black forms were appropriated, adapted and vulgarized by whites" in "advertisements, painting, sculpture, photography, popular music, dance and theatre, literature, journalism, furniture design, fashion and *objets d'art*" (9). She notes that for the avant-garde, "The reality of the black man and the mystery of the land he represented became fertile psychological landscapes in which the white man could create and satisfy his desires. The line of demarcation between the real and the unreal became increasingly blurred. For Europeans, Africa and the black man were framed in notions of high adventure, savagery, fear, peril and death" (13). For the Surrealist group centered on the ethnographic journal *Documents*, founded by Georges Bataille after his split from Breton in 1929, "The negrophilia they advocated was far more transgressive than popular sentiment allowed. They went beyond a frivolous aestheticising towards a 'hard primitivism' involving an interest in

sexual deviance, fetishism, magic, ritual practices and cannibalism as a way of critiquing and transgressing the norms of European society" (135).

35 In addition to Archer-Straw's excellent discussion of European primitivism, on the use of primitivist and often racist stereotypes employed by white critics of American jazz, see Maureen Anderson "White Reception" and Ted Gioia, "Jazz and the Primitivist Myth."

36 See the discussion of Cunard and Loy in Rosenbaum, "Topsy-Turvy Aesthetics," MLNAG.

37 As additional evidence for Loy's interest in Josephine Baker, Linda Kinnahan argues that Loy's poem "Negro Dancer," published in 1961 but possibly written in Paris, "recalls the theatrics of Josephine Baker, who performed the 'danse sauvage' in Paris during the years of Loy's residence there. Indeed, the poem's attention to the dance as performance, in the poem's final lines, recasts the racialized (and racist) visual signifiers to suggest the dancer's conscious appropriation of white expectations. In 'posturing' the 'aboriginal innocencies' [*sic*] of 'an overwrought eros,' the dancer performs blackness 'in the glare of a theater,' both a 'Puppet' to cultural stereotypes and also, the poem arguably suggests, exceeding them in the 'cosmic spasm' that mitigates the 'glare' of an artificial racial lens, circulated within a visual set of signifiers" (*Mina Loy, Twentieth-Century Photography* 62). After her move from Paris to New York, Loy created a "Study for Monument to Basketball" (n.d.), a tribute to the sport's African American heritage that depicts an arm and hand reaching skywards with a basketball (MLSII 90), and a collage construction of "Untitled (Black Dancers)," echoing the theme of "Negro Dancer" (MLSII 177).

38 Loy's representation draws on widely circulated stereotypes of the pickaninny, which first arose during the antebellum period and were popularized through minstrel shows, and a variety of media forms including postcards, books, objects, and film (see David Pilgrim, "Picaninny Caricature"). While she likely alludes to Josephine Baker's performance, Loy's depiction of the figure's upside-down head suggests that she may also have been drawing on the racial symbolism of the topsy-turvy doll. See Rosenbaum, "Topsy-Turvy Aesthetics." Archer-Straw discusses a photograph with Baker and Count Pepito Abatino holding a bare-breasted Josephine Baker doll: "Allusions to puppetry are all too obvious: what are more difficult to discern in this photograph are the motives and scars entailed in such cultural and racial denudation" (96–97).

39 Dalton and Gates describe Baker's role in *The Chocolate Dandies*, which opened in September 1924: "Topsy Anna, the part created especially for

Baker, was straight out of the racist minstrel tradition: she was a ragamuffin in blackface wearing bright cotton smocks and clown shoes" (911). *La Revue nègre*, which originated in New York but opened in Paris in October 1925, "would be transformed from a vaudeville show, replete with stereotypes and conceived for a white American public raised on segregation and racism, into a music-hall performance tailored for openly curious, somewhat voyeuristic Parisians" (911). In the opening number, a "Mississippi River Dock Scene" (913), "Josephine Baker entered the tableau in blackface leaps, wearing plaid dungarees, with knees bent, feet spread apart, buttocks thrust out, stomach sucked in, cheeks puffed out, eyes crossed. She appeared to be part animal—Colin saw a kangaroo, others a giraffe—and part human. Her movements were just as astonishing: shaking, shimmying, writhing like a snake, contorting her torso, all this while emitting strange, high-pitched noises. Then, almost before the audience could comprehend what this apparition might possibly be, she burst offstage on all fours, stiff-legged, derriere extended into the air, hands spanking the boards as she scuttled into the wings" (914). The finale was the "danse sauvage," set in a Harlem nightclub, and described by Janet Flanner thusly: "She made her entry entirely nude except for a pink flamingo feather between her limbs; she was being carried upside down and doing the split on the shoulder of a black giant. Midstage, he paused, and with his long fingers holding her basket-wise around the waist, swung her in a slow cartwheel to the stage floor, where she stood like his magnificent discarded burden, in an instant of complete silence" (qtd. in Dalton and Gates 914).

40 Archer-Straw emphasizes Baker's astute performance of "The fantasy that whites create for her" in *La Revue nègre* (94). Suzanne Churchill's analysis of Gwendolyn Bennett's response to Josephine Baker emphasize Baker's, and in turn Bennett's, satirical remaking of racist stereotypes: "Bennett's language both describes and adopts the Revue's strategy of exploiting and subverting Primitivist stereotypes by recalibrating them in a distinctly modern, ironic, energetic style" ("Whole Ensemble" 9). Bennett's response to Baker's performance in *La Revue nègre* demonstrates this shared strategy: "The heightened artifice produces a beauty of its own, Bennett suggests, even as Baker's hyperbolic gestures expose the artificiality of the racist stereotypes. [...] Bennett recognizes in Baker the inherently performative nature of womanliness, particularly as it intersects with Blackness: the social imperative to perform within a pre-set gendered, racialized vocabulary, and the power that can be wielded from distortions and exaggerations of those cultural scripts" (13).

41 K. Allison Hammer discusses the famous banana skirt that Baker wore in "la danse des bananes": "With its comedic playfulness, associations with bigness (as in 'top banana') and references to plantations in the French Antilles, the banana itself became an ideal metaphor for colonial hierarchies in Baker's performances. Much of Baker's skillful dethroning of the white colonizer occurred through covert and nuanced comic subversion" (175). Hammer discusses the banana belt as used by Baker in performance as a sexual hybrid, "a female phallus—a 'monstrous' hybridity that is neither Black, phallic, and maternal, nor Black, phallic and masculine," generating a "crisis in categorization" (174).

42 On the widespread sentiment that Baker embodied the spirit of African American jazz in late 1920s Paris, see Terri J. Gordon, "Synesthetic Rhythms."

43 Alex Goody argues that through representations of dance and dancers throughout her long career, "Loy questions gendered stereotypes that restrict women as creative individuals" ("Dance" 151). She adds "The traces of dance are tenuous and the authenticity or purity of its meanings vulnerable to exploitation. Dance like Duncan's performs significance, but the body is also a performance, one that can be directed and invested with sense by the embodied subject but that also can be taken over and ascribed particular connotations by others. It is this co-optation of dance and its possible meanings that Loy resists" (151).

44 See Sadiah Qureshi, "Displaying Sara Baartman"; see also Mae G. Henderson's discussion of Baker and Baartman in her chapter "Josephine Baker and *La Revue Nègre*" in *Speaking in Tongues*.

45 Similarly, David Chinitz comments of Langston Hughes's engagement with primitivism, "Hughes's position was of course complicated by his racial identity, which made him an object and not merely an observer of primitivist representation" (60). Churchill's discussion of Gwendolyn Bennett's response to Josephine Baker emphasizes a shared racial identity: "In her interartistic responses to Josephine Baker, Bennett adopts strategies from verbal, visual, and performing arts to extricate the dancer from the racist arena of minstrelsy and Primitivism and position her within an ensemble of talented artists on a sophisticated, urban, international stage"; Bennett "counters stereotypes of racial otherness and affirms a Black, female 'we'" ("Whole Ensemble" 5).

46 In *Passion Projects*, Micir makes visible what she calls a "diverse archive of biographical acts—published and unpublished books, drafts, outlines, fragments, letters, annotation, collections, objects, and ephemera." She argues that queer feminist writers undertook these biographical acts as "passion

projects" that came at personal cost without social reward, to "resist the marginalization and exclusion of their friends, colleagues, lovers, companions, and wives from dominant narratives of literary history" (3).

47 Loy signaled that *Lunar Baedecker* marked the beginning of a new era deeply informed by a "Futurist" past through the collection's reverse chronology. In choosing to begin the book with her most recent poems (1921–1922) written during her travels in New York-Florence-Paris-Vienna-Berlin, followed by the poems she wrote in Florence while associated with Futurist circles (1914–15), Loy presented a genealogy of her poetic career, even as this chronology indicated the continuing importance of both Dada and Futurism.

48 Irene Gammel singles out the Baroness Elsa von Freytag-Loringhoven, Loy, Djuna Barnes, Stein, and Edna Millay as those who "vigorously pushed the boundaries of female sexual expression in poetry" (9–10), writing that the Baroness "tore down post-Victorian gender codes by poeticizing decidedly unpoetic subject matter, including birth-control devices such as condoms [...] sex toys [...] and specific sex acts including oral sex" (9). After *Travels with Mina Loy* was complete, Sara Crangle published her two-volume study of Loy, which includes an extensive, fascinating analysis of Loy's career-long engagement with eros; see in particular *Elevated Realms*, chapter 1, "Hearts Absented and Newborn: Loy's Esoteric Eros." In brief, Crangle argues that "esotericism is Loy's primary means of cohering the subject; in turn, it is by Eros that Loy unites self with world. Loy's esoteric Eros is the requisite counterpart to her satire; as a binary, satire and Eros cohere and structure Loy's oeuvre" (*Elevated Realms* 9). Esotericism for Loy "is also a methodology, a committed pursuit to the metaphysical, transcendent, or gnostic" (15), which Crangle demonstrates was informed by Loy's lifelong interest in various spiritual practices—"Loy was a spiritualist magpie" (19)—enlivened by her engagement with "psychoanalytical, mystical, and ideological thinking" (51), and fueled by her feminism (50).

49 Duchamp worked on the *Large Glass* from 1912 to 1923: he started his "Notes" on the *Glass* in Paris, continued work on the *Glass* after his move to New York in 1915, and declared it "definitively unfinished" in 1923. A selection from the "Notes" was published in English translation in the Surrealist number of *This Quarter* (1932), edited by Breton. The 1942 Duchamp issue of *View* would also feature the *Large Glass*.

50 In 1934, Duchamp published *La Mariée mise à nu par ses célibataires même* (commonly known as the "Green Box"), a collection of notes (begun in 1912) about the *Glass*, and in his words, "The final product was to be a wedding of mental and visual elements" (qtd. in Tomkins 296). The pun on

wedding reveals that the only marriage of Bride and Bachelors would be a conceptual one, involving the play of word and image, written notes and artwork.

51 Judovitz points out that the *Glass*'s refusal of consummation coupled with its resistance to the Bride's visual allure creates a "Delay in Glass," inviting an intellectual, verbal engagement (*Drawing* 40–41). Kinnahan argues that Loy's poetry, visual art, and visual poetics were profoundly influenced by her engagements with photography and film, forms of media that came to increasing prominence over the course of her career (see her *Mina Loy, Twentieth-Century Photography*).

52 Burke writes, "one wonders whether she saw in this self-consciously modern pendant a comment upon her emotional temperature. Since the mercury remained at the bottom of the 'earring,' it is possible that, from his perspective, she had gone cold with the loss of Cravan. In a way, Man Ray's portrait was as objectifying as his nude photography of the Baroness, and the joke, quite possibly, was on his subject" (*Becoming* 299). If Man Ray's photo comments on Loy's erotic "temperature" due to the loss of Cravan, "Lunar Baedeker" critically dismantles the mischaracterization of female eros in works by Duchamp and Man Ray. This commentary continued in New York. MLSII includes a photograph by Denise Brown Hare, "Marcel Duchamp Wearing 'Sexy' Crown, Designed by Mina Loy" (1955 or 1959) (MLSII 93). Hare has photographed Duchamp with the phallic front-piece of the hat juxtaposed against a rendition of the Bachelors from his *Large Glass*, revealing Loy's ironic commentary. Loy also depicted and commented on Duchamp in a number of her late assemblages; see Churchill et al., "Handiwork."

53 Burke dates this work to New York 1948–53 (*Becoming* 422–23). Crangle has recently published an extensive discussion of "History of Religion and Eros," including Loy's criticisms of Freud, in *Elevated Realms* (33–43). Crangle argues that "Seeking the harmonies of an esoteric Eros, Loy finds Freudian psychoanalysis insufficient to the truth of women's conditioning, or the actual cause of women's anatomical dissatisfaction. As importantly for Loy, the Freudian inner self is too vivisected" (39). Crangle points out that "Loy nevertheless follows psychoanalysis in coming to rely upon the cohering force of Eros" (40) and "In this regard, Freud might thus be seen as another of Loy's coronary bypasses, another evaded circulatory centre" (41).

54 As Whitney Chadwick observes, "The cultivation of eros in Surrealism made woman into an active sexual force in the world and in man's creative life, but the language of love, whether expressed in the romantic visions of Breton and Éluard or in the perverse images of Dalí and Bellmer, was a

male language. Its subject was woman, its object woman, and even while proclaiming woman's liberty, it defined her image in terms of man's desires" (103). Suzanne Hobson argues that for Loy, "By over-intellectualizing and over-exposing the act of procreation, Freud had turned a mysterious life-force into a dogmatic duty" ("Mina Loy's 'Conversion'" 252).

55 See Paul Peppis, "Rewriting Sex." In "Havelock Ellis" Loy recounts a 1920 conversation in which Ellis told her that "Ninety percent of the women in England [...] found no pleasure in marriage" (SE 235). In "The Library of the Sphinx," circa early 1920s, Loy, inspired by Ellis, tackles the male modernists' misconceptions. The sphinx figures the representation of woman in writing by men, and whose actual experience thus remains veiled and enigmatic: "'Woman—' said Havelock Ellis to the sphinx, 'put up with what she got and she got nothing!' [...] Your literature—let us examine it your literature — / It was written by the men—" (SE 254). Surveying Joyce, Frank Harris, D. H. Lawrence, and T. S. Eliot, Loy concludes that "Practically the whole of our psychological literature written by men might be lumped together as the unwitting analysis of the unsatisfied woman" (SE 256–57). Loy's "Library of the Sphinx" explores the Anglo-American tradition, but she would also engage Surrealist depictions of the sphinx, as in her painting *The Green Sphynx* (MLSII 109). As Alyce Mahon argues, for the male Surrealists, "The myth of the sphinx was especially attractive, providing the perfect metatext for an exploration of forbidden desire, as well as encompassing the fantasy of the femme fatale, the potential of the city for the marvelous encounter, and a means of self-questioning by which logic and riddle could be set against each other" (1).

56 Loy's ongoing interest in windows echoes her earlier Florentine writing, which, as Kinnahan argues in chapter 2, presents figures gazing out literal, historical, and metaphorical windows at the urban streets, forming a complex "interaction of vision and place."

57 The "wing shows" anticipate Loy's paintings of celestial winged beings, exhibited at the Levy Gallery in 1933. On this exhibition, see Gross, "Truant," MLSII 70–77.

58 See Burke, *Becoming* 339. More information can be found in the Carolyn Burke Collection on Mina Loy and Lee Miller, Yale Collection of American Literature, Beinecke Rare Book and Manuscript Library, YCAL MSS 778, box 6, folder Brown, Susan, correspondence regarding Mina Loy and "Jaded Blossoms," 1978. At this time, Loy carefully studied the *Exhibition of Decorative and Industrial Arts in Paris* (Apr.–Oct. 1925) (Burke, *Becoming* 339–40).

59 For excellent discussions of Loy and fashion see Jessica Burstein, *Cold Modernism*; Susan Dunn, "Fashion Victims" and "Mina Loy, Fashion"; Kinnahan, chapter 1 of *Travels with Mina Loy*, and chapter 2 of *Mina Loy, Twentieth-Century Photography*.

60 Helena Rubinstein advertised her perfumes in *View*, Charles Henri Ford's magazine that featured Surrealist (and surrealist-influenced) art and writing. Loy included the poem, which she typed in a letter dated July 15, 1940, to Mr. Titus at the Helena Rubenstein company. The poem follows:

> Fragrance is harmonious on the air
> as music is a fragrance to the ear
> The very silence of Perfume offsets it's [*sic*] subtlety
> Rubinstein of sound made melody
> Helena Rubinstein presents: —
> The scented symphony of her silent Syrinx
> To whisper, from behind your ear,
> To Everyman
> ALLURE
> As once the pipes of Pan ———

Loy addressed the poem's "two interlacing themes," which she identified as "the musics [*sic*] of the two Rubinsteins" and the "silence of perfume," adding "The first obviously could only be used by your firm but may not fit in with your firm's policy, in which case I might transpose the poem; or you might care to purchase the third line as a Perfume slogan. I would require any firm using this poem to allow me to submit an illustration for it, should one be needed, before the firm decided on an illustration by any other artist." Burke notes that Loy sold the Pipes of Pan design but the Helena Rubinstein company changed the name to Syrinx. See, Carolyn Burke Collection on Mina Loy and Lee Miller, Yale Collection of American Literature, Beinecke Rare Book and Manuscript Library, YCAL MSS 788, box 1, Inventions.

61 See in particular Kinnahan's discussion of Loy's "Mass Production on 14th Street" as a feminist engagement with Surrealism and the fashion economy (*Mina Loy, Twentieth-Century Photography* 90–107).

62 On Loy's lampshade shop see Burke, *Becoming* 341–44; Burstein 187–89; Gross, "Truant," MLSII 57–66; Rosenbaum, "Mina Loy's Lamp Shop," MLNAG.

63 Although the found object may be mass-produced, the manner of its finding, as in Giacometti's case, is subject to chance, unconscious desire, and unplanned intuition (Hopkins 90–91). Loy's gleaning anticipates the film

Les Gleaners et la Glaneuse by Agnès Varda (2000). As Virginia Bonner argues, "Varda explores gleaning out of sympathy with those who glean to survive, and Varda considered her art as a kind of gleaning," revaluing "the used, the aged, even the unsightly," a stance consistent with Loy's. Julien Levy as an aspiring filmmaker recorded Loy as "La Glaneuse"; beginning in 1932, Levy made "short experimental films of artists in action" including one of Loy at the Paris flea market (Burke, *Becoming* 378; "Loy-alism" 69). In doing so, Levy initiated a transatlantic connection between Loy and Joseph Cornell: on his trips with Loy to the flea market, Levy bought boxes and watch parts that he gave to Cornell, who made them into small surrealist objects that Levy exhibited at his New York Gallery (Burke, *Becoming* 379).

64 Hayden reads Mrs. Jones's "alternately solicitous and cruel policing" of Insel's body as Loy's response to the Surrealists' one-sided treatment of eros (*Curious Disciplines* 156).

65 Discussing Loy as a designer across media, Burstein coins the term "domestica" so as "to emphasize the household elements in Loy, crossed as they are with a rigid eroticism that makes strange the recognizable circuits of the everyday" (*Cold Modernism* 152)." This insight can be applied to many of Loy's lamps, which denaturalize "the recognizable circuits of the everyday."

66 Mina Loy's letters to Julien Levy from Paris indicate that she enjoyed representing Dalí for the Levy Gallery, although this arrangement ended in 1935. The correspondence between Loy, Julien Levy, and Joella Levy involving Loy's representation of Dalí can be found in the Carolyn Burke Collection on Mina Loy and Lee Miller, Yale Collection of American Literature, Beinecke Rare Book and Manuscript Library, YCAL MSS 778, box 1 (Correspondence) and box 9 (Carolyn Burke Correspondence 1999–2004). Loy discusses Dalí in *Insel*; the protagonist Mrs. Jones states "Dalí, for instance, is fated to the most extravagant of publicities. He is inclined to accept my theory, for some of the shrillest gags in his already fabulous advertisement were the result of sheer coincidence" (27). Mrs. Jones describes Insel in Dalí-esque terms: "he shifted the part of a hard roll sandwich he was eating, out of the way, horrifyingly developing a Dalí-like protuberance of elongated flesh with his flaccid facial tissue" (30).

67 For Loy's lists of her bottles, see the Carolyn Burke Collection on Mina Loy and Lee Miller, Yale Collection of American Literature, Beinecke Rare Book and Manuscript Library, box 6, folder "Paris: Mina Loy's Bottle Collection."

68 On the installation photograph as an important form of museal display as well as historical documentation for Dada and Surrealism, see Kathryn Floyd, "Writing the Histories."

69 This woman-chair may allude to and comment on the couch-body hybrid in Cocteau's film *Blood of a Poet* (1930), which Dalí would later respond to with his *Mae West Lips Sofa* (1936).

70 Objects by women were included in important Surrealist exhibitions, including the 1933 *Exposition Internationale du Surréalisme* at the Pierre Colle Gallery; the 1936 *Exposition Surréaliste d'Objets* at the Charles Ratton Gallery; the 1938 *Exposition Internationale du Surréalisme*; the 1936 *International Surrealist Exhibition* in London; and at the 1936–7 *Fantastic Art, Dada, Surrealism* exhibition at MoMA.

71 Man Ray used a glass snow globe in his circa 1935 object *Snowball*, and Joseph Cornell often used glass bell jars as containers for objects, as in his *Untitled (Glass Bell)*, circa 1932, published in *Minotaure* 10 (Winter 1937) (Guigon 51).

72 As Kinnahan argues in chapter 2, Loy's visit to Carrara and its marble quarries informed her poem "The Mediterranean Sea" (1928) and specifically her depiction of Carrara as a "marble sentinel" (LLB96 101–02) standing at the "liminal meeting space of mountain and sea." Loy draws on feminine and masculine, maternal and military, human and amphibian qualities in her depiction of Carrara and its surroundings, inviting comparison to her *Lobster Boy* object.

73 See Churchill, *Little Magazine*.

74 On Loy's role as Levy's agent see Burke "Loy-Alism" 67–74 and *Becoming* 377; Elizabeth Arnold "Afterword" 182; Gross "Truant," MLSII 68–70. Duchamp—like Loy, a pivotal figure in the transatlantic migration of Surrealism—played a key role in introducing Loy to Levy. Duchamp met Levy in New York when Duchamp learned that Levy's father Edgar had purchased Brâncuși's *Bird in Space*. Loy's poem "Brancusi's Golden Bird," originally published in *The Dial*, no. 73 (Nov. 1922), and republished in *Lunar Baedecker* (1923), had accompanied the 1926 exhibition of *Bird in Space* at the Brummer Gallery in New York (Januzzi, "Bibliography" 523). With Duchamp and Robert McAlmon, Julien Levy traveled to Paris in February 1927, where he met Loy and her daughter Joella at Peggy Guggenheim's. Levy married Joella in August 1927 and remained entranced by his mother-in-law's beauty and artistic gifts; he would help to promote Loy's poetry and visual art throughout her career (Burke, *Becoming* 346; "Loy-alism" 62).

75 In Paris, Loy negotiated acquisitions with the Bermans, Giacometti, Tchelitchew, de Chirico, and Massimo Campigli, and commissioned work from Ernst, Dalí, and Magritte; she also worked with Pierre Colle and Léonce Rosenberg who had galleries showing Surrealist work in Paris. Loy's dealings on behalf of the Levy Gallery with the German surrealist painter Richard Oelze in 1935–36 would inspire her loosely autobiographical novel *Insel*.

76 On the exhibitions of Loy's artwork at the Levy Gallery, see Burke, "Loy-alism" 70–71; Jacobs, "Chronology of Exhibitions" in Schaffner and Jacobs 175, 180; Burke, *Becoming* 377–79; and Gross, "Truant" MLSII 70–81. The contemporary reviews of Loy's 1933 exhibition compared her paintings to the poetic paintings of Blake, Apollinaire, Éluard, and Cocteau.

77 Barr, Levy, and Arthur Everett Austin, Jr. (head of the Wadsworth Atheneum) were all students of Paul Sachs at Harvard, who taught museum administration (Schaffner and Jacobs 12); Steven Watson, "Julien Levy" 80–83). The MoMA acquired many works through the Levy Gallery, including its collection of Atget photos (Schaffner, "Alchemy" 29; Watson, "Julien Levy" 89).

78 Levy's innovative approach to exhibitions shaped his plans with Woodner-Silverman for a Surrealist House for the 1939 New York World's Fair (Kachur 106), which became Salvador Dalí's *Dream of Venus* pavilion (Kachur 111–29). Levy began his gallery to exhibit the work of Atget and other photographers (Kinnahan, *Mina Loy, Twentieth-Century Photography* 77–82; Schaffner, "Alchemy" 26–28). Also notable were the number of women artists and photographers who received solo exhibitions at the Levy Gallery (see Jacobs, "Chronology of Exhibitions" in Schaffner and Jacobs 173–89).

79 See Schaffner, "Alchemy" 36; Jacobs, "Chronology" in Schaffner and Jacobs 179, 188–89.

80 Sarah Hayden notes that Loy understood *Insel* as part of her "immense experimental prose work" *Islands in the Air*, which Hayden describes as "an ambitious, categorically unstable project to encompass the entirety of her autobiography in a fictionalized prose form" ("Introduction," *Insel* 2014, xiv). On Julien Levy's instructions, Loy contacted Oelze who had lived in Paris since 1933; Levy told Loy to "draw him out, offer moral and financial support, and select those canvases that seemed suited to America" (Burke, "Loy-alism" 73). Oelze was isolated and poor, and Burke writes that "few outside the Surrealist inner circle—Breton, Dalí, and Oelze's compatriot Max Ernst—knew much about him" (*Becoming* 381). Elizabeth Arnold postulates that "it may have been this shared aversion to wholehearted membership in groups that drew Loy and Oelze together" ("Afterword," *Insel* 183). Loy's protagonist Mrs. Jones sees Insel as "too surrealistic for the surrealists" (125) and notes his "distinction" as someone who like herself "'popped up' from nowhere at all—as if all my life I had lacked a crony of my 'own class'" (59). Loy's ability to speak German and a shared affinity for an art of "incipient forms" contributed to her interest in Oelze.

81 The novel is both a framing of Surrealist art and a critical engagement with Oelze/Insel as a Surrealist muse. For varied interpretations of this complex

relationship, see Arnold, Armstrong, Ayers, Bozhkova, Bronstein, Gaedtke, Hayden, Christanne Miller, and Walter. On the importance of Christian Science as it mediates Mrs. Jones' relationship to Insel and Surrealism, see the essays by Tim Armstrong ("Loy and Cornell" 204–20), David Ayers (221–47), Hayden (*Insel* 2014; *Curious Disciplines* 152–53), and Lara Vetter, "Theories of Spiritual Evolution."

82 Sarah Hayden argues that Loy raises Insel's morphine addiction in the novel as a possibility that Mrs. Jones ultimately rejects, while in the alternate unpublished ending "The Visitation of Insel," Mrs. Jones accepts the fact of Insel's addiction and casts Insel's Surrealism as an effect of morphine ("Introduction," *Insel* 2014, xxvii–xxxi).

83 Key scenes in the novel that involve the framing and display of Insel include: Mrs. Jones's transformation of her apartment into a Surrealist installation featuring Insel as a sleeping sea creature; Mrs. Jones's critical response to Insel's painting *Die Irma*; and Mrs. Jones's use of analogies to Surrealist film and photography to "develop" her images of Insel as they stroll around Paris. Loy's writerly techniques in these scenes allude to and draw on Surrealist art in varied media, including photographic superimposition (38–39, 63, 117), the Surrealist object (44–45), Surrealist film (51, 61–62, 84), and Surrealist painting (50–51). At times Loy adopts Oelze's artistic method—one of shading in "invisible myriads [...] so passionately with the overfine point of his pencil" (109)—to describe Insel and his art, as if to beat Oelze at his own game. Insel seems to embody the Surrealist image: Mrs. Jones comments, "He was so at variance with himself, he existed on either side of a paradox" (34); "He possessed some mental conjury enabling him to infuse an actual detail with the magical contrariness surrealism merely portrays" (51–52).

84 Christina Walter has persuasively argued for this connection between *Die Irma* and *Frieda* (682–83).

85 MoMA's 1937 *Fantastic Art, Dada, Surrealism* exhibition catalogue mentions the Frieda/Kafka connection (228) and states that the sketch was "given anonymously," although MoMA's provenance research suggests that the museum purchased the sketch. In a January 24, 1937 letter to Alfred Barr, Oelze states, "I was in such a bad condition this last month in Paris—especially psychically—so that I could not finish the picture, Frieda, and at the end destroyed it. I am very sorry for it—because I promised it to you—but I do hope you understand and will forgive me" (Oelze). In his correspondence with Oelze about the exhibition, Barr refers to Mina Loy's role as agent, suggesting that Oelze's inclusion was facilitated by Loy (Museum of Modern Art Archives).

86 See Susan Rosenbaum's discussion of Loy's correspondence with James Laughlin in "I'm Not the Museum," MLNAG. Hayden emphasizes that in December 1953 Laughlin turned down *Insel* (*Insel* 2014, xviii).

87 Micir understands the archive "as a site of bio-critical action" (9), with such archives taking the form of "experiments in biographical life writing" (8) that challenged and sought to transform "cultural and generic norms" (7). In this light, Loy's autobiographical and biographical writing can be approached as modernist archives. Burke comments at the start of her biography that she "relie[d] on Mina Loy's 'subconscious archives,' the trove of her lightly veiled fiction and autobiography constituting her memoirs" (*Becoming* ix); however, Sandeep Parmar in her study of Loy's autobiographies, cautions that the disordered nature of Loy's archival drafts, combined with Loy's deliberate crafting of her personae, complicate any reading of her autobiographical works for documentary truth ("Introduction," *Reading* 1–20).

88 Though Loy's 1933 paintings did not sell, Levy wrote Loy in 1934 about the "possibility of another Loy exhibition for next year," but advised her, however, to "[add] color this time." See Gross, "Truant," MLSII 81–81, 106–09. Loy's unexhibited paintings focus not on the heavens but on the sea, and many are painted in shades of green and blue. These paintings appear darker in theme: the opening sequences, titled *Drift of Chaos* and *The Styx*, along with the painting titled *Sentinel*, suggest Loy's apprehension of impending doom, akin to the sense of foreboding in Oelze's painting *Expectation*, discussed by Burke ("Loy-alism" 74). See Gross, "Truant," MLSII 81, 106–09; Lauterbach, "Art of the Unbeautiful," MLSII 125–27. Lauterbach discusses the *Drift of Chaos* paintings' interest in fragments and "indeterminate shapes," signifying "remnants, or beginnings," often of a "nascent female form" (MLSII 126).

89 *Drift of Chaos III (Venus)* precedes the *Drift of Chaos IV (Oyster Woman)* painting in the series numbered by Loy, confirming that Loy was reflecting on Venus in these works (see MLSII 107, 126).

90 As Elizabeth Arnold states, "Loy uses *Insel* to set herself not just apart from but far above the Surrealists while at the same time guarding against this quintessential Surrealist's instability and misogyny" ("Afterword," *Insel* 186).

91 On the Surrealists in New York during World War Two, see in particular the studies by Martica Sawin, *Surrealism in Exile*; Dickran Tashjian, *Skyscraper Primitives* and *Boatload of Madmen*; Jed Perl, *New Art City*; and Sandra Zalman, *Consuming Surrealism*. On Surrealism in American little magazines see Tashjian, *Boatload of Madmen*; Rosenbaum, "Exquisite Corpse."

92 Loy lived on 13th Street near Union Square from 1941 to 1944. Thus, she was close to Third Avenue, which as it continues south, turns into the Bowery. The Third Avenue elevated train ran over the Bowery until it was taken down in 1956. In 1948 Loy moved to Second Street, then later that year to Stanton Street, where she lived until she moved to Aspen. See Burke, *Becoming* chapters 18 and 19 (385–424).

93 Deirdre Egan argues that the drafts of the poem "confirm a link between the poet and her down-and-out subjects" (982). Loy scholars have provided excellent readings of this poem and the new vision that it explores; see in particular Maeera Shreiber, "Divine Women"; Kinnahan, *Mina Loy, Twentieth-Century Photography*; Deirdre Egan, "Mina Loy's Modern Long Poem"; and Tara Prescott, *Poetic Salvage*.

94 Loy may have had in mind the 1932 film *The Mummy*. *The Mummy* had no official sequels, but rather was reimagined in *The Mummy's Hand* (1940), *The Mummy's Tomb* (1942), *The Mummy's Ghost* (1944), and *The Mummy's Curse* (1944). Loy's interest in horror films and mummies is apparent in the novel *Insel*, when Loy's protagonist Mrs. Jones states that Insel "reminded one of those magically animated corpses described by William Seabrook" (51); to help Insel with "money-making devices," Mrs. Jones suggests that "The most practical [was] to star him in a horror film" (76).

95 Loy, like Cornell, was drawn to popular entertainments and film and created "museums" of the street that had much in common with lower Manhattan's dime museums and wax museums. Tim Armstrong suggests that the "sugar-coated box-office" "is a less than celebratory image: indeed, it would be quite easy to read these lines as [an] indirect critique of Cornell and his rituals of enclosure" ("Loy and Cornell" 207–08).

96 See in particular Kinnahan's detailed, insightful discussion of Loy's Bowery poems and Abbott's photography in her chapter 3, "Portraits of the Poor: The Bowery Poems and the Rise of Documentary Photography" (*Mina Loy, Twentieth-Century Photography*). Abbott's 1939 collection *Changing New York* "chimes with Loy's late Bowery poems [...] grouped as a series she entitled 'Compensations of Poverty'" (134). Both poet and photographer share "serial tactics of juxtaposition, framing, and perspective" and often employed these techniques to capture "surreal looking displays" (138, 139). In this merging of Surrealism with realist documentary modes, Loy explores the ethical implications of seeing; Kinnahan argues, "Loy's late urban poems join in a documentary effort to make the modern city visible to itself and to promote that visibility as a necessary commentary on socio-economic conditions, ideologies of progress, and histories of modern urban change"

(124), a crucial frame for reading the subjects and style of the poetry and assemblages Loy created in New York. Kinnahan points out that, in their documentary focus, "the late poems do become more direct and simplified in linguistic arrangement and form. These late poems take up less formally radical experimentalism than her earlier poems and, as a group, follow more syntactical and linear regularity, direct referentiality, and singular focus, in contrast to more extensive uses of collage, abrupt juxtaposition, multiplicity of perspective, and eliding gaps of her earlier work" (124). On modernist documentarians' merging of realist documentary modes with modernist experiment, see Jeff Allred, *American Modernism and Depression Documentary*.

97 One of the key guidebooks published around the time of Loy's return was the 1939 *New York City Guide* sponsored and published by the Federal Writers Project. This guidebook contains a section on the Bowery (119–21) that addressed the problem of homelessness.

98 "Dust to dust" alludes to the burial service from the Anglican *Book of Common Prayer*, and emphasizes mortality and bodily "remains," which are ironically "scrapped," Loy's punning play with "remain" and "scrap" indicating both the remnants of the body and the cultural desire to erase them.

99 As Amy Elkins notes, "The photographs are the only truly contemporary images of Loy's assemblages that show them the way Loy herself chose to display them, revealing Loy's particular orientation of her artwork" (1095).

100 In visual-verbal collaborations, patriarchy and its associated hierarchies, including the conventional antagonism between a masculinized word and feminized image, were challenged and opened up: responses across media like Loy's response to *The Large Glass*, often served as a means of exploring new configurations of gender and desire, beyond the limits imposed by Breton and the Surrealist movement. Renée Hubert points out that in Surrealist circles, while men collaborated with other men, and women occasionally collaborated with other women, the most common collaborative grouping was the heterosexual couple; collaborative works created by gay or lesbian couples were less common (1, 6). Collaborative works involving women not only commented on and refigured notions of original authorship, but also explored and challenged social relationships defined by gender, sex, race, class, and power (Hubert 4, 10, 27). The works of Claude Cahun (born Lucy Schwob) and her partner Marcel Moore (born Suzanne Malherbe) were groundbreaking in this respect, as was the collaboration between Surrealist painters Remedios Varo and Leonora Carrington (see Arcq et al., *Surreal Friends*).

101 See the detailed discussion of Loy and collaboration in the introduction, note 12. We distinguish Loy's involvement in artistic networks from the related concept of collaboration, and discuss how other Loy scholars use this terminology.

102 On this connection between Cornell's *Soap Bubble Set* and Loy's "Lunar Baedeker," see Rosenbaum, "Sidewalk Surrealism," MLNAG.

103 Although Loy and Cornell had established a relationship through exchanges of letters, materials, and artwork, and had likely met at the Levy Gallery prior to 1943, this year marked a new stage in their friendship. Cornell would visit Loy on his trips into Manhattan; they also talked on the phone and exchanged letters. Loy recommended books to Cornell including Alain-Fournier's novel *The Wanderer* (1913; translated 1928) and Mary Webb's 1924 novel *Precious Bane* (Burke, *Becoming* 405–07), both of which would influence Cornell's work. His letter of August 1, 1943, was itself an epistolary collage, with a cutout Chinese figurine glued onto blue starred paper. In a 1944 letter Loy thanked Cornell for sending his *Crystal Cage*, which had appeared in Charles Henri Ford and Parker Tyler's Americana Fantastica issue of *View* (January 1943). Cornell invited Loy to his exhibitions in New York, including the 1945 Museum of Modern Art exhibition of *Portrait of Ondine* (Burke, *Becoming* 407). He asked for photos of Mina for his "romantic museum," which he exhibited in 1946 at MoMA as *Romantic Museum, Portraits of Women, Constructions and Arrangements*; although Cornell did not include Loy's photo, he quoted lines from *Precious Bane* in the program (Burke, *Becoming* 406–07).

104 A copy of the November 21, 1946, letter from Cornell to Loy can be found in the Carolyn Burke Collection on Mina Loy and Lee Miller, Yale Collection of American Literature, Beinecke Rare Book and Manuscript Library, box 4, folder Joseph Cornell.

105 Joseph Cornell papers, 1804–1986, bulk 1939–1972, Archives of American Art, Smithsonian Institution.

106 Carolyn Burke Collection on Mina Loy and Lee Miller, Yale Collection of American Literature, Beinecke Rare Book and Manuscript Library, box 4, Joseph Cornell folder.

107 Cornell had thought to ask Marianne Moore rather than Loy for an appreciation of his *Aviary* show; Donald Windham wrote the appreciation that was published in the exhibition catalog. A shared interest in collage as well as spirit and grace connect Cornell and Moore, but also Cornell and Loy: both Moore and Loy functioned as Cornell's poetic muses at this moment. Tellingly, it was Loy not Moore whose "winged words" (Cornell) would

best articulate the method, aims, and effects of Cornell's *Aviary*. Loy drew Moore in 1928 on a visit to Joella and Julien Levy in New York, and as Burke has discussed, these two poets and their careers were often compared by male critics (see Burke, *Becoming* 221, 403). On Moore and Cornell, see Ellen Levy's excellent discussion in *Criminal Ingenuity*.

108 See Ashley Lazevnick, "Impossible Descriptions." Brâncuși was a friend of Loy's in Paris, but she also greatly admired his art. Her poem "Brancusi's Golden Bird" was additionally exhibited alongside Brâncuși's sculpture at the Brummer Gallery in New York in 1926, solidifying the connection between word and image at the center of Loy's art. The Levy family's purchase of *Bird in Flight* after seeing it at the Brummer Gallery initiated Julien Levy's trip to Paris with Duchamp, where he met Loy and married her daughter Joella, and eventually facilitated the dialogue and friendship between Loy and Cornell. Thus, the history Loy records is both personal and aesthetic.

109 See Loy's "Gate Crashers of Olympus" (SE 230–01) on Braque and Picasso, or as Loy puns, "P.O. Casse (cf. French breakage)."

110 Cornell wrote to Alfred Barr in fall 1936 as Barr was preparing the catalog for the *Fantastic Art, Dada, Surrealism* exhibition that "I would appreciate your saying that I do not share in the subconscious and dream theories of the Surrealists. While fervently admiring much of their work I have never been an official Surrealist, and I believe that Surrealism has healthier possibilities than have been developed. The constructions of Marcel Duchamp who the surrealists themselves acknowledge bear this out, I believe" (qtd. in Solomon 84). Cornell similarly wrote to Charles Henri Ford in 1939 of his "total lack of interest in psycho-analysis and the current preoccupation with sex" (qtd. in Solomon 95).

111 Tim Amstrong questions Loy's paradoxical interest in embodiment and in Christian Science, "a religion which dismisses mere physical existence," arguing that "one answer to the question involves seeing that Christian Science does not so much abolish the object as replace it with something different: a transfigured reality" ("Loy and Cornell" 206). Armstrong emphasizes that Christian Science and Surrealism share "the abolition of the world in favour of a transfigured reality, a universe of desire" (210–11). Maeera Shreiber similarly argues that Loy's late poems find that "holiness is necessarily a broken thing—to be found in the bodies and in the faces of society's outcasts, otherwise known to her as 'angel bums'" ("Divine Women" 468). Shreiber argues that Loy's interest in the sexual body in her late work "may be understood as an interpretation of Christian Science's view of the spiritual value of the physical" (469).

112 Here Loy echoes her signature "Compiled by Mina Loy" in "O Marcel – – – otherwise I Have Also Been to Louise's" (see Figs. 3.11 and 3.12), but the mechanical gesture has been elevated and rendered spiritual, signaling Loy's awareness of the evolving role of the modern artist.

113 See Rosenbaum, "Sidewalk Surrealism," MLNAG. Yasna Bozhkova has subsequently developed the connection between Walter Benjamin and Loy, arguing that Loy's allusive poetics are a key to her "dialectical" practice of layering images, allusions, and aesthetics "in tension with one another" (279), a practice similar to Benjamin's use of the "dialectical image" (7–8).

114 This aesthetic of surprise is indebted to Apollinaire, "L'Esprit nouveau et les poètes" (1918) a foundational document for the Surrealists.

115 Loy's oeuvre suggests that "ekphrasis "and "collaboration" are concepts that need to be expanded; ekphrasis as employed by Loy in her essay extends into collage and collaboration. In collage we can track a shifting relation between artist and muse, curator and artist, subject and object: Loy and Cornell, like the Surrealists, put into action a collaborative and reciprocal rather than antagonistic relationship between word and image. Although ekphrasis is a concept conventionally applied to literature, scholars have approached it in the context of the museum (Heffernan; Bergmann Loizeaux; Fischer; Paul; Yacobi) and have usefully extended it to film and music (Clüver; Bruhn; Sager Eidt).

116 Lévêque-Claudet argues that Cornell conflates "the feminine voice and the song of a bird" (142). Similarly, Deborah Solomon writes that Cornell "associated birds with female performers. Birds are curvaceous, clad in feathers, and capable of song, qualities which Cornell's Aviaries, with their colorful cutouts and actual music boxes, abundantly suggest" (187). Both Solomon and Ellen Levy offer astute analyses of gender and erotic desire in Cornell's boxes. Many Surrealist poets and artists used the crossing and mixing of media to dramatize the gendered play of difference and affinity, competition and union, that animates desire. In his discussion of the celebrated Lautréamont's proto-Surrealist image of "the chance meeting upon a dissecting table of a sewing-machine with an umbrella," Ernst stated that "umbrella and sewing-machine will make love" ("Inspiration" 81). Ernst and other male Surrealists emphasized the erotics of bringing together disparate realities through the surrealist image, collage, frottage, and collaboration (Lydenberg 272). As Kinnahan argues, Lautréamont's sewing machine became a privileged icon in the visual art of Dalí, Man Ray, and Cornell, with women's bodies the materials that are pierced, produced, and sewn by the machine, reflecting the gendering of sewing, the consumer, and fashion, a complex that Mina Loy would critically engage (*Mina Loy, Twentieth-Century Photography* 93–94).

117 André Masson created this work for the "rue Surrealiste" featuring seventeen altered mannequins (see Altshuler, *Avant-Garde in Exhibition* 126–28).

118 We can chart the trajectory of the romantic to modern lyric through the changes in its iconic birds: from Keats's nightingale to Baudelaire's swan to Hardy's thrush and Frost's Oven Bird, Stevens's blackbird, Bishop's rooster, and Moore's and Loy's pigeons. Loy keeps the origins of the lyric as song in mind: as Jim Powell notes, Loy pays attention to the pigeons' "irritant, alluring / music" and the poem's subtle use of rhyme and sound mimics the "cooing" of the pigeons (16).

119 Jim Powell argues that Loy's concern is to bring the pigeon's nature into the poem, and only "by implication the life of their observer [...] as an instance of a common urban humanity and fate realizing itself in the terms and gestures of a companionable portrait of these creatures with whom it shares the city" (16).

120 Neiman published "Impossible Opus," "Photo after Pogrom," "Negro Dancer," and "Property of Pigeons" in the spring/summer 1961 issue of *Between Worlds*; he published "Faun Fare" and "In Extremis" ("Show Me a Saint Who Suffered") in fall/winter 1962. "Ephemerid," "Hilarious Israel," "Aid of the Madonna," and "Chiffon Velours" were published in *Accent* in the 1940s; "Hot Cross Bum" was published in *New Directions* in 1950; and "Idiot Child on a Fire-Escape" was published in *Partisan Review* in 1952 (LLB96, "Notes"). Deirdre Egan has argued that Loy's drafts that list poems from this era under the title "Compensations of Poverty" indicate her conception of these poems as a carefully arranged sequence (970, 985).

121 Cornell would collaborate on nine films with Rudy Burckhardt. They filmed *The Aviary* in November and December 1955 over three Sundays; as Burckhardt filmed, Cornell directed where to film (Solomon 228).

122 We have no record of an exchange about Loy's poem, and it's possible that these two like-minded artists independently took the pigeon as muse. Marianne Moore's "Pigeons" (1935) may have been a further influence, and Wallace Stevens's "Sunday Morning" concludes with "casual flocks of pigeons" that "make / Ambiguous undulations as they sink, / Downward to darkness, on extended wings."

123 Although Cornell's boxes capture and display exotic birds rather than pigeons, they too emphasize the mysteries of avian life through their stacks of small drawers, whose contents are blocked from the viewers' eyes.

124 As Kinnahan argues, Loy's play with horizontal versus vertical perspectives, light and shadow in these assemblages was influenced by Umbo's photograph *Uncanny Street* (1928), owned by Julien Levy (*Mina Loy, Twentieth-Century*

Photography 42). Gross also discusses this connection in "Truant" MLSII, 78–81. In Paris, Loy had also explored "topsy-turvy" perspective in her 1935 painting *Surreal Scene* and in *Insel*. Insel's protagonist Mrs. Jones comments on a similar play with perspective: "Again I received a strictly lateral invitation to wholly exist in a region imposing a supine inhabitance. A region whose architecture, being parallel to Paradise, is only visible to a horizontal gaze. Should one stand up to it, it must disappear" (*Insel* 110). "Supine" means lying face upward, or failing to act or protest as a result of moral weakness or indolence. The bum lying on the sidewalk, too easily dismissed as indolent, perhaps searches for or sees "Paradise."

CODA

1 Roger Conover, in an email dated January 7, 2026, explains that a recent inspection of Loy's handwriting on the verso sides of *Prospector 1* and *Prospector 2* reveals that the titles for these pieces have been erroneously reversed in previous scholarship and that the dates of composition are 1957 (*P1*) and 1959 (*P2*). The Bowdoin exhibit catalogue *Mina Loy: Strangeness is Inevitable* (Gross, ed.), published before this discovery, includes these errors. The dates and titles we have cited accord with Conover's recent conclusion.

2 See Carolyn Burke's biography for information about Loy's years in Aspen. Jennifer R. Gross notes in "Truant of Heaven" that "the aspirational gold prospector became Loy's final subject, in *Prospector 1* and *Prospector 2*. These paintings are brilliant distillations of Loy's lifelong preoccupation with hands and faces" (MLSII 103).

3 See note 1 in this chapter.

4 Joseph Cornell letter to Mina Loy, July 3, 1951, Joseph Cornell papers, 1804–1986, Archives of American Art, Smithsonian Institution, https://www.aaa.si.edu/collections/items/detail/joseph-cornell-letter-to-mina-loy-8261.

5 Loy, letter to Carl Van Vechten, 54 Costa San Giorgio, undated [circa summer 1916], Carl Van Vechten papers, series 1, box 76, folder 1082–83, image 48.

6 Both Roger Conover and Cristanne Miller have remarked on the small number of poems that Loy published in New York. Conover states, "Mina Loy was never interested in administering her own poems [...], and from the 1920s on, she rarely did. She published only ten poems in the last thirty-five years of her life, all solicited" (LLB82, "Introduction" xxx). Miller points out that "Loy published no poetry at all between 1931 and 1946 and began to write again only in 1941" (193).

7 Loy's repeated yet unsuccessful attempts to get James Laughlin, founder of *New Directions*, to publish her surrealist novel *Insel*, is a good example (see Sarah Hayden, "Introduction," *Insel* 2014). Loy struggled to exhibit her artwork from the mid-1930s onwards, as discussed in chapter 4 and at length in "Collecting Mina Loy," MLNAG, https://mina-loy.com/chapters/surrealism-on-the-move-new-york-1937-1953/3-collectingminaloy/.

8 Levy's informal role as agent began in the early 1930s. Conover quotes from Loy's 1930 letter to Joella and Julien Levy about her failure to place her 1930 poem "Jules Pascin" with *Hound and Horn* editor Bernard Handler, who had invited a submission but passed on the poem (LLB96 207). Levy arranged two of Loy's Paris publications "Lady Laura in Bohemia" and "The Widow's Jazz" in *Pagany* in 1931, after Loy had sent the poems to Joella with the request that Joella take them to Thayer and Marianne Moore at *The Dial*. See Roger Conover's editor's note in LLB96 (203–05); see also Linda Kinnahan's discussion of the circumstances of this publication, which involved Levy's agreement to permit publication of some Atget photos in *Pagany* if Loy's poems were also published (*Mina Loy, Twentieth-Century Photography* 152). In a June 21, 1951, letter to Mina Loy, Levy states that he showed her poem "Hot Cross Bum" (*New Directions*, 1950) to his neighbor Philip Rahv who thought it magnificent, and asked for a poem for *Partisan Review* (Carolyn Burke Collection on Mina Loy and Lee Miller, Yale Collection of American Literature, Beinecke Rare Book and Manuscript Library, box 3, folder Mina Loy to Joella and Julien Levy, circa 1950–54). Levy subsequently submitted "Idiot Child on a Fire-Escape" to *Partisan Review* where it was published in 1952 (LLB96 209).

9 In letters from Julien Levy to Joella Bayer dated December 17, 1963, and January 18, 1964, Levy states that he has stored the works in his barn, covered in plastic. In an April 18, 1969, letter to Joella Bayer, Julien Levy mentions that his barn has collapsed and asks whether he should ship or store the two cases of Loy paintings. In a letter dated May 6, 1969, Joella Bayer refers to their phone conversation and reiterates her permission to have the artwork crated and stored (Carolyn Burke Collection on Mina Loy and Lee Miller, Yale Collection of American Literature, Beinecke Rare Book and Manuscript Library, "Correspondence" box 3).

10 See "Mina Loy papers: Collection Overview," Mina Loy Papers, Yale Collection of American Literature, Beinecke Rare Book and Manuscript Library.

11 See Laura Scuriatti's discussion of the Mina Loy papers, "Fragmentary, Elusive, Modernist."

12 https://mina-loy.com/chapters/

EXHIBIT 1

1 This biography and timeline are indebted to the following works of scholarship: Carolyn Burke's biography, *Becoming Modern: The Life of Mina Loy*, provides an overview of Mina Loy's life and career built on scrupulous research and interviews with Loy's family, friends, and acquaintances. It is an invaluable resource for the history, context, publication, and exhibition of Loy's writing and art. Marisa Januzzi's annotated bibliographies of works published by and about Loy, published in *Mina Loy: Woman and Poet*, provide a detailed publication and reception history of the poet, and are necessary reading for any student of Loy trying to understand the arc of her public career. Roger Conover's timetable in LLB82 and the introductions to both LLB82 and LLB96, along with his detailed notes on the editorial, publication, and reception history of the poems in LLB96, are a crucial resource. Sara Crangle's introduction and notes to *The Stories and Essays of Mina Loy* contain detailed histories of drafts of unpublished works, and for published texts, histories of their publication and reception. Suzanne Hobson and Rachel Potter's *The Salt Companion to Mina Loy* includes a concise Loy chronology (12–16), and Rochel L. Gasson and Jesse Riley created interactive timelines of various spans of Loy's life for the Mina Loy website (https://mina-loy.com/timeline/).

2 For discussion and illustrations of Mina Loy's evolving signature style, see Churchill, "Loy's Signature Style."

3 Recorded by Paul Blackburn, Black Mountain poet and editor of *The Black Mountain Review*, these conversations are accessible on *PennSound*: https://writing.upenn.edu/pennsound/x/Loy.php.

EXHIBIT 2

1 This survey hits highlights and patterns in Loy scholarship, rather than striving to be comprehensive. See Marisa Januzzi's annotated bibliography in *Mina Loy: Woman and Poet* (ed. Shreiber and Tuma, 1998).

2 Published by Black Sparrow Press, *Insel* went out of print before being more recently reprinted, with a new introduction and material by Sarah Hayden and edited by Elizabeth Arnold, by Melville House in 2014.

3 Januzzi's dissertation *"Reconstru[ing] Scar[s]": Mina Loy and the Matter of Modernist Poetics* (1997) usefully constructs a proposed "critical edition" of Loy's poetry that offers an extensive set of archival notes on Loy's work, based upon final manuscript copy-texts, beginning with "Supplement: Introduction

to a Critical Edition of Mina Loy" (97–137) and including a range of edited poems and annotations reflecting Januzzi's archival work and decisions (138–576). Completed just as Conover's *Lost Lunar Baedeker* appeared, the dissertation asserts that Conover's edition should be "adopted as the standard," while also distinguishing itself in its use of final manuscripts (when extant), rather than first publications as copy-text, and in striving to produce "an edition that reflects [...] the archival and historical record" through a "systematic collation of variants" and the editorial apparatus of a critical edition (Januzzi, *"Reconstru[ing]"* 100). The supplement includes annotations and full copy-texts of Loy's 1925 "Anglo-Mongrels and the Rose," many previously unpublished and published poems, and usefully documented histories of the two books Loy published in her lifetime and the 1982 posthumous collection edited by Conover.

4 *Mina Loy: Strangeness is Inevitable* opened in April 2023 at the Bowdoin Museum of Art, under the direction of Anne Collins Goodyear, the curatorship of Jennifer R. Gross, and the guidance and collection support of Roger Conover. The exhibit moved to the Arts Club of Chicago, March–June 2024.

5 *Mapping Mina Loy Studies* was organized by Jade French (Loughborough University), Jennifer Ashby (European University Institute), and Julia Heinemann (Leipzig University). *Mina Loy and Her Networks* was organized by Yasna Bozhkova (Université Sorbonne Nouvelle), Diane Drouin (Sorbonne Université), and Juliette Utard (Sorbonne Université).

6 "International Psycho-Democracy" (LLB82 276).

7 Conover discusses these musical artists in "Mina Loy, 'I'm Not the Museum'," included in the exhibit catalog for *Strangeness Is Inevitable*. A recording of Conover's talk is hosted on the Bowdoin College Museum of Art's Loy site: https://calendar.bowdoin.edu/event/mina-loy-strangeness-is-inevitable-lecture. Final events for the art exhibit included a performance of his song "Mina Loy" by Busterwolf (musician, visual artist, photographer), followed by a public discussion between the artist, Conover, and Ross Cisneros (artist and composer): https://www.bowdoin.edu/art-museum/exhibitions/2023/mina-loy.html.

8 For a bibliography of Loy's published artworks through 1996, see Burke, *Becoming*; for reproductions of Loy's art, helpful sources include Gross, *Strangeness*; Caws, *Mina Loy*; Elkins (Berenice Abbott's photographs of assemblages from the Bodley exhibit). Photos taken by Maurice Poplin housed with Loy's papers at the Beinecke Library (labeled "Julien Levy Gallery 1933") document a sequence of sixteen paintings from 1933, titled "Drift of Chaos."

9 See: http://www.francisnaumann.com/daughters%20of%20dada/loy.html.

10 The international team included Alison Dobbins, Alex Goody, Alexis Bacon, Alyssa Ridder, Laura Scuriatti, Janet Haley, Megan Heeres, Suzanne Churchill, and Melissa Thompson. See the description of the project: https://theatre.msu.edu/news/mina-loys-trailblazing-feminism-takes-center-stage-at-msu/.

11 For discussion of Corgan and Moore, see Conover, "Mina Loy, 'I Am Not the Museum'," 197; on Short Fictions, see "Project Blog, February 28, 2020" on *Mina Loy: Navigating the Avant-Garde*, https://mina-loy.com/news-events/. Other listings of creative original performances on this list were provided by Roger Conover.

Works Cited

Abrams, M. H. *A Glossary of Literary Terms*. 6th ed., Harcourt Brace, 1993.

Ades, Dawn. "From Rogue to Rags." *Mina Loy: Strangeness Is Inevitable*, edited by Jennifer R. Gross, Princeton UP, 2023, pp. 144–73.

Alfandary, Isabelle. "Becoming American, Becoming Agrammatical: Reading Stein with Deleuze." *Gertrude Stein in Europe: Reconfigurations Across Media, Disciplines, and Traditions*, edited by Sara Posman and Laura Luise Schultz, Bloomsbury Academic, 2017, pp. 129–44.

Allmer, Patricia, editor. *Intersections: Women Artists/Surrealism/Modernism*. Manchester UP, 2016.

Allred, Jeff. *American Modernism and Depression Documentary*. Oxford UP, 2009.

Altshuler, Bruce. *The Avant-Garde in Exhibition: New Art in the 20th Century*. University of California Press, 1994.

Anderson, Maureen. "The White Reception of Jazz in America." *African American Review*, vol. 38, no. 1, 2004, pp. 135–145. *JSTOR*, https://doi.org/10.2307/1512237.

Archer-Straw, Petrine. *Negrophilia: Avant-Garde Paris and Black Culture in the 1920s*. Thames & Hudson, 2000.

Arcq, Tere, Joanna Moorehead, and Stefan Van Raay, editors. *Surreal Friends: Leonora Carrington, Remedios Varo and Kati Horna*. Lund Humphries/ Pallant House Gallery, 2010.

Armstrong, Tim. "Loy and Cornell: Christian Science and the Destruction of the World." *The Salt Companion to Mina Loy*, edited by Rachel Potter and Suzanne Hobson, Salt Publishing, 2010, pp. 204–20.

Armstrong, Tim. *Modernism, Technology, and the Body: A Cultural Study*. Cambridge UP, 1998.

Arnold, Elizabeth. "Afterword." *Insel*, by Mina Loy, Black Sparrow Press, 1991.

Asukile, Thabiti. "J. A. Rogers' 'Jazz at Home': Afro-American Jazz in Paris during the Jazz Age." *The Black Scholar*, vol. 40, no. 3, fall 2010, pp. 22–35. https://doi.org/10.1080/00064246.2010.11413518.

"Avant-garde, N., Senses 1 and 2." *Oxford English Dictionary*. 2nd ed., Oxford UP, 1989.

Ayers, David. "Mina Loy's *Insel* and its Contexts." *The Salt Companion to Mina Loy*, edited by Rachel Potter and Suzanne Hobson, Salt Publishing, 2010, pp. 221–47.

Bäckström, Per, and Benedikt Hjartarson, editors. *Decentring the Avant-Garde*. Rodopi, 2014.

Bacon, Alexis, Suzanne Churchill, Alison Dobbins, Alex Goody, Laura Scuriatti, and Melissa Thompson. "Dramaturgical Notes." Proceedings of the Loy Play Group workshop, Boston, Apr. 2023.

Baedeker, Karl. *Italy: Handbook for Travelers, Northern Italy*. 13th ed., Dulau and Co./Charles Scribner's Sons, 1906.

Balla, Giacomo. "Futurist Manifesto of Men's Clothing." 1914. *Reading Design*, https://www.readingdesign.org/futurist-manifesto-mens-clothing.

"Bandbox Theatre." *Internet Broadway Database (IBDB)*, https://www.ibdb.com/theatre/bandbox-theatre-1051. Accessed 1 July 2025.

Barbie. Directed by Greta Gerwig, Warner Bros. Pictures, 2023.

Barr, Alfred H., Jr., editor. *Fantastic Art, Dada, Surrealism.* Museum of Modern Art, 1936.

Barrett Browning, Elizabeth. *Casa Guidi Windows: A Poem*. Chapman & Hall, 1851.

Bay-Cheng, Sarah. "Modernist Poetic Drama: A Critical Introduction." *Poets at Play: An Anthology of Modernist Drama*, edited by Bay-Cheng and Barbara Cole, Susquehanna UP, 2010.

Benjamin, Walter. *The Arcades Project*. Translated by Howard Eiland and Kevin McLaughlin, Belknap Press of Harvard UP, 1999.

Benjamin, Walter. *Reflections: Essays, Aphorisms, Autobiographical Writings*. Edited by Peter Demetz, translated by Edmund Jephcott, Schocken Books, 1986.

Benson, Timothy O., and Éva Forgács, editors. *Between Worlds: A Sourcebook of Central European Avant-Gardes, 1910–1930*. MIT Press, 2002.

Bentivoglio, Mirella, and Franca Zoccoli. *The Women Artists of Italian Futurism: Almost Lost to History*. Midmarch Arts Press, 1997.

Bergmann Loizeaux, Elizabeth. *Twentieth-Century Poetry and the Visual Arts*. Cambridge UP, 2009.

Bishop, Elizabeth. *Poems, Prose, and Letters*. Edited by Robert Giroux and Lloyd Schwartz, Library of America, 2008.

The Blind Man, no. 1, Apr. 10, 1917. https://collections.library.yale.edu/catalog/15245295.

The Blind Man, no. 2, May 1917. https://collections.library.yale.edu/catalog/15245296.

Bohn, Willard. *Modern Visual Poetry*. U of Delaware P, 2001.

Bohn, Willard. *Reading Visual Poetry*. Fairleigh Dickinson UP, 2011.

Bonner, Virginia. "Beautiful Trash: Agnès Varda's *Les Glaneurs et la glaneuse*." *Senses of Cinema*, no. 45, Nov. 2007, https://sensesofcinema.com/2007/feature-articles/glaneurs-et-glaneuse/.

Bozhkova, Yasna. *Between Worlds: Mina Loy's Aesthetic Itineraries.* Clemson UP, 2022.

Braggiotti, Gloria. *Born in a Crowd*. Thomas Y. Crowell Company, 1957.

Braun, Emily. "Futurist Fashion: Three Manifestoes." *Art Journal*, vol. 54, no. 1, spring 1995, pp. 34–41. https://doi.org/10.1080/00043249.1995.10791674.

Breton, André. *André Breton: Selections*. Edited by Mark Polizzotti, U of California P, 2003.

Breton, André. *Mad Love*. 1937. Translated by Mary Ann Caws, U of Nebraska P, 1987.

Breton, André. *Manifestoes of Surrealism*. Translated by Richard Seaver and Helen R. Lane, U of Michigan P, 1969.

Breton, André. *Nadja*. Translated by Richard Howard, Grove Press, 1960.

Breton, André. "Surrealism: Yesterday, To-day and To-morrow." *This Quarter*, vol. 5, no. 1, Sept. 1932, pp. 7–44.

Breton, André. *What is Surrealism? Selected Writings*. Edited and translated by Franklin Rosemont, Monad Press, 1978.

Bronstein, Hilda. "Mina Loy's *Insel* as Caustic Critique of the Surrealist Paradox." *How2*, vol. 1, no. 4, Sept. 2000.

Bruhn, Siglind. *Musical Ekphrasis: Composers Responding to Poetry and Painting*. Pendragon Press, 2000.

Bull, John [J. B.]. "Illustrations for a Marionette Theatre." *The Mask*, vol. 5, no. 2, Oct. 1912, pp. 150–53. https://bluemountain.princeton.edu/bluemtn/?a=d&d=bmtnaau191210-01.1.67.

Bürger, Peter. *Theory of the Avant-Garde*. Translated by Michael Shaw, foreword by Jochen Schulte-Sasse, U of Minnesota P, 1984.

Burke, Carolyn. *Becoming Modern: The Life of Mina Loy*. Farrar, Straus and Giroux, 1996, reprinted by U of California P, 1997.

Burke, Carolyn. Carolyn Burke Collection on Mina Loy and Lee Miller. Yale Collection of American Literature, Beinecke Rare Book and Manuscript Library, https://archives.yale.edu/repositories/11/resources/1801.

Burke, Carolyn. "Mina Loy." *Dictionary of Literary Biography 4: American Writers in Paris, 1920–1939*, edited by Karen Lane Rood, Gale Research Co., 1980, pp. 259–61.

Burke, Carolyn. "Mina Loy & *Househunting*, or Biography as Restoration." *Mina Loy: Navigating the Avant-Garde*, 2020, https://mina-loy.com/mina-loy-househuntingor-biography-as-restoration/.

Burke, Carolyn. "The New Poetry and the New Woman: Mina Loy." *Coming to Light: American Women Poets in the Twentieth Century*, edited by Diane Wood Middlebrook and Marilyn Yalom, U of Michigan P, 1985, pp. 37–57.

Burke, Carolyn. "Loy-alism: Julien Levy's Kinship with Mina Loy." *Julien Levy: Portrait of an Art Gallery*, edited by Ingrid Schaffner and Lisa Jacobs, MIT Press, 1998, pp. 60–79.

Burstein, Jessica. *Cold Modernism: Literature, Fashion, Art*. Pennsylvania State UP, 2012.

Caws, Mary Ann. *Mina Loy: Apology of Genius*. Reaktion Books, 2022.

Caws, Mary Ann, Rudolf E. Kuenzli, and Gwen Raaberg, editors. *Surrealism and Women*. MIT Press, 1991.

Chadwick, Whitney. *Women Artists and the Surrealist Movement*. Little, Brown and Company, 1985.

Chinitz, David. "Rejuvenation Through Joy: Langston Hughes, Primitivism, and Jazz." *American Literary History*, vol. 9, no. 1, spring 1997, pp. 60–78. *Oxford Academic*, https://doi.org/10.1093/alh/9.1.60.

Churchill, Suzanne W. *The Little Magazine* Others *and the Renovation of Modern American Poetry*. Ashgate, 2006.

Churchill, Suzanne W. "Loy's Signature Style." *Mina Loy: Navigating the Avant-Garde*, 2020, https://mina-loy.com/loys-signature-style/.

Churchill, Suzanne W. "The Lying Game: *Others* and the Great Spectra Hoax of 1917." *Little Magazines and Modernism: New Approaches*, edited by Suzanne W. Churchill and Adam McKible, Ashgate, 2007, pp. 177–95.

Churchill, Suzanne W. "Mina Loy, 'Maison des Bains a Forte dei Marmi' (c. 1909-1915)." *Mina Loy: Navigating the Avant-Garde*, 2020, https://mina-loy.com/art-exhibits/maison-des-bains-a-forte-dei-marmi/.

Churchill, Suzanne W. "'The Whole Ensemble': Gwendolyn Bennett, Josephine Baker, and Interartistic Exchange in Black American Modernism." *Humanities*, vol. 11, no. 4, June 2022. *MDPI*, https://doi.org/10.3390/h11040074.

Churchill, Suzanne W., Linda A. Kinnahan, and Susan Rosenbaum. "Digital Baedeker: A Feminist Experiment with Mina Loy's Archive." *The Contemporary Poetry Archive: Essays and Interventions*, edited by Linda Anderson, Edinburgh UP, 2019, pp. 63–79.

Churchill, Suzanne W., Linda A. Kinnahan, and Susan Rosenbaum. "Feminist Designs: Modernist Digital Humanities & *Mina Loy: Navigating the Avant-Garde*." *Feminist Modernist Studies*, vol. 1, no. 3, 2018, pp. 243–56. https://doi.org/10.1080/24692921.2018.1505255.

Churchill, Suzanne W., Linda A. Kinnahan, and Susan Rosenbaum. "Handiwork: Mina Loy, Collage, and the En Dehors Garde." *Modernism/modernity Print Plus*, vol. 5, cycle 2, 21 Oct. 2020, https://modernismmodernity.org/forums/posts/handiwork.

Clüver, Claus. "Quotation, Enargeia, and the Functions of Ekphrasis." *Pictures Into Words: Theoretical and Descriptive Approaches to Ekphrasis*, edited by Valerie Robillard and Els Jongeneel, Vrije Universiteit UP, 1998, pp. 35–52.

Coaston, Jane. "The Intersectionality Wars." *Vox*, 20 May 2019, https://www.vox.com/the-highlight/2019/5/20/18542843/intersectionality-conservatism-law-race-gender-discrimination.

Conley, Katharine. *Automatic Woman: The Representation of Woman in Surrealism*. U of Nebraska P, 1996.

Conover, Roger L. "Arthur Cravan." *4 Dada Suicides: Selected Texts of Arthur Cravan, Jacques Rigaut, Julien Torma, and Jacques Vaché*. Atlas Press, 1995, pp. 14–88.

Conover, Roger L. "Introduction." *The Last Lunar Baedeker*, edited by Conover, Jargon Society, 1982.

Conover, Roger L. "Introduction"; "Notes on the Text." *The Lost Lunar Baedeker*, edited by Conover, Farrar, Straus and Giroux, 1996.

Conover, Roger L. Introduction, "Mina Loy, *Prospector 2* (1959)." *Mina Loy: Navigating the Avant-Garde*, 2020, https://mina-loy.com/art-exhibits/storymap-of-bowery-construction/.

Conover, Roger L. "Mina Loy, 'I'm Not the Museum'." *Mina Loy: Strangeness Is Inevitable*, edited by Jennifer R. Gross, Princeton UP, 2023, pp. 182–98.

Conover, Roger L. "Opening Lecture." *Mina Loy: Strangeness Is Inevitable exhibition*, 27 Apr. 2023, Visual Arts Center, Kresge Auditorium, Bowdoin College, Brunswick, Maine. Exhibition lecture.

Conover, Roger L. "(Re)Introducing Mina Loy." *Mina Loy: Woman and Poet*, edited by Maeera Shreiber and Keith Tuma, National Poetry Foundation, 1998, pp. 245–70.

Cornell, Joseph. Joseph Cornell papers, 1804–1986, bulk 1939–1972. Archives of American Art, Smithsonian Institution. https://www.aaa.si.edu/collections/joseph-cornell-papers-5790.

Cornell, Joseph, and Rudy Burckhardt. *The Aviary*. 1955. 16mm film, 11 minutes, black and white, silent.

Cornell, Joseph, and Rudy Burckhardt. *Nymphlight*. 1957. 16mm film, 7 minutes, color, silent.

Craig, Gordon. "The Futurists." *The Mask*, vol. 4, no. 4, Apr. 1912, pp. 277–80. https://bluemountain.princeton.edu/bluemtn/?a=d&d=bmtnaau191204-01.1.17.

Craig, Gordon. "The Game of Marionettes: Letters to a Friend, from Gordon Craig." *The Mask*, vol. 5, no. 2, Oct. 1912, pp. 145–50. https://bluemountain.princeton.edu/bluemtn/?a=d&d=bmtnaau191210-01.1.59.

Craig, Gordon. "Gentlemen, The Marionette!" *The Mask*, vol. 5, no. 2, Oct. 1912, pp. 95–97. https://bluemountain.princeton.edu/bluemtn/?a=d&d=bmtnaau191210-01.2.5.

Craig, Gordon. "On Futurismo and the Theatre: Some Notes." *The Mask*, vol. 6, no. 3, Jan. 1914, pp. 194–200. https://bluemountain.princeton.edu/bluemtn/?a=d&d=bmtnaau191401-01.1.14.

Crangle, Sara. *Elevated Realms: An Anatomy of Mina Loy*. U of Edinburgh P, 2024.

Crangle, Sara. "Introduction." *Stories and Essays of Mina Loy*, edited by Crangle, Dalkey Archive Press, 2011, pp. vii–xxiv.

Crangle, Sara. *Nethered Regions: An Anatomy of Mina Loy*. U of Edinburgh P, 2024.

Crenshaw, Kimberlé. "Kimberlé Crenshaw on Intersectionality, More Than Two Decades Later." *Columbia Law School*, 8 June 2017, https://www.law.columbia.edu/news/archive/kimberle-crenshaw-intersectionality-more-two-decades-later.

Crenshaw, Kimberlé. "Mapping the Margins: Intersectionality, Identity Politics, and Violence against Women of Color." *Stanford Law Review*, vol. 43, no. 6, July 1991, pp. 1241–99. *JSTOR*, https://doi.org/10.2307/1229039.

Crowninshield, Frank. "From a Friend." *The Blind Man*, no. 2, May 1917, p. 10. Yale Collection of American Literature, Beinecke Rare Book and Manuscript Library, https://collections.library.yale.edu/catalog/15245296.

Cunard, Nancy, editor. *Negro: An Anthology*. Wishart & Co., 1934.

Dalton, Karen C. C., and Henry Louis Gates, Jr. "Josephine Baker and Paul Colin: African American Dance Seen Through Parisian Eyes." *Critical Inquiry*, vol. 24, no. 4, summer 1998, pp. 903–34. https://doi.org/10.1086/448901.

Davis, Alex, and Lee M. Jenkins. *Locations of Literary Modernism: Region and Nation in British and American Modernist Poetry*. Cambridge UP, 2000.

Davis, Natalie Zemon. "Foreword." *The Allure of the Archives* by Annette Farge, translated by Thomas Scott-Railton, Yale UP, 2013.

"Do You Strive to Capture the Symbols of Your Reactions? If Not You Are Quite Old Fashioned." *New York Evening Sun*, 13 Feb. 1917, p. 10.

Drake, William. *The First Wave: Women Poets in America, 1915–1945*. Macmillan Publishing Co., 1987.

Duchamp, Marcel. *Notes and Projects for* The Large Glass. Edited by Arturo Schwarz. Harry N. Abrams, 1969.

Dunn, Susan. "Fashion Victims: Mina Loy's Travesties." *Stanford Humanities Review*, vol. 7, no. 1, 1999, pp. 101–17.

Dunn, Susan E. "Mina Loy, Fashion, and the Avant-Garde." *Mina Loy: Woman and Poet*, edited by Maeera Shreiber and Keith Tuma, National Poetry Foundation, 1998, pp. 443–56.

DuPlessis, Rachel Blau. *Blue Studios: Poetry and Its Cultural Work*. U of Alabama P, 2006.

DuPlessis, Rachel Blau. *Genders, Races, and Religious Cultures in Modern American Poetry, 1908–1934*. Cambridge UP, 2001. *Cambridge Core*, https://doi.org/10.1017/CBO9780511549632.

Eburne, Jonathan. "Afrosurrealism as Counterculture of Modernity." International Society for the Study of Surrealism Conference, Bucknell University, 1–4 Nov. 2018. Conference presentation.

Edwards, Brent Hayes. *The Practice of Diaspora: Literature, Translation, and the Rise of Black Internationalism*. Harvard UP, 2003.

Egan, Deirdre. "Mina Loy's Modern Long Poem: New York and the *Compensations of Poverty*." *Literature Compass*, vol. 6, no. 5, Sept. 2009, pp. 968–88. https://doi.org/10.1111/j.1741-4113.2009.00648.x.

Eliot, T. S. "John Marston." 1934. *Essays on Elizabethan Drama*, Harcourt Brace, 1956, pp. 162–78.

Eliot, T. S [T. S. Apteryx]. "Observations." *The Egoist*, vol. 5, no. 5, May 1918, pp. 69–70.

Elkins, Amy E. "From the Gutter to the Gallery: Berenice Abbott Photographs Mina Loy's Assemblages." *PMLA*, vol. 134, issue 5, Oct. 2019, pp. 1094–1103. *Cambridge Core*, https://doi.org/10.1632/pmla.2019.134.5.1094.

Ernst, Max. "Inspiration to Order." *This Quarter*, vol. 5, no. 1, Sept. 1932, pp. 79–85. Surrealist number, guest editor André Breton.

Federal Writers Project. *New York City Guide: A Comprehensive Guide to the Five Boroughs of the Metropolis—Manhattan, Brooklyn, the Bronx, Queens, and Richmond*. Random House, 1939.

Feinstein, Amy. "Goy Interrupted: Mina Loy's Unfinished Novel and Mongrel Jewish Fiction." *Modern Fiction Studies*, vol. 51, no. 2, summer 2005, pp. 335–53. *Project MUSE*, https://doi.org/10.1353/mfs.2005.0038.

Fields, Kenneth. "The Poetry of Mina Loy." *Southern Review*, vol. 3, no. 3, July 1967, pp. 597–607.

Fischer, Barbara K. *Museum Mediations: Reframing Ekphrasis in Contemporary American Poetry*. Routledge, 2006. https://doi.org/10.4324/9780203959244.

Flint, Lucy. "Alberto Giacometti: *Woman with Her Throat Cut (Femme égorgée)*." *The Solomon R. Guggenheim Foundation*, 1 May 2016, https://www.guggenheim.org/artwork/1424.

Floyd, Kathryn M. "Writing the Histories of Dada and Surrealist Exhibitions: Problems and Possibilities." *Exhibitions and Display in Dada and Surrealism*, special issue of *Dada/Surrealism*, edited by Floyd, vol. 21, no. 1, fall 2017. https://pubs.lib.uiowa.edu/dadasur/article/29361/galley/137792/view/.

Ford, Lauren Moya. "The World Is Finally Ready for Mina Loy." *Hyperallergic*, 12 Apr. 2023, https://hyperallergic.com/814518/the-world-is-finally-ready-for-mina-loy/.

Fort, Ilene Susan, and Tere Arcq, editors. *In Wonderland: The Surrealist Adventures of Women Artists in Mexico and the United States*. Los Angeles County Museum of Art/Museo de Arte Moderno, Mexico City/DelMonico/Prestel, 2012.

France, Anatole. "The Marionettes of M. Signoret." *The Mask*, vol. 5, no. 2, Oct. 1912, pp. 98–102. https://bluemountain.princeton.edu/bluemtn/?a=d&d=bmtnaau191210-01.1.10.

Frank, Adam. "The Expansion of Setting in Gertrude Stein's Landscape Theater." *Modernism/modernity Print Plus*, vol. 3, cycle 1, 9 Mar. 2018, https://doi.org/10.26597/mod.0045.

Freud, Sigmund. *The Interpretation of Dreams*. 3rd ed. Translated by A. A. Brill, Macmillan, 1913.

Friedman, Susan Stanford. "When a 'Long' Poem Is a 'Big' Poem: Self-Authorizing Strategies in Women's Twentieth-Century 'Long Poems.'" *Dwelling In Possibility: Women Poets and Critics on Poetry*, edited by Yopie Prins and Maeera Shreiber, Cornell UP, 1997, pp. 13–37.

"Frieze." *Oxford Dictionaries*. Oxford UP, n.d., https://premium.oxforddictionaries.com/definition/english/frieze.

Frost, Elisabeth A. *The Feminist Avant-Garde in American Poetry*. U of Iowa P, 2003.

Gaedtke, Andrew. "From Transmissions of Madness to Machines of Writing: Mina Loy's *Insel* as Clinical Fantasy." *Journal of Modern Literature*, vol. 32, no. 1, fall 2008, pp. 143–62. *Project MUSE*, https://doi.org/10.2979/jml.2009.32.1.143.

Gammel, Irene. *Baroness Elsa: Gender, Dada, and Everyday Modernity—A Cultural Biography*. MIT Press, 2002. https://doi.org/10.7551/mitpress/1517.001.0001.

Genauer, Emily. "The Fur-Lined Museum." *Harper's Magazine*, July 1944, pp. 129–38.

Gilbert, Alan. "Looking Anew at Mina Loy, From Paris to the Bowery." *Hyperallergic*, 11 Sept. 2023, https://hyperallergic.com/843370/looking-anew-at-mina-loy-bowdoin-college-from-paris-to-the-bowery/.

Gilmore, Susan. "Imna, Ova, Mongrel, Spy: Anagram and Imposture in the Work of Mina Loy." *Mina Loy: Woman and Poet*, edited by Maeera Shreiber and Keith Tuma, National Poetry Foundation, 1998, pp. 271–318.

Gioia, Ted. "Jazz and the Primitivist Myth." *The Musical Quarterly*, vol. 73, no. 1, 1989, pp. 130–43. *Oxford Academic*, https://doi.org/10.1093/mq/73.1.130.

Girdwood, Megan. "'Puppet of Skeletal Escapade': Dance Dialogues in Mina Loy and Carl Van Vechten." *Modernist Cultures*, vol. 16, no. 2, 2021, pp. 265–88. https://doi.org/10.3366/mod.2021.0331.

Goody, Alex. "'The Dance of the Intelligence'?: Dancing Bodies in Mina Loy." *Tulsa Studies in Women's Literature*, vol. 37, no. 1, spring 2018, pp. 131–56. *Project MUSE*, https://doi.org/10.1353/tsw.2018.0006.

Goody, Alex. "Empire, Motherhood, and the Poetics of the Self in Mina Loy's *Anglo-Mongrels and the Rose*." *Life Writing*, vol. 6, no. 1, 2009, pp. 61–76. https://doi.org/10.1080/14484520802550338.

Goody, Alex. *Modernist Articulations: A Cultural Study of Djuna Barnes, Mina Loy, and Gertrude Stein*. Palgrave Macmillan, 2007.

Gordon, Terri J. "Synesthetic Rhythms: African American Music and Dance Through Parisian Eyes." *The Scholar and Feminist Online*, vol. 6, nos. 1–2, fall 2007/spring 2008, https://sfonline.barnard.edu/baker/print_gordon.htm.

"Grande Serata Futurista," *Lacerba* (periodico quindicinale), Florence, 15 Dec. 1913, vol. 1, no. 24. pp. 281–96.

Greenberg, Clement. "Avant-Garde and Kitsch." *Partisan Review*, vol. 6, no. 5, fall 1939, pp. 34–49.

Gross, Jennifer R. "Truant of Heaven: The Artist Mina Loy." *Mina Loy: Strangeness Is Inevitable*, edited by Gross, Princeton UP, 2023, pp. 2–103.

Gross, Jennifer R., editor. *Mina Loy: Strangeness Is Inevitable*. Princeton UP, 2023.

Guggenheim, Peggy. *Out of This Century: The Informal Memoirs of Peggy Guggenheim*. Dial Press, 1946.

Guggenheim, Peggy, editor. *Art of This Century: Objects, Drawings, Photographs, Paintings, Sculpture, Collages, 1910 to 1942*. Art Aid Corporation, 1942.

Guigon, Emmanuel. "With Hidden Noise." *Joseph Cornell and Surrealism*, edited by Matthew Affron and Sylvie Ramond, Fralin Museum of Art at the University of Virginia, 2015, pp. 48–57.

Hammer, K. Allison. "'Doing Josephine': The Radical Legacy of Josephine Baker's Banana Dance." *Women's Studies Quarterly*, vol. 48, nos. 1–2, spring/summer 2020, pp. 165–81. *Project MUSE*, https://doi.org/10.1353/wsq.2020.0010.

Harding, James Martin. *Cutting Performances: Collage Events, Feminist Artists, and the American Avant-Garde*. U of Michigan P, 2010.

Harris, Rowan. "Futurism, Fashion, and the Feminine: Forms of Repudiation and Affiliation in the Early Writing of Mina Loy." *The Salt Companion to Mina Loy*, edited by Rachel Potter and Suzanne Hobson, Salt Publishing, 2010, pp. 17–46.

Hartigan, Lynda Roscoe. "Joseph Cornell, le Chasseur d'Images." *Joseph Cornell and Surrealism*, edited by Matthew Affron and Sylvie Ramond, Fralin Museum of Art at the University of Virginia, 2015, pp. 74–83.

Hartley, Marsden. "The Importance of Being 'Dada'." *Adventures in the Arts: Informal Chapters on Painters, Vaudeville, and Poets*. Boni & Liveright, 1921, pp. 247–54.

Hauptman, Jodi. "Sweepings." *Joseph Cornell and Surrealism*, edited by Matthew Affron and Sylvie Ramond, Fralin Museum of Art at the University of Virginia, 2015, pp. 84–103.

Hayden, Sarah. *Curious Disciplines: Mina Loy and Avant-Garde Artisthood*. U of New Mexico P, 2018.

Hayden, Sarah. "Introduction." *Insel*, by Mina Loy. Melville House Publishing, 2014.

Heffernan, James A. W. *Museum of Words: The Poetics of Ekphrasis from Homer to Ashbery*. U of Chicago P, 1993.

Henderson, Mae G. *Speaking in Tongues and Dancing Diaspora: Black Women Writing and Performing.* Oxford UP, 2014.

Hobson, Suzanne. "Mina Loy's 'Conversion' and the Profane Religion of Her Poetry." *The Salt Companion to Mina Loy*, edited by Rachel Potter and Hobson, Salt Publishing, 2010. pp. 248–65.

Hong, Cathy Park. "Delusions of Whiteness in the Avant-Garde." *Lana Turner*, no. 7, 2014, reposted at https://shc.stanford.edu/arcade/interventions/delusions-whiteness-avant-garde.

Hopkins, David. *Dada and Surrealism: A Very Short Introduction*. Oxford UP, 2004.

Hubert, Renée Riese. *Magnifying Mirrors: Women, Surrealism, and Partnership*. U of Nebraska P, 1994.

Januzzi, Marisa. "Bibliography: Published Works by Loy, in Order of Appearance, Including Artworks in Reproduction and Significant Posthumous Publications." *Mina Loy: Woman and Poet*, edited by Maeera Shreiber and Keith Tuma, National Poetry Foundation, 1998, pp. 516–39.

Januzzi, Marisa. "Dada Through the Looking Glass, or: Mina Loy's Objective." *Women in Dada: Essays on Sex, Gender, and Identity*, edited by Naomi Sawelson-Gorse, MIT Press, 1998, pp. 578–612.

Januzzi, Marisa. *"Reconstru[ing] Scar[s]": Mina Loy and the Matter of Modernist Poetics*. 1997. Columbia University, PhD dissertation.

Johns, Margaret. "Free Footed Verse Is Danced in Ridgefield, New Jersey." *The New York Tribune*, 25 July 1915, p. 7.

Judovitz, Dalia. *Drawing on Art: Duchamp and Company*. U of Minnesota P, 2010.

Judovitz, Dalia. *Unpacking Duchamp: Art in Transit*. 1995. U of California P.

Julius, Emanuel. "This Summer's Style in Poetry, or the Elimination of Corsets in Versifying." *The New York Call*, 16 May 1915, section 2, p. 3.

Kachur, Lewis. *Displaying the Marvelous: Marcel Duchamp, Salvador Dalí, and Surrealist Exhibition Installations*. MIT Press, 2001.

Kamenish, Paula K. *Mamas of Dada: Women of the European Avant-Garde*. U of South Carolina P, 2015.

Kinnahan, Linda A. "Economics, Nation, and Family in Mina Loy's 'Anglo-Mongrels and the Rose'." *Resistance and Reform: Modernist Women and American Social Engagement*, edited by Jody Cardinal, Deirdre Egan-Ryan, and Julia Lisella, Lexington Books/Rowman & Littlefield, 2019, pp. 245–72.

Kinnahan, Linda A. "Loy's Italian Baedeker: Mapping a Feminist En Dehors Garde." *Mina Loy: Navigating the Avant-Garde*, 2020, https://mina-loy.com/chapters/italy-italian-baedeker/.

Kinnahan, Linda A. "Mina Loy, Fashion Designs (c. 1914)." *Mina Loy: Navigating the Avant-Garde*, 2020, https://mina-loy.com/art-exhibits/mina-loy-fashion-designs-c-1914/.

Kinnahan, Linda A. "Mina Loy, 'The Beach' (c. 1909–1915)." *Mina Loy: Navigating the Avant-Garde*, 2020, https://mina-loy.com/art-exhibits/storymap-of-the-beach/.

Kinnahan, Linda A. *Mina Loy, Twentieth-Century Photography, and Contemporary Women Poets*. Routledge, 2017.

Kinnahan, Linda A. *Poetics of the Feminine: Authority and Literary Tradition in William Carlos Williams, Mina Loy, Denise Levertov, and Kathleen Fraser*. Cambridge UP, 1994.

Konkol, Margaret. "Prototyping Mina Loy's Alphabet." *Feminist Modernist Studies*, vol. 1, no. 3, 2018, pp. 294–317. https://doi.org/10.1080/24692921.2018.1505273.

Kouidis, Virginia M. *Mina Loy: American Modernist Poet*. Louisiana State UP, 1980.

Krantz, Larry. "Three Neglected Poets." *Wagner Literary Magazine*, 1959, pp. 2–63.

Kreymborg, Alfred. *Troubadour: An American Autobiography*. Sagamore Press, 1957.

Kuhl, Nancy. "Mina Loy Papers Online." *Beinecke Rare Book and Manuscript Library*, 5 Dec. 2017, https://beinecke.library.yale.edu/article/mina-loy-papers-online.

Lauterbach, Ann. "Mina Loy: Art of the Unbeautiful True." *Mina Loy: Strangeness Is Inevitable*, edited by Jennifer R. Gross, Princeton UP, 2023, pp. 112–41.

Lazevnick, Ashley. "Impossible Descriptions in Mina Loy and Constantin Brancusi's *Golden Bird*." *Word & Image*, vol. 29, no. 2, 2013, pp. 192–202. https://doi.org/10.1080/02666286.2013.787809.

Lehmann, Ulrich. "Dame Not Dada." *Mode and Mode* 8: "Rogue," Oct. 2020, https://eight.modeandmode.com/page/8.

Lévêque-Claudet, Camille. "Joseph Cornell's Music Box." *Joseph Cornell and Surrealism*, edited by Matthew Affron and Sylvie Ramond, Fralin Museum of Art at the University of Virginia, 2015, pp. 135–49.

Levertov, Denise. "Notes of Discovery." *Lunar Baedeker & Time-Tables*, by Mina Loy, Jonathan Williams/Jargon Society, 1958.

Levy, Ellen. *Criminal Ingenuity: Moore, Cornell, Ashbery, and the Struggle Between the Arts*. Oxford UP, 2011.

Levy, Julien. *Memoir of an Art Gallery*. Putnam, 1977. MFA Publications, 2003.

Levy, Julien. *Surrealism*. Black Sun Press, 1936.

Linett, Maren. "All Winged Their Supermen: Mina Loy, Olive Moore, and the Transhumanist Imagination." *ELH*, vol. 90, no. 4, winter 2023, pp. 1159–86. *Project MUSE*, https://doi.org/10.1353/elh.2023.a914019.

Loy, Mina. "Biography of Songge Byrd." Mina Loy papers. Yale Collection of American Literature, Beinecke Rare Book and Manuscript Library, box 5, folder 130. 1952. https://collections.library.yale.edu/catalog/11700590.

Loy, Mina. *Brontolivido*. Drafts, Mina Loy papers. Yale Collection of American Literature, Beinecke Rare Book and Manuscript Library, https://archives.yale.edu/repositories/11/archival_objects/674898. Accessed 15 Apr. 2025.

Loy, Mina. Carolyn Burke Collection on Mina Loy and Lee Miller. Yale Collection of American Literature, Beinecke Rare Book and Manuscript Library, https://archives.yale.edu/repositories/11/resources/1801. Accessed 3 July 2025.

Loy, Mina. *Crystal Pantomime*. Directed by Lin Hixson, Every house has a door, 9 May 2024, The Arts Club of Chicago; 16 May 2024, The Jane Addams Hull-House Museum, Chicago.

Loy, Mina. *Esau Penfold*. Fragments, Mina Loy papers. Yale Collection of American Literature, Beinecke Rare Book and Manuscript Library, https://digital.library.yale.edu/catalog/11138823. Accessed 15 April 2025.

Loy, Mina. "First Costa Visit." Drafts, Mina Loy papers. Yale Collection of American Literature, Beinecke Rare Book and Manuscript Library, https://collections.library.yale.edu/catalog/11173003. Accessed 15 Apr. 2025.

Loy, Mina. *Futurism, Feminism, and the Right to "Genius": Mina Loy's* The Sacred Prostitute *and Other Plays*. Edited by Alison Dobbins, Michigan State University Libraries, 2025. https://openbooks.lib.msu.edu/minaloy/. Accessed 15 April 2025.

Loy, Mina. "Gloria." Drafts, Mina Loy papers. Yale Collection of American Literature, Beinecke Rare Book and Manuscript Library, https://collections.library.yale.edu/catalog/11124035. Accessed 15 Apr. 2025.

Loy, Mina. "In...Formation." *The Blind Man*, no. 1, "Independents' Number," 10 Apr. 1917, p. 7. https://collections.library.yale.edu/catalog/15245295. Accessed 15 April 2025.

Loy, Mina. *Insel*. Edited by Elizabeth Arnold, Black Sparrow Press, 1991.

Loy, Mina. *Insel*. Edited by Elizabeth Arnold and Sarah Hayden, Melville House, 2014.

Loy, Mina. "Interview with Mina Loy and Paul Blackburn, with Robert Vas Dias, 1965." *PennSound*, https://writing.upenn.edu/pennsound/x/Loy.php. Accessed 15 April 2025.

Loy, Mina. *The Last Lunar Baedeker*. Edited by Roger L. Conover, Jargon Society, 1982.

Loy, Mina. Letters to Carl Van Vechten, Carl Van Vechten papers. Yale Collection of American Literature, Beinecke Rare Book and Manuscript Library, https://collections.library.yale.edu/catalog/2043789. Accessed 3 July 2025.

Loy, Mina. Letters to Mabel Dodge Luhan, Mabel Dodge Luhan papers. Yale Collection of American Literature, Beinecke Rare Book and Manuscript Library, https://collections.library.yale.edu/catalog/10000282. Accessed 3 July 2025.

Loy, Mina. *The Lost Lunar Baedeker: Poems of Mina Loy*. Edited by Roger L. Conover, Farrar, Straus and Giroux, 1996.

Loy, Mina. *Lost Writings: Two Novels by Mina Loy*. Edited by Karla Kelsey, Yale UP, 2024.

Loy, Mina. *Lunar Baedecker*. Contact Publishing Co., 1923.

Loy, Mina. *Lunar Baedeker & Time-Tables*. Jonathan Williams/Jargon Society, 1958.

Loy, Mina. "O Marcel – – – otherwise I Also Have Been to Louise's." *The Blind Man*, no. 2, May 1917, pp. 14–15. https://collections.library.yale.edu/catalog/15245296. Reprinted with explanatory note in *View*, vol. 5, no. 1, Mar. 1945, pp. 35, 51. https://www.duchamparchives.org/pma/archive/component/MDR_B014_F006_001/. Accessed 15 April 2025.

Loy, Mina. *The Pamperers*. *The Dial*, vol. 69, no. 1, July 1920, pp. 65–78. https://babel.hathitrust.org/cgi/pt?id=uva.x000020944&seq=79. Accessed 15 April 2025.

Loy, Mina. *The Pamperers*. *Stories and Essays of Mina Loy*, edited by Sara Crangle, Dalkey Archive Press, 2011, pp. 162–87.

Loy, Mina. *The Pamperers*. Directed by Siobhán Scarry, 12 Nov. 2010, The Open Space Gallery, Victoria, BC, Canada.

Loy, Mina. "The Pamperers." Fragment, Mina Loy papers. Yale Collection of American Literature, Beinecke Rare Book and Manuscript Library, https://collections.library.yale.edu/catalog/11859518. Accessed 3 July 2025.

Loy, Mina. "Pas de Commentaires! Louis M. Eilshemius." *The Blind Man*, no. 2, May 1917, pp. 11–12. https://collections.library.yale.edu/catalog/15245296. Accessed 15 April 2025.

Loy, Mina. "Phenomenon in American Art (Joseph Cornell)." *The Last Lunar Baedeker*, edited by Roger L. Conover, Jargon Society, 1982, pp. 300–02.

Loy, Mina. Poems and Plays [contains *Collision* and *Cittábapini*]. 1914, 1915. Mina Loy papers. Yale Collection of American Literature, Beinecke Rare Book and Manuscript Library, https://collections.library.yale.edu/catalog/2112213. Accessed 15 April 2025.

Loy, Mina. *The Poetic Dramas of Mina Loy*. Produced by Alison Dobbins and directed by Melissa C. Thompson, 7 Dec. 2023 at Michigan State University Broad Art Museum, East Lansing; and 8 Dec. 2023 at Michigan State University, Flint. https://minaloy.dobbinsa.msu.domains/. Accessed 15 April 2025.

Loy, Mina. "Rome." Drafts, Mina Loy papers. Yale Collection of American Literature, Beinecke Rare Book and Manuscript Library, https://collections.library.yale.edu/catalog/11134427. Accessed 15 Apr. 2025.

Loy, Mina. *The Sacred Prostitute*. *Stories and Essays of Mina Loy*, edited by Sara Crangle, Dalkey Archive Press, 2011, pp. 188–215.

Loy, Mina. *The Sacred Prostitute*. Mina Loy papers. Yale Collection of American Literature, Beinecke Rare Book and Manuscript Library, https://collections.library.yale.edu/catalog/12154402. Accessed 25 July 2025.

Loy, Mina. *The Sacred Prostitute*. Illustrated by CF. *Triple Canopy*, 13 Sept. 2011, https://canopycanopycanopy.com/contents/the_sacred_prostitute. Accessed 15 April 2025.

Loy, Mina. *The Sacred Prostitute and Other Plays by Mina Loy*. Directed by Melissa C. Thompson, 4–7 Apr. 2024, UMF Theatre, Performance Space, Emery Community Arts Center, University of Maine at Farmington. https://wpsites.maine.edu/emerycommunityartscenter/2024/03/13/the-sacred-prostitute-and-other-plays/. Accessed 15 April 2025.

Loy, Mina. *The Sacred Prostitute and Other Tales from the Home of a Mad Woman*. Directed by Anja Klock, 11–13 Nov. 1999, Rarig Center Xperimental Theatre at the University of Minnesota.

Loy, Mina. "Second Costa Visit." Drafts, Mina Loy papers. Yale Collection of American Literature, Beinecke Rare Book and Manuscript Library, https://collections.library.yale.edu/catalog/11134835. Accessed 15 April 2025.

Loy, Mina. *Stories and Essays of Mina Loy*. Edited by Sara Crangle, Dalkey Archive Press, 2011.

Loy, Mina. *Two Plays* [*Collision* and *Cittàbapini*]. *Rogue*, vol. 1, no. 6, 15 June 1915, pp. 15–16. https://collections.library.yale.edu/catalog/17374476. Accessed 15 April 2025.

Luhan, Mabel Dodge. *Intimate Memories*. Harcourt, Brace and Company, 1933. 2 vols.

Lusty, Natalya. "Sexing the Manifesto: Mina Loy, Feminism and Futurism." *Women: a cultural review*, vol. 19, no. 3, 2008, pp. 244–60. https://doi.org/10.1080/09574040802413834.

Lusty, Natalya. *Surrealism, Feminism, Psychoanalysis*. Ashgate, 2007.

Lydenberg, Robin. "Engendering Collage: Collaboration and Desire in Dada and Surrealism." *Collage: Critical Views*, edited by Katherine Hoffman, U of Michigan P, 1989, pp. 271–86.

Lyon, Janet. "Mina Loy's Pregnant Pauses: The Spaces of Possibility in the Florence Writings." *Mina Loy: Woman and Poet,* edited by Maeera Shreiber and Keith Tuma, National Poetry Foundation, 1998, pp. 379–402.

Mahon, Alyce. "La Feminité triomphante: Surrealism, Leonor Fini, and the Sphinx." *Dada/Surrealism*, vol. 19, no. 1, 2013. https://doi.org/10.17077/0084-9537.1274.

Malraux, André. *Museum without Walls*. Translated by Stuart Gilbert, Pantheon Books, 1949.

Mao, Douglas, and Rebecca L. Walkowitz. "The New Modernist Studies," *PMLA*, vol. 123, no. 3, May 2008, pp. 737–48. *Cambridge Core*, https://doi.org/10.1632/pmla.2008.123.3.737.

Marinetti, F. T. "Dynamic and Synoptic Declamation." 11 Mar. 1916. *Futurism: An Anthology*, edited by Lawrence Rainey, et al., Yale UP, 2009, pp. 219–24.

Marinetti, F. T. "The Founding and Manifesto of Futurism." 20 Feb. 1909. *Futurism: An Anthology*, edited by Lawrence Rainey, et al. Yale UP, 2009, pp. 49–53.

Marinetti, F. T. "Mafarka's Discourse on Futurism." *Mafarka the Futurist. Critical Writings by F. T. Marinetti*, edited by Günter Berghaus, translated by Doug Thompson, Farrar, Straus and Giroux, 2006, pp. 32–42.

Marinetti, F. T. "Technical Manifesto of Futurist Literature." *Critical Writings by F. T. Marinetti*, edited by Günter Berghaus, translated by Doug Thompson, Farrar, Straus and Giroux, 2006, pp. 107–19.

Matthews, J. H. *An Introduction to Surrealism.* Pennsylvania State UP, 1965.

McAuley, James. "The Artists and Their Alley, in Postwar France." *The New York Times*, 22 Sept. 2016, https://www.nytimes.com/2016/09/22/t-magazine/art/impasse-ronsin-artists-montparnasse-constantin-brancusi.html.

McBride, Henry. Foreword. "Modern Forms." *The Dial*, vol. 69, no. 1, July 1920, pp. 61–64, https://babel.hathitrust.org/cgi/pt?id=uva.x000020944&seq=75.

McClenathan, Erin. "Loy in View (1945)." *Mina Loy: Navigating the Avant-Garde*, 2020. https://mina-loy.com/art-exhibits/loy-in-view/.

McHale, Brian, and Randall Stevenson, editors. *The Edinburgh Companion to Twentieth-Century Literatures in English*. Edinburgh UP, 2006.

Mell, Leah. "3D Animation: Loy's 'Collision'." *Mina Loy: Navigating the Avant-Garde*, 2020. https://mina-loy.com/new-frequencies/mina-loys-collision-3d-animation/.

Meynell, G. G. "Freud Translated: An Historical and Bibliographical Note." *Journal of the Royal Society of Medicine*, vol. 74, no. 4, Apr. 1981, pp. 306–09. https://doi.org/10.1177/014107688107400414.

Michel, Jean-Claude. *The Black Surrealists*. Peter Lang, 2000.

Micir, Melanie. *The Passion Projects: Modernist Women, Intimate Archives, Unfinished Lives*. Princeton UP, 2019.

Miki, Roy. *The Prepoetics of William Carlos Williams: Kora in Hell*. U of Michigan Research P, 1983.

Miller, Cristanne. *Cultures of Modernism: Marianne Moore, Mina Loy, and Else Lasker-Schüler*. U of Michigan P, 2007.

Miller, Tyrus. *Late Modernism: Politics, Fiction, and the Arts Between the World Wars*. U of California P, 1999.

Milton, John. *Paradise Lost*. *Complete Poems and Major Prose*. Edited by Merritt Y. Hughes. Macmillan, 1985.

Mina Loy: Navigating the Avant-Garde. Edited by Suzanne W. Churchill, Linda A. Kinnahan, and Susan Rosenbaum. University of Georgia, 2020. https://mina-loy.com.

"Mina Loy Papers: Collection Overview." Mina Loy papers. Yale Collection of American Literature, Beinecke Rare Book and Manuscript Library, https://archives.yale.edu/repositories/11/resources/1681. Accessed 14 May 2025.

Mina Loy: Strangeness Is Inevitable. 6 Apr.–17 Sept. 2023, curated by Jennifer R. Gross, Bowdoin College Museum of Art, Brunswick, ME, https://www.bowdoin.edu/art-museum/exhibitions/2023/mina-loy.html.

Mina Loy: Strangeness Is Inevitable. 19 Mar.–8 June. 2024, curated by Jennifer R. Gross, Arts Club of Chicago, https://www.artsclubchicago.org/exhibition/mina-loy-strangeness-is-inevitable/

Mina Loy's Feminist Futurist Dramas. Directed by Alison Dobbins, 7–8 Dec. 2023, Michigan State University Broad Art Museum and University of Michigan-Flint North Bank Dance Studio.

Morse, Samuel French. "The Rediscovery of Mina Loy and the Avant Garde." *Wisconsin Studies in Contemporary Literature*, vol. 2, no. 2, spring/summer 1961, pp. 12–19. *JSTOR*, https://doi.org/10.2307/1207316.

Motherwell, Robert, editor. *The Dada Painters and Poets*. Wittenborn Schultz, 1951.

Nadeau, Maurice. *The History of Surrealism*. Translated by Richard Howard, Harvard UP, 1989.

Naumann, Francis M. *New York Dada: 1915–23*. Harry N. Abrams, 1994.

"Necropolis, *N.*, Etymology." *Oxford English Dictionary*, Oxford UP, Sept. 2025. https://doi.org/10.1093/OED/5987115966.

North, Michael. *Camera Works: Photography and the Twentieth-Century Word*. Oxford UP, 2005.

Norton, Louise. "Buddha of the Bathroom." *The Blind Man*, no. 2, May 1917, pp. 5–6. https://collections.library.yale.edu/catalog/15245296.

Oelze, Richard. Letter to Alfred Barr, 24 Jan. 1937. Registrar exhibition files, exhibit 55, Museum of Modern Art Archives, New York.

Parmar, Sandeep. "Mina Loy's 'Colossus' and the Myth of Arthur Cravan." *Jacket*, no. 34, Oct. 2007, http://jacketmagazine.com/34/parmar-loy.shtml.

Parmar, Sandeep. *Reading Mina Loy's Autobiographies: Myth of the Modern Woman*. Bloomsbury, 2013.

Paul, Catherine E. *Poetry in the Museums of Modernism: Yeats, Pound, Moore, Stein*. University of MI Press, 2002.

Peppis, Paul. "Rewriting Sex: Mina Loy, Marie Stopes, and Sexology." *Modernism/modernity*, vol. 9, no. 4, Nov. 2002, pp. 561–79. *Project MUSE*, https://doi.org/10.1353/mod.2002.0075.

Perl, Jed. *New Art City: Manhattan at Mid-Century*. Vintage, 2007.

Perloff, Marjorie. "English as a 'Second Language': Mina Loy's 'Anglo-Mongrels and the Rose.'" *Mina Loy: Woman and Poet*, edited by Maeera Shreiber and Keith Tuma. National Poetry Foundation, 1998, pp. 131–48.

Pilgrim, David. "The Picaninny Caricature." *Jim Crow Museum*, Oct. 2000, https://jimcrowmuseum.ferris.edu/antiblack/picaninny/homepage.htm.

Pilsch, Andrew. *Mina Loy Online*. https://oncomouse.github.io/loy/. Accessed 14 Nov. 2024.

Poggi, Christine. "Dreams of Metallized Flesh: Futurism and the Masculine Body." *Modernism/modernity*, vol. 4, no. 3, Sept. 1997, pp. 19–43. *Project MUSE*, https://doi.org/10.1353/mod.1997.0056.

Poggi, Christine. "*Folla/Follia*: Futurism and the Crowd." *Critical Inquiry*, vol. 28, no. 3, spring 2002, pp. 709–48. https://doi.org/10.1086/343236.

Poggioli, Renato. *The Theory of the Avant-Garde*. Translated by Gerald Fitzgerald, The Belknap Press of Harvard UP, 1968.

Pollock, Griselda. "Moments and Temporalities of the Avant-Garde 'in, of, and from the feminine.'" *New Literary History*, vol. 41, no. 4, autumn 2010, pp. 795–820. *Project MUSE*, https://doi.org/10.1353/nlh.2010.0030.

Posman, Sara, and Laura Luise Schultz, editors. *Gertrude Stein in Europe: Reconfigurations across Media, Disciplines, and Traditions*. Bloomsbury Academic, 2017.

Potter, Rachel, and Suzanne Hobson, editors. *The Salt Companion to Mina Loy*. Salt Publishing, 2010.

Pound, Ezra. "Others." *The Little Review*, vol. 4, no. 11, Mar. 1918, pp. 56–58.

Powell, Jim. "Basil Bunting and Mina Loy." *Chicago Review*, vol. 37, no. 1, winter 1990, pp. 6–25.

"A Power-House as a Futurist Painter Sees It." *Popular Science Monthly*, vol. 90, no. 4, Apr. 1917, p. 538. https://archive.org/details/sim_popular-science_1917-04_90_4/page/538/mode/1up.

Prescott, Tara. *Poetic Salvage: Reading Mina Loy*. Bucknell UP, 2016.

"Pug Debs Make Society Bow." *New York Dada*, Apr. 1921, https://www.monoskop.org/images/4/41/New_York_Dada.pdf.

Qureshi, Sadiah. "Displaying Sara Baartman, the 'Hottentot Venus'." *History of Science*, vol. 42, no. 2, June 2004, pp. 233–57. https://doi.org/10.1177/007327530404200204.

Rainey, Lawrence, Christine Poggi, and Laura Wittman, editors. *Futurism: An Anthology*. Yale UP, 2009.

Rasula, Jed. *Destruction Was My Beatrice: Dada and the Unmaking of the Twentieth Century*. Basic Books, 2015.

Re, Lucia. "Mina Loy and the Quest for a Futurist Feminist Woman." *The European Legacy*, vol. 14, no. 7, 2009, pp. 799–819. https://doi.org/10.1080/10848770903363896.

Rexroth, Kenneth. "Les Lauriers Sont Coupés, No. 2: Mina Loy." *Circle*, vol. 1, no. 4, 1944, pp. 69–70.

Ribemont-Dessaignes, George. "In Praise of Violence." *The Little Review*, vol. 12, no. 1, spring/summer 1926, pp. 40–41. Surrealist number. https://babel.hathitrust.org/cgi/pt?id=gri.ark:/13960/s29232d45pg&seq=66.

Richardson, Michael, editor. *Refusal of the Shadow: Surrealism and the Caribbean*. Translated by Krzysztof Fijałkowski and Michael Richardson, Verso, 1996.

Roberts, Andrew Michael. "Rhythm, Self and Jazz in Mina Loy's Poetry." *The Salt Companion to Mina Loy*, edited by Rachel Potter and Suzanne Hobson, Salt Publishing, 2010. pp. 99–128.

Roché, Henri Pierre. "The Blind Man." *The Blind Man*, no. 1, 10 Apr. 1917, pp. 3–6. https://collections.library.yale.edu/catalog/15245295.

Rosemont, Franklin, and Robin D. G. Kelley, editors. *Black, Brown, & Beige: Surrealist Writings from Africa and the Diaspora*. U of Texas P, 2009.

Rosemont, Penelope, editor. *Surrealist Women: An International Anthology*. Athlone Press, 1998.

Rosenbaum, Susan. "Brides Stripped Bare: Surrealism, the *Large Glass*, and U.S. Women's Imaginary Museums." *Exhibitions and Display in Dada and Surrealism*, special issue of *Dada/Surrealism*, edited by Kathryn Floyd, vol. 21, no. 1, fall 2017. https://pubs.lib.uiowa.edu/dadasur/article/29356/galley/137787/view/.

Rosenbaum, Susan. "The 'Do It Yourself' Avant-Garde: American Women Poets and Experiment." *A History of Twentieth-Century Women's Poetry*, edited by Linda A. Kinnahan, Cambridge UP, 2016, pp. 323–38. *Cambridge Core*, https://doi.org/10.1017/CBO9781316488560.021.

Rosenbaum, Susan. "Elizabeth Bishop and the Miniature Museum." *Journal of Modern Literature*, vol. 28, no. 2, winter 2005, pp. 61–99. *Project MUSE*, https://doi.org/10.1353/jml.2005.0030.

Rosenbaum, Susan. "Exquisite Corpse: Surrealist Influence on the American Poetry Scene, 1920–1960." *Oxford Handbook of Modern and Contemporary American Poetry*, edited by Cary Nelson, Oxford UP, 2012, pp. 268–300. *Oxford Academic*, https://doi.org/10.1093/oxfordhb/9780195398779.013.0011.

Rosenbaum, Susan. "'I'm not the Museum': Mina Loy, the Julien Levy Gallery, and Trans-Atlantic Surrealism." *Mina Loy: Navigating the Avant-Garde*, 2020, https://mina-loy.com/chapters/surreal-scene/4-loy-surrealism-the-levy-gallery/.

Rosenbaum, Susan. "Sidewalk Surrealism: Loy's and Cornell's Aviaries." *Mina Loy: Navigating the Avant-Garde*, 2020, https://mina-loy.com/chapters/surrealism-on-the-move-new-york-1937-1953/2-sidewalk-surrealism-loys-and-cornells-aviaries/.

Rosenbaum, Susan. "Surrealist Histories." *Mina Loy: Navigating the Avant-Garde*, 2020, https://mina-loy.com/chapters/surreal-scene/2-surrealist-histories-loy-the-parisian-avant-garde/.

Rosenbaum, Susan. "Topsy-Turvy Aesthetics: Mina Loy, Jazz, Surrealism, and Race." *Mina Loy: Navigating the Avant-Garde*, 2020, https://mina-loy.com/loy-surrealism-race/.

Rothfuss, Joan. "Mina Loy Has Finally Arrived." *Chicago Reader*, 18 Apr. 2024, http://chicagoreader.com/arts-culture/mina-loy-arts-club-strangeness-is-inevitable/.

Sacher-Masoch, Leopold von. *Venus in Furs*. Translated by Joachim Neugroschel, Penguin, 2000.

Sager Eidt, Laura M. *Writing and Filming the Painting: Ekphrasis in Literature and Film*. Rodopi, 2008.

Sawelson-Gorse, Naomi, editor. *Women in Dada: Essays on Sex, Gender, and Identity*. MIT Press, 1998.

Sawin, Martica. *Surrealism in Exile and the Beginning of the New York School*. MIT Press, 1995.

Scarry, Siobhán. "Introduction." Poets Theatre production: *The Pamperers*, Open Space Gallery, Modernist Studies Association Conference, Victoria, BC, 12 Nov. 2010.

Schaffner, Ingrid. "Alchemy of the Gallery." *Julien Levy: Portrait of an Art Gallery*, edited by Ingrid Schaffner and Lisa Jacobs, MIT Press, 1998, pp. 20–59.

Schaffner, Ingrid, and Lisa Jacobs, editors. *Julien Levy: Portrait of an Art Gallery*. MIT Press, 1998.

Schaum, Melita. "'Moon-flowers Out of the Muck': Mina Loy and the Female Autobiographical Epic." *Massachusetts Studies in English*, vol. 10, no. 4, 1986, pp. 254–76.

Schmid, Julie. "Mina Loy's Futurist Theatre." *Performing Arts Journal*, vol. 18, no. 1, Jan. 1996, pp. 1–7. *JSTOR*, https://www.jstor.org/stable/3245807.

Scuriatti, Laura. "Fragmentary, Elusive, Modernist: The Mina Loy Papers at the Beinecke Rare Book and Manuscript Library." *The Bloomsbury Handbook of Modernist Archives*, edited by Jamie Callison, Matthew Feldman, Anna Svendsen, and Erik Tonning, Bloomsbury, 2024, pp. 55–69.

Scuriatti, Laura. *Mina Loy's Critical Modernism*. UP of Florida, 2019.

Scuriatti, Laura. "Transnational Modernist Encounters in the Provinces: *Lacerba*, Mina Loy, and International Debates on Sexual Morality in Florence." *Forum for Modern Language Studies*, vol. 53, no. 3, 2017, pp. 303–13. *Oxford Academic*, https://doi.org/10.1093/fmls/cqx014.

Sedgwick, Eve Kosofsky. *Between Men: English Literature and Male Homosocial Desire*. Columbia UP, 1985.

Seita, Sophie. "The Politics of the Forum in Feminist Avant-Garde Magazines After 1980." *Journal of Modern Literature*, vol. 42, no. 1, fall 2018, pp. 163–82. *Project MUSE*, https://doi.org/10.2979/jmodelite.42.1.11.

Seita, Sophie. *Provisional Avant-Gardes: Little Magazine Communities from Dada to Digital*. Stanford UP, 2019.

Semar, John [J. S.]. Introduction to "Gentlemen, the Marionette!" *The Mask*, vol. 5, no. 2, Oct. 1912, p. 95. https://bluemountain.princeton.edu/bluemtn/?a=d&d=bmtnaau191210-01.1.7.

Sergeant, Adeline. *In Vallombrosa: A Sequence*. F. V. White & Co., 1897.

Sheringham, Michael. *Everyday Life: Theories and Practices from Surrealism to the Present*. Oxford UP, 2006.

Shin, Ery. *Gertrude Stein's Surrealist Years*. U of Alabama P, 2023.

Shreiber, Maeera. "Divine Women, Fallen Angels: The Late Devotional Poetry of Mina Loy." *Mina Loy: Woman and Poet*, edited by Shreiber and Keith Tuma, National Poetry Foundation, 1998, pp. 467–86.

Shreiber, Maeera, and Keith Tuma, editors. *Mina Loy: Woman and Poet*. National Poetry Foundation, 1998.

Sica, Paola. *Futurist Women: Florence, Feminism, and the New Sciences*. Palgrave Macmillan, 2016. https://doi.org/10.1057/9781137508041.

Solomon, Deborah. *Utopia Parkway: The Life and Work of Joseph Cornell.* Farrar, Straus and Giroux, 1997.

"Some Notes upon Ancient Puppets, by 'Yorick' with an Introductory Word by the Translator." *The Mask*, vol. 4, no. 4, Apr. 1912, pp. 301–03. https://bluemountain.princeton.edu/bluemtn/?a=d&d=bmtnaau191204-01.1.41.

"Sometimes We Dread the Future." *Every Week*, vol. 4, no. 14, 2 Apr. 1917, p. 14. https://everyweek.unl.edu/assets/images/large/ew.issue.19170402.p014.jpg.

Spackman, Barbara. "Mafarka and Son: Marinetti's Homophobic Economics." *Modernism/modernity*, vol. 1, no. 3, Sept. 1994, pp. 89-103. *Project MUSE*, https://doi.org/10.1353/mod.1994.0064.

Stauder, Ellen Keck. "The Irreducible Surplus of Abstraction: Mina Loy on Brancusi and the Futurists." *Mina Loy: Woman and Poet*, edited by Maeera Shreiber and Keith Tuma, National Poetry Foundation, 1998, pp. 357–78.

Stein, Gertrude. *Geography and Plays*. The Four Seas Co., 1922.

Stein, Gertrude. *Selected Writings of Gertrude Stein*. 1946. Edited by Carl Van Vechten, Vintage Books, 1990.

Stillman, Steel. "Ulrike Müller on Humiliation, Repetition, and Painting with Enamel." *Art News*, 4 Nov. 2019, https://www.artnews.com/art-in-america/interviews/ulrike-muller-interview-enamel-painting-humiliation-63667/.

Suzanne, Nichelle. "En Dehors, Out the Door." *Dance Advantage*, 12 Jan. 2010, https://www.danceadvantage.net/en-dehors-dedans/.

Symons, Arthur. "A Word on Puppets." *The Mask*, vol. 5, no. 2, Oct. 1912, p. 103. https://bluemountain.princeton.edu/bluemtn/?a=d&d=bmtnaau191210-01.1.15.

Tashjian, Dickran. *A Boatload of Madmen: Surrealism and the American Avant-Garde, 1920–1950*. Thames and Hudson, 1995.

Tashjian, Dickran. *Skyscraper Primitives: Dada and the American Avant-Garde, 1910-1925*. Wesleyan UP, 1975.

Taylor, Michael R. "Blind Man's Bluff: Duchamp, Stieglitz, and the *Fountain* Scandal Revisited." *Mirrorical Returns: Marcel Duchamp and the 20th Century Art*, edited by Yukihiro Hirayoshi, National Museum of Art, Osaka, 2004, pp. 206–13.

Tomkins, Calvin. *Duchamp: A Biography*. Henry Holt, 1996.

Tuma, Keith. *Fishing by Obstinate Isles: Modern and Postmodern British Poetry and American Readers.* Northwestern UP, 1998.

Twitchell-Waas, Jeffery. "'Little Lusts and Lucidities': Reading Mina Loy's Love Songs." *Mina Loy: Woman and Poet*, edited by Maeera Shreiber and Keith Tuma, National Poetry Foundation, 1998, pp. 111–28.

Van Vechten, Carl. *Sacred and Profane Memories*. Alfred A. Knopf, 1932.

Vendler, Helen. "The Truth Teller." *The New York Review of Books*, 19 Sept. 1996, https://www.nybooks.com/articles/1996/09/19/the-truth-teller/.

Vetter, Lara. *Modernist Writings and Religio-Scientific Discourse: H.D., Loy, and Toomer*. Palgrave Macmillan, 2010.

Vetter, Lara. "Theories of Spiritual Evolution, Christian Science, and the 'Cosmopolitan Jew': Mina Loy and American Identity." *Journal of Modern Literature*, vol. 31, no. 1, 2007, pp. 47–63. *Project MUSE*, https://doi.org/10.2979/jml.2007.31.1.47.

Volt [Vincenzo Fani]. "Futurist Manifesto of Women's Clothing." *Roma Futurista*, 1920. *Everything2*, https://everything2.com/title/Futurist+Manifesto+of+Women%2527s+Fashion.

Voyce, Stephen. "'Make the World Your Salon': Poetry and Community at the Arensberg Apartment." *Modernism/modernity*, vol. 15, no. 4, Nov. 2008, pp. 627–46. *Project MUSE*, https://doi.org/10.1353/mod.0.0039.

Walter, Christina. "Getting Impersonal: Mina Loy's Body Politics from 'Feminist Manifesto' to *Insel*." *Modern Fiction Studies*, vol. 55, no. 4, winter 2009, pp. 663–92. *Project MUSE*, https://doi.org/10.1353/mfs.0.1635.

Watson, Steven. "Julien Levy: Exhibitionist and Harvard Modernist." *Julien Levy: Portrait of an Art Gallery*, edited by Ingrid Schaffner and Lisa Jacobs, MIT Press, 1998, pp. 80–95.

Watson, Steven. *Strange Bedfellows: The First American Avant-Garde*. Abbeville, 1991.

Watz, Anna. *Surrealist Women's Writing: A Critical Exploration*. Manchester UP, 2021.

Webster, Michael. *Reading Visual Poetry after Futurism: Marinetti, Apollinaire, Schwitters, Cummings*. Peter Lang, 1995.

White, John. "Italian Futurism and Russian Cubo-Futurism." *The Routledge Companion to Experimental Literature*, edited by Joe Bray, Alison Gibbons, and Brian McHale, Routledge, 2012, pp. 21–35.

Williams, Jonathan. "Things Are Very Far Away." *The Nation*, 27 May 1961, pp. 461–62.

Williams, William Carlos. "Mina Loy." *Lunar Baedeker & Time-Tables*, edited by Jonathan Williams, Jargon Society, 1958.

Winters, Yvor. "Mina Loy." *The Dial*, vol. 80, no. 6, June 1926, pp. 496–99. https://babel.hathitrust.org/cgi/pt?id=uc1.31175013759686&seq=612.

Wood, Beatrice. "Dream of a Picture Hanger." *The Blind Man*, no. 1, 10 Apr. 1917, p. 7. https://collections.library.yale.edu/catalog/15245295.

"Would You Be 'Different?' Madame Loy Shows How." *Pittsburgh Press*. 3 Apr. 1921, https://www.newspapers.com/clip/15430648/mina_loy_fashion_designs/.

Yacobi, T. "Ekphrastic Double Exposure and the Museum Book of Poetry." *Poetics Today*, vol. 34, no. 1–2, 2013, pp. 1–52, https://doi.org/10.1215/03335372-1894487.

Yorick [P. Ferrigni]. "A History of Puppets: A Few Statistics." *The Mask*, vol. 6, no. 1, July 1913, pp. 27–29. https://bluemountain.princeton.edu/bluemtn/?a=d&d=bmtnaau191307-01.1.31.

Zalman, Sandra. *Consuming Surrealism in American Culture: Dissident Modernism.* Routledge, 2015.

Zelazo, Suzanne. "Roger Conover: Conjurer, Cartographer, Curator." *Mina Loy: Navigating the Avant-Garde*, 2020, https://mina-loy.com/roger-conover-conjurer-cartographer-curator/.